McGraw-Hill Series in Political Science

Joseph P. Harris, *Consulting Editor*

IDEAS AND ISSUES
IN PUBLIC ADMINISTRATION
A Book of Readings

McGRAW-HILL SERIES IN POLITICAL SCIENCE

Joseph P. Harris, Consulting Editor

‌ ‌ ‌

Adrian · Governing Urban America: Structure, Politics, and Administration

Bone · American Politics and the Party System

Chase · The United Nations in Action

Ebenstein · Political Thought in Perspective

Ferguson and McHenry · The American Federal Government

Ferguson and McHenry · The American System of Government

Ferguson and McHenry · Elements of American Government

Field · Governments in Modern Society

Frank · Cases on the Constitution

Gosnell, Lancaster, and Rankin · Fundamentals of American Government: National, State, and Local

Gosnell, Lancaster, and Rankin · Fundamentals of American National Government

Gross · The Legislative Struggle

Haas and Whiting · Dynamics of International Relations

Hartmann · Basic Documents of International Relations

Hartmann · Readings in International Relations

Holloway · State and Local Government in the United States

Leonard · Elements of American Foreign Policy

Leonard · International Organization

Mangone · A Short History of International Organization

Millett · Management in the Public Service

Neumann · European and Comparative Government

Pierson and Gil · Governments of Latin America

Riemer · Problems of American Government

Roche and Stedman · The Dynamics of Democratic Government

Rodee, Anderson, and Christol · Introduction to Political Science

Strausz-Hupé and Possony · International Relations

Svarlien · An Introduction to the Law of Nations

Turner · Politics in the United States: Readings in Political Parties and Pressure Groups

Vandenbosch and Hogan · The United Nations: Background, Organization, Functions, Activities

Waldo · Ideas and Issues in Public Administration: A Book of Readings

Wilson · The American Political Mind

Wilson · Police Administration

IDEAS AND ISSUES
IN
PUBLIC ADMINISTRATION

A Book of Readings

Edited by
DWIGHT WALDO

Department of Political Science
University of California at Berkeley

New York   Toronto   London
McGRAW-HILL BOOK COMPANY, INC.
1953

Preface

This book of readings has been designed primarily for use with a textbook in a general course in public administration, though I believe it will also stand by itself as an introduction to the major areas of the subject. In constructing the book I have tried to follow these principles:

1. Coverage of the subjects embraced in most general courses in public administration, as evidenced by textbooks and course outlines.

2. An exploration at greater length than textbook permits—or time or library may allow—of some major trends, theories, and controversies.

3. Some representation of differing points of view on matters about which intelligent and experienced men may—and do—disagree.

4. Quotation of passages of sufficient length—often entire essays—to convey adequately the sense and spirit of the author.

This principle of relatively long selections has meant that not all subjects discussed in the textbooks appear in the Table of Contents of this book. However, many subjects (communication, for example) which have been denied separate treatment because of limitations of space are discussed at various places under other headings, as reference to the index will disclose. After all, an administrative system in being does not obviously reflect conventional subject headings, and the classification of materials in public administration is largely arbitrary.

As the book is designed primarily as a supplement to a textbook, I have not included bibliographies, with which the textbooks abound. In the interests of space and simplicity, I have omitted authors' footnotes from the selections.

All books are autobiographical, reflecting the experience of the author or editor. These readings and their introductory notes reflect, for good or ill, the knowledge and tastes of the editor. They reflect a strong interest in theoretical problems which have come increasingly to the fore in administrative study in the past decade, and they reflect in several ways my several years of varied administrative experience. I can only hope that others may find that my experience was instructive and that my predilections are their own.

DWIGHT WALDO

BERKELEY, CALIF.
MARCH, 1953

Contents

Chapter 1

The Role of Administration in Modern Society

The following account of a mine disaster was written by a journalist. But it is not only superb journalism, it is one of the best essays on administration in any language. For the writer has not only told the "human" story of the violent deaths of 111 men; he has also—soberly, fairly, and carefully—tried to answer the questions: How did the disaster happen? Why?

In his attempt to find the cause of the blast at Centralia No. 5 the journalist lays bare the administrative vitals of our society. Time after time a person who has participated in administration finds himself saying as he reads, "Yes, that's the way it is—how often have I seen that!" Again and again there is faithfully pictured a typical administrative procedure or relationship.

What caused the fatal blast? The socialist will find in the analysis strong support for his belief that private ownership of such things as mines is evil. The men died, he will conclude, because the owner and managers were more interested in profits than in lives. Is this really true? Perhaps, in part. But if it is true in part, certainly it is *only* in part. For what is brilliantly illuminated by Mr. Martin's essay is that the problems of how to run our large-scale, technological society transcend economic systems.

Even if it were to be admitted—and most people do not believe it—that such impulses as greed would be abolished or held in check by the abolition of private ownership of the means of production, the problems of administration clearly transcend the problems of evil impulse. These problems involve, for example, human ignorance and human inertia. They involve problems in social mechanics and personal relations. The experienced student of administration will find it hard to believe that the administrative

1

problems that are passed in review in this essay would be much altered under any economic system.

The central truth revealed by this essay is that all of us in a modern society work in the tunnels of Centralia No. 5. The welfare, happiness, and very lives of all of us, that is to say, rest in significant measure upon the performance of administrative mechanisms that surround and support us. From the central matters of food and shelter to the periphery of our intellectual activity, the quality of administration in modern society touches our daily lives. Today your life may depend upon the administration of purity controls in a pharmaceutical house, tomorrow it may depend upon the decisions of a state department of motor vehicles, next week it may rest with the administrative wisdom of an official in the Department of State. Willy-nilly, administration is everyone's concern. If we wish to survive, we had better be intelligent about it.

The Blast in Centralia No. 5 :
A Mine Disaster No One Stopped *

John Bartlow Martin

Already the crowd had gathered. Cars clogged the short, black rock road from the highway to the mine, cars bearing curious spectators and relatives and friends of the men entombed. State troopers and deputy sheriffs and the prosecuting attorney came, and officials from the company, the Federal Bureau of Mines, the Illinois Department of Mines and Minerals. Ambulances arrived, and doctors and nurses and Red Cross workers and soldiers with stretchers from Scott Field. Mine rescue teams came, and a federal rescue unit, experts burdened with masks and oxygen tanks and other awkward paraphernalia of disaster. . . .

One hundred and eleven men were killed in that explosion. Killed needlessly, for almost everybody concerned had known for months, even years, that the mine was dangerous. Yet nobody had done anything effective about it. Why not? Let us examine the background of the explosion. Let us study the mine and the miners, Joe Bryant and Bill Rowekamp and some others, and also the numerous people who might have saved the miners' lives but did not. The miners had appealed in various directions for help but got none, not from their state government nor their federal government nor their employer nor their own union. (In threading the maze of officialdom we must bear in mind four agencies in author-

* From *Harper's Magazine*, Vol. 196 (March, 1948), pp. 193–220. A substantial part of the essay is omitted in this abridgment, largely material on the lives of the miners and their families. Copyright, 1948, by John Bartlow Martin. Reprinted by permission of Harold Ober Associates.

ity: The State of Illinois, the United States Government, the Centralia Coal Company, and the United Mine Workers of America, that is, the UMWA of John L. Lewis.) Let us seek to fix responsibility for the disaster. . . .

The Centralia Mine No. 5 was opened two miles south of Centralia in 1907. Because of its age, its maze of underground workings is extensive, covering perhaps six square miles, but it is regarded as a medium-small mine since it employs but 250 men and produces but 2,000 tons of coal daily. It was owned by the Centralia Coal Company, an appendage of the Bell & Zoller empire, one of the Big Six among Illinois coal operators. . . . The Bell & Zoller home office was in Chicago (most of the big coal operators' home offices are in Chicago or St. Louis) ; no Bell & Zoller officers or directors lived at Centralia.

There are in coal mines two main explosion hazards—coal dust and gas. Coal dust is unhealthy to breathe and highly explosive. Some of the dust raised by machines in cutting and loading coal stays in suspension in the air. Some subsides to the floor and walls of the tunnels, and a local explosion will kick it back into the air where it will explode and, in turn, throw more dust into the air, which will explode; and as this chain reaction continues the explosion will propagate throughout the mine or until it reaches something that will stop it.

The best method of stopping it, a method in use for some twenty-five years, is rock dusting. Rock dusting is simply applying pulverized stone to the walls and roof of the passageways; when a local explosion occurs it will throw a cloud of rock dust into the air along with the coal dust, and since rock dust is incombustible the explosion will die. Rock dusting will not prevent an explosion but it will localize one. Illinois law requires rock dusting in a dangerously dusty mine. Authorities disagreed as to whether the Centralia mine was gassy but everyone agreed it was exceedingly dry and dusty. The men who worked in it had been complaining about the dust for a long time—one recalls that "the dust was over your shoetops," another that "I used to cough up chunks of coal dust like walnuts after work"—and indeed by 1944, more than two years before the disaster, so widespread had dissatisfaction become that William Rowekamp, as recording secretary of Local Union 52, prepared an official complaint. But even earlier, both state and federal inspectors had recognized the danger.

Let us trace the history of these warnings of disaster to come. For in the end it was this dust which did explode and kill one hundred and eleven men, and seldom has a major catastrophe of any kind been blueprinted so accurately so far in advance.

Driscoll O. Scanlan (who led the rescue work after the disaster) went to work in a mine near Centralia when he was 16, studied engineering at night school, and worked 13 years as a mine examiner for a coal company until, in 1941, he was appointed one of 16 Illinois state mine inspectors by Governor Green upon recommendation of the state representative from Scanlan's district. Speaking broadly, the job of a state inspector is to police the mine operators—to see that they comply with the state mining law, including its numerous safety provisions.

But an inspector's job is a political patronage job. Coal has always been deeply enmeshed in Illinois politics.

Dwight H. Green, running for Governor the preceding fall, had promised the miners that he would enforce the mining laws "to the letter of the law," and however far below this lofty aim his administration fell (as we shall see), Scanlan apparently took the promise literally. Scanlan is a stubborn, righteous, zealous man of fierce integrity. Other inspectors, arriving to inspect a mine, would go into the office and chat with the company officials. Not Scanlan; he waited outside, and down in the mine he talked with the miners, not the bosses. Other inspectors, emerging, would write their reports in the company office at the company typewriter. Not Scanlan; he wrote on a portable in his car. Widespread rumor had it that some inspectors spent most of their inspection visits drinking amiably with company officials in the hotel in town. Not Scanlan. Other inspectors wrote the briefest reports possible, making few recommendations and enumerating only major violations of the mining law. Scanlan's reports were longer than any others (owing in part to a prolix prose style), he listed every violation however minor, and he made numerous recommendations for improvements even though they were not explicitly required by law.

Scanlan came to consider the Centralia No. 5 mine the worst in his district. In his first report on it he made numerous recommendations, including these: "That haulage roads be cleaned and sprinkled. . . . That tamping of shots with coal dust be discontinued and that clay be used. . . ." Remember those criticisms, for they were made February 7, 1942, more than five years before the mine blew up as a result (at least in part) of those very malpractices.

Every three months throughout 1942, 1943, and 1944 Scanlan inspected the mine and repeated his recommendations, adding new ones: "That the mine be sufficiently rock dusted." And what became of his reports? He mailed them to the Department of Mines and Minerals at Springfield, the agency which supervises coal mines and miners. Springfield is dominated by the Statehouse, an ancient structure of spires and towers and balconies, of colonnades and domes; on its broad front steps Lincoln stands in stone. Inside all is gloom and shabby gilt. The Department of Mines and Minerals occupies three high-ceilinged rooms in a back corner of the second floor. The Director of the Department uses the small, comfortable, innermost office, its windows brushed by the leaves of trees on the Statehouse lawn, and here too the Mining Board meets. In theory, the Mining Board makes policy to implement the mining law, the Director executes its dictates; in practice, the Director possesses considerable discretionary power of his own.

In 1941 Governor Green appointed as Director Robert M. Medill, a genial, paunchy, red-faced man of about sixty-five. Medill had gone to work in a mine at sixteen; he rose rapidly in management. He had a talent for making money and he enjoyed spending it. He entered Republican politics in 1920, served a few years as director of the Department of Mines and Minerals, then returned to business (mostly managing mines) ; and then, after working for Green's election in 1940, was rewarded once more with the directorship. Green reappointed him in 1944 with, says Medill, the approval of "a multitude of bankers and business men all over the state. And miners. I had the endorsement of all four factions." By this he means the United Mine Workers and its smaller rival, the Progressive Mine Workers, and the two associations of big and little operators; to obtain the endorsement of all four of these jealous, power-seeking groups is no small feat. As Director, Medill received $6,000 a year (since raised to $8,000) plus expenses of $300 or $400 a month. He lived in a sizable country house at Lake Springfield, with spacious grounds and a tree-lined driveway.

To Medill's department, then, came Driscoll Scanlan's inspection reports on Centralia Mine No. 5. Medill, however, did not see the first thirteen reports (1942–44) ; they were handled as "routine" by Robert Weir, an unimaginative, harassed little man who had come up through the ranks of the miners' union and on recommendation of the union had been appointed Assistant Director of the Department by Green (at $4,000 a year, now $5,200). When the mail brought an inspector's report, it went first to Medill's secretary who shared the office next to Medill's with Weir. She stamped the report [with date of receipt] . . . and put it on Weir's desk. Sometimes, but by no means always, Weir read the report. He gave it to one of a half-dozen girl typists in the large outer office. She edited the inspector's recommendations for errors in grammar and spelling, and incorporated them into a form letter to the owner of the mine, closing:

"The Department endorses the recommendations made by Inspector Scanlan and requests that you comply with same.

"Will you please advise the Department upon the completion of the recommendations set forth above?

"Thanking you . . ."

When the typist placed this letter upon his desk, Weir signed it and it was mailed to the mine operator.

But the Centralia company did not comply with the major recommendations Scanlan made. In fact, it did not even bother to answer Weir's thirteen letters based on Scanlan's reports. And Weir did nothing about this. Once, early in the game, Weir considered the dusty condition of the mine so serious that he requested the company to correct it within ten days; but there is no evidence that the company even replied.

This continued for nearly three years. And during the same period the federal government entered the picture. In 1941 Congress authorized the U.S. Bureau of Mines to make periodic inspections of coal mines. But the federal government had no enforcement power whatever, the inspections served only research. The first federal inspection of Centralia Mine No. 5 was made in September of 1942. In general, the federal recommendations duplicated Scanlan's—rock dusting, improving ventilation, wetting the coal to reduce dust—and the federal inspectors noted that "coal dust . . . at this mine is highly explosive, and would readily propagate an explosion." In all, they made 106 recommendations, including 33 "major" ones (a government official has defined a "major" hazard as one that "could . . . result in a disaster"). Four months passed before a copy of this report filtered through the administrative machinery at Washington and reached the Illinois Department at Springfield, but this mattered little: the Department did nothing anyway. Subsequent federal reports in 1943 and 1944 showed that the "major" recommendations had not been complied with. The federal bureau lacked the power to force compliance; the Illinois Department possessed the power but failed to act.

What of the men working in the mine during these three years? On November 4, 1944, on instructions from Local 52 at Centralia, William Rowekamp, the recording secretary, composed a letter to Medill: "At the present the condition of those roadways are very dirty and dusty . . . they are getting dangerous. . . . But the Coal Co. has ignored [Scanlan's recommendations]. And we beg your prompt action on this matter."

The Department received this letter November 6, and four days later Weir sent Inspector Scanlan to investigate. Scanlan reported immediately:

"The haulage roads in this mine are awful dusty, and much dust is kept in suspension all day. . . . The miners have complained to me . . . and I have wrote it up pretty strong on my inspection reports. . . . But to date they have not done any adequate sprinkling. . . . Today . . . [Superintendent Norman] Prudent said he would fix the water tank and sprinkle the roads within a week, said that he would have had this work done sooner, but that they have 20 to 30 men absent each day." (This last is a claim by the company that its cleanup efforts were handicapped by a wartime manpower shortage. This is controversial. Men of fifty-nine—the average wartime age at the mine—do not feel like spending weekends removing coal dust or rock dusting, a disagreeable task; winter colds caused absenteeism and miners are always laying off anyway. On the other hand, the company was interested in production and profits: as Mine Manager Brown has said, "In the winter you can sell all the coal you can get out. So you want top production, you don't want to stop to rock dust.")

At any rate, Rowekamp's complaint got results. On December 2, 1944, he wrote Scanlan: "Well I am proud to tell you that they have sprinkled the 18th North Entry & 21st So. Entry and the main haulage road. . . . Myself and the Members of Local Union #52 appreciate it very much what you have done for us." It is apparent from this first direct move by Local 52 that Scanlan was working pretty closely with the Local to get something done.

But by the end of that month, December 1944, the mine once more had become so dirty that Scanlan ended his regular inspection report: ". . . if necessary the mine should discontinue hoisting coal for a few days until the [cleanup] work can be done." But all Weir said to the company was the routine "The Department endorses . . . ."

Early in 1945 it appeared that something might be accomplished. Scanlan, emerging from his regular inspection, took the unusual step of telephoning Medill at Springfield. Medill told him to write him a letter so Scanlan did:

"The haulage roads in this mine are in a terrible condition. If a person did not see it he would not believe. . . . Two months ago . . . the local officers [of Local Union 52] told me that . . . if [the mine manager] did not clean the mine up they were going to prefer charges against him before the mining board and have his certificate canceled. I talked them out of it and told them I thought we could get them to clean up the mine. But on this inspection I find that practically nothing has been done. . . . The mine should discontinue hoisting coal . . . until the mine is placed in a safe condition. . . . The coal dust in this mine is highly explosive. . . ."

This stiff letter was duly stamped "Received" at Springfield on February 23, 1945. A few days earlier a bad report had come in from Federal Inspector Perz. And now at last Medill himself entered the picture. What did he do? The Superintendent at Centralia had told Scanlan that, in order to clean up the mine, he would have to stop producing coal, a step he was not empowered to take. So Medill bypassed him, forwarding Scanlan's letter and report to William P. Young, Bell & Zoller's operating vice-president at Chicago: "Dear Bill. . . . Please let me have any comments you wish to make. . . . Very kindest personal regards." From his quiet, well-furnished office near the top of the Bell Building overlooking Michigan Avenue, Young replied immediately to "Dear Bob" [Medill]: "As you know we have been working under a very severe handicap for the past months. The war demand for coal . . . we are short of men. . . . I am hopeful that the urgent demand of coal will ease up in another month so that we may have available both the time and labor to give proper attention to the recommendations of Inspector Scanlan. With kindest personal regards. . . ."

A week later, on March 7, 1945, Medill forwarded copies of this correspondence to Scanlan, adding: "I also talked with Mr. Young on the phone, and I feel quite sure that he is ready and willing. . . . I would suggest that you ask the mine committee [of Local 52] to be patient a little longer, inasmuch as the coal is badly needed at this time."

The miners told Scanlan they'd wait till the first of April but no longer. On March 14 Medill was to attend a safety meeting in Belleville. Scanlan went there to discuss Centralia No. 5 with him. According to Scanlan, "When I went up to his room he was surrounded with coal operators . . . all having whiskey, drinking, having a good time, and I couldn't talk to him then, and we attended the safety meeting [then] went . . . down to Otis Miller's saloon, and I stayed in the background drinking a few cokes and waited until the crowd thinned out, and went back up to his hotel room with him. . . . It told him that the mine was in such condition that if the dust became ignited that it would sweep from one end of the mine to the other and probably kill every man in the mine, and his reply to me was, 'We will just have to take that chance.' " (Medill has denied these words but not the meeting.)

On the first of April the president of Local Union 52 asked Scanlan to attend the Local's meeting on April 4. The miners complained that the company had not cleaned up the mine and, further, that one of the face bosses, or foreman, had fired explosive charges while the entire shift of men was in the mine. There can be little doubt that to fire explosives on-shift in a mine so dusty was to invite trouble—in fact, this turned out to be what later caused the disaster—and now in April 1945 the union filed charges against Mine Manager Brown, asking the State Mining Board to revoke his certificate of competency (this would cost him his job and prevent his getting another in Illinois as a mine manager). Rowekamp wrote up the charges: ". . . And being the Mine is so dry and dusty it could of caused an explosion. . . ."

Weir went to Centralia on April 17, 1945, but only to investigate the charges against Brown, not to inquire into the condition of the mine. He told the miners they should have taken their charges to the state's attorney. Nearly a month passed before, on May 11, Weir wrote a memorandum to the Mining Board saying that the company's superintendent had admitted the shots had been fired on-shift but that this was done "in an emergency" and it wouldn't happen again; and the Board refused to revoke Manager Brown's certificate.

Meanwhile, on April 12 and 13, Scanlan had made his regular inspection and found conditions worse than in February. He told the Superintendent: "Now, Norman, you claim Chicago won't give you the time to shut your mine down and clean it up. Now, I am going to get you some time," and he gave him the choice of shutting the mine down completely or spending three days a week cleaning up. The Superintendent, he said, replied that he didn't know, he'd have to "contact Chicago," but Scanlan replied: "I can't possibly wait for you to contact Chicago. It is about time that you fellows who operate the mines get big enough to operate your mines without contacting Chicago." So on Scanlan's recommendation the mine produced coal only four days a week and spent the remaining days cleaning up. For a time Scanlan was well satisfied with the results, but by June 25 he was again reporting excessive dust and Federal Inspector Perz was concurring: "No means are used to allay the dust." Following his October inspection Scanlan once more was moved to write a letter to Medill; but the only result was another routine letter from Weir to the company, unanswered.

Now, one must understand that, to be effective, both rock dusting and cleanup work must be maintained continuously. They were not at Centralia No. 5. By December of 1945 matters again came to a head. Scanlan wrote to Medill, saying that Local 52 wanted a sprinkling system installed to wet the coal, that Mine Manager Brown had said he could not order so "unusual" an expenditure, and that Brown's superior, Superintendent Prudent, "would not talk to me about it, walked away and left me standing." And Local 52 again attempted to take matters into its own hands. At a special meeting on December 12 the membership voted to prefer charges against both Mine Manager Brown and Superintendent Prudent. Rowekamp's official charge, typed on stationery of the Local, was followed next day by a letter, written in longhand on two sheets of dime-store notepaper, and signed by 28 miners. . . . At Springfield this communication too was duly stamped "Received." And another Scanlan report arrived.

Confronted with so many documents, Medill called a meeting of the Mining Board on December 21. Moreover, he called Scanlan to Springfield and told him to go early to the Leland Hotel, the gathering place of Republican politicians, and see Ben H. Schull, a coal operator and one of the operators' two men on the Mining Board. In his hotel room, Schull (according to Scanlan) said he wanted to discuss privately Scanlan's report on Centralia No. 5, tried to persuade him to withdraw his recommendation of a sprinkling system, and, when Scanlan refused, told him "you can come before the board." But when the Mining Board met in Medill's inner office, Scanlan was not called before it though he waited all day, and after the meeting he was told that the Board was appointing a special commission to go to Centralia and investigate.

On this commission were Weir, two state inspectors, and two members of the Mining Board itself, Schull and Murrell Reak. Reak, a miner himself, repre-sented the United Mine Workers of America on the Mining Board. And Weir, too, owed his job to the UMWA but, oddly, he had worked for Bell & Zoller for twenty years before joining the Department, the last three as a boss, so his position was rather ambiguous. In fact, so unanimous were the rulings of the Mining Board that one cannot discern any management-labor cleavage at all but only what would be called in party politics bipartisan deals.

The commission had before it a letter from Superintendent Prudent and Manager Brown setting forth in detail the company's "absentee experience" and concluding with a veiled suggestion that the mine might be forced to close for good (once before, according to an inspector, the same company had abandoned a mine rather than go to the expense entailed in an inspector's safety recom-mendation). Weir wrote to Prudent, notifying him that the commission would visit Centralia on December 28 to investigate the charges against him and Brown; Medill wrote to the company's vice-president, Young, at Chicago ("You are being notified of this date so that you will have an opportunity to be present or designate some member of your staff to be present"); but Medill only told Rowekamp, "The committee has been appointed and after the investiga-tion you will be advised of their findings and the action of the board"—he did not tell the Local when the commission would visit Centralia nor offer it opportunity to prove its charges.

Rowekamp, a motorman, recalls how he first learned of the special commis-sion's visit. He was working in the mine and "Prudent told me to set out an empty and I did and they rode out." Prudent—remember, the commission was investigating charges against Prudent—led the commission through the mine. Rowekamp says, "They didn't see nothing. They didn't get back in the buggy runs where the dust was the worst; they stayed on the mainline." Even there they rode, they did not walk through the dust. Riding in a mine car, one must keep one's head down. In the washhouse that afternoon the men were angry. They waited a week or two, then wrote to Medill asking what had been done. On January 22, 1946, Medill replied: the Mining Board, adopting the views of the special commission, had found "insufficient evidence" to revoke the certificates of Prudent and Brown.

He did not elaborate. Next day, however, he sent to Scanlan a copy of the commission's report. It listed several important violations of the mining law: inadequate rock dusting, illegal practice in opening rooms, insufficient or improperly placed telephones, more than a hundred men working on a single split, or current, of air. In fact, the commission generally concurred with Scanlan, except that it did not emphasize dust nor recommend a sprinkling system. Thus in effect it overruled Scanlan on his sprinkling recommendation, a point to remember. It did find that the law was being violated yet it refused to revoke the certificates of the Superintendent and the Mine Manager, another point to remember. Weir has explained that the board felt that improvements requiring construction, such as splitting the airstream, would be made and that anyway "conditions there were no different than at most mines in the state." And this is a refrain that the company and the Department repeated in extenuation after the disaster. But actually could anything be more damning? The mine was no worse than most others; the mine blew up; therefore any might blow up!

The miners at Centralia were not satisfied. "It come up at the meeting," Rowekamp recalls. Local 52 met two Wednesday nights a month in its bare upstairs hall. The officers sat at a big heavy table up front; the members faced them, sitting on folding chairs which the Local had bought second-hand from an undertaker. Attendance was heavier now than usual, the men were aroused, some were even telling their wives that the mine was dangerous. They wanted to do something. But what? The state had rebuffed them. Well, why did they not go now to the higher officials of their own union, the UMWA? Why not to John L. Lewis himself?

One of them has said, "You have to go through the real procedure to get to the right man, you got to start at the bottom and start climbing up, you see? If we write to Lewis, he'll refer us right back to Spud White." Spud White is Hugh White, the thick-necked president of the UMWA in Illinois (District 12), appointed by Lewis. Now, Lewis had suspended District 12's right to elect its own officers during the bloody strife of the early 1930's, when the members, disgusted with what they called his "dictator" methods and complaining of secret payrolls, expulsions, missing funds, stolen ballots, and leaders who turned up on operators' payrolls, had rebelled; in the end the Progressive Mine Workers was formed and Lewis retained tight control of the UMWA. A decade later the Illinois officers of UMWA demanded that he restore their self-government, but Lewis managed to replace them with his own men, including

Spud White. By 1946 President White, a coal miner from the South, was consulting at high levels with Lewis, he was receiving $10,000 a year plus expenses (which usually equal salary), and he was maintaining a spacious home on a winding lane in the finest residential suburb of Springfield, a white house reached by a circular drive through weeping willows and evergreens.

Evidently the perplexed miners at Centralia already had appealed to District 12 for help, that is to White. Certainly Murrell Reak, the UMWA's man on the Mining Board and a close associate of White's, had asked Weir to furnish him with a copy of the findings of the special commission: "I want them so I may show the district UMWA. So they in turn may write Local Union down there, and show them that their charges are unfounded or rather not of a nature as to warrant the revocation of mine mgr. Certificate. . . ." Jack Ripon, the bulky vice-president of District 12 and White's right-hand man, said recently, "We heard there'd been complaints but we couldn't do a thing about it; it was up to the Mining Department to take care of it."

And yet in the past the UMWA has stepped in when the state failed to act. One unionist has said, "White could have closed that mine in twenty-four hours. All he'd have had to do was call up Medill and tell him he was going to pull every miner in the state if they didn't clean it up. It's the union's basic responsibility—if you don't protect your own wife and daughter, your neighbor down the street's not going to do it."

Perhaps the miners of Local 52 knew they must go it alone. They continued to address their official complaints to the State of Illinois. On February 26 Rowekamp wrote once more to Medill: "Dear Sir: At our regular meeting of Local Union 52. Motion made and second which carried for rec. secy. write you that the members of local union 52 are dissatisfied with the report of the special investigation commission. . . ." No answer. And so the members of Local 52 instructed Rowekamp to write to higher authority, to their Governor, Dwight H. Green.

It took him a long time. Elmer Moss kept asking if he'd finished it and Rowekamp recalls, "I'd tell him, Elmer, I can't do that fast, that's a serious letter, that'll take me a while." He wrote it out first in pencil and showed it to a couple of the boys and they thought it sounded fine. Then, sitting big and awkward at his cluttered little oak desk in the living room of his home outside town, he typed it, slowly and carefully—"anything important as that I take my time so I don't make mistakes, it looks too sloppified." He used the official stationery of the Local, bearing in one corner the device of the union—crossed shovels and picks—and in the other "Our Motto—Justice for One and All." He impressed upon it the official seal—"I can write a letter on my own hook but I dassn't use the seal without it's official"—and in the washhouse the Local officers signed it. Rowekamp made a special trip to the post office to mail it. It was a two-page letter saying, in part:

Dear Governor Green:

We, the officers of Local Union No. 52, U. M. W. of A., have been instructed by the members . . . to write a letter to you in protest against the negligence and unfair practices of your department of mines and minerals . . . we want you to know that this is not a protest against Mr. Driscoll Scanlan . . . the best inspector that ever came to our mine. . . . But your mining board will not let him enforce the law or take the necessary action to protect our lives and health. This protest is against the men above Mr. Scanlan in your department of mines and minerals. In fact, Governor Green this is a plea to you, to please save our lives, to please make the department of mines and minerals enforce the laws at the No. 5 mine of the Centralia Coal Co. . . . before we have a dust explosion at this mine like just happened in Kentucky and West Virginia. For the last couple of years the policy of the department of mines and minerals toward us has been one of ignoring us. [The letter then recited the story of the useless special commission.] We are writing you, Governor Green, because we believe you want to give the people an honest administration and that you do not know how unfair your mining department is toward the men in this mine. Several years ago after a distaster at Gillespie we seen your pictures in the papers going down in the mine to make a personal investigation of the accident. We are giving you a chance to correct the conditions at this time that may cause a much worse disaster. . . . We will appreciate an early personal reply from you, stating your position in regard to the above and the enforcement of the state mining laws.

The letter closed "Very respectfully yours" and was signed by Jake Schmidt, president; Rowekamp, recording secretary; and Thomas Bush and Elmer Moss, mine committee. Today, of these, only Rowekamp is alive; all the others were killed in the disaster they foretold.

And now let us trace the remarkable course of this letter at Springfield. It was stamped in red ink "Received March 9, 1946, Governor's Office." In his ornate thick-carpeted offices, Governor Green has three male secretaries (each of whom in turn has a secretary) and it was to one of these, John William Chapman, that the "save our lives" letter, as it came to be called, was routed. Two days later Chapman dictated a memorandum to Medill: ". . . it is my opinion that the Governor may be subjected to very severe criticism in the event that the facts complained of are true and that as a result of this condition some serious accident occurs at the mine. Will you kindly have this complaint carefully investigated so I can call the report of the investigation to the Governor's attention at the same time I show him this letter?" Chapman fastened this small yellow memo to the miners' letter and sent both to Medill. Although Medill's office is only about sixty yards from the Governor's, the message consumed two days in traversing the distance.

The messenger arrived at the Department of Mines and Minerals at 9:00 A.M. on March 13 and handed the "save our lives" letter and Chapman's memorandum to Medill's secretary. She duly stamped both "Received" and handed them to Medill. He and Weir discussed the matter, then Medill sent the original letter back to the Governor's office and dictated his reply to Chapman, blaming the war, recounting the activities of the special commission, saying: "The complaint sounds a good deal worse than it really is. The present condition at the mine is not any different than it has been during the past ten or fifteen years. . . . I would suggest the Governor advise Local Union No. 52, U. M. W. of A., that he is calling the matter to the attention of the State Mining Board with instructions that it be given full and complete consideration at their next meeting."

This apparently satisfied Chapman for, in the Governor's name, he dictated a letter to Rowekamp and Schmidt: "I [*i.e.*, Governor Green] am calling your letter to the attention of the Director of the Department of Mines and Minerals with the request that he see that your complaint is taken up at the next meeting of the State Mining Board. . . ." This was signed with Governor Green's name but it is probable that Green himself never saw the "save our lives" letter until after the disaster more than a year later. Nor is there any evidence that the Mining Board ever considered the letter. In fact, nothing further came of it.

One of the most remarkable aspects of the whole affair was this: An aggrieved party (the miners) accused a second party (Medill's department) of acting wrongfully, and the higher authority to which it addressed its grievance simply, in effect, asked the accused if he were guilty and, when he replied he was not, dropped the matter. A logic, the logic of the administrative mind, attaches to Chapman's sending the complaint to the Department—the administrative mind has a pigeonhole for everything, matters which relate to law go to the Attorney General, matters which relate to mines go to the Department of Mines and Minerals, and that is that—but it is scarcely a useful logic when one of the agencies is itself accused of malfunction. Apparently it did not occur to Chapman to consult Inspector Scanlan or to make any other independent investigation.

And Jack Ripon, Spud White's second-in-command at the District UMWA, said recently, "If I get a letter here I turn it over to the department that's supposed to take care of it, and the same with Governor Green—he got some damn bad publicity he shouldn't have had, he can't know everything that's going on." Ripon's sympathy with Green is understandable—he must have known how Green felt, for he and Spud White received a copy of the same letter. Ripon says, "Oh, we got a copy of it. But it wasn't none of ours, it didn't tell us to do anything. So our hands was tied. What'd we do with it? I think we gave it to Reak." Perhaps Murrell Reak, the UMWA's man on the Mining Board, felt he already had dealt with this matter (it was Reak who, to Scanlan's astonishment, had joined the other members of the special commission in upholding the Superintendent and Mine Manager in their violations of the law and then had been so anxious to help White convince the members of Local 52 "that their charges are unfounded"). At any rate, Reak apparently did not call the Board's attention to the "save our lives" letter, even though it was a local of his own union which felt itself aggrieved. And White took no action either.

As for Medill, on the day he received the letter he called Scanlan to Springfield and, says Scanlan, "severely reprimanded" him. According to Scanlan, Medill "ordered me to cut down the size of my inspection report," because Medill thought that such long reports might alarm the miners, "those damn hunks" who couldn't read English (Medill denied the phrase); but Scanlan took this order to mean that Medill wanted him to "go easy" on the operators— "it is the same thing as ordering you to pass up certain things." And one day during this long controversy, Medill buttonholed Scanlan's political sponsor in a corridor of the Statehouse and said he intended to fire Scanlan; Scanlan's sponsor refused to sanction it and but for this, Scanlan was convinced, he would surely have lost his job.

But now hundreds of miles away larger events were occurring which were to affect the fate of the miners at Centralia. In Washington, D.C., John L. Lewis and the nation's bituminous coal operators failed to reach an agreement and the miners struck, and on May 21, 1946, President Truman ordered the mines seized for government operation. Eight days later Lewis and Julius A. Krug, Secretary of the Interior, signed the famous Krug-Lewis Agreement. Despite strenuous protests by the operators, this agreement included a federal safety code. It was drawn up by the Bureau of Mines (a part of the U.S. Department of the Interior). And now for the first time in history the federal government could exercise police power over coal mine safety.

Thus far the efforts of the miners of Local 52 to thread the administrative maze in their own state had produced nothing but a snowfall of memoranda, reports, letters, and special findings. Let us now observe this new federal machinery in action. We shall learn nothing about how to prevent a disaster but we may learn a good deal about the administrative process.

"Government operation of the mines" meant simply that the operators bossed their own mines for their own profit as usual but the UMWA had a work contract with the government, not the operators. To keep the 2,500 mines running, Secretary Krug created a new agency, the Coal Mines Administration. CMA was staffed with only 245 persons, nearly all naval personnel ignorant of coal mining. Theirs was paper work. For technical advice they relied upon the Bureau of Mines plus a handful of outside experts. More than two months passed before the code was put into effect, on July 29, 1946, and not until November 4 did Federal Inspector Perz reach Centralia to make his first enforceable inspection of Centralia No. 5. Observe, now, the results.

After three days at the mine, Perz went home and wrote out a "preliminary report" on a mimeographed form, listing 13 "major violations" of the safety code. He mailed this to the regional office of the Bureau of Mines at Vincennes, Indiana. There it was corrected for grammar, spelling, etc., and typed; copies then were mailed out to the Superintendent of the mine (to be posted on the bulletin board), the CMA in Washington, the CMA's regional office at Chicago, the District 12 office of the UMWA at Springfield, the UMWA international headquarters at Washington, the Bureau of Mines in Washington, and the Illinois Department at Springfield. While all this was going on, Perz was at home, preparing his final report, a lengthy document listing 57 violations of the safety code, 21 of them major and 36 minor. This handwritten final report likewise went to the Bureau at Vincennes where it was corrected, typed, and forwarded to the Bureau's office in College Park, Maryland. Here the report was "reviewed," then sent to the Director of the Bureau at Washington. He made any changes he deemed necessary, approved it, and ordered it processed. Copies were then distributed to the same seven places that had received the preliminary report, except that the UMWA at Springfield received two copies so that it could forward one to Local 52. (All this was so complicated that the Bureau devised a "flow sheet" to keep track of the report's passage from hand to hand.)

We must not lose sight of the fact that in the end everybody involved was apprised of Perz's findings: that the Centralia Company was violating the safety code and that hazards resulted. The company, the state, and the union had known this all along and done nothing, but what action now did the new enforcing agency take, the CMA?

Naval Captain N. H. Collisson, the Coal Mines Administrator, said that the copy of the inspector's preliminary report was received at his office in Washington "by the head of the Production and Operations Department of my headquarters staff . . . Lieutenant Commander Stull. . . . Lieutenant Commander Stull would review such a report, discuss the matter with the Bureau of Mines as to the importance of the findings, and then . . . await the final report"—unless the preliminary report showed that "imminent danger" existed, in which case he would go immediately to Captain Collisson and, presumably, take "immediate action." And during all this activity in Washington, out in Chicago at the CMA's area office a Captain Yates also "would receive a copy of the report. His duty would be to acquaint himself with the findings there. If there was a red check mark indicating it fell within one of the three categories which I shall discuss later, he would detail a man immediately to the mine. If it indicated imminent danger . . . he would move immediately." The three categories deemed sufficiently important to be marked with "a red check mark" were all major hazards but the one which killed 111 men at Centralia No. 5 was not among them.

These, of course, were only CMA's first moves as it bestirred itself. But to encompass all its procedures is almost beyond the mind of man. Let us skip a few and see what actually resulted. The CMA in Washington received Perz's preliminary report November 14. Eleven days later it wrote to the company ordering it to correct one of the 13 major violations Perz found (why it said nothing about the others is not clear). On November 26 the CMA received Perz's final report and on November 29 it again wrote to the company, ordering it to correct promptly *all* violations and sending copies of the directive to the Bureau of Mines and the UMWA. Almost simultaneously it received from Superintendent Niermann a reply to its first order (Niermann had replaced Prudent, who had left the company's employ): "Dear Sir: In answer to your CMA8-gz of November 25, 1946, work has been started to correct the violation of article 5, section 3c, of the Federal Mine Safety Code, but has been discontinued, due to . . . a strike. . . ." This of course did not answer the CMA's second letter ordering correction of all 57 violations, nor was any answer forthcoming, but not until two months later, on January 29, 1947, did the CMA repeat its order and tell the company to report its progress by February 14.

This brought a reply from the company official who had been designated "operating manager" during the period of government operation, H. F. McDonald. McDonald, whose office was in Chicago, had risen to the presidency of the Centralia Coal Company and of the Bell & Zoller Coal Company through the sales department; after the Centralia disaster he told a reporter, "Hell, I don't know anything about a coal mine." Now he reported to CMA that "a substantial number of reported violations have been corrected and others are receiving our attention and should be corrected as materials and manpower become available." For obvious reasons, CMA considered this reply inadequate and on February 21 told McDonald to supply detailed information. Three days later McDonald replied ("Re file CMA81-swr"): He submitted a detailed report—he got it from Vice-President Young, who got it from the new General Superintendent, Walter J. Johnson—but McDonald told the CMA that this report was a couple of weeks old and he promised to furnish further details as soon as he could get them. The CMA on March 7 acknowledged this promise but before any other correspondence arrived to enrich file CMA81-swr, the mine blew up.

Now, the Krug-Lewis Agreement set up two methods of circumventing this cumbersome administrative machinery. If Inspector Perz had found what the legalese of the Agreement called "imminent danger," he could have ordered the men removed from the mine immediately (this power was weakened since it was also vested in the Coal Mines Administrator, the same division of authority that hobbled the state enforcers). But Perz did not report "imminent danger." And indeed how could he? The same hazardous conditions had obtained for perhaps twenty years and the mine hadn't blown up. The phrase is stultifying.

In addition, the Krug-Lewis Agreement provided for a safety committee of miners, selected by each local union and empowered to inspect the mine, to make safety recommendations to the management, and, again in case of "an immediate danger," to order the men out of the mine (subject to CMA review). But at Centralia No. 5 several months elapsed before Local 52 so much as appointed a safety committee, and even after the disaster the only surviving member of the committee didn't know what his powers were. The UMWA District officers at Springfield had failed to instruct their Locals in the rights which had been won for them. And confusion was compounded because two separate sets of safety rules were in use—the federal and the state—and in some instances one was the more stringent, in other instances, the other.

Meanwhile another faraway event laid another burden upon the men in the mine: John L. Lewis' combat with Secretary Krug. It ended, as everyone knows, in a federal injunction sought at President Truman's order and upheld by the U.S. Supreme Court, which forbade Lewis to order his miners to strike while the government was operating the mines. (Subsequently Lewis and the UMWA were fined heavily.) The members of Local 52 thought, correctly or not, that the injunction deprived them of their last weapon in their fight to get the mine cleaned up—a wildcat strike. A leader of Local 52 has said, "Sure we could've wildcatted it—and we'd have had the Supreme Court and the government and the whole public down on our necks."

The miners tried the state once more: Medill received a letter December 10, 1946, from an individual miner who charged that the company's mine examiner (a safety man) was not doing what the law required. Earlier Medill had ignored Scanlan's complaint about this but now he sent a department investigator, who reported that the charges were true and that Mine Manager Brown knew it, that Superintendent Niermann promised to consult Vice-President Young in Chicago, that other hazards existed, including dust. Weir wrote a routine letter and this time Niermann replied: The examiner would do his job properly. He said nothing about dust. This letter and one other about the same time, plus Young's earlier equivocal response to Medill's direct appeal, are the only company compliance letters on record.

There was yet time for the miners to make one more try. On February 24, 1947, the safety committee, composed of three miners, wrote a short letter to the Chicago area office of the Coal Mines Administration: "The biggest grievance is dust. . . ." It was written in longhand by Paul Compers (or so it is believed: Compers and one of the two other committee members were killed in the disaster a month later) and Compers handed it to Mine Manager Brown on February 27. But Brown did not forward it to the CMA; in fact he did nothing at all about it.

And now almost at the last moment, only six days before the mine blew up, some wholly new facts transpired. Throughout this whole history one thing has seemed inexplicable: the weakness of the pressure put on the company by Medill's Department of Mines and Minerals. On March 19, 1947, the St. Louis Post-Dispatch broke a story that seemed to throw some light upon it. An Illinois coal operator had been told by the state inspector who inspected his mine that Medill had instructed him to solicit money for the Republican Chicago mayoralty campaign. And soon more facts became known about this political shakedown.

Governor Dwight H. Green, a handsome, likeable politician, had first made his reputation as the young man who prosecuted Al Capone. By 1940 he looked like the white hope of Illinois Republicans. Campaigning for the governorship, Green promised to rid the state of the Democratic machine ("there will never be a Green machine"). He polled more votes in Illinois than Roosevelt; national Republican leaders began to watch him. Forthwith he set about building one of the most formidable machines in the nation. This task, together with the concomitant plans of Colonel Robert R. McCormick of the Chicago *Tribune* and others to make him President or Vice-President, has kept him occupied ever since. He has governed but little, permitting subordinates to run things. Reelected in 1944, he reached the peak of his power in 1946 when his machine succeeded in reducing the control of the Democratic machine over Chicago. Jubilant, Governor Green handpicked a ward leader to run for mayor in April of 1947 and backed him hard.

And it was only natural that Green's henchmen helped. Among these was Medill. "Somebody," says Medill, told him he was expected to raise "$15,000 or $20,000." On January 31, 1947, he called all his mine inspectors to the state mine rescue station in Springfield (at state expense), and told them—according to Inspector Scanlan who was present—that the money must be raised among the coal operators "and that he had called up four operators the previous day and two of them had already come through with a thousand dollars . . . and that he was going to contact the major companies, and we was to contact the independent companies and the small companies." Medill's version varied slightly: he said he told the inspectors that, as a Republican, he was interested in defeating the Democrats in Washington and Chicago, that if they found anybody of like mind it would be all right to tell them where to send their money, that all contributions must be voluntary.

After the meeting Scanlan felt like resigning but he thought perhaps Governor Green did not know about the plan and he recalled that once he had received a letter from Green (as did all state employees) asking his aid in giving the people an honest administration: Scanlan had replied to the Governor "that I had always been opposed to corrupt, grafting politicians and that I wasn't going to be one myself; and I received a nice acknowledgement . . . the Governor . . . told me that it was such letters as mine that gave him courage to carry on. . . ." Scanlan solicited no contributions from the coal operators.

But other inspectors did, and so did a party leader in Chicago. So did Medill: he says that his old friend David H. Devonald, operating vice-president of the huge Peabody Coal Company, gave him $1,000 and John E. Jones, a leading safety engineer, contributed $50 (Jones works for another of the Big Six operators and of him more later). No accounting ever has been made of the total collected. The shakedown did not last long. According to Medill, another of Governor Green's "close advisers" told Medill that the coal operators were complaining that he and his inspectors were putting pressure on them for donations and if so he'd better stop it. He did, at another conference of the inspectors on March 7.

Since no Illinois law forbids a company or an individual to contribute secretly to a political campaign we are dealing with a question of political morality, not legality. The Department of Mines and Minerals long has been a political agency. An inspector is a political appointee and during campaigns he is expected to contribute personally, tack up candidates' posters, and haul voters to the polls. Should he refuse, his local political boss would have him fired. (Soliciting money from the coal operators, however, apparently was something new for inspectors.) Today sympathetic Springfield politicians say: "Medill was just doing what every other department was doing and always has done, but he got a tough break." But one must point out that Medill's inspectors were charged with safeguarding lives, a more serious duty than that of most state employees, and that in order to perform this duty they had to police the coal operators, and that it was from these very operators that Medill suggested they might obtain money. A United States Senator who investigated the affair termed it "reprehensible."

What bearing, now, did this have on the Centralia disaster? Nobody, probably, collected from the Centralia Coal Company. But the shakedown is one more proof—stronger than most—that Governor Green's department had reason to stay on friendly terms with the coal operators when, as their policeman, it should have been aloof. As a miner at Centralia said recently: "If a coal company gives you a thousand dollars, they're gonna expect something in return."

Here lies Green's responsibility—not that, through a secretary's fumble, he failed to act on the miners' appeal to "save our lives" but rather that, while the kingmakers were shunting him around the nation making speeches, back home his loyal followers were busier building a rich political machine for him than in administering the state for him. Moreover, enriching the Green machine dovetailed nicely with the personal ambitions of Medill and others, and Green did not restrain them. By getting along with his old friends, the wealthy operators, Medill enhanced his personal standing. Evidence exists that Bell & Zoller had had a hand in getting him appointed Director, and remember, Weir had worked as a Bell & Zoller boss. By nature Medill was no zealous enforcer of laws. As for the inspectors, few of them went out of their way to look for trouble; some inspectors after leaving the Department have obtained good jobs as coal company executives. Anyway, as one inspector has said, "If you tried to ride 'em, they'd laugh at you and say, 'Go ahead, I'll just call up Springfield.' " As one man has said, "It was a cozy combination that worked for everybody's benefit, everybody except the miners." And the miners' man on the Board, Murrell Reak of the UMWA, did not oppose the combination. Nor did Green question it.

As the Chicago campaign ground to a close, down at Centralia on March 18 Federal Inspector Perz was making another routine inspection. General Superintendent Johnson told him the company had ordered pipe for a sprinkler system months earlier but it hadn't arrived, "that there would be a large expenditure involved there . . . they had no definite arrangements just yet . . . but he would take it up with the higher officials of the company" in Chicago. Scanlan and Superintendent Niermann were there too; they stayed in the bare little mine office, with its rickety furniture and torn window shades, till 7:30 that night. No rock dusting had been done for nearly a year but now the company had a carload of rock dust underground and Scanlan got the impression it would be applied over the next weekend. (It wasn't.) Perz, too, thought Johnson "very conscientious . . . very competent." Scanlan typed out his report—he had resorted wearily to listing a few major recommendations and adding that previous recommendations "should be complied with"—and mailed it to Springfield. Perz went home and wrote out his own report, acknowledging that 17 hazards had been corrected but making 52 recommendations most of which he had made in November (the company and the CMA were still corresponding over that November report). Perz finished writing on Saturday morning and mailed the report to the Vincennes office, which presumably began processing it Monday.

The wheels had been turning at Springfield, too, and on Tuesday, March 25, Weir signed a form letter to Brown setting forth Scanlan's latest recommendations: "The Department endorses. . . ." But that day, at 3:26 P.M., before the outgoing-mail box in the Department was emptied, Centralia Mine No. 5 blew up. . . .

The last of the bodies was recovered at 5:30 A.M. on the fifth day after the explosion. On "Black Monday" the flag on the new city hall flew at half staff and all the businesses in town closed. Already the funerals had begun, 111 of them. John L. Lewis cried that the 111 were "murdered by the criminal negligence" of Secretary Krug and declared a national six-day "mourning period" during this Holy Week, and though some said he was only achieving by subterfuge what the courts had forbidden him—a strike and defiance of Krug—nonetheless he made the point that in the entire nation only two soft coal mines had been complying completely with the safety code; and so Krug closed the mines.

Six separate investigations began, two to determine what had happened, and four to find out why. Federal and state experts agreed, in general, that the ignition probably had occurred at the extreme end, or face, of the First West Entry, that it was strictly a coal-dust explosion, that the dust probably was ignited by an explosive charge which had been tamped and fired in a dangerous manner—fired by an open-flame fuse, tamped with coal dust—and that the resulting local explosion was propagated by coal dust throughout four working sections of the mine, subsiding when it reached rock-dusted areas. . . .

And what resulted from all the investigations into the Centralia disaster? The Washington County Grand Jury returned no-bills—that is, refused to indict Inspector Scanlan and five company officials ranging upward in authority through Brown, Niermann, Johnson, Young, and McDonald. The Grand Jury did indict the Centralia Coal Company, as a corporation, on two counts of "wilful neglect" to comply with the mining law—failing to rock dust and working more than 100 men on a single split of air—and it also indicted Medill and Weir for "palpable omission of duty." The company pleaded *nolo contendere*—it did not wish to dispute the charge—and was fined the maximum: $500 on each count, a total of $1,000 (or less than $10 per miner's life lost). The law also provides a jail sentence of up to six months but of course you can't put a corporation in jail.

At this writing the indictments against Medill and Weir are still pending, and amid interesting circumstances. Bail for Medill was provided by Charles E. Jones, John W. Spence, G. C. Curtis, and H. B. Thompson; and all of these men, oddly enough, are connected with the oil and gas division of the Department from which Medill was fired. And one of them is also one of Medill's defense attorneys. But this is not all. Medill and Weir filed a petition for a change of venue, supported by numerous affidavits of Washington County residents that prejudice existed. These affidavits were collected by three inspectors for the oil and gas division. They succeeded in getting the trial transferred to Wayne County, which is dominated by a segment of Governor Green's political organization led locally by one of these men, Spence. Not in recent memory in Illinois has the conviction of a Department head on a similar charge been sustained, and there is little reason to suppose that Medill or Weir will be convicted. Medill performed an act of great political loyalty when he shouldered most of the blame at Centralia, in effect stopping the investigation before it reached others above him, and this may be his reward.

Why did nobody close the Centralia mine before it exploded? A difficult question. Medill's position (and some investigators') was that Inspector Scanlan could have closed it. And, legally, this is true: The mining law expressly provided that an inspector could close a mine which persisted in violating the law. But inspectors have done so very rarely, only in exceptional circumstances, and almost always in consultation with the Department. Scanlan felt that had he closed the Centralia mine Medill simply would have fired him and appointed a more tractable inspector. Moreover, the power to close was not his exclusively: it also belonged to the Mining Board. (And is not this divided authority one of the chief factors that produced the disaster?) Robert Weir has said, "We honestly didn't think the mine was dangerous enough to close." This seems fantastic, yet one must credit it. For if Scanlan really had thought so, surely he would have closed it, even though a more pliable inspector reopened it. So would the federal authorities, Medill, or the company itself. And surely the miners would not have gone to work in it.

Governor Green's own fact-finding committee laid blame for the disaster upon the Department, Scanlan, and the company. The Democrats in the Illinois joint legislative committee submitted a minority report blaming the company, Medill, Weir, and Green's administration for "the industrial and political crime. . . ."; the Republican majority confessed itself unable to fix blame. After a tremendous pulling and hauling by every special interest, some new state legislation was passed as a result of the accident, but nothing to put teeth into the laws: violations still are misdemeanors (except campaign solicitation by inspectors, a felony) ; it is scarcely a serious blow to a million-dollar corporation to be fined $1,000. Nor does the law yet charge specific officers of the companies—

rather than the abstract corporations—with legal responsibility, so it is still easy for a company official to hide behind a nebulous chain of command reaching up to the stratosphere of corporate finance in Chicago or St. Louis. It is hard to believe that compliance with any law can be enforced unless violators can be jailed.

As for the Congress of the United States, it did next to nothing. The Senate subcommittee recommended that Congress raise safety standards and give the federal government power to enforce that standard—"Immediate and affirmative action is imperative." But Congress only ordered the Bureau of Mines to report next session on whether mine operators were complying voluntarily with federal inspectors' recommendations. . . .

After the Centralia disaster each man responsible had his private hell, and to escape it each found his private scapegoat—the wartime manpower shortage, the material shortage, another official, the miners, or, in the most pitiable cases, "human frailty." Surely a strange destiny took Dwight Green from a federal courtroom where, a young crusader, he overthrew Capone to a hotel in Centralia where, fifteen years older, he came face to face with William Rowekamp, who wanted to know why Green had done nothing about the miners' plea to "save our lives." But actually responsibility here transcends individuals. The miners at Centralia, seeking somebody who would heed their conviction that their lives were in danger, found themselves confronted with officialdom, a huge organism scarcely mortal. The State Inspector, the Federal Inspector, the State Board, the Federal CMA, the company officials—all these forever invoked "higher authority," they forever passed from hand to hand a stream of memoranda and letters, decisions and laws and rulings, and they lost their own identities. As one strives to fix responsibility for the disaster, again and again one is confronted, as were the miners, not with any individual but with a host of individuals fused into a vast, unapproachable, insensate organism. Perhaps this immovable juggernaut is the true villain in the piece. Certainly all those in authority were too remote from the persons whose lives they controlled. And this is only to confess once more that in making our society complex we have made it unmanageable.

———

The two following selections present what might be called a "philosophy of administration." Despite some obvious differences in approach the two authors give similar answers to a common problem. The problem is: How are our individual and collective lives to be given meaning and direction in the middle of the twentieth century? The authors unite in a belief that *administration*, broadly conceived, can help us both to define our goals clearly and to realize them fully.

The essence of the matter is that the defining of our ends and the devising of means of achieving them must take place under conditions new in the experience of the human race. A myriad of interrelated factors, but chiefly the development of modern science and technology, have created a new "condition of man." Never before the twentieth century has man existed in numbers approaching the present figure of two and a third billions. Never before in his history has man's method of living—economic, social, political, cultural—been so complex, so swiftly changing. The small, tradition-bound societies of history and prehistory are now replaced by the world-wide, dynamic Great Society.

Devised in the "last five minutes" of man's experience on earth, there is no a priori reason why this Great Society should be permanent. It may be consumed in the fires of war or simply fall apart from lack of wit and determination to maintain it. Even if it continues to exist, there is in turn no a priori reason why it must be "good." If not properly managed, it may accentuate traditional human ills and add some new ones.

How to maintain the Great Society and how to transform it into a Good Society? Both authors feel that administration is the answer—or a large part of the answer—to this question. Administration is thus broadly conceived; it is man rising above the blind and aimless forces of his physical and social environment and imposing upon these forces a meaningful pattern.

This point of view is not—to say the least of it—to be accepted uncritically. But these essays are good statements of the "faith of the administrator." They challenge those who respond sympathetically to high achievement. They challenge those who respond negatively to find a better answer. Query, is the position taken by the authors ethically acceptable? Is it realistic?

The first essay, on administration as a fine art, is by Ordway Tead. Mr. Tead is a man of varied and outstanding achievement in private and public affairs who has also found time to pen a number of useful books in the fields of psychology, education, and administration. The themes which Mr. Tead has emphasized in his writings on administration are *democracy* and *leadership;* these two principles, he believes, can be successfully synthesized—indeed must be if the Good Life is to be realized. Query, is there an element of incompatibility between democracy and leadership which no formula can eliminate?

This essay is the first chapter in Mr. Tead's most recent book, *The Art of Administration*. It is addressed primarily to private rather than to public administrators, but the truth or falsity of Mr. Tead's theses presumably would not be affected seriously if the emphasis were reversed.

Administration—a Fine Art *

ORDWAY TEAD

Fly over New York City imaginatively in an airplane, and remove the roofs from successive buildings in your mind's eye. What do you see? You see people, tens of thousands of them, at work. You see top executives in quiet offices thinking, planning, conferring, issuing orders which affect people in distant localities where their companies have plants. You see boards of directors hearing reports and adopting policies which may mean more or less employment in Akron, Detroit, Pittsburgh. You see department store heads in conference with merchandise managers. You see office managers in insurance companies, banks, investment houses, wholesaling firms, facilitating the labors of many. You see huge hospitals in which doctors, nurses and auxiliary staffs are working to restore health. You see universities, colleges and schools in which administrators and teachers are providing education. You see governmental bureaus—Federal, state and municipal—in all of which some phase of the public welfare is being served.

Everywhere there are people managing and there are people being managed. This is taking place in organizations, large or small, and for all kinds of purposes.

If you start your day in a restaurant, the employees of an organization serve you. Transportation to your office by subway, bus or trolley, is provided by highly organized resources. If you go to an evening movie or play, or listen to the radio, an elaborate organization is ministering to you.

We in America live and move and have our being—a vast segment of us—in, and through, and with, the benefit of organizations of people. For New York City is only a larger sample of scores of other places where if we raised the roof we would see the same thing.

Relatively, this is a new situation, both in the number and in the size of the organizations in operation. Anything like this was unknown two hundred years ago. And if, historically, we wanted to look at human associations which brought large numbers of people into action together, we would have to observe military bodies or the church, although armies were only sporadically assembled and the clerical officers of the church were geographically scattered. Nevertheless, this historic experience is not without helpful lessons for us, many of which have already been incorporated into the body of accepted knowledge and practice we employ in other kinds of agencies.

There is a common factor running through the activities of all organizations. . . . This common factor is that people are closely associated together under direction to accomplish certain stipulated purposes. There are administrators, managers, lesser executives, and there are those who are managed. Those who

* By permission from *The Art of Administration*, by Ordway Tead. Copyright, 1951, McGraw-Hill Book Company, Inc.

are managed are related to a position or job, to a group of similarly occupied workers, to an immediate supervisor, and to the organization as a whole.

At first blush it might seem that this is so usual and prevalent that it hardly needs to be a matter of remark or concern. But my primary assumption is that the human relationships involved in all these organized dealings do not spontaneously result in harmonious or productive outcomes. People do not naturally and eagerly work shoulder to shoulder or as between one group and another in happy ways. There are frictions and strains; there are misunderstandings; there is indifference to productive results; there is an actual sense of conflict among individuals and groups. There is cooperation of sorts, or no productive outcomes would result; but it is often what someone has aptly described as "antagonistic cooperation."

Indeed, as compared with the previous modes of human activity—in hunting, pastoral, agricultural, or handicraft societies—the present physical intensification of human relations and their pervasive actuality throughout the waking life of people have created an intensely artificial situation and problem. This in itself puts a tax upon the adjustive powers of persons which is essentially a new demand on human nature. To assume that these new kinds of confining and continuing relations can carry on without benefit of thought and planning for good and productive results would surely be an astonishing hope. It is a hope contrary to the facts.

In addition to the personal adjustments required, there are the divergent or conflicting group relations which arise and which have to be taken into account. We are made dramatically aware of these on the occasion of strikes, lockouts, publicized limitations on output, "feather-bedding" or other forms of "spreading the work." All who know associated action at first hand will agree that high corporate morale is not universal, that eager and informed cooperation is not typical, that corporate loyalty and "partnership" are more talked of than attained. . . .

. . . Administration is the comprehensive effort to direct, guide and integrate associated human strivings which are focused toward some specific ends or aims. . . . Administration is conceived as *the necessary activities of those individuals (executives) in an organization who are charged with ordering, forwarding and facilitating the associated efforts of a group of individuals brought together to realize certain defined purposes.* . . .

A common need in all organizations is that these appropriate activities of administration be analyzed, be understood and be applied. Our understanding of a general body of principles which would warrant the name of a science is still less than adequate. . . . However, . . . there may be a common body of attitudes, approaches, and methods of attack which can be useful, if not, indeed, essential, in many kinds of organizations and situations.

Application of these points of view to specific situations surely comprises an *art* requiring great skill, discernment and moral fortitude. Indeed, so pervasive in influence, so valuable, so adroitly constituted is this skill that it deserves to be recognized as a *fine art*. If work with paints or clay, with combinations of sounds in music, with combinations of words and ideas in literature—if these are fine arts, we are certainly entitled to call that labor also a fine art which would bring closer together in purpose the organized relationships of individuals and groups to each other. It is, indeed, an art of the highest order to be able to bring about the most fruitful possible collaboration in a world where associated effort is the typical expression of individuals who seek to be productively alive. And this art becomes in all good sense a social undertaking of fundamental public importance.

Moreover, if an important attribute of a fine art is to enhance insight into new areas of reality to which human feelings respond with a direct satisfaction, then administrative effort can result in creating associated human relationships which without question exemplify a fine art. An art, as Whitehead somewhere says, "exhibits for consciousness a finite fragment of human effort achieving its own perfection within its own limits."

Administration at its best exhibits a finite fragment of human creativity striving toward its own kind of perfection in good associated performance and achievement.

But administration at its worst can be a grave social liability. For it can be humdrum, routine, impersonal and domineering; and when it is thus corrupted it becomes ugly and soul-destroying. It can, indeed, so change its aspect by willful, arrogant and arbitrary behavior as to become dangerously antisocial in its fruits.

This is what was in the mind of a discerning social observer when he wrote:

"Never has the general scheme of existence weighed more heavily upon men, reducing them—by means of time-tables, by all kinds of physical impacts upon their senses, by the demand for speed, by compulsory imitation, by the abuse of mass production, and so on—to the level of being mere products of a certain organization which aims at rendering them as similar as possible even in their very tastes and amusements. We are the slaves of a machine whose interference does not stop increasing, thanks to the means we create of impinging more and more widely on the common environment of life. The devotee of speed obstructs the devotee of speed, and it is the same with the devotees of the ether waves; devotees of the beaches and mountains. If we add to these constraints, which arise from interference with our pleasures, those which the modern disciplines of labour impose on the majority, we will find that dictatorship merely completes the system of pressures and bonds of which modern men, in those countries which are politically most free, are the more or less conscious victims."

This characterization of society's condition puts into words some of the dangers here under scrutiny. And if the "general scheme of existence" is to weigh less heavily, if modern men in politically free societies are not to be "victims," if the disciplines which labor imposes on the majority are not to be soul-destroying, good administration will have to bear a considerable share of the burden of the corrective effort. It will have to be practiced on a wide scale, with a considered philosophy, and with consummate art. . . .

. . . Let it be recalled that an art requires a *medium* for its expression. And in the case of administration the medium seems to be threefold. Its full expression takes place in and through *organization, human beings,* and a certain kind of wide social and cultural setting, which for us in America is a *democratic society.* . . .

Administration is, in short, a fine art because it summons an imposing body of special talents on behalf of a collaborative creation which is integral to the conduct of civilized living today. This creation is comprised of the ongoing operation of numerous organizations through which human individuals are hopefully gaining many of their necessary and rightful satisfactions.

Finally, since the wisest artist would be in command both of general principles and of ways of applying them, some combination of these two approaches is necessary to supply the foundation for a mastery of the art of administration.

———◆———

The following selection is abridged from an essay on "American Society and Public Administration" by Professor John M. Gaus, a leading contemporary student of administration. Better than any other writer on public administration Professor Gaus has woven the theories and techniques of administration together with the trends and problems of twentieth-century America. Owing in large measure to his influence, there is presently a trend to study administration in relation to its setting, its "ecology."

In this selection the emphasis is upon public rather than private administration, and the role of public administration is construed in relation to particular American problems. Written in the thirties in the midst of the Great Depression, the essay bears some of the distinguishing marks of the day. But though the contours of particular problems may have changed, the emphasis of the essay is upon change itself as the clue to the role of public administration: good administration facilitates change but cushions its effect; permits—even encourages—change in society, but protects meanwhile "the individual's sense of security, and his sense of purpose."

Query, what different emphases might Professor Gaus have, what new trends or problems might he address himself to, if he were applying his theme of "controlled change through administration" to America in the fifties?

American Society and Public Administration *

JOHN M. GAUS

What comes first . . . in our . . . search for the true basis of public administration in American society? It is an examination, necessarily brief, of change and its incidental consequences—change, so to speak, in the abstract. The direct consequences of any given and specific change do not concern us here. The development of the bicycle, and later of the automobile, are direct causes, for example, of the wide adoption of hard-surfaced roads. But the point is that such changes in general, in the unpremeditated, seldom predicted, and subtle influence which they have upon the tastes and resulting daily life of individuals, strike at two vital points: the individual's sense of security, and his sense of purpose.

An idea of the indirect consequences of change is basic to an understanding of the United States. As J. F. Jameson remarks:

"The movement of westward expansion . . . is one of the most familiar facts of American history. But perhaps we do not always remember how peculiar it is, nor take notice of all its consequences. Is there any other great country whose center of population moves over the country many miles each decade, as does ours, which in a hundred and thirty years moved westward from the Chesapeake to Illinois? But what are the social results? A nation's center of population is, in a way, its center of gravity. A shifting center of gravity forces a nation into perpetual readjustment of its life. That which was the center of the merchant's particular branch of business ten years ago is no longer its center now; the farmer, the commercial traveller, the engineer, the speculator, must learn anew, every ten years, the social geography of his country. Restless change, increasing adaptation to new conditions, will be the characteristic of such a nation."

But this will not be the only characteristic, nor is the westward movement of population the only major factor illustrating and comprising change in American society. At least, these others deserve mention as of equal importance: the changing cultural mixtures due to immigration from so many nations; the rise of great urban centers and their repercussion on rural life; the great mobility of life within a locality, within the United States, and from employment to employment.

The clash of cultures in this country which immigration from so many nations has produced is familiar. It was noted in the Colonial period, when there was worry over the influx, for example, of the Germans; in the middle of the last

* From *The Frontiers of Public Administration* (Chicago: 1936), essays by John M. Gaus, Leonard D. White, and Marshall E. Dimock. Abridged. Reprinted by permission of the University of Chicago Press.

century, when a strong political movement arose in protest against the new Irish immigration; and in the more recent decades, when we had first the Americanization movement, and then the movement which resulted in the immigration-restriction laws. We cannot estimate the cost, concealed in many ways, of what these attitudes have been and continue to be to the national life. But one of the most serious results has been the wiping out, for millions of people, of the support and protection given by a culture which their parents brought from the Old Country before any adequate provision of the culture of the new country had been made. This is not to despise or neglect the existence and development of a new culture in this country. Indeed, many critics of what was conceived to be Puritanism, the Old South, the Frontier, or the way of life of substantial middle-class business families in the United States in the past century, for example, reveal a costly ignorance of these matters, and exercise a wholly evil influence. We need very much to discover, reveal, and develop our "usable past" for the enhancement of our own future, despite the dangers thus offered of an ossified conception of it present in the travesties associated with some "patriotic" societies. But deliberately to create both contempt for an Old World culture and to frustrate the reception of newcomers into that which is native to this land is to court—and win —disasters long noted by social workers in our great cities.

Not only is such an absence of a supporting cultural medium responsible for individual maladjustments, but it also is a cause of degradation of political life. The cultural group whose Old World traits are despised, but whose members have had no initiation into a wholesome American tradition, turn to the kind of racial leader whose chief appeal is the prostitution of racial or national pride, and whose chief activity is the use of his power for private gain.

But the disruption of the neighborhood, the ebb and flow of population from country to city and back again, from one industry or job to another, is also costly. The hillbilly who comes to Detroit to work in the automobile plants at wages beyond his reach at home, who is cast off in slack times to wander back to the hills to live off the relatives; the country boys and girls who dwell in the vast impersonal lodging-house districts of our great cities; the crowds of unskilled or semi-skilled workers who now have a brief job in a city factory and now turn back to the submarginal farms exhausted by the tenancy of submarginal farmers— these only casually and by accident come to participate easily and naturally in anything that can be called a community life. The history of the settlement movement in this country supplies eloquent testimony of the need for some network of institutions to replace, for the time being, those aids to the individual and family in critical moments of their lives which were supplied as a matter of fact in the old self-contained stable neighborhood of the countryside or town. Sickness, death, accident, unemployment, the terrors of the unknown when among strangers in faith, custom, and language—all destroy security and the sense of purposefulness in life.

The destruction of neighborhood stability and all that it implies both reflects and is caused by the dependence upon a sensitive interdependent economic system in which far-flung ties of communication, extreme division of labor, large-scale organization of financing, and a complex price system play their parts. Nor are the prices equally flexible; some stick, others give. To manipulate the system, increasing proportions of paper-workers are required, situated at increasing distances from the source of ultimate wealth production in mine, field, forest, and shop. The objective becomes blurred, the place of the individual part in the organism obscured. The counters in the game—money and credit—seem to behave, too, in terms of other disturbing factors incidental to their own genius.

This problem of insecurity has been well stated by a student of urbanization, Arthur Pollard, as follows:

"The man who does not live on a farm must in general have money every day to live, while the man on a farm can go for days and sometimes weeks without money. In the past he has needed money only for a very few days in the year. Back in 1800 only 15 per cent of the population did not live on farms. The great majority then did not need to save much money in the form of cash or liquid credits, but saved it rather in the form of land and equipment. To-day 77 per cent do not live on farms. The only security that this city population can have must be provided largely in the form of cash or liquid credits. The difference is enormous, and it has a bearing on our social and financial organization that has scarcely been appreciated, and certainly has received far too little attention. . . . How to provide real security for an urban population such as ours is probably the most difficult problem that civilization faces."

Social instability and insecurity are by no means confined to the cities. With increasing specialization in agriculture the farmer has become more directly influenced—through the markets, the banks, transport, and communication—economically and culturally by the forces affecting the city dweller than formerly. As his soils become exhausted from a process of "mining" the fertility, as his fixed charges continue despite the fluctuations of prices and the value of money, aids from the larger political units have to be pumped into the rural areas to maintain roads and schools; proposals are advanced for zoning land to prevent further agricultural use of areas less fitted for agriculture, to encourage the growing of forest crops, and to develop recreational uses. With the shrinking of markets overseas, with shifts in consumer tastes and declines in urban purchasing power, an emergency program to enable commodity growers to adapt their output to available markets is devised. We have hitherto thought that the problems of government and control in our industrial and urban world were of great importance and complexity; but the administrative aspects of the new rural policies now rival them in the challenge to foresight, accurate analysis, comprehensiveness, and administrative capacities generally. . . .

Thus both in city and in country the only hope which the individual can have today for securing some stable basis from which to survey his world and set about making something of his capacities is that he can, with his fellows, organize institutions through which the arbitrary forces which affect him may be in some degree mitigated or controlled.

Change, resulting in the kind of obvious and surface insecurity mentioned above, has deeper consequences. It forces itself upon the attention of the psychologist and psychiatrist. They have had to search beyond the individual to isolate the causes of his maladjustments. Thus Elton Mayo has traced, in his studies of employees of a Chicago factory, their problems into the city neighborhoods in which these workers reside, and has drawn upon analyses of these neighborhoods made by sociologists. He finds the primary social disruptions of family and neighborhood life of basic importance in the problems that arise in working life in the factory. He concludes:

"Just as our political and economic studies have for two hundred years tended to take account only of the economic functions involved in living, so also in our actual living we have inadvertently allowed pursuit of economic development to lead us into a condition of extensive social disintegration. . . . One suspects that the Chicago researches are significant not only for criminal and suicide inquiry, but significant for students of industrial relations, of psychoneurosis and of education."

This truth was strongly stressed at least fifty years ago by the settlement pioneers in the United States such as Jane Addams, Robert A. Woods, and others. Mayo continues:

"The imposition of highly systematized industrial procedures upon all the civilized cultures has brought to relative annihilation the cultural traditions of work and craftsmanship. Simultaneously the development of a high labor mobility and a clash of cultures has seriously damaged the traditional routine of intimate and family life in the United States. Generally the effect has been to induce everywhere a considerable degree of social disorganization; the comfortable non-logic of every social code has been reduced, at least in part, to irrational exasperation—without any prospect of development towards a better understanding for the average citizen."

Frankwood Williams, diagnosing the ills of the college youth, records also the devastating effect upon the individual student of the social forces, reflected in the home, which Mayo has found to be so influential also in the factory. After describing conversations with students whose parents had become alarmed at their waste of the college years, he remarks:

"But what underlay all these things, as one sees it now, and what I believe is more important now for the youth of the country generally than the immediate difficulties due to the 'depression,' and accountable not only for the symptomatic behavior mentioned here, but for the deep cynicism that seems to pervade both the universities and the secondary schools, is that youth, full of energy and ideal-ism, finds no purpose (except as he may have a personal ambition which repre-sents the working out of a conflict within him) to which he can tie, and lacks, therefore, motivating power. He finds no purpose to take over from us. Insofar as he finds a purpose in us at all, he finds it without sense. The very lives of his parents are evidence of the senselessness of their purposes."

Change which we have found to be so characteristic of American life, change that has disrupted neighborhoods, that has destroyed cultural stabilities, that has reflected a sweep across the continent, the restless migration to city and back to farm, from one job to another, has brought its widely hailed merits. Its merits have been of so spectacular a nature, indeed, that we speak of it as progress. Striking individuals emerge. Vast works are accomplished. Excitement and stimu-lus are in the atmosphere. All things are possible to some men. Its costs are also becoming clearer, registered in the great dramatic collapses of the depression, more subtly in the defeat, disintegration, and frustration of individuals, the sense of void where once, in the conquering of a continent, there was purpose. The very challenge of the continent is reflected in Emerson and Whitman. Can it be recaptured?

We seem to have wandered far from the topic of public administration. Yet my thesis is that through public instruments some new institutional basis which will enable the individual to find development and satisfaction can be created, and some sense of purpose may again flower. In the total drift of social institu-tions during a century, indeed, a new institutional pattern can be discerned, and watchful eyes already make it out. As Gardiner Means says:

"Economic developments during the past hundred years have played an out-rageous trick on the economic fraternity. Gradually but steadily great segments in the organization of economic activity have been shifted from the market place to administration. . . . In 1929 approximately 49 per cent of all corporate wealth —excluding the duplication of financial corporations—was controlled by two hundred corporations. The controls of nearly half of industrial activity had be-come an administrative matter for two hundred great administrative units. . . . This shift from organization through the market place to organization by admin-istrative action has gone so far that the market place appears to have become rather a disorganizing than an organizing influence. . . . Either we must make the market place a satisfactory coordinator or supplement the market place by other coordinating devices."

In the efforts to find some new sense of control, of opportunity for the indi-vidual to assert some influence on the situation in which he finds himself, the individual has associated his efforts with others in like predicament. As investor, he has pressed for collective instruments wherewith he may offset his incapacity alone in dealing with banking, insurance, credit, and the issuance and exchange of securities. As worker, he has devised public and collective instruments for bargaining or regulations concerning hours, wages, and other factors; he has similarly grappled with problems of industrial accident and disease, and unemployment. As consumer, he secures agents wherewith to investigate the quality of his milk supply. As resident and citizen, he has established collective services such as paved roads that are cheaper than he could supply individually, or that could otherwise not be provided at all yet are essential for life in crowded urban centers, such as water supply, sewage and waste disposal, or fire prevention. He presses for new services as their value to him in preserving or enhancing his way of life is demonstrated; thus he attempts to preserve the amenities of his home by zoning land, by parks, and by traffic controls. His wife is told that her place is in the home. She agrees. But she points out that the functions thus assigned her have moved from the farmhouse of 1800 to the playground, nursery school, food industry, movie, and many other places today; that she must, for duty's sake, follow the home there; and that to do the job properly she must hire adequate agents such as health officers, playground directors, factory inspectors, movie censors, or else the home is left defenseless. Both husband and wife may find, indeed, that these neighborhood services which extend their effectiveness to something approaching the scope of the forces which they must control must sometimes extend very far indeed into the state, the region, the nation.

Nor is this all. When Chicago set out to provide itself with an adequate water supply, geography required it to establish some means of disposing of its sewage also; this involved it with disputes with other cities in the state, then other states, and finally with a foreign state. We are learning in an expensive school that arms are not a problem that can be solved by a single state; adequate armaments are relative to what the others have, and they in turn are relative to the kinds of disputes which may call for their use, and thus we find our local issues leading into the international society of which we are a part, and requiring here, also, agents to serve us all. Here the task of breaking through commitments to old symbols is most difficult of all—yet must be solved if we are to achieve what our interdependent system makes possible. . . .

To speak of these new organizations as extending the range of individual effort in some degree proportionate to the otherwise irresponsible coercive power of the natural forces and human organizations with which the individual must deal may seem evasive. It may be more intelligible to say that we are submerging the individual, and theories of his place in society, beneath the state and theories of socialism. This is to forget that these, too, are tested ultimately by their enrichment of the individuals who comprise the state. It is true that to speak of the individual as investor, producer, and consumer is to overstress one aspect of his life. Despite theories of economic interest he is first of all a person, a human being, whose needs are first supplied in the family circle and then in the community whose degree of civilization influences the quality of family life directly. Hence it is primarily the citizen, the member of the public, whose place in the new society demands greatest consideration. If during the critical years of infancy the family surrounding the child is characterized by poverty and insecurities of all sorts, and presents an environment of conflict, worry, and strain; if during childhood the provision of schooling, of play, of group life, prohibits the kind of development of the individual through which good habits are formed and potential capacities developed—the basis of a citizenship adequate for thinking through its challenging problems is never provided.

The task of predicting the consequences of contemporary actions, of providing the requisite adjustments, is immensely difficult in individual or family life. The difficulties increase with the size and complexity of the unit and the expansion of the range of variables. Nevertheless, the large organization of commanding authority may be able to reduce the variables by inserting dikes which canalize future action. True, if the dikes break, the loss to those who have built homes assured of their protection is the greater. When a price-fixing agreement in an industry collapses, the ruin is more devastating for the industry than the losses in competition spread over a long period. But other dikes—if properly cared for—may release the energies of people for more constructive tasks than the fighting of floods. A fairly enforced system of weights and measures, of regulation of utility rates, or of banking standards eliminates the waste effort harmful to the consumer, the shipper, or the depositor. The business man, indeed, constantly presses upon governments for too great an extension of planning, of dike-building, of elimination of uncertainties than is good for the rest of us. He has come to take these government policies favorable to him so much for granted that they no longer appear to him to be special favors. Thus the establishment by law and administration of a system of property (not really private, but essentially created by a public act) and of tariffs are creative acts of government that establish certainty in some activities and eliminate the uncertainties, for example, arising from brute force or foreign goods.

All such certainties—whether property rights, tariffs, labor laws—are, we have seen, possible shock absorbers against the excessive costs of change. They are dangerous instruments to use; yet we constantly expand their range as one interest presses to obtain a counterbalancing protection against another, and as the uncertainties inherent in our interdependent price system increase. The task which falls upon the administrators, whether in political or financial, commercial or industrial government, is therefore steadily growing more difficult and important. Can we obtain administrators who will be competent to undertake these tasks? What qualities must they possess? Can they be developed through education? Is there, indeed, a common, public interest for which we require such agents and trustees? Must we, to be honest, accept the spoils system and the pressure group as the complete, and the essential, theory of political society?

No American family has contributed more to a solution of this central problem of using the public services so that the citizen may realize his best self than the Adams family. J. Q. Adams was one of the few members of the governing class of the early years of our republic who had some imaginative conception of what our natural resources might do for us. His grandson, Henry, saw how decisive a public service of good quality would be in the new America, and worked mightily to achieve it. Charles Francis Adams, another grandson, was a founder of the public utility regulation movement, and with the younger Charles Eliot invented a metropolitan planning and park system for Boston. Brooks Adams, brother of Henry and Charles, in his writings, analyzed penetratingly the role of the administrator in a world of social change. In his *The Degradation of the Democratic Dogma* he interpreted the teachings of his grandfather and revealed the dream—and disappointment—of that amazing man. In his *The Theory of Social Revolutions* he remarks:

"It is in dealing with administration, as I apprehend, that civilizations have usually, though not always, broken down, for it has been on administrative difficulties that revolutions have for the most part supervened. Advances in administration seem to presuppose the evolution of new governing classes, since apparently, no established type of mind can adapt itself to changes in environment, even in slow-moving civilizations, as fast as environments change. . . . The most distressing aspect of the situation is that social acceleration is progressive in proportion to the activity of the scientific mind which makes mechanical discoveries, and it is therefore a triumphant science which produces those ever more rapidly recurring changes in environment to which men must adapt themselves at their peril."

The requisite quality for directing the necessary readjustments to new scientific application so that social change due to material developments will not be too great is to be found, he urges, in administrators with "a high order of generalizing mind—a mind which can grasp a multitude of complex relations." Do we attempt to secure such minds for our public services, and do we attempt to develop them in our educational system?

Chapter 2

The Matter of "Bureaucracy"

On few things are Americans as agreed as they are on the opinion that bureaucracy is bad. It is castigated again and again—and at length—by the organs of public opinion; and "bureaucrat" is a term of disdain or even deep opprobrium.

But what is bureaucracy and who is a bureaucrat? If one tries to answer this by examining popular usage, he arrives quickly at a state of thorough confusion. He quickly learns that there is more emotional warmth than conceptual content in customary usage. He quickly learns that usage shifts with the tides of politics and business, and that attitudes depend upon the position of the user with respect to an office or position—particularly whether he views it from the outside or the inside.

A student of administration needs a keen ear for the uses and abuses of bureaucracy in political forensics. He needs also a sharp and well-trained mind to deal with conditions of administrative pathology that are the hard core of truth in the "cuss word" use of bureaucracy. (Some of these conditions of administrative pathology were clearly pictured in the "Centralia" story.) The student of administration needs also the clarity to see that the word bureaucracy can be used objectively and precisely by the student of administration, to denote certain general aspects of organization in modern society, whether the organization is public or private.

Presented below are two sharply contrasting interpretations of bureaucracy. The first is what might be called a scholarly elaboration of the popular notion of bureaucracy. "Bureaucratic" so used connotes arbitrariness, officiousness, formalism, unimaginativeness, and so forth. The connotations of the term are so various, in fact, that some of them seem to contradict others. For example, "bureaucratic" may be used to mean "power hungry"; but it may also be used to imply timidity, a shrinking not only from power but from responsibility. This type of ambiguity in the popular, opprobrious use of the term is discernible even in the following essay prepared for the *Encyclopaedia of the Social Sciences* by the late distinguished British social scientist, Harold J. Laski.

Bureaucracy *

H. J. LASKI

Bureaucracy is the term usually applied to a system of government the control of which is so completely in the hands of officials that their power jeopardizes the liberties of ordinary citizens. The characteristics of such a regime are a passion for routine in administration, the sacrifice of flexibility to rule, delay in the making of decisions and a refusal to embark upon experiment. In extreme cases the mem-

* From *Encyclopaedia of the Social Sciences*, Vol. 3, pp. 70–73. Somewhat abridged. Copyright 1930, by The Macmillan Company, publishers, and used with the permission of The Macmillan Company.

bers of a bureaucracy may become a hereditary caste manipulating government to their own advantage.

Until quite modern times bureaucracy seems to have arisen as a by-product of aristocracy. In the history of the latter a disinclination on the part of the aristocracy for active government has in some cases led to the transfer of power into the hands of permanent officials. In other cases the origin of bureaucracy may be traced to the desire of the crown to have a body of personal servants who may be set off against the appetite of the aristocracy for power. In the latter event the bureaucrats themselves may have developed into an aristocracy, as happened in eighteenth century France. Previous to the nineteenth century bureaucracies have always sought, wherever possible, to become a privileged caste. When they have succeeded they have attempted to obtain for themselves either the same powers as the aristocracy or access to that superior class. . . .

The advent of democratic government in the nineteenth century overthrew in the western world the chance of maintaining a system whereby officials could constitute a permanent and hereditary caste. But for the most part the new conditions which accompanied democracy made bureaucracy possible in a new phase. It was essential to have a body of experts surrounding the minister in charge of a particular service. The latter was an amateur who remained in office for at most a few years. It was therefore almost a condition of successful administration that the officials who surrounded him should hold office permanently. And since democracy implied also publicity, it was important too that there should be a uniform body of precedents, a consistent tradition, to which reference could be made in order to justify before a legislative assembly the action that was taken.

The tendency accordingly has been toward a certain suspicion of experimentalism, a benevolence toward the "safe" man. There develops almost insensibly an *esprit de corps* with canons of conduct, observance of which becomes the test of promotion. Administrative codes grow up and are applied simply from the conservatism of habit. When rules have been long in operation or when they have been made by men of considerable experience it is very difficult to resist their authority. Because they are old it is held that they embody necessary experience; and officials are not easily persuaded to abandon them. A bureaucracy, moreover, because it is open to public criticism in a democratic state is always anxious to secure a reputation for accuracy. It prides itself on not making mistakes. It insists on seeing questions from every point of view. This results not seldom in a slowness in taking action, a multiplication of *paperasserie*, in which the negative side of some proposed course of action is easily magnified as against its possible advantages. Because mistakes will lead to criticism a bureaucracy is easily tempted to persuade a timid minister that the statute he contemplates is probably destined to fail.

Under modern conditions these problems are magnified still further. The scale of the modern state and the vastness of the services it seeks to render make expert administration inevitable. To control the expert in such conditions is an unenviable task. The necessary knowledge of detail is as a rule concentrated in his department alone. The need to be impersonal means uniformity of administration; and this in its turn means a code of precedents through which it is difficult to cut one's way to the recognition of a new principle. Experts, moreover, naturally tend to push the field they administer to its furthest confines; the appetite for power grows by what it feeds on. In England, for example, the last thirty years have seen the increasing abandonment by Parliament of any effective control over departmental action. Even judicial control has had to surrender to the need for administrative discretion rendered necessary because the processes of law are too cumbrous to deal effectively with the delicacy of the technical issues involved. Where the legislative machinery still attempts interference, as in the United States, the result is fatal to expert and adequate administration.

We have reached, in short, a position in which certain simple principles may be laid down. (1) In countries built upon the English parliamentary model the legislature cannot because of the extent and pressure of its business do more than accept or reject the conclusions of ministers. (2) The conclusions of ministers based, as they must be, upon information which requires experts for its formulation and interpretation are very largely those of the higher officials of the departments in their charge. (3) In the department there is a constant pressure toward caution. The minister has to assume responsibility for the mistakes of his subordinates and it is a point of honor with his subordinates that these be minimal; the simplest way to this end is to minimize the sphere of novelty. (4) The system of appointment by competitive examination, adopted as a necessary precaution against the evils of patronage, means that the young official grows up in the department and that his promotion depends largely upon the recommendation of his seniors. In this sense a high reward may too easily be won for conformity to the departmental code. In any case appointment from without is deeply resented and it will be found that most officials favor promotion by seniority; this, as a rule, is to mistake antiquity for experience. (5) In the United States there is hardly a bureaucracy in the European sense of the term; the small salaries and the operation of the spoils system prevent the continuity of service known in Europe. But the disadvantages of this system are great: the failure to attract able men to the civil service and the consequent low level of quality in the administrative performance. Discontinuity at the top of the departments involves a price perhaps even heavier than that paid for excessive continuity.

It should be pointed out that these undesirable characteristics of bureaucracy are not in the least confined to the service of the state; they operate wherever there is large scale organization. Trade unions, churches, institutions for social work, great industrial corporations, all these are compelled by the very size of the interests they represent and by their complexity to take on the same habits of bureaucracy. The familiarity of officials with the technical details of their work involves the accretion of power in their hands. The need for rules makes for stereotyped regulation. Innovation is distrusted because it means a departure from the wonted routine. The problem, for example, of influencing a great political party to adopt a new outlook frowned upon by its leaders; the effort to persuade, say, a great shipbuilding firm to turn from iron to steel; the difficulty of inducing case workers in a charitable organization to skepticism of their inquiries; these are merely examples of the power of habit over those who specialize in a particular department. It is rarely difficult in a trade union congress for the officials to "steam roller" the delegates into acceptance of policies about which as individuals the majority may be dubious. A great business corporation, as long as it earns a dividend, never has to bother itself about its shareholders. It is the boast of the Roman Catholic church that it has not changed since its foundation; and innovators have always been driven either to schism or submission. Even in a comparatively new state like the Soviet Republic the proceedings of the Communist party are full of accusations of this kind against officials.

In all large scale enterprise men who are desirous of avoiding great responsibility (and the majority of men is so desirous) are necessarily tempted to avoid great experiments. In a political democracy this obviously becomes an official habit where there is a tendency to a bureaucratic system. Nothing will be undertaken for the public for which it is not clamant. The difficulties of meeting the demands made will be exaggerated out of all proportion. Information necessary to the making of policy will be withheld, sometimes on the ground that it is not in the public interest to reveal it, sometimes by the argument that its collection would be unjustifiably expensive. Decisions will be made without the assignment of reasons for making them, or postponed until, in Bacon's phrase, the questions "resolve of themselves." The result is discretion, secrecy, conservatism, and all these minister to the preservation of power.

In modern times bureaucracies have, outside of Russia under the czarist regime, rarely been corrupt in a crude sense. Most of the advantages they obtain for themselves (security of tenure, superannuation, incremental salaries, annual vacation) are recognized as the necessary accompaniments of sound work. Nor has there been the tendency to nepotism which distinguished earlier types. Of course there have been scandals; in France notably there have been some sordid exposures worthy of the *ancien régime*. But it is in a broad sense just to say that in its political context the economic morality of the modern civil service, where it has had the advantage of permanence, has been far higher than that of private enterprise.

Its faults clearly arise from the difficulty of controlling experts in any department where action depends upon special knowledge which as a rule they alone possess and where mistakes of innovation may entail serious consequences. The size of the modern state in fact tends to make its government an oligarchy of specialists, whose routine is disturbed by the occasional irruption of the benevolent amateur. In England it may be said that the technical efficiency of the civil service has made it possible to avoid many of the larger evils of bureaucracy because the long period of service of outstanding statesmen gives to them a power of control not easily obtainable elsewhere. In Germany, on the other hand, at least until 1916, the statesman in office tended to be the supreme bureaucrat who could avoid the consequence, to be faced in England, of having to meet a popular verdict. Moreover the English system of fairly constant and thorough inquiry into the whole condition of the civil service has made possible the introduction of a genuine flexibility of organization at comparatively frequent intervals. But it still remains true in England as elsewhere that the contact between the civil service, on the one hand, and the legislative assembly and the general public, on the other, is far too haphazard and incoherent. . . .

"Bureaucracy" has a meaning in contemporary social science much different from that given it in the above essay. To understand this other meaning is to take an important step toward understanding the society in which we live.

Bureaucracy in contemporary social science is used to denote a *general type* of human organization, distinguishable by significant criteria from other types of human organization. As a type of organization bureaucracy has both good and bad characteristics. Its "bad" characteristics are among those included when the term is used in its popular, opprobrious sense; so there is a measure of overlapping between the two uses of the term. But the two usages remain clearly distinguishable. One, the popular, is connotative, emotional, imprecise. The other is denotative, analytical, precise.

The writer of the following passages, Max Weber (a German, who died in 1920), was one of the great scholars of history, and these passages are part of what one of Weber's translators accurately calls "a classic formulation of the characteristics of bureaucratic organization." Other scholars would—and do—insist that in this or that aspect Weber erred in his analysis of bureaucracy as a type of human organization. But in the main his analysis is accepted as true and significant.

Weber's scholarship ranged across cultures and up and down the centuries. He sought to see human society as a whole, to develop a system for classifying and analyzing all human institutions. This is not the place to attempt to present even the outlines of his system of sociology, but it is desirable to comment on two or three aspects of his ideas in order that the passages below may be seen in perspective.

In Weber's analysis there are three main types of authority or principles of "legitimacy" in human organization. One of these is "traditional authority," authority sanctioned simply by time and the accepted status of its claimant. This type of authority tends to characterize primitive societies, or "civilized" societies in which law and science are rudimentary. Another type of authority is "charismatic authority." This is authority based on personal qualities of leadership or magnetism; there may be an accompanying belief that the charismatic leader is superhuman. This type of authority is exemplified in the war hero or religious prophet. The third type of authority is "rational" or "legal authority." This is authority based on a set of rules accepted by the members of an organization as "legitimate." Legal authority inheres in the office, not the man, and anyone may exercise it if he has come into the office "according to the rules."

This third type of legitimate authority in human organization is associated with bureaucracy: bureaucracy is the "typical" way in which rational or legal authority is institutionalized. More or less well-developed bureaucratic organizations have appeared here and there in history, but it is in Western civilization during the past several hundred years that bureaucracy has had its flowering. In fact, our civilization is characteristically bureaucratic in its organization, and this is no less true of private organization than it is of government. Much of Weber's wide-ranging studies was given to probing the causes and bases of bureaucratic organization. His conclusions were that bureaucratic organization has necessary ideological and technological conditions that must be fulfilled before it can flourish. It is associated, for example, with the growth of legal and monetary systems. Organizations as well as organisms have environments, in other words; and just as organisms must be studied in relation to their environments, so must organizations—if they are to be understood.

Some of what Weber has to say in the extracts below will seem childishly obvious, some of it needlessly formal and abstract. For he is presenting an analysis of what we have lived with all our lives. But it is the nature of genius to show us in a new light and really for the first time what is obvious.

Bureaucracy *

MAX WEBER

Characteristics of Bureaucracy

Modern officialdom functions in the following specific manner:
I. There is the principle of fixed and official jurisdictional areas, which are generally ordered by rules, that is, by laws or administrative regulations.

1. The regular activities required for the purposes of the bureaucratically governed structure are distributed in a fixed way as official duties.

2. The authority to give the commands required for the discharge of these duties is distributed in a stable way and is strictly delimited by rules concerning the coercive means, physical, sacerdotal, or otherwise, which may be placed at the disposal of officials.

3. Methodical provision is made for the regular and continuous fulfilment of these duties and for the execution of the corresponding rights; only persons who have the generally regulated qualifications to serve are employed.

In public and lawful government these three elements constitute "bureaucratic authority." In private economic domination, they constitute bureaucratic "management." Bureaucracy, thus understood, is fully developed in political and ecclesiastical communities only in the modern state, and, in the private economy, only in the most advanced institutions of capitalism. Permanent and public office authority, with fixed jurisdiction, is not the historical rule but rather the exception. This is so even in large political structures such as those of the ancient Orient, the Germanic and Mongolian empires of conquest, or of many feudal structures of state. In all these cases, the ruler executes the most important measures through personal trustees, table-companions, or court-servants. Their commissions and authority are not precisely delimited and are temporarily called into being for each case.

II. The principles of office hierarchy and of levels of graded authority mean a firmly ordered system of super- and subordination in which there is a supervision of the lower offices by the higher ones. Such a system offers the governed the possibility of appealing the decision of a lower office to its higher authority, in a definitely regulated manner. With the full development of the bureaucratic type, the office hierarchy is monocratically organized. The principle of hierarchical office authority is found in all bureaucratic structures: in state and ecclesiastical structures as well as in large party organizations and private enterprises. It does not matter for the character of bureaucracy whether its authority is called "private" or "public."

When the principle of jurisdictional "competency" is fully carried through, hierarchical subordination—at least in public office—does not mean that the "higher" authority is simply authorized to take over the business of the "lower." Indeed, the opposite is the rule. Once established and having fulfilled its task, an office tends to continue in existence and be held by another incumbent.

III. The management of the modern office is based upon written documents ("the files"), which are preserved in their original or draught form. There is, therefore, a staff of subaltern officials and scribes of all sorts. The body of officials actively engaged in a "public" office, along with the respective apparatus of material implements and the files, make up a "bureau." In private enterprise, "the bureau" is often called "the office."

In principle, the modern organization of the civil service separates the bureau from the private domicile of the official, and, in general, bureaucracy segregates official activity as something distinct from the sphere of private life. Public monies and equipment are divorced from the private property of the official. This condition is everywhere the product of a long development. Nowadays, it is found in public as well as in private enterprises; in the latter, the principle extends even to the leading entrepreneur. In principle, the executive office is separated from the household, business from private correspondence, and business assets from private fortunes. The more consistently the modern type of business management has been carried through the more are these separations the case. The beginnings of this process are to be found as early as the Middle Ages.

It is the peculiarity of the modern entrepreneur that he conducts himself as the "first official" of his enterprise, in the very same way in which the ruler of a specifically modern bureaucratic state spoke of himself as "the first servant" of the state. The idea that the bureau activities of the state are intrinsically different in character from the management of private economic offices is a continental European notion and, by way of contrast, is totally foreign to the American way.

IV. Office management, at least all specialized office management—and such management is distinctly modern—usually presupposes thorough and expert training. This increasingly holds for the modern executive and employee of private enterprises, in the same manner as it holds for the state official.

V. When the office is fully developed, official activity demands the full working capacity of the official, irrespective of the fact that his obligatory time in the bureau may be firmly delimited. In the normal case, this is only the product of a long development, in the public as well as in the private office. Formerly, in all cases, the normal state of affairs was reversed: official business was discharged as a secondary activity.

VI. The management of the office follows general rules, which are more or less stable, more or less exhaustive, and which can be learned. Knowledge of these rules represents a special technical learning which the officials possess. It involves jurisprudence, or administrative or business management.

The reduction of modern office management to rules is deeply embedded in its very nature. The theory of modern public administration, for instance, assumes that the authority to order certain matters by decree—which has been legally granted to public authorities—does not entitle the bureau to regulate the matter by commands given for each case, but only to regulate the matter abstractly. This stands in extreme contrast to the regulation of all relationships through individual privileges and bestowals of favor, which is absolutely dominant in patrimonialism, at least in so far as such relationships are not fixed by sacred tradition.

The Position of the Official

All this results in the following for the internal and external position of the official:

I. Office holding is a "vocation." This is shown, first, in the requirement of a firmly prescribed course of training, which demands the entire capacity for work for a long period of time, and in the generally prescribed and special examinations which are prerequisites of employment. Furthermore, the position of the officials is in the nature of a duty. This determines the internal structure of his relations, in the following manner: Legally and actually, office holding is not considered a source to be exploited for rents or emoluments, as was normally the case during the Middle Ages and frequently up to the threshold of recent times. Nor is office holding considered a usual exchange of services for equivalents, as is the case with free labor contracts. Entrance into an office, including one in the private economy, is considered an acceptance of a specific obligation of faithful management in return for a secure existence. It is decisive for the specific nature of modern loyalty to an office that, in the pure type, it does not establish a relationship to a *person,* like the vassal's or disciple's faith in feudal or in patrimonial relations of authority. Modern loyalty is devoted to impersonal and functional purposes. . . .

II. The personal position of the official is patterned in the following way:

1. Whether he is in a private office or a public bureau, the modern official always strives and usually enjoys a distinct *social esteem* as compared with the governed. His social position is guaranteed by the prescriptive rules of rank order and, for the political official, by special definitions of the criminal code against "insults of officials" and "contempt" of state and church authorities.

The actual social position of the official is normally highest where, as in old civilized countries, the following conditions prevail: a strong demand for administration by trained experts; a strong and stable social differentiation, where the official predominantly derives from socially and economically privileged strata because of the social distribution of power; or where the costliness of the required training and status conventions are binding upon him. The possession of educational certificates—to be discussed elsewhere—are usually linked with qualification for office. Naturally, such certificates or patents enhance the "status element" in the social position of the official. . . .

Usually the social esteem of the officials as such is especially low where the demand for expert administration and the dominance of status conventions are weak. This is especially the case in the United States; it is often the case in new settlements by virtue of their wide fields for profit-making and the great instability of their social stratification.

2. The pure type of bureaucratic official is *appointed* by a superior authority. An official elected by the governed is not a purely bureaucratic figure. Of course, the formal existence of an election does not by itself mean that no appointment hides behind the election—in the state, especially, appointment by party chiefs. Whether or not this is the case does not depend upon legal statutes but upon the way in which the party mechanism functions. Once firmly organized, the parties can turn a formally free election into the mere acclamation of a candidate

designated by the party chief. As a rule, however, a formally free election is turned into a fight, conducted according to definite rules, for votes in favor of one of two designated candidates.

In all circumstances, the designation of officials by means of an election among the governed modifies the strictness of hierarchical subordination. In principle, an official who is so elected has an autonomous position opposite the super-ordinate official. The elected official does not derive his position "from above" but "from below," or at least not from a superior authority of the official hierarchy but from powerful party men ("bosses"), who also determine his further career. The career of the elected official is not, or at least not primarily, dependent upon his chief in the administration. The official who is not elected but appointed by a chief normally functions more exactly, from a technical point of view, because, all other circumstances being equal, it is more likely that purely functional points of consideration and qualities will determine his selection and career. As laymen, the governed can become acquainted with the extent to which a candidate is expertly qualified for office only in terms of experience, and hence only after his service. Moreover, in every sort of selection of officials by election, parties quite naturally give decisive weight not to expert considerations but to the services a follower renders to the party boss. This holds for all kinds of procurement of officials by elections, for the designation of formally free, elected officials by party bosses when they determine the slate of candidates, or the free appointment by a chief who has himself been elected. The contrast, however, is relative: substantially similar conditions hold where legitimate monarchs and their subordinates appoint officials, except that the influence of the followings are then less controllable. . . .

3. Normally, the position of the official is held for life, at least in public bureaucracies; and this is increasingly the case for all similar structures. As a factual rule, *tenure for life* is presupposed, even where the giving of notice or periodic reappointment occurs. In contrast to the worker in a private enterprise, the official normally holds tenure. Legal or actual life-tenure, however, is not recognized as the official's right to the possession of office, as was the case with many structures of authority in the past. Where legal guarantees against arbitrary dismissal or transfer are developed, they merely serve to guarantee a strictly objective discharge of specific office duties free from all personal considerations. In Germany, this is the case for all juridical and, increasingly, for all adminis-trative officials. . . .

4. The official receives the regular *pecuniary* compensation of a normally fixed *salary* and the old age security provided by a pension. The salary is not measured like a wage in terms of work done, but according to "status," that is, according to the kind of function (the "rank") and, in addition, possibly, according to the length of service. The relatively great security of the official's income, as well as the rewards of social esteem, make the office a sought-after position, especially in countries which no longer provide opportunities for

colonial profits. In such countries, this situation permits relatively low salaries for officials.

5. The official is set for a *"career"* within the hierarchical order of the public service. He moves from the lower, less important, and lower paid to the higher positions. The average official naturally desires a mechanical fixing of the conditions of promotion: if not of the offices, at least of the salary levels. He wants these conditions fixed in terms of "seniority," or possibly according to grades achieved in a developed system of expert examinations. Here and there, such examinations actually form a character *indelebilis* of the official and have lifelong effects on his career. To this is joined the desire to qualify the right to office and the increasing tendency toward status group closure and economic security. All of this makes for a tendency to consider the offices as "prebends" of those who are qualified by educational certificates. The necessity of taking general personal and intellectual qualifications into consideration, irrespective of the often subaltern character of the educational certificate, has led to a condition in which the highest political offices, especially the positions of "ministers," are principally filled without reference to such certificates. . . .

———◆———

The passage above is primarily an analysis and description of bureaucratic organization as a type. In the passage below Weber argues the "superiority" of bureaucratic organization and develops the thesis that, indeed, the modern world is dependent upon bureaucracy. Large-scale, technologically advanced society, that is to say, depends for its existence upon the superior "efficiency" of the bureaucratic type of organization. Bureaucracy is no less an aspect of capitalist institutions than of governmental institutions—contrary to a widely held belief. And while socialists no less than capitalists have historically condemned bureaucracy, socialism no less than capitalism—perhaps more than capitalism—is dependent for its execution on bureaucratic forms.

These are challenging ideas. Are they true? If the thesis is correct that bureaucratic organization is a must for any society that seeks to live in the accustomed manner of modern, Western civilization, then the great historical argument about "capitalism" and "socialism" as abstractions has been largely a meaningless disturbance of the air.

What of the argument that bureaucracy is "technically superior"? With this point of view most American students of administration of the past generation have been in general agreement. Perhaps in some sense bureaucracy *is* superior. But in that case, what about the democracy in which we profess to believe? Is bureaucracy superior to democracy? American students of public administration have, paradoxically, held to a strong belief in democracy at the same time they have been firmly convinced of the superiority of "the monocratic type of bureaucratic administration." Much ingenious thinking has gone into the reconciliation of two points of view that seem at first glance to clash. In the essay by Woodrow Wilson, which opens the chapter "The Study of Public Administration," some of this ingenious thinking is displayed.

The Monocratic Type of Bureaucratic Administration *

MAX WEBER

Experience tends universally to show that the purely bureaucratic type of administrative organization—that is, the monocratic variety of bureaucracy—is, from a purely technical point of view, capable of attaining the highest degree of efficiency and is in this sense formally the most rational known means of carrying out imperative control over human beings. It is superior to any other form in precision, in stability, in the stringency of its discipline, and in its reliability. It thus makes possible a particularly high degree of calculability of results for the heads of the organization and for those acting in relation to it. It is finally superior both in intensive efficiency and in the scope of its operations, and is formally capable of application to all kinds of administrative tasks.

The development of the modern form of the organization of corporate groups in all fields is nothing less than identical with the development and continual spread of bureaucratic administration. This is true of church and state, of armies, political parties, economic enterprises, organizations to promote all kinds of causes, private associations, clubs, and many others. Its development is, to take the most striking case, the most crucial phenomenon of the modern Western state. However many forms there may be which do not appear to fit this pattern, such as collegial representative bodies, parliamentary committees, soviets, honorary officers, lay judges, and what not, and however much people may complain about the "evils of bureaucracy," it would be sheer illusion to think for a moment that continuous administrative work can be carried out in any field except by means of officials working in offices. The whole pattern of everyday life is cut to fit this framework. For bureaucratic administration is, other things being equal, always, from a formal, technical point of view, the most rational type. For the needs of mass administration to-day, it is completely indispensable. The choice is only that between bureaucracy and dilettantism in the field of administration.

* From *The Theory of Social and Economic Organization*, translated by A. M. Henderson and Talcott Parsons. Copyright, 1947, by Oxford University Press, Inc.

The primary source of the superiority of bureaucratic administration lies in the role of technical knowledge which, through the development of modern technology and business methods in the production of goods, has become completely indispensable. In this respect, it makes no difference whether the economic system is organized on a capitalistic or a socialistic basis. Indeed, if in the latter case a comparable level of technical efficiency were to be achieved, it would mean a tremendous increase in the importance of specialized bureaucracy.

When those subject to bureaucratic control seek to escape the influence of the existing bureaucratic apparatus, this is normally possible only by creating an organization of their own which is equally subject to the process of bureaucratization. Similarly the existing bureaucratic apparatus is driven to continue functioning by the most powerful interests which are material and objective, but also ideal in character. Without it, a society like our own—with a separation of officials, employees, and workers from ownership of the means of administration, dependent on discipline and on technical training—could no longer function. The only exception would be those groups, such as the peasantry, who are still in possession of their own means of subsistence. Even in case of revolution by force or of occupation by an enemy, the bureaucratic machinery will normally continue to function just as it has for the previous legal government.

The question is always who controls the existing bureaucratic machinery. And such control is possible only in a very limited degree to persons who are not technical specialists. Generally speaking, the trained permanent official is more likely to get his way in the long run than his nominal superior, the Cabinet minister, who is not a specialist.

Though by no means alone, the capitalistic system has undeniably played a major role in the development of bureaucracy. Indeed, without it capitalistic production could not continue and any rational type of socialism would have simply to take it over and increase its importance. Its development, largely under capitalistic auspices, has created an urgent need for stable, strict, intensive, and calculable administration. It is this need which gives bureaucracy a crucial role in our society as the central element in any kind of large-scale administration. Only by reversion in every field—political, religious, economic, etc.—to small-scale organization would it be possible to any considerable extent to escape its influence. On the one hand, capitalism in its modern stages of development strongly tends to foster the development of bureaucracy, though both capitalism and bureaucracy have arisen from many different historical sources. Conversely, capitalism is the most rational economic basis for bureaucratic administration and enables it to develop in the most rational form, especially because, from a fiscal point of view, it supplies the necessary money resources.

Along with these fiscal conditions of efficient bureaucratic administration, there are certain extremely important conditions in the fields of communication and transportation. The precision of its functioning requires the services of the railway, the telegraph, and the telephone, and becomes increasingly dependent on them. A socialistic form of organization would not alter this fact. It would be a question whether in a socialistic system it would be possible to provide conditions for carrying out as stringent bureaucratic organization as has been possible in a capitalistic order. For socialism would, in fact, require a still higher degree of formal bureaucratization than capitalism. . . .

Bureaucratic administration means fundamentally the exercise of control on the basis of knowledge. This is the feature of it which makes it specifically rational. This consists on the one hand in technical knowledge which, by itself, is sufficient to ensure it a position of extraordinary power. But in addition to this, bureaucratic organizations, or the holders of power who make use of them, have the tendency to increase their power still further by the knowledge growing out of experience in the service. For they acquire through the conduct of office a special knowledge of facts and have available a store of documentary material peculiar to themselves. While not peculiar to bureaucratic organizations, the concept of "official secrets" is certainly typical of them. It stands in relation to technical knowledge in somewhat the same position as commercial secrets do to technological training. It is a product of the striving for power.

Bureaucracy is superior in knowledge, including both technical knowledge and knowledge of the concrete fact within its own sphere of interest, which is usually confined to the interests of a private business—a capitalistic enterprise. The capitalistic entrepreneur is, in our society, the only type who has been able to maintain at least relative immunity from subjection to the control of rational bureaucratic knowledge. All the rest of the population have tended to be organized in large-scale corporate groups which are inevitably subject to bureaucratic control. This is as inevitable as the dominance of precision machinery in the mass production of goods.

Chapter 3

How Do Private and Public Administration Differ?

The shift from the previous chapter to the present is in part but a change in focus on the same subject. Certainly the word "bureaucracy" is the key word in the next selection.

However, the question now is not, "What is bureaucracy?" but, "What are the differences between private and public administration?" That they have much in common is now clear and could not be denied even by the writer of the following selection, even though his purpose is precisely to emphasize that there are crucial differences. In turn, that there are differences and that the differences are significant would be denied by few. Certainly there is much room for disagreement as to the identity, the dimensions, and the implications of the differences.

The writer of the next selection, Ludwig von Mises, represents an important school of thought among economists. In his book *Bureaucracy*, from which this selection comes, he states in strong—even extreme—form a thesis that has much support among economists and among the population at large. As will become quickly evident, this thesis is one which the student of public administration is likely to find at best a half-truth, at worst a perilous falsehood. But it is a point of view which must be taken seriously. Anyone who wishes to reject it should be prepared with reasons, if he is concerned either with his intellectual honesty or his effectiveness in the political process.

The crux of von Mises' argument is that the difference between business management and bureaucratic management is fundamental because business management has an incentive and method of calculation—namely, money profit—unavailable to public administration. In result, not only is efficiency "an entirely different thing" in the two types of operations, but there is no real method of calculating efficiency or success in public administration. It thus is adrift without compass or anchor.

Bureaucracy, used here to describe this type of management to which money profit does not apply, is no doubt a necessary evil. In one sense it is even a good. Government has no choice but to use bureaucratic management; and government of the proper type and in proper and limited areas is better than no government. But government should never be extended beyond a small, "necessary" area.

Whatever the position taken on these matters, most students of administration, public or private, would find that von Mises' argument suffers from overstatement. For example, is any business branch nowadays turned over to a newly appointed director "with one directive only: Make profits"? Or is the new director made subject to a whole body of "company policy" and the branch's operation perhaps even prescribed in great detail by centrally promulgated regulations?

Query, are there similar statements which the facts will not sustain?

Bureaucratic Management *

LUDWIG VON MISES

It is frequently asserted that bureaucratic management is incompatible with democratic government and institutions. This is a fallacy. Democracy implies the supremacy of the law. If it were otherwise, the officeholders would be irresponsible and arbitrary despots and the judges inconstant and capricious cadis. The two pillars of democratic government are the primacy of the law and the budget.

Primacy of the law means that no judge or officeholder has the right to interfere with any individual's affairs or conditions unless a valid law requires or empowers him to do so. *Nulla poena sine lege,* no punishment unless ordered by a law. . . .

It is in fact an awkward thing if a scoundrel evades punishment because a law is defective. But it is the minor evil when compared with judicial arbitrariness. If the legislators acknowledge that the law is inadequate they can substitute a more satisfactory law for a less satisfactory. They are the mandatories of the sovereign, the people; they are, in this capacity, supreme and responsible to the voters. If the voters disapprove of the methods applied by their representatives, they will, at the next election, return other men who know better how to adjust their actions to the will of the majority.

It is the same with the executive power. In this field too there is only the alternative between the arbitrary rule of despotic officeholders and the rule of the people enforced by the instrumentality of law abidance. It is a euphemism to call a government in which the rulers are free to do whatever they themselves believe best serves the commonweal a *welfare state,* and to contrast it with the state in which the administration is bound by law and the citizens can make good in a court of law their rights against illegal encroachments of the authorities. This so-called welfare state is in fact the tyranny of the rulers. (Incidentally we have to realize that even a despotic government cannot do without regulations and bureaucratic directives if it is not to degenerate into a chaotic regime of local caciques and to disintegrate into a multitude of petty despotisms.) The aim of the constitutional state also is public welfare. The characteristic feature that distinguishes it from despotism is that not the authorities but the duly elected people's representatives have to decide what best serves the commonweal. This system alone makes the people sovereign and secures their right of self-determination. Under this system the citizens are not only sovereign on election day but no less so between elections.

The administration, in a democratic community, is not only bound by law

* From *Bureaucracy* (New Haven: 1944), pp. 40–56. Abridged. Reprinted by permission of the Yale University Press.

but by the budget. Democratic control is budgetary control. The people's representatives have the keys of the treasury. Not a penny must be spent without the consent of parliament. It is illegal to use public funds for any expenditures other than those for which parliament has allocated them.

Bureaucratic management means, under democracy, management in strict accordance with the law and the budget. It is not for the personnel of the administration and for the judges to inquire what should be done for the public welfare and how the public funds should be spent. This is the task of the sovereign, the people, and their representatives. The courts, the various branches of the administration, the army, and the navy execute what the law and the budget order them to do. Not they but the sovereign is policy-making. . . .

The assertion that bureaucratic management is an indispensable instrument of democratic government is paradoxical. Many will object. They are accustomed to consider democratic government as the best system of government and bureaucratic management as one of the great evils. How can these two things, one good, the other bad, be linked together? . . .

To these objections we must answer again that bureaucracy in itself is neither good nor bad. It is a method of management which can be applied in different spheres of human activity. There is a field, namely, the handling of the apparatus of government, in which bureaucratic methods are required by necessity. What many people nowadays consider an evil is not bureaucracy as such, but the expansion of the sphere in which bureaucratic management is applied. This expansion is the unavoidable consequence of the progressive restriction of the individual citizen's freedom, of the inherent trend of present-day economic and social policies toward the substitution of government control for private initiative. People blame bureaucracy, but what they really have in mind are the endeavors to make the state socialist and totalitarian.

There has always been bureaucracy in America. The administration of the customs and of the foreign service has always been conducted according to bureaucratic principles. What characterizes our time is the expansion of the sphere of government interference with business and with many other items of the citizenry's affairs. And this results in a substitution of bureaucratic management for profit management.

The Essential Features of Bureaucratic Management

The lawyers, the philosophers, and the politicians look upon the supremacy of the law from another angle than does this book. From their point of view the main function of the law is to limit the power of the authorities and the courts to inflict evils upon the individual citizen and to restrict his freedom. If one assigns to the authorities the power to imprison or even to kill people, one must restrict and clearly circumscribe this power. Otherwise the officeholder or judge would turn into an irresponsible despot. The law determines under what conditions the judge should have the right and the duty to sentence and the policeman to fire his gun. The law protects the people against the arbitrariness of those in office.

The viewpoint of this book is somewhat different. We are dealing here with bureaucracy as a principle of administration technique and organization. This book looks upon the rules and regulations not merely as measures for the protection of the people and for safeguarding the citizen's rights and freedom but as measures for the execution of the will of the supreme authority. The need to limit the discretion of subordinates is present in every organization. Any organization would disintegrate in the absence of such restrictions. Our task is to investigate the peculiar characteristics of bureaucratic management as distinguished from commercial management.

Bureaucratic management is management bound to comply with detailed rules and regulations fixed by the authority of a superior body. The task of the bureaucrat is to perform what these rules and regulations order him to do. His discretion to act according to his own best conviction is seriously restricted by them.

Business management or profit management is management directed by the profit motive. The objective of business management is to make a profit. As success or failure to attain this end can be ascertained by accounting not only for the whole business concern but also for any of its parts, it is feasible to decentralize both management and accountability without jeopardizing the unity of operations and the attainment of their goal. Responsibility can be divided. There is no need to limit the discretion of subordinates by any rules or regulations other than that underlying all business activities, namely, to render their operations profitable.

The objectives of public administration cannot be measured in money terms and cannot be checked by accountancy methods. Take a nation-wide police system like the F.B.I. There is no yardstick available that could establish whether the expenses incurred by one of its regional or local branches were not excessive. The expenditures of a police station are not reimbursed by its successful management and do not vary in proportion to the success attained. If the head of the whole bureau were to leave his subordinate station chiefs a free hand with regard to money expenditures, the result would be a large increase in costs as every one of them would be zealous to improve the service of his branch as much as possible. It would become impossible for the top executive to keep the expenditures within the appropriations allocated by the representatives of the people or within any limits whatever. It is not because of punctiliousness that the administrative regulations fix how much can be spent by each local office for cleaning the premises, for furniture repairs, and for lighting and heating. Within a business concern such things can be left without hesitation to the discretion of the responsible local manager. He will not spend more than necessary because it is, as it were, his money; if he wastes the concern's money, he jeopardizes the branch's profit and thereby indirectly hurts his own interests. But it is another matter with the local chief of a government agency. In spending more money he can, very often at least, improve the results of his conduct of affairs. Thrift must be imposed on him by regimentation.

In public administration there is no connection between revenue and expenditure. The public services are spending money only; the insignificant income derived from special sources (for example, the sale of printed matter by the Government Printing Office) is more or less accidental. The revenue derived from customs and taxes is not "produced" by the administrative apparatus. Its source is the law, not the activities of customs officers and tax collectors. It is not the merit of a collector of internal revenue that the residents of his district are richer and pay higher taxes than those of another district. The time and effort required for the administrative handling of an income tax return are not in proportion to the amount of the taxable income it concerns.

In public administration there is no market price for achievements. This makes it indispensable to operate public offices according to principles entirely different from those applied under the profit motive.

Now we are in a position to provide a definition of bureaucratic management: Bureaucratic management is the method applied in the conduct of administrative affairs the result of which has no cash value on the market. Remember: we do not say that a successful handling of public affairs has no value, but that it has no price on the market, that its value cannot be realized in a market transaction and consequently cannot be expressed in terms of money.

If we compare the conditions of two countries, say Atlantis and Thule, we can establish many important statistical figures of each of them: the size of the area and of the population, the birth rate and the death rate, the number of illiterates, of crimes committed, and many other demographical data. We can determine the sum of the money income of all its citizens, the money value of the yearly social product, the money value of the goods imported and exported, and many other economic data. But we cannot assign any arithmetical value to the system of government and administration. That does not mean that we deny the importance or the value of good government. It means only that no yardstick can measure these things. They are not liable to an expression in figures.

It may well be that the greatest thing in Atlantis is its good system of government. It may be that Atlantis owes its prosperity to its constitutional and administrative institutions. But we cannot compare them with those of Thule in the same way as we can compare other things, for instance, wage rates or milk prices.

Bureaucratic management is management of affairs which cannot be checked by economic calculation.

The Crux of Bureaucratic Management

The plain citizen compares the operation of the bureaus with the working of the profit system, which is more familiar to him. Then he discovers that bureaucratic management is wasteful, inefficient, slow and rolled up in red tape. He simply cannot understand how reasonable people allow such a mischievous system to endure. Why not adopt the well-tried methods of private business?

However, such criticisms are not sensible. They misconstrue the features peculiar to public administration. They are not aware of the fundamental difference between government and profit-seeking private enterprise. What they call deficiencies and faults of the management of administrative agencies are necessary properties. A bureau is not a profit-seeking enterprise; it cannot make use of an economic calculation; it has to solve problems which are unknown to business management. It is out of the question to improve its management by reshaping it according to the pattern of private business. It is a mistake to judge the efficiency of a government department by comparing it with the working of an enterprise subject to the interplay of market factors.

There are, of course, in every country's public administration manifest shortcomings which strike the eye of every observer. People are sometimes shocked by the degree of maladministration. But if one tries to go to their roots, one often learns that they are not simply the result of culpable negligence or lack of competence. They sometimes turn out to be the result of special political and institutional conditions or of an attempt to come to an arrangement with a problem for which a more satisfactory solution could not be found. A detailed scrutiny of all the difficulties involved may convince an honest investigator that, given the general state of political forces, he himself would not have known how to deal with the matter in a less objectionable way.

It is vain to advocate a bureaucratic reform through the appointment of businessmen as heads of various departments. The quality of being an entrepreneur is not inherent in the personality of the enterpreneur; it is inherent in the position which he occupies in the framework of market society. A former entrepreneur who is given charge of a government bureau is in this capacity no longer a businessman but a bureaucrat. His objective can no longer be profit, but compliance with the rules and regulations. As head of a bureau he may have the power to alter some minor rules and some matters of internal procedure. But the setting of the bureau's activities is determined by rules and regulations which are beyond his reach.

It is a widespread illusion that the efficiency of government bureaus could be improved by management engineers and their methods of scientific management. However, such plans stem from a radical misconstruction of the objectives of civil government.

Like any kind of engineering, management engineering too is conditioned by the availability of a method of calculation. Such a method exists in profit-seeking business. Here the profit-and-loss statement is supreme. The problem of bureaucratic management is precisely the absence of such a method of calculation.

In the field of profit-seeking enterprise the objective of the management engineer's activities is clearly determined by the primacy of the profit motive. His task is to reduce costs without impairing the market value of the result or to reduce costs more than the ensuing reduction of the market value of the result or to raise the market value of the result more than the required rise in costs. But in the field of government the result has no price on a market. It can neither be bought nor sold.

———◆———

The author of this selection agrees with Ludwig von Mises that "government is different." But he disagrees sharply as to the nature, and particularly as to the need and value, of the differences. Here is an interpretation friendly toward public administration—without being unfriendly toward private administration.

A journalist and editor before 1933, Paul H. Appleby, the author, went to Washington with the New Deal administration as an assistant secretary of the Department of Agriculture. He experienced the tumultuous events of depression and world war in high Federal office, and has since become Dean of the Maxwell School of Citizenship and Public Affairs, of Syracuse University, a pioneer and leading institution in the teaching of public administration.

This selection is the first chapter of a book titled *Big Democracy,* published in 1945, the first of a number of writings in which Dean Appleby has tried to distill the essence of his experience in public administration. To his many admirers these writings are a unique combination of significant observation, acute perception, and balanced judgment.

Dean Appleby would be quick to admit that in some ways and in some manner government is not subject to a dollars-and-cents measuring stick. Indeed, this is precisely what he insists upon in his writings on administration—and on politics as well. Public administration is consciously and directly focused on the "public interest." This to him makes it of highest importance and greatest difficulty. He does not deny that private administration focused on profit serves the public interest. He refuses, however, to dismiss the problem of public administration as unimportant, as von Mises seems to do. Instead, for him public administration must do its job properly in order that the benefits of private administration may in fact be realized.

Query, to what extent must the theses advanced by Ludwig von Mises be qualified in the light of Dean Appleby's presentation?

Government Is Different *

PAUL H. APPLEBY

It is exceedingly difficult clearly to identify the factors which make government different from every other activity in society. Yet this difference is a fact and I believe it to be so big a difference that the dissimilarity between government and all other forms of social action is greater than any dissimilarity among those other forms themselves. Without a willingness to recognize this fact, no one can even begin to discuss public affairs to any good profit or serious purpose.

Analysis of Differences

Some of the less important of these differences are generally acknowledged and accepted. For example, the public recognizes without much thought or question that a good lawyer will not necessarily make a good judge. Dimly, except by those who have paid special attention to the matter, it is seen that the function of a judge, even though it has to do with law, is very different from the function of a lawyer. Attorneys treat specific situations in terms of the interests of their clients except only for the making of necessary adjustments to legal, ethical, and public-relations considerations. To have a society made up entirely of persons thinking like lawyers and clients, no matter how well intentioned, would be plainly impractical if not impossible. We must also have persons thinking and acting like judges. Yet many of us fail to recognize the need of having persons thinking and acting like government officials. To elevate an excellent lawyer to the bench will not guarantee society even a tolerably good judge. It should be equally patent that men with excellent records in private business will not necessarily make competent government officials.

In both cases, particularly in the lower brackets, there is through self-selection a certain automatic correction that limits the number of major errors in appointments. Many lawyers are not attracted to the bench. Their disinterest usually reflects some missing qualification. Should an opportunity for appointment to a very high court be offered, there would be some tendency for the thought of honor and prestige to outweigh other considerations. But, in general, individual tastes and interests furnish material evidence of qualification and play a positive role in the process of selection. So in the choosing of government personnel. In ordinary periods many persons have little inclination to enter government, while others are strongly attracted to it. These inclinations and disinclinations are significant, and sometimes controlling, factors in the determination of the general result. In extraordinary times, however, new factors such as patriotism, desire for adventure, or other considerations may come into play and cause propor-

* From *Big Democracy* (New York: 1945), pp. 1–10. Reprinted by permission of Alfred A. Knopf, Inc.

tionately a far greater number of people to aspire to positions in the public service. Many of these persons will, by reason of temperament, outlook, and experience, be utterly unqualified for government work. Others will be qualified only to advise; in government they are technicians—experts in specific non-governmental enterprises. By and large, those who do not normally and consistently feel a great interest in government will not be good prospects. In general, the more they have succeeded in non-governmental fields, the more they have developed interests and habits of thought that will unfit them for government. Obviously the more delicate and difficult distinctions have to do with upper-bracket positions. There, surely, patriotism, zeal, and intelligence could never be enough—any more than they could be accepted as adequate criteria in selecting candidates for the bench from the ranks of the bar, or in selecting army generals from non-military ranks.

Admittedly there are many positions in government in which persons may function very much as they would outside of government. This is true chiefly in such lower-bracket jobs as those of charwomen, elevator operators, messengers, clerks, and typists. Yet even with respect to these there are countless instances where the employee works for the government because he definitely prefers public employment and where that preference has served the public interest. The public would be gratified and moved if it could know of them. Some day it will. For, sooner or later, regard for self-interest, coupled with a sense of justice, will cause the public to be concerned far beyond what it is today over contemptuous attitudes toward lowly government "clerks" and bureaucrats.

Government is not different, however, simply in respect of personnel. The temperament and attitude of a judge do not furnish a complete basis for understanding the character and functioning of our judicial system. Courts are not simply assemblages of judges. Neither are they simply a succession of judicial procedures. Both of these and something over are required to make a judicial *system*. Hence the importance of popular attitudes regarding what is expected in and from a judge. All these things together, expressed in individually well-selected judges, are essential to an effective judiciary. So it is with government in general. It, too, is a *system* and the system cannot be understood except in terms of the public employees themselves, their conceptions of their positions, and the attitudes of the public about what is required in and from our civil servants. These elements together are what make government a system, for in combination they comprise what we call a bureaucracy.

The qualifications for judges differ from those for other governmental people because their functions differ. Yet these qualifications may be used to illustrate a fundamental distinction between governmental and non-governmental tasks. In common speech reference is made to the "judicial temperament." One might similarly refer to the governmental temperament. But temperament seems to me to be less satisfactory as a common denominator than attitude. Consequently I shall speak of the "governmental attitude."

Significance of Attitudes

In my judgment no one can serve the public as it should be served by a governmental official unless he has a public-interest attitude with certain special characteristics. The carrying on of government involves action. No matter how many studies may be required, government in the final analysis is action—organized action. Persons in high positions must have a sense of action. They must have a feeling of the need for decisions to get things done. They must be able to organize resources whether of personnel, material, or information so that contemplation of objectives will be translated into accomplishment.

What has been said with reference to action is familiar to the field of business no less than government. I have, one might say, portrayed the executive, particularly the big business executive. But what I have said up to this point is, of itself, no more adequate to make a governmental administrator than knowledge of the law alone is adequate qualification for a judge. Even possessed of patriotism and zeal, the most capable business executive in the country might be a most dismal failure in government. Indeed, in actual fact many such persons do fail in government. The press, however, ordinarily treats them with such special favor, and their prestige generally is so great, that the public rarely learns of their failure. Strangely enough, their actual induction into government is often political rather than the opposite, as is commonly supposed. Frequently they are appointed to official positions as a means for securing additional support for governmental action. Or they are sought for their prestige, which, since government has the job of maintaining and developing political unity, is always a factor for legitimate consideration.

This feeling for action and this ability to organize resources for action do, of course, resemble corresponding talents that are essential for non-governmental executives. There are business executives who can serve government well, and vice versa. But just as there are successful business executives who could not do well in government, so it is true that some governmental executives who are able to administer public affairs with distinction would probably fail if transferred to private enterprise.

It is instructive to observe that big businessmen who have inherited large business interests seem, on the average, to be better bets for government service than those of the self-made variety. This is probably the result of the development of a special attitude of public responsibility inculcated by parents who were especially conscientious or concerned about what inherited wealth might do to their children. It may derive, too, from some special stimulation to self-questioning and reflection forced by their station of privilege on especially responsible young people. Or it may be the result of their being able or, for that matter, obliged to deal with their affairs more *generally*—that is, with less concentration on the ordinary objective of managing things with an eye to monthly earnings and profits.

Many businessmen, especially those of the self-made variety, have the disadvantage for government service of being prima donnas, with strong personalities too little adjustable to situations other than the ones they have come to dominate. This is true also, to be sure, of some types of vivid politicians who are effective as spokesmen but unable to function as administrators. It seems to be true both of businessmen and politicians that the spread of their activity—their participation in more than one field, and preferably in many more than one—has something to do with their ability to *manage* governmental organizations. Politicians inevitably rub up against more considerations; they tend to be more broadly stimulated. Thus any man of political inclinations who has had organizational and executive experience would be a superior prospect for success as a public official for the reason that he would, almost inevitably, have developed breadth of view and a public-interest attitude.

How Business Looks at Government

It may be unfortunate, but it is nevertheless a fact that, because of factors beyond its control, no industry can realize its own social aspirations. It is also true that no industry can regard public interest equally with industrial interest. That cannot be its function; it must have a different and narrower one. Governments exist precisely for the reason that there is a need to have special persons in society charged with the function of promoting and protecting the public interest.

People tend to develop a sense of responsibility with respect to the functions for which officially they are responsible. Ordinary people brought into government tend to develop some special degree of public responsibility. Yet there are wide ranges of differences in this respect, as everyone knows. Long concentration on other functions unfits a great many people for governmental service. I have seen scores of businessmen in government who were not able to sense the differences between government and business. Without being venal, some thought their positions in government simply a fortunate special privilege, like being the cousin of a purchasing agent. Others again had the fixed idea that the best possible way of promoting the public welfare would be to help private business and assumed accordingly that doing favors for private business was their simple governmental duty.

Business itself, however, does not feel that way in its general attitude toward government. In all things other than those that make for its own profit, a business concern expects government to be guided by a public-interest point of view. The brevity of cabled news sometimes makes such things clearer than does the lengthier reporting of news at home. Consider, for example, this dispatch in the Paris edition of the *New York Herald-Tribune* for the year 1934:

"U.S. Investment Bankers Endorse Roosevelt Policy. White Sulphur Springs, W. Va., Oct. 31—The Convention of the Investment Bankers Association, meeting here, offered today its full assistance to President Roosevelt in his recovery program.

"A resolution was passed in which it was stated that the members of the association would stand behind the President *in all measures which were not calculated to infringe on their own interests.* The bankers offered Roosevelt their *whole-hearted support in particular in all his efforts on their behalf."*

The italics are mine.

Since most governmental actions affect other persons more than they do us as individuals, we all wish governmental action to be what it needs to be with respect to others, while yet, of course, being considerate of us. The truly governmental official in a democracy comes in the course of time to appreciate this. Under the impact of popular demands and lamentations he comes to realize that he must try to operate in a governmental way; that is, through action which is as fair as possible, and as uniform as possible, and which can be taken publicly and publicly explained.

Essential Character of Government

In broad terms the governmental function and attitude have at least three complementary aspects that go to differentiate government from all other institutions and activities: breadth of scope, impact, and consideration; public accountability; political character. No non-governmental institution has the breadth of government. Nothing the national government does in New England can be separated from what it does in New Mexico. Other enterprises may ignore factors remotely related to their central purposes but not the government of the United States; it is supported, tolerated, or evicted on the basis of a balance involving the sum total of everything in the nation. No other institution is so publicly accountable. No action taken or contemplated by the government of a democracy is immune to public debate, scrutiny, or investigation. No other enterprise has such equal appeal or concern for everyone, is so equally dependent on everyone, or deals so vitally with those psychological intangibles which reflect popular economic needs and social aspirations. Other institutions, admittedly, are not free from politics, but government *is* politics.

Government administration differs from all other administrative work to a degree not even faintly realized outside, by virtue of its public nature, the way in which it is subject to public scrutiny and public outcry. An administrator coming into government is struck at once, and continually thereafter, by the press and public interest in every detail of his life, personality, and conduct. This interest often runs to details of administrative action that in private business would never be of concern other than inside the organization. Each employee hired, each one demoted, transferred, or discharged, every efficiency rating, every assignment of responsibility, each change in administrative structure, each conversation, each letter, has to be thought about in terms of possible public agitation, investigation, or judgment. Everything has to be considered in terms of what any employee anywhere may make of it, for any employee may be building a file of things that could be made publicly embarrassing. Any employee who later may be discharged is a potentially powerful enemy, for he can reach the press and Congress with whatever charges his knothole perspective may have invited. Charges of wrongdoing on the part of a government official are always news, no matter who makes the charge, for every former employee is regarded as a source of authoritative and inside information.

In private business the same employee would be discredited by the very fact of having been discharged. Government employees number far less than nongovernmental employees, but the cases of discharged government workers getting into the public prints with denunciations of their former chiefs must be at least a thousand times more frequent. A person discharged is always offended. But whereas a person discharged from a private job is of little interest to the press, the dismissal of a person from a public job is regarded as public business.

This is not to say that I would have it otherwise. I am simply calling attention to it as a fact that greatly differentiates government from business. But the public would do well in judging such reports to consider them in perspective with similar, unaired situations in non-governmental fields.

Because of these circumstances, every governmental executive lives and moves and has his being in the presence of public dynamite. Every action he may take is influenced by this condition—whether before or after an explosion.

Millions of dollars are spent every year in government because of this situation—millions that would not have to be spent in private organizations. In a narrow sense government tends therefore to be less efficient because of its public nature. But since government operates more in the public interest because of such special attention and scrutiny, the net effect is to make it more efficient in terms of its central purpose.

As an illustration of the way in which disgruntled or dismissed employees cause expenditures of millions of dollars a year, let me cite the case of a man whom I have never seen, but whose activities I had occasion to follow for a full decade. During this entire period (and also for ten years preceding it) he carried on a continuous series of campaigns against a half-dozen of the ablest executives in the government. He talked ad hominem and ad infinitum to writers of gossip columns. He wrote to the Director of the Bureau of the Budget, to other administrative officials, and to members of the Congress. He made hundreds of charges of misconduct, not one of which was warranted. Each one, however, had to be carefully investigated and duly reported. His superiors were reluctant to discharge him for communicating with members of Congress because to do so would perhaps have convinced hostile Congressmen of the truth of the charges. He cost the government hundreds of times more than his salary, and he stayed on the job until he reached retirement age.

The public nature of the government's business thus makes for a great difference in organizational discipline. Government employees often discuss their work with others in a way that would cause immediate discharge were they on the payroll of a private organization. Press and public both expect and induce that kind of talk. Business executives coming into government with no experience to prepare them for such a situation often find it extremely hard to adjust themselves to it. Yet some adjustment is an absolute necessity.

Generally the bigger a corporation, the more complex it is. An outsider can easily get lost in any of its fields of operations—raw materials, marketing, production, labor relations, finance, and management. Yet in relation to the United States government even the very largest corporation is small and simple. And the more big corporations we have, the more complex must the government become. Government, dealing in one way or another with almost everything, requires in its highest officials a special competence in handling relationships among all the varied and powerful forces, activities, and elements in the country. At the top the job is that of managing relationships between the complex parts of the entire nation, of giving both form and leadership to the life of the whole people. At that level it is an art—the art of politics. Only a politician can be President. The President needs economic understanding, but he should not function as an economist; he needs legal understanding, but he should not function as a lawyer; he needs business understanding, but he should not function as a businessman; he needs social understanding, but he should not function as a sociologist; he needs understanding of research, but he should not function as a scientist; he needs understanding of agriculture, labor, finance, but he should not function as a farmer, laborer, or banker. He needs to understand these *broadly* in order to understand politics: his success or failure as President depends on how he functions as a politician. At its best, politics is statesmanship.

Statecraft—government—is different from all other professions because it is broader than anything else in the field of action. Purely speculative thought and emotion may range a wider field, yet even this may be doubted, for government must be concerned with intellectual and emotional outreachings too. Government is different because it must take account of all the desires, needs, actions, thoughts, and sentiments of 140,000,000 people. Government is different because government is politics.

Chapter 4
The Study of Public Administration

There would probably be considerable agreement among contemporary professional students of public administration that the following essay by Woodrow Wilson is the most distinguished essay—of such brief compass, at least—in the history of American public administration. Published early in Wilson's career, in 1887, it proved a remarkably accurate prediction of the shape of things to come.

Through the essay Wilson sought to aid in the establishment of public administration as a recognized field of study. As it happened, nearly forty years passed before public administration (as we think of it today) as a field of study had developed to the point at which the first textbooks for college use were published. But when they did appear they were developed along lines that Wilson's essay clearly foreshadowed. Doctrine after doctrine which public administration accepted as valid was first clearly enunciated by Wilson in 1887.

Some of these doctrines were suggested above in the comment upon the selection from Weber. They concern the reconciliation of democracy, with its beliefs in popular control and participation, with the idea of professional, efficient administration, subject to its own criteria and procedures. The reconciliation was achieved by conceiving of government as divided between "politics" and "administration." The realm of politics is the proper realm for the exercise of democracy. And politics should have a general superintendency over administration. But administration itself should be free from political "meddling."

This general point of view became widely accepted among administrative students, and it is still, in one form or another, widely held. Is it a valid doctrine? This is one of the vital theoretical problems of current administrative study. Most writers now argue that any strict distinction between politics and administration is unrealistic or undesirable. But the older point of view still holds many redoubts of theory and practice.

In connection with the "politics-administration" doctrine and the attacks upon it, there is a curious detail in Wilson's essay. You will note that in the opening paragraph Wilson states that the first object of administrative

study is to discover "what government can properly and successfully do."
Now, this is a description of the central concern of *politics*; but the essay
is devoted largely to arguing the separability of politics and administration.
Certainly this seems to be a serious inconsistency. Probably Wilson's answer
would be that the politics from which administration should be free is the
activities of political parties, not the process of public policy formulation.
Query, is this a realistic distinction?

Whether or not this is an inconsistency, the foreign literature on administration to which Wilson refers—and from which American students borrowed heavily—certainly is as much concerned with what government
should do as with how it should be done. And significantly, one of the
strongest trends today in the study of administration is to include "public
policy" in the curriculum.

The Study of Administration *

WOODROW WILSON

I suppose that no practical science is ever studied where there is no need to
know it. The very fact, therefore, that the eminently practical science of administration is finding its way into college courses in this country would prove that
this country needs to know more about administration, were such proof of the
fact required to make out a case. . . . It is a thing almost taken for granted
among us, that the present movement called civil service reform must, after the
accomplishment of its first purpose, expand into efforts to improve, not the
personnel only, but also the organization and methods of our government offices:
because it is plain that their organization and methods need improvement only
less than their *personnel*. It is the object of administrative study to discover, first,
what government can properly and successfully do, and, secondly, how it can
do these proper things with the utmost possible efficiency and at the least possible
cost either of money or of energy. On both these points there is obviously much
need of light among us; and only careful study can supply that light.

Before entering on that study, however, it is needful:

I. To take some account of what others have done in the same line; that is
to say, of the history of the study.

II. To ascertain just what is its subject-matter.

III. To determine just what are the best methods by which to develop it, and
the most clarifying political conceptions to carry with us into it.

Unless we know and settle these things, we shall set out without chart or
compass.

* From *Political Science Quarterly*, Vol. 2 (June, 1887), pp. 197–222. Abridged.

I.

The science of administration is the latest fruit of that study of the science of politics which was begun some twenty-two hundred years ago. It is a birth of our own century, almost of our own generation.

Why was it so late in coming? Why did it wait till this too busy century of ours to demand attention for itself? Administration is the most obvious part of government; it is government in action; it is the executive, the operative, the most visible side of government, and is of course as old as government itself. It is government in action, and one might very naturally expect to find that government in action had arrested the attention and provoked the scrutiny of writers of politics very early in the history of systematic thought.

But such was not the case. No one wrote systematically of administration as a branch of the science of government until the present century had passed its first youth and had begun to put forth its characteristic flower of systematic knowledge. Up to our own day all the political writers whom we now read had thought, argued, dogmatized only about the *constitution* of government; about the nature of the state, the essence and seat of sovereignty, popular power and kingly prerogative; about the greatest meanings lying at the heart of government, and the high ends sets before the purpose of government by man's nature and man's aims. The central field of controversy was that great field of theory in which monarchy rode tilt against democracy, in which oligarchy would have built for itself strongholds of privilege, and in which tyranny sought opportunity to make good its claim to receive submission from all competitors. Amidst this high warfare of principles, administration could command no pause for its own consideration. The question was always: Who shall make law, and what shall that law be? The other question, how law should be administered with enlightenment, with equity, with speed, and without friction, was put aside as "practical detail" which clerks could arrange after doctors had agreed upon principles.

That political philosophy took this direction was of course no accident, no chance preference or perverse whim of political philosophers. The philosophy of any time is, as Hegel says, "nothing but the spirit of that time expressed in abstract thought"; and political philosophy, like philosophy of every other kind, has only held up the mirror to contemporary affairs. The trouble in early times was almost altogether about the constitution of government; and consequently that was what engrossed men's thoughts. There was little or no trouble about administration,—at least little that was heeded by administrators. The functions of government were simple, because life itself was simple. Government went about imperatively and compelled men, without thought of consulting their wishes. There was no complex system of public revenues and public debts to puzzle financiers; there were, consequently, no financiers to be puzzled. No one who possessed power was long at a loss how to use it. The great and only question was: Who shall possess it? Populations were of manageable numbers;

property was of simple sorts. There were plenty of farms, but no stocks and bonds: more cattle than vested interests.

I have said that all this was true of "early times"; but it was substantially true also of comparatively late times. One does not have to look back of the last century for the beginnings of the present complexities of trade and perplexities of commercial speculation, nor for the portentous birth of national debts. Good Queen Bess, doubtless, thought that the monopolies of the sixteenth century were hard enough to handle without burning her hands; but they are not remembered in the presence of the giant monopolies of the nineteenth century. When Blackstone lamented that corporations had no bodies to be kicked and no souls to be damned, he was anticipating the proper time for such regrets by full a century. The perennial discords between master and workmen which now so often disturb industrial society began before the Black Death and the Statute of Laborers; but never before our own day did they assume such ominous proportions as they wear now. In brief, if difficulties of governmental action are to be seen gathering in other centuries, they are to be seen culminating in our own.

This is the reason why administrative tasks have nowadays to be so studiously and systematically adjusted to carefully tested standards of policy, the reason why we are having now what we never had before, a science of administration. The weightier debates of constitutional principle are even yet by no means concluded; but they are no longer of more immediate practical moment than questions of administration. It is getting to be harder to *run* a constitution than to frame one. . . .

There is scarcely a single duty of government which was once simple which is not now complex; government once had but a few masters; it now has scores of masters. Majorities formerly only underwent government; they now conduct government. Where government once might follow the whims of a court, it must now follow the views of a nation.

And those views are steadily widening to new conceptions of state duty; so that, at the same time that the functions of government are every day becoming more complex and difficult, they are also vastly multiplying in number. Administration is everywhere putting its hands to new undertakings. . . .

This is why there should be a science of administration which shall seek to straighten the paths of government, to make its business less unbusinesslike, to strengthen and purify its organization, and to crown its duties with dutifulness. This is one reason why there is such a science.

But where has this science grown up? Surely not on this side the sea. Not much impartial scientific method is to be discerned in our administrative practices. The poisonous atmosphere of city government, the crooked secrets of state administration, the confusion, sinecurism, and corruption ever and again discovered in the bureaux at Washington forbid us to believe that any clear conceptions of what constitutes good administration are as yet very widely current in the United States. No; American writers have hitherto taken no very important part in the advancement of this science. It has found its doctors in Europe. It is not of our making; it is a foreign science, speaking very little of the language of English or American principle. It employs only foreign tongues; it utters none but what are to our minds alien ideas. Its aims, its examples, its conditions, are almost exclusively grounded in the histories of foreign races, in the precedents of foreign systems, in the lessons of foreign revolutions. It has been developed by French and German professors, and is consequently in all parts adapted to the needs of a compact state, and made to fit highly centralized forms of government; whereas, to answer our purposes, it must be adapted, not to a simple and compact, but to a complex and multiform state, and made to fit highly decentralized forms of government. If we would employ it, we must Americanize it, and that not formally, in language merely, but radically, in thought, principle, and aim as well. It must learn our constitutions by heart; must get the bureaucratic fever out of its veins; must inhale much free American air.

If an explanation be sought why a science manifestly so susceptible of being made useful to all governments alike should have received attention first in Europe, where government has long been a monopoly, rather than in England or the United States, where government has long been a common franchise, the reason will doubtless be found to be twofold: first, that in Europe, just because government was independent of popular assent, there was more governing to be done; and, second, that the desire to keep government a monopoly made the monopolists interested in discovering the least irritating means of governing. They were, besides, few enough to adopt means promptly. . . .

On this side the sea we, the while, had known no great difficulties of government. With a new country, in which there was room and remunerative employment for everybody, with liberal principles of government and unlimited skill in practical politics, we were long exempted from the need of being anxiously careful about plans and methods of administration. We have naturally been slow to see the use or significance of those many volumes of learned research and painstaking examination into the ways and means of conducting government which the presses of Europe have been sending to our libraries. Like a lusty child, government with us has expanded in nature and grown great in stature, but has also become awkward in movement. The vigor and increase of its life has been altogether out of proportion to its skill in living. It has gained strength, but it has not acquired deportment. Great, therefore, as has been our advantage over the countries of Europe in point of ease and health of constitutional development, now that the time for more careful administrative adjustments and larger administrative knowledge has come to us, we are at a signal disadvantage as compared with the transatlantic nations; and this for reasons which I shall try to make clear.

Judging by the constitutional histories of the chief nations of the modern world, there may be said to be three periods of growth through which government has passed in all the most highly developed of existing systems, and through which it promises to pass in all the rest. The first of these periods is that of absolute rulers, and of an administrative system adapted to absolute rule; the second is that in which constitutions are framed to do away with absolute rulers and substitute popular control, and in which administration is neglected for these higher concerns; and the third is that in which the sovereign people undertake to develop administration under this new constitution which has brought them into power.

Those governments are now in the lead in administrative practice which had rulers still absolute but also enlightened when those modern days of political illumination came in which it was made evident to all but the blind that governors are properly only the servants of the governed. In such governments administration has been organized to subserve the general weal with the simplicity and effectiveness vouchsafed only to the undertakings of a single will.

Such was the case in Prussia, for instance, where administration has been most studied and most nearly perfected. Frederic the Great, stern and masterful as was his rule, still sincerely professed to regard himself as only the chief servant of the state, to consider his great office a public trust; and it was he who, building upon the foundations laid by his father, began to organize the public service of Prussia as in very earnest a service of the public. His no less absolute successor, Frederic William III, under the inspiration of Stein, again, in his turn, advanced the work still further, planning many of the broader structural features which give firmness and form to Prussian administration to-day. Almost the whole of the admirable system has been developed by kingly initiative.

Of similar origin was the practice, if not the plan, of modern French administration, with its symmetrical divisions of territory and its orderly gradations of office. The days of the Revolution—of the Constituent Assembly—were days of constitution-*writing*, but they can hardly be called days of constitution-*making*. The Revolution heralded a period of constitutional development,—the entrance of France upon the second of those periods which I have enumerated,—but it did not itself inaugurate such a period. It interrupted and unsettled absolutism, but did not destroy it. Napoleon succeeded the monarchs of France, to exercise a power as unrestricted as they had ever possessed.

The recasting of French administration by Napoleon is, therefore, my second example of the perfecting of civil machinery by the single will of an absolute ruler before the dawn of a constitutional era. No corporate, popular will could ever have effected arrangements such as those which Napoleon commanded. Arrangements so simple at the expense of local prejudice, so logical in their indifference to popular choice, might be decreed by a Constituent Assembly, but could be established only by the unlimited authority of a despot. The system of the year VIII was ruthlessly thorough and heartlessly perfect. It was . . . in large part, a return to the despotism that had been overthrown.

Among those nations, on the other hand, which entered upon a season of constitution-making and popular reform before administration had received the impress of liberal principle, administrative improvement has been tardy and half-done. Once a nation has embarked in the business of manufacturing constitutions, it finds it exceedingly difficult to close out that business and open for the public a bureau of skilled, economical administration. There seems to be no end to the tinkering of constitutions. Your ordinary constitution will last you hardly ten years without repairs or additions; and the time for administrative detail comes late. . . .

The English race . . . has long and successfully studied the art of curbing executive power to the constant neglect of the art of perfecting executive methods. It has exercised itself much more in controlling than in energizing government. It has been more concerned to render government just and moderate than to make it facile, well-ordered, and effective. English and American political history has been a history, not of administrative development, but of legislative over-sight,—not of progress in governmental organization, but of advance in law-making and political criticism. Consequently, we have reached a time when administrative study and creation are imperatively necessary to the well-being of our governments saddled with the habits of a long period of constitution-making. That period has practically closed, so far as the establishment of essential principles is concerned, but we cannot shake off its atmosphere. We go on criticizing when we ought to be creating. We have reached the third of the periods I have mentioned,—the period, namely, when the people have to develop administration in accordance with the constitutions they won for themselves in a previous period of struggle with absolute power; but we are not prepared for the tasks of the new period.

Such an explanation seems to afford the only escape from blank astonishment at the fact that, in spite of our vast advantages in point of political liberty, and above all in point of practical political skill and sagacity, so many nations are ahead of us in administrative organization and administrative skill. Why, for instance, have we but just begun purifying a civil service which was rotten full fifty years ago? To say that slavery diverted us is but to repeat what I have said—that flaws in our constitution delayed us.

Of course all reasonable preference would declare for this English and American course of politics rather than for that of any European country. We should not like to have had Prussia's history for the sake of having Prussia's administrative skill; and Prussia's particular system of administration would quite suffocate us. It is better to be untrained and free than to be servile and systematic. Still there is no denying that it would be better yet to be both free in spirit and proficient in practice. It is this even more reasonable preference which impels us to discover what there may be to hinder or delay us in naturalizing this much-to-be-desired science of administration.

What, then, is there to prevent it?

Well, principally, popular sovereignty. It is harder for democracy to organize administration than for monarchy. The very completeness of our most cherished political successes in the past embarrasses us. We have enthroned public opinion; and it is forbidden us to hope during its reign for any quick schooling of the sovereign in executive expertness or in the conditions of perfect functional balance in government. The very fact that we have realized popular rule in its fulness has made the task of *organizing* that rule just so much the more difficult. In order to make any advance at all we must instruct and persuade a multitudinous monarch called public opinion,—a much less feasible undertaking than to influence a single monarch called a king. An individual sovereign will adopt a simple plan and carry it out directly: he will have but one opinion, and he will embody that one opinion in one command. But this other sovereign, the people, will have a score of differing opinions. They can agree upon nothing simple: advance must be made through compromise, by a compounding of differences, by a trimming of plans and a suppression of too straightforward principles. There will be a succession of resolves running through a course of years, a dropping fire of commands running through a whole gamut of modifications. . . .

So much, then, for the history of the study of administration, and the peculiarly difficult conditions under which, entering upon it when we do, we must undertake it. What, now, is the subject-matter of this study, and what are its characteristic objects?

II

The field of administration is a field of business. It is removed from the hurry and strife of politics; it at most points stands apart even from the debatable ground of constitutional study. It is a part of political life only as the methods of the counting-house are a part of the life of society; only as machinery is part of the manufactured product. But it is, at the same time, raised very far above the dull level of mere technical detail by the fact that through its greater principles it is directly connected with the lasting maxims of political wisdom, the permanent truths of political progress.

The object of administrative study is to rescue executive methods from the confusion and costliness of empirical experiment and set them upon foundations laid deep in stable principle.

It is for this reason that we must regard civil-service reform in its present stages as but a prelude to a fuller administrative reform. We are now rectifying methods of appointment; we must go on to adjust executive functions more fitly and to prescribe better methods of executive organization and action. Civil-service reform is thus but a moral preparation for what is to follow. It is clearing the moral atmosphere of official life by establishing the sanctity of public office as a public trust, and, by making the service unpartisan, it is opening the way for making it businesslike. By sweetening its motives it is rendering it capable of improving its methods of work.

Let me expand a little what I have said of the province of administration. Most important to be observed is the truth already so much and so fortunately insisted upon by our civil-service reformers; namely, that administration lies outside the proper sphere of *politics*. Administrative questions are not political questions. Although politics sets the tasks for administration, it should not be suffered to manipulate its offices.

This is a distinction of high authority; eminent German writers insist upon it as of course. Bluntschli, for instance, bids us separate administration alike from politics and from law. Politics, he says, is state activity "in things great and universal," while "administration, on the other hand," is "the activity of the state in individual and small things. Politics is thus the special province of the statesman, administration of the technical official." . . .

There is another distinction which must be worked into all our conclusions, which, though but another side of that between administration and politics, is not quite so easy to keep sight of: I mean the distinction between *constitutional* and administrative questions, between those governmental adjustments which are essential to constitutional principle and those which are merely instrumental to the possibly changing purposes of a wisely adapting convenience.

One cannot easily make clear to every one just where administration resides in the various departments of any practicable government without entering upon particulars so numerous as to confuse and distinctions so minute as to distract. No lines of demarcation, setting apart administrative from non-administrative functions, can be run between this and that department of government without being run up hill and down dale, over dizzy heights of distinction and through dense jungles of statutory enactment, hither and thither around "ifs" and "buts," "whens" and "howevers," until they become altogether lost to the common eye not accustomed to this sort of surveying, and consequently not acquainted with the use of the theodolite of logical discernment. A great deal of administration goes about *incognito* to most of the world, being confounded now with political "management," and again with constitutional principle. . . .

A clear view of the difference between the province of constitutional law and the province of administrative function ought to leave no room for misconception. . . . Public administration is detailed and systematic execution of public law. Every particular application of general law is an act of administration. The assessment and raising of taxes, for instance, the hanging of a criminal, the transportation and delivery of the mails, the equipment and recruiting of the army and navy, *etc.*, are all obviously acts of administration; but the general laws which direct these things to be done are as obviously outside of and above administration. The broad plans of governmental action are not administrative; the detailed execution of such plans is administrative. Constitutions, therefore, properly concern themselves only with those instrumentalities of government which are to control general law. Our federal constitution observes this principle in saying nothing of even the greatest of the purely executive offices, and speaking only of that President of the Union who was to share the legislative and policy-making functions of government, only of those judges of highest jurisdiction who were to interpret and guard its principles, and not of those who were merely to give utterance to them.

This is not quite the distinction between Will and answering Deed, because the administrator should have and does have a will of his own in the choice of means for accomplishing his work. He is not and ought not to be a mere passive instrument. The distinction is between general plans and special means.

There is, indeed, one point at which administrative studies trench on constitutional ground—or at least upon what seems constitutional ground. The study of administration, philosophically viewed, is closely connected with the study of the proper distribution of constitutional authority. To be efficient it must discover the simplest arrangements by which responsibility can be unmistakably fixed upon officials; the best way of dividing authority without hampering it, and responsibility without obscuring it. And this question of the distribution of authority, when taken into the sphere of the higher, the originating functions of government, is obviously a central constitutional question. If administrative study can discover the best principles upon which to base such distribution, it will have done constitutional study an invaluable service. Montesquieu did not, I am convinced, say the last word on this head.

To discover the best principle for the distribution of authority is of greater importance, possibly, under a democratic system, where officials serve many masters, than under others where they serve but a few. All sovereigns are suspicious of their servants, and the sovereign people is no exception to the rule; but how is its suspicion to be allayed by *knowledge?* If that suspicion could but be clarified into wise vigilance, it would be altogether salutary; if that vigilance could be aided by the unmistakable placing of responsibility, it would be altogether beneficent. Suspicion in itself is never healthful either in the private or in the public mind. *Trust is strength* in all relations of life; and, as it is the office of the constitutional reformer to create conditions of trustfulness, so it is the office of the administrative organizer to fit administration with conditions of clear-cut responsibility which shall insure trustworthiness.

And let me say that large powers and unhampered discretion seem to me the indispensable conditions of responsibility. Public attention must be easily directed, in each case of good or bad administration, to just the man deserving of praise or blame. There is no danger in power, if only it be not irresponsible. If it be divided, dealt out in shares to many, it is obscured; and if it be obscured, it is made irresponsible. But if it be centred in heads of the service and in heads of branches of the service, it is easily watched and brought to book. If to keep his office a man must achieve open and honest success, and if at the same time he feels himself intrusted with large freedom of discretion, the greater his power the less likely is he to abuse it, the more is he nerved and sobered and elevated by it. The less his power, the more safely obscure and unnoticed does he feel his position to be, and the more readily does he relapse into remissness.

Just here we manifestly emerge upon the field of that still larger question,—the proper relations between public opinion and administration.

To whom is official trustworthiness to be disclosed, and by whom is it to be rewarded? Is the official to look to the public for his meed of praise and push of promotion, or only to his superior in office? Are the people to be called in to settle administrative discipline as they are called in to settle constitutional principles? These questions evidently find their root in what is undoubtedly the fundamental problem of this whole study. That problem is: What part shall public opinion take in the conduct of administration?

The right answer seems to be, that public opinion shall play the part of authoritative critic.

But the *method* by which its authority shall be made to tell? Our peculiar American difficulty in organizing administration is not the danger of losing liberty, but the danger of not being able or willing to separate its essentials from its accidents. Our success is made doubtful by that besetting error of ours, the error of trying to do too much by vote. Self-government does not consist in having a hand in everything, any more than housekeeping consists necessarily in cooking dinner with one's own hands. The cook must be trusted with a large discretion as to the management of the fires and the ovens. . . .

The problem is to make public opinion efficient without suffering it to be meddlesome. Directly exercised, in the oversight of the daily details and in the choice of the daily means of government, public criticism is of course a clumsy nuisance, a rustic handling delicate machinery. But as superintending the greater forces of formative policy alike in politics and administration, public criticism is altogether safe and beneficent, altogether indispensable. Let administrative study find the best means for giving public criticism this control and for shutting it out from all other interference.

But is the whole duty of administrative study done when it has taught the people what sort of administration to desire and demand, and how to get what they demand? Ought it not to go on to drill candidates for the public service?

There is an admirable movement towards universal political education now afoot in this country. The time will soon come when no college of respectability can afford to do without a well-filled chair of political science. But the education thus imparted will go but a certain length. It will multiply the number of intelligent critics of government, but it will create no competent body of administrators. It will prepare the way for the development of a sure-footed understanding of the general principles of government, but it will not necessarily foster skill in conducting government. It is an education which will equip legislators, perhaps, but not executive officials. If we are to improve public opinion, which is the motive power of government, we must prepare better officials as the *apparatus* of government. If we are to put in new boilers and to mend the fires which drive our governmental machinery, we must not leave the old wheels and joints and valves and bands to creak and buzz and clatter on as best they may at bidding of the new force. We must put in new running parts wherever there is the least lack of strength or adjustment. It will be necessary to organize democracy by sending up to the competitive examinations for the civil service men definitely prepared for standing liberal tests as to technical knowledge. A technically schooled civil service will presently have become indispensable.

I know that a corps of civil servants prepared by a special schooling and drilled, after appointment, into a perfected organization, with appropriate hierarchy and characteristic discipline, seems to a great many very thoughtful persons to contain elements which might combine to make an offensive official class,—a distinct, semi-corporate body with sympathies divorced from those of a progressive, free-spirited people, and with hearts narrowed to the meanness of a bigoted officialism. Certainly such a class would be altogether hateful and harmful in the United States. Any measures calculated to produce it would for us be measures of reaction and of folly.

But to fear the creation of a domineering, illiberal officialism as a result of the studies I am here proposing is to miss altogether the principle upon which I wish most to insist. That principle is, that administration in the United States must be at all points sensitive to public opinion. A body of thoroughly trained officials serving during good behavior we must have in any case: that is a plain business necessity. But the apprehension that such a body will be anything un-American clears away the moment it is asked, What is to constitute good behavior? For that question obviously carries its own answer on its face. Steady, hearty allegiance to the policy of the government they serve will constitute good behavior. That *policy* will have no taint of officialism about it. It will not be the creation of permanent officials, but of statesmen whose responsibility to public opinion will be direct and inevitable. / . .

The ideal for us is a civil service cultured and self-sufficient enough to act with sense and vigor, and yet so intimately connected with the popular thought, by means of elections and constant public counsel, as to find arbitrariness or class spirit quite out of the question.

———◆———

The following selection is the body of a speech delivered in 1939 by the late Charles A. Beard, addressing a governmental research group. Well known for his historical writings, Beard was also a commanding figure in American political science. He took an active part in the growth of the public administration movement, both as an organizer and as a writer. Toward the end of his career he made several thoughtful and moving statements of his firm belief in the importance of administrative study. This is one of these statements.

At the center of Beard's address are the assertion and development of the thesis that administration is a "science." Generally speaking, there has been and still is agreement among administrative students on the line taken here by Beard. In an age in which science is highly esteemed, this attitude is understandable; and the case which Beard and others make is persuasive. Still, this position must not be accepted without challenge. Even if it should be essentially correct, *uncritical* acceptance of it will lead to unsound theory and practice. For example, will Beard's comparison of economics and economic theory with administrators and administrative theory stand the test of critical examination? The judgment on economics may not be too severe, but are the "principles of administration" really on better or other foundations? Much of what was believed by students of Beard's generation to be firm scientific truth is believed by many today to have been but hasty generalization based on incomplete observation.

One should bear in mind too the point of view of many students of administration that what we are dealing with here is not a science but an art—recall Mr. Tead's essay above on administration as a "fine art." Query, can these two points of view be reconciled? Is the distinction between pure science and applied science useful?

Incidentally, Beard's plea, near the end of his speech, for a "crowning organization of officials and private persons concerned with the whole science of administration" was followed very shortly after by the organization of the American Society for Public Administration, which is just such an organization.

Philosophy, Science and Art of Public Administration *

CHARLES AUSTIN BEARD

The word science of administration has been used. There are many who object to the term. Not long ago one of the most distinguished British writers on government and politics ridiculed the idea in my presence. He said that there is no such thing as a science of administration, that trying to teach it is folly, and that the very notion of training anybody in it is ridiculous. Observing the heat of the eminent gentleman on the subject, I let it drop. In my later years I have become somewhat like Esther Johnson. Of her Dean Swift remarked: "Whether from

* Address delivered before the Annual Conference of the Governmental Research Association, Princeton, N. J., Sept. 8, 1939.

easiness in general, or from her indifference to persons, or from her despair of mending them . . . , when she saw any of the company very warm in a wrong opinion, she was more inclined to confirm them in it than to oppose them. It prevented noise, she said, and saved time."

Now if by science is meant a conceptual scheme of things in which every particularity covered may be assigned a mathematical value and all particularities covered and in process may be exactly expressed in a differential equation, then administration is not a science. In this sense only astro-physics may be called a science and it is well to remember that mechanical laws of the heavens tell us nothing about the color and composition of the stars and as yet cannot account for some of the disturbances and explosions which seem accidental.

If, on the other hand, we may rightly use the term science in connection with a body of exact knowledge, derived from experience and observation, and a body of rules or axioms which experience has demonstrated to be applicable in concrete practice, and to work out in practice approximately as forecast, then we may, if we please, appropriately and for convenience, speak of a science of administration. It is as much a general science as economics or psychology or biology, more of a science than history or politics. Once, when the great French mathematician, Poincaré, was asked whether Euclidean geometry is true, he replied that the question had no sense but that Euclidean geometry is and still remains the most convenient. The Oxford English dictionary tells us that a science is, among other things, a particular branch of knowledge or study; a recognized department of learning.

The more modest writers of distinction among contemporary scientists, such as E. W. Hobson, have surrendered the mechanical materialism of the mid-nineteenth century, which insisted that all things—both physical objects and organic life, including human beings—are subject to law and can be described in mechanical terms. They do not deny that all things material and human may be subject to law. They just honestly confess that they do not know it. They are content with finding what they call "deterministic tracts" of matter and force which may be correctly called deterministic sequences. The engineer deals with such a tract when he takes a given volume of water at a given elevation and directs it downward against a given type of water wheel geared to a dynamo. His science enables him to determine in advance, by a knowledge of the factors involved, that the operation will produce a given result which can be counted upon with decided assurance. Scientists also proceed by analysis and classification and some of their sciences have not advanced very far beyond the stage of classification. Even that is useful. We use classifications when we choose ginger ale instead of corn whiskey.

I should myself prefer to limit the term science to bodies of knowledge which are wholly deterministic in their rules or axioms. But that would exclude most natural sciences and, besides, the human race, as demonstrated by the dictionaries, persists in using the term science in its etymological and broader sense. I bow to the verdict of usage, and, besides, I find no word more convenient and exact than the term science to cover the body of knowledge and practice called administration.

Administration, Economics and Physics

I have said that administration is as much of a science as economics. It is, in my opinion, far more of a science. Economics has been and still is primarily descriptive. It seeks to describe the actual economic conduct of vast masses of human beings operating within and between nations and the movement of such phenomena as prices, wages, and exchanges. The calculations of the economist are constantly subject to the violent changes introduced by politics—changes which are unpredictable and incalculable. The English body of economic knowledge is not very applicable in Germany or Russia. Moreover, the economist is not an operator. He does not operate railways and factories, and test out his theories in practice. He is not at all concerned with the concrete problems of starting an operation or system. Save in rare cases, the economist is a mere observer.

The case of administration is different in fundamental respects. The economist is dealing with what is sometimes called, erroneously, I think, a natural order of things, at least, with things that operate, it is said, unconsciously and automatically. The administrator is more like the engineer who constructs a power plant, that is, he is concerned with the realization of conscious human purposes by the conscious use of human beings and materials. It is true that the mere student of administration may be just an observer, but he does not merely observe natural, unconscious, and automatic operations. He observes the formulation of human purposes, consciously and deliberately, and operations designed to effect given results. And he sees calculations of results in advance realized later in practice with a high degree of approximation. The degree of approximation between advance calculations and results is not often, if ever, as exact as in the case of a hydro-electric plant, but it is constantly exact enough for practical purposes.

In other words, there are in administration things analogous to, if not identical with, the mechanical tracts or deterministic sequences of physics. If, for example, it is decided by government to accomplish the purpose of providing compensation at given rates for men and women employed in industry who sustain injuries in connection with their occupations, the administrator can, like the engineer, estimate in advance the probable cost of such a design, indicate the types of officers and employees necessary to administer the design, and the administrative procedures appropriate to the whole process from beginning to end. And, as in the case of the hydro-electric engineer, the administrator later sees the results of his operations and can compare them with his advance estimates. There are more variables and incalculables in human affairs than in hydro-electric affairs, but even so administration achieves predetermined results with an approximation which is often amazing for its exactness. If administrative designs and estimates were not realized in practice with a high degree of exactness, both industry and government would collapse.

And if the experience of natural science is any guide, then as the science of administration advances, we may reasonably expect it to take on an increasingly deterministic character. As research, scientific societies, and the exchanges of knowledge and hypotheses by natural scientists have advanced the exactness of knowledge in the domain of natural science, so we may expect research, administrative societies, and the exchanges among administrators to advance the exactness of knowledge in the domain of administration.

Already, we may truly say, we have an enormous body of exact and usable knowledge in the domain of administration. It would be easy to list thousands of volumes and articles on the subject, from the hands of high competence. I have seen this body of literature grow from a few items in 1898 to an enormous mass in 1939. Every informed and competent person in the field of administration knows this to be a fact. During this period I have seen the number of research workers increase from a mere handful to hundreds. This is a fact also, at least for informed and competent persons. During this period the opportunities for life work in administration have multiplied many times. This is also a fact, for informed and competent persons. I dare say, though I shall not try to prove it, that the body of exact literature in administration is many times larger than the body of exact literature in natural science when Bacon, Galileo, and Newton began the revolution in natural science three hundred years ago, and is at least as exact as the literature of history, politics, economics, and classics, now widely used in our colleges and universities. During this same period I have seen the number of societies and organizations among administrators, local and general, increase from nothing to fifty or sixty.

Training and Research in Administration

Now anything that is known can be communicated, can be imparted to youth. In other words, this body of administrative literature can be taught to young men and women; perhaps also to the aged, if they are not hopeless. And it is possible by tests to discover whether or how far the process of communicating and imparting administrative knowledge has been successful, not precisely in all cases, but certainly as precisely as in any of the subjects dealing strictly with the humanities. Moreover, and this is highly important, young men and women who had more or less mastered the principles, maxims, and axioms of administrative science can now, by what is called in-service training, fortify their formal knowledge by living experiences in and with administration. There is, then, a science of administration, in the sense in which I have used the term, and it can be taught, learned, and used. There is nothing in anything that determines whether it must be taught in universities, but, if universities have a warm and living interest in the future of our government and civilization they will teach it, and public officials and politicians will take note of it, profit by it, and improve the public services as a result of it. . . .

Besides extending our training in the science of administration, we must increase our provisions for research in administration. We must do this in our universities, special institutions, and in the great divisions of government. I shall refer particularly to the last. Slowly our administrators and politicians are realizing the importance of research and planning as adjuncts to the successful administration of any complicated affairs, especially where constantly changing circumstances alter the situation. From the very beginning of scientific management, advance planning has been deemed the clue to successful results and research has been deemed indispensable to planning and execution. Great administrators and students of the subjects know how vital this is to effective administration, and I need make no exposition of the topic. As administration becomes more and more scientific, that is, as it advances in exactness of projection, forecast, and results, it will raise planning and research to a top position in thought and practice. Natural science and technology have done this with amazing effectiveness. Without the inquiry into relevant facts and without the blueprint, they would be on the level of astrology.

Organization

One more phase of the subject and I have finished. From the establishment of the Royal Society in England in the seventeenth century to the present, with increasing emphasis, it has been demonstrated that societies of scientific workers have contributed to the advancement of science in every direction. They have provided formal exchanges of knowledge and hypotheses. They have afforded opportunities for the contact of individuals, which is a vitalizing stimulus to individual activities. They have enlisted public interest in, and support for, scientific work. Already various associations of persons interested in administration, private and official, have been formed in the United States and have proved their usefulness. The time is now ripe for a crowning organization of officials and private persons concerned with the whole science of administration in its broadest reaches—a society concerned with administration in itself, as distinguished from the administration of particular functions, such as highways or public health. It would by no means neglect the specific and the concrete, but it would concentrate on the development of the methods, procedures, and axioms common to all branches of the public service and by rigorous general thinking stimulate and guide thought about single specialties. It could serve the science of administration as scientific societies have served natural science.

In all this I have not been unmindful of the great context of history and civilization in which administration works. I am not among those simple souls that can find the simple causes of national grandeur or sublime civilizations or the decline of nations. But I do observe in the histories of Greece and Rome records which show that incompetence of administration and the breakdown of administration accompanied the disintegration of the state and civilization. And I am sure that, if we are to bring our resources, skills, and powers into full and noble use, if we are to build a public and private economy that can sustain an enduring society, if we are to provide the conditions necessary to the full flowering of civilization in America, we shall have to rely upon the constant advancement of administrative science. Thus, we may be worthy of our heritage and our opportunities.

Chapter 5

Theory of Organization: The Genus

Nothing seems more appropriate in introducing the subject of theory of organization than a reference to the fable of the blind men and the elephant. Each of the blind men, you will recall, touched with his hands a different part of the elephant, and as a result there was among them radical difference of opinion as to the nature of the beast.

Similarly, there is so much divergence between different theories of organization (not all of which can be represented in a book of this scope) as to be startling. How is the diversity to be accounted for? Which theories are correct, which in error?

Our fable has relevance here. The various students who have written so differently have approached administration with different preconceptions and purposes. Since "the eye is blind to what the mind does not see," organization seems to vary according to the mind with which it is approached. When viewed from inside, it looks much different than from the outside; viewed by an economist it looks much different than when viewed by a psychologist; the private's army is not the general's army. It is perhaps not so much that some theories of organization are right and some wrong as that the differing theories present, with varying degrees of adequacy, different aspects of the truth. Query, is the important thing about a theory of organization not so much its truth as its *usefulness*?

The writings on theory of organization do not have any very close counterparts in the writings of any previous period of history. This is partly because what they are most concerned with—the phenomena of large-scale, formal organization—tends to be modern. This is due also, however, to the fact that only recently in man's history has he tried to subject organization itself to abstract, comprehensive, and detailed analysis. Partly, no doubt, this recent disposition for man to subject organization itself to objective analysis is due to the spread of the "scientific spirit," which has induced us to look with new and penetrating eyes at what had before been taken for granted. Human institutions and personal relations are increasingly studied in a way once thought possible or desirable only for the study of "the natural order."

The following selection is an abridgment of the opening chapters of *The Principles of Organization,* by James D. Mooney, a book of wide use and great popularity in recent decades. In these chapters the general principles of all organization are, it is alleged, set forth analytically, and the remainder of the book is devoted to demonstrations of these principles in military, religious, and other organizations.

The Principles of Organization is from the literature of business administration rather than public administration. There is a large area of overlapping interest and ideas between the two fields, however, and in the matter of organizational analysis public administration has been heavily indebted to business administration. Until a decade or so ago students of public administration accepted without important modification most of the organizational ideas and techniques of business administration. Lately, however, public administration has tended to modify and supplement the more abstract and "technical" approach to organization with concepts from such fields as sociology and psychology—as will appear in some later selections. Meanwhile, however, business administration has forged ahead too, and its present frontiers of organizational theory are beyond the point represented by Mr. Mooney's *Principles.*

But though the frontiers of research and speculation are far advanced over a decade or two ago, most of the ideas presented in this essay are still working ideas of current professional work in organization. Its vocabulary is still current coin. "Scalar principle," "delegation of authority"—such concepts still play an active role in current thought and action.

Perhaps the most interesting and controversial idea of traditional organization theory is that a good organizational structure is one that conforms to the proper design for a good organization, one fitted to "the enduring types of mind found among all individuals at all times," rather than conforming to the actual characteristics and peculiarities of the individuals who happen to "inhabit" the organization at a particular time. Query, is this sensible? Is it proper scientific method, as it is represented to be? Or is it a dogmatic presumption, a misreading of the meaning of scientific method?

From one point of view the selections from Max Weber in Part I might be classified as "theory of organization." Query, to what extent are Weber and Mooney in conflict, to what extent complementary?

Is Mooney's analysis logically sound and empirically valid?

The Principles of Organization *

JAMES D. MOONEY

When any group combines for a given purpose, even if the group consists of only two persons or more, we have the psychic fundamentals of organization, plus the principle which must underlie all associated effort. Let us here employ the simplest illustration. Two men unite their strength to move some object that is too heavy or bulky to be moved by one. Here we have associated effort, which is synonymous with organization, and likewise *coordination*, the first principle that underlies all such effort.

This illustration indicates the exact definition of organization. *Organization is the form of every human association for the attainment of a common purpose.*

This definition does not mean that all forms of human association are alike, for these are as numerous as the variety of human aims and motives. . . . But at least it is axiomatic that any motive calling for associated human action must express itself in organization. These forms, of course, will vary according to the nature of the aim; it is only through the finding of certain features essential to all forms that we can justify the claim that we have found a principle. Before we proceed, however, in the effort to identify such principles it is necessary to review some of the considerations implicit in our definition of organization.

The first point is that this definition identifies organization as a pure process. This indicates a dual relation; on the one hand, to the people who create and use the process and, on the other, to the aim or object of the process. Our purpose is the study of organization simply as a process, which means the study of its internal structure. . . .

Organization has been termed the formal side of administration, likewise the machinery of administration, the channel through which the measures and policies of administration become effective. There is truth in these descriptions, but not the whole truth. Again, organization has been called the framework of every group moving toward a common objective. Here also the simile is sound as far as it goes. It seems to imply that organization refers only to the differentiation of individual duties, as set forth in the familiar organization charts. But duties must relate to procedure, and it is here that we find the real dynamics of organization, the motive power through which it moves to its determined objective.

Organization, therefore, refers to more than the frame of the edifice. It refers to the complete body, with all its correlated functions. It refers to these functions as they appear in action, the very pulse and heartbeats, the circulation, the respiration, the vital movement, so to speak, of the organized unit. It refers to the coordination of all these factors as they cooperate for the common purpose.

* Revised ed. (New York: 1947), pp. 1–45. Abridged. Reprinted by permission of Harper & Brothers, Publishers.

This description of the relation between organization and administration also indicates what is meant by *system* in organization. As organization relates to procedure, involving the interrelation of duties as well as duties in themselves, so system may be described as the technique of procedure.

The introduction of the word "technique" gives us another slant on the relation of administration to organization. It might appear that organization is in some way subordinated to administration. In a practical sense, so it is, for the instrument must always appear subordinate to that of which it is the instrument, and one duty of administration is to provide its own administrative instrument, which means to organize. Yet in another sense the relation is reversed. If the building presupposes the builder, or organizer, the function of administration also presupposes the building, or something to administer. Let us, therefore, compare these two in terms of technique.

The art or technique of administration, in its human relations, can be described as the art of directing and inspiring people, which must be based on a deep and enlightened human understanding. The technique of organization may be described as that of relating specific duties or functions in a coordinated whole. This statement of the difference between organizing and administering clearly shows their intimate relation. It shows also, which is our present purpose, that the technique of organizing is prior, in logical order, to that of administering. A sound organizer may be a poor leader or administrator, because his temperamental qualities may not fit him for the latter task. On the other hand, it is inconceivable that a poor organizer can ever make a good leader, if he has any real organizing work to do.

The prime necessity in all organization is harmonious relations based on integrated interests, and, to this end, the first essential is an integrated relation of the duties, considered in themselves. This means that the sound coordination of the activities of all the people on the jobs demands, as its necessary antecedent, the sound coordination of the jobs as such. It is evident, therefore, that a good job of organizing is a necessity antecedent to efficient administration. Administration always presupposes something tangible to administer, and this something only organization can supply. . . .

The Coordinative Principle

Organization begins when people combine their efforts for a given purpose. We have shown this by the simple illustration of two people uniting their efforts to lift and move some weighty object. This combination, however, is not the first principle of organization. It is only an illustration of organization itself.

To find the first principle, let us carry the illustration a step further. The efforts of these two lifters must be coordinated, which means that they must act together. If first one lifted, and then the other, there would be no unity of action, and hence no true organization of effort. Coordination first appeared in organization when one of those hairy, slow-witted ancestors of ours assumed authority and gave the guttural equivalent of "Heave ho!" *Here, then, we find the first principle of organization.*

Coordination, therefore, is the orderly arrangement of group effort, to provide unity of action in the pursuit of a common purpose.

When we call *coordination* the first principle, we mean that this term expresses the principle of organization *in toto*; nothing less. This does not mean that there are no subordinated principles; it simply means that all the others are contained in this one of coordination. The others are simply the principles through which coordination operates and thus becomes effective.

As coordination contains all the principles of organization, it likewise expresses all the purposes of organization, in so far as these purposes relate to its internal structure. To avoid confusion we must keep in mind that there are always two objectives of organization, the *internal* and the *external*. The latter may be anything, according to the purpose or interest that calls the group together, but the internal objective is coordinative always.

Authority. In some spheres of organization the external objective is not continuous. This is true of army organizations in peacetime, when all external objectives are in abeyance, and the army merely waits for mobilization day, for the day of action. In every form of organization, however, the internal objective must be constant. This internal objective is organized efficiency, and everything that is essential to such efficiency is expressed in the single word "coordination." There can be no waiting for "M-day" in coordination. It is a constant necessity in organization, essential to the existence of the organization itself.

As coordination is the all-inclusive principle of organization, it must have its own principle and foundation in *authority*, or the supreme coordinating power. Always, in every form of organization, this supreme authority must rest somewhere, else there would be no directive for any coordinated effort.

The term "authority," as here used, need not imply autocracy. Where true democracy prevails, this authority rests with the group as a whole, as it rests in our government with the people of the United States. In the simplest and most compact forms of democratic organization it is represented in the entire group, assembled at one time, in one place. Examples in secular government are separated as widely in time as the ecclesia of ancient Athens and the present New England town meeting.

In whatever form it may appear, this supreme coordinating authority must be conceived simply as the source of all coordination, and not necessarily as the coordinating directive that runs through the entire organization. In a democracy like our own this authority rests with the people, who exercise it through the leaders of their choice. . . .

Mutual Service. Community of interest is the legitimate basis of every organization. In searching for its psychic fundaments we find that it can mean only *mutuality of interest.* This in turn implies mutual duties, which means the obligation to *mutual service.* This obligation is universal, transcending, therefore, the sphere of organization. As expressed in the ancient Roman juridical maxim *do ut des* (I give that thou mayest give), it is the manifest basis of all human relations.

In a special sense, however, it has an application within the sphere of organization. Here it is the moral phase of the principle of coordination. It is for this reason that organizations of all kinds, whether governmental, religious, military, or industrial, furnish our best human examples of the spirit of mutual service.

Although the formal technique of organization has, until recent years, received but scant attention, the humanistic phases of organization have an extensive literature. In this literature the obligation to mutual service is called by various names, among them cooperation, integration, functional relating, and integrated functioning. All these terms suggest the formal as well as the human side of coordination, which shows how impossible it is to separate them. We must keep in mind that organizations are the creations of people, and hence that everything that is formal in organized forms must rest on psychic fundaments.

A true coordination must be based on a real community of interest in the attainment of the desired object. It is equally true that a community of interest that is real, not only in the objective sense but likewise in everybody's consciousness, can come only through a real community of understanding. This means not merely that administration and members must understand each other, but that each and all must understand what the real purpose is and, furthermore, that every group represented in the organization must understand how and why the attainment of this purpose is essential to the welfare of all.

The reason, we think, is obvious. Mutuality of interest or, let us say, a common interest, does not, so far as human consciousness is concerned, constitute an *identity* of interest. The only conceivable means of attaining a true integration of all group interests in organization is through administrative policies that will make this community of interest a more tangible reality to every member of the group.

It is evident that every element of psychic coordination is a necessity in the establishment of harmony in all internal relations. Even this statement, however, does not include everything necessary in a truly coordinated efficiency. Before we leave this subject of coordination, therefore, let us consider one more element, especially conspicuous in church and military organization, which has its lessons for organizers in every sphere.

Doctrine. Coordination implies an aim or objective. But it does not follow, even where there is a true mutual interest, a mutual understanding, and a degree of mutual participation, that each and every member of the organization does in fact carry in his mind a deep understanding of the objective and how it may be attained. Among the higher officials, those who are responsible for results, this understanding should be ever present. They should know, furthermore, that the more this understanding seeps down through all ranks and grades, until all are permeated with it, the greater will be the coordinated effort and the greater the strength of the organization for the accomplishment of its purpose. It is the necessary means to this end that brings us in contact with the significant word "doctrine."

To most people this word has a religious flavor, and well it may, for, of all forms of organization, religious associations are the ones that are most deeply imbued with its spirit. But the word itself has a broader meaning. We see this illustrated in the various applications of the title "doctor," which means simply the teacher, representative, or practitioner of a doctrine. There is, indeed, a doctrine for every conceivable form of collective human effort.

Doctrine in the primary sense means the *definition of the objective*. In religious associations this doctrine is based on faith, as formally stated in the *creed*. In industrial organizations it is the attainment of a *surplus through service*. In governmental organization we find different and constantly changing doctrines, but always a doctrine of some sort, however varied its interpretations by the leaders and statesmen of history. In this primary sense doctrine is synonymous with the objective.

When we consider, however, the *procedure necessary to attain the objective* we encounter the secondary meaning of the word, which it seems a misnomer to call secondary, for it often transcends the primary meaning in practical importance. This fact the following examples will show.

With a physician or surgeon the doctrine of the objective is obvious. It is to make the patient well. But the doctrine of procedure and its application call for a thorough training and wide experience. Likewise, the doctrine of the military objective is simple. According to the school of Foch and Napoleon, it is the forcing of a decision through the overthrow of the adversary. The necessary procedure, however, constitutes a highly technical art, in which all the principles of military strategy and tactics are involved.

This point is vital in all forms of coordinated effort. Always there is sure to be a doctrine of procedure of some kind, but it is not enough to have such a doctrine, nor is it sufficient for the doctrine to be a sound one. Above all, it is essential that this doctrine shall, in the popular phrase, be "sold" to everyone concerned. Every member of an organization should not only know its doctrine, but he should feel it and absorb it until he lives in its atmosphere and makes it the guide of all his acts.

A doctrine of procedure does not mean a body of set rules that must be accepted as though they were articles of faith. . . .

To find a simpler illustration of unity of doctrine, and its necessity in the attainment of any group objective, we may turn to the field of sports, such as our national games of baseball and football, where groups are competing and where success in the attainment of the purpose depends on coordinated effort. In these sports there is a real functional differentiation of duties. In the formal sense, however, the problems of organization are all predetermined by the rules of the game. The primary objective also is so simple that the shortest word will state it. It is to *win*.

When we come, however, to procedure, in other words, to the means necessary to win, we find emerging in each case a real doctrine which accounts for the high importance of the baseball manager and the football coach. Tracing each doctrine through all the intricacies of baseball and football strategy we find that it rests, as it must, on the first principle of organization, namely, coordination of effort. This coordination, so essential to victory in any sport where a number of players combine their efforts for a common purpose, has given us the splendid word "teamwork." . . .

The Scalar Principle

Coordination must contain in its essence the supreme coordinating authority. It is equally essential to the concept of organization that there be a formal process through which this coordinating authority operates from the top throughout the entire organized body. This process is a tangible reality, observable in every organization. It appears in a form so distinct that it practically names itself.

Scalar Principle. The scalar principle is the same form in organization that is sometimes called hierarchical. But, to avoid all definitional variants, scalar is here preferred.

A scale means a series of steps, something graded. In organization it means the grading of duties, not according to different functions, for this involves another principle of organization, but according to degrees of authority and corresponding responsibility. For convenience we shall call this phenomenon of organization the scalar chain.

The common impression regards this scale or chain merely as a "type" of organization, characteristic only of the vaster institutions of government, army, church, and industry. This impression is erroneous. It is likewise misleading, for it seems to imply that the scalar chain in organization lacks universality. These great organizations differ from others only in that the chain is longer. The truth is that wherever we find an organization even of two people, related as superior and subordinate, we have the scalar principle. This chain constitutes the universal process of coordination, through which the supreme coordinating authority becomes effective throughout the entire structure.

The scalar process has its own principle, process, and effect. These are: (1) *Leadership*, (2) *Delegation*, (3) *Functional Definition*, and they will be considered in this order.

Leadership. In the consideration of leadership in organization, two things are essential. We must define how it relates to the supreme coordinating authority, and then how it relates to the two other forms of the scalar process.

Leadership represents authority, and it must possess all the authority necessary to the exercise of its leadership, but this does not mean that leadership and supreme authority are identical. It is true that there are and have been organizations where the supreme coordinating authority exercises its own leadership. This is characteristic of all absolutist forms. It appeared in the autocratic empires of antiquity. In recent years it has reappeared in the so-called totalitarian states. The usual procedure, however, is for the supreme coordinating authority, wherever it may rest, to appoint, elect, or otherwise designate its leaders. Such designation is itself a process; one that gives us the key to the true definition of leadership in organization.

Leadership is the form that authority assumes when it enters into process. As such it is the determining principle of the scalar process, existing not only at the source, but projecting itself through the entire scalar chain until it effectuates the formal coordination of the entire structure.

The importance of efficient leadership increases with the growth of an organization. Such growth demands leaders who know the principles of organization and how to apply them. But the qualities of leadership involve more than the capacities of the organizer; they demand the psychic qualities of the leader. This phase of leadership is as vital as the spirit of coordination itself. It is in fact the operating phase of this process, since it is the leader who must coordinate not only the jobs but the people by whom the jobs are filled. . . .

The next point to be noted is that the scalar process emanating from leadership must have its own movement through which the scale is formed. It is this process that we shall now consider.

Delegation. Delegation means the conferring of a specified authority by a higher authority. In its essence it involves a dual responsibility. The one to whom authority is delegated becomes responsible to the superior for doing the job, but the superior remains responsible for getting the job done. This principle of delegation is the center of all processes in formal organization.

Delegation appears in organization as a necessary consequence of processive authority or leadership. It is inherent in the very nature of the relation between superior and subordinate. The moment the objective calls for the organized effort of more than one person, there is always leadership, with its delegation of duties. This is true even of the simplest and most compactly organized unit, where there is always face-to-face leadership. It might appear to some that the foreman of a section gang on a railroad delegates no duties. In reality, unless he takes pick or shovel in hand and works with his men, he delegates everything except the one thing he cannot delegate, namely, the authority inherent in his own job and the responsibility that goes with it for getting the work done.

Another point to be noted is that delegation always means the conferring of authority, and can never mean anything else. The term "authority" is frequently taken to mean authority over people, but this is not its necessary meaning in organization. Even the foreman of a section gang delegates an authority to his men, an authority to do certain things, which carries with it the responsibility for doing what is thus authorized. Always, in every job, even an office boy's job, there must be a delegated authority of this kind, otherwise responsibility would have no logical basis.

The responsibility of leadership for getting the job done does not exhaust this point. We must still consider the human factors implied in this responsibility. It is not alone what the leader must do but, above all, what he must be. The exercise of leadership presupposes, as its first necessity, the power of understanding. The true leader must know in its entirety what is intended, and know it so clearly that he can see the end from the beginning. Such knowledge is a necessity even in the boss of a section gang. Again, the leader may be directing the collective efforts of a group of men of the highest intelligence, each of whom is the complete master of the task to which he has been assigned. In each case there must be a leader whose duty it is to coordinate each factor with every other factor in the attainment of the common purpose.

When an organization outgrows the possibility of face-to-face leadership, there must ensue that feature of organization which we may call subdelegation. This means that the leader begins to delegate an authority similar to his own. In other words, he delegates the right of delegation itself, involving the same kind of authority over others. Thus, we have the lengthening of the scalar chain, which appears in larger organizations of every kind. Whatever the length of the chain, however, the same principle must run through the whole structure. The subordinate is always responsible to his immediate superior for doing the job, the superior remains responsible for getting it done, and this same relationship is continued up to the top leader, whose authority makes him responsible for the whole.

It should be observed that when authority delegates powers similar to its own, this may or may not mean the delegation of the right actually to appoint subordinates. In the case of appointments to important key positions, the higher authority may reserve this right. This, however, does not alter the relation between superior and subordinate in the scalar chain. The superior begins at once to delegate to the subordinate duties which carry with them their own authority; hence coordinated responsibility is implicit in all such relations. . . .

When we examine the process of delegation, as it reveals itself in historical forms, we shall find it appearing in several phases other than the simple one just described. The form we have here considered is the one where leadership delegates to subordinates something of its own authority, in other words, *delegation downward.* Among historical forms we shall find the phenomenon of *delegation upward,* in which there is delegated an actual authority over the delegator, likewise of *delegation outward,* where a measure of authority is delegated to some outside organization. We shall also find a distinction between the *direct,* or *immediate,* forms of delegation and those that are *indirect,* or *mediate.* Another phenomenon, observable in the judicial sphere of government, is that the scalar gradations of the judiciary do not represent successive links of delegated authority, but that all of them derive directly from a higher authority. The reason for this will become evident when we come to consider the character of the judicial function in organization.

All forms of delegation have one feature in common. They indicate an authority of some kind that does the delegating and has the right to delegate. The sum of it is that delegation, as a form, possesses that universality in organization which identifies it as a principle. Without this principle no organization can function.

Functional Definition. The third and effectuating principle of the scalar process is *functional definition.* This principle is not synonymous with functionalism, which is a separate principle of organization. Functional definition is antecedent to all functions because it is the form in organization that assigns all functions. It is the scalar form through which leadership delegates to each subordinate his own specific task.

In order to make clear the distinction between functional definition and functions as such it may be well to expand this point. What we have termed functional definition is simply the final end and aim of the entire scalar process. We have defined the scalar principle as the *processive* form, and the functional principle as the *effective* form of coordination. It is evident, therefore, that in this scalar process there must be some ultimate form that produces the functional effect, otherwise the connection between the process and the effect would not be established. When a superior delegates any duty to a subordinate he defines the function of that subordinate, which only scalar authority can do. Thus, functional definition is the end, the aim, and the finality of the entire scalar process.

This truth may be demonstrated by a study of the scalar chain in any form of organization. In a small, compact organization, with only two links in the chain, those of leader and subordinates, the functional definition is direct and immediate. When the organization grows the chain lengthens, and subdelegation appears. This means simply an extension of the process. But the process itself is always the same. And functional definition is always its aim and object. . . .

The Functional Principle

By the term "functionalism" we mean the *distinction between kinds of duties.* Thus, it is clearly distinguished from the scalar principle. To employ a military illustration, the difference between generals and colonels is one of gradations in authority and is, therefore, *scalar.* The difference between an officer of infantry and an officer of artillery, however, is *functional,* because here we have a distinct difference in the nature of these duties.

This definition of functionalism is justified by current usage. But it is an invented meaning, due, like all such inventions, to the inadequacies of our language. Strictly speaking, the word "function" means the act of performance or execution, and may designate any activity that appears in organization, even to supreme authority itself. It is necessary, therefore, to emphasize the point that when we speak of functionalism in organization we mean *functional differentiation* between kinds of duties.

Functions may be innumerable in variety according to the procedure necessary to attain the given purpose. This is observable in modern manufacture, where the technique of mass production has introduced such minute divisions of labor that nearly every individual job has become a separate function. Here arises the question whether these great varieties of functions have any common denominators. Are there any universal principles of functionalism, in which are included the sum of all functions, and, if so, can we identify in them the same logical order that we have already observed in the scalar process? There are such principles of functionalism, and they follow the same order.

Principle of Functionalism. In every organized undertaking there must be some function that determines its objective, another that moves to its attainment, and a third that makes interpretative decisions in accordance with those rules of procedure that have been predetermined. These functions, which may be called the *determinative,* the *applicative,* and the *interpretative,* are related as a principle, process, and effect. In secular government they are known as the *legislative,* the *executive,* and the *judicial* functions.

Each of these primary or universal functions presupposes the coordinative and scalar principles of organization, although in absolutist forms of government this dependency is obscured by the fact that the supreme coordinating authority usually exercises its own leadership. Hence it usually appears in the threefold guise of supreme legislator, executive, and judge, and likewise makes no functional distinctions in the delegation of these duties.

In a constitutional form of government, however, all these functions are separately delegated. Under the American system the people elect their legislators, their higher executives, and in many states their judges. When not elected directly by the people, these judges receive their appointments through a procedure we shall describe as *mediate delegation.* The determinative or legislative function, because of its usual collective character, appears more like a single unit than either of the others, yet even here is subdelegation of legislative authority. Even such common, everyday matters as the police rules regulating street traffic represent the exercise of a subdelegated legislative function.

The judicial function, like the legislative and the executive, is scalar in its organization, with the graduated authority of higher and lower courts, but here we do not find the subdelegation downward of judicial authority. This is explained by the nature of the judicial function, in which the authority to decide confers no right of initiative. This absence of initiative also explains all that is distinctive in judicial procedure. In the determinative and executive spheres the highest authority initiates, which means that it has the *first word*. In the judicial sphere the highest authority has only the *last word*. Hence procedure in the courts, unlike procedure in the two other functional spheres, moves not downward but upward.

We have here described the three universal or primary functions as they appear in government. Their universality as functions, however, must be apparent. There is no conceivable duty, function, or individual job of any kind that does not involve one of three things: the determination of something to be done, the doing of that something, the decision of questions that may arise in the course of the doing in conformity with predetermined rules and practice. It may happen that all three functions are represented in the same job.

Here enters another vital point. The frequent presence of all three primary functions in the same job indicates how much less we may expect to find these functions completely separated in the general structure of organization. At most this separation is relative. In secular government, where it appears more distinctly than in other forms, it has been mainly a development of modern times, and such segregation is never complete even in modern government.

In our own Constitution the legislative arm retains the judicial right of trial through impeachment. Likewise the Senate, in its authority to confirm or reject appointments to office, possesses an executive function. Thus, when the Senate sits behind closed doors, to consider the fitness of such appointments, it is said to go into "executive session." On the other hand, the chief executive, through his advisory function, backed by the right of veto, possesses a degree of authority in the legislative sphere. The truth is that the ideal of organized efficiency is not the complete segregation, but the integrated correlation of the three primary functions.

Functional Correlation. Here it may be urged that the ultimate purpose of every organizer is the integrated correlation of all functions. True enough, and such correlation, to be truly scientific, must be based on the principles of organization. The organizer should know the three primary distinctions that underlie all functionalism. He should know that these functional principles are universal in organization; that even the adhering function we call "staff" must relate in some way to all of them. He should know that, as the three scalar forms constitute the principle of *processive coordination,* so the three universal functional forms must be the basis of all *effective coordination.* He must identify these functional principles, as they appear in every job, and make them the basis of his correlation.

The history of functionalism in organization may be briefly traced, in its broad outlines. We have seen that the functional principle is always present in every organized undertaking, but the highly diversified functionalism of present-day factory organization, for example, is a development of modern times. Even in older forms of organization, however, we may trace through the ages an increasing diversity in functional duties. This was due not only to the growth of these organizations, but mainly to the advance in the range of human knowledge, and especially of technical knowledge. In a primitive age, relatively destitute of such knowledge, the functional differences were bound to be few and of a simple kind, but the growth of technology introduces another and supplementary functionalism. This technical functionalism first appeared in military organization, where the use of different weapons introduced real functional distinctions between different arms of the service.

Specifying Duties. The importance of an exact specification of all individual duties, in its effect on the morale of an organization, may be shown by examples that are familiar in all human experience. How often do we hear it said of organized institutions of every kind that they are all "shot through with politics." A superficial thinker might take this as a reflection on the personnel. If he should become acquainted with this personnel he might be surprised to find how good it really is. Ten to one, we must go to organization, rather than to personnel, to find the real cause of the trouble.

To say that such conditions, when they exist, are the fault of administration is true but not sufficiently explicit. They are due to the administrative neglect of the necessities of formal organization and the application of its principles.

When a member of an organization is placed in a position with duties ill defined in their relation to other duties, what happens? Naturally he attempts to make his own interpretation of these duties and, where he can, to impose this view on those about him. In this process he encounters others in similar cases, with friction and lack of coordination as the inevitable result.

On the positive side orderly procedure gives way to the practice of "cutting across lots"; in its negative phase it results in the shirking of responsibilities or, in popular phrase, "passing the buck." Such conditions become aggravated when leadership itself takes short cuts without considering the long-time consequences. The two conditions usually go together, for the leadership that is careless in the specification of subordinate duties is likely to be disorderly in the exercise of its own. True coordination in the formal sense can be effectuated only through exact definition of duties, and this must begin at the top. Without it there will be friction even at the top, and under these conditions it is futile to look for harmony down the line.

The opposite type of leader, the one who regards the exact specification of the duties pertaining to every function, in their relation to other functions, as of first importance, may sometimes appear formalistic, but in the results he is justified by all experience.

Reason and evidence combine to prove that exactitude in the specification of tasks is a necessity in the creation of a true collective harmony. Harmony in this phase may be merely passive, however, expressed in the absence of friction. To translate this passive harmony into an active and efficient harmony, something more is needed, and here we are reminded of the dictum of Marshal Foch, that active obedience always presupposes understanding. The employee who is charged with some duty or function, if he conceives it only as such, may perform his duties passively. But when he sees its relation to other functions all about him, and the relation of all to the total purpose, there ensues a mental process that relates him personally to that object and helps to transform him from a passive into an active participator in the common purpose. When all the members of an organization attain this attitude, the result is a unity of spirit, the mainspring of efficient cooperative effort.

Formal correlation of functions is the task of the organizer. His job is to correlate duties as such. Correlation of spirit is the responsibility of the leader. He correlates the people who perform these duties. These facts show the importance of an understanding of the formal principles of organization. But not until there is a true and general understanding of the common purpose do we have that real and active *horizontal correlation* which is the final test of a truly efficient organization.

Writers on administration distinguish between the principles of *perpendicular* and *horizontal* correlation. Expressing the same thought in the terms here used, these two forms relate to the scalar and functional principles. We have called it the duty of leadership to achieve a complete correlation of functions. Leadership, however, represents the scalar principle in organization. This scalar relation, alone, through the contact of command cannot provide the universal understanding of the common purpose, the relation of each individual to this purpose and to every individual through it, which are necessary to true functional correlation.

Leadership must create and employ horizontal contacts to supplement the perpendicular, so that this understanding may be properly disseminated throughout the organization. This service must be used by the scalar authority not only for its subordinates, but for itself.

Only in this way can the unity of spirit, the real power of cooperative efficiency, be developed.

The Staff Phase of Functionalism

Staff service in organization means the service of *advice* or *counsel,* as distinguished from the function of authority or command. This service has three phases, which appear in a clearly integrated relation: the *informative,* the *advisory,* and the *supervisory.*

The informative phase refers to those things which authority should know in framing its decisions; the advisory, to the actual counsel based on such information; the supervisory, to both preceding phases as applied to all the details of execution. It is through this last phase that the informative and advisory phases become operative throughout an entire organization. If authority needs all the information that is requisite in making its decisions, those down the line, to whom is delegated the carrying out of orders, need the information requisite to a truly intelligent execution. Staff service, in this phase, may be called a service of knowledge, and, as such, it supplies the final necessity in a true horizontal coordination of organized effort.

Here arises a vital question. How are we to distinguish in psychic terms between the functions of line and staff? In terms of organization the answer is simple. It is the function of the staff merely to counsel; that of the line, and the line only, to command. But these terms may be too simple. They leave unanswered the main question. Why should the line commander need the services of a staff of counselors? Why, as commander, assuming him to be fit for command, should he not be in counsel sufficient unto himself?

It would be easy to reply that, in every large organization, the information the line leader needs in framing his decisions requires more than mere individual counselors; it requires nothing less than organized staff counsel. But when we advance to the next phase of staff service—from the *informative* to the *advisory*—we encounter another aspect of the line and staff relation. Here we find the staff function exercising an authority of its own, an authority that is no less real than line authority, even though it includes no right of command.

The point is that the line represents the authority of *man;* the staff, the authority of *ideas.* The true value of a staff official has only one measure—his ability to generate ideas that are of value to line authority, and his efficiency in imparting these ideas to the whole organization. Through this authority, inherent in sound and workable ideas, the staff official may frequently advance to important line command. Likewise, advancement in line leadership may often depend on the leader's capacity to generate workable ideas, quite as much as anything inherent in his own right of command.

The term "staff phase of functionalism" is used by us advisedly. The familiar expression, borrowed from military terminology, is "line and staff." The almost invariable use of these terms in conjunction is intended to distinguish between the right of command and the function of counsel. To the layman, however, it may be misleading in its implications. It may suggest that the structure of organization is like a double-track railroad, consisting of line and staff as two co-ordinated functions.

There could be no more erroneous conception. The structure of organization is single-track only, and can never be anything else. What is known in military organization as the line is synonymous with what we have called the scalar chain, and there can be but one chain of line authority. Any duty in organization that cannot be identified as an actual link in the scalar process is an auxiliary function, adhering to the line like the sidings along the main track. This means that every staff function must adhere to the line in some dependent relation, and could not otherwise exist. If we find in staff organization a counterpart of the same scalar gradations that appear in the line, this is implicit in the fact of its adherence. It must, of necessity, follow the gradations of that to which it adheres.

Auxiliary Service. The staff is purely an auxiliary service. Its function is to be informative and advisory with respect to both plans and their execution. This is implicit in the meaning of the word "staff," which is something to support or lean upon but without authority to decide or initiate. In the case of the execution of plans the only difference is that staff service becomes informative and advisory with respect to plans already formed, and in that sense *supervisory*. Hence, in the sphere of execution, the staff functionary, though he has no right of command inherent in his own function, may and usually does speak in the name of higher authority. To avoid confusion of ideas it is always essential to identify functions as such, without regard to the shifting relations through which such functions may be exercised. Above all, it is essential to keep in mind that the difference between staff and line is not the difference between thinking and doing, for these two faculties are present in every activity. The term "staff" is strictly one of formal organization, to distinguish the function of counsel from the scalar right of command.

Taking organizations concretely, we shall find the same characteristics in staff service that we have already noted in our study of functionalism. We have observed that even the three primary functions—planning, performing, and deciding according to plans—are never completely segregated in any organization. We must not expect, therefore, to find complete segregation of individual staff as distinguished from line duties.

To illustrate: the head of some department that is distinctly staff in the nature of its service to the organization as a whole must, nevertheless, possess a line authority within his department. Again, in organizations we find departments that have both line and staff duties. The heads of such departments may have an advisory relation to the top leadership, but they have line authority with respect to the performance of their own particular function.

This is generally true of organizations that are departmentally functionalized at the top. It is always the case in secular government, and appears in the relation of cabinet officers to the premier or president. In army organization such departmentalized functions are always classed as staff, yet even here there are some duties which, strictly speaking, are auxiliary line functions. This is true of the so-called staff troops, whose duties are mainly concerned with communication, supply, and transport. However, in tracing historically the origin of such duties we find that they have all grown originally out of some informative and advisory service, and this explains why they are still included under the general term of "staff."

Another possible source of confusion on the historical side is the word "staff" itself, which has not always had its present and generally accepted meaning. In older military forms the term was applied in a collective sense to all officers, whatever their functions, who were in immediate contact with the commander in chief. The present meaning of the term in military organization is hardly older than the eighteenth century. It remains true, however, that military organization was the first to use the term in its present sense.

Staff Evolution. The history of the staff phase of functionalism, as it appears in various kinds of organizations, with differing objectives, will be reserved for later consideration. For the present it will suffice to indicate in broadest outline the general character of this evolution.

We have already noticed, in tracing the general history of functionalism, that it is always present in its three primary forms—the determinative, the applicative, and the interpretative—and that a supplementary functionalism, strictly technical in character, evolves only with advancing human knowledge. A similar evolution appears in the history of the staff function. Technical staff functionalism probably made its first appearance in military organization, for technical differences in line duties, owing to variety of weapons, first appear in this sphere. Where there are different line functions it is reasonable to assume corresponding differences in staff service, but we can find no such functions actually described in the organization of ancient armies. There is one staff function, however, that is always present in every organization, ancient or modern, namely, the staff service of collective counsel.

The collective character of early staff service accorded with the needs of a primitive age. The primitive leader neither needed nor could command technical counsel, for of technical knowledge there was little or none. But one need he had in common with every leader, ancient or modern, namely, the broad wisdom drawn from the well of human experience, and for such help and guidance he depended on the collective counsel of those about him. The importance of this staff function is proved by the fact that it was not informal or occasional. It had become formal as far back as we can trace it.

Among ancient examples are the Homeric chiefs, on whom the king depended for counsel, and the *witenagemot*, literally council of wise men, of the Anglo-Saxon kings. An advisory council of some sort is as old as organization itself. It is equally modern, for no advance in human knowledge will ever remove the leader's need for the help of elemental human wisdom, and especially of collective wisdom, in the making of all-important decisions.

Another lesson of history is the constant flux or movement of staff functions, ever contracting, expanding, or changing their form according to times and conditions. A classic example is the senate of ancient Rome. This body, which under the ancient kings and the consuls of the early Republic had been purely advisory, with no legislative authority, gradually usurped line powers until, in one period of Roman history, it exercised the highest authority of the state.

The contrary examples are equally notable. We have in history instances of important staff functions which, through either atrophy or the transformation of staff duties, retain their original character in name only. The usual tendency in such cases is for the council, or collective staff function, to become departmentalized, a trend that is inherent in specialization of every kind. In ecclesiastical organization we find an example in the consistory of cardinals, as distinguished from the conclave; in secular government, in the British privy council. Both these bodies, in their origin, were collective advisory councils to the sovereign authority, and such in theory they remain. In both cases, however, the growth of specialization has done its work. In the Catholic Church today these functions are exercised mainly by the different congregations of the Curia Romana; in Great Britain, by a relatively modern committee of the privy council known as the cabinet. In each case the meetings of the complete body have become merely formal and ceremonial.

In the history of the staff function in military organization we find still another trend. It begins with individual staff services, and evolves into a departmentalized and coordinated staff service. This difference is explained by the fact that, unlike church or secular government, warfare, in its very essence, is a technical matter. In the early days, however, when military weapons were the simple bow, sword, and spear, and when battles were fought under the immediate eye of the commander, the staff services were relatively few and minor. The changing conditions of warfare that began with the invention of gunpowder, the revolution in arms and equipment, and the resulting problems of supply and transport led to an increase in the number and importance of these staff functions until their coordination became imperative. Out of these necessities has evolved the modern *general staff*, a true advisory council, departmentalized but still a unit, which advises concerning all plans and supervises their execution, from every phase of departmental service to the military strategy which determines the total movement, and assembles all these elements in a coordinated whole.

Throughout all this change, two factors only appear constant. One is the ever-present staff principle, which in some form is always operative. The other is the constant movement in the relation between line and staff duties.

Is it possible, in these changing line and staff relations, to identify any definite cycle? The only one that has appeared in modern industrial organization is involved in the application of the principle of delegation, with its tendency toward either centralization or decentralization.

Line and Staff Relations. Undue centralization always tends to confer a measure of line authority on the staff. Centralization favors the maximum of technical staff efficiency, but the extreme of this tendency may sacrifice other things of equal moment; above all, the decentralized initiative that may be necessary in many cases.

The psychics of the line and staff relation involve simply a broader restatement of the psychics of leadership. The leader is the head of the line, and it is the line, in every form of organization, that represents its real fighting strength. The leader must be strong not only in movement, but in the planning that precedes the movement. The value of staff service presupposes a leader who is competent to appraise such counsel.

The individual staff official is concerned with the special phase of the situation that pertains to his own staff function. This phase must relate to other phases, however, and for this reason individual staff services must be coordinated in a complete staff service. But the line leader is, after all, the final coordinator. General Summerall, formerly Chief of Staff, U.S. Army, expressed the psychics of the line and staff relation in words that apply to organization in every sphere. "The commander," he said, "must know the art of staff support, and each member of the staff must know the art of command. Yet no commander can be replaced by any staff, however able the latter may be. The responsibility for decision and initiative must rest with him, and he must have the attributes, the character, and the knowledge to be worthy of the confidence and the service of the staff."

It may be asked why the leader who can qualify under these exacting specifications should need a functionalized and coordinated staff service? The answer is to be found in the complexities of modern life, which are reflected in all forms of organization. Always there are are too many things to think about, too many factors to consider, too diversified a knowledge required for their solution, for the unaided capacity of one leader to compass. Though all decisions must remain with the directing head, it is imperative that these problems should come to him predigested, with all the thought and research that organized staff service can bestow upon them. The staff is an expansion of the personality of the executive. It means more eyes, more ears, and more hands to aid him in forming and carrying out all his plans.

When we come to the psychic attitude of leadership toward staff counsel, we find the same types of leaders which we have already observed in the delegation of authority.

First is the leader who leans too hard on his staff, which means that he is prone to rely on others for his own thinking. Such leaders have been common enough in the past, especially in the realm of government. The monarchical system, with its principle of leadership through inheritance, has in past ages given the world far too many leaders who were unfit to rule. Under such leadership, if long continued, either of two things usually happens. In the first instance, the functionalized staff counselors gradually assume line authority in their own departments. The result is what is called a bureaucracy, where each department tends to become a law unto itself, with little coordination through centralized control.

In the other case, some one counselor gradually usurps the function of leadership until the previous leadership becomes merely titular. Conspicuous historical examples were the mayors of the palace under the later Merovingian kings in the seventh and eighth centuries, and the more recent shogunate in Japan. In such cases, either the titular authority reasserts its leadership, as it did in Japan, or the actual leadership becomes formal, as it did in Central Europe with the founding of the Carlovingian dynasty. Another example of titular leadership, entirely different in its origin, is found in modern constitutional monarchies. Here the gradual transfer of authority to counselors, who, as ministers, acquire a real line responsibility, is due to the transition from autocracy to constitutionalism. The ancient form survives in the modern substance.

Another type of leader survives more frequently in modern organizations. This is the leader whose confidence in his own strength renders him impervious to staff counsel. Leadership of this sort, to be successful, must manifest surpassing genius. Only a Napoleon can act thus and, in the popular idiom, "get away with it." The long-term effects of such leadership must be destructive of organized efficiency. Staff service always tends to atrophy when its counsels are ignored.

The third and truly modern type of leader need not be described, for we have already indicated his main qualities. This leader represents the real balance between the two extremes, and for the same reason achieves a true balance between the line and staff functions.

Principles of Staff Service. It is evident that there are two prime necessities in an efficient staff service: *coordination* and *infiltration.*

The importance of staff coordination has already been indicated. Without such coordination the practical result would be only a confusion of counsel. What line authority requires of its staff is a complete and correlated picture, for such a picture is an absolute necessity in the making of sound decisions. This necessity explains the purpose of the departmentalized *general staff* in armies, where the staff activities are so coordinated that the contributions of all departments are made to fit together in a complete picture.

The term "coordination" describes the necessary method of sound staff procedure, but *infiltration* of knowledge is the ultimate purpose of all staff activities. Staff service is not alone for the top leader. It comes to him first, for he needs it in the making of his own decisions, but the subordinates in the scalar chain, down to the rank and file, likewise need it in the intelligent execution of all plans. Even in military organization, where the nature of the objective requires a greater rigidity of discipline, and consequently a stronger emphasis on the function of command, the fact that efficient procedure cannot be insured through the contacts of command alone has been demonstrated by all military experience. To insure the completely unified structure, unified both in form and in the spirit of the common purpose, there must likewise be horizontal coordination, based on contacts that provide a true service of knowledge. Every enlightened leader knows this. How often do we find the leader, laying aside for the time his function of command, and assuming the role of staff counselor to his subordinates! Anyone who has had the fortune to serve under such a leader knows the inspiration and the indoctrination, of both purpose and procedure, that is infused by this type of leadership.

This kind of indoctrination, issuing directly from the leader, must, through physical necessity, be confined largely to what we have called face-to-face leadership. In a vast institution such direct contacts throughout the entire organization are impossible; hence an informative and advisory service, establishing these contacts throughout the whole structure, must itself be organized. In military organization we find this necessity provided for in the scalar gradations of the staff, with complete general staffs attached to each unit down to the division, and individual staff services attached even to the smaller units of command. This form of organized and infiltrated staff service is now becoming paralleled in our most advanced industrial institutions.

This service of knowledge in the sphere of execution has been defined by us as the *supervisory* phase of staff service. The term means more than mere general oversight. Detailed supervision is what is meant, and for such supervision *in-*

spection is a better name. So important is this service of inspection that some organizers distinguish between the *planning* staff, the *operating* staff, and the *inspection* staff. Inspection, however, pertains mainly to operations and may, therefore, be included in the operating or supervisory staff function.

One other aspect of this service of knowledge remains to be considered, and some may regard this as the most important of all. It is not alone the leader who has important things to tell his subordinates, either directly or through organized staff service. These subordinates may have important things to tell the leader, things that he should know in the exercise of his leadership. They have important things to tell each other also, and this mutuality of things to be made known runs through all relations of superiors, subordinates, and equals, in every link of the scalar chain. The infiltration of a true service of knowledge cannot be conceived as merely moving from the top downward. No organization can be truly unified in spirit until it has evolved a similar service moving from the bottom upward. It is well in organization that all should have the right to be heard, for it is only through this right, an organized machinery for its expression, and a stimulus to its exercise that a truly informed leadership becomes conceivable or possible.

———◆———

The previous selection was a careful summary statement of much traditional organizational theory. The following selection is included to indicate the nature of some current trends.

The two terms that describe the older organizational theory in comparison with the newer are "rational" and "management-oriented." By rational is meant that it tended to emphasize the power of human reason to master the facts of human relationships and to manipulate these relationships in logically designed ways to achieve predetermined goals. This abstract, formal approach is symbolized by the organization chart, on which "people are square boxes." By management-oriented is meant that it stressed the role of the executive, the "managers," concentrating rather heavily on techniques by which those in authority could manipulate the organization. On the whole it was optimistic as to the degree of manipulation possible by the managers.

The newer theory departs from the older in a greatly increased recognition of nonrational factors in human nature. It stresses the emotional, even the subconscious. It directs attention also to the large area of our lives not directed, normally and easily at least, to achieving the goals of organizations of which we may happen to be members. The newer theory seeks to bring within its system of concepts the emotional and social factors thought to be neglected in earlier theory. It does not so much abandon rationalism, as seek to achieve a higher and broader rationalism, a rationalism which brings the non- and irrational within its scope and control.

The newer theory departs from the older somewhat, however, in a decrease in manager orientation. While the "higher rationalism" is partly aimed at and results in more perfect managerial control of an organization and the people in it, one of the important results of recent study has been a depreciation of the role of the executive—a clearer recognition that the grouping of humans we call an organization is not comparable to clay on the potter's wheel, to be shaped in any fashion pleasing to the potter. The role of the "nonmanagerial member" and the effects of social groupings in and surrounding an organization now receive much attention. There are even beginnings of what might be called democratic administrative theory, in contrast to theory that has been authority-oriented.

Both cause and consequence of the recent trends are emphasis upon the data and concepts of psychology and sociology. Both psychologists and sociologists have become increasingly interested in formal organization and in administrative problems, and their studies in turn have helped to bring about a broadened approach on the part of administrative students.

The following essay was written in a spirit of meaningful jest. Ostensibly, it is a treatment of the organization and functioning of the bureau as a type or species of organization. Actually, most of what is said applies (so far as it is valid) to organization in general, whether in bureau or some other form.

Professor Earl Latham, the author, writes to amuse, but his jests are pointed and his purpose is serious. He has fun at the expense of his professional colleagues, he makes solemn but irreverent gestures before the "idols" of traditional organization theory. But his aim is clearly not frivolous or malicious, but pedagogical.

His thesis is that the older theory of organization is not science, as often claimed, but "theology" in the sense that it is a set of beliefs accepted on faith, not on demonstration of empirical reality. Real organization, he claims, is something quite different from the textbook model of the manner in which organization "ought" to behave.

Query, are his strictures too severe? Does he himself go beyond what the empirical evidence will support?

Hierarchy and Hieratics *

EARL LATHAM

This is an essay on the organization of a bureau. . . . The nomenclature is not entirely satisfactory but there are visible differences between bureaus on the one hand, and departments and divisions on the other. The department is usually a holding company of assorted services and functions organized by bureaus. Divisions perform activities designed to achieve the functions of the bureaus. . . .

It is certainly not unusual to launch an exposition of such problems by scanning the literature, the hieratics or sacred writings of commentators, on the subject. There one can learn that bureaus should be organized by function or clientele, when they are not organized by accident or malice. When circumstance and accident beget bureaus, a light touch of coordination here and there is said to be important. Very nice things are also said about integration. Staff services almost always get favorable notices and a central place in the discussion, although the line may be mentioned sympathetically, as lords and ladies might refer with gracious pity to the "working classes," useful but dirty. . . .

What are the principal tenets of the theology of administration? . . . There are two principal tenets—an epic myth and a principle. The epic myth postulates a first cause in the person of a creator—in this case the chief of the bureau. It is the creator who fashions his particular bureaucratic world out of the void. As this godchief breathes the gift of life into his creation, there springs into being a structure of serried ranks, held in the confines of their accustomed bounds by his will and command. The mind of this secular divinity is the mind of the universe he begets, and his will is its will, his law, its law. In this mythic conception of the creation of the administrative universe, the creator may sometimes eat his children like Chronos in the Greek fable. For what the creator giveth, the creator may take away.

Having brought the administrative universe into being, the godchief fixes its eternal form. The principle that maintains this form is the concept of hierarchy. Hierarchy is an ordered structure of inferior and superior beings in an ascending scale. The godchief dwells at the apex, from which, with his terrible eye, he can search out the hearts of his lowliest subordinates and mold their deed to his command. The graphic picture of this mythic form is the triangular shape associated with pyramids and pup tents. Hierarchy is the linchpin that locks the form. With the mythic creation to bring the bureau into being and the principle of hierarchy

* From *Employment Forum*, Vol. 2 (April, 1947), pp. 1–6. Somewhat abridged. Subtitled in the original "A Note on Bureaus." Reprinted by permission of the author and the International Association of Personnel in Employment Security.

to fix its structure, the principal elements of the bureaucratic theology are complete. A vertical godchief fathers an orderly universe, and by his will, fixes the orbits of every star in his administrative galaxy.

Is this fanciful? Of course it is. But these assumptions are related to a science of administration, based upon observable data, as magic is to medicine. In fact our knowledge of what goes on in administration is roughly at about the stage medicine was in when the cure for typhoid was a ritual dance by a man with deer horns and a rattle. A book comes to mind in connection with these theological assumptions of administration. It is SOUTH WIND by Norman Douglas and has nothing to do with the "principles" of administration, being a novel and therefore admittedly fictional. It does however have something to do with available varieties of gods, and therefore bears upon our subject. At one point in the book Mr. Keith, a man of wealth, speaks his views about theology to Mr. Heard the Bishop of Bampopo. Of the classic gods, he says that they

". . . were invented by intellectualists who felt themselves capable of maintaining a kind of comradeship with their deities. Men and gods were practically on a level. They walked hand in hand over the earth. These gods belonged to what one might call the horizontal or downstairs variety."

"And those others?"

"Oh, they are the upstairs or vertical type. They live overhead . . ."

The theologians of administration deal with the upstairs or vertical variety. They live overhead. The use of the word "hierarchy" to describe these relationships is particularly apt, since hierarchy originally meant (and still does) a rank or order of holy beings. But perhaps enough has been said to indicate that the parallel between standard theologies and the theology of administration is close. It is close enough to be fraternal, at least, if not filial.

What of it? To answer these three words it is necessary to ask at least twice three questions. What is the fact if the mythic conception is a fiction? What is organization? What is the grain of sense and truth in hierarchy as a frame of relations? What is the function of the chief, if not command? Are agency communications ever anything else than a "troublesome code of verbal signals, unintelligible to ordinary folk"? And, finally, what is the nature of the administrative universe, if not the extended will of the chief? These questions are the basic questions about bureaus, and they bring us to the subject, although in truth we have never left the subject. Because administration as a systematic body of knowledge is at the magic and not the medicine stage, it is more important to raise these first questions than to proceed on the basis of fictions and semantic exercises.

The following sections will discuss each of these questions and provide some answers, at least, if not conclusions.

II

First, as to organization. It is often stated to be the arrangement of men and materials for the accomplishment of some given purpose. That is one way of looking at organization, to be sure, but there is another way of stating it. Can you see it, feel it, taste it? Does it have weight, size, and density? Does it have personality? Where would you look to find an organization? The spectators at a baseball game are arranged by architects and engineers for the purpose of watching the game. Are they an organization? Clearly not, but why not? The answer, it may be suggested, is that the spectators don't think they are.

Organization is an idea, not a thing. It is an idea that men have about their relation to each in the accomplishment of common objectives. It does not exist anywhere but in the minds of people. It has not independent existence apart from the thoughts and understanding of men. Imagine two men, unknown to each other, trying to put out a brush fire. The first goes to a stream for a pail of water, returns and throws it on the flames. While he is at the fire, the second is at the stream. When the second is at the fire the first is at the stream. Each of them thinks that he is alone in the effort to put out the fire. Between them they extinguish it. They are nevertheless not an organization, for they have no idea of their relation to each other. Neither is combining his muscle with the other. Each is working without relation to the other. There is no identification of each with respect to each, and together, with respect to the common object. Without this identification, organization does not exist.

Certain consequences follow from the view that organization basically is the idea that men have about their relationships to each other in joint undertakings. First, the common possession of such an idea helps to produce and maintain a sense of belonging. This sense of belonging tends to keep a group together. Second, it tends to develop a sense of not belonging that works to exclude "outsiders." The sum of these two senses is a sense of jurisdiction that is one of the elemental facts of bureaucratic life. In the establishment of a bureau or any larger or smaller unit of organization, this sense of jurisdiction has to be faced and dealt with. Within the organization, it tends to breed cults and factions. With respect to those outside the organization, it tends to breed rivalry and competition, both of the high order and the low order.

Consider the internal problem first. The bureau is going to need, say, lawyers and economists. Both of these groups show a remarkable clannishness. They exhibit a selective awareness of professional identity, and a tendency to exclude aliens to the craft. Unless regulated and controlled in the general interest, they may become clots in the blood stream of the agency. They must usually be so arranged with respect to the executive and the "line" that they serve without dominating. As staff technicians their function is to serve, not order. That is, they generally serve and do not order. Much depends upon whether the staff function is, as Pfiffner classifies them, general, technical, or auxiliary. Some of these, like the last, are "operations" themselves.

The propensity of the general and technical staff services to expand and control is a kind of internal imperialism that has to be limited else order is defeated and confusion prevails. In an excess of enthusiasm for their specialties, and a simple-minded belief that all men would be good and could be trusted if they were only lawyers, or economists, or whatever the private medicine is, they struggle for power in a high-minded way, for the good of the order. In so doing, and to the extent that they are successful, they split and diffuse the power of the agency, and prevent it from coming to a focus.

Consider next the external problem. With respect to other agencies, the sense of jurisdiction (that is, of excluding others) produces most of the inter-bureau fights in Washington. A corollary of this attitude is the desire to become self-sufficient, the effect of which may be observed in both the internal and external relations of a bureau. The desire to be self-sufficient is based in the impulse to remain unique and to exclude others. Thus the War and Navy Departments have maintained separate procurement services for the same kinds of supplies and services. Bureaus and even divisions within bureaus recruit most of their personnel themselves, in effect maintaining their own personnel offices. The numerous housing agencies and housing services among the Federal agencies bespeak the urge to be self-sufficient in the matter of housing.

The key to organization is the understanding that each individual has of his relation to others in the achievement of the common purpose. But that understanding does not come to pass until the common purpose is defined. For what purposes are bureaus created? To fulfill some item of public policy stated in law, it may be said. But these statements of purpose are ordinarily very general and vague. These general purposes have to be defined more sharply, and that is where the bureau comes in. The bureau devises means to achieve these ends, techniques to fulfill these purposes. Bureaus exist to perform functions that will promote the realization of the general purposes of the agency of which it is a part. Within the bureau, the function may be broken into activities that will accomplish the function.

Purposes, functions, and activities then—this trinity contains the elements which must be understood by the members of a bureau if their relationship to each other is to be clear. Without this orientation of the parts to the whole, the members of an agency run the risk of acting at cross purposes and not as an efficient purposive unity. Without continuous orientation, the parts tend to break away from the hub. Technique becomes divorced from purpose and exists for its own sake. The bureau disintegrates and separates. Its divisions become independent satrapies. The work of the agency is done by treaty among the division chiefs. The cure for common ignorance about common purposes is instruction. Where the disintegration of a bureau's parts occurs because of common ignorance about the inter-connections of purpose, function, and activity, then it is clear that there should be instruction on these points. This matter will be discussed further as an aspect of communications.

III

Organization, then, is an idea. If so, what is hierarchy? It also is an idea. It is the idea men have about whom they follow and whom they lead. Pfiffner's definition (he calls it the "scalar process") is as follows:

"There is supreme leadership represented by the person, or persons, at the apex of the hierarchical pyramid, but in order to exercise this leadership it is necessary to delegate both authority and responsibility to the subleaders on the various subordinate steps of the scale."

In so saying, he restates a belief and a manner of expressing it that has won the approval of Urwick, Fayol, Mooney, and Reilley. It is held to be so self-evident that Urwick in his *Elements of Administration* remarks that it "is unnecessary to comment on this obvious requirement except to utter a warning against the common assumption that the necessity for a scalar chain of authority implies that every action must climb painfully through every link in the chain, whether its course is upwards or downwards." Here is all of the familiar symbolism of the theology of administration including the mystic sign of the pyramid. It is abstract and formalistic. It is metaphor, not science. It is a figure of speech, not a representation of observed characteristics.

Like an article of faith in a religious creed, hierarchy is a symbol of the belief in the mythic form of administrative organization. And again, like an article of religious faith it is believed in spite of the lack of evidence to support and confirm it and often in the face of evidence that disputes the truth of the article. At the most the notion of hierarchy is a symbol of relationships believed to be desirable, in which some impose themselves upon others in a serried order. The organization chart is the conventional emblem of the cult. The godchief rides his solitary peak, and his subordinates fall away below him on either side, with faces turned to the radiance of authority which they themselves cannot generate, but can only reflect. There is usually no room on the organization chart for the 40–90% of the staff not in the front office, or the headquarters, or the central office. A truer representation would turn the conventional pyramidal organization chart upside down, with the most numerous part given central place.

It is a bold presumption to contradict so much piety. But the conventional expression of the organization of authority and the practice of leadership in administrative organizations is not always symbolically accurate or factually true. The grain of truth is the need for order in the administrative universe. But it need not be an authoritarian order. The gods, to use the phrase of Norman Douglas, need not be vertical gods. The picturization need not be a pyramid of boxes. If the pictographs of geometry are to be used, perhaps a circle would be more appropriate and relevant, with the parts arranged in an orderly way around the center. New knowledge about the structure of molecules, atoms, and electrons can supply other diagrams. Each of them is a cosmos, a microcosm that reproduces the solar system, in which the elemental parts are held in orderly relationship to the center. If metaphor is to color speech, perhaps the native form of administrative organization is to be found in nuclear physics instead of theology.

The structure of authority and the practice of leadership in an administrative organization, bureau or department can both be at variance with the formal pattern. Often there is an informal and invisible government of the agency that mocks the abstract formalism of the charts and the printed rules. Administration is a limited system of governance and exhibits the characteristic problems of other political structures. One of these is the contrast between the legal form and the practical fact. In Britain, for example, the prime minister is responsible to the king in legal form and to the electorate in practical fact. In America, the President and Congress fix public policy, in legal form, but it is frequently done by private groups, in fact. As for example, when in 1946 the cattlemen and feeder lot operators in effect abolished the price controls on meat by striking against the public policy stated in the statutes. So it is within administrative agencies. The distribution of actual power and influence in the operations of an agency may be completely at variance with the formal or legal distribution. The "natural" leaders of the group need not be the formal office-holders. The informal bureaucracy may shape the course and destinies of the agency despite the formal bureaucracy.

To repeat, the germ of truth in the insistent use of the concept hierarchy is the need for order. But how is order contrived? The theology of administration makes it a function and by-product of the will of the godchief expressed in command. There is order because he wills order. His command proceeds from the top of the Olympian chart and rules the entire structure below him. But if hierarchy is the idea that each member of the organization has of whom to lead and whom to follow, it must be clear that order is rather a by-product of the leader-follower relationship. In short, it is the individuals that make up the organization who generate the will to order. Chester Barnard says the same thing in another way when he observes that authority "is the character of a communication (order) in a formal organization by virtue of which it is accepted by a contributor or 'member' of the organization as governing the action he contributes. . . ." He concludes that "the decision as to whether an order has authority or not lies with the persons to whom it is addressed" and does not reside elsewhere. In brief, authority is the idea of him who receives orders and not him who makes them.

This notion turns upside down the administrative universe of bureaucratic theology. Hierarchic authority is a fiction and the gods are horizontal, not vertical. What is the fact? The fact is that human beings in a social group, be it government bureau or workshop, have a vitality and motive force which are independent of the speeches and advices of the nominal head. As individuals in a group they have an impulse or will to cooperate with the members of the group in common actions. They want to behave *socially*, that is, to act in concert with others. This impulse or will is not called into being by the godchief. It exists without him. In fact, the iron hand, the rigorous application of hierarchic notions, the frustration of social expression, produce tensions that may defeat the object of the group. The hierarchic conception assumes that the group innately is a rabble of unorganized individuals and that order, when it appears, is a reflection of the godchief's creative logic. But unless the administrator sees his group as a coherent social unit, he is likely to develop, not harmony and order, but disorder and discouragement.

IV

If hierarchic authority is a theological fiction, what is the function of the front office of the bureau? It is to provide leadership and judgment. Leadership is essentially guidance not command. The distinction is important. Guidance assumes an independent motion in the thing guided. This is the case with social groups including bureaus. As Elton Mayo has indicated, there is an internal motion of the members of a group toward joint action, an impulse to cooperate and work together. It exists whether it is oriented or not. Command on the other hand implies that independence of motion does not exist but that motion is provided originally by the commander. In this view, inert particles draw life and action from the moving cause, which is outside them. Leadership then directs the will to cooperate.

But, as indicated above, there is also a function of judging. What is the function of judging? It is the making of choices between alternative courses of policy or action. Where do these choices come from, and how are they stated? They come from within the organization. It has been suggested that one of the principal functions of bureaucratic organization is to restrict the number of alternative choices, so that the front office of the bureau or agency may choose from a few instead of many. In this conception the function of organization is to sift the available choices to reduce their number.

There is something to this view, although it needs qualification. It is objectionable in part because it concentrates unduly on the front office of the bureau at the expense of the rest of the bureaucratic group. It makes it appear as though the group existed for the front office when they should exist for each other. But it does point out that some of the work of the front office is that of judging. And it indicates further that the alternatives are worked over within the organization. In short, once the impulse to cooperate and work together is organized, its internal motion does not cease. There is a pressure upon the front office to act. This is certainly not the way the godchief's empire treats him, in the mythic fiction. Pressure is put on the front office by the organization to act or not to act. The pressure appears in the form of alternatives which the front office accepts or rejects. Whichever way it decides, it performs a function of judgment.

It is clear then that, once oriented by the front office, the bureau exhibits a velocity of its own. Under these circumstances, the front office, the leadership, serves another social function besides that of guiding and judging. The head is the symbol of the central idea that animates the group. Indeed after the functions of guiding and judging have been performed for a specific project, say, there is often nothing for the leader to do but let the group-in-motion take its course. And in enterprises of great complexity and vast interdependence, it may be impossible for the leader to divert the group-in-motion from its given course and object, once started. In the greatest over-the-water invasion in the history of the world, for example, Eisenhower, after giving the final assault command, was impotent for the duration of the assault.

V

Several paragraphs ago, the subject of communications was taken up briefly and then deferred. It was there said that the cure for common ignorance about the common purpose of the bureaucratic group was instruction, and that instruction was an aspect of communications. The godchief in the epic myth about the administrative universe is a vertical god who experiences all of the difficulties of communication that Norman Douglas describes. Being perpendicularly overhead at a vast distance, it is necessary to devise a "troublesome code of verbal signals, unintelligible to common folk, for the expression of mutual desires." In the conception of the bureau as a social group, however, communication is a functional process which moves throughout the whole body, like blood which carries food and air to the tissues. If any part of the social organism is shut off from the sources of its enrichment and nourishment, it quickly shows the signs of bureaucratic paralysis.

Communication should inform. If it is true that organization and hierarchy are ideas and that their location is not external to, but in the minds of men, it is important that these ideas reflect the common purpose. The only way that this can be accomplished is by a well designed system of communication. The system cannot be a one way street of orders, advices, instructions, rules, regulations, and commands. This is not communication but verbal archery, in which many of the arrows must fly wide of the mark. Successful orientation of the will of the group to cooperate depends upon the understanding of the common objective. Leadership involves constant guidance. The success of both depends upon the understanding men have of the purposes they are to share and the directions in which they are to move. Understanding needs to be kept informed. Communication is the very vitality of a living and moving organism. . . .

Free communication is closely associated with the achievement of the social and individual satisfactions of group existence. . . . The identification of the self with the group is promoted when the sense of participation in the purposes of the group is fostered by free exchange of information. In the organization and establishment of a bureau it is certainly as important for the planners to provide complete forms of expression for the individual as it is to get green pile rugs for the brass hats. Lawrence Appley has said that the whole art of administration is the development of people. Free communication is a sovereign method to promote this end. The Training Within Industry programs made it clear that great reservoirs of energy and information were to be tapped if the potentialities of the individual worker were released. . . .

VI

The bureau has a special problem, perhaps, in that it is usually the size of administrative organization that contains a field service. And that brings to the front a special application of the views expressed. By an unselective choice of reading, it is easy to come to the conclusion that administration deals almost exclusively with the behavior of CAF–14's or better, in Washington, or other central office headquarters. This is a by-product of the theology of administration, and its preoccupation with the godchief and his works. Viewed in its totality, the most numerous part of a bureau may not be in the headquarters city at all but in the field.

The theological coloration of the conception of hierarchy frequently tints speculation and practice where central office-field relationships are involved. There is a semi-religious sense in which it is often said that the central office is the top and the field is the bottom, the first "above" and the second "below." The relation of superior to inferior is here implied as when we say that a man is high-born or low-born. The military pattern exhibits this association of rank and status with regrettable fidelity. Many complications follow this habit of view where the field is involved. It is much easier for example to maintain the theological fiction of a godchief who never appears to his humble ministers in the line but whose will is interpreted to them by intermediary clerics. The difficulty of communication is enhanced by factors of time and distance. The very remoteness of the relationship breeds confusion.

It is important within the frame of a bureau, where all are within easy distance of each other, to devise arrangements of communication that inform. It is doubly important to do so when geography separates the center from the rest of the organization. The field and only the field can inform the headquarters of the problems of the bureau as they appear at the margin of deed and accomplishment where the agency meets the customers. The headquarters alone can provide the leadership that directs the internal motion of the group towards the common purpose. Even this division of labor is somewhat artificial for the headquarters has no monopoly of policy and the field no monopoly of action. The relationship is mutual and reciprocal and each area of competence shades imperceptibly into the other. The field should participate in the formulation of policy and both central office and field should share in the action.

The verbal archery conception of headquarters communications is utterly inadequate for the management of large enterprises in the field. The arrow makers in the central office satisfy a certain lust in fondling lethal missiles and there is pleasure in flexing the bow that drives them out of sight. But the arrow makers and bow benders are acting a fantasy. Frequently they commit the group to ill considered and rash enterprises because of insufficient knowledge of the facts in the field. Or, as has often happened, the field first learns about important policy changes by reading the newspapers. The fault is a failure of communications. The remedy is in the hands of the central office. A bureau which sets up a field establishment without heeding this need vitiates the strength and effectiveness of the group.

VII

The sum of these observations can be quickly stated. The theology of administration is a less satisfactory explanation of what goes on in the bureau form of group life than the sociology of administration. Not structure but people are the stuff of which a bureau is made. And its motive force is not mechanics but dynamics. Because bureaus are groups of people, they exhibit the common patterns of behavior of groups of people. There is no science of "bureau" administration, narrowly conceived, that is different from the science of group behavior in other forms of administrative groups. What is relevant and true about the behavior of bureaus is relevant and true about the behavior of departments and divisions, the next larger and the next smaller forms of administrative organization.

New approaches to bureaucracy, both public and private, need to be considered. Empirical study of the ways in which human beings behave in shop, factory, and office is needed to counteract the pernicious effect of the slogans and mottoes which pass as explanations of how people act. Society at this moment in history is neurotic and disintegrated. Before we return to the arboreal life, we should try once to see if we can be as smart about people as we have been about engines, if indeed it isn't too late.

Chapter 6

Theory of Organization: Some Species

Unfortunately, there is no precise and agreed meaning for the various terms used to designate different types and sizes of organizational entities. Department, bureau, division, branch, section, unit, office—these and other terms are used variously, depending upon the custom of a particular organization, the accidents of history, the purposes of a certain writer, and so forth. Even a single organization, if large, is likely to show inconsistency in the use of such labels.

No doubt the lack of precise and agreed meaning is due in part to the fact that human relations which are the "stuff" of organization are intangible and fluid, hard to classify with neat labels. It should be recognized too that organizational labels are meant at least as much to *prescribe* as to *describe*, that is to say, a label placed upon a part of an organization may be intended not merely to describe what it *is* but to fix what its role and function with regard to the whole *ought* to be; particularly, the label may be meant to indicate where the organizational part fits into the hierarchy of formal authority, the "chain of command."

The following essay is on the construction of a "department." Fortunately this term, as compared with some of the others, has a fairly well agreed-upon meaning and common use in public administration. As generally used, departments are the largest parts or subdivisions of an organization or jurisdiction; their "heads" are immediately "below" the chief executive in the chain of authority. The Federal Department of Agriculture, a state Department of Natural Resources, a municipal Police Department, are examples; their heads report to the President, the governor, the mayor (or city manager), respectively.

In the following essay "department" is used in this sense, but not restricted to this sense. By this is meant that what the author has to say applies for the most part of the construction of any type of public organization, at least any "line" organization, whatever its label. The concepts of organization that are used, namely, organization according to (1) function, (2) work process, (3) clientele or matériel, and (4) territory, were brought into widespread use in public administration in the mid-1930's in an essay by Professor Luther Gulick. It has been widely accepted that in departmental construction, function or "major purpose" should be considered as the "first principle." Much of the organizational reconstruction that has recently taken place in American public administration has been justified in terms of establishing an organization with a recognizable, defensible, major purpose.

The author of this essay is Professor Schuyler C. Wallace; the essay appears as a chapter in a book titled *Federal Departmentalization* and subtitled *A Critique of Theories of Organization*. The book grew out of the widespread discussion of organization of the Federal government, following publication of the famous Report of the President's Committee on Administrative Management in 1937. As the word "critique" in the subtitle indicates, however, the book is devoted more to the criticism of old theories than the presentation of new.

Query, is Professor Wallace too critical toward this fourfold scheme of analysis—as some have suggested? Or is he too charitable in concluding that it constitutes "an exceedingly useful frame of reference for further thinking"—as some now hold? What precisely *is* its value to the student or practitioner of administration?

Considerations Which Enter into the Construction of a Department *

SCHUYLER C. WALLACE

Among the difficult problems connected with the process of departmentalization is the determination of the criteria by which the subordinate administrative units should be grouped together in a departmental structure. At various times and in diverse places a multiplicity of factors have entered into decisions. For the most part, however, these factors fall into a series of categories from which a limited number of generalizations have been drawn. As a result of these generalizations it is commonly asserted that the process of departmentalization rests upon four major concepts of organization: (1) function; (2) work processes; (3) clientele; and (4) territory.

On the surface the fundamental character of these several modes of organization may seem to be self-evident, yet such is far from the case. Before turning to the question of their application, it might be well, consequently, to examine the nature of the concepts themselves.

The difficulty of so defining these concepts as to render them capable of automatic application is strikingly revealed in connection with the "principle" of functionalism itself. The term is usually thought to denote the grouping together in a departmental organization of those subordinate administrative units which are dedicated to the same or similar purposes—the solution of the same or similar problems. Upon the basis of this hypothesis, the several military units concerned with land defense are commonly grouped together in a Department of War; the naval units in a Department of Navy.

This definition is perfectly satisfactory as far as it goes, but unfortunately it does little more than indicate the dominant characteristic of the concept. Its exact boundaries remain to be delineated. The difficulties inherent in this definition can, perhaps, best be indicated by a series of questions.

Should the various military and naval units of the government be grouped together in separate military and naval establishments as suggested previously?

* From *Federal Departmentalization* (New York: 1941), pp. 91–146. Abridged. Reprinted by permission of the Columbia University Press.

Or should they be integrated into a single Department of National Defense? Both modes of organization would, in the light of the definition given above, be functional in character. In consequence, the mere enunciation of a general "principle of administration" is of little or no help in settling the problem.

Still another aspect of the definition which gives rise to uncertainty is the difficulty of determining the purpose to which the several administrative units are actually dedicated. What, for example, is the primary purpose of the German system of transport, civil or military? Is it the same in time of war as it is in time of peace? Obviously not. In time of war the transportation system of Germany— or for that matter of any other country—is an integral part of the system of national defense. Should it therefore, along with the army, navy, and air force, be consolidated with the Ministry of National Defense? Or should it be permitted to retain an autonomous position? What should be done in time of peace? Would the conclusions relative to the proper situs of these agencies as a result of a study of the German situation be equally applicable to the United States?

The answers to these questions will not be discovered by a microscopic analysis of the definition given above. Instead they will be found by an investigation of the political, economic, administrative and military conditions surrounding each given situation. One answer might be given in time of war; another, in time of peace. One solution might be proper for the German Reich, another for the United States. Nevertheless, until we have ascertained the fundamental purposes to which the activities of the several subordinate administrative units have been directed, little or no progress can be made in the application of the concept. To give meaning to the concept these purposes must be discovered.

At times the objectives to which the several administrative units are directed are clearly set forth in the fundamental law of the land. Illustrations of this fact can be found in the constitution of practically every state in the American union. More frequently, however, they are to be found in legislative enactments, administrative decrees and court decisions; often as in the event of war, they are to be found in the nature of the situation itself. Any attempt to apply the concept of functionalism to a concrete situation consequently necessitates not merely a survey of the administrative activities of the several units of administration but an examination of the actions of constituent assemblies, legislative and judicial bodies as well. For only after an analysis of the decisions of all the policy-determining bodies directly or indirectly concerned with the activities of the several administrative units is it possible to arrive at the underlying legislative intent. And only after the discovery of the legislative intent in relation to the specific situations under discussion is it possible to implement the meaning of the concept to the point of practical applicability.

No less disconcerting than the inadequacy of the definition, as it has been indicated in the paragraphs immediately preceding, is the difficulty—under certain circumstances at least—of differentiating some of these organizational concepts from others. Superficially the distinction between them is clear. Thus, as has already been pointed out, departmentalization according to function has been defined as the grouping of subordinate administrative units in a departmental pattern upon the basis of the underlying purpose to which they have each been dedicated. Departmentalization according to work processes seems even more simple. It has as its primary *raison d'être* the bringing together in a single department of those who have had similar professional training or who make use of the same or similar equipment. Departmentalization upon the basis of clientele is also apparently self-explanatory, and should result in the concentration in a single department of those subordinate administrative units which are designed to serve some particular segment of the body politic.

Without question each of these definitions reveals the essential qualities of the mode of organization it purports to define. Undoubtedly also, on the basis of these definitions, it is possible to characterize many of the administrative departments as they exist in the various countries in the world today. No less indubitable is it, however, that these definitions fail to delineate clearly the boundaries between the several concepts themselves, and are in consequence responsible for a considerable measure of the obscurity and confusion which characterizes much of the abstract discussion of the subject.

The point may be clarified by means of illustration. The primary object of the Department of War is the military defense of the nation. It is, in consequence, quite evidently organized upon a functional basis. Under its aegis, there has been brought together a tremendous personnel with similar professional training who make use of similar equipment. But this by definition is organization upon the basis of another concept—work processes. The question inevitably arises: Upon what basis is the Department of War actually organized? The answer in this case is reasonably clear—and in any case does not make much difference. The paramount consideration which has governed the development of the department has been that of function or purpose at least in the minds of fundamental thinkers as distinguished from routineers—everything else has been incidental.

Such, however, is not the case in connection with the oft-proposed Department of Public Works. Ostensibly such a department might be organized around a single purpose: the construction of all such public works as the policy-determining body might authorize. An incidental result of the development of such a department would be the concentration in a single department of the vast majority of the civilian engineering staffs now employed by the government. Would the fact that such a unit was called a Department of Public Works justify its characterization as a functionally organized department? What if the title of such a department were changed to that of Engineering? Obviously the mere nomenclature of the department would not be decisive in the matter. It would be necessary to investigate the internal organization of the department to discover whether the department was primarily oriented to the solution of a congeries of problems in all their ramifications or whether its *raison d'être* was the economies and efficiencies which might be effected through the closer integration of the engineering activities of the administration. In point of fact both considerations might well play a part in the creation of such an administrative agency.

The illustration clearly indicates the shadowy line which delineates the concepts of function and process. . . .

In the light of this analysis the question inevitably arises as to the utility of discussing such ill-defined and poorly delineated concepts in the abstract.

The question implies a far greater degree of confusion than actually exists. For although it must be conceded that the generally accepted definitions are somewhat unsatisfactory both in their failure to supply concrete criteria as to their applicability and in the twilight zones which characterize their boundaries, there is, nevertheless, connected with each of these concepts, a real core of meaning. Thus, although these generalizations scarcely deserve the characterization of "principles of administration," they must nevertheless be given a prominent place among the factors which must be weighed in the construction of a departmental organization.

Under what conditions should emphasis be laid upon one of these considerations rather than another? In what circumstances should similarity of purpose or function dominate the development of a departmental structure? When are the services rendered to a particular segment of the body politic of paramount importance? What weight, if any, should be given to factors of professional advantage or technical efficiency? How significant is the mere matter of place or territory? These are weighty matters in the creation of a departmental structure and as such deserve extended consideration.

In connection with any analysis of these several concepts, however, a preliminary caution should be emphasized. No one has ever advocated the construction of departments solely upon the basis of function, or work processes, or clientele or territory. Instead, in the very nature of things, functional, technical, clientele, and territorial factors enter into the construction and operation of all national or large-area departments. Such considerations vary from division of work to division of work, and practice and common sense take them into account as existing departmental organizations demonstrate. Back of all technical considerations, however, lie large questions of national policy and purpose which have a bearing upon present practices and proposed innovations. Given a particular set of assumptions respecting public policy—*e.g.*, the desirability of maintaining constitutional government, the normal judicial processes, legislative control over the administration, etc.—the problem then is the emphasis which should be laid upon one relevancy rather than another, *i.e.*, function, clientele, etc., in a given social context and the particular devices which can be adopted to offset any disadvantages to efficiency accruing from a given emphasis. . . .

Function

The most widely utilized basis of departmental integration is that of function or purpose. In whole or in part the Departments of State, War, Navy, Post

Office, Agriculture, Commerce, Labor, and Treasury in the United States rest upon this foundation. . . . The simple fact is that a considerable number of departments, perhaps a majority, in every major unit of government in the world are dominated to some degree by this principle.

Possibly the greatest advantage which this basis of departmental organization possesses is the fact that it expedites the performance of a given task, the solution of a given problem.

Obviously if all the administrative units concerned with a particular job are integrated in a single department, subject to the direction of a single supervisory officer, the task ought to be accomplished more expeditiously than if these same administrative units are scattered hither and yon throughout the administration. No energy need be wasted working out agreements with other branches of the administration. Interdepartmental frictions can be minimized. Priorities can be decided upon the needs of the situation rather than upon the basis of departmental loyalties. The proper timing of the activities of the various administrative units involved can be worked out. Orders can be issued and action assured.

The point can be made clearer, perhaps, through the use of an illustration. It would seem axiomatic, for example, that the various military units connected with land operations—the General Staff, Office of the Adjutant General, Inspector General, Judge Advocate General, Quartermaster General, Surgeon General, Engineers, Ordnance, Signal Officer, Air Corps, Field Artillery, Coast Artillery, Infantry, etc.—should be concentrated in a single department rather than scattered throughout the administrative structure. The primary objective of these military forces is to meet, check, and defeat the enemy. Supplies and munitions must arrive at a given place at a given time. The air corps must warn of the massing of enemy troops. Tanks and artillery must support the infantry when their support is needed. In other words, the machinery must exist for an almost instantaneous coordination of the activities of all the military units engaged in active warfare.

This is only possible if these various and sundry units have been integrated into a single department under a unified command. To scatter these units among the civilian departments, thus necessitating not only a tremendous waste of time in the negotiation of interdepartmental agreements at some crucial moment, or worse still, making possible interdepartmental friction and deadlock, would be so inconceivably fantastic that in fact it is never done. All active military units connected with land warfare are everywhere component parts of a single Department of War or of National Defense. Any alternative form of organization would be almost synonymous with military suicide. . . .

Integration by function thus not only insures unity of action but it contributes considerably to a more completely rounded consideration of all aspects of a given problem or congeries of problems than is likely under any other form of organization.

Another advantage inherent in the integration of the subordinate administrative units of government upon the basis of purpose is that this mode of departmentalization contributes somewhat to a reduction of the degree of overlapping and duplication which otherwise appears to be inevitable.

Owing to the fact that the United States Employment Service, the Social Security Board, the Public Works Administration, and the Works Progress Administration (now Works Projects Administration) were formerly independent units rather than integral parts of a single agency dedicated to the solution of the unemployment problem, friction rather than cooperation has more than once characterized their relationships. Similarly, only continuous consultation and an attitude of the utmost willingness to cooperate and to accommodate prevented the Social Security Board and the Department of Labor from unnecessarily duplicating each other's statistical services. . . .

Equally advantageous, in the opinion of certain students of public administration at any rate, is the fact that integration according to function conforms best with "the objectives of government as they are recognized and understood by the public. The public sees the end result and cannot understand the methodology. It can therefore express its approval or disapproval with less confusion and more effectiveness regarding major purposes than it can regarding the processes." This might be expressed in other terms. Since the public is primarily interested in the solution of particular problems or the discharge of certain public duties, rather than in the administrative techniques or procedures by which the solutions are worked out or duties discharged, the grouping of the various administrative units in a series of departments organized around the operations in a given field of human endeavor is distinctly advantageous in that, to some extent at least, it fixes the responsibility for performances, and in so doing focuses public attention upon the responsible officials. Under some circumstances it may marshal the support of a powerful segment of the community behind the administrative units involved in working out a problem or conducting given operations. Such, for example, has been the position of the Department of Agriculture both in connection with the formulation of its plans for crop control and in their administration. Alternatively this procedure may concentrate such a battery of criticism on a departmental program as to cause its modification or even abandonment.

The simple fact is that integration according to function radically reduces the number of situations in which administrative officials can engage in the time-honored pastime of "buck-passing." This, it should be remarked parenthetically, is not an exclusive attribute of integration on the basis of function since organization on the basis of clientele frequently produces a similar result.

No less important in the minds of many observers is the influence which this simplification of the machinery of government may be expected to exert in connection with the less spectacular but more frequent day-to-day relations existing between the administration and particular segments of the body politic over the interpretation of the detail of various statutes. Thus the manufacturer who is both annoyed and embarrassed by the fact that diverse information called for by the Bureau of Internal Revenue and the Bureau of Customs unnecessarily complicates the keeping of his books can appeal the whole question to the Treasury with the full knowledge that the problem can be settled intradepartmentally, and that it will not have to undergo the slow and tedious process of interdepartmental negotiation or be bogged down in a morass of interdepartmental jealousy and negligence. . . .

Yet, despite the advantages inherent in the principle of functionalism as a basis of departmental integration, a number of defects are clearly apparent.

The first is the difficulty of differentiating the illusion of functionalism from the reality thereof. For example, in connection with the recent proposal to change the name of the Department of Interior to the Department of Conservation on the ground that the latter name more accurately describes its purpose, the question inevitably arises: conservation of what? Of our territorial boundaries? The Departments of State, War, and Navy have, presumably, some slight interest in the question. Of our human resources? The Departments of Labor, Agriculture, and Commerce might all insist that such a department would encompass many, if not all, of their activities. Of our natural resources? The Department of Agriculture has already protested, and protested rather vigorously, that the effective utilization of agricultural lands is part and parcel of any program dedicated to the conservation of our natural resources.

In other words, the term functionalism is, seemingly, capable of such broad interpretation, or misinterpretation, that it can be used to justify the creation of a department which would encompass the entire government. Needless to say, in this sense the concept of functionalism is totally valueless as a basis of departmental integration.

But the difficulty of differentiating the illusion from the reality of functionalism does not end here. If it did the task would be relatively simple. The real problem is presented in such suggestions as the proposed consolidation of the Departments of War and Navy into a Department of National Defense, already referred to in pages preceding; the integration of the health, education and welfare units into a Department of Public Welfare; or alternatively, the combination of the labor, social security, and welfare units into a single Department of Social Affairs. Which suggestion truly embodies the principle of organization according to function? . . .

More disadvantageous in its effects upon departmental operations is the fact that the grouping of the subordinate administrative units into a series of departments upon the basis of function frequently produces an attitude of self-sufficiency on the part of the departmental managers which results both in administrative astigmatism and an unwillingness to cooperate with other departments. The mere fact that the departmental managers have under their direction all of the units of government directly concerned with performances and the solution of the problems to which the department is dedicated is frequently conducive to the development of a departmental bias or emphasis likely to interfere with the capacity of the departmental managers to view their affairs in a broad perspective. For instance, the Department of Agriculture is very apt to think of the development of our water resources largely from the angle of soil erosion, with little or no regard for the utilization of those resources either from the point of view of power or of navigation. Similarly, the creation of a Department of Public Utilities would entail the risk that the development of our water resources would be viewed essentially as a problem of power, rather than one of navigation or soil erosion. Still another bias would in all probability characterize the proposed Department of Transportation which might well view the development of our river systems exclusively from the point of view of their potentialities as arteries of commerce. . . .

Scarcely less deleterious than any of the disadvantages thus far cited in its influence upon the process of administration is the fact that the rigid application of the principle of functionalism to the administrative structure unnecessarily complicates the number of contacts between the public and the government. If the Indian Bureau, for example, were segmented into its constituent parts, and the various parts were allocated to a series of functional departments, a portion of its activities would go to the Treasury, another portion to a Department of Public Welfare, a third, to the Department of Agriculture, and the remaining activities here, there, and elsewhere. In so far as "the poor Indian" is concerned, the result would be confusion thrice confounded. It would be necessary for each individual Indian to take up his various and sundry problems with a multiplicity of governmental agencies, instead of dealing with a single office. Similarly, if the Veterans Administration were reorganized on the basis of function, its diverse activities would be scattered among a number of departments. Certain aspects of its work would be assigned to the Treasury, and others to a Department of Public Welfare; the balance would be divided among administrative subdivisions in still other parts of the departmental structure. The inevitable consequence would be a multiplication of the offices through which the veteran would of necessity transact his business. Whether the advantages which are attainable through a rigid application of the principle of functionalism would more than offset the inconveniences which would result is certainly controversial.

A still further result of a universal application of the functional principle would be the dismissal from consideration of a whole congeries of political factors which in a democracy certainly cannot be overlooked.

Process

An alternative method of departmental integration is on the basis of work processes, whether dictated by personnel or equipment. Thus there would be brought together in a single department all those who practice a given or related profession, *e.g.*, engineering, teaching, medicine, law, military or naval science, or who make use of similar complicated equipment. The adoption of this principle, heedless to say, would necessitate a radical shift in the foci of many departments as they are organized today. A Department of Health would include all doctors, and all nurses, bacteriologists, psychologists, etc., as well. Not only would it handle all the general public-health work for the government but the health services now carried on by the schools and the various welfare units; and, if the principle were vigorously applied, the medical work of the army and navy would similarly fall within its jurisdiction. Members of the legal profession would be attached to the Department of Justice or, as it might more accurately be called, the Department of Law, and detailed therefrom to specific assignments. Similarly, the engineers would have their headquarters in a Department of Engineering and would likewise be assigned to other units as the need arose. Here, too, if the principle were pushed to its logical conclusion, the engineering work of the army and navy might conceivably be handled by a detail from the Department of Engineering.

This principle of organization, it is asserted, is conducive to "the maximum utilization of up-to-date technical skill, and by bringing together in a single office a large amount of each kind of work (technologically measured) makes it possible in each case to make use of the most effective divisions of work and specialization." Thus if school doctors were attached to the health department instead of the Department of Education, they would be in constant touch with their professional colleagues and should in consequence be the recipients of professional stimuli not otherwise probable. Moreover, they would have access to much better equipped laboratories than are otherwise available. Finally, the increased volume of medical work canalized to a Department of Health from all sources would make possible an otherwise unattainable degree of specialization within the Department both in connection with diagnosis, prevention, and treatment.

The utilization of this basis of departmental integration would also make possible a considerable measure of economy both as a result of a more extensive use of labor-saving machinery and as a result of mass production. Thus the concentration of all printing in the hands of the Government Printing Office has undoubtedly avoided the duplication not only of linotype machines and printing presses by each of the departments but has also radically reduced a duplication of personnel. In this vein, the President's Committee on Administrative Management argued that the concentration of all engineering units now maintained by the government into a single Department of Public Works would materially lessen the existing duplication of the very expensive construction machinery made inevitable by the present organization of engineering work. At the moment much of this machinery is used only upon a part-time basis.

Organization by process, it is insisted furthermore, makes possible much more effective coordination in all of the technical and skilled work of an enterprise, "because all of those engaged in any field are brought together under the same supervision instead of being scattered in the several departments as is the case when organization is based upon some other principle." Such, for example, has been the heart of the argument in behalf of the centralization of the statistical work now being carried on by the functionalized departments. The Central Statistical Board, it should be remarked parenthetically, was essentially a compromise between concentration upon the basis of process and the decentralization which is necessary under a functionalized departmental system. In similar fashion, it is argued, the concentration of all legal talent in a single department, whether of Justice or of Law, would *ipso facto* produce more careful legal work and certainly a greater degree of uniformity in the preparation of executive orders, departmental regulations, and drafts of proposed legislation.

Organization by process, it is contended, greatly facilitates cost analyses in the several fields and therefore makes more readily available comparative data respecting unit costs. In consequence, it affords a useful basis for the organization of certain particular services such as budgeting, accounting, purchasing, etc., even when it is not utilized throughout the entire administrative field.

Perhaps the strongest argument in behalf of departmentalization on this basis, however, is the fact that in many respects at least it is best adapted to the development of a career service for government employees, especially if the present basis of recruitment, with its strongly marked vocational element, continues. In a departmental organization based upon process, the school doctor need not feel that he is in a dead end professionally. If the Department of Health is properly organized, he can clearly see the rungs of the ladder up which he may make a professional ascent. The engineer attached to the Office of Education need not feel that he is merely an incident in the educational system. . . .

Despite the very real economies and operating efficiencies which may accrue from the grouping of the subordinate administrative units into departments upon the basis of process, conflicts and frictions are also inherent in the procedure.

In the first place, if this principle were applied universally or even generally, the burden of coordination imposed upon the chief executive in any large system would be beyond his physical and mental capacity. As Dr. Gulick has pointed out, "purpose departments must be coordinated so that they will not conflict but will work shoulder to shoulder. But whether they do, or do not, the individual major purposes will be accomplished to a considerable extent and a failure in any service is limited in its effect to that service. Process departments must be coordinated not only to prevent conflicts, but also to guarantee positive cooperation. They must work hand in hand. They must also time their work so that it will fit together, a factor of lesser significance in the purpose departments. A failure in one process affects the whole enterprise, and a failure to coordinate one process division may destroy the effectiveness of all of the work that is being done."

Recurring to an illustration used earlier, the activities of the commissary, the engineering units, the medical corps, the office of ordnance, etc., simply must be coordinated with those of the infantry, tanks, and artillery, or else an entire campaign may be lost. The rigid utilization of process as a basis of departmental organization would allocate certain of these units to positions in the administrative structure outside the Department of War. In the events of hostilities, this would necessitate a rapidity of interdepartmental coordination which would in all probability be unattainable. The sheer logic of necessity would force a grouping of these units immediately under the chief executive. . . .

The maximum utilization of up-to-date skill . . . is not an inevitable concomitant of organization according to process. Indeed, the health officers assigned to school work, or the naval officers detailed to transport service, or the lawyers allocated to the Department of Interior may either be youngsters just beginning their professional careers assigned to these various posts for the simple reason that from the point of view of the department as a whole they appear to be relatively unimportant, or they may be misfits whom the heads of the various departments have been too tenderhearted to discharge. A system of detail from the process departments to subsidiary services may actually enable the head of each of these various departments to keep their youngsters employed while they are gaining maturity and experience in aspects of the administration in which he, the department head, is least interested, or alternatively, to locate misfits in positions in which from his point of view they will do the least harm. In both cases, however, the result may be inefficiency in so far as the administration of these subsidiary functions is concerned.

A further criticism brought against this method of organization is that it tends to make means more important than ends. This may easily result in the development of a red-tape bureaucracy. Even today there are "accountants who think that the only reason for running a government is the keeping of books." And one sometimes suspects that many of the complicated aspects of legal procedure are due to the reverence of the legal profession for form rather than for content. Organization according to process would, it is asserted, definitely accentuate the influence of the ritualists.

Moreover, such a pattern of organization is weighted on the side of financial extravagance. The fact that the Bureau of Reclamation has been guided by engineers rather than by agriculturalists has, so it is charged, been partly if not primarily responsible for the development of a number of reclamation projects which have not been self-sustaining. Errors have been made, so the criticism runs, which could not conceivably have been committed had the Bureau been subject to the supervision of a department fundamentally concerned with the problem of agriculture, and only incidentally interested in keeping its staff of engineers employed. This, it is argued, is the great danger in creating a Department of Engineering or Public Works. The head of such a department, so it is claimed, will feel morally obligated to keep his staff employed, and will, in consequence, countenance the construction of engineering projects another department head might disapprove. . . .

Another undesirable consequence which frequently flows from this mode of departmental organization is the development of an attitude of professional arrogance on the part of the departmental managers and an irritation at any and all attempts to impose popular control not found elsewhere. That the professional man should develop a measure of impatience or even contempt for the laity is natural. Many of the things which appear obvious to him must be explained step by step to the uninitiated. In consequence this ignorance seems simply appalling. Moreover, by virtue of his superior knowledge the professional man knows, or thinks he knows, what should be done in a given situation better than the uninformed public—or its political representatives. Thus professional educators insist that education is too important or too mysterious to be subject to the supervision of our politically elected municipal executives or even municipal legislatures. Instead, our educational systems must occupy an independent or quasi-independent status, one, incidentally, which professional educators will be able to dominate nine times out of ten. . . .

Integration on this basis frequently leads to the appointment of narrow specialists as department heads. The result is frequently unfortunate both intra- and inter-departmentally. The appointment of a narrow specialist to the headship of a large administrative department may well result in departmental narrowness rather than in efficiency. Thus the appointment of a physicist to the head of a Department of Science may lead to an overemphasis of the mathematical sciences and the neglect of the organic sciences. . . .

The appointment of a specialist to the head of a department, it is urged, moreover, is likely to be conducive to promotions within the department upon the basis of technical efficiency rather than administrative ability. Technical ability is undoubtedly important; nevertheless, the management of a department calls for other and equally significant qualities—a breadth of vision and a capacity for leadership frequently not possessed by the mere technician.

The assignment of a specialist to the leadership of a department is very likely to accentuate the very difficulties of interdepartmental coordination that organization upon the basis of process itself precipitates. As has been indicated previously, a long career of specialization is very apt to produce loyalties to a particular profession, primary interest in the problems of that profession, and the neglect of most problems falling outside the bounds of that profession. Such a background, to put it mildly, scarcely tends to promote that interdepartmental understanding and sympathy which is imperative in the solution of interdepartmental problems. . . .

Finally, the development of these specialized departments with their emphasis upon means rather than ends will, so it is argued, have a disintegrating influence upon the chief executive's cabinet. Here more than anywhere breadth of view is imperative. The ends to which the energies of government should be dedicated are paramount over the technical procedures which should be followed in the attainment of those ends; but, in so far as the department exerts any influence upon its politically appointed head, it will be likely to emphasize the means rather than the ends. Stimuli for broad thinking relative to the purpose of government action will be lacking or appear only fortuitously.

Clientele or Matériel

A third possible method of departmental integration is upon the basis of clientele or matériel. This principle is, perhaps, best illustrated in the organization of the Veterans Administration "which deals with all the problems of the veterans, be they in health, in hospitals, in insurance, in welfare, or in education." The Immigration and Naturalization Service, the Children's Bureau, and the Office of Indian Affairs constitute still other illustrations. Each of these deals with its clientele in various relations. The Immigration and Naturalization Service handles the immigrant problem not from one side but from three—legal, financial, and medical. The Children's Bureau insists that just as the individual child cannot be divided into component parts but must instead remain a single entity, so its work must encompass all aspects of child welfare—health, education, and vocational guidance. The jurisdiction of the Office of Indian Affairs is even more sweeping, embracing practically all the governmental activities—health, educational, and financial—which relate to these wards of the nation. To some degree at least, it may be asserted that the Departments of Agriculture, Labor, and Commerce have been organized upon a similar pattern, in that they each serve the particular needs of some large segment of the body politic. In consequence, the Agricultural Extension Service, which from a functional point of view might well be placed under the Office of Education, is, in fact, part and parcel of the Department of Agriculture. For a long time the Federal Board for Vocational Education was attached to the Department of Labor. The Department of Commerce aspires to be the agency to which businessmen of the nation can come and feel certain of a friendly reception. The heads of these three departments look upon themselves more or less as spokesmen for their respective clienteles in the chief executive's cabinet. . . .

Departmental integration on the basis of clientele has the great advantage of simplifying the relationship of the administration with the public. Veterans desirous of information relative to the various services which the government is prepared to render participants in the World War may ascertain the answer to any problem which may confront them directly from the Veterans Administration without being shunted from office to office. Similarly, the farmer interested in obtaining advice relative to any one of a number of problems which may arise in the conduct of his industry may do so at the Department of Agriculture. In this way the confusion and irritation so frequently attendant upon the public's transaction of business with the government is avoided.

Unquestionably the grouping of the subordinate administrative units into a departmental structure on the basis of clientele makes possible a coordination of the activities of the government with regard to particular segments of the public to a degree not attainable under any other form of organization.

The Office of Indian Affairs, for example, insists quite correctly that the Indians constitute a peculiar people who find it difficult if not impossible to adapt themselves to the demands of modern industrial civilization, that if they were left to themselves they would shortly be reduced to destitution, if not extinction. The Commissioner of Indian Affairs asserts consequently that it is the function of his office to protect the Indian in his existing status, and to effect, if possible, a gradual transformation of Indian habits and characteristics so that the Indian may at some future date take his place upon a plane of equality with his Caucasian contemporaries. This inevitably involves not only the temporary administration of Indian property but also instruction in at least the primary principles of personal and community hygiene, formal instruction in the schools, and vocational training in agriculture, the trades, and contemporary business practices.

Inevitably the question arises as to whether this task could not be more effectively accomplished if it were broken down into its component parts and the parts allocated to their various places in the administrative structure upon a functional basis. If this were done, the administration of Indian property would be turned over to one or other of the fiscal agencies of the government; the development of health standards to the United States Public Health Service; the educational activities to the Office of Education, and so on.

Such a proposal has more than once received serious consideration. But the answer both of the Indian administrators and of the leading students of Indian affairs has in each case been in the negative. In their opinion, the problems concerning the Indian tribes are so peculiarly related to Indian characteristics and so interrelated with each other that if they are to be solved at all they must be solved by a single agency. For these reasons it would be difficult to separate tutelage in personal hygiene from the formal instruction given in the schools; it would be no less difficult to separate the administration of Indian property from the endeavor both to effect a transformation in Indian character which will make the Indian self-sustaining, more or less sophisticated in the ways of a modern financial and industrial world, and at the same time to conserve enough tribal life to preserve the best of Indian culture. . . .

Over against these distinct advantages inherent in departmental integration on the basis of clientele or matériel have been set a number of definite drawbacks.

In the first place, the principle is clearly incapable of universal or even general application. Any such attempt would lead to such a multiplicity of departments as to frustrate the primary purpose of departmentalization—coordination. As Viscount Haldane pointed out in his justly famous *Report on the Machinery of Government*, a vigorous application of the principle would lead to a Department of Youth, a Department of the Aged, a Department of Urban Dwellers, a Department of Agriculture, a Department of Manufacturers, a Department of Miners, a Department of College Professors, a Department of Doctors, and so on. The result would be such a multiplicity of small departments and administrations that the problem of interdepartmental coordination would be indistinguishable from that which now exists at the bureau level.

Any such departmental pattern, moreover, would inevitably lead to jurisdictional conflict and duplication. Just what should constitute the jurisdictional bounds, for example, of a Department of the Aged? Would it undertake to furnish those services which are the peculiar need of the aged—(pensions, hospitalization, and the rest), or would it also encompass within its jurisdiction water supply and fire protection? If it did the latter, the complexities of administration would become insurmountable.

If, on the other hand, the constituents of the Department of the Aged are to be the recipients of services from a Water Department, a Health Department, a Department of Education, a Police Department, a Fire Department, *et al.*, what becomes of the principle of integration on the basis of clientele? To say that the recipients of water, health, and educational services or of police and fire protection constitute the clientele of these several departments, is, of course, a mere juggling of words. Each and every individual in the entire community makes use of these several services. The plain truth is that the principle of integration on the basis of clientele possesses validity only when the congeries of problems which relate to a particular segment of the population are so evidently real and so closely interrelated that they can be solved effectively only if approached as a single complex rather than through the medium of their constituent elements. . . .

Also significant from the point of view of administrative efficiency is the fact that departments organized upon the basis of clientele or matériel, in contrast to those based upon work processes, rarely provide a sufficient volume of work of a given sort to make possible a completely satisfactory division of labor, or equally important, to provide satisfactory careers upon the basis of which capable persons will be attracted into the government service.

Finally, under certain circumstances at least, this pattern of departmental integration is said to render administration unduly subservient to the demands of the pressure groups. The Veterans Administration is generally conceded to be very sympathetic to the Veterans' Lobby, throwing the weight of its influence behind the demands of King Legion in season and out. . . .

Territory

A fourth method of departmental organization is that based upon place or territory. This technique has long been used as a basis of intradepartmental organization both in the national government and in the state and local areas. In the Department of State, for example, there is a Division of Western European Affairs, of Eastern European Affairs, of Far Eastern Affairs, of Near Eastern Affairs, of Mexican Affairs, of Latin American Affairs, and so on. In many of the larger cities, the police department is divided into precincts; almost complete supervisory authority is delegated to the precinct captain through whom all communications both from and to headquarters must go. A similar situation is frequently found in connection with the construction and maintenance of streets, sewers, and various public works.

This technique has been applied at the departmental level principally in connection with overseas possessions. In Great Britain the Indian administration is placed in the India Office, matters affecting Dominion relations in the Dominion Office, and the management of the Crown colonies in the Colonial Office. . . .

In the United States, the Bureau of Insular Affairs and the Division of Territories, formerly in the Departments of Navy and Interior, respectively, represent similar developments. But the relative insignificance of our overseas empire, together with the fact that the larger proportion of that empire is in such close proximity to the United States as to be practically a part of our continental domain, makes any immediate application of the principle upon a departmental scale inexpedient.

Departmentalization upon the basis of place or territory has not been wholly confined to administrative units dealing with overseas possessions, however. This is evidenced not only by the continued existence of a Secretary of State for Scotland in Great Britain, but—radically different though it is—by the recent creation of the Tennessee Valley Authority and the further proposal to create seven additional regions similar in character centering around the great river valleys of the United States.

To some extent departmental integration upon this basis partakes of the nature of the geographic decentralization discussed previously. The two concepts, however, are distinct and separate. The governmental decentralization, analyzed earlier, generally involves not merely the delegation of administrative power but legislative and political authority as well. Once these powers have been delegated, they can usually be abrogated only by legislative, or under certain circumstances, constitutional action. By contrast, departmentalization on the basis of place or territory is concerned only with the organization and distribution of administrative power. And, under all circumstances, the Chief Executive will legally continue to exercise the same degree of control over the subordinate administrative units, grouped in such a department, as he would had they been grouped together upon any other basis. . . .

The infrequent utilization of the principle in internal administrative organization in contrast to its general use in connection with overseas possessions inevitably raises a question as to its applicability to internal affairs. It is certainly hard to believe that the burden of administration in the smaller countries of the world—Switzerland, Sweden—will ever become such as to render decentralization in this fashion imperative. In countries possessing vast stretches of territory, however, the factor of distance may be just as complicating administratively as it is in connection with the administration of an overseas empire. The problem may, of course, be solved through some form of federalism. Nevertheless, as we have already discovered, federalism has the tremendous disadvantage of failing to provide a mechanism of coordination adequate to the exigencies of a complicated national economy. Under these circumstances, consequently, it may well be that departmentalization upon the basis of place or territory may be that exact compromise between the advantages of decentralization and centralization which is thought desirable. . . .

Departmental integration upon this basis permits a greater coordination of the services rendered and control exercised within a given area than would otherwise be possible. Thus the concentration of the development of the Tennessee River Valley in the hands of a single federal agency has made possible an integration of the various engineering, power, navigation, housing, and agricultural projects which would have been unattainable under any other form of organization.

Internally as well as externally this pattern facilitates the special adaptation of governmental policies to the needs of the areas affected. Thus the tremendous power resources of the Tennessee Valley have impelled the T.V.A. to concentrate upon the construction of dams and the development of electrical energy. Elsewhere the emphasis might have been quite different.

No less important than either of the preceding advantages is the fact that this mode of departmentalization also furnishes an effective medium through which the needs and aspirations of the people of the different sections can be presented to the administration. This is true not only of the day-to-day detail of administration which can be influenced by the direct impacts of local residents upon the departmental managers, but also in connection with these larger aspects of public policy in which the regions have a distinctly sectional point of view. The mechanism will, of course, be all the more effective if the heads of these regional departments are natives of the regions over which they preside. Thus the existence of a Secretary of State for Scotland has undoubtedly created the feeling and perhaps the actuality that the peculiar needs of this northern non-English section of the British Isles are being more effectively looked after than would otherwise be the case. The substitution of a single agency of government operating over a large area for ten or twelve functional departments, moreover, should simplify intergovernmental relations. Thus a single regional department of the federal government covering New England or the Old South should not only simplify the working out of intergovernmental agreements, but should also minimize those interdepartmental conflicts which inevitably contribute to intergovernmental confusion and irritation under a federal form of government.

Incidentally, this form of departmental organization, so it is asserted, should result in numerous economies of operation, even in a country like the United States. Although the distance from New York to Seattle is not as great as that from London to Calcutta, it is nevertheless of significant proportions. The delegation of broad supervisory authority to administrative officers located on the West coast should consequently cut radically both travel and communication costs, minimize paper work, and permit the more effective disposition of the regional personnel.

If, however, the application of this principle of departmentalization domestically possesses distinct advantages, it also has inherent in it certain serious drawbacks. In the first place, it should be obvious that it inevitably increases the difficulties in the way of developing and administering uniform national policies. Although the maintenance of uniform policies is by no means universally desirable, nevertheless, there are certain fields in which they are imperative. There is, for example, a minimum below which the administration of the health laws of the nation cannot be allowed to fall.

Similarly, if the military defenses of the country are to be maintained in a reasonable state of efficiency it is apparent that there must not only be uniformity of drill and equipment, but unity of command as well. If the navy is to be of any significance in the defense of either our continental or overseas empire, it must operate as a unit and not as a series of disjointed segments. In so far, consequently, as this mode of departmentalization undermines the unity of administration in those spheres in which unity is imperative, it *ipso facto* impairs its own *raison d'être*. . .

A further disadvantage inherent in departmentalization upon the basis of place or territory is that it may well be conducive to an overemphasis upon regional in contrast to national thinking.

One of the great differences between the executive and the legislative departments of the government of the United States as they are now organized is that the former is inclined to think in national terms, the later in terms of their respective states or constituencies. At times, *e.g.*, the period from 1861 to 1865, it has been the executive which has held the country together. Departmental integration on the basis of place or territory would, it is charged, radically weaken the centrifugal influence of the executive and greatly enhance the tendency toward sectionalism, both economic and political. And in so doing it might easily lead to disturbing consequences. In any event, a reduction in national thinking is not an end to be desired, for, with the increasing integration of our economic life, more and more of our problems are becoming national, fewer and fewer regional in character. . . .

The mere matter of drawing the geographic boundaries of these regional departments would itself be a difficult and complex task. A survey of administrative decentralization as it now exists within the functional and process departments reveals almost as many distinct administrative areas as there are departments. The Department of War, for example, is organized into nine army corps; the Federal Reserve Board into twelve Federal Reserve Districts; the Rural Electrification Administration centers everything in Washington and operates directly from the national capital; by contrast, the Department of Agriculture utilizes each of the forty-eight states. Even where two or more departments use the same geographic area, experience has often dictated the utilization of different foci. Thus while a number of federal agencies operating in Michigan have located their headquarters in Detroit, an equal number whose work necessitates close cooperation with the state government have centered their activities in Lansing. In short, there are no "natural boundaries" for administrative devolution which encompass at one and the same time all the administrative activities of the federal government. Instead, the boundaries vary according to the nature of the work being carried on. Any attempt to delineate such boundaries, therefore, would not only encounter a multiplicity of difficulties, but might indeed necessitate the sacrifice of so many advantages inherent in other departmental patterns as to much more than offset any possible gains. . . .

No less important than any of the foregoing is the fact that this form of departmental organization might also lead to the domination of these regional departments by local politicians and local pressure groups.

The American party system has been defined as a "federation of local machines held together by the cohesive power of public plunder." The definition is obviously unfair and inaccurate, nevertheless it illustrates a point. The party organization in the United States is predominantly state or regional in character, so much so, that despite the theoretically national character of our administrative organization, the statutes themselves provide that assignments to the civil service shall be proportionate to the population of the various states. Nor does the regional pressure stop here. The system of senatorial courtesy enables the senators, particularly if they are from the majority party, to dictate appointments to many offices not embraced by the civil service laws. If, then, this situation exists in the face of an allegedly nationalistic form of departmentalization, what would take place if the departments were organized on an avowedly regional basis? . . .

Closely allied to, and indeed an inseparable part of, the demands of the local politicians would be the efforts of the local pressure groups. Needless to say, pressure-group activities are not necessarily pernicious. In a sense, the Constitution of the United States may be said to have been the work of pressure groups. In like fashion, our tariff policy has been the resultant of pressure-group activities. The Civil Service Reform League can claim at least partial credit for the adoption of the merit system. But in each of these cases the policy finally adopted has been the result of the play of forces in the national arena. To some extent at least, selfish local interests have canceled each other or have led to beneficial compromises. No such corrective would exist if the administration were departmentalized along regional lines. Instead, The Associated Manufacturers of New England might conceivably dominate the administration of the Department of New England, with the result that in New England the enforcement of the national labor law might easily become difficult if not impossible. Similarly, the "Cotton Growers Association" might dictate the broad lines of the enforcement in the Department of Southern Affairs, thereby frustrating all efforts to alleviate the condition of the tenant farmers. The simple fact is that vested interests of this character occasionally become more or less dominant even in the nationally organized departments. It seems highly probable, consequently, that their influence would be even more radical in departments organized upon a regional rather than a national basis.

So serious are these defects that except for the recent suggestion that the seven great river valleys of the United States be so organized, one might be inclined to dismiss quite categorically the concept of departmentalization upon the basis of place or territory.

Indeed, if the preceding analysis has revealed anything, it is that the study of administration has not as yet developed a set of scientific principles relative to the problem of departmental integration capable of precise application. Instead, it is evident that the concepts we have been discussing are at best a series of generalizations deduced from past experience. Down to date the exact nature of these concepts has not been carefully defined, nor have their boundaries been accurately delineated. Moreover, the advantages which each of these several modes of organization is sometimes said to possess are, under certain circumstances at least, offset by a multiplicity of weaknesses. To a very considerable extent the utilization of one of these modes of departmental organization rather than another turns upon the objective sought. . . . Thus it is evident that the controlling factor in determining the foundation upon which a departmental structure should rest is not some abstract concept of administration but the paramount objective to which the department is dedicated. Equally obvious is it, however, that the mere application of one of these concepts will not *ipso facto* produce the desired grouping. Instead, the advantages and disadvantages of each of these modes of departmental integration must be weighed in connection with each addition to the departmental structure. . . .

The mere fact that these several concepts have not as yet attained the precision of a scientific formula does not, however, render them valueless. Far from it, for vaguely defined and poorly delineated as they are, subject to all the qualifications, limitations, and exceptions that have been noted in the preceding pages, they constitute nevertheless an exceedingly useful frame of reference for further thinking upon the subject.

One organizational problem that is of much greater concern to public than to private administration is "independence." Actual operating independence of various kinds, and theories justifying such independence, are by no means unknown to private administration. But the special theories and conditions under which government is carried on raise special problems of independence in public administration.

In private administration independence, when it is considered at all as an issue, is likely to be considered in terms of "efficiency": will independence of some type for an operating unit or branch manager "pay off" in

terms of greater production or less expense? In government, similar problems of efficiency are also frequently present. But government in the United
States is carried on under a political philosophy that makes efficiency in its
usual sense a secondary or irrelevant consideration. Our political theories,
embodied in constitutions and laws, even place a premium upon ensuring
that some things not be done at all or, if done, be done in ways that place
first emphasis upon "proper form," protection of rights, equality of treatment, and securing of the public interest. It is in connection with attaining
these ends that independence of some kind in public administration is most
frequently proposed and defended.

This type of independence in administration is closely related, as are
many things in American public administration, to a principle of constitutional construction that lies at the base of our Federal and state constitutions: namely, the separation of powers. According to this theory the proper
ends of government are best attained when its powers and functions are
divided among persons and organs that counterbalance and curb each
other, so that none shall become overmighty. In practice this means chiefly
that the powers of government are divided in the main into three parts,
with a legislative body to make laws, an executive to execute the laws, and
a court system to interpret the laws. There is not complete separation,
however, and in fact, in pursuing the idea of checks and balances, each of
the three parts is given some of the powers that would under rigorous
separation go to one of the other two. Thus the President is Chief Executive and must see that the laws are faithfully executed, but he is also given
constitutional means of participating in lawmaking. Conversely, the Congress is primarily concerned with lawmaking, but it shares as of constitutional right control of many aspects of administration of the law.

This system of government is obviously complex, fraught with possibilities not only for disagreement on the issues of the day but for doubt and
heated argument on how the powers of government themselves should be
related and exercised. Our constitutional history concerns in large part the
conflicting interpretations of the separation of powers and the ebb and flow
of actual power among the three branches. First one branch, then another,
seems in a position of dominance.

The rise of modern public administration has added new aspects to old
arguments. Generally speaking, those identified with public administration
as a field of study have tended to be partisans of the executive in the un-
ending struggle with the legislative and judicial—a natural tendency. This
natural tendency toward identification with the executive has probably been
accented, however, by the fact that the doctrines and techniques that public

administration has taken from various sources, chiefly business administration, tend to emphasize executive power and responsibility. It is significant too that business administration, from which so much has been borrowed, has emphasized efficiency to the exclusion of the other criteria with which, as noted above, government in the United States is historically and constitutionally concerned.

In 1887 occurred an event of great importance in constitutional and administrative development. The event was the establishment of the Interstate Commerce Commission, charged with preventing abuses in our developing nation-wide rail system. Two organizational features of the Commission were of great moment. One was that it was set up "independent" of any of the regular executive departments. The other was the fact that it was headed not by a single person but by a board. These precedents were followed again and again in following decades when Congress determined that the Federal government should undertake some new activity but that it should not be entrusted to an established executive department.

The result has been the establishment of a wide range of government activities carried on outside the executive branch proper—and certainly outside the other two branches. And the result of this has been highly complex and sometimes heated controversy. Some have claimed that this development in effect has subverted the Constitution, which clearly intended that there should be three and only three branches of government. Others, waiving the constitutional issue, have argued that this development is "inefficient," "unsound," and so forth. Still others, however, have found reason to believe that this new development is wholly in accord with the constitutional principle of divided and balanced powers; and that when the legitimate constitutional ends of government are considered, the independence of the new agencies is more likely to achieve them efficiently than would be the case if the functions of the independent agencies were carried on by executive departments.

In the mid-thirties President Roosevelt appointed a committee, the President's Committee on Administrative Management, to conduct a study of "administrative management" in the Federal government. The Committee, composed of distinguished political scientists, and its staff of eminent students of public administration, prepared and presented in 1937 a series of recommendations supported by special studies. These recommendations and special studies have significantly affected our constitutional development. Several major administrative developments are undoubtedly attributable to the Commission's work, and the end of the influence of its philosophy is not in sight.

The selection below is an adaptation of one of the studies prepared under the President's Committee on Administrative Management. Its author is Professor Robert E. Cushman, who has made a professional specialty of independent regulatory commissions. Professor Cushman's proposals for reform have been included in this adaptation only in briefest form, and without their supporting argument, so that more of the very excellent general factual and theoretical material might be included.

The proposals of Professor Cushman, as will be seen, represent an attempt to secure the legitimate advantages of independence without what he considers the illegitimate disadvantages. These proposals were not accepted as the basis for reorganization at the time, but there has been a slow evolutionary movement in their direction in the intervening years. In the period ahead there will probably be heated controversy over proposed further changes in the independent regulatory commissions. The interests affected are substantial, and feelings run deep.

Is Professor Cushman's treatment of the constitutional issues adequate and fair? Does his formula give due weight to all the factors which by his own analysis are relevant? Is his formula simpler than his analysis of the facts warrants?

The Problem of the Independent Regulatory Commissions *

ROBERT E. CUSHMAN

Statement of the Problem. By "independent," as applied to a commission or board, is meant that it is wholly outside any regular executive department. It is not subject to control by any Cabinet secretary or by the President. The members of some "independent" commissions can be removed from office by the President in his discretion, whereas in other cases such removals may be made only for causes set out in the statutes. "Independence," as the term is used in this study, does not mean independence of Presidential removal, but merely a status of isolation from the major executive departments. The term "regulatory" implies governmental control over private conduct or property interests, and distinguishes such a body as the Federal Trade Commission, which is supposed to police interstate commerce in behalf of fair competition, from the independent Farm Credit Administration, which carries on the work of lending Government money. The

* Adapted from *The Problem of the Independent Regulatory Commissions*, in Report with Special Studies, President's Committee on Administrative Management (Washington: 1937).

Federal Trade Commission regulates, the Farm Credit Administration does not.

The independent regulatory commissions present a challenging problem in any program of Federal administrative reorganization. They stand actually and potentially for decentralization. Though they do not escape supervision by the courts, they are wholly free from control by the President. Experience has evolved no practical means of making them responsible to the Congress. As someone has said, they are a sort of "fourth department" in the National Government.

Beginning with the Interstate Commerce Commission in 1887, Congress has used the independent commission technique in more than a dozen cases for the handling of various regulatory jobs. But in fully as many cases Congress has given the same kind of regulatory functions to bureaus in the executive departments, especially in the Department of Agriculture. If Congress has followed any consistent principle in choosing between these two methods, it has failed to disclose what that principle is. Sometimes the same function has been set up in both ways successively, as in the case of the Shipping Board, which began as an independent commission, later became a bureau in the Department of Commerce, and in 1936 emerged again in the guise of the new independent Maritime Commission.

The whole problem may be stated thus: There is high respect, based on experience, for the independent commission as a device for Federal regulation. There exists a strong inclination to use this method for handling new regulatory jobs as they emerge. At the same time, the multiplication of these independent bodies tends inevitably toward a decentralized and chaotic administrative system. They are areas of unaccountability. They occupy important fields of administration beyond the reach of Presidential direction and responsibility. Is there any logical point at which to stop creating them? If not, is there any alternative or compromise plan by which the major advantages of the independent commission technique may be kept, and at the same time the administrative confusion that comes from setting up numerous independent bodies avoided?

The Development of Independent Commissions

Congress began 50 years ago to create independent commissions to handle Federal regulatory functions. This movement in the field of national administration is the result of much legislative groping—much reliance upon trial and error. It has developed its own philosophy as it has gone along. Its major principles have never been followed with complete consistency and the commissions set up have varied widely in form and function. A good deal is known about some of the commissions, but the commission movement as such has never been explored. Important questions concerning it have remained unanswered. Among these are the following: What motives or reasons led Congress to create independent commissions? Why have those commissions varied so widely in organization and duties? What relationships were the commissions supposed to bear to the three departments of the Government? Why has Congress created independent commissions to handle some regulatory functions, whereas in other cases it has given the same sort of functions to the regular executive departments? The following brief survey of the commission movement, based mainly upon its legislative history, attempts to throw some light on these questions.

It is obvious that the full story of the creation of the major regulatory commissions would comprise vital chapters in the Nation's economic history. There is not space for that story here, but no account of the commission movement however brief can ignore the following facts: First, the decline of *laissez faire* and the growth of governmental regulation of business that followed upon the heels of the Civil War and Reconstruction. Second, the emergence of vitally important economic problems demanding Federal rather than State regulation. Third, the growth of the technique of governmental regulation through the legislative formulation of "standards" of business conduct to be applied in concrete cases by the quasi-judicial decisions of administrative agencies. Fourth, the emergence of the idea that governmental regulation of business should not be confined to the enforcement of criminal penalties but should partake of continuous and not unfriendly supervision.

It may be noted that early congressional experimentation with the independent commission was influenced by the experience of the States. Twenty-five State commissions were already regulating railroads when the Interstate Commerce Act was passed in 1887. The seeds were being rapidly sown for the growth of the multitude of State boards and commissions that were ultimately to produce the almost complete decentralization of executive power in the American State.

The Interstate Commerce Commission, 1887.[1] Someone has said that had it not been for the Supreme Court's decision in 1869 (*Paul* v. *Virginia*, 8 Wallace 168) that interstate insurance business is not interstate commerce, the first Federal commission would probably have been an insurance commission. Be that as it may, the Court unquestionably precipitated the action that created the Interstate Commerce Commission by holding, in *Wabash, St. Louis and Pacific Railway Co.* v. *Illinois* (118 U.S. 557), decided in 1886, that the interstate railroad business was subject to exclusive Federal control under the commerce clause and that abuses in it could not be corrected by State law. If the railroads were to be regulated, Congress must do it.

The Interstate Commerce Act was directed against concrete abuses—pooling, discriminations, rebates, and the like. Congress had been considering the problem of regulation for over a decade and numerous bills had been introduced. As the discussions progressed, the issue was drawn between the House and the Senate over the creation of an independent commission. The House, led largely by Mr. Reagan from Texas, favored laws that would punish rate abuses and rebates, and that would be enforced by the Department of Justice in the regular courts. To set

[1] While the original Report contains histories of all the independent commissions, only one is reproduced here, for illustrative purposes.—The Editor.

up a commission, it was urged, would be to provide a substitute for action, a sop thrown to the public in lieu of direct and responsible enforcement of laws that had real teeth. A commission would not be large enough, nor honest enough, to exercise wide powers of control over the railroad system. Such a commission, further, would involve an unconstitutional delegation of legislative power.

The commission idea was sponsored in the Senate by Senator Cullom. He urged that the mere existence of a commission would prevent a large number of abuses; many cases would be settled out of court, and the cost and delay of litigation would thus be saved; the shipper with a prima facie case against the railroad would have that case prosecuted by the Government; and the commission would be able, as a body of experts, to study and report back to Congress on all phases of the problem of railroad regulation.

The compromise between these two positions, hastened by the decision in the Wabash Railway Co. case, already mentioned, resulted in setting up a commission and in putting into the act drastic prohibitions against railroad abuses. It is clear that the new commission was not to "manage" or "regulate" the railroads in any positive or constructive way. It was not looked upon as a court with authority to decide anything finally. It was to investigate complaints and start action in the courts. It was to keep Congress informed as to the progress of the whole job and recommend legislation that might be needed.

Congress does not seem to have had any clearly worked out philosophy as to where the new Interstate Commerce Commission fitted into the governmental structure. In some ways it was to aid the process of legislation, in other ways the process of law enforcement. It had no direct relations with the President, nor had he figured in the movement that led to its creation. The details of its structure and organization escaped serious discussion. The new commission was to send its annual report to the Secretary of the Interior who was instructed to provide the commission with offices and supplies and to approve its expense vouchers and the appointment and compensation of its employees. The Secretary of the Interior almost immediately asked to be relieved of these responsibilities and the commission was made completely independent in 1889.

The new commission got off to an inauspicious start. It was viewed as a natural enemy by the railroads. The courts looked upon it with suspicion because of its hybrid powers and by decision after decision reduced its meager authority. But Congress watched its work closely, considered with care its numerous legislative proposals, and ultimately strengthened it by legislation. By degrees it became a powerful regulatory body. It has been given many of its later functions not because it is important to have them handled by an independent body, but because the Commission could take them over more easily than any other agency. It has earned the respect of the courts, which now extend it a deference withheld from some of the younger and less powerful commissions.

The first Federal regulatory commission stands out as the most conspicuous and successful. . . . It regulates and manages the land transportation system of the Nation. Its powers are legislative, administrative, and judicial. It has a responsibility to the courts to keep within its statutory powers. It has a vague responsibility to the Congress with respect to its whole job, but there is no way of making that responsibility effective except by additional statutory instructions. It has no formal responsibility to the President, though its paths cross his at numerous points. It is, in short, a little government in itself, set up for the purpose of governing the railroads—a sort of fourth department for the administration of a single function of vast importance. Small wonder that Congress has looked upon its handiwork with satisfaction and has been strongly impelled to follow the same technique for the handling of new regulatory functions as they have emerged. . . .

Regulatory Functions in the Executive Departments

The establishment of independent commissions has been only one of the techniques used by Congress to organize regulatory functions. In many cases it has given to bureaus or divisions in the regular executive departments the same type of duty that has been given to the independent commissions. The Department of Agriculture has been the one to receive most of these delegations of powers.

The movement seems to have begun with the enactment in 1906 of the Food and Drug Act. The same year saw the passage of the 28-hour law for the transportation of livestock, and in 1907 the Meat Inspection Act went into effect. Though these functions were established on a modest basis at the outset, they have come to be highly important and to affect a very large number of persons subject to control. In 1912 important powers of regulation were granted in the Plant Quarantine Act; in 1916 the Cotton Futures Act and the Warehouse Act were passed. In 1921, as a result of the Federal Trade Commission's investigation of the packing industry, Congress passed the Packers and Stockyards Act. Instead of placing the enforcement of this statute in the Federal Trade Commission, it was given to the Secretary of Agriculture, who still administers it. Under the act the Secretary exercises a rate-making authority very similar to that of the Interstate Commerce Commission and has other important powers as well. In the same year Congress passed the Grain Futures and Commodities Exchange Act, which has since been amended several times. In 1923 the Cotton Standards Act was passed. These are some of the more conspicuous instances in which regulatory authority, involving not only administrative policy but quasi-judicial power, has been turned over to bureaus or divisions in the Department of Agriculture. A more thorough examination of the statutes reveals more than 40 of these acts.

Why has Congress followed this policy in these particular cases? In the first place, the Department of Agriculture, created to provide adequate representation of the agricultural industry, has always enjoyed a prestige which exceeds that of most of the other executive departments. Set up under very auspicious circumstances, it developed quickly a tradition for sound administration and career service that has not been duplicated in equal measure in the other departments. Consequently there does not arise in Congress the same objection to placing an important regulatory function in this Department that would have to be met if it were suggested that such a job be given to some of the other departments.

In the second place, most of the regulatory functions mentioned above affect primarily the agricultural industry. The Department itself has large forces in the field. It is equipped in personnel to take on with a minimum of expense and effort a new regulatory job. Though there were political reasons involved in the decision, it is also true that one of the reasons why the Packers and Stockyards Act of 1921 was given to the Secretary of Agriculture for enforcement was because that Department already had the facilities for administering it.

In the third place, the regulatory work that has been mentioned here is somewhat narrower in its scope and stirs up much less controversy and antagonism than work such as that of the Federal Trade Commission. These regulatory functions are, in the main, policing functions and they are in a broad sense helpful to the very interests that are subject to them. Any opposition that might arise from those immediately affected would be overshadowed by the advantages that were brought to the agricultural industry as a whole.

Segregation of Judicial or Appellate Aspects of Administration

In dealing with the broad subject of this study, some attention should be given to the evolution of an administrative technique connected with the regulatory problem that is quite different from the techniques so far discussed. This is the segregation either in appellate administrative bodies or in boards or courts of review of the function of reviewing the decisions of administrative officers who perform regulatory duties, or the establishment on a more formal plane of administrative or legislative courts to do the same type of work. This development may be explored along three separate lines.

In the first place, it has seemed desirable in a number of instances to provide some kind of appellate body in a department or commission to review the decisions made by the administrative officers. These appellate bodies are not courts, and many of them operate without the formalities of a strictly judicial procedure. The following are the more conspicuous examples of this arrangement. There has long been in the Department of the Interior a Board of Appeals to review cases coming up in the public land divisions. The Civil Service Commission has a Board of Appeals and Review for the hearing of cases passed upon by the staff of the Commission. There is a Board of Appeals in the Patent Office which handles a large volume of business within the Department of Commerce. . . .

This technique has most often been employed where the volume of administrative business is so large that a vast number of individual decisions must be made. It is important that they be handled with speed. A great many of them are purely routine matters in respect to which no review would be asked, but it is important to provide a way of correcting the mistakes that are likely to creep into the handling of such a mass of business.

A second and more formal device for separating out the judicial phases of the regulatory process leans in the direction of an administrative court. In 1910 Congress established the Commerce Court for the purpose of relieving the circuit courts of the task of reviewing the decisions of the Interstate Commerce Commission. It was felt that a body of men who gave exclusive attention to railroad problems would acquire an expertness that would facilitate the handling of these important cases. This experiment merits closer study than has yet been given to it. The court was curiously organized; its judges were drawn from the Federal circuit bench, with selection by the Chief Justice of the United States. They were to serve for five-year terms, at the end of which they were to go back to their circuit court duties. The Commerce Court did not grasp the significance of the experiment which was being tried. It insisted upon trying *de novo* practically every case brought before it from the Interstate Commerce Commission and its own decisions were reversed by the Supreme Court on appeal. The impeachment and removal from office of one of its members, Judge Archbald, accentuated the unpopularity which it had earned on other grounds. It was abolished in 1912.

In 1924 Congress established the United States Board of Tax Appeals to take over the functions that had previously been performed by the Committee on Appeal and Review in the Treasury. The Board of Tax Appeals is practically a legislative court. Its functions are judicial in character. It exercises no discretion other than that exercised by any court of law. Its members are appointed for 12-year terms and may be removed by the President only for causes stated in the statute. It is not in the Department of the Treasury but is declared to be an independent establishment in the Executive Department. There was strong congressional opposition to having it in any way subject to Treasury influence. It handles a vast volume of business coming to it from the various bureaus and divisions of the Treasury involving problems of tax law.

In the third place, Congress has set up certain legislative courts for reviewing particular classes of administrative decisions. These courts are not organized under the judiciary article of the Constitution but are set up by Congress in the exercise of its various delegated powers. The Court of Claims was set up in 1855, and somewhat changed as to its procedure and power in 1866. In 1909 Congress created the Court of Customs Appeal, to take over the work that had been handled by the Board of General Appraisers in the Treasury. It created the Customs Court in 1922, and in 1930 converted the Court of Customs Appeal into the Court of Customs and Patent Appeals. The judges of all of these courts have life tenure and perform no administrative duties.

This whole movement in the direction of segregating the judicial aspects of the administrative or regulatory process is well worth exploring. It has been easy to create these tribunals where the administrative functions involved are in the main of a routine character and where the questions presented are essentially questions of law involving no substantial amount of administrative discretion.

Where the plan has been tried it has, on the whole, worked well. It provides a review of administrative action by an impartial and yet expert tribunal.

Reasons for the Establishment of Independent Regulatory Agencies

From this review of the history of the regulatory commissions it is possible to summarize the more important reasons that have led Congress from time to time to set up independent commissions. It is apparent that these reasons are not in every case arguments. In some instances they are merely explanations of why Congress acted as it did. They may be listed as follows:

1. Independent regulatory commissions have been given important judicial or quasi-judicial duties. It is not easy to defend the turning of judicial work over to responsible administrative officers. The judicial function should be performed by independent and impartial persons. Therefore when the quasi-judicial element in any regulatory job is of primary importance, it has seemed plausible to suggest that the function be handled by an independent agency.

2. It has seemed desirable to have the important regulatory functions kept free from the pressures and influences of political domination. Sometimes it has been feared that an important task would be turned over to persons selected for partisan reasons and be left subject to definitely partisan control. Sometimes the very magnitude of the regulatory job has made it seem dangerous to place it in a department subject to the normal political controls that must have free play there. Underlying this reason has been a conviction that more honest and efficient administration will be secured if the task is placed in the hands of an independent body.

3. Many of the tasks of regulation are complicated and technical in the extreme. It has seemed easier to secure the services of experienced experts for the handling of such jobs if they were freed from the political pressures that normally prevail in the departments.

4. The adequate handling of some problems has seemed to require regional representation. This was an important element in the organization of the Radio Commission and the Shipping Board. Geographical representation could be more readily secured in independent commissions than in executive departments.

5. Congress has set up some of the independent commissions because it has not known what else to do with new regulatory jobs. There was no logical place in the Executive Branch of the Government in 1887 in which to put the task of railroad regulation. It was much easier to create a new and independent agency. In some instances there has been no department performing any functions which had any connection with a particular regulatory task. In other cases such departments existed but were felt to be biased or partisan with reference to the job to be done.

6. Some regulatory tasks have been experimental in the extreme. Congress itself has not known exactly how the job ought to be done and has not been able to set forth any very specific instructions. It has seemed easy and natural to solve

the problem temporarily by creating a commission with authority to investigate and explore the whole field, develop standards of regulation, and report back to Congress on legislative changes that might seem desirable.

7. Some regulatory tasks involve important rule-making authority. This sub-legislative power has often been of great importance and has vitally affected the interests of business and industry. There is a popular belief that important rule-making functions ought to be performed by a group rather than by a single officer, by a commission rather than by a department head.

8. Finally, the prestige and the traditions of the Interstate Commerce Commission and the general success with which it is commonly supposed to have handled its important job have undoubtedly influenced Congress to set up other commissions modeled upon it. The most cursory examination of legislative debates upon the various regulatory acts under review indicates the extent to which the Interstate Commerce Commission model has weighed in the minds of Members of Congress.

The Inherent Problem of the Independent
Regulatory Commissions—A Basic Dilemma

No clear analysis of the job done by the regulatory commission, viewed in the light of its complete independence, can fail to emphasize a sharp conflict of principle involved in its make-up and functions. It suffers from a sort of internal inconsistency. The Commission has imposed upon it important duties of administration and policy-determination. The vast powers of the new Maritime Commission in the managing of shipping subsidies are of this sort. For the doing of such work the Commission ought to be clearly and effectively responsible and that responsibility, if it is to exist at all, must be to the President. The Commission has other duties of a judicial nature for the proper performance of which it needs, not responsibility, but complete independence. An example is found in the power of the Interstate Commerce Commission to decide reparations cases. Then it is given another class of duties called quasi-judicial because they are both discretionary and judicial. The commission determines policy by the same process by which it judges the rights of parties. The vast bulk of the regulatory commission job is of this kind. It is illustrated by the cease-and-desist order of the Federal Trade Commission, through which the businessman learns from the same act of the Commission what the law of unfair competition is and that he has violated it. Here the Commission does work with respect to which it ought to be at the same time both *politically responsible* and *judicially independent*.

This seems to be a dilemma. If the regulatory commissions, present and future, are wholly independent they are completely irresponsible for the doing of very important policy-determining and administrative work. The mixing of discretionary and judicial duties in the same hands and even in the same task encourages pressures and influences that tend to impair complete judicial neutrality. On the other hand, to rob the commissions of their status of independence is seriously to menace the impartial performance of their judicial and quasi-judicial work. If there is no escape from this dilemma, no middle course or alternative principle, then the problem of the independent commission simmers down to a balancing of the disadvantages of the status of complete independence against the potential dangers of political domination. In that event it is pretty clear that the choice would be to keep the commissions independent.

But before exploring the possibility of any middle-ground proposal for dealing with the commissions, it will be profitable to analyze the actual disadvantages of giving complete independence to commissions that must do so many and such "mixed" jobs. This leads to a study, first, of the extent to which the "independence" of the commissions obstructs effective over-all management in the Federal administration; second, of the extent to which the merging in the commissions of judicial, nonjudicial and "mixed" functions tends to undermine the neutrality with which the judicial work is done.

The Obstruction of Effective Over-all Management

The President is the general manager of the United States. The very purpose of an Executive Department under the Constitution is to center upon a unified and powerful Executive responsibility for a coordinated policy of administration and its efficient execution. Congress, by its very nature, is incapable either of doing administrative work or of holding accountable in any effective way the many officers or agencies engaged in administration. The President's duties and responsibilities in this field are not routine in nature, but carry with them broad discretionary powers.

At the same time the Constitution gives the President a share in the law-making process. More important than his power to veto bills or to call special sessions of Congress has come to be his power to advise Congress on legislative matters and to make legislative proposals. The Constitution declares that he "Shall from time to time give to the Congress Information of the State of the Union, and recommend to their Consideration such Measures as he shall judge necessary and expedient." (Art. II, sec. 3.) Congress has by law given to the President a vitally important power of legislative initiation by commanding him to formulate and submit the annual budget. The exigencies of party leadership have, of course, broadened his responsibilities in this regard. In short, Congress and the country at large definitely expect the President to have a legislative program; they have become dependent upon his having such a program. It is necessary, therefore, to study the impact of the policy-determining functions of the independent commissions upon the President's responsibilities in the field of legislation, as well as upon his administrative policies.

Relation to Legislative Responsibilities of the President. Heavy responsibilities have been placed on the President in the field of legislative proposal. Congress and the Nation look to him for broad programs of national policy as well as the initiation of detailed measures, such as the budget. His responsibility in this field comes not merely from his position as leader of his party. It comes also from the fact that from his vantage point as head of the administration he has a better opportunity to know, to appraise, and to coordinate national policy proposals than any other officer or group of officers. What the President strives to do is to provide a leadership that prevents conflicts and confusion. Insofar, then, as substantial powers of policy-determination and legislative proposal are scattered about among a growing crop of independent bodies to be exercised in "insulated chambers," to that extent are conflict and confusion of policy encouraged and the President's effectiveness and responsibility weakened. The commissions vary a good deal in the degree to which they affect the President in this regard. But all of them interfere some; some interfere a good deal; and the independent commission movement as such interferes, potentially, with the President's authority and responsibility in this field. This interference occurs in connection with broad policy proposals and also in the more restricted field of initiation and sponsorship of specific measures.

The extent to which the independent commissions interfere, actually or potentially, with the President's responsibility in the field of broad policy proposal will depend on how much discretion they enjoy in matters of policy. Some enjoy very little, others a good deal. The actual extent to which the President has been bothered in this regard by the independence of the commissions is perhaps of less interest here than are the potentialities of interference. The President and the commissions have had their disagreements, but they are not chronically at loggerheads, and the commissions can probably be counted upon to cooperate with the President most of the time. The important fact is, however, that they do not need to cooperate unless they wish, and the President cannot, therefore, depend upon that cooperation. A few illustrations will show the nature and importance of this problem.

The Interstate Commerce Commission has broad control over the whole transportation system. The Transportation Act of 1920 placed on the Commission the "duty of taking steps toward development and maintenance of an adequate national transportation service." This is, and is intended to be, policy-determination in its broadest sense. And since the maintenance of a transportation system intimately concerns nearly every other phase of the economic life of the Nation, it is clear that policy-determinations by the Commission impinge at many points upon any well-conceived program affecting national social and economic problems. It is certainly hard to defend on any basis of theory a status of independence for such vast policy-determining functions free from any directing authority to integrate them into the general legislative program of the Nation. . . .

Interference with Presidential Management in the Field of Administration. The President is the responsible head of the national administration, but the independent commissions, by their very nature, undermine his administrative authority and responsibility. To them has been parceled out complete independence in several important fields of administration. This has not been inadvertent. Congress has definitely intended to place the commissions beyond the reach of Presidential management. It is sometimes said that they are responsible to Congress in respect to their administrative duties—that they are "agents" of Congress. The Supreme Court has so referred to them. In reality, however, this "agency" is confined to making investigations and reports to Congress. Congress has no effective means of supervising the administrative activities of the commissions and has shown little desire to do so. The net result is that in the field of administration the commissions are not held accountable to anyone. And yet to them is entrusted the administration of laws dealing with some of the most vital economic and social interests of the Nation. The Constitution commands the President to "take Care that the Laws be faithfully executed" (Art. II, sec. 3) ; but obviously he cannot see that the Interstate Commerce Act or the Federal Trade Commission Act is faithfully executed, because the job has been given to someone else. In forming and carrying out his own administrative policies he must reckon with the administrative policies of a dozen or more wholly independent bodies, whose activities overlap his own sphere of responsibility at many points. The results, actual and potential, of this decentralization in the administrative system may be considered more closely.

In the first place, the aggressiveness and effectiveness of the President's general law-enforcement program will be impaired by any lack of vigor on the part of the independent commissions. This may be illustrated from the history of the Federal Trade Commission. It has important duties in discovering violations of the Sherman and Clayton Acts as well as in ferreting out and suppressing unfair competitive trade practices. The enforcement of the anti-trust laws and other laws regulating business is not an automatic process. Vital questions of administrative policy are bound up in it. The Trade Commission Act recognizes this by instructing the Commission to move in the case of an unfair competitive practice "if it shall appear to the Commission that a proceeding by it in respect thereof would be to the interest of the public." One President may adopt a policy of noninterference with business and confine the activities of his administration to violations of law too obvious to escape notice. Another President may be a "trust-buster" and push with vigor the regulation of business and the discovery and punishment of business crimes. These are matters of policy so important that they sometimes become issues in Presidential campaigns. No one denies the right of the President to determine which policy he will follow, or his responsibility for it. But a President who is a militant "trust-buster" will find his policy of business regulation seriously crippled if the Federal Trade Commission is composed of men who believe business ought to be let alone. This was exactly the belief of Commissioner William E. Humphrey, appointed to the Commission by President Coolidge in 1925. Until his removal by President Roosevelt in 1933 he was able to cast a deciding vote and thus to dominate the policy of the Commission. He openly announced a policy of friendly toleration toward business, embarrassing investigations were cut to the minimum, and a more lenient regulatory policy was pursued. This attitude was not in serious conflict with the policies of Presidents Coolidge and Hoover, but when President Roosevelt took office he requested the resignation of Mr. Humphrey on the ground that "your mind and my mind do not go along together on either the policies or the administering of the Federal Trade Commission."

In the second place, effective coordination of national administrative policy is obstructed by the independent commissions. This obstruction is, again, both actual and potential. The commissions frequently deal with problems certain aspects of which are handled by other agencies. There is considerable overlapping of functions and even conflict of jurisdiction, not only between the commissions and the departments but also between the commissions themselves. The dividing line between the jurisdiction of the Power Commission and the Securities and Exchange Commission over power companies is badly confused and full of potential conflict. Yet each is independent and the conflicts will have to be ironed out either by diplomatic negotiations or by an act of Congress. Several agencies besides the Federal Trade Commission have authority over unfair trade practices, but there is no central authority that can whip conflicting policies into line. Many of the commissions have large powers of issuing rules and regulations on various subjects, but there is no authority to require any central clearance for these or to see that they harmonize with the President's policies in the same or closely related fields. It seems clear that the important managerial and administrative duties of the new Maritime Commission will impinge at many points upon the administrative policies of the Interstate Commerce Commission, not to mention the policies of the State Department, in the field of foreign trade.

Then, too, independent commissions are inclined to strive for a high degree of self-sufficiency. Since they are independent they are indisposed in many cases to utilize the services already existing in the departments, but establish their own statistical, economic, and legal divisions. They, of course, need these services, but they are under no obligation to integrate them into the larger administrative structure, with the result that there is some needless duplication of staff and much overlapping of function.

It may be admitted that the administrative confusion resulting from any single independent commission may not in itself be serious. Furthermore, the evil is abated by the cooperative spirit that the commissions show some of the time. But if more of these independent bodies are created the disintegration of effective and responsible administrative management by the President will be increased.

Danger to the Impartial Handling of Judicial Work

The most important work done by the independent commissions is either judicial or quasi-judicial. Such work calls for the highest measure of impartiality in order that justice may be done and public confidence may be maintained. To secure such impartiality has been the most important and cogent single reason for making independent commissions independent. Were it not for their judicial and quasi-judicial work it would be hard to find any intelligent reason for their independent status. And yet, in the very nature of the work the commissions do, there are inherent elements that menace the neutrality and impartiality with which their judicial and quasi-judicial functions are performed. Two of these undermining influences may be considered.

The first danger to the neutrality of the independent commission lies in the fact that it must combine its judicial work with work of policy-determination. Courts protect themselves by refusing to do nonjudicial work. The independent commissions cannot so protect themselves. They must add to the duties of the judge those of the lawmaker and the administrator. This is not inadvertent or accidental; it is inherent and inescapable. It is true that the commissions have some duties that are pretty clearly legislative, some that are purely administrative, and others that are quite definitely judicial. These may be separate and distinct. But the vast bulk of the duties given to independent commissions are "mixed" functions. They contain, in varying degrees, the qualities that are associated with legislation, administration, and adjudication. The best example of a "mixed" function is the application by an administrative body of "standards" to the conduct of individuals or business. The method is to incorporate in a statute a "standard" that is to be applied by the commission to concrete cases. "Unfair competitive trade practices" is such a standard; "just and reasonable rate" is another. The application of such a standard is an interesting process by which the commission at the same time determines policy and prosecutes violations of that policy. It is performing in the same act the duties of lawmaker, prosecutor, and judge.

This merging in the commission's work of elements that are discretionary with elements that are judicial subjects the commission to pressures from many sources. It is not objectionable to try to influence policy by honest and open methods. But when policies are being determined by a body also doing judicial work, it is impossible to influence policy without danger of demoralizing the impartiality of the judge. In most of the cases in which "pressure" has been brought to bear on the independent commission the purpose has been to influence the discretion of the commission rather than the judicial part of its duty. On occasion the President has exerted pressure when the commission's policies have impinged upon his own. Private interests have exerted pressure, sometimes directly, sometimes through the intervention of members of Congress, and this pressure has not always been confined to commission policy but has sometimes sought to influence adjudication. The commissions are being asked to perform judicial tasks interwoven with determinations of policy which at times are the subjects of acute partisan controversy or economic class antagonisms. This is not the atmosphere in which the rights of individuals ought to be judged. It is a vital and inherent weakness of the independent commission system that it makes this necessary.

A second danger to the neutrality of the independent commission lies in the fact that in handling some of its most important work it acts both as prosecutor and as judge. This not only undermines judicial fairness; it weakens public confidence in that fairness. This unfortunate situation exists in the work of the Federal Trade Commission. An important part of the Commission's job is to ferret out unfair competitive trade practices and issue cease-and-desist orders against them. There is a first stage in the proceeding in which the Commission, with the aid of its staff, makes an investigation and draws up a complaint. The second stage is a formal hearing before the Commission in which it decides whether the charges in the complaint have been proved and either issues a cease-and-desist order or dismisses the action. The temptation for the Commission to decide that it has proved its own case must be very strong, and the businessman not unnaturally resents having his rights settled by an "interested" tribunal. As is clearly brought out in Gerard Henderson's study of the Federal Trade Commission, one of the reasons why the Supreme Court paid such scant respect to the Commission's findings of fact is because the records showed a disposition in many of the Commission's cases to "build up" a record that would support its orders. The Court was suspicious of this bias and ruthlessly reexamined the evidence for itself. . . .

It appears, therefore, that the independent commission, as an institution or technique, obstructs effective administrative management by giving important policy-determining functions to independent bodies. It also appears that this same combination of functions imperils the judicial neutrality of the commissions. It appears further that the difficulty is inherent, since the same functions are at once policy-determining and judicial. To put the independent commissions, as they now exist, into the executive departments and subject them to direct political and administrative control would still further threaten the impartiality with which they do their judicial work. . . .

Legal Aspects of Presidential Control Through Removal Power

Whatever power of control the President has over the independent commissions will spring from his power to remove members from office. The present status of that removal power will therefore be explored.

But a word may be said, first, about the practical aspects of the removal power. It is indispensable to effective administrative management. There is no way in which an officer may effectively control or direct his subordinates unless he can dismiss them. The importance of the removal power is not measured by the frequency with which it is used. If the power exists, that very fact makes its frequent use unnecessary.

If the President had power to remove the members of the independent commissions, certain practical results would follow. First, the power would probably be used very sparingly. During the years when it was supposed that the President did have this power, few removals were made or attempted, and those only when the President felt acutely the conflict between the commission's policy and his own. President Coolidge tried to avoid the necessity of removals, in one or two cases, by asking commissioners for undated letters of resignation. This reflected the common Presidential reluctance to appear to be interfering with agencies which the public thinks of as quasi-judicial.

In the second place, if the President could remove independent commissioners, he would, as a result of the impact of that relationship, get from the commissions a greater degree of cooperation in matters of policy and administration. This would be due less to fear of removal than to the subtle sense of accountability to the President resulting from the mere existence of the power.

In the third place, the removal power would enable the President to secure from the commissions compliance with Executive orders. The power of the President to issue Executive orders comes from several sources. But whatever the source, the problem of securing compliance with the orders is the same. They can be enforced where the removal power exists. They cannot be enforced where it does not.

The present law as to the President's power of removal may now be examined.

Present Law as to Presidential Removals. Though the law with respect to the President's power of removal is uncertain and confused at many points, three things have been pretty definitely settled by the Supreme Court.

First, the President cannot be restricted by Congress in his power to remove executive officers whom he appoints with the consent of the Senate, or presumably, without that consent. He gets this power of removal from the grant of Executive power in Article II, sec. 1, of the Constitution. Congressional interference with it would, therefore, violate the separation of powers. This was decided in 1926, in the case of *Myers* v. *United States* (272 U.S. 52). This decision strengthened the hand of the President in his responsible management of the Executive Branch of the Government.

Second, Congress may properly provide that the members of commissions set up to perform quasi-legislative and quasi-judicial work, rather than "purely executive" work, shall be removable by the President only for the causes stated in the statute. This was the Court's decision in *Rathbun* (*Humphrey*) v. *United States* (295 U.S. 602), decided in 1935 in a case involving a member of the Federal Trade Commission.

Third, if Congress sets up no restriction, the President may remove any officer whom he appoints, even if he is not a "purely executive" officer. The removal power of the President is implied not only from Article II of the Constitution, as above noted, but also from the power to appoint. This has been law ever since the case of *Ex parte Hennen* (13 Peters 230) was decided in 1839. Though Congress may protect a regulatory commission from the President's discretionary removal power, it must do so by positive legislation. If the statute is silent as to removal, as in the case of several of the boards and commissions reviewed in this study, the President has full power of removal.

A Suggested Solution

The historical background of the independent regulatory commission problem in the Federal Government has been briefly reviewed and the legal and practical difficulties involved in making these commissions independent of the Executive Branch have been pointed out. The problem of the independent commission arises, as has been indicated, from the merging in the same body of administrative and policy-determining functions with respect to which it ought to be accountable to the President, and quasi-judicial functions in the performance of which it ought to be wholly independent. A solution is needed that will establish responsibility for the administrative and policy-determining aspects of the regulatory job, and at the same time will guarantee the neutrality of the judicial and quasi-judicial part of the work. It should facilitate administrative management without lessening judicial independence.

It is very probable that there is no one solution of this problem. Certainly a careful investigation, preferably conducted by a quasi-judicial body, should precede any material alteration of the organization of the independent commissions, particularly of those that have been in existence for many years. In some instances it might be decided to make no change in the existing organization, whereas in other instances it might be found advisable to place a commission within one of the executive departments and to separate its administrative activities from those of a quasi-judicial character.

With this possibility in view, the following plan is suggested for consideration. It is a plan that may be modified greatly to fit the particular situation, and should be regarded as a general rather than a specific proposal. Other and better ways of meeting the problem may be discovered. The plan is outlined as one possible solution.

Essential Features of the Plan

The main features of the suggested solution of the independent commission problem will be set forth briefly before examining in detail the major problems involved in putting it into operation. The plan would put independent commissions into regular executive departments if "suitable" departments now exist or can be provided. "Suitable" departments are those that have functions relevant to those of the commission, and that are neutral with respect to the regulatory duties of the commission rather than "promotional" or otherwise biased. If suitable departments cannot be provided, commissions should be independent.

The commission, in being put into a department, would be broken down into two sections. One of these would be the Judicial Section, which would be "in" the department for purposes of "administrative housekeeping," but otherwise completely independent. Its members would be removable by the President only for incompetence or misconduct, and neither the Cabinet Secretary nor the President could review its decisions. This section would handle the judicial and quasi-judicial aspects of regulation. Alongside it would be set up an Administrative Section, which would be a bureau or division in the department and fully responsible as such to the Secretary and the President. The bureau chief, as well as the staff, should be on a career basis under appropriate civil service rules. To this section would be given the rule-making, administrative, and, in general, the policy-determining aspects of regulation. To assure internal flexibility, changes in the structural details of these sections and the division of duties between them might be made by Executive order of the President. Such Executive orders, however, like those authorized in the Economy Act of 1933 for the reallocation of administrative agencies and functions, might be made subject to congressional disallowance within a fixed time (60 days).

———————◆———————

As it was in the case of the independent regulatory commissions, the primary issue in the following selection on government corporations is their "independence" of the regular executive departments. But the case for the independence of the government corporation rests on different grounds. For the central argument in favor of the government corporation is that "business-type" activities should, when carried on publicly, be carried on by a form of organization of tried and proved business efficiency, not by regular departments and according to routines appropriate for strictly governmental functions.

The government corporation, like the independent regulatory establishment, is a relatively new type of governmental organization. The Federal government's ownership and operation of its first corporate organization dates from soon after the turn of the century, and most of its corporate organizations were brought into existence to meet emergency conditions during the two world wars and the depression of the 1930's.

As this suggests, the corporate form was not adopted for governmental administration in the United States in accordance with a well-developed constitutional or administrative theory. But rather, after governmental corporations had appeared upon the scene in numbers, they were subjected to scrutiny by students of administration, their advantages and disadvantages assessed, and a body of theory concerning them developed. Among students of administration there has been some argument, even enthusiasm, for the corporation as an administrative instrument. On the other hand, the "independence" of the corporation has conflicted with strong tendencies in administrative theory toward unity, simplicity, and integration.

Dr. Harold Seidman, author of this essay, has been since 1943 a member of the staff of the U. S. Bureau of the Budget. Since 1945 much of his work has related to government corporations, in which field he has developed an *expertise* that has received international recognition.

Dr. Seidman has reached what will seem to many persons rather negative conclusions on the present worth and future potentialities of the government corporation. Query, has he treated fairly the theory and assessed properly the accomplishments of the government corporation? Is his interpretation of constitutional doctrine correct? Is his closing reference to the government corporation in Latin America relevant and fair?

The Theory of the Autonomous Government Corporation : A Critical Appraisal *

HAROLD SEIDMAN

The industrial boom of the 1870's marked the beginning of what has often been described as the "era of the corporate revolution" in the United States. Prior to the Civil War, use of the corporate form in the industrial field was confined almost entirely to the textile industry. But the transition from an agricultural to an industrial economy, accompanied as it was by the rapid growth of "big business," greatly stimulated the use of the corporate form because of the advantages it offered in the way of limited liability and pooled investment. Today the corporation has virtually become a way of life in America, and Harold J. Laski went so far as to say that it is regarded as "almost an object of religious devotion."

A development comparable to the corporate revolution in industry is found in the history of the United States government during and after World War I. The United States acquired the Panama Railroad Company in 1904 when it purchased the assets of the French Canal Company, but it was not until World War I that the first wholly owned government corporations were created. Of the World War I corporations, only the Federal Land Banks have survived to the present day. With the coming of the "New Deal" and the final stages of the transition from the "laissez-faire" state to the "positive" state, the government assumed responsibility for a wide variety of social and economic programs, many of which required it to engage in business-type operations. It soon became apparent that the traditional government organization did not readily lend itself to the effective administration of programs of this type. Recourse was therefore had to the form of organization which had proved so successful in private industry—the corporation. The corporation has now come to be accepted as the appropriate instrument for administering programs of an industrial or commercial character. This fact is reflected in President Truman's statement in his 1948 Budget Message

* From *Public Administration Review*, Vol. 12 (Spring, 1952), pp. 89–96. Reprinted by permission of the author and the *Public Administration Review*.

that "experience indicates that the corporate form of organization is peculiarly adapted to the administration of governmental programs which are predominantly of a commercial character—those which are revenue producing, are at least potentially self-sustaining, and involve a large number of business-type transactions with the public."

There are at the present time thirty-nine active wholly government-owned corporations in the United States, including twelve Intermediate Credit Banks and twelve Production Credit Corporations which are parts of the Farm Credit System. In addition, there are twenty-four mixed-ownership corporations, those whose capital stock is owned in part by others than the federal government, namely the Central Bank for Cooperatives, twelve Banks for Cooperatives, and eleven Home Loan Banks. These corporations conduct a wide variety of enterprises such as making and guaranteeing loans of private institutions to businessmen, farmers, home owners, foreign governments, and other borrowers; insuring private individuals against loss from crop failures, price declines, and other hazards; operating power and synthetic rubber plants, tin smelters, railroads, canals, hotels, steamship and barge lines, and terminal and harbor facilities; distributing electric power; and purchasing and selling commodities in foreign and domestic markets.

William A. Robson has called the government corporation "one of the most significant institutional innovations of our time." Robson might well have added that the government corporation is also one of the most controversial institutional innovations of our time. The rise of the government corporation has stirred strongly ambivalent emotions in the breast of conservatives and liberals, centralists and decentralists. It has produced a literature which is replete with contradictions and strange paradoxes.

Thus, we find banker Winthrop A. Aldrich and conservative Republicans in the forefront of the group which vehemently argued that a corporation was necessary to assure "business-like" administration of the Marshall Plan, despite the fact that a few short years before other conservatives, including the United States Chamber of Commerce, were urging with equal vehemence that "no more government corporations be created [and] that existing corporations be liquidated as soon as possible. . . ." Dwight Waldo has noted:

"The example of private corporate practice has been one of the favorite weapons in the dialectic armory of those who have been interested in deprecating legislative or judicial influence and in aggrandizing executive power. On the other hand a number of persons have found in the practices of corporate interrelationships a hope that society can be planned and managed in the requisite degree without the disadvantages and dangers of great concentration of authority. . . ."

The key to the paradox is to be found in a fundamental divergence concerning the nature and role of the government corporation. The public as well as the private corporation has gained adherents who view it with almost religious devotion. A relatively small but highly prolific group of writers appear to accept the corporate form of organization as a desirable end in itself, regardless of the purpose which it serves. To them the corporation is an institution which is inherently different from other organs of government. They have projected a "pure" form of government corporation with two minimum characteristics—a board of directors and autonomy, particularly from direction and control by the executive branch. The inner essence of the corporation is considered to be completely destroyed by any serious deviations from the "pure" form.

Other writers reject in whole or in part the theory of the autonomous corporation. They contend that the corporation is merely another instrument for accomplishing governmental purposes—that while business programs should be accorded such operating and financial flexibility as may be required for efficient administration, the fact of incorporation does not in and of itself confer a special status. They conclude that the basic relationship of a corporation to the executive and the legislative should be much the same as that of any other government agency.

This cleavage in basic approach to government corporations is not an expression of conflicts in economic ideologies, although these may be motivating factors in individual cases. Rather, it represents a difference in philosophy of government.

If there is a single underlying theme in the literature of corporate autonomy, it is distrust of government. Harold Laski points out that "most Americans have a sense of deep discomfort when they are asked to support the positive state. . . . They tend to feel that what is done by a governmental institution is bound to be less well done than if it were undertaken by individuals, whether alone or in the form of private corporations." If a service cannot be performed by private enterprise, then obviously the next best thing is something which looks as nearly as possible like a private institution and which has as little as possible to do with government. Thus the feeling of discomfort is somewhat alleviated when services are provided by a public corporation and the corporation is so organized that it is of but not in the government.

II

The theory of corporate autonomy finds its earliest expression in the works of W. F. Willoughby. To relieve the staggering burden of business, both in the executive branch and the Congress, Willoughby proposes the adoption by the government of the "holding corporation" form of organization. All of the revenue-producing services of the government would be organized as public corporations and given "complete financial autonomy. . . . In this manner only is it possible to determine accurately the extent to which the service is paying its way, producing a profit, or running up a deficit."

In addition to financial autonomy, Willoughby would also give the corporations administrative and, to an extent, legislative autonomy. The relationship between the general government and the corporations would be much the same as that between a state and a municipal corporation. The advantages cited for the holding corporation arrangement are that it would (1) reduce the burden on the Congress; (2) provide continuity and freedom of action which cannot be obtained in the Congress; (3) take purely business and technical services of the government outside the domain of politics; (4) encourage the development of career services; and (5) relieve the corporations of compliance with regulations and procedures applicable to governmental services. Willoughby emphasizes that the central feature of his proposal is "the adoption by Congress of the policy of delegating to a subordinate board of directors the direct responsibility for the exercise of the function of general direction, supervision, and control." In two respects, Willoughby does not go so far as some of the later theorists of corporate autonomy. His plan would retain an annual budget review by the Congress and would provide for an annual audit by the comptroller general.

It is significant that nowhere in Willoughby's discussion is there any reference to the President. This omission stems from his belief that constitutionally the President of the United States possesses no administrative authority and that the line of authority runs directly from the administrative services to the legislature, except where the latter has expressly provided otherwise. It is his view that the President cannot even give orders to heads of executive departments with respect to the performance of their duties. For Willoughby the theory of corporate autonomy is a logical outgrowth of his interpretation of the Constitution.

The theory of corporate autonomy has been most fully developed by Marshall E. Dimock and C. Herman Pritchett. While implicit in Dimock's argument is an interpretation of the President's function comparable to that advanced by Willoughby, his case is based principally on what he believes to be inherent characteristics of the corporate form of organization. Although acknowledging that there is no innate magic in the term corporation, Dimock distinguishes between "authentic" corporations and others which have not been established along "principled" lines and, consequently, are not worthy of the name. The one essential attribute of an authentic corporation is autonomy, the right to manage its own affairs. Dimock defines autonomy to mean "concentrating managerial powers in the hands of competent people and giving them enough free rein to achieve the desired results. It is the privilege of being left alone so long as you do not overstep the rules laid down in advance."

Dimock also enumerates certain other organizational, financial, and operating characteristics which distinguish an "authentic" government corporation. The first is self-contained finance and financial freedom. This means removal from the necessity of annual appropriations; power to borrow money; ability to retain earnings as working capital or for reserves; freedom, in the matter of expenditures, from general governmental regulations and restrictions; and freedom, in auditing and accounting, from control of regular government accounting officials. Dimock notes that it is in this area that corporations in the United States have been losing ground in recent years. The second is an effective board of directors, "the key to program success." The weakening of boards of directors is considered "one of the principal evidences of corporate weakness" and is attributed possibly to "some fancied jealousy" by the Congress. Dimock argues along much the same lines as Willoughby that while the Congress may be the over-all board of directors, the corporation's own board is the *operating* board of directors. However, the corporation's board should confine itself to policy and checking on results and not engage in detailed administration. The third and final characteristic is unity of management which grows out of and is closely related to the idea of autonomy. Unity requires that the internal management have "a single, coordinated leadership under which all elements needed for success are combined in a manner conducive to efficiency and flexibility."

C. Herman Pritchett also embraces the concept of an "authentic" corporation. He laments that "government corporations remain and even increase in number while *the* government corporation is passing away." In Pritchett's view, "the original corporate concept embodied not only independence from Congress but also a certain degree of autonomy with respect to the executive branch of the government." This he finds has "fallen afoul of the prevailing trend toward integration." He concludes that it is "unwise to talk about 'the government corporation,' for the attributes which marked the earlier federal corporations and made them representatives of a distinctive type of administrative organization have been disappearing before our eyes, like the Cheshire cat. Soon there may be nothing left but a smile to mark the spot where the government corporation once stood."

Dimock and Pritchett have allowed themselves to become so fascinated by the frosting on the cake that they have neglected adequately to analyze what is underneath. This has led to a preoccupation with relatively superficial manifestations of the corporate form, such as boards of directors and organizational autonomy. Neither of these constitutes the vital force of a government corporation.

Dimock in particular stresses the essentiality of an independent board of directors. "Let federal bureaucrats ponder the loss of corporate identity if representative boards are not reinstated," he warns. Dimock does not explain why calling a commission or advisory committee a "board of directors" endows it with special virtues which it would not otherwise possess. Yet the functions and composition of a board, depending upon whether the directors serve full or part time, are no different from those of a commission or advisory committee. The Senate investigation of the Reconstruction Finance Corporation demonstrates that a full-time board of directors is by no means immune from the ills generally associated with plural executives.

There is no doubt that to many the board of directors is the trade-mark of a government corporation. But this is more or less of an historical accident resulting from the fact that many state incorporation laws require the establishment of boards of directors elected by the stockholders. A board of a private corporation nominally has the duty to act for the stockholders in formulating basic policies and checking on the results of operations. In government this role in the final analysis is performed not by the board, but by the President and the Congress, especially the appropriations committees. Government corporations have existed and operated effectively without a board of directors. The Brookings Institution has correctly stated that "there appears to be nothing inherent in the corporate form of organization to require a board instead of a single administrator. . . . Similarly there appears to be nothing inherent in the noncorporate form to require a single administrator instead of a board." A board of directors may well be found advisable and useful under some circumstances, but it is not the *sine qua non* of a government corporation.

Part of the confusion undoubtedly arises from the use of the term "corporation." It might have been preferable if the government corporation had not borrowed its name from a private prototype. While government and private corporations in the United States do possess certain common characteristics, there are and always have been fundamental differences. Both have a legal personality, can sue and be sued, and generally have boards of directors. Here the resemblance ends. Private corporations, with the obvious exceptions, are organized for profit and the corporate form is utilized primarily to take advantage of limited liability, pooling of investment, transferability of securities, and perpetuity. These benefits are of little or no significance for a government corporation.

Pritchett and V. O. Key, Jr., are concerned by the apparent diversity of form which exists among United States government corporations. Key concludes: "It is thus misleading to speak of 'the' government corporation. No uniformity of powers or of form is apparent; about all that government corporations have in common is the name." Here again outward appearances are deceiving. While there is considerable variety in the kinds of programs administered by government corporations, nonetheless they exhibit a high degree of uniformity as to purpose, nature of activity, and powers.

III

Government corporations are organized to achieve a public purpose authorized by law. This fact is often forgotten. So far as purpose is concerned, a corporation cannot be distinguished from any other government agency. This view was vigorously stated by the United States Supreme Court in the case of *Cherry Cotton Mills* v. *U.S.* (327 U.S. 536) when it held that the fact "that the Congress chose to call it a corporation does not alter its characteristics so as to make it something other than what it actually is, an agency selected by the government to accomplish purely governmental purposes."

With the sole exception of the Institute of Inter-American Affairs, all United States government corporations administer programs which are predominantly of a commercial or industrial character. These programs are revenue producing and potentially self sustaining. They involve a large number of business transactions with the public. Although it would appear to be self evident, it is necessary to note that government corporations do not perform quasi-judicial or quasi-legislative functions. Popular writers have been confused by the apparent similarity in structure between government corporations and independent regulatory commissions. Thus David Lawrence writes: "Basically the RFC is supposed to be an 'independent agency' and not a part of the executive department or the White House, but a creature of Congress, as are all other independent Boards and Agencies." This view cannot be supported either by law or by practice. In the Morgan Case the Supreme Court ruled that a TVA director is not comparable to a member of a regulatory commission and, like any other officer of the executive branch, serves at the pleasure of the President. The functions of a corporation are the same as those of any administrative agency; the difference between the two is in the *method* employed to perform the functions.

Since there is no federal law of corporations, a government corporation possesses only those powers which are enumerated in the act of Congress creating it. Despite this fact, there is remarkable uniformity in the powers granted to government corporations by the Congress. With some minor variations, government corporations can sue and be sued; acquire property in their own name; use their revenues; obtain funds either by borrowing from the Treasury or from revolving funds, instead of by securing annual appropriations; and determine the character and necessity of their expenditures and the manner in which they are incurred, allowed, and paid, subject to laws specifically applicable to government corporations rather than to general statutes controlling the expenditure of public funds. These are the vital ingredients which give a government corporation its distinctive character and without which it cannot operate successfully.

The objective to be sought is not freedom from all governmental regulations and controls, but freedom from those which are unsuited to a business operation and stifle operations. Prior to the enactment of the Government Corporation Control Act in 1945, the only alternative to applying regulations devised for traditional governmental activities was often to apply no controls at all. But absence of controls was due to failure to develop new techniques, not to the inherent nature of the corporate form. As the U.S. Bureau of the Budget reported to the Congress:

"Within recent years it has been increasingly recognized that financial controls generally applicable to government-type programs, such as civil government, health and sanitation, cannot satisfactorily be employed in the case of programs which are essentially of a business nature. This is reflected by the enactment in 1945 of the Government Corporation Control Act, which provides for new types of controls, such as business-type budget and commercial-type audit, specially designed to meet the needs of programs of a business character."

The Corporation Control Act is one of the most significant developments in the art of public administration. With it the government corporation can be said to have come of age in the United States. Experience during the past seven years has not substantiated Pritchett's gloomy prediction that the Corporation Control Act "goes far toward completing the task of eliminating the features which have made government corporations useful instruments for enterprise purposes."

Organizational autonomy neither enhances nor detracts from the essential attributes of a government corporation. It may result, however, in so isolating the corporation that it does not have any choice in the formulation of broad public policies affecting its sphere of activity. Autonomy is two edged. It means not only freedom from outside direction and control, but also exclusion from the "official family" and close working relationships with top policy-making officials. These informal day-to-day associations afford an official the most favorable opportunity to influence policy determinations.

Making corporations full-fledged members of the government team is to the advantage both of the corporation and of the government as a whole. Corporate programs are generally closely interrelated with those of traditional agencies having the same major purposes. Each is dependent upon the other for the successful accomplishment of its mission. For example, the economic development program of the Virgin Islands Corporation must be geared into the education, health, and other programs of the Virgin Islands Government and the Department of the Interior. Otherwise the corporation might be attempting to industrialize the Islands while the other agencies were concentrating on the training of agricultural workers. Leonard White obviously has situations of this type in mind when he states that coordination and control of policy of the corporations is required "to the end that the policy of the government as a whole shall be free from contradiction."

Dimock believes that the Congress, not the executive branch, should be relied on to correct such conflicts and inconsistencies. He contends that integration is unnecessary because "in theory and in practice the supervisory function is adequately performed by the corporate board of directors, its paid management, and Congress." Policy control "is established through charter powers, legislation, appropriations [although Dimock elsewhere says corporations should be free from appropriations], and surveillance." The hypothetical illustrations given by Dimock, however, are examples not of policy coordination but of repeal or negation of congressional enactments. He asserts that if the President were given executive control over corporations, he might turn the TVA over to old line agencies, refuse to pay agricultural subsidies, or direct the Export-Import Bank to make loans to nationals of the United States rather than to foreign countries. No one, of course, has ever proposed that the President should have such authority. What the President or other supervisory official must have is authority to assure that actions taken by corporations, within the powers granted to them by the law, are consonant with the policies of the government. Certainly, it is not

the responsibility of the Export-Import Bank to formulate the foreign policy of
the United States.

The only concession that Dimock is willing to make to proponents of integration is a liaison relationship between a Secretary and a corporation. The Secretary's sole function would be "to keep informed" of the corporation's program
objectives "in order better to advise Congress and the cabinet on large policy
questions arising in his area of public policy." The Secretary would have no directive authority, and criticisms of the corporation's efficiency and achievements
would be dealt with directly by the board and the management. "If the cabinet
official were allowed to rule with a heavy hand," Dimock concludes, "the corporation might as well be a bureau because its corporate character would be
lost. . . ."

IV

Unless Willoughby's interpretation of the President's role is accepted, the
theory of the autonomous corporation cannot be reconciled with the American
constitutional system. The President as chief executive cannot, even if he so
desires, relieve himself of responsibility for the activities of government corporations. The Hoover Commission proclaimed as a fundamental principle: "The
President, and under him his chief lieutenants, the department heads, must be
held responsible and accountable to the people and the Congress for the conduct
of the executive branch." As a corollary to this principle, the commission stated:
"Responsibility and accountability are impossible without authority—the power
to direct." The power to direct must extend to all components of the executive
branch, including corporations.

The theory of the autonomous corporation is rejected both by the President's
Committee on Administrative Management and by the Hoover Commission. The
President's Committee recommended that "each 'governmental corporation'
should be placed under a supervisory agency in an appropriate department." The
President should be authorized to place corporations under such "over-all governmental controls as may be found advisable in each case. . . ." The penetrating analysis by Commissioners Acheson, Pollock, and Rowe reaches the very
heart of the matter. Their separate statement appended to the Hoover Commission report on *Federal Business Enterprises* recognizes that

"The significant differences between business enterprises and other Government activities do not relate to purpose, but are to be found in the nature of the
activity, operating practices, method of financing and internal organization. . . .
Business enterprises do not and should not derive any special organizational
status from the fact that they are business enterprises and not some other type of
governmental activity. . . . Any attempt to deal with them as a thing apart can
create serious organizational problems."

The weight given to the theory of the autonomous corporation has never been justified by practice in the United States. The "authentic" government corporation is largely a fictional creation. The Panama Railroad Company, which was succeeded by the Panama Canal Company on July 1, 1951, is most often referred to as a classic example of a "pure" government corporation. Yet it failed to meet the most important criteria prescribed by Dimock. From almost the very beginning the company was managed and operated as an integral part of a government agency, The Panama Canal. Over-all supervisory authority was vested in the Secretary of War, now the Secretary of the Army, as stockholder. Directors were appointed by the Secretary and served at his pleasure. Most of them were former governors of The Panama Canal or officials of the corporation. The board rarely met more than three or four times a year. The company was not organizationally autonomous, but it possessed the operating and financial flexibility common to most present-day corporations. Another of the early "pure" corporations, the Inland Waterways Corporation, was at the time of its establishment made subject to the direction and control of the Secretary of War and did not even have a board of directors.

The theory of the autonomous corporation can be more easily reconciled with the parliamentary form of government. But the current trend in both Canada and Great Britain is away from earlier concepts of corporate autonomy. J. E. Hodgetts reports that in Canada government corporations are employed primarily to obtain "autonomy in establishment control." There is an increasing tendency in Canada to make full-time civil servants directors of corporations. The Minister is now much more than a pipeline between the corporation and the Parliament. Public corporations in Great Britain, according to Herbert Morrison,

"are accountable to Parliament through Ministers on matters for which Ministers are themselves responsible. . . . [This list includes] research; capital development; education and training; borrowing by the Boards; forms of accounts and audits; annual reports, pension schemes; the appointment of, and other matters connected with, Consumers' Councils. And, of course, the fact that Ministers appoint the Boards, and their powers of general direction are fundamental to the question of public accountability."

Ministers have directive authority and can, for example, order a board to remedy defects to which consumers' councils have drawn attention. Robson has noted that in establishing recent public corporations Great Britain has provided for a much greater degree of ministerial intervention than was applied to similar prewar institutions. It is his view that "Parliament will not be able to exercise effective control or supervision over the operations of the public corporations. . . . For the task of general supervision and direction on questions of major policy we must look to ministers and their departments."

It is significant that the theory of the autonomous government corporation has taken hold principally in those countries in which the central government is weak or unstable, or in which there is deep-seated distrust of government. More "authentic" corporations probably can be found in Latin America than in any other area of the world. The autonomous corporation has been seized upon as a panacea for inefficient or even corrupt government. However, the proliferation of autonomous corporations has in many instances merely served to aggravate a chaotic administrative system. Autonomy has been carried to the extreme, with the appointment of directors frequently being vested in private groups rather than in the government. With the draining off of major government programs, both of a business and a nonbusiness character, into autonomous public corporations, the ministries in some countries have become hollow shells. In some parts of Latin America public corporations can be said literally to constitute a headless and irresponsible fourth branch of government.

Latin American experience provides both a lesson and a warning. Properly understood for what it is, a tool of government which is well adapted to the administration of certain types of public programs, the government corporation has a definite and constructive role to play in modern government. Once the mechanism is sanctified and for that reason alone accorded a status different from that of other government agencies, it loses its utility.

Chapter 7

Levels and Interrelations

The problem of how the powers and functions of an organization should be divided is fundamental and persistent. Indeed, whatever else it may be, organization *is* division of powers and functions.

From one viewpoint the division of powers and functions is a technical problem, needing for its solution whatever "science" we may have achieved in administrative study. From another viewpoint, however, the division of powers and functions reaches beyond the technical to the philosophical. For the divisions that are made are likely to be justified ultimately in terms of theories of government, economics, social life, and so forth.

The most common problem of division of powers and functions is the "functional" one: how to divide the task to be done into meaningful, manageable powers and functions and assigned to those most competent to execute them. In any organization of significant size, however, there are soon problems of "levels and interrelations." As powers and functions are divided and redivided, the hierarchical principle is used to ensure that there shall be order and unity. But the principle of hierarchy is never more than half the solution to an organizational problem—usually much less. For in itself it does not answer crucial questions: At what level in the hierarchy should a given function be performed? What are the proper interrelations between the levels of the hierarchy?

Moreover, in large organizations there is another prominent and important problem of division of powers and functions. This is the geographic or area problem: How shall powers and duties be divided when the area of the organization is so large that single individuals cannot be responsible (except formally) for any power or function for the whole area? Here the principle of hierarchy again serves the purpose of ensuring at least a minimum of order and unity, by marking out official "lines of responsibility" from the periphery to the center of the organization. But there remain crucial questions: How many times does geography require the redivision of powers and functions? How are the proper areas to be determined? What is the appropriate hierarchical level for any given power or function? What are the proper interrelations between levels of the hierarchy?

Function and area are logically quite distinguishable principles of organization, and in large organizations there is an abiding tendency toward conflict between the proponents of the two ways of dividing powers and functions—because a division of powers and functions is also a division of rewards and satisfactions, penalties and dissatisfactions. On the other hand, while logically contrary, organization by function and organization by area blend into each other and are sometimes indistinguishable in operation—as Professor Wallace demonstrated above. Actual organizations selected at random display different patterns of levels and interrelations according to a host of factors, including—but not limited to—constitutional and administrative theory, personalities, geography, economics, and communications.

As has been previously indicated, students of public administration in America have been historically much concerned with hierarchy and centralization of power. This general predisposition toward hierarchy and centralization is an understandable response to what was seen as a need for order and efficiency in accomplishing the tasks of government in the twentieth century. Democratic control as well as efficiency and economy, it was felt, would be advanced by making the administrative world more of a cosmos and less of a chaos.

There have always been a number of students of administration, however, who felt that the emphasis upon hierarchy and centralization was misplaced and even dangerous. They have argued that democratic control and even efficiency and economy are best ensured by "decentralization," by a

fuller and freer exercise of administrative powers and functions at the
periphery of an organization. In this view, overcentralization means
"anemia in the extremities, apoplexy at the center."

The picture of two contesting schools of thought, however, is somewhat
misleading. While some students of administration are identified with an
emphasis upon either centralization or decentralization, many cannot be so
identified and there is a great deal of agreement on administrative means
and ends even between the extreme positions. For most students, the amount
and types of decentralization, the problems of levels and interrelations, are
to be solved for each organization in terms of its own purposes and peculiar
circumstances, after study, and with a willingness to change the pattern of
organization with changing circumstances.

The following essay is an abridgment of the first chapter of a study of
administrative decentralization in the U.S. Department of Agriculture, by
Professor David B. Truman. It is an excellent review, set in a broad perspective, of the main reasons for and the obstacles to a policy of decentralization. While some of the discussion applies only to the conditions of Federal
government in the United States, most of the factors reviewed are of general
importance in organization.

Query, what theories and practices of organization in public administration conduce to the realization of democracy? Is this a meaningful question?
What is the relationship, if any, between the issues raised in this essay and
those presented by the independent regulatory commission and the government corporation?

The Problem of Decentralization *

DAVID B. TRUMAN

Primary among the recurring and persistent problems of government is that of
so arranging the constituent elements of the body politic that its human resources
may be employed to the full, that no single group shall be so poorly articulated
with the whole as to desire the destruction of the established equilibrium, and
that the entire organism may adjust to change without violent rupture or dissolu-
tion. A host of philosophers and statesmen through the ages have wrestled with
the problem in its general aspects or have faced its difficulties in the heat of particular political crises.

* Chapter I in *Administrative Decentralization; A Study of the Chicago Field
Offices of the United States Department of Agriculture* (Chicago: 1940). Abridged.
Reprinted by permission of the University of Chicago Press.

This question of centralization and decentralization, which has been aptly characterized as "the zoning of power," has a number of different aspects—territorial, group, and personal. As changes in the physical and ideological environment make the satisfaction of new demands upon the holders of power the price of their continuance, the problem must be solved again, and a new equilibrium is produced whose value will be modified in turn. . . .

It has been repeatedly shown that a centralized administration, heaping on itself an intolerable measure of responsibility, invites collapse in periods of stress. A recent study of the development of four revolutionary crises reaffirms this point by indicating that the presence of administrative entanglements and confusions was a common element in the background of the English, American, French, and Russian revolutions. While it would be ridiculous to maintain that the entire, or even the major, responsibility for the avoidance of violent upheaval lies with the executors of policy, it is nonetheless clear that administration, and especially administrative organization, is a vital factor. E. Pendleton Herring states the position clearly when he says:

"The administrative branch of the government cannot maintain a balance in a dynamic society, but it can do much toward clarifying and effectuating the purposes declared by our legislators. The caliber of our officials and the efficiency of their organization will largely determine the successful application of those policies designed to promote the general welfare."

But the requirement of decentralized administration can be indicated in narrower, less dramatic terms than those of violent social upheaval. Conditions of administrative inadequacy producing frustration and failure in legislative policy are equally to be avoided. The factors which demand decentralization if such inefficiency is to be minimized can be discussed under three general headings.

The Problem of Popular Control over the Newer Functions of the National Government. The persistent increase in the number of functions performed by the national government of the United States has been amply described, and the increased responsibility which this growth has placed upon the shoulders of the federal officials has been discussed at length. It is sometimes forgotten, however, that not only has the number of federal functions been augmented, but the nature of these newer duties is far different from that of those which characterized the national government two generations ago. Federal authority now makes demands upon the individual farmer and businessman, performs services and enforces requirements in countryside and market place which bring it into contact with the citizen with an intimacy which but recently was unknown even in times of war.

At the same time we have witnessed an integration and centralization within the federal administrative structure. As John A. Fairlie pointed out many years ago, the early conception of a department head in England and the United States considered him without authority to direct the actions of his subordinate officers, "but as the result of a century of development the national administration has become centralized in spirit and practice as well as in form." To complicate the picture still further we find that the newer administrative preoccupations encompass a widening group of technical and professional operations understood only by small segments of those affected by these activities. . . .

The Conflict between Administrative Effectiveness and the Theory of Rigid Federalism. Much of the criticism of the increase in the functions of the national government has been based upon fear of the destruction of the federal system in the United States, anticipation of the complete eclipse of the states. The following quotation is typical of the more extreme partisans of this view:

"The equilibrium of power between the Federal and State Governments cannot stand the meddlesome activity of the Board of Vocational Rehabilitation and the Department of Agriculture, as their greedy fingers reach into millions of American homes, developing in the youth of the land the belief that they should look to the Federal, rather than to their State governments."

Such protestations, following a tradition as old as the *Federalist*, are based on the assumption of an inherent and essential conflict of interest between the Union and the several states. However, the increasing difficulty of classifying the functions of government as of either local or national concern tends to rob the assumption of much validity. With government activity expanding into such fields as public health, the provision of security against the ravages of economic fluctuations, the facilitation of marketing agricultural and industrial produce, the protection of natural resources, and the like, the question involves less the division of function between the state and national governments than the co-ordination of the efforts of both toward the efficient prosecution of all such functions. The problem is less to maintain the independence of the two levels than to realize and to instrument their patent interdependence. . . .

Adjusting National Policies to Local Peculiarities. Closely related to the two aspects of the need for administrative decentralization which have just been discussed is a final point dealing with the adjustment of national policy to local physical and economic peculiarities. To say that a problem is of sufficiently broad scope or is so critical as to make it of national importance is to employ a type of generalization which, though accurate, is subject to qualification by those intrusted with transforming the resulting broad national policy into action. To establish by legislative declaration a policy in favor, for example, of soil conservation is to recognize a need which may be national both in geographical extent and in importance, but it of necessity does not recognize the "dust bowl," the corn belt, and the Great Lakes "cutover" region as such different aspects of the question that they almost constitute separate problems. The same may be said of a policy of market regulation where one center carries on such a volume of the total trading and the resulting effect of its activities upon "the market" is so great that it constitutes a problem different in almost every respect from that in the smaller center. Rivers, lakes, mountains, soil peculiarities, climatic variations, transportation facilities, types of agricultural and industrial specialization, and even social customs combine to give particular areas, whose exact boundaries may not be easily identifiable, the aspect of separate problems.

When a national policy affecting such areas is adopted, the administrators of the legislation must consider that the success of the national determination depends upon the successful adaptation of administration to the peculiarities of all these problem areas. The effectiveness of the whole plan cannot be divorced from the success or failure of its application in all the regions which make up the total problem.

The Difficulties Obstructing Administrative Decentralization

Despite the importance of the need for decentralization in the national administrative structure, the difficulties in the way of its satisfaction are numerous and imposing. The persistence of the problem through time and its emergence today in most large organizations, both governmental and nongovernmental, strikingly indicate the influence of these obstacles. While many of these are peculiar to the functions performed by particular organizations, there are four which appear to be common to all, namely, (1) the influence of tradition and the lack of conscious adaptation to the factors of a changing environment, (2) the exigencies of central control, (3) the related question of the influence upon decentralized subdivisions of localized pressure groups, and (4) the difficulty of co-ordinating decentralized functions.

The Influence of Tradition. No one who has observed the struggles throughout the past thirty years to effect a thorough reorganization of the executive branch of the federal government can fail to appreciate the importance of tradition as an obstacle to the intelligent adaptation of public administration to changes in other spheres of society. A similar situation exists in many state and local governments.

Some students have realized the value of administrative flexibility, as the following quotation from one of the leaders in the recent effort at federal reorganization indicates: "An organization is a living and dynamic entity. Each activity is born, has its periods of experimental development, of vigorous and stable activity, and, in some cases, of decline. A principle of organization appropriate at one stage may not be appropriate at all during a succeeding stage. . . ." The failure of administrators to appreciate this view of organization and their reluctance to revise customary methods may be due in part, as Brooks Adams suggested a quarter of a century ago, to the intellectual isolation attendant upon specialization. The same point was made by the regional experts of the National Resources Committee in discussing the disinclination of administrative officers, who are concerned first with questions of control, to recognize the reality of the region.

Whatever the causes of such resistance may be, its existence is a matter of concern when the conditions of government demand the flexibility of decentralization, for, as Merriam has pointed out, ". . . in the end the overcentralized system kills itself, crushed down by the impossible burdens it has tried to carry. All its good intentions will not avert catastrophe."

The Requirements of Central Control. Most of the advantages of establishing a national policy concerning the problems to which the federal government gives its attention are likely to be lost if the means of top control are destroyed by excessive decentralization. Yet the very idea of central control in a large organization assumes a degree of selection of the matters which are of such importance as to merit the continuous scrutiny of the chief officials. The crux of the problem is to decide what questions shall be handled at the central office and to devise means of following the use of delegated authority so as to provide adequate uniformity without stifling initiative and flexibility on the periphery. But between the extremes of deciding everything at headquarters and of leaving the field offices virtually independent there is a wide twilight zone through which a dividing line must be drawn in terms of the varying needs of each organization.

To complicate the problem further there are conditions in public administration which make its difficulties in this respect greater than those under which other organizations must operate. The public servant must guide his every action by the law as it is declared by the legislature, the courts, and such officers as the comptroller-general of the United States. Under such circumstances it is not surprising that the department head or bureau chief who will be held accountable is reluctant to have his field subordinates in a position to invite the censure of these guardians of the law. The necessity of accountability in the public service, then, involves not only maintaining a consistent administrative policy but also being legally correct.

The means of checking on the use of delegated authority by field subordinates fall under the two general heads of authorization in advance and review of completed action. The former includes regulations and the sanction of decisions on unusual questions not covered by regulation. The latter covers reports, accounts, audits, and the like. Where the work of the organization is capable of being reduced to measurable units, control of the second type is greatly facilitated. Despite these methods of control, however, and their facilitation by the use of the telephone, the telegraph, statistical machines, and personal conferences, what has been called "the general hesitancy of central administrative heads to delegate sufficient real power" is a persistent obstacle to decentralization.

Decentralization and the Influence of Local Pressure Groups. Where considerable authority is devolved upon field officials, there is always the danger—accentuated when central control is weak—that policy will be unduly influenced by those private individuals and groups who are in closer and more intimate contact with the field than are the superior officers. Such danger comes not only from localized groups but also from the local representatives of the more powerful national groups.

While on first thought one may question whether pressures would be any more effective in the field than at headquarters, further examination suggests this possibility. Field officers, even when they have considerable authority, are subordinates and are usually paid on that assumption. Moreover, the prestige of any localized official is likely to be less than that of a man whose responsibility covers a larger territory. For these reasons field officers—with many personal exceptions, of course—may be considered less well placed to resist pressure or influence, particularly when it takes the more subtle forms of flattery, extreme deference, personal assistance, and social favors.

The consequences of successful pressure upon the units of a decentralized system as compared with similar influence upon a central office may also be more serious. While the modification of a national administrative policy to suit the wishes of an organized group may limit the effectiveness of a program, it will, at least, probably not destroy desirable geographical uniformity. Moreover, if the group is really representative of a large segment of opinion in the country, such influence may even be desirable. Localized influence, however, if carried to any great lengths, is likely to beget such differences of policy between field offices that national policy will be a fiction.

While these considerations refer to possibilities rather than to any specific cases known to the author, it is nonetheless true that they constitute a sizable difficulty in the way of efforts for decentralization. They are probably not in themselves sufficient cause for embracing a centralized system, but they do demand the exercise of ingenuity in developing safeguards for decentralization through control mechanisms, positive personnel work, personal conferences with superior officers, and the like.

Co-ordinating Decentralized Units. In any large organization the equitable balancing of all divisions of the enterprise in such a way that the whole will operate as a unit becomes the central concern of administration. Means must be provided, at one or more points in the hierarchy, of reviewing the range of activities performed, of avoiding or eliminating conflicts of policy or procedure, and of facilitating the harmonious meshing of all elements in the large program. This co-ordination can be achieved in a centralized organization covering a small area, where the responsible division heads are in frequent contact with one another and their superior officer and where the evidences of conflict can be readily noticed. When the element of physical isolation is injected, however, the problem is seriously complicated, especially if any considerable amount of authority is devolved upon field officers. Contradiction and duplication may become so general that the semblance of a nation-wide policy will be destroyed, and the evidences of such lack of co-ordination may be slow to appear to the central authorities. Where the subdivisions of the organization are made in terms of problem areas which are not uniform either in size or in location of their field headquarters, the likelihood of such developments is even greater.

Under such circumstances central co-ordination must be maintained, and authority can be delegated to the field only in such matters as will permit no conflict with other units or only to the extent that means can be developed for assuring adequate co-ordinating authority in the field. The latter may be attempted by having the functional or process services, like personnel, report and adjust conflicts affecting their particular duties, by providing a standardized procedure for appeals from the decisions made by field officers, by standardizing jurisdictional boundaries and limiting the number of headquarters cities, by providing for regional and local co-ordinating committees of an informal sort, or by delineating co-ordinating regions headed by a regional co-ordinator with authority to promote co-operation and eliminate conflicts. Other devices or combinations of these devices may be employed. The fact that each of these has its shortcomings further emphasizes the co-ordination problems presented by the decentralization of administration. The regional co-ordinator, for example, may subvert the principle of unity of command.

The Assets and Liabilities of Decentralization

While the above discussion covers the major reasons for pursuing a policy of administrative decentralization and indicates the principal difficulties presented, it is appropriate to point out briefly its possible advantages and disadvantages, by way both of a summary and of an addition of other points which, though not of primary importance, are nevertheless a part of the problem.

Administrative decentralization can be expected to facilitate popular control and participation, as has been argued above. Particularly where a national policy intimately affects the lives of a large number of people, the executors will also be in contact with the demands of those affected. Moreover, freedom from restrictive rulings by a central authority will permit a degree of flexibility in the application of legal favors and restraints, and it should foster a spirit of healthy experimentation. The greater discretionary authority of field officials and their more vigorous representation of local needs at the central headquarters should result in the adaptation of national aims to peculiar local conditions.

At the same time, decentralization in federal administration should, as has been noted before, promote the effective co-operation of all three governmental levels in the prosecution of interrelated or interdependent functions. Close personal contact combined with the freedom to improvise should do much to eliminate artificial barriers among the various jurisdictions. Also, if decentralization can be applied to a majority of departments or functions in the national government, all those activities related to a particular problem area can be co-ordinated in the field.

There is the further possible advantage of eliminating various types of delay and red tape by doing away with the requirement of frequent reference to central authorities before action can be taken in the field. Similarly, such provisions would relieve the congestion of work at the central point and, by cutting down the amount of detailed work, would tend to emphasize planning and policy activities at the top of the hierarchy. Moreover, where the capital is crowded with people and lack of office space has become a serious problem, decentralization will allow them to be moved to points where physical congestion is not so serious. Further, where responsible officials are located in or close to the objects of administration, travel costs and similar expenses could be greatly reduced.

Finally, it should be pointed out that decentralization affords an opportunity to improve the morale of a large section of the civil service by breaking down the sharp distinction which tends to develop between the departmental service and the much larger field staff. Real decentralization . . . necessitates the delegation of a large amount of discretionary authority, and this in turn increases the opportunities for initiative and responsibility in the field. Such developments would inevitably increase the prestige and morale of all those located outside of the capital.

The primary disadvantage of decentralization, as noted above, is the increased difficulty of maintaining a nation-wide policy—of preserving the uniformity necessary to the effective administration of a policy affecting the country as a whole. Central control may be so weak that a program may differ seriously in its execution from the purposes it was intended to achieve, and co-ordination of geographical subdivisions may be so far handicapped as to invite duplication or even contradictory policy.

Moreover, where the outlook of officials becomes localized, it is not unlikely that their management policies will be short-sighted as far as the national welfare is concerned. This, of course, is a possibility inherent in any plan of geographical subdivision, but it is far more serious where authority is decentralized as well. Further, where an administrative structure is made up of a number of small geographical units, it is possible that their size may prevent their making full use of the technical services and the high degree of specialization which promote efficiency in larger, centralized organizations.

Since a decentralized system requires a high degree of competence on the part of the principal supervisory officials in the field, it is likely that the establishment of such a system will increase the costs of supervisory personnel. The need of this type of man in these positions, combined with the limited prestige enjoyed by local officials and their possible susceptibility to local pressures, as we have already indicated, presents a personnel problem which may discredit efforts toward decentralization. There is the further objection that freedom of field officials from central restraints will invite a variety of local abuses in such matters as purchasing, recruitment, and promotion which will at best present a difficult problem and at worst render the system unworkable.

Finally, it can be argued that the problem of delimiting geographical jurisdictions presents such obstacles as to restrict seriously the possibilities of decentralization. Areas which are established for one function will differ considerably from those required for the administration of another program. Those activities which rely heavily upon co-operation with the states, for example, may have to use the state lines for their boundaries, while those projects which can be carried on independently by the federal authorities and whose problems cannot be confined within political boundaries may require a totally different type of area. Yet co-ordinated planning and policy formation may necessitate uniformity of geographical subdivision. Under such circumstances decentralization may have to be confined within a very limited sphere.

This summary of assets and liabilities of a policy of administrative decentralization indicates that it is one which must be adopted with considerable caution. Its hazards may be as great as those associated with its opposite. It appears likely, moreover, that an administrative organization in action will present some of the characteristics of both tendencies and that, as both are to be regarded not as ends but merely as means to the end of efficient administration, both should be present in any organization in such proportions as will assure a minimum of inefficiency.

———◆———

The following selection is distinctly different in tone and approach from the preceding one, though it is addressed to the same subject: the problem of "levels and interrelations." Prepared and delivered as a lecture at the Department of Agriculture's Graduate School during the Second World War, it is one of a distinguished series dealing with Washington-field relationships. Its author is Donald C. Stone, who has had a varied experience in important administrative positions.

As might be expected, since it was delivered by a practicing administrator to a group with administrative experience, the lecture is a down-to-earth treatment of the subject. The dialogues which compose the fore part of the lecture may not catch the precise rhythm of colloquial speech, but they convey the authentic feeling of the administrative problems they illustrate.

As Mr. Stone's lecture was the first in the series and introductory in character, it touches only lightly many important subjects. But it does offer a splendid review of many of the problems of levels and interrelations as they present themselves to a Federal administrator.

Washington-Field Relationships *

DONALD C. STONE

I propose to begin my discussion of Washington-field relationships by taking you on a tour of Federal offices in the field and in Washington. Rather than engaging in a recitation of administrative theory, I have enlisted the help of some of my staff to guide us in an on-the-scene inspection of some sore spots in this adminis-

* In *Washington-Field Relationships in the Federal Service* (Washington: 1942), lectures and papers by Donald C. Stone and others. Somewhat abridged.

trative area. Let us hear a few of these field and Washington officials express the manner in which some of their problems arise.

Life in the Field

A staff meeting of regional officials is in progress at Atlanta. They are discussing a new field bulletin defining responsibilities of the field staff. Tom Technical is speaking: "I think this bulletin is clear insofar as my duties are concerned. It says that representatives in the field are responsible to the technical divisions in Washington on technical matters, but are subordinate to the regional director for administrative matters. All of my work is concerned with advising the district units on their programs and methods. That is all technical work. This means I report to and take my orders from Washington." Regional Director: "Oh, yes?"

* * * *

Officials from several districts in the Rocky Mountain region are convened in Denver for a conference. In a hotel room after the day's sessions are over, three district managers are letting off steam. The man from Pocatello is saying, "These guys in Washington have no sense of reality. The District of Columbia isn't the United States. Procedures written there just don't fit—they don't take into account operating realities—I can't follow them and get the job done. They complain if Congress tries to pass a bill tying an administrator's hands on administrative detail and then they go ahead and write procedures in such detail that we're supposed to act like robots. It's one thing to sit in a swivel chair in Washington and dictate a new procedure, and quite another thing to apply it in Pocatello."

The man from Salt Lake chimes in: "Another thing—there are a hundred swivel-chair experts in Washington concerned with a hundred angles of our program. Each thinks his piddling little compartment is the most important— the only important aspect—and that full time should be devoted to it."

"What you're saying," observes the man from Montana, "is that we're over-functionalized—that's a Washington 50-cent word—anyway we're over-functionalized to the extent that line authority over us doesn't exist. We have not one, but a hundred bosses who can't agree among themselves. Most of the disorganization in the field exists in the minds of the Washington officials and their cross relationships."

* * * *

While we are in St. Louis, let's see what they are doing in the Purities and Derange Commission. I think if you listen you can hear the Chief answering his assistant who has suggested another visit by the Washington personnel director.

"A lot of good it would do, unless he spent more time than he did last year. First time anyone from the Washington Personnel Division had been around for two years. He showed up Friday morning about ten o'clock, took up two hours of my time talking about the war, and then at noon he suddenly excused himself saying he had to catch the one o'clock to New Orleans. Never reached our Personnel Section, where Ross was waiting, loaded with questions . . . Nice place, New Orleans, for a weekend!"

*   *   *   *

In the corn belt we find ourselves in the home of a field officer in charge of a large region. He has a big job to do and receives a goodly salary . . . to do it. He is sitting at his desk poring over office papers as his wife asks, "John, how did things go at the office today? You seem in low spirits."

"Oh, not so good," he replies. "You know that plan I submitted to Washington for carrying on the fall program? Well, I got a letter today from Mullins, the Director, telling me to drop it. He said the people out here wouldn't like it. Out *here*, mind you! A lot he knows about out here. What burns me up is that no one who knows anything about these matters makes the decisions. Mullins didn't write that letter, I know. Such things get passed down the line without serious consideration to where some $2,000 youngster struts his budding genius over it. This one was probably overtired from night law classes!"

*   *   *   *

In Cansville, Kansas, a director of a State agency has been carrying on protracted negotiations through his regional office and Washington to have appointed a "Supervisor of Migratory Labor." Negotiations have proceeded leisurely, while crops ripen and groups of migrant laborers storm local offices seeking work in response to the widespread publicity that the State-Federal program would provide such service. He is on the phone listening to a frantic local manager saying: "There are 500 men here asking for jobs; I was to be told where I should direct them. What shall I do?"

"Tell them there's a pink tea party on in Washington and all the classification experts are gazing into a crystal ball to see whether the classification sheet for 'Supervisor of Migratory Labor' should say he exercises *wide* discretion or *broad* discretion." . . .

*   *   *   *

Moving North, we find Smith, the crack operator in the Wabasha office of the Barn Debit Administration, waving a fat, official-looking circular.

"Listen, Chief, we might as well shut up shop if we have to adopt this new loan policy. It may apply to New England farmers, but it'll never work with our farmers here in South Dakota. It sure shows the loan chief's mind has never been out of New England, although they transplanted his body to Washington for that nice big desk in Room 210."

*   *   *   *

Swinging down to Dallas, we find the local claims examiner in the Bulova office of the Survival of the Fittest Benefit Administration to be very overwrought and purple in the face. He is saying to the manager,

"What can I tell that poor old lady today? This is the seventh return appointment she's kept to find out what the status of her claim is. The first week we were deciding whether the question had to be settled in Washington. The second week the Regional Office was tracing the claim because they had no record of receiving it. The third week the Regional Director and the Regional Attorney were fighting as to whether it should be returned here or sent on to Washington. The fourth week it was going through the mill of the receiving and recording unit in Washington, and the fifth week there was a disagreement between the claims adjudicators and the claims reviewers as to what amount the lady was entitled to. Then the sixth week the Washington lawyers got hold of it and questioned her eligibility to any benefit at all. They tell me this week that the claim has been brought to the attention of one of the Board members who's particularly interested in this claims eligibility question. Now what can I tell this lady? She's pretty intelligent; she's got a copy of the Act and she just keeps pointing to Sec. 103q and saying, 'It seems quite clear to me; I can't understand what the trouble is.' "

Life in Washington

And what is life like in Washington? First we'll go down to the Exterior Department to see the Assistant to the Under Secretary. We find John Weary, Chief of the Chorus Service, also there. He is saying to the impatient Assistant to the Under Secretary, "I am sorry, but I really can't give you that information. I wired our office at Denver for it a week ago and I just now received a wire back saying that the Superintendent was away and that he had not authorized his assistant to release such important information during his absence." The Assistant to the Under Secretary: "My, oh my, I always wondered why the Secretary wanted the Chorus Service transferred from the Horticulture Department."

*   *   *   *

Suppose we next stop at the V Street building of the D.P.Q. Administration for just one moment—the eighth habitation for the Administration in the 1942 fiscal year and the fifth of its 13 buildings. There we see I. M. Harassed, hardworking Chief of the Field Division. He leans back in his chair, lights his pipe, and philosophizes to his new stenographer, "To all these field offices, I'm a louse. I'm the guy who denies Keokuk a new rug, Fort Wayne a new supply cabinet, Dallas a bookcase, Spokane a water cooler, and so on. Each field office thinks it's the most important one and that each of its eccentricities are perfectly justifiable. As if the Bureau of the Budget and the Appropriations Committee will give us the money we think necessary to run our field offices! Where would we be if we let this money dribble out on silk window drapes and mahogany double desks?

And since I have to decide what takes precedence, I guess I'm as popular as Frankenstein."

*   *   *   *

In another agency the chief of a service division is speaking to the Administrator:

"You'll have to put the blame in the right place. The Chief of Operations didn't refer those Cincinnati papers to me. How can I be responsible for the recruitment program if I am short-circuited by his men out in the field?"

*   *   *   *

The Director of CRA has a number of his field men in for a conference. They have accused him point blank of working in a vacuum in preparing instructions to the field and issuing orders impossible to carry out because of ignorance of field conditions. Says the Director,

"What have we got field officials for, if not to tell us of conditions in the field? That's one reason you're in here now and another reason why we spend so much time trying to develop a work reporting program. For two years now I've been hopping on this, and the idea hasn't even dented the surface."

*   *   *   *

The treasurer of the R.F.D. is bawling out the chief statistician. "Here it is the tenth of the month and the reports from six regions are still missing. Can't you do something about this?"

"My dear Roberts, if you have any idea of how to make those fellows in the field realize that every month is bound to end sooner or later, let me have it. I have circularized them again and again to prepare the reports promptly, but each time they seem to be taken completely by surprise when the month drops out from under them. Now, don't tell me that we ought to fire them—the new ones would be just the same."

Organization of Field Offices

In developing an organization to carry out a program, it is necessary first to determine just what kind of activities are to be carried on and how the work will be performed. Only after this clarification can the type of organization units, centers of coordination, and staff services be determined. While this, to my mind, is the rational approach, most organizations are developed from the top going down, rather than at the level of operations working upward. The whole purpose of the existence of Federal agencies is to perform public services, to benefit or serve individual citizens, and this means dealing with citizens where they are, that is, in the field. The administrative pattern of regions and districts and of field operating units must, therefore, be established in specific relation to the particular job to be done. Unfortunately, this is not always the practice. Regional boundaries are often drawn without consideration of the realities of operating factors but rather on the basis of a pattern carved out in somewhat of a vacuum in Washington or transplanted from another program of dissimilar character. Once established, generally in the early stages of a program, there seems no consciousness that administrative experience or change in direction of program with the passage of time may necessitate changes in organization or administrative procedure.

Responsible top officials in Washington tend to think it impossible to delegate authority to field offices to act unless there is a rigid check-control from headquarters. Field officers, no matter how well they are picked, will make mistakes—so do we all—and they will not always perform as the headquarters official would if he were in the field; and vice versa. That must be taken for granted. But this does not mean that a much better job will not be done in the field if field directors are given authority commensurate with their responsibilities. By keeping transactions *out* of Washington and approaching the Washington relation to the field as one of setting policies and standards and of giving help on difficult matters, the policy of freedom of action will produce much better results than regimented circumscription.

A correlated question is the need for unity of command in individual field offices. Anarchy results if a field office has no head, with the chiefs of the various functions or services reporting administratively to their functional equivalents in the Washington set-up. Unity of command presents no problem where the field office is carrying out a unified purpose program, like the WPA, the Wage and Hour Division, and the Veterans Administration; here you can readily place a region or a State office under the full direction and authority of one person. But the problem becomes more difficult as you get into multiple purpose agencies like the War Production Board and the Federal Security Agency. It would not be easy, for instance, to place all of the Agriculture Department operations within a region under single direction. When the programs are so diverse, persons responsible for a particular program in the field become too far removed by channels and needs of clearances, and so on, from the subdivision of the department in Washington which has responsibility for the particular program. Nevertheless, the correlation of activities in the field is necessary to some degree. The responsibility of regional officers for achieving this correlation will vary greatly according to the extent to which the activities or agencies comprise a single or a multi-purpose program. In any event, our administrative ingenuity needs to be applied with full vigor to the department and refining of devices to coordinate the work of a department and of its various branches as it flows out to the field.

Finally, I should like to emphasize the need for providing field offices with the necessary management tools to carry on their responsibilities. The manager of a large field office must engage in budgetary planning and follow-up, personnel management, and program planning, and he must have staff to assist him in the general task of direction and coordination of operations. He can't rely on budget and personnel staffs in Washington to perform his management job, as seems too often to be the prevailing view in Washington. They may help, they may set policies and procedures, they may give him other kinds of direct aid, but if he is to be manager he must have his kit of management tools within arm's reach for use on all parts of his working organization. The common disposition to bind regional operations by rigid procedures through such attempts to provide all of the staff resources from Washington must be resisted if effective field administration is to result.

Organization of Headquarters to Serve Field

The organization of Washington headquarters to serve the field—notice the word serve—is of great importance to effective field administration. The various functional program groups into which an agency is organized inevitably result in a constant pull by each group away from the general agency focus into special functional foci. Each of these functional or program groups, in dealing with the field, similarly provides a centrifugal force pulling away from the central job to be done. The big problem of headquarters' administration is how to tie together all of the technical branches to bring about a unified impact on field offices.

The functional or technical branches always insist that they must deal directly with the field offices. However, an over-all agency approach, at least insofar as single-purpose programs are concerned, requires that these technical specialties be unified into some single stream of contact with the field. This means that the line of authority to the field must be down a central chain of command flowing from the head of the agency through a general administrative official or officials to the heads of the field offices. Some operating official in the line of command must be responsible for the *whole* field program.

This doesn't mean that all contacts by personnel in the various technical and functional branches must flow through this main channel. If it did, impossible bottle-necks, delay, and irritations would result. The major proportion of business which functional staff in the field carry on with functional and technical staff at headquarters is of a routine character, and there is no reason why such contacts cannot be conducted directly. However, they are to be conducted with the consent of the main line of command. The Washington chief of field operations, or whatever he may be called, has as one of his most important duties the task of determining continuously what types of actions, what kind of reports, what procedural or technical matters can be handled directly between field office staff and functional units at the Washington headquarters, without going all the way up and down the main line of authority. It is his job to see that this segregation of routine and non-routine is current and observed, that the field office receives the specialized help, guidance, policies, and plans which it needs. Similarly, it is his responsibility to assure that field directors set up organizations and carry out programs in accordance with the policies laid down by the agency's technical staff in Washington.

Leadership Versus Check-control Approach by Washington

I have mentioned the evils of the transaction-checking approach of controlling, rather than supervising, field operations. This point warrants some elaboration, since it is one of the principal sore spots in Washington-field relations. In Bureau of the Budget studies of the administration of departments and agencies we find this common characteristic: headquarters' officials cannot believe that field officers can be controlled unless a review or check is made, transaction by transaction, of the work carried on out in the field. There are, of course, notable exceptions.

Let me repeat—and it needs continuous reiteration—under programs which are essentially of a field service character, the job of Washington staff is to formulate the programs, establish policy, develop standards and some of the principal procedures, and to create a field organization which is competent to administer and permitted to administer the programs. These things cannot be done remotely by the Washington staff; field staff must participate all along the line. Policy, programs, and procedures must be developed and constantly re-valued in terms of operating and administrative experience, and, with a few exceptions, this experience is taking place in the field. It is futile to set up policy that won't stand up on the firing line; it is wasteful to develop specimen organization plans for field offices unless they are custom-made to the realities and meas-urements of a particular situation. It is useless exercise to establish standards of operation if they do not fit the conditions in a particular area, or to establish such a rigid standard or pattern that it cannot be adapted to conditions varying throughout the country. It is a waste of effort to prepare regulations or instruc-tions which field staff aren't in sympathy with or don't understand. Obviously, field staff must participate in all of these matters. If an agency sends out bulletins dealing with basic policies and procedures which hit the field "cold," that agency can chalk up a black mark on its administrative ledger.

The real job of the Washington staff is to help the field staff do its job, not to do the field job itself. This means elimination of the "directive" approach, line item budgets, transaction reviews, preaudits of cases, and, what is worst of all, the writing of voluminous letters and memoranda prior to taking action that is urgently needed. All these things kill initiative. They stifle administration. They give a black eye to Government. Delegation of authority must be real, not just on paper. Such delegation of authority must follow the spirit of a top official in one of the Federal agencies who recently told his field managers to go ahead and act when action was needed, even violating regulations, if necessary, and to tell their agency about it afterward. Only with this kind of administration can we expect to attract capable, responsible, broad-gauged officials in the field service.

This approach would eliminate instances of field agencies imperiled by budgets which have been prepared for them without giving them a chance to set forth their needs. Under such a philosophy, it could not happen that a new employee would walk into the office of a field executive who had never seen or heard of him and say, "I have been sent by Mr. So and So, your Personnel Director in Washington, who tells me I am to be your executive assistant." No longer would field representatives from Washington come into regional headquarters and field offices to carry on an investigation as the principal part of their technique of reviewing progress in the field. Nor would field officials report that all goes well and that they have no problems, upon the visit of headquarters' staff. . . .

Rotation of Personnel

In the illustrations given earlier, you will note the frequent situation where field staffs have little knowledge of the problems faced by the Washington officials and the Washington staff in turn lacks appreciation of the job in the field. As one remedy to this difficulty, I strongly urge more extensive adoption of the practice of rotating personnel. Washington staff should be acquainted with field realities by tours of duty in the field to the fullest possible extent. Field officials in turn should be brought into Washington for extended assignments. Furthermore, staff in one district office should periodically be moved to other district offices. The dividends of these practices are rich, both in terms of benefit to individual employees and of contributions to the operations and administration of the agency.

In most agencies field employees are not given the same attention for promotion as are employees in Washington. The latter are closer to top officials and the personnel officers who decide such matters. A systematic plan for reviewing field personnel for promotion, reassignment, and rotation will aid in bringing about more equitable treatment of all employees.

The Art of Communication

Another area for improving Washington-field relationships is that of communication—communication from the field to Washington and from Washington to the field. This is only one segment, but the most difficult segment, of the general question of communication between persons and units within an organization.

The purpose of communication, as I see it, is to *inform*, convey ideas, educate. Administration depends for its life blood upon the adequacy of communication, whether it be in the form of direct discussion between superior and subordinate, or of conferences, telephone calls, letters, memoranda, orders, circulars, manuals, or what not. Information must go from the line of operations up to the top in order that top leadership and policy may be sound, and decisions and thinking at the top must flow to the very roots of the organization, if well planned, productive action is to result.

This free flow of information from bottom to top and from top to bottom is vital to effective management. Frequently the basis for criticisms of field officers that Washington staff does not know field problems results from the failure of the field staff to inform them. In a few agencies, and I think the number is growing, top management has established an environment and a chain of relationships with the staff which encourages the transmission upwards of suggested changes in procedure, problems to be resolved, difficulties encountered, and proposed remedies. Conversely, in many agencies the top officials have willingly succeeded in locking themselves in an ivory tower. Sensitivity to this communications problem on the part of the top leadership, enlightened personnel policies, and the pursuance of the consultative management approach at all levels will break down obstacles to proper conveyance of information in large agencies. They will also lead to more intelligible administrative instructions, bulletins, letters, and memoranda.

This problem of communications is equally important in government relations to citizens. If the field employee is well informed about administrative matters as well as programs, he can deal more intelligently with the citizens—and that means the Federal Government in the eyes of those citizens. Since administrative departments are not subject directly to popular control, there rests great responsibility on administrators to find out what the people are thinking and how they are reacting. This means citizens generally, not just those who may benefit most by specific programs. The head of every agency dealing with the citizen has a real job in training his employees in the art of communicating and dealing with the public.

One of the greatest barriers to clear understanding of objectives and methods by both officials and employees, and the citizen public, is the growing tendency of administrative officials to clothe their thoughts and directives in a specialized language. The deeper we get into this specialized language, this jargon of high-sounding words, the farther we remove the intent of the ideas from the understanding of most readers. This was rather well illustrated sometime back by a member of Parliament who wrote to the London Times that if Lord Nelson were alive today he would never say, "England expects every man to do his duty." The famous admiral's statement probably would run something like this:

"England anticipates that as regards the current emergency, personnel will face up to the issues and exercise appropriately the functions allocated to their respective occupation groups."

In trying to combat this tendency, I have often wondered what could be the impelling motives toward the use of this jargon. Is it an attempt to make administration sound mysterious, difficult, and complicated? Does it spring from the prevailing reverence attached to something termed "technical"? Do officials think they will dignify their status, perhaps securing higher civil service classifications, if they place an impenetrable veil of words over their work? I sometimes think we might justly be accused of being an adolescent professional group sowing the wild oats of high sounding terminology in a vain expectation that administration will thus be made more scientific. I think we are mature enough and advanced enough to see through any such faulty reasoning. Administration must stand on its own feet—and its feet, in fact its heart, brain, and blood, must be the aiding of understanding of ideas by employees within an agency and by the general public. I submit that one infallible precept toward accomplishing this end is the simplification, rather than the compounding, of the written and spoken word which is the main vehicle of administrative action.

PART THREE : PERSONNEL

Chapter 8

Conflicting Values and Emerging Trends

Commentaries on the history of the personnel movement in the United States customarily make a distinction between an early phase designated as "a crusade for the merit principle" and a later phase designated as "the transition from negative 'police' concepts to positive 'managerial' concepts." An appreciation of the techniques and problems that are the subject and concern of modern personnel administration is dependent upon an understanding of these two phases and the differing and sometimes conflicting forces that they have set in operation.

The crusade for the merit principle was based upon a repugnance to the low tone of American political life in the post Civil War decades. It sought to rescue "republican institutions" from the gross corruption and sorry ineptitude then resulting from the political application of the formula that "to the victors belong the spoils." It sought to "keep the rascals out," and its merit principle was conceived as much a test of honesty and purity as of competence.

The transition from this negative emphasis upon preventing dishonesty to the newer positive emphasis—indeed, the very notion of "personnel administration"—results from forces set in motion, on the whole, several decades later. These forces are chiefly those associated with Scientific Management and the rise of business administration. From business administration (and to a lesser extent from such sources as constitutional and foreign study) students of public administration took a great deal of conceptual and technical baggage, adapting it more or less to the public area. They took from business administration a positive emphasis: the idea of personnel *management*, under or by the executive; a new stress upon competence, efficiency, and the full utilization of all "human resources."

The newer, positive emphasis is superimposed upon, it does not replace, the older, negative emphasis. The two became mixed together, ideologically and professionally, with resulting stresses and anomalies. There is a tendency nowadays to deprecate the earlier ideas, and "progressives" in personnel management feel that outmoded attitudes and techniques are a serious obstacle to achievement of good modern personnel management in government. But at the same time the crusade for the merit principle has not yet been wholly won. Indeed, political appointment to "non-policy-making" positions still is the practice in substantial areas of Federal, state, and local government despite more than three-quarters of a century of organized effort to eradicate it.

This section begins, therefore, with a brief but direct look at the "patronage" issue. The two selections presented were written more than a decade ago. But it is a measure of the persistence and depth of the issues involved that, apart from references to contemporary names and dates, they might have appeared either a generation ago or last month.

While to most people it seems as obvious as an axiom from Euclidean geometry that appointments should be upon a merit basis—and professional students of administration are almost as unlikely to declare themselves in favor of political appointment as ministers are to come out for sin—the matter is not so simple as it seems at first glance. The defense of the patronage system presented below is not included as a mere foil. It bristles with issues worth more serious attention than customarily accorded them. The weight of evidence and expert opinion are strongly against spoils; but does the persistence of political appointment over a wide area after three generations of reform indicate that the reformers have failed to account for all the facts?

Certainly the questions involved reach to the heart of the American constitutional system. Is patronage necessary to compensate for the "defect" of the separation of powers, the division between branches of government? Could political parties—generally conceded to be essential to democracy—exist in America without patronage? Would they, as some argue in contrary, be actually strengthened by the complete elimination of patronage, thus enabled to perform their function of presenting issues without irrelevant distractions?

Another set of questions clusters around the meaning and methods of democracy. Can merit be determined wholly apart from political responsiveness? If the Jacksonian methods of ensuring political responsiveness are obsolete and dangerous in the twentieth century, what is to replace them? Has public administration squarely faced and adequately answered this question?

The first of the two selections is a defense of patronage as a principle productive of both democracy and efficiency. It is presented under the name William Turn, though the editor is informed that this is a pseudonym. Whoever the author, the piece is well done; the idiom as well as the argument is authentic. The author of the second selection, presenting a case against patronage, is Betsy Knapp, an administrative student with practical experience in public life. Both selections are substantially abridged.

In Defense of Patronage *

WILLIAM TURN

In an era which places a great deal of emphasis on the value of so-called "expert" opinion, there is something unreasonable in the hysterical indictments of political patronage which are made today with little or no actual knowledge of what it is about.

Almost thirty years of practical political experience have given me a real insight into the subject, and to my way of thinking, the attackers of the patronage systems are guilty of an unpatriotic act against an inherent and necessary part of our American political system. The true cause for the introduction of the spoils system was the triumph of democracy. Today it remains the one realistic device for permitting the majority of the people to mold the policies of government.

Why Party Workers Are Needed

If the people as a whole are to have a real voice in the conduct of the government, they must be organized. What is more (and this is going to be a terrible shock to the starry-eyed reformers), they have to be pushed around and coaxed or dragged to the polls to exercise the hard-won privilege of the franchise. Thousands of people never vote because the registration dates pass before the campaign gets exciting, and they are not interested enough to make the effort to qualify. Others get wildly excited about issues or candidates between election days and damn the government from first to last, but forget all about their objections on election day. To prod these lazy ones into action, to insure that our democratic form of government will remain truly democratic and representative of a majority of *all* the people and not just of a selfish few, militant party organizations are essential. There must be drilling and training, hard work with the awkward squad, and an occasional dress parade.

This work requires the labor of many men. There must be precinct captains and ward leaders and district representatives. On registration days and on election

* From "Improved Personnel in Government Service," *Annals*, Vol. 189 (January, 1937), pp. 22–28. Reprinted by permission of *The Annals of the American Academy of Political and Social Science*. Abridged.

days there must be telephone squads and free transportation and wide-awake generalissimos. Every day of the year there must be party leaders actively concerned with the business of the organization—keeping in close touch with the great masses of "average folks" whose participation is vital to any truly democratic process, learning what they are thinking, and interpreting for them the policies which are being put into effect.

Now, some men labor for love and some for glory. But glory comes only to a few of the most outstanding leaders; it cannot serve as a general inducement, and even those who love must live. It is an essential idea of democracy that the leaders shall be of the people. They must belong to the class that makes its own living. What then could be more reasonable than for good citizens who have displayed their ability and their devotion to the principles of democracy within their party to be picked for responsible service with the government when there are positions to be filled? I have heard it suggested that we need more training in our schools in preparation for public service; but I wonder what better training there could be than the practical lessons which are a part of the orderly and disciplined advancement in the organization? Recognition in party organizations, like recognition anywhere else, comes in proportion to good service rendered.

My own experience has been a clear record of this principle. After an apprenticeship which included such routine chores as the distribution of handbills and tacking up campaign posters, I began to learn the fundamentals of party organization as a precinct leader, and I can report my activities here with no embarrassment. The idea was simply this: I went out and got acquainted with my neighbors! When a new family moved into the neighborhood, I made myself known to them at the earliest possible moment and saw to it that they got acquainted and were taken into the activities of our community. On registration days I was an early and persistent caller, ready with information about where and how to register, helping to arrange for time off if necessary, and making up schedules to take care of those who needed transportation or someone to mind the baby.

As I proved my sincerity and ability, I was allowed to sit in on the party councils. Here I found men who were leaders in the community and who honestly believed that the policies of our party would further the welfare of our people. They were frequently profane, but never treacherous. They met together and considered seriously the choice of candidates who would earnestly support the policies of the party and who seemed to have the confidence of the largest number of people in our community.

When election time approached, it was perfectly natural that my neighbors and I should talk about the candidates, and since my participation in the councils of the party had given me a better acquaintance with some of the candidates than most of them had, they were glad to hear what I could tell them. Some of the candidates spoke at meetings in our neighborhood, and it pleased both my neighbors and myself to follow these meetings with introductions and more informal conversations which gave them an opportunity to express their opinions and talk face to face with men who had their interests at heart. People in general are not very interested in just abstract ideas. But when those ideas are associated with Joe or Sam or Frank, whom they know as friends and leaders, then there is flesh upon the bones of democracy, and government is something which has interest and meaning.

The success of a candidate is much more than a chance to pull a plum out of the patronage pie; it is the satisfactory knowledge that the public affairs are in the hands of colleagues in whom it is possible to have confidence. When new policies are being developed, this is of tremendous importance. It is human nature to be suspicious of any change in the way of doing things, whether it is the way the new preacher begins the service, or a city ordinance allowing right turns on red lights. Without the confident and sympathetic support of the rank and file, there is a great deal of waste motion before people are ready to give the new ideas a fair trial.

Business Methods in Government

And that reminds me of the old chestnut about "What business man would run his plant like the government?" People can get pretty excited about that, but most of them don't stop to figure out that the only condition under which that question would be pat is, for example, if a private utility company were taken over by public ownership. We have all had ample opportunity during the past few years to get a reasonably clear idea of the sentiments these two camps have about each other. Keeping that in mind, I ask you to consider what the general manager for the public ownership outfit should do about personnel. According to the reformers, he shouldn't fire any of the people in the business he took over, because some of them would have been around for thirty or forty years and knew just how their jobs should be done.

Now isn't that a pretty idea? We can assume that every employee in the business had been campaigning vigorously against the change in management. Department heads, brought up to look upon public ownership as an unwarranted invasion of private property rights, would be so hopping mad and so absolutely sure that the new plan couldn't work that they wouldn't bother to open their mail. Some of the boys who had to take salary cuts would get together on the side and start figuring out how they could spoil the show and return the business to the hands of their friends. A fine way to do business!

For the benefit of those who think "the spoils system" is something which Andrew Jackson turned loose on a previously pure and unsuspecting world, I should like to point out that the desire of leaders to surround themselves with loyal and trustworthy supporters is a perfectly natural and understandable phenomenon which is as old as time itself. The very founding of our Nation depended on the unswerving loyalty of a few daring men, and the administration of our first great President, George Washington, took into consideration the importance of placing in office those who were "supporters of the system." There is evidence, too, that this famous statesman made his appointments with an eye to geographic distribution, realizing that such action was both fair and wise. When he had appointments to make from areas in which he was personally unacquainted, he asked for recommendations from the Congressmen from those districts, because as he very properly believed, their local knowledge gave their words special weight.

Patronage appointments for demonstrated party loyalty seem to me most likely to promote efficiency. Too light weight is given to the protection which patronage gives the government against bureaucratic sabotage, which its enemies naïvely deny on the theory that "the spoils" are distributed in grab-bag fashion, with those having the longest reach taking home the prizes. The occasional administrations which have ignored the principles of loyalty and fair play in distributing patronage have been short-lived. It is only common sense for an organization which wants to maintain unity and strength in its own ranks to grant recognition on a completely democratic basis.

As for the quality of the appointments, it should be borne in mind that while patronage is a reward to those who have worked for party victory, it is also the test of a party's fitness to remain in office. Every bad appointment weakens the party's power. Dr. Carl J. Friedrich, of Harvard University, reported for the Commission of Inquiry on Public Service Personnel:

"You cannot take offices with vast powers attached to them 'out of politics' for politics is not a bottle or any other variety of container. Politics is the struggle for power. Where there is power, there is politics. What you can do, and what you must do, is to make politics responsible."

That is just what patronage does.

Civil Service Employees

A good measure of the value of patronage is the nature of the alternatives which are offered in its place. The greatest of these is civil service! This is a unique system under which it is assumed that people are simple organic compounds, subject to laboratory methods. Examinations are given to these specimens, and on the basis of the results they are neatly catalogued and filed until needed. Orders are filled on the general understanding that short of an Act of God there will be no returns or exchanges. The finished product is a pale, quiet individual, faithful in a dim sort of way, disinclined to originality, but capable within a limited field of an insolence that makes one wonder why it is called "civil."

The chief advantage of the civil service system appears to be that it offers regular, light employment at a moderate remuneration. This undoubtedly attracts large numbers of steady-going, unimaginative people, but I question whether their services are of any greater value to the public than the less routine but more lively efforts of patronage appointees who have a personal stake in the business. Men and women who stay in one place too long get in a rut. Like a horse with blinders, they see in only one direction, and too often that direction is not toward the taxpayers who pay their salaries. I think it is significant that when people speak of "government employees" they almost always have in mind a roomful of clerks.

It has been my experience that a dull level of mediocrity is likely to be encountered in civil service, and it was doubtless this same feeling which led Andrew Jackson to say, "I cannot but believe that more is lost by the long continuance of men in office than is generally to be gained by their experience." A more violent friend of mine refers to the "Snivel Servants" who are so afraid of doing any original thinking that it is only after long persuasion that you can get them to agree with you that Christmas will probably be on the 25th of December next year. This man is a real friend of government workers and has done a lot for them, but their shilly-shallying ways and their unwillingness to work together for any purpose whatever try his patience.

Of course the civil service policy of forbidding all political activity to government employees is largely responsible for this attitude, and I think it is a dangerous threat to democracy. Here is a large group of the very people who should have an active voice in party councils, and they are so hedged about with restrictions that they shy like a frightened horse at the mere mention of the words "Democrat" and "Republican." . . .

Room for Improvement

The enemies of the patronage system are willing occasionally to admit that their systems are not the perfect answer, and I will be equally magnanimous and admit that the patronage system could be improved. A great forward step has already been taken in the distribution of patronage. In the old days, there was an element of gamble in the assignment of jobs. There was more of the "first come, first served" philosophy, and a good-natured rivalry between leaders occasionally resulted in extra portions for the more aggressive. But closer organization and better discipline have led to a merit policy which seems to me to offer the best possible service to the public. The most important single factor in its betterment would be a more active participation in party councils by the people who are doing most of the talking about what is wrong! Our government is not going to get any simpler as time goes on, and the need for experts in the field will increase; but if their contribution is to be realistic *and responsible*, they must first learn the elementary lessons of democratic control as exemplified in the political party.

Is Patronage Necessary? *

BETSY KNAPP

Patronage not only hampers the development of parties based on issues, it also interferes with the administration of government services. After an election public officials not infrequently find themselves so harassed by job-seekers that there is little time to carry on the public business. Thus government fails in its most important function—service to the public. Postmaster General James A. Farley has given a vivid description of what this pressure for jobs was like in Washington in 1933:

"I had anticipated quite a rush of deserving patriots who were willing to help F.D.R. carry the burden. But, to be frank, I had never had the slightest conception of what was about to happen. They swarmed in and flocked in by the hundreds and thousands until it seemed as though they must have been arriving by special trainloads. They hurried to the headquarters of the National Committee and, when they learned that it was impossible to see me there, they hurried over to the Post Office Department to demand an audience with me at once. I may as well confess—because everyone knows it to be a fact—that for two or three months I was compelled to hand over the running of the Post Office Department to my worthy assistants, Joseph C. O'Mahoney, William C. Howes, Clinton B. Eilenberger, Silliman Evans, and other capable aides.

"Untold dozens of the job aspirants discovered where I lived and haunted the hotel corridors in the effort to catch up with me. As a result, even though my working day usually extended to midnight or even after, I virtually had to slip back and forth to the office like a man dodging a sheriff's writ. When the pressure let up a bit, I was about the happiest individual on earth." . . .

The same sort of pressure is felt in state and local governments when there are large numbers of jobs to be distributed among the faithful. In Michigan, after the passage of an act by the 1939 legislature reducing the number of positions subject to the Michigan civil service law, one of the state officials remarked: "There will be so much confusion around here for the next two weeks that we won't be able to get anything done." . . .

Patronage puts the public official on the horns of a dilemma. There are some, like former Senator Robinson of Arkansas, who think there is no solution. He once confessed he did not know of ". . . any method by which senators may escape devoting a material and substantial part of their time, which is really required in connection with official duties, in the attempt to reward their supporters and friends, their party associates, by securing for them political jobs." . . .

* Chapter I in *The Awkward Age in Civil Service* (Washington: 1940). Abridged. Reprinted by permission of the League of Women Voters of the United States.

In spite of the logic of the argument for getting rid of patronage, as a benefit both to the political parties and to government officials, this outworn method of filling government positions does not lack for forthright defenders.

There are some who argue that patronage is necessary for the maintenance of democracy:

"I know a number of people who sincerely think that this appointment system is wrong simply because so much reliance is placed upon members of Congress and other elected officials. To my way of thinking that is the *most democratic way of all* and, in the long run, the best way of getting competent people." [1]

"Patronage is *essential to the maintenance of democracy*. The hope of recognition and reward to party workers has long been a stimulus without which parties have been unable to function."

"We believe it is a healthy condition for a public employee to know that his party must win for him to retain his job. Then he is going to do his level best to make his party's administration efficient and deserving. *We are against lifetime jobs for a class which turns up its nose at politics*. Many jobholders under the merit system don't take the trouble to vote."

These comments reveal confusion about the meaning of democracy, not to mention confusion about the nature of the public service. They imply that the will of the people will not be carried out unless legislative candidates who are successful at the polls have the opportunity to put their supporters in government jobs, and that the public service belongs to the parties and not to the people as a whole. The will of the people as expressed in elections will more likely be accomplished if administrative positions are filled on the basis of ability without regard to political conviction, and if a public service is developed which will loyally carry out the policies of whatever party is in power.

Another contingent of patronage defenders are confused about the relationship of the representative function to the selection of government employees:

"*This is a representative government, and a legislator is a direct representative of his constituents.* He knows, or should know, them and their desires. They trust him to be better informed regarding the affairs of government than they are, at least until they learn he is not, because he can devote his whole time to keeping informed regarding them. If they do not trust him to make appointments, then they certainly should not trust him to enact legislation. The representatives of the people should have, at the least, a positive check upon Government employees and their appointment."

Representative democracy means that the people, through persons elected by them, shall have the ultimate control over government, but it does not follow from this, that the people's elected representatives should attempt to do everything

[1] The italic type in these quotations was added by the author. The first in this series, incidentally, is from James A. Farley, quoted above.—The Editor.

that pertains to government or even to supervise everything. Legislative bodies are suited for deliberation on important matters of public policy, but not for the solution of day to day administrative problems, nor in many cases for the selection of administrative officers. Legislators require some method of reviewing the activities of the executive branch of the government in order to assure themselves that policies, once decided upon, are carried out. The powers of appropriation and investigation are adapted to this purpose, but the selection of personnel is not. This task requires specialized training and is better performed by others than lawmakers. Senator Norris of Nebraska, speaking from his long experience in the United States Congress, said on this point:

". . . I did assert, I again assert, and I do not apologize for it, that when the Members of the Senate of the United States seek to pass on the qualifications of tens of thousands and hundreds of thousands of officials of the United States, they are undertaking a job which they never can properly finish. They cannot do it. It is impossible. . . .

"One cannot be a successful Senator and take care of the public interests which are confided to him if all his time is taken up in getting jobs for people, or seeing whether applicants are competent to fill positions. It is common knowledge that Members of Congress can do better if they have men who can search out and look up qualifications of applicants for positions."

And then there are those who claim that patronage is part of the system of checks and balances set up in the federal Constitution and in most of the state constitutions. When the method of appointing postmasters was under consideration in the Congress in 1937 this defense of the patronage system was made:

". . . this method of appointing postmasters is ideal, [*i.e.*, on recommendation of the Congressmen] and it is one that has been tried out through all the years. *It follows our constitutional system of checks and balances.* It is the rarest thing that a postmaster goes wrong. Postmasters are responsible to the Congressman, or to the Senators where the office is in the Senator's home town, and, as a rule, they are a competent and efficient body of men."

The system of checks and balances is designed to protect us against too great a concentration of power in the hands of any one group of public officials. As a part of this system the President must seek the advice and consent of the Senate on important appointments. It is appropriate that Congress should participate in the appointment of the officers, department heads and a few others, who must make the major decisions about how best to put congressional policies into effect. Certainly, however, the point cannot be sustained that congressional advice on appointments to positions that are strictly administrative in character protects the people from the irresponsible exercise of power. Such protection comes rather when administrative officers are selected by a method which assures systematic investigation of their qualifications, and when their tenure of office is made dependent on the quality of service they render rather than on the fortunes of the political parties.

All of these defenses of patronage reflect confusion about the difference between policy and administration. The administrative staff of a government agency is responsible for putting into effect the policies of the party in power. Although this work involves discretion, and although administrators have functions of investigation and recommendation that affect the formulation of policy, they are not responsible for the final decisions which determine new action. There is, therefore, no reason for the Congress to participate in the selection of such officers or for partisan political considerations to affect the choices made.

Nevertheless, there are some people who think that practically every officer with other than routine responsibilities is intimately associated with policy, and that there must be a fairly large turnover of administrative personnel whenever there is a political turnover. Mr. James A. Farley is one proponent of this point of view:

"It is simply impossible for a President of the United States, or a Cabinet member, or the head of an independent government establishment, to put his policies into operation with the maximum effectiveness unless his key employees are fully in sympathy with what he is endeavoring to accomplish. Take my word for it, no matter how conscientious an employee may be, or how loyal he thinks he is, if he is basically at odds with the policies of the department in which he works, that fact will show itself in his labors sooner or later."

As Mr. Farley suggests, persons who render poor service or who sabotage the policies of their superiors should be dismissed. The basic problem that he describes would be solved to a great extent at the outset, if officers were selected primarily for their capacity for administrative work and their enthusiasm for the public service rather than their enthusiasm for a particular set of policies.

But quite apart from this point there are objections to Mr. Farley's view of government administration. In the first place, when there is frequent and large turnover of administrative personnel, there are corresponding difficulties in trying to find satisfactory people for the posts. It is not easy to find persons who have the requisite qualifications and who are also acceptable politically, who can afford to leave their business or profession to take over an important public position for a short period of time only. The experience of the United States Treasury Department in filling one Under Secretaryship and three Assistant Secretaryships between 1933 and 1940 is a good illustration. In that period there were six Under Secretaries and eight Assistant Secretaries, and only in two instances was the change the result of a promotion.

In the second place, turnover of administrative personnel for political reasons implies rejection of the idea that government service can be made a career, with the possibility of promotion to positions of responsibility and importance. Even Mr. Farley, as a proponent of turnover, recognizes the value of making top departmental positions available to career employees. The first New Deal appointee for the position of Fourth Assistant Postmaster General, in charge of expenditures for new buildings, was a prominent Democrat. When he resigned "to accept a more lucrative position in private business," a civil service employee of many years' experience was appointed as his successor.

If a clearer distinction were made between policy and politics on the one hand, and administration on the other, career men could more frequently attain top administrative positions, and the public service would be improved. It would also be easier to rout the patronage defenders whose ideas about the nature of democratic institutions are confused. . . .

Patronage has been used to meet another important need by providing one source of support for party organizations. Public jobs have become a substitute for cash in compensating the thousands of workers who help the parties win elections. In addition, those who get the jobs become a source of cash contributions to the party treasury. The explanation given by Senator Minton of Indiana of the "Two Percent Club" in that state describes the system in common usage:

"It is a Democratic organization, and the purpose of it is to keep the Republicans out of power in Indiana, and may God prosper it. . . .

"Let us now take a look at this Two Percent Club which the Senator has seen fit to characterize as political racketeering. We all know that in running a political party you must have the wherewithal to do it. You have to have sinews of war. You must have money with which to conduct a political campaign. In all seriousness I ask Senators, 'Where do you want to get your money? You have got to get it some place. Where do you want to turn to get it?' The Democratic Party simply says, 'We elect to go to our people who hold offices under the Democratic Party and who are responsible for the administration in the Democratic Party's lease of power, and ask them to contribute of their funds in order to defray the expenses of the Democratic Party.' What could be fairer than that, Mr. President?"

Apart from the fact that such a system makes a private vested interest out of the public service, the question Mr. Minton raises is a fair one: "Where do you want to get your money?" No one has ever provided a completely satisfying answer.

In the last fifty-six years, however, the efforts of merit system proponents have resulted in an intermittent but increasing withdrawal of public positions from the patronage arena, and the parties still thrive. There is every indication that they would continue to thrive even if no public positions were bought and sold in the market place. Mr. Frank Kent suggests that one of the chief results would be the reduction in the number of people who could make a living in machine politics.

Another result might well be an increase in the number of people willing to do political work on a volunteer basis, particularly as an increase in emphasis on issues might be expected to follow a decrease in emphasis on jobs. As long as party organization and finance are geared to the philosophy that those who help parties win elections are entitled to "honest rewards," it will not be easy to attract support on any other basis.

Moreover, patronage is not an unmitigated blessing even to the parties. Mr. Farley has pointed out that patronage can tear parties apart as well as bind them together:

"I think the objection of most people to the present system is that patronage jobs are used to build political machines. That is a fact, and it would be a senseless falsehood to deny it. Moreover, I am perfectly conscious of the fact that when political organizations begin thinking about jobs and nothing else, when they forget that the public business should come first, they have commenced their own death chant without realizing it. History shows very plainly that a lust for jobs on the part of shortsighted leaders has broken up more political organizations, both Republican and Democratic, than any other single cause. That is a danger that must be guarded against; in fact, it is something that is inherent in every kind of organization. The protest of the public is the best way to discipline an organization against that sort of thing.

"But those people who are inclined to imagine that patronage, and patronage alone, is the only thing that keeps a political party knit together are off on a tangent that is about as far wrong as anything humanly could be. I am convinced that with the help of a few simple ingredients like time, patience, and hard work, I could construct a major political party in the United States without the aid of a single job to hand out to deserving partisans."

When an expert in political organization, such as Mr. Farley, says that patronage is not necessary, there would seem to be little need for the layman to worry lest the parties be unable to survive without it.

———◆———

The title of the following selection, "Let's Go Back to the Spoils System," suggests that it is a close companion of "In Defense of Patronage." But instead of a serious proposal to return to the patronage system it is instead a strong indictment of the manner in which civil service is administered by the Federal government, and a request for improvement. It is a journalistic account of the negative civil service approach to personnel matters, and a plea for more of a positive, "managerial" approach.

The author, John Fischer, is a journalist by profession, and this essay was written for *Harper's Magazine* soon after the Second World War. But Mr. Fischer had had several years' experience in Federal employment as well as journalistic training, and he felt strongly about his subject. The result is lively reading.

Of Mr. Fischer the editors of *Harper's* remark that he "bears the scars of a seven-year struggle with Civil Service in a number of government agencies. He is not an unbiased observer." Perhaps not. Undoubtedly there is a certain striving for journalistic effect. And Mr. Arthur S. Flemming, then one of the three Commissioners, made reply in a following issue; there are two sides to the story. But the references in the essay to Professor Floyd W. Reeves indicate that there is competent professional opinion in close support of the case presented. Nearly everything that Mr. Fischer alleges has been said soberly and at length in the professional literature. (The editor is not an unbiased observer either. He also "bears scars.")

The nub of the matter is the conflict between older and newer values, procedures, personages, and institutions. There is a cultural and institutional lag. With the battle for civil service reform not yet fought to a successful conclusion, students and practitioners in the field of personnel must meanwhile try to adapt the apparatus of "positive" personnel work to the new governmental environment at a time when social and technical change takes place with ever-increasing acceleration. And the governmental environment seems often and in many ways unaccommodating. What is easy and manifest in business seems impossible of acceptance in government, at least in the short run.

Query, should Mr. Fischer lay part of the blame on the Founding Fathers instead of on the Civil Service Commission? Is he failing to take account of the thesis of Dean Appleby that "government is different"?

Let's Go Back to the Spoils System *

JOHN FISCHER

The good citizens slapped each other on the back on the evening of January 16, 1883, and their hosannahs were heard throughout the land. A reluctant Congress had just passed the Civil Service Act, which would guarantee an honest, efficient, and economical government forevermore. The corrupt political bosses finally had been routed; their thieving henchmen would be shooed away from the public trough; and from then on federal jobs would be filled strictly on merit by the ablest men the country could produce. It was a major victory for Righteousness, Liberalism, and Good Government.

But somehow, in the sixty-two years since that glad day, the Great Reform has gone sour. Today Washington is filled with good citizens who lie awake nights

* From *Harper's Magazine*, Vol. 191 (October, 1945), pp. 360–368. Somewhat abridged. Reprinted by permission of Harper & Brothers, Publishers.

thinking up new and sulphurous curses to hurl at Civil Service. Nearly every agency pays a large staff to figure out ingenious schemes for carrying on the public business in spite of Civil Service regulations. (These rules and regulations, couched in language that would gag a Philadelphia lawyer, fill a 524-page book, plus 46 pages of reference tables. Probably no living man wholly understands them; but they govern every waking hour of the three and a half million people in the federal service, including—*especially* including—their behavior off the job.) Thousands of typists, who might be doing useful work in a hand laundry, waste their dreary lives filling out stacks of Civil Service forms, usually in quintuplicate. A responsible executive officer in the War Department recently offered (very privately) his considered judgment that the Civil Service system had been the greatest single obstacle to the war effort. . . .

II

What's gone wrong with Civil Service is easy enough to find out. You can get the story, in almost identical terms, from anybody who has ever held an executive job in Washington.

First of all, it's too slow. If you were an administrator in urgent need of a new assistant, you might hope to get somebody on the job—with luck and infinite finagling—in six or eight weeks. (He wouldn't be the man you want, of course.) In wartime the pace was a little faster—there were even cases in which a man was hired within a week—but even then par for the course was at least a month. If you wanted to beat that, you had to "hand process" the appointment, personally carrying the sheaf of papers through the maze of the agency personnel office and the Civil Service Commission, and mobilizing all the pressure you could, including telephone calls from the applicant's congressman.

When you want to fire a man, the procedure naturally is more tedious. In theory, it is as easy to get rid of an incompetent in the government service as it is in private industry; in practice, the ordeal may drag on for six or eight painful months. If you are an experienced administrator, you will never try to fire anybody—you will foist him off on some unsuspecting colleague in another bureau, or transfer him to the South Dakota field office, or reorganize your section to abolish his position.

I once spent a whole winter trying to "terminate," as Civil Service puts it, an elderly female clerk who had become so neurotic that no other woman could work in the same room with her. This involved written charges, interviews with my tearful victim, protests from her senator, indignant union delegations, and formal hearings before a panel of personnel experts. In the end I gave up and arranged for her transfer, with a raise in pay, to the staff of a trusting friend who had just joined the government. She is there to this day, chewing paper clips, frightening secretaries, and muttering to herself as she misfiles vital documents; I think of her every time I pay my income tax. My friend, who no longer speaks to me, is trying to get her transferred to the Veterans Administration. . . .

202 PART THREE: PERSONNEL

Even worse than the Civil Service Commission's leisurely gait is its delight in harassing the operating officials who are responsible for running the government. The typical administrator may spend as much as a third of his time placating the commission and the hordes of minor personnel specialists who infest Washington. He draws organization charts, argues with classification experts, fills out efficiency ratings, justifies the allocation of vacancies, and listens to inspiring lectures on personnel management until he has little energy left for his real job. He may search for hours for those magic words which, properly recited in a job description, will enable him to pay a subordinate $4,600 instead of $3,800. (The phrase "with wide latitude for exercise of individual initiative and responsibility" is nearly always worth $800 of the taxpayers' money; but it took me two years to find that out.)

No bureaucrat can avoid this boondoggling. If he fails to initial a Green Sheet or to attach the duplicate copy of Form 57, the whole machinery of his office grinds to a halt. If he deliberately flouts the established ritual, or neglects to show due respect for the personnel priesthood, his career may be ruined and his program along with it. In a thousand subtle ways the personnel boys can throw sand in the gears. They can freeze appointments and promotions, block transfers, lose papers, and generally bedevil any official who refuses to "co-operate." If they bog down a government project in the process, that is no skin off their backs—nobody can ever hold them responsible.

Nor can the administrator escape the Civil Service investigators, who drop in once or twice a week to question him about the morals, drinking habits, and possibly treasonable opinions of some poor wretch who has applied for a federal job. These investigators often are amusing fellows. I got well acquainted with one who formerly had been a small-town private detective; he had an uncommonly prurient mind, which led him to handle every case as if he were working up adultery charges for a divorce suit. Nearly all of them operate on the theory that anybody willing to work for the government must be a scoundrel, probably with Communist tendencies, who could never hold a job anywhere else. They have a boundless appetite for gossip, and they waste a lot of other people's time. What purpose they serve is obscure, because their investigations often are not completed until five or six months after the new employee starts work. If he actually were as villainous as they seem to suspect, he would have plenty of time to sell the country's secrets to a sinister foreign power before the investigators caught up with him.

These are minor indictments, however. The really serious charge against the Civil Service system is that it violates the most fundamental rule of sound management. That rule is familiar to every businessman: when you hold a man responsible for doing a job, you must give him the authority he needs to carry it out. Above all, he must be free to hire his own staff, assign them to tasks they can do best, and replace them if they don't make good.

In peacetime, at least, no agency operating under the trammels of Civil Service has this authority. Suppose, for example, that Congress sets up a special Flood Control Agency, with urgent orders to harness the rampaging Ohio River. The new FCA administrator, full of zeal, asks the Civil Service Commission to give him the best chief engineer the merit system can supply.

After some argument whether a first-class engineer—capable of earning $30,000 a year in private practice—is worth $6,500 to the government, the commission finally tells the administrator to take his choice of three men. They head its list of people who once took a Civil Service engineering examination. All the best men on the list have already been snapped up by other agencies, of course, because the last examination was held five years ago. And it wasn't a very good list in the first place, because few people in the profession knew that such an examination was being held. (It had been announced in a bulletin, printed in the kind of type used for Bible footnotes and displayed on postoffice notice boards between the Marine recruiting posters and the FBI photos of escaped kidnappers.)

Of the three "referrals," one turns out to be a professor at Freshwater Academy who never poured a yard of concrete in his life. The second is afflicted with a personality which makes it impossible for him to work in any organization. The third actually has had some practical experience—he once designed a garbage disposal plant—but he has no sympathy with the flood control program; he is a firm believer in Free Enterprise and non-interference with acts of God. The administrator has to take him anyway, although he personally knows a dozen better-qualified men who are eager to tackle the job.

During the next six months, while the administrator tries desperately to recruit the rest of his staff from Civil Service registers, the chief engineer surveys the Ohio River. He reports that flood control is neither practical nor desirable, and that in any case it should be left to private industry. Meanwhile, a flood wipes out Cincinnati, Louisville, and Paducah. With one voice the press denounces the administrator as a bungling bureaucrat, and a Senate investigating committee demands his head.

The Civil Service Commission, of course, is unperturbed. It has done its duty in preserving the merit system free from all taint of patronage. The sacred regulations have been kept intact. If a few thousand unfortunates have been drowned in the Ohio Valley, that is none of its concern.

Fantastic? Not in the least. In the past twelve years a number of government programs have been hobbled in precisely this fashion.

III

Although the defects of Civil Service are plain enough, the reasons for them are not so easy to find.

By no means all the blame rests on the Civil Service Commissioners. They are three earnest, well-meaning people, who grieve sincerely over the flaws in their organization. . . .

The commission's permanent staff [is] the most inbred, tradition-ridden clique in Washington. These veteran bureaucrats know that their bosses come and go, while they endure forever. They are skilled in the art of passive resistance, and they have no intention of letting any upstart commissioner tamper unduly with their time-hallowed procedures. Their idol is Theodore Roosevelt, the only Civil Service commissioner who ever attained national prominence—his desk is enshrined in the central hall of their F Street lair—and they look with grave suspicion on any ideas which he did not sanction in 1895.

The tight inner circle of the permanent staff is made up of men who started with the commission as messengers or clerks some twenty years ago, and rose to positions of power on the seniority escalator. Few of them have had any experience in private business or other government departments; they have little conception of the problems of an operating agency.

They have two guiding principles. The first is Keep the Rascals Out. Civil Service, in their view, is a kind of police force designed to keep political patronage appointees from creeping into federal jobs. This they do well—but they rarely feel any responsibility for positive action to make the government work, or to persuade the best possible men to enter the federal service.

The second aim of the commission bureaucracy is to increase the dignity and power of the personnel profession. To this end, they have developed a special jargon which no outsider can understand, plus an elaborate structure of regulations, red tape, and ritual which can be mastered only after years of study. They demand of the whole government what Dr. Floyd W. Reeves, professor of administration at the University of Chicago, has described as "an almost idolatrous worship" of the commission's "detailed and antiquated rules."

It is hard to blame them for this—after all, they are only doing what the legal and medical professions did centuries ago. The result, however, is a vested interest in complexity and formalism which is largely responsible for the ill-repute of the Civil Service system.

But the greatest share of guilt falls on Congress. Lacking any real enthusiasm for the Civil Service idea, it has never bothered to work out comprehensive legislation for a modern, effective system of personnel administration. Instead, over the course of years it has encrusted the original act of 1883 with scores of piecemeal amendments and special statutes. This has resulted in a legal patchwork which would baffle even the ablest and most aggressive commissioners. One law, for example, sets up special qualifications for coal mine inspectors; another provides that employees of the Farmers' Home Corporation must be residents of the states where they work; a third specifies that superintendents of national cemeteries must be disabled Army veterans—no sailors or Marines need apply. All of these laws, and many more like them, undermine the principle that the best man ought to get the job; each one is intended to confer special preference on some particular group of job-hunters. They are simply devices for legalizing favoritism and patronage on a large scale.

In addition, Congress has steadfastly refused to give the commission enough money to hire a proper staff or to run its business efficiently. (Until a few years ago, one of the field offices got along with a single telephone and borrowed chairs from the federal jail whenever it had to hold an examination.) Nor have there ever been funds to develop scientific testing methods, or to keep the registers fresh with frequent examinations.

It is true, of course, that the commission seldom fights aggressively for the money it needs, and that it sometimes has actually encouraged Congress to pass bad legislation. Only a few months ago, for example, the commission managed to have written into law one of its most hampering regulations—the so-called "Rule of Three," which limits choice in appointments to the three names at the top of the register. Dr. Reeves, a leading authority in the field of public administration, characterized this step as "a major disaster."

Nevertheless, such blunders would be impossible if Congress took an intelligent interest in the problems of federal employment. Of all the present congressmen, only one—Robert Ramspeck of Georgia—has shown such an interest. The attitudes of the rest range from indifference to frank contempt. As a result, government pay scales are notoriously low, and any bill designed to harass or discriminate against government workers is almost sure to pass with whoops of glee.

Worst of all, Congress has perpetuated the basic flaw in the original Civil Service Act. The commission is still an independent agency, entirely divorced from the normal structure of government. Although it wields great power it is responsible to no one. It serves only as a kind of decrepit watch-dog, which growls at the regular departments, but seldom tries to help them get their job done.

IV

It can be argued, in all seriousness, that Congress would do well to wipe out Civil Service, hide, horns, and tallow, and go back to the old-fashioned spoils system. . . .

Such a forthright return to the patronage system would, however, be a pretty drastic step—probably more drastic than is actually necessary. Before junking Civil Service entirely, maybe Congress should consider replacing the 1883 jalopy with a 1945 model.

The blueprint for a modern and workable Civil Service is already at hand. It was drawn up in 1937, after months of careful study, by a group of experts from outside the government known as the Committee on Administrative Management. The committee's suggestions were warmly endorsed by most of the recognized authorities in this field, and the President urged Congress to put them into effect immediately. As usual, Congress wasn't interested, and nothing happened.

These proposals are still as sensible as they were eight years ago and even more urgently needed. They call for four major reforms:

1. The present commission should be abolished, along with its whole collec-

tion of red tape and the senescent bureaucrats who weave it. (These gentlemen should be permitted to leave Washington quietly, in spite of a widespread demand among other government workers that they be tarred, feathered, and ridden out of town on their own filing cabinets.)

2. Each agency should be permitted to hire its own help. They should be chosen strictly on merit, with all political influence ruled out, on the same basis which TVA now is using so successfully. Every department would then be able to get a competent personnel staff to replace its present herd of second-raters—it could attract good men because it could give them real responsibility.

3. A single Federal Personnel Administrator, responsible directly to the President, would lay down over-all policies for the various agencies, and see to it that they are carried out. (He would *not* try to enforce a multitude of petty rules.) His office also could carry on the few functions of the present commission which really need to be centralized—such as handling retirement funds, arranging transfers, and pooling the recruitment of minor employees.

4. A part-time, unpaid, non-political board should be set up to keep a wary eye on the administrator and on the personnel operations of the agencies. From time to time it might suggest general policies or standards. Its main job, however, would be to look out for the public interest, and make sure that the new, decentralized merit system actually worked with a minimum of political interference. (It would of course be impossible, and probably undesirable, to get a scheme which would be entirely free of politics. The present setup certainly is not—the whims of a senator now are treated with religious deference by nearly all Washington personnel men, from the commission down.)

These changes, plus a number of minor reforms suggested by the Committee on Administrative Management, should result in an immediate and substantial saving for the taxpayer. By eliminating the present overlapping and duplication between the functions of the Civil Service Commission and those of the agency personnel offices, it should make possible a sharp reduction in the total number of personnel men in Washington. What Dr. Reeves describes as the "elaborate, time-consuming, and costly reports" now prepared at the commission's behest could be dispensed with; every week, according to my rough estimates, this should save 1,328,772 forms, Green Sheets, affidavits, and classification charts, thus releasing from bondage whole regiments of typists. Moreover, many an expensive subterfuge could be abandoned. A department could put a new man on the regular payroll the day it needed him, for example, instead of hiring him as a "temporary consultant" at $25 a day during the months it takes for his appointment papers to trickle through the commission.

Far more important, however, would be the gains in speed and efficiency throughout the entire government. Offices no longer would be demoralized by the annual ordeal of efficiency ratings. Transfers and promotions might come through on schedule. Administrators could spend their time administering, instead of practicing the mumbo-jumbo of the Civil Service liturgy. Men of stature might then be more willing to enter the public service, and the machinery of government perhaps could cope a little more adequately with the unprecedented loads which are being thrust upon it.

———◆———

In the midst of the Second World War a group of former students of Professor Charles E. Merriam, a great seminal mind in American political science, cooperated in producing a book of essays honoring the teacher who had inspired them. In tribute to the firm faith in the future of the "values of democracy" taught them by Professor Merriam the theme and title of the book was *The Future of Government in the United States.*

One of the essays included in the book is by Professor Leonard D. White, who for nearly a generation has been an outstanding writer in public administration—in fact, he had much to do with its establishment as an independent field of study. This essay, titled "The Public Service of the Future," is an attempt to project the development of the public service in coming decades. The following selection is one of the seven parts of this essay, the part dealing with the personnel aspects of the public service.

Professor White's prediction of "the shape of things to come" can now be compared to the shape which is actually in process of emerging. Does it "stand up"? Query, to what extent, if at all, is Professor White's essay a statement of what he *hopes* will happen, rather than simple prediction?

The essay is rich fare, and many paragraphs could be—in fact, are—the subject of volumes. Two matters, however, may be singled out for special attention (some are dealt with more fully below).

One of these is the proper role of the lawyer in administration. By long tradition the lawyer has great weight in public administration in America, and he often is in a position of high administrative authority. Ought the lawyer's role in administration be reduced in importance? Are the claims to authority of the one trained in public administration superior to the lawyer's? For what manner of position? Why?

The other matter is the status and function of civil service unions. Is the *unionization* of government service inconsistent with its *professionalization?* By what principles can a civil service union's right to strike be determined? What implications does civil service unionization have for the political system of a country—and vice versa?

The Public Service of the Future *

LEONARD D. WHITE

It is clear that the American public service will continue to be affected by . . . tendencies which have been at work for many years—tendencies that are largely indigenous and only indirectly related to or affected by the international scene or the shifting balance between the center and the extremities of our federal system. Science, the professions, technology, and management press steadily toward the technical improvement of public administration; localism, humanitarianism, and "politics" tend to delay the emergence of forms of organization which seem technically superior but which run counter to deep-seated American preferences. The effect of world-competition, military and commercial alike, will be to favor the technicians in the decades to come.

In this section are recounted some of the probable impacts of present forces on the public service of the next ten or twenty years—the further extension of the merit system, the gradual demarcation of broad categories of responsibility, and the proportionate increase in numbers and influence of the scientists, professional men, and managers; the confirmation and progressive acceptance of a career service; and the steady increase in the importance of civil service unions, leading to a re-examination of their place in the administrative system.

1. *Extension and evolution of the merit system.* The formal acceptance of the doctrines of the merit system will progress against the persistent, if misguided, hostility of most active politicians and with not infrequent local retrogressions. This drive is in full stream, energized by the National League of Women Voters, the Junior Chamber of Commerce, and other groups which have joined their strength to the National Civil Service Reform League and to organized public service employees. New impetus will be given by the exigencies of defense, war, and reconstruction. The goal was set in 1937 in the words of the President's Committee on Administrative Management—to extend the merit system "upward, outward and downward" to cover all but policy-determining positions. By 1941 this goal had been substantially achieved in the national government. By 1950 we may expect that all sections of state and local governments receiving federal funds will also be firmly settled under the aegis of a merit system, required as a condition of federal aid. At least thirty-five states should have adopted state-wide merit systems by 1950, perhaps more; for the states cannot much longer refuse to see the fatal implications to their statehood of incompetence, partisanship, and inertia. Most middle-sized and large cities now have a merit system; by

---

* From *The Future of Government in the United States*, Leonard D. White (ed.) (Chicago: 1942), part IV, pp. 192–217 (pp. 200–209 reprinted here). Reprinted by permission of the University of Chicago Press.

1950 the exceptions will be rare, and standards of administration will have improved.

By 1960 some backward areas will still cling obstinately to "partisan and personal administration"; they will be enclaves—objects of curiosity and contempt; and when they have gone, in Merriam's phrase, "they will not be missed. No monuments will be erected to them."

The consequences of this achievement will be great. They will involve the proper recognition of skill and competence; they will create an instrument for the execution of policy ever more adequate to its tasks; they will obviate the dangers of a weak administration, which "can neither advance nor retreat successfully [but] can merely muddle"; they will require new foundations for the political party and a type of political leadership still too uncommon; they will assure to the executive "the chief means by which an intelligent and sustained initiative" can be maintained—"a relatively permanent and experienced corps of administrators associated with the executive."

Along with the extension of the merit system there will be an increasing proportion of scientific, professional, and technical personnel in the public service. Their proportion in the whole mass of public employees was very small in 1900 but has been steadily mounting. We may predict with confidence that it will continue to expand. In the decade 1930–40 the economists were firmly established in the government service; future decades may see rising groups of professional administrators, professional public relations experts, broadcasting technicians, experts in administrative referenda, planning consultants, public opinion poll experts, "personnelists," budgeteers, and others in government service. Some of them may fail to achieve respectability or congressional confidence, but the number, variety, and importance of the professional, scientific, and technical groups are certain to increase disproportionately to the clerical and manipulative corps.

It is to be expected also that new types of organizational lines will be drawn in the large public services of the future, reflecting the major levels of responsibility involved in conducting the public business. These differentials will be of slow growth. The process may be initiated by the recognition of an administrative corps as a functional branch—a corps whose membership will be derived from varied sources but whose responsibilities will be segregated in theory and practice in the interest of effective administration. This evolution may be anticipated with some confidence, although it will not occur at once or rapidly; there may be stubborn opposition. The eventual consequences for the improvement of the managerial corps are great.

The gradual segregation of an administrative corps will set in motion other differentials. The business-administration group (purchasing, printing, contracting for office services, selling, management of real estate, and the like) will be comprehended as performing a special function different from that of overhead management, requiring special skills but different from those of overhead management—or, to use the term coined by Messrs. Brownlow, Gulick, and Merriam, "administrative management."

The place of the professional group in this gradual clarification of function in the total task of administration is far from clear now, and its future trends are obscure. That each of the professions (excepting perhaps theology) will place its special competence at the service of government in larger measure seems certain. That the tone of the public service will be elevated as the professions impress more and more upon it their professional ideals is clear. But the extent of the contribution of the several groups to overhead management is not clear, and present trends give no conclusive clue to the future.

It is also likely that the function of middle management will be more sharply differentiated in the future public service. The function can be readily identified, midway between the manifold clerical and specialist operations dealing with individual cases, on the one hand, and, on the other, the operations of top management dealing with generalized situations. It is a sector or zone of responsibility well marked in most national public services. Its personnel is often immobilized in other countries but has never been and is unlikely to be in the United States by other than considerations of personal competence and adaptability.

In short, it seems probable that a slow and gradual differentiation of function in the public service may develop, leading to a clearer recognition of the special tasks of higher administration, of business management, of the professions, of middle management, and possibly of other management zones. This trend will not carry with it any implication of barriers between these respective groups other than those naturally flowing from the nature of the work to be done. Much needless and ill-founded apprehension has been stirred by failure to appreciate that a zone of operations can be specialized and attention given to its improvement without introducing a closed personnel system which smacks of caste or artificiality. In order to keep open the door of opportunity in harmony with cherished American ideals it is not necessary to oppose the effective organization of different governmental tasks.

2. *Development of public service careers.* Closely related to differentiation of function is the further evolution and general acceptance of a public service career system, eventually on a genuinely national scale and contributory to an international public service. The concept was formulated in 1933 by the Commission of Inquiry on Public Service Personnel, of which Charles Merriam was an active member: "We recommend . . . that steps shall be taken to make public employment a worthwhile life work, with entrance to the service open and attractive to young men and women of capacity and character, and with opportunity of advancement through service and growth to posts of distinction and honor." Some branches of the service, especially the scientific and professional corps, have already quietly achieved this status and exemplify the rich assets which a responsible career service provides to a democratic government.

Two other branches of the national service are now ripe for action: the higher administrative and the legal. Recommendations of the President's Committee on Civil Service Improvement (1941) for career-service organization at these two vital points drew their inspiration from the Commission of Inquiry on Public Service Personnel and the President's Committee on Administrative Management. Top management is especially suited for a career service; its function is essentially the same in headquarters and field, in federal, state, and metropolitan governments; and, with its outposts in planning, budget, personnel, and procedures, it perhaps might become one of the first truly national career services. It seems likely that great strides will be taken in this direction in the next decade and that the goal might be substantially achieved at the end of two decades. Certain it is that the "forward march of American democracy at this point of our history depends more upon effective management than upon any other single factor"—words written in the Report of the President's Committee on Administrative Management in 1937, while the world-crisis could still be thought avoidable.

A career service in higher administration will be facilitated by the successful outcome of the experiments now in process under the direction of L. L. Thurstone for the purpose of identifying the mental traits that constitute administrative ability. If it may be assumed that such traits exist, that they can be identified, and that individuals can be tested to discover to what degree they are possessed, the foundation is then laid for the scientific selection of a future administrative corps. To this corps would be admitted at an early age for training and development persons who demonstrably had promise of administrative success; from it would be excluded persons who by claim of seniority or friendship might aspire to middle- and higher-bracket management and directing positions.

With respect to the place of lawyers in the future administrative corps, we cannot speak with confidence. Law and politics have traditionally been close companions, thus bringing lawyers to the very seat of authority. Law and administration are inseparable; the legal adviser must be consulted by the administrator at every important turn. A lawyer's veto of a proposed course of action on grounds of illegality forces fresh consideration by the administrative staff. Both lawyers and administrators find it difficult to put limits to the role of the lawyer in the public service.

The gradual formation of a body of administrators marked by tested native endowment and special training may therefore encounter the contrary tendency (inspired by propinquity, authority, and personal competence) toward the acceptance of the lawyer as a principal source of top administrative personnel. From other professions and from the law many high officials will always be drawn—that is taken for granted. But only the lawyers among the many professions (excluding the special case of public education) seem likely to be able to challenge successfully the gradual establishment of a specialist corps of administrators. Without derogation to the ability, loyalty, and idealism of the legal profession, we may hope that as a group they will not monopolize the top administrative positions in 1950 or 1960.

With respect to both top administrators and high-ranking lawyers the problem of assignment (or disposition) subsequent to a change in administration may become bothersome, unless new ideas are put into circulation. If one party remains steadily in control of national affairs, the problem is minimized; but, if there should occur a rapid alternation of parties or sharp fluctuations in national policy, an intolerable strain may be put on the capacity of administrators and lawyers to adjust. The country ought not to lose the services of these highly trained and experienced experts, but a party bearing contradictory policies to its predecessor is unlikely to accept fully the loyalty and reliability of the principal advisers of its opponents.

The issue has been resolved in England, within the framework of a basically homogeneous policy pursued by all parties, by depending upon a long-established tradition of loyal service to the government of the day. It is doubtful whether even in England this tradition could withstand major breaks in policy. In our immediate future, permanence of tenure of these two top-ranking groups should be assured by law and respected by all parties. No party, however, need feel obliged to keep each such official in the identical post which he occupied by appointment under another party. This pool of talent, legal and administrative, is at the disposition of the whole government, not merely a department or other agency; transfer should be easy and flexible, both to conserve the intellectual integrity of individuals and to provide to politically responsible officials advisers with whom they can work effectively.

There may remain instances in which no appropriate use can be made of officials in the highest administrative and legal classifications. To meet this situation we may suggest the usefulness of a legal and administrative group acting in the role of "His Majesty's Opposition," for the time being in a nonactive status known analogously to the French as *en disponibilité*. That they could be useful in an advisory and critical capacity there can be no doubt. They would thus remain in close contact with public affairs and in due course of time would resume an active status—not necessarily only subsequent to a further change of party. The purpose is to conserve an administrative resource in which a substantial investment has been made and to strength the career service by emphasizing its continuity of achievement.

3. *Civil service unions*. Correlative with the augmented importance of the scientific, professional, and administrative corps there will be during the next decade or two a steady increase in the importance of civil service unions. Variously looked upon as threats to the sovereignty of the state or as pillars of a new type of social organization, they are not likely in the next twenty years to depart far from their immediate task of conserving the economic status of their members. In this area they will play a considerable, if relatively restricted, role. At times they will speak belligerently, and in some instances they may act belligerently, but in general their influence will be exerted along conservative lines. Most of what they want can be had only from appropriating bodies; these popular assemblies can-

not safely be antagonized; and consequently the more extreme types of union pressure on management are unlikely to develop.

Civil service unions are now harassed and weakened by the divisions in the American labor movement and by schisms indigenous to their own ranks. One of their principal problems in the next decade—perhaps much longer—will be to harmonize their internal differences and present a common program backed by the full weight of their members and their affiliations. The history of civil service unions in other countries confirms over a half-century of experience in the United States—that such unity of purpose and organization is a teasing will-o'-the-wisp.

The extension of public ownership and management over utilities already unionized is certain to present perplexing problems, of which the New York subway system is only an early example. We shall probably first attempt to develop the distinction between a governmental and a business enterprise, following the example of France in the decade 1890–1900. The collapse of this solution in France does not presage success among a people less dialectically gifted than the French. Whither the course of events thereafter, no man can now predict.

More imaginative prophets may profess to visualize the day when organized workers in government will seek and receive a formal share in management. I cannot share this expectancy, at least within the next two decades. In settling employment matters, workers will doubtless be consulted in increasing measure, and forms of consultation will become more firmly established. Organized workers may secure representation on the official agencies which administer their conditions of employment and may thus acquire advantageous observation posts from which better to protect their interests; they may be called upon as an interest group to elect their representatives to agencies dealing with their employment problems; but they are unlikely to acquire a controlling voice in the official bodies where they sit.

Less likely is it that organized civil service employees as such will seek for power in the settlement of the great substantive issues of public policy. Peace, war, or neutrality; aid to farmers, business, or exporters; regionalism, nationalism, or state rights; the stabilization of the economic cycle—these are problems which organized public employees are likely to eschew. The risks of embarking upon their public discussion are great: diversion of effort, internal conflict, outside criticism, and waste of resources. The possible gains are correspondingly slender. Such hazardous ventures are usually the outcome of irresistible urges or great ambitions on the part of a few "leaders" and consequently may not be avoided in full. But that organized civil service employees as a group and over the years will seek to determine substantive public policy unconnected with conditions of employment is not to be anticipated. A consultative voice in management problems, a deep concern with employment conditions, yes; but not more.

From time to time in our history as a nation the loyalty of public officers and employees has been a political issue and a problem in public administration (could it be one without being the other also?). In the period since the Second World War this problem has developed new dimensions and has entered an acute phase. As this is written, the problem is one of great gravity in our national life.

In the following brief selection the recent developments are neatly outlined and some of the major issues delineated. The author is Professor William Seal Carpenter of Princeton University, who was for seven years administrator of New Jersey's civil service system. The selection is from a recent book on *The Unfinished Business of Civil Service Reform*.

The issues are thorny. Is the distinction between "disloyal and subversive" *thoughts* and disloyal and subversive *actions* a realistic distinction? What different principles should apply in the public realm than in the private realm—remembering how "public" and "private" blend together in the Great Society, particularly in time of crisis? Do the determining principles differ in a democracy from in a dictatorship, or does the problem of security make the problem the same regardless of the official theory of government?

The "Loyalty" Issue *

WILLIAM SEAL CARPENTER

A . . . threat to the recruitment of the best young people for public employment looms on the horizon in the loyalty program sponsored by the federal government and now being duplicated in part by a number of the states. The federal government and the governments of at least forty-one states have long carried on their statute books laws covering subversive activities. Generally these laws dealt with sedition, and covered oral or printed utterances in which the state or the government is held in contempt and the people are encouraged to refuse obedience to its commands. A new and different policy was inaugurated in the Hatch Act of 1939 and reached its full flowering in Executive Order No. 9835, issued by President Truman on March 21, 1947. This policy undertakes to treat employees of the government as a special group with respect to the question of political loyalty.

The loyalty program which emerged under the aegis of the Hatch Act was designed to exclude from public employment any person who held "membership in any political party or organization which advocates the overthrow of our con-

---

* From *The Unfinished Business of Civil Service Reform* (Princeton: 1952), pp. 23–26. Reprinted by permission of the Princeton University Press.

stitutional form of government in the United States." Under the pressure of war conditions, Congress authorized the War and Navy Departments to dismiss summarily employees considered by the departments to be "bad security risks." In 1946 the same authority was extended to the Department of State. The Atomic Energy Act of 1946 contained a provision that no person should be employed by the agency until the Federal Bureau of Investigation had made an investigation and report upon the character, associations, and loyalty of the individual. Thus in peace and war the employees of certain "sensitive agencies" were to be subjected to special conditions of employment which were not applied to other federal employees and which were not related to the prohibitions contained in the Hatch Act. The way was thereby paved in legislative policy for the executive order of President Truman, which requires a loyalty investigation of every person entering the civilian employment of any department or agency of the executive branch of the government and which holds the head of each department and agency personally responsible for eliminating disloyal employees.

Executive Order No. 9835 was declared to have a two-fold objective: first, to afford the United States maximum protection against the infiltration of disloyal persons into the ranks of its employees; and second, to afford equal protection to the loyal employees of the government against unfounded accusations of disloyalty. Subsequently, on April 28, 1951, the President issued an executive order which recites: "The standard for the refusal of employment or the removal from employment in an executive department or agency on grounds relating to loyalty shall be that, on all the evidence, there is a reasonable doubt as to the loyalty of the person involved to the Government of the United States." Although the loyalty program grants the suspected employee a hearing, it does not provide that he shall be confronted by his accusers or afford him an opportunity to cross-examine them. Indeed, he may be refused an exact statement of the charges against him if for reasons of security specific charges are deemed unwise. The process is not a judicial process.

Nevertheless, the United States Supreme Court on April 30, 1951, upheld in the case of *Bailey v. Richardson* a decision of the United States Circuit Court of Appeals for the District of Columbia (122 Fed. Rep. 2nd Series, 46). The court vindicated the procedures pursued in the loyalty program and adhered to the doctrine that, except to ensure compliance with statutory requirements, the courts will not review the action of federal executive officials in dismissing executive employees. On the same day the Supreme Court in another case ruled that the Attorney General could make no public listing of organizations declared to be communistic without affording them a hearing. "This is the first time," said Mr. Justice Jackson, "this court has held rights of individuals subordinate and inferior to those of organized groups. It is justice turned bottom-side up."

From the standpoint of recruitment for public employment, the question is not whether the loyalty program is legally sound but whether it is politically and administratively desirable. There can be no dissent from the preamble to Executive

Order No. 9835 that "it is of vital importance that persons employed in the federal service be of complete and unswerving loyalty to the United States." At the same time, the government requires for the performance of its services the most capable and intelligent citizens obtainable. There has already been much criticism that government service tends largely to attract unimaginative men and women who lack the resources for any kind of work except routine tasks under supervision. While this criticism is unfair to thousands of public employees, it must be admitted that administrative policies which impose restraints upon the freedom of thought and expression will divert from government employment the very people whose loss can be least afforded. The dissenting opinion in *Bailey v. Richardson* remarked: "No doubt some [loyalty] boards are quite aware that unconventional views and conduct have no tendency to indicate disloyalty. But the fact remains that some boards imagine the contrary. This fact is only too well known. It puts government employees under economic and social pressure to protect their jobs and reputations by expressing in words and conduct only the most orthodox opinions on political, economic, and social questions."

The government of the United States and the governments of the eight or more states which have enacted laws requiring loyalty oaths already have ample statutory authority to refuse employment to persons who are guilty of disloyal conduct. Actions which are subversive in character can be punished readily under existing laws whether the perpetrators are already public employees or merely candidates for public employment. What the loyalty program seeks to accomplish is punishment for harboring thoughts which are disloyal and subversive. The development of administrative procedures which will accurately evaluate and appraise the thoughts of men has thus far defied human ingenuity.

It is a fantastic situation in which an organization is entitled to a judicial hearing before it can be branded as subversive while an employee can be removed and stigmatized as disloyal without being confronted by his accusers or being furnished with specific charges. The right to public employment is not drawn into question, because no such right exists. But the right to reputation is cherished by everybody. Unless the procedures of the loyalty program in federal and state governments can be so constructed that the reputations of loyal citizens will be adequately safeguarded, there will be little inducement for able and intelligent men and women to enter public employment.

———————◆———————

In many ways the following selection is a close companion of the preceding one. It too deals with the question of loyalty. It is focused, however, not upon the problem of ideological defection, but upon ordinary moral honesty and pecuniary integrity. Like the ideological problem, it has plagued the public service throughout our history. Like the ideological problem, it has recently been magnified and intensified. In either case, it is no exaggeration to say that the future of American democracy will depend upon its satisfactory resolution.

Mr. Herbert Emmerich, the author, has been director of the Public Administration Clearing House since 1945. He is an outstanding figure in American public administration, having served with distinction in many and varying positions and having written a long list of significant essays and books. Mr. Emmerich addresses this essay to the members of the American Society for Public Administration through the medium of its official organ. As will be seen, the essay goes beyond its subject to sketch perceptively recent trends in the public service.

Query, has Mr. Emmerich, in his plea for perspective, achieved a true perspective, a genuinely balanced view? Or is he himself too close to the scene, too much a partisan, to achieve the objectivity he seeks? Has he left unstated any significant issues bearing upon his subject? Are his observations and suggestions in Part III sound?

A Scandal in Utopia *

HERBERT EMMERICH

The recent disclosures of serious irregularities in the management of our national revenue collection system should not pass unnoticed in the pages of this journal. The American Society for Public Administration, which publishes this *Review*, is dedicated to the advancement of the standards of honest and efficient public administration. We who constitute its membership cannot fail to be aroused by the apparent deterioration of a service which for many years has enjoyed a high reputation. When we add to these disclosures those made by the Senate committee headed by Senator Kefauver inquiring into the effect on local and state law enforcement agencies of commercialized interstate gambling syndicates, we must feel that a pretty thorough stock-taking is in order. It is appropriate for us to ask ourselves some searching questions about the state of American public administration in these critical times. It is important not only to put these occurrences in their proper perspective but to bend our energies to building upon the current interest in these matters to obtain lasting improvements in the public service in directions which many of us have been advocating for a long time. . . .

In approaching this unpleasant topic it seems to me that those engaged in government service must, in the interest of their profession, avoid two pitfalls. One pitfall is to allow government work as a vocation to be libeled by failing to supply facts when exaggerated and sensational generalizations are drawn from

* From *Public Administration Review*, Vol. 12 (Winter, 1952), pp. 1–9. Abridged. Reprinted by permission of the author and the *Public Administration Review*.

specific instances of wrongdoing. The other pitfall is to fail to admit the serious nature of these occurrences, the need for their correction, and the threat they constitute to the reputation and prestige of public administration.

Unfortunately these revelations come at an embarrassing time from both the domestic and the foreign points of view. At home we are engaged in a large mobilization effort to defend ourselves and the rest of the free world against a dangerous threat. The volume of public administration is expanding enormously. We are drafting young men for military service, spending great sums on defense and foreign aid, and taxing and regulating our citizens and private institutions to an extent never before attempted except in a period of all-out war. In the extraordinarily difficult task of administering these programs we need the best people we can get. It is a time which calls for confidence of citizens in their government so that they will be ready to accept the necessary sacrifices and prepared to render public service in the national effort. Not the least serious result of these disclosures, particularly when they are blown up into blanket defamations of the government service, is that they make harder the already difficult job of attracting and retaining the able people that the present great effort requires. . . .

The most serious danger of a wholesale castigation of the integrity of American democratic government at this stage of world history is the effect it will have on other countries. We cannot sell the extension of democratic government if we recklessly assert that its entire machinery is corrupt. Having pledged our resources to assist other nations in a common enterprise to resist aggression and to spread the areas of freedom and well-being by means of money, materials, and the exchange of skills and know-how through technical assistance, we find ourselves in a new role of telling other peoples how to manage their affairs and, indeed, how to govern themselves. The assumption has grown in the underprivileged nations that the United States, having demonstrated such great technical prowess and productivity, such a high standard of living, such generosity and dynamic leadership in world affairs, must have things pretty well managed at home. The fact is that we have an abundant supply of good things to export in addition to our industrial, scientific, and military skills and products. In the last fifty years we have made great improvements in the techniques of our public administration, and in this field we have many sound methods that other lands need and can profitably adapt to their own institutions. I refer not only to the techniques in general administrative management, but also to those in special fields such as education, health, and agriculture, in all of which we have very special, though not exclusive, contributions to make. Neither we nor the other free nations can afford to turn off this rich source of help because of what may seem to be "A Scandal in Utopia" to peoples who look with envy on our abundance and efficiency.

It is important to put the current revelations in proper perspective not only to insure a fair interpretation of their meaning abroad but also to gain the maximum benefit for the improvement of the public service. Robert Ramspeck, chairman of the United States Civil Service Commission, is rendering a valuable service by his "campaign of facts." He is insisting that while the necessary steps are taken to correct the situation, the revelations not be allowed to become a wholesale castigation of the federal service, which is preponderantly honest, able, and industrious.

It occurs to me that three approaches may be helpful in getting a proper perspective in our thinking about the current scandals in the government. One is the historical approach, another is through analysis of the environment in which government operates, and a third is through an assessment of postwar trends in American public administration.

II

I believe the point can be made that we have come a long way in increasing the respect of citizens for the public service and in raising the standards which they expect it to uphold. The very things that are now causing surprise and indignation as deviations from the standard were at many times in our history unfortunately taken for granted and considered normal operating procedure. We have only to remember the low standards prevailing in the latter part of the nineteenth century to perceive the great change that has come about. In the period of westward expansion, with its ruthless exploitation of immigrant labor and natural resources, predatory interests bought state legislatures, which in turn elected United States senators, who in turn "appointed" unqualified political hacks to government posts. The federal service, with some notable exceptions, was generally held in low esteem—a place for hangers-on and incompetents who were supposed to run the errands and do the favors for special interests through a system of political brokerage. As the big cities grew and as frontier towns sprang up there was a similar decline in the moral tone of local government. It took the assassination of President Garfield to dramatize to the nation the evils of the patronage system and to give the pioneer reformers a chance to get their plans adopted.

The British as usual were ahead of us in governmental reform, but lest we get an inferiority complex we may recall that the British patronage and rotten borough systems lasted into the nineteenth century and were not eliminated until after the Civil Service and the Reform Acts were passed. Even in more recent times there have been occasional lapses on the part of British public men, but when these occur we do not jump to the conclusion that because of individual transgressions everyone in His Majesty's magnificent service is venal and corrupt.

To compare the present state of public indignation to the relative callousness of bygone days we need not go back to the scandals of the Grant administration, or the "embalmed beef" disclosures after the Spanish American War, or the Teapot Dome revelations involving two Cabinet officers in the Harding administration. Most of us can still recall the nightmare of the prohibition era of the 1920's when corruption in large segments of all levels of government was ac-

companied by a general spirit of lawlessness in our communities and a general
cynicism among citizens toward government. All levels of government and of
society were besmirched in this disgraceful era in our history. Not the least of the
good results of the Twenty-first Amendment were the tremendous improvements
it brought about in the local, state, and federal services and in the reversal of
attitude of citizens toward law-enforcement and other government officials. The
fact that we have reacted so indignantly to the present crop of disclosures is evidence of the high standard of expectation we have reached in regard to the integrity of public servants. We are shocked not because we have a low regard for
public officials, but because we expect them to have so high a standard of
integrity.

On the positive side, it may be noted that in the period of greatly enlarged
governmental activities and expenditures of the New Deal and World War II
there was evidence of a greatly improved standard of public administration. In
spite of the large delegations of authority to the executive during the Roosevelt
administration, both in peace and in war, dozens of investigating committees disclosed practically no scandals and none of major national proportion. . . .

A brief examination of the environment in which public administration operates in our democracy will also help to put the current examples of official misconduct in proper perspective. In a country that is committed to the largest possible measure of individual freedom and initiative and variety in its private enterprises, public administration cannot operate in a vacuum. It must touch, and be
touched by, private interests. Indeed, with the growth of big government, which
regulates, taxes, finances, and contracts with private enterprise and litigates with
private interests, these contacts are more pervasive and important than ever
before. In some instances the government service is a training ground for, and
steppingstone to, remunerative private careers. Government in the United States
operates in a "business civilization," as James Truslow Adams has described our
culture. Men going into government from business must understand that certain
practices that are accepted in large parts of the business world, such as liberal
entertainment and exchange of gifts, are not accepted in the official world. It is
essential that persons working for the government at all times be above suspicion of favoritism to their friends, to their political backers, or to persons who
might advance their future careers.

In a democracy the public service must operate in a political atmosphere. It is
right and proper that members of Congress and congressional committees should
be interested in facts regarding government policies and procedures. They have
the right and the duty to scrutinize and review both policy and practices. In the
determination of policy, the special needs of industrial and occupational interest
groups and of widely varying localities and regions cannot be ignored; but in the
application of policy to particular cases, these special claims frequently cannot
be granted. Here there is need for continuing vigilance and for perhaps a degree
or kind of administrative awareness we have not yet demonstrated

In considering the environment in which government operates, we must look at the problems created by the organized professions and guilds, their pressures for representation and for special exemptions from the merit system. The lawyers have enjoyed some special exemptions from civil service rules, but they are by no means the only group that needs to reconsider its relationship to government service.

It has also become a part of the environment of our democracy for many persons to serve their government part-time or for short tours of duty. There is need in a free society for this kind of mobility between public and private employment. It is particularly important in times of crisis. Today we are again begging persons whose skills are particularly needed in the defense effort to come into the government service. In recruiting such persons for short periods of service or for part-time consulting work, we must insure that merit and fitness are the sole criteria in selection. Such appointments, however, do not involve tenure rights, and they do not need to be made through formal competitive tests. Once a person of this type has entered on duty, however, he should no more represent an interest group than he should represent a local political club. He is in the service of the government of the United States and while in that service he owes his undivided loyalty to it and to the standards which have come to characterize it. There is a much more subtle form of disloyalty and corruption than the obvious forms that we generally hear about, and it is to a degree an unconscious one. It is a lack of loyalty to the general interest resulting from conflicting specialized loyalties.

A third way of getting a better perspective on the significance of current scandals in the government service is to try to measure or assess the postwar trends in American public administration. There are two distinct postwar trends that can be identified; the first gets on the front page, the second rarely gets any notice of importance.

Although there has been less "letdown" after World War II in the standards of public service and in citizen morale than after other wars in our history, there has been a trend in this direction. In addition to the government scandals, there have been athletic scandals and an unusual number of bank defalcations. We are still reaping some of the fruits of the prohibition days, and the scions of the bootleggers have turned to commercialized gambling and other shady businesses which have sought and sometimes found special protection through bribing hitherto honest but underpaid police departments and undermanned law-enforcement agencies. There has been an abundance of private employment at higher rates of pay and with less danger to health and reputation than the hazardous government service offers. This situation has naturally drawn off talented men from Washington. There have been cases where the President, who has made earnest and persistent efforts to find good men to fill important jobs, has mistakenly shown the same loyalty to persons deficient in a proper sense of public deportment that he has shown to outstanding men of high character that he thought were being unfairly attacked. Some of the young New Dealers may have been

fanatically hostile toward business in the excitement of the early relief and recovery days. As a reaction to this feeling, in the postwar period the pendulum in
some cases may have swung too far to the other extreme.

But when one considers the enormous expansion of governmental services in
every field, the amount of delegated discretion, the vast sums of money for loans,
guarantees, contracts, and subsidies, and the extent to which governmental action
touches private interest at every point, it is remarkable how free federal officials
have been of wrongdoing and favoritism in comparison with previous times. The
sensational emphasis given to the backsliding trend is partly because it has news
value, partly because of partisan considerations; but I believe the indignant reaction is also an evidence of the higher standard of public morality and expectation of governmental integrity to which we have become accustomed.

The positive and less glamorized and publicized trend in postwar public administration in the United States is as clearly identifiable as the negative one.
This is the trend of a really astonishing amount of improvement at all levels of
government that has taken place since 1945.

In our cities there has been a veritable upsurge of administrative and governmental improvement. Citizen organizations and professional associations of public officials have both contributed to this progressive trend by the interchange of
information on improved methods and by the stimulation of continuing programs of improvement. In city after city citizen campaigns have led to new
charters and improved forms of government. The number of cities with the
council-manager form of government has doubled since 1945; today 1060 cities
are operating under this plan. Other cities have adopted new charters with interesting innovations; Philadelphia and Boston are the most recent examples of large
cities that have made thoroughgoing changes in both structure and personnel.
Every big city but Chicago has eliminated the ward system. Important steps have
been taken in city-county consolidation and in improved metropolitan and regional
governmental arrangements. Between the last two censuses over 10,000 small
local taxing units were abolished. Great forward strides in the quality of
municipal service have resulted from the adoption of better techniques in many
specialized fields.

The states have not lagged in undertaking administrative improvement. In
recent years a number have completely renovated outmoded constitutions or have
adopted amendments to open the way to improvements in administration. Some
thirty-five states have had their Little Hoover Commissions; their recommendations are resulting in many reforms.

In recent years there has been a further great decline in the patronage system
at the state and local levels and a great improvement in the way in which the
merit system is administered. In spite of the headline rackets that the Kefauver
Committee has uncovered, today, in 1952, we need no longer apologize with
Lincoln Steffens for "the shame of the cities," or deplore with James Bryce the
failure of local government in the American commonwealth. . . .

Even at the much flagellated federal level the postwar period has been, on balance, one of progress. The work of the President's Committee on Administrative Management (the Brownlow Committee) and of the Commission on Organization of the Executive Branch (the Hoover Commission) has provided the impetus for continuing executive and legislative action for improvement. It is not generally appreciated what earnest cooperation President Truman gave to ex-President Hoover's work and the extent to which he has continued to follow up on the recommendations of the Hoover Commission. A large percentage of these recommendations has been adopted and installed according to the testimony of the Citizens' Committee on the Hoover Report—testimony that cannot be said to be biased in favor of the present administration. In addition to reforms in the fields of administrative management, fiscal operations, procurement, and personnel, there has been real progress in the centralization of policy and decentralization of day-to-day work. Department after department and bureau after bureau have made managerial studies and have followed them up with reorganizations and the installation of improved methods and procedures. The modernization of procedures in such agencies as the Patent Office, the Bureau of Land Management, the Customs Bureau, Bureau of Reclamation, and the Coast Guard may be cited as just a few examples of this trend. The archaic federal accounting system is in the process of being thoroughly renovated through the joint accounting project, in which the General Accounting Office is working with the cooperation of the Treasury Department and the Bureau of the Budget to accomplish one of the biggest managerial reforms in federal executive history. In all of these reforms, the responsible officials have taken the initiative and have enlisted the help of advisory committees, task forces, special consultants, management engineers, and professional associations.

There is still, of course, vast room for improvement at all levels, and day-by-day efforts of citizen associations and professional organizations of officials, working with the aid of an enlightened press, will be needed to achieve it. . . .

III

In the light of these perspectives, what can we do about the current scandals in government? How can we emphasize the positive trend in public administration and arrest the negative trend? I think the answer lies in two directions. One is to accelerate the rate of putting into practice the things we already know about the art and science of administration and the other is to accelerate the rate of practical research and invention on the points about which we are ignorant. This article does not pretend to exhaust the avenues of approach, but the story would not have an ending if I did not give one or two examples of what I mean.

The tone of the front office sets the tone of any administration, and I cannot refrain from criticizing from an administrative point of view some of the things that have happened in the front office in the Truman administration that have generally been attacked from a political point of view. I have served the government during the Truman administration as a consultant and as a member of the President's Advisory Committee on Management and have come to respect the many good things that have been done. But the tone in some sections of the front office has not been good.

After 150 years without help, the President of the United States in 1939 was given a White House Staff and an Executive Office to assist him, and they, like Caesar's wife, must be above suspicion. Even more important than the obvious improprieties which have been publicized is the danger that the top office will intervene in departmental operations. It is not enough that the Executive Office should set a tone and create an atmosphere for the departments and agencies to emulate in respect to honesty; the members of the Executive Office must lean over backward to be sure of "operating at the proper level," as Dean Paul Appleby puts it. The Executive Office and the White House staff cannot escape having political duties and responsibilities. But in the main these responsibilities must be confined to the policy field and the President must insist that his staff refrain from becoming centers of influence or back doors for special pressures in individual cases. Nor should the President have a gestapo at his disposal for gumshoe work or surveillance in the departments and agencies of the government. The fine work that this administration has done to foster management improvement and to decentralize responsibility must not be impaired by intrusions from above into day-to-day operations for which department and agency heads are responsible.

The Secretaries of the departments, in turn, have a duty to create an atmosphere which the bureaus and agencies should emulate and to avoid interfering in detailed operations. As the managerial heads of large operating staffs, they also need a system of managerial audits of the performance of the agencies under their supervision. Here again I do not advocate a kind of detective service to uncover irregularities that a good current accounting audit should uncover, but constructive managerial surveys, audits, and inspections carried on by a qualified staff at the department or large bureau level. Such surveys should come to the attention of the bureau chiefs and department heads and should serve to encourage good practices and to discourage poor practices.

I think it has been amply demonstrated that at the operating level the patronage system is obsolete and dangerous. A regional or field office is particularly susceptible to political pressures, and the revelations in the Bureau of Internal Revenue have once more indicated that even career people with civil service status are not immune to temptation when the collector or the deputy collector, who are their bosses, have political loyalties other than to their chief in Washington. Whatever the shortcomings of our present civil service system, recent events lead me to conclude that we need to extend civil service at the regional and field level.

Perhaps the time has come also for another special review of the status of lawyers in the government, both in Washington and in the field. It may be that we are ready for the forward steps of selecting United States attorneys and their staffs through a merit system and of giving them permanent status.

Better methods are needed in recruiting and training temporary and part-time executive and technical personnel, both for home assignments and for overseas missions. Hit-and-miss recruiting and inadequate briefing methods are now used for such personnel. Increasingly, attention is being given to the suggestion that a United States civilian reserve corps be established to secure and develop this kind of talent.

On the side of research and invention, I believe we need a thorough reconsideration of the training and indoctrination that government employees receive upon entrance into the public service and at critical periods in their careers. I know of no governmental in-service training program that discusses the environment in which government operates or the points of ethics involved in standards of good government practice. The code of ethics that has been recommended by the Subcommittee on the Establishment of a Commission on Ethics in Government would be useful as a starting point, but each agency has special problems the answers to which are not so obvious as one might think, and even within an agency ethical problems vary among the various fields of work. I have seen many pure scientists and rigid executives enter the government service determined to "have nothing to do with politics or politicians," and I have seen many inexperienced persons enter the government service assuming that it was smart and accepted governmental practice to do favors for elected officials and their friends. New government officials are presumed to know the rules, and there is surprising lack of indoctrination on proper conduct. There are surprisingly few departmental conferences to develop or to teach desirable standards of conduct. Here there is room both for research and for invention. We need new methods to overcome these unrealistic assumptions, for the good government servant must have an unusual combination of flexibility and firmness. He must understand the principle of compromise that underlies the policy-making processes of a democratic state and appreciate that it does not involve a compromise of principle in the application of policy to individual cases.

Chapter 9

Education and Recruitment

A bureaucracy tends to reflect the society of which it is a part and which it serves and governs. The society's morals and manners, its class and family structure, its economic and educational systems, can be read in the mirror of its civil service by the careful observer.

Nearly the entire range of professions, occupations, and specializations characteristic of modern society is represented in the civil service of the modern state. The performance of most of the great variety of public employees is much the same in public as in private employment—surveyors survey, welders weld, and typists type. The problem of "education for the public service," then, spans nearly the breadth of society, in the sense that no public service can rise far above its educational base. On the other hand, in a society that is predominantly "private enterprise" education has many other aspects, interests, and objectives than training persons for public employment.

In recent years, accompanying the rise of public administration as a separate field of study—and indeed inseparable from it—is the question whether it is possible and desirable to train persons for the public service as such. Granting the large area of overlapping between public and private education and occupations, is there nevertheless a separate, specific governmental or administrative function? If so, in what sense and precisely how can persons be educated, in advance of performance, to perform the function well?

A great deal of controversy, much of it heated, has raged around the issues involved here. The issues themselves are highly complex, and the area of confusion is at least as large as the area of controversy. A listing of some of the major questions indicates the possibilities for both confusion and controversy: Is there a difference between education and training? To what extent ought these to be performed in the schools? To what extent after entering employment? Granting that leadership and vision ought to characterize administrators, can these qualities be taught? If there is in high administration a synthesizing or "generalist" function as against the specialization typical of large-scale enterprise, what is it? Can people be taught to be "generalists"—paradoxically, specialists in generalization? If there is a separate, specific generalist or administrative function, in what respects does it differ between public administration and private administration?

The following two brief essays introduce and review some aspects of these questions. In them, two distinguished figures argue opposite sides of the question, "Shall we train for public administration?" Arguing for such training is the late William E. Mosher, Dean of the Maxwell School of Citizenship and Public Affairs. Arguing against the attempt is Robert M. Hutchins, through the thirties and forties President of the University of Chicago and long a controversial figure in American education because of his strong emphasis upon general and cultural education as against specialized and professional training.

Shall We Train for Public Administration? *
"Impossible"

ROBERT M. HUTCHINS

I hold that it is impossible for a college to prepare men directly and specifically for public life. This is partly the result of the nature of public life and partly the result of the nature of a college. Public life is concerned with action adapted to immediate concrete situations. It is impossible to learn how to deal with immediate concrete situations except by dealing with them. It is impossible to import these situations into a college curriculum.

The medical schools have had a bad effect on educational theory. Whenever anybody wants to train somebody for something in college, he says he wants to do for that field what the medical schools have done for medicine. In the medical schools one learns by doing precisely the things one does in practice. The patients are sick. The professors and their students are trying to cure them. To accomplish the same thing in public administration we should have to have the professors actually engaged in the public service and the students learning as their assistants.

I am, for my sins, an educational administrator. I ask myself what I would do if I were called on to give a course that would make my pupils good college administrators. I might tell them anecdotes of my harrowing experiences. This might while away a week or so. I might give them my impressions of professors and trustees. This might amuse them a little longer. I might recite the glorious past and amazing present of American education, something they could read in any standard text over the weekend. But if I wanted to teach them anything that had intellectual content and required intellectual effort (and these surely are the tests of a curriculum) I would have to teach them something that was not educational administration and which consequently I was not qualified to teach. The fact is that educational administration is not a subject-matter. And neither is public administration. There is, therefore, nothing that can be taught that can be called public administration as such.

It is not an answer to say that public life is important. When there are so many important things to teach we must select those that have the following characteristics: (*a*) they must be subjects that are, as nearly as we can determine, fundamental; and (*b*) they must be subjects that can be taught. I have already shown

* These essays appeared in the first issue of the *Public Administration Review,* March, 1938, a publication of the Maxwell School, Syracuse University.

that public administration can't be taught. It is easy to show that it is not funda-mental. Public life deals with action upon organizations, in particular situations. The ends of action, the nature of organizations, and the qualities of men are all prior, from the standpoint of understanding, to the actions that constitute the alleged subject-matter of courses designed to prepare men directly for public life.

Nor is it an answer to say that there is a lot of information about the public service. I do not doubt it. To take the Post Office alone, we could define the duties of all the officers of the department. We could trace the department's history. We could describe the organization, its operation, and its difficulties. We could compare our postal service in every detail with the British, French, German, Swiss, Italian, Japanese, and Czechoslovakian systems. We could do this for the Post Office Department. We could then do it for every other branch of the Federal government. And in our remaining time we could follow the same plan for all state governments, county governments, city governments, town govern-ments, village governments, and all other political subdivisions whatever. But what contribution should we be making to the preparation of men for public life? The information, insofar as it was useful, could be acquired without coming to college to get it. And it is almost impossible to tell whether it is useful until the individual in question has got a job in the Post Office or some other Depart-ment and has discovered what he needs to know.

Now if public administration is not a subject-matter that can be taught in college, are the colleges helpless to assist the country through the preparation of men and women who will be intelligent public servants? By no means. The col-leges have a direct and conspicuous service to perform in this connection. They can give their students an education. If they should do this, they would find that they had done the very best thing that could be done for the country and for the public service.

Of course I do not refer to the kind of education that we give our students now. That might be useful in providing the insignia necessary to gain entrance to professional schools and university clubs. But since we cannot claim that our graduates can even read or write, the less we boast about the education we give them, the better. What kind of education can we give them that will not only help them to lead happy and effective lives but will also contribute to make them leaders of men? I take it that we are not interested in qualifying petty office holders for routine positions. We want our graduates to exert some influence in the formulation as well as the execution of policy. The course of study, too, should be one that the student cannot master without our aid. It should be one where teaching, instruction, and guidance are of some help. And finally it should be a course of study which, instead of being composed of little fake experiences, is made up of material which the student cannot learn from living, or if he can, only after a long period of trial and error which we should wish to spare him.

I suggest that we try to communicate to our students the traditional wisdom of the race. Much of this deals with public life, public service, and public administration. A student who studied it might therefore be educated and he might be prepared for public life as well. One objection I have to courses of study in public administration is that they may displace education. I cherish the notion that students ought to be educated. The proposal I am making can prepare them for public life without interfering with their education. In fact, the materials studied with a view to public life would contribute to their education.

For a large part of the accumulated wisdom of the race has to do, as I have suggested, with the organization and management, the birth, progress, and death of political institutions. The great works of history beginning with Herodotus and Thucydides and coming down to the present day are full of penetrating analyses of actions in immediate concrete situations. The greater the works the more penetrating the analysis. And so in the realm of what used to be called practical philosophy, the field of ethics and politics, we have in Plato's Republic, in the Ethics and Politics of Aristotle, and in writers since then, like William James and John Dewey, subtle and sophisticated analyses of the ends of political societies and the means by which they may be attained. It seems to me self-evident that the best educational equipment for public life is a thorough knowledge of the moral and political wisdom accumulated through our intellectual history. This young people cannot acquire either in their idle hours or in the hurly-burly of practical life. This is something the colleges can give them. It is, I venture to think, the only thing the colleges can give them that will qualify them for the public service; for as an ancient sage remarked, "The same education and the same habits will be found to make a good man and a good statesman and king."

"Schools Can Do Much"

WILLIAM E. MOSHER

In this issue will be found . . . [an article] by President Robert Hutchins of Chicago University emphasizing the futility of anything in the way of pre-entry training apart from the development of intelligence and character. . . . [This article prompts] the writer to make the following observations. In the first place, a line should be drawn between training on the undergraduate and on the graduate level. President Hutchins was evidently considering only the former, although on other occasions he is reported as having expressed himself adversely on the latter as well.

With respect to a training course for undergraduates, a review of curricula in a number of schools will go to show that such courses are rather of an incidental than a specific character. In not a few cases the curriculum consists of the grouping together of the courses that are given as a matter of course in a liberal arts program. The number of offerings in the departments of government, sociology, and economics may have a contribution to make to the student who plans to seek a position in government, but neither from the point of view of content nor teaching method would one be justified in considering them pre-entry training courses for government positions. The same thing may be said for courses in chemistry, physics, bacteriology and other courses of this character. The student who has majored in chemistry will obviously have some advantage from this work if he makes application for a vacancy in the Division of Chemistry in the Agriculture Department or Bureau of Standards. That is he may go into the public service on the basis of such training, but equally well into private industry. If he combines the basic courses with one in governmental administration, he might profit from this combination should he seek a government position. However, none of these courses has probably been designed with reference to the peculiarities of the public service. On the whole it may be said that there are probably very few schools which have systematically developed pre-entry training courses that definitely look toward a governmental career.

When it comes to the graduate level a different situation arises although here something of the same sort of observation may in the opinion of the writer be made, namely that a large number of institutions announcing offerings which profess to prepare for government service are providing the same sort of advanced work which would be offered even though none of the graduates were interested in seeking a government position. A technician such as a graduate chemist or a graduate statistician will obviously be better qualified for a vacancy on a governmental staff where advanced chemistry and advanced statistics are essential, than would one with no graduate work in these fields. Under a strict definition of pre-entry training *for the public service* such courses would hardly qualify.

It will surely be granted that the public service involves certain peculiarities which distinguish it from private industry or from work in the academic field. It is our thesis that if one is trained for the public service he should be acquainted with such peculiarities. He should have some understanding of public law, of the administrative discretion which is exercised under such law because finally the scope of a public official's activity is circumscribed by law. He should have some understanding of governmental organization and relationships under such organization. He should appreciate how budgets of public authorities are set up and controlled. Further, he should have a pretty good comprehension of personnel controls and the law affecting public officials. Matters of this sort are essential to intelligent behavior in the work-life of a public employee.

For the limited number of young people who are ambitious to enter the field of public administration a more thoroughgoing acquaintaince with so-called staff functions is to be prescribed. It is held by a number of political scientists and at least by implication by President Hutchins that it is quite out of the question to offer pre-entry training on such functions with any effectiveness. It is further maintained that the only way to acquaint oneself with these peculiarities of public administration is through work on the job. To this the present writer would take exception and on the ground that the majority of officials to whom novitiates would necessarily go to school are themselves lacking the administrative skill, administrative knowledge, and perspective. If one would learn how not to carry on administrative functions he would do well to sit at the feet of almost any administrator selected by chance. A young man who has even a fair background in administrative techniques with little or no experience can make contributions of a substantial character to many administrators, who, because of a lack of perspective and special study, are thoroughly entangled in the traditional ways of doing things.

Furthermore, in view of the large body of knowledge now available concerning administrative practices and methods it is possible for one to equip himself for an administrative career in much the same way as physicians and engineers are equipped for the practice of their professions. Practitioners in these fields must obviously learn by doing and can become adept in their calling only through doing. This would not, however, justify the argument that they should not acquaint themselves with approved techniques and methods before undertaking to practice in their chosen calling.

The parallel might be pressed further by comparing the administrator who necessarily must have acquaintance with a variety of techniques and the ways in which special technicians may be used, and the young medic who likewise has to utilize the services of technicians without himself being a master in each of the fields of those whose aid he must utilize. Although the administrator should know something about public law, public finance, accounting, and the like, he can hardly be a specialist in these several fields any more than a medical man can be a bacteriologist, a pharmacologist, a neurologist, and an orthopedist. One has only to sit in the office of an administrator for a week to discover that he is somewhat comparable to an orchestra leader who produces volumes of harmonious sound with the aid of twenty or thirty different instruments, the majority of which he cannot himself play.

In conclusion it must be taken for granted that an administrator will develop the judgment and skill—shall we say the art—so necessary for the handling of his rather complicated job *by doing*. But to assume that he will not be a more successful actor in the administrative scene because of a broad background in procedures and criteria with respect to such procedures, runs contrary to logic and contrary to experience. No one would argue that it is possible to produce full-fledged administrators on a college campus any more than full-fledged medical or engineering practitioners can be produced on a college campus. The medical students devote their first two years, and parts of their last two, to the learning of their "science"; and the engineers ordinarily devote a longer period to the same task. A long term of internship and apprenticeship is prescribed in both instances before the graduates in these callings are accepted as practitioners. If this same need is once recognized for prospective administrators, and opportunities are opened up for internes and apprentices with an understanding of administrative processes, definite progress in one of the most neglected fields of governmental management may be looked for with considerable confidence.

———◆———

As its title suggests, the following essay, "An American Administrative Class?" bears on the issues raised in the preceding selections. Its author is Professor Rowland Egger, who has in addition to high professional competence a gift for the well-turned phrase.

In 1946 as a part of Princeton University's bicentennial there was held a Conference on University Education and the Public Service. Professor Egger's essay is one of a distinguished series resulting from the Conference.

The phrase "Administrative Class" as used in the title of the essay refers to the small group of permanent civil servants, so named, at the apex of the British civil service. To American students of public administration, the British Administrative Class has long been an engaging spectacle, an object of frequent study and often envious comparison. In a governmental and administrative system much like our own, the education, recruitment, and performance of the British Administrative Class differs greatly from American practice in filling high administrative positions. Its members are recruited almost exclusively from highly able graduates of the universities; it is a career service entered early or not at all; its members fill the great majority of high administrative positions. There is considerable agreement among administrative students that the British Administrative Class is on the whole a "successful" administrative institution. The education of the members of it has been, however, in the traditional liberal arts curriculum of the British university, not in public administration in the professional sense.

Obviously, in the differences between British and American practice there is room for much speculation and argument. In the Princeton Bicentennial Conference, the implications of the differences were at the center of the discussions. For the British experience was there reviewed and defended by distinguished British public figures. The American participants in turn tried to view the British experience in the light of American institutions and necessities, to determine wherein the "administrative class" idea is good and adaptable, wherein bad or irrelevant. Professor Egger's essay comes near to being a summary, not only of the American point of view as expressed at the Conference, but of most recent well-informed opinion among administrative students.

Query, to what extent is the administrative experience of one country relevant to another? What problems are raised by the attempt to transfer or copy administrative institutions?

An American Administrative Class? *

ROWLAND EGGER

The basic issue raised by the conference—the need for a trained administrative class in the civil service—is one that reaches to the very bedrock of social, governmental, administrative, and educational organization. If the universities can do little about the development of a corps of trained generalists on their own motion—since they do not control their market—it is equally true that nothing can be done unless the universities participate, either in bending the concept of administrative class preparation to academic notions of the content of a general education, as in Britain, or in accommodating themselves to the developing substance of the generalist function in a contemporary society, as is more likely to be the case in the United States. It is the purpose of this essay, therefore, to examine the possibility of the development of an administrative class "in harmony," as James Forrestal has phrased it, "with American traditions and fully recognizing the democratic spirit of American institutions." . . .

The emphasis which has latterly come to be placed upon the civil servants of the generalist variety proceeds from two sources: (1) admiration for the truly notable achievements of the "elite corps" of the British civil service known as first division or administrative class employees, a group which numerically has never exceeded in normal times more than 1,500, which is less than 0.35 per cent of the prewar British civil service, and less than 2.5 per cent of the so-called "treasury" or general classes of the civil service; (2) a critical reappraisal of developments within the American bureaucracy which reveals important deficiencies with respect to continuity and consistent development in top management *expertise* and administrative policy. . . .

The problems and difficulties incident to the lack of an institutionalized administrative class in the American civil service were not discovered at Princeton. The deficiency has from time to time been remarked by scholars and commentators; de Tocqueville was the first, but by no means the last, to criticize systematically this defect in American administrative arrangements. More recently the Commission of Inquiry on Public Service Personnel made an exhaustive investigation of the problem. In many respects, the report of this commission in 1935 is comparable to the Macaulay report of 1854, for the clarity of its diagnosis and the simplicity and straight-forwardness of its therapeutics. The findings of the Commission of Inquiry with respect to the need for an administrative class in the American civil

* From *The Public Service and University Education* (Princeton: 1949), Joseph E. McLean (ed.), pp. 205–233. Abridged. Reprinted by permission of the Princeton University Press.

service were strongly buttressed by the investigations of the President's Committee on Civil Service Improvement, headed by Justice Stanley Reed, which in 1941 emphatically reiterated the need for recognition of and institutionalization of recruitment for a generalist group in the federal service. . . .

It is, I think, pertinent at this point to look at the substance of the generalist function in modern government. . . . The Association of First Division Civil Servants submitted a statement to the British Royal Commission on the Civil Service in 1931 which summarizes the matter with great clarity from the British standpoint:

"The business of government, if it is to be well done, calls for the steady application of long and wide views to complex problems; for the pursuit, as regards each and every subject matter, of definite lines of action, mutually consistent, conformed to public opinion and capable of being followed continuously while conditions so permit and of being readily adjusted when they do not. Almost any administrative decision may be expected to have consequences which will endure or emerge long after the period of office of the Government by which or under whose authority it is taken. It is the special function of the civil service and the special duty of the administrative class of that service in their day-to-day work to set these wider and more enduring considerations against the exigencies of the moment, in order that the Parliamentary convenience of today may not become the Parliamentary embarrassment of tomorrow. . . . Vacillation, uncertainty, and inconsistency are conspicuous symptoms of bad administration. . . .

"Thus the efficient performance of the administrative work of the various departments calls in all cases for a trained mental equipment of high order, while in the particular case powers developed in some particular direction are needed. In some spheres what is most wanted is judgment, *savoir-faire*, insight and fair-mindedness; in others, an intellectual equipment capable of the ready mastery of complex and abstruse problems, for instance, taxation or other economic subjects; in others, imagination and constructive ability."

Writing against the distinctive background of the particularly American scene, the Commission of Inquiry on Public Service Personnel stated the problem in these clear and cogent terms in its 1935 report:

"Under the American system of self-government, the voters elect legislative bodies and chief executives, and various other special officers, to make the laws, adopt the budgets, vote the taxes, and determine the general public policies. The actual doing of the work of government in accordance with these laws and policies is entrusted to appointed men and women. As it is impossible for the chief executive or for the legislative committees to deal with these men and women individually all the way down the line, each major activity is organized as a department, headed by an appointed or elected officer (called secretary, commissioner, or the like). The duties of this department head fall into two categories, political and administrative. Politically he is responsible to the chief executive or the electorate for carrying out in the work of his department the general political program of the dominant party. Administratively he is responsible for (*a*) interpreting the laws and regulations under which his department operates, (*b*) distributing the work of the department in such a way that the policies which have been determined may best be carried out, (*c*) maintaining consistency in the work of the department as between its various bureaus and activities and with other departments as well, (*d*) preserving continuity as between the past, the present, and the future of the work of the department, except of course where policy has been consciously altered, (*e*) keeping the department efficient and its personnel 'on its toes,' (*f*) reporting to the public, and being prepared to explain the work of the department. These latter duties are what the Commission means by administrative work. Since they are non-political, they could and should be assigned to career men in the administrative service. . . . In the federal government, we need only to recognize what has actually developed in certain departments at various times, and create in each department the definite position of Permanent Under Secretary and place this position in the career service. . . .

"The administrator is the link between the elective and appointive political service, on the one hand, and the professional and the clerical services on the other. He is differentiated from the political official, the 'executive' under our law, in that he does not make the important final decisions on political policy, does not advocate such policies before the electorate, and does not rise or fall on the basis of the acceptance or rejection of 'his' policies by the electorate or their elected representatives. These are the functions of the elected officials, who are therefore political and 'responsible.' The political officials serve as a buffer between the public and the administrators, interpreting public opinions and decisions and forcing them on the administration. If the elected official fails in his endeavors to lead the democratic procession, or at least to keep in front, he is dropped and another elected in his place.

"To the elected official the administrator is indispensable. The latter knows intimately the entire machine of government, is acquainted with its possibilities and limitations, and, through those who work with him, has command of the scores of technical and scientific facts and skills which must be correlated for the development and execution of any policy. And after a policy has been adopted, it is the administrator who translates the decision into reality through planning, organizing, and delegating, staffing, directing, coordinating and budgeting for the execution of the program within the limits assigned. In this process there are many important decisions of administrative policy to be made. These fall to the administrator to make, in harmony with the general program. If matters arise for which the general policy is no guide, or which may raise new or different political questions, these he must refer to the superior political official. Under a career administrative service, the administrator becomes extremely skillful in making the nice distinctions between political questions of policy and administrative questions of policy, because he rises in a service devoted to these matters.

"The relation of the administrator to the technical services is as follows. It is the administrator's responsibility to understand and coordinate public policy, and interpret it to the operating services. While he will have deep appreciation of and considerable intimate acquaintance with the operations of the technical and business departments, he cannot know their technology or science. No man can now be an expert in all fields. For the same reason, the technical and professional heads of these services can seldom if ever know the technologies or problems of their neighbors, or have a balanced view of the entire picture of government, or see what is necessary in their own work to produce in the end a correlated public service. In insisting on this correlation and conformity of work to the policies which have been adopted, the administrator is not interfering in technical work, which must of course be left to the technicians. He is, rather, applying to the technical field decisions of public policy, which, equally, are beyond the competence or responsibility of the technician." . . .

It would, however, be misleading to infer that among the commentators and investigators there is anything like agreement or unanimity with respect to the practicability of establishing an administrative class in the American civil service. Lewis Meriam, in his *Public Personnel Problems*, raises a number of objections to the notion of the administrative class. He suggests that the federal system in the United States has resulted in the allocation of general staff functions to the national authorities in many segments of governmental activity, while operations remain at the state level and subject to state policy within broad limits. The functions of the federal official tend to be the collection of facts and statistics, research, investigation, propaganda, promotion, and largely advisory supervision. These, he thinks, are not the functions of an administrative class official, and he points to the inadequate development of the research and investigatory function in British administration as evidence of the failure of the administrative class in this area. He is likewise of the opinion that at this late date we will never in the United States be able to superimpose an "administrative class" on the professional, technical, and scientific employees, because our reaction from the spoils system has exalted the professional and scientific group at the expense of the "administrative" group formerly composed mainly of spoils appointees. Moreover, if the services traditionally administered by scientists-turned-executive are excluded, there would be, he says, only about 1,000 administrative class positions in the entire federal service, which means that the number of new appointments per annum necessary to maintain it would be infinitesimal—or anyway too small to interest American universities.

Moreover, Lewis Meriam questions bluntly the assumption that administrative ability is inconsistent with professional competence. Staff agencies of the research, investigational, and promotional type, he points out, are small and present few large problems of general organization and management. On the other hand, they do require a large measure of professional competence and standing. He goes on to name a group of officials in which professional competence is implicit in their titles—the Surgeon General of the Public Health Service, the Commissioner of Education, the Director of the Bureau of Agricultural Economics, the Director of the Bureau of Standards, the Director of the Geological Survey, etc. He continues:

"Proponents of a special administrative class sometimes contend that scientific and technical men lack administrative ability. . . . Ability to cite some cases in which scientific and technical men lack administrative ability does not prove that all scientific and technical men lack administrative ability, any more than ability to cite some cases in which scientific and technical men were outstanding administrators proves that all such men are excellent administrators. No evidence has yet been adduced to prove that in America, under our educational system, a general academic education produces better administrators than a more vocational education, or that graduates of general arts who do not go on into professional fields are superior in administrative ability to graduates in arts who subsequently get professional education. In the absence of sound statistics one must resort to observation. Observation suggests that administrative ability and interest are something rather separate and distinct from fields of learning and that good administrators and poor administrators may be found in almost any field."

Meriam makes a good deal of the psychological handicaps of junior administrators, inducted as heirs apparent to administrative empires, and of the difficulties which a favored position throws in the way of securing cooperation and effectively leading an organization. He sums up his position on this point as follows:

"The English system works because the members of the administrative division constitute a caste which occupies all the positions from top to bottom within that division. It is highly questionable whether it would work if it were not a caste and if there were real competition among two or more divisions for upper positions. If the caste ever loses full and complete control of the upper positions, its own days are probably numbered."

Differences in recruitment theory and policy, the broadening of technical and professional education and of civil service examinations for technical and professional positions, and the alleged inapplicability in Great Britain of the "administrator" principle to smaller agencies and smaller governments are also cited, but his main indictment of the administrative class proposal rests upon the grounds which have been outlined.

The essentials of the British approach to administrative class education and recruitments have been thoroughly covered in Sir James Grigg's essay, and need not be labored here. Professor Woodward sums it up by saying that "one of the most remarkable achievements of the English in the nineteenth century was to devise a mode of education which gave to the English upper middle class the qualities of an old governing aristocracy." Nor was he hesitant to urge strongly the case for classical learning—instruction in Latin and Greek—as an important base for the type of education required by an administrator, although he recognizes, albeit with a certain reluctance, the trends in English education which are tending to place increased emphasis upon "newer" subjects such as economics, public administration, and the history and working of institutions, the educational value of which in his opinion is by no means well established. While Sir James Grigg skillfully avoided commitment with respect to the appropriate subject matter for an administrative class education—beyond observing that if he had it to do over again he would not submit to the unholy alliance of mathematics and natural science—he is completely unequivocal in his support of subject-matter irrelevancy in administrative class preparation.

The completely charming essays of Professor Woodward and Sir James Grigg actually demonstrate most of all how profoundly educational traditions can diverge within a general *milieu* of cultural similarity, and how drastically different social and administrative patterns may become under the aegis of a common legal system. Even those who have been privileged to participate at first hand in the absorbing educational processes of an English university cannot but realize that the game is being played under a set of rules all but incomprehensible to outsiders—and whether the rules are for Lilliputians or Brobdingnagians only time can tell.

On the whole, I am inclined to the view that American experience tends to sustain Lewis Meriam's view that administrative ability and interest are something rather separate and distinct from fields of learning. For my own part, and speaking as one subjected to the rigors of an exceptionally drastic classical education, I can affirm that more often than not in America, and occasionally at Oxford itself, Aristophanes and Aeschylus are taught by mere linguistic grease-monkeys, and their educational and cultural content is somewhat below that of a good course in horseshoeing. On the other hand, and I apologize again for a personal reference, the university course which affected me most profoundly and opened up vistas of humanistic knowledge which I had completely overlooked before was a lecture series in the School of Engineering dealing with the history of sewage disposal in ancient and medieval times. Here it was that Catullus, Livy, Tacitus, Horace, Petronius, Juvenal, Plautus, and Terence came to life—here the real significance of Roman engineering and legal genius became apparent—and here the elementary connection between the development of urban civilization (which is to say the development of civilization) and the growth of man's ingenuity in disposing of animal waste became clear and I began to understand and appreciate its decisive influence in the cultural development of modern man.

Moreover, and with no more than a fleeting regret for the terrific waste which this confesses, it may be observed that there is very little Aristotle ever wrote that Jowett did not improve substantially in the translating.

The Meriam postulate that administrative ability and interest are apart and distinct from subject matter fields implies that the art of managing men probably cannot be taught through formal instructional mechanisms. Sir James Grigg would, of course, agree with this position. From this point, however, the argument diverges sharply. Since the art of managing men cannot be taught, Sir James and Professor Woodward proceed to the position that only a cultural education (phrase of argument-begging import) imparting a sense of form and facile perception of relativities constitutes a proper administrative class education. The Commission of Inquiry and the Reed Committee would respond that even if the art of managing men cannot be imparted by formal instructional methods, the principles and practices involved in the scientific use of the tools of management can be taught. Lewis Meriam would insist that between the politicians on the one hand and the professional and technical staff on the other there is no place for an administrative class, and no need for one even if a place could be found, so why bother trying to educate one.

Let us take the evidence, before closing this phase of the argument, of one of the professional scientists whose ghosts Lewis Meriam invokes so freely and casually. Dr. W. W. Stockburger, one of the great career officials of the federal service, started out as an instructor in botany at Denison University, later became physiologist in charge of drug and related plants in the Bureau of Plant Industry, and eventually wound up as director of personnel of the United States Department of Agriculture. Out of his long, rich, and varied experience as scientist and as administrator Dr. Stockburger writes as follows:

"Specialized training in the law or the sciences is an adequate foundation upon which to build an administrative career. . . . Administration, although not separate and apart from the activity administered, involves a series of relationships not inherent in what is to be administered, but superimposed upon it. The understanding of the nature of these relationships and of the art of utilizing them effectively will be facilitated by a mastery of the principles of public administration and an exploration of the content of the social sciences. If government is to secure for the public service recruits who have the capacity to become satisfactory administrators, our educational institutions must be induced to afford selected students an opportunity to acquire a perspective of the relations of governmental operations to the public interest much broader than that usually developed in the standardized technical courses."

The evidence is easier to recite than to apply. Stockburger the plant physiologist, which is the dominant *motif* of his career, is to a considerable degree the proof of Lewis Meriam's assertion that technical and administrative ability are not incompatible and are frequently encountered in the same person. But Stockburger the humanist and student of administration, a facet only imperceptibly inferior to his scientific side, would be the first to deny Meriam's conclusions with respect to administrative class education and is, in fact, our most positive witness and ardent advocate in behalf of the systematic preparation of administrative personnel.

Of all the proposals which have been made for the establishment of an administrative career service in the United States government, that of the Commission of Inquiry on Public Service Personnel is at once the most comprehensive, the best documented, and the most knowledgeable with regard to the immediate and long-run implications of the undertaking. The pertinent portions of the commission's report merit our careful attention at this point.

The Commission of Inquiry proposed that the public service be organized in five major groups or divisions: (1) the administrative group, comprehending the personnel involved in general management, including organizing, staffing, directing, coordinating, planning, budgeting, and reporting; (2) the professional group, including those who use the special techniques and knowledge mastered by the recognized professions, such as medicine, engineering, law, architecture, chemistry, social work, and teaching; (3) the clerical group, covering those who perform the office work of handling the business and papers and records and reports which every large scale enterprise must maintain; (4) the skilled and trades group, including carpenters, plumbers, masons, steel workers, mechanics, electricians, painters, printers, etc.; (5) the unskilled group, covering ordinary day labor.

These five groups, the commission felt, constituted the basis for reasonably self-contained, though by no means air-tight, separate career services, within which entrants would climb their appropriate career ladders and work out their proper destinies. The commission emphasized certain specific conditions which must be met in order to establish and maintain any of the proposed career services. "There must be public acceptance, acknowledgment and general understanding of the career services, and an appreciation on the part of professional and scientific groups, the learned societies and the press of the distinctions between the services and the nature of the contributions of each of the total work of government." For each of the five services the commission proposed that there should be "an appropriate method of entrance based solely on the characteristics and capacities of the applicant, and so defined that the conditions of entrance would be relatively stable and easily understood." The commission points out that

"inasmuch as a 'career' presupposes a lifetime of work of growing knowledge and skill, entrance should be limited, in the ordinary course of events, to the lowest positions within each service and to a young group of entrants. A career cannot be said to exist if top positions are generally recruited from outside, from men who do not understand the work, and in such a way as to create an effective bar to advancement from the bottom to the top of the service itself."

It particularly emphasizes that

"opportunity for advancement and promotion within each career service must be open to all within the service on the basis of work alone and capacity for the higher post. Each service must be viewed in the broadest possible light so that the top posts may be filled from a wide base and so that those who enter at the bottom may have the opportunity of reaching great eminence." The commission draws particular attention to its view that

"wherever careers in the public service are virtually identical with careers in private life, the definition of the service, the system of training, the method of entrance, the opportunities for advancement, and the compensation should be definitely related, and opportunities for transfer back and forth should be provided. But where the nature of the public work is clearly unique, or governed by different or conflicting motives, the method of recruitment and the conditions of service should be different, and transfers back and forth should be scrutinized with care."

The establishment of professional, scientific, and other associations within the service, as well as organizations for considering conditions of service and for ministering to the social life of the group is strongly encouraged by the commission.

Obviously, the recruitment policies embraced condition more than any other single factor the outworking of the program. The commission is quite fearless in "laying it on the line" in this respect as well. It suggests:

(1) The unskilled group would be "recruited without reference to education, on the basis of fitness for the work, determined entirely by practical tests, usually on the job. While most men would enter the service after grade school, or perhaps after two years of high school, there would be no particular age limit."

(2) The skilled and trades group would be recruited "after education, which normally would not extend beyond high school, on the basis of the mastery of particular skills and trades. Admission should be competitive through practical tests, with entrance age limits so computed as to bring the examination soon after the completion of apprenticeship."

(3) The clerical group is divided into two sub-groups, the strictly clerical and the clerical-executive divisions. The clerical group "would be recruited after not less than two years of high school and be trained for the special techniques of their jobs after entry. Age limits would thus be set at possibly sixteen to seventeen, and the examination would deal primarily with general intelligence and with the subjects these young men and women have been taking in school. . . . The clerical-executive group would be taken at a later stage, that is, after general high school education. The age limit should be set at eighteen to nineteen, and the examination should be related to high school subjects. If special training in business colleges is required, it should be given after selection."

(4) The professional group would be "recruited after special training, but before practical experience. The appropriate age limits are from twenty-three to twenty-eight, and the examinations should deal almost exclusively with the mastery of the special training. An extremely useful device in the recruitment of professional service is the requirement that the candidate shall possess the

certificate of the appropriate accredited professional or scientific bodies or associations."

(5) The administrative group would be selected from

"those with an advanced general education immediately upon the completion of that education. The appropriate examination is one which will seek to determine which of the young men and women who present themselves during a given year have at that stage of development attained an outstanding position among their fellows of the same age group in the pursuit of general knowledge. The examination should determine primarily what the candidates are, not what they know about the work for which they are to be trained in the future."

The commission reiterates at a number of points in the course of its report that it is not proposing a closed career service. There will be times, it believes, when it may be necessary to bring from outside the particular career service persons with extensive practical experience into advanced posts which require such practical experience; there is no abrogation of the career principle, the commission says, provided the normal course of promotion is retained on a career basis. Moreover, the commission views the system which it proposes as providing not a series of pigeonholes on an organization chart, but rather a series of ladders, starting at different ages and after different periods of education and experience, and arriving eventually at different points. The commission believes it to be a matter of prime importance that the ladders should not be so far apart that the unusual employee will be unable to pass from one ladder to another on the basis of additional education or experience.

The chapter dealing with administrative and management personnel in the report of the President's Committee on Civil Service Improvement, submitted in 1941, was undoubtedly the high point of the committee's work. Unfortunately, it had fallen so "flat on its face" in the teapot tempest over the status of lawyers in the federal service that it never thereafter really recovered its dignity or self-confidence, so that even at its boldest it is a little less than incisive. Gordon Clapp has summed up with both clarity and charity the committee's proposals in the following words:

"The Committee's recommendations visualize the creation of an administrative group with or without professional or scientific specializations consisting of incumbents having administrative responsibilities in positions occupying grades CAF-11, P-4, and higher.[1] This administrative career service corps would be replenished largely by promotion or transfer from within the service with primary reliance as to method of selection placed in the hands of examining committees and the discriminating judgments of superior administrative officers and departmental personnel officers. Furthermore, the Committee urges recogni-

[1] These were "medium" grades in the then-existing Federal classification system.— The Editor.

tion of the role of general management in the career service directly below the policy-making heads, the general managers constituting the top rank of the administrative corps. It is significant to note that the Committee does not participate directly in the time-worn controversy as to whether persons for administrative responsibility should be drawn from among those of professional or technical training and experience or from among those whose training and experience are devoid of such specialization. The Committee wisely accepts the fact that higher administrative positions are and will be occupied by persons from both backgrounds. They rightly identify the higher administrative group upon the basis of the common denominator of administrative skill and responsibility."

The committee, in choosing to avoid the difficult political and social problems inherent in the establishment of an administrative class through the creation of a selection procedure and the provision of a definite career ladder leading to the top management positions, ignored the central problem of how to secure subordinate personnel competent to assume the management responsibilities of the upper echelons. The administrative capacities of the people in CAF-11, P-4, and higher exercising administrative responsibility will be no better than the potential administrative capacity recruited at the entrance levels. In and of themselves, the committee's recommendations do nothing to improve the administrative potentialities of the input at the bottom. It is not denied, of course, that the recognition of a managerial corps in the civil service which the committee proposes would have a salutary effect. But this recognition is not the heart of the matter, and I am not reassured even by Clapp's subsequent reference to the mitigating effects of "existing mysteries of human potentiality" in overcoming inadequate selection procedures.

The events which have transpired in the twelve years since the Commission of Inquiry on Public Service Personnel reported have served in large measure to validate and reemphasize the recommendations then made. Despite a very considerable expansion in the numbers of employees with general administrative abilities produced by the successive federal relief and public works programs, including the inauguration of the social security program, the war found us with an alarming deficiency in the administrative group. During the war an enormous administrative machine was hastily put together, composed mainly of recruits from business and the professoriate, built in many cases around general administrators who themselves had barely had time to get their rough edges smoothed off in the relief, works, and social security programs. Since the war all of the businessmen, most of the professors, and a goodly number of the trained administrators have left. It will be an interesting, but probably not very edifying, spectacle to watch the organization of ERP, and we may be virtually assured that a new group of appointees will recapitulate *in toto* every mistake that was ever made from FERA to the present, in addition to inventing a large number of new and unique errors. This is one of the minor costs of not having an administrative class with a well-established and generally accepted role in federal top management.

The proposals of the commission, it should be noted, involve no deemphasis of professional education and training, which is a special characteristic of American education. Nor is the administrative service ladder closed to those who start off their careers in professional and technical fields. There is no reason to think that a career system such as the commission contemplates would not produce its W. W. Stockburgers, its William Alanson Whites, and its Ellen C. Potters, or that any of them would encounter difficulty in switching over from the professional to the administrative ladder, and perhaps back again, as the occasion required. On the other hand, the commission's proposals would assure a reservoir of generally educated employees in junior administrative positions throughout the service from which the higher administrative echelons would normally be renewed. After all, most M.D.'s had rather practice medicine than hold the moist hands of nervous politicians.

The objection to the establishment of an administrative class based upon social grounds—the creation of a privileged class of bright young college graduates in the government—never actually had much foundation, and at the present time, when a college education is literally within reach of everyone who desires one, is a factor of no consequence whatever. Moreover, as the lack of continuity in federal topside management clearly indicates, the democratic ideal is not applied in the public service today to the extent that uncritical opinion supposes. As Harold Dodds pointed out a decade ago:

"There exists a practical deadline in our national and local governments between, say, the position of chief clerk and the position of directing head of a bureau or agency. Unfortunately, however, it is politics that too often enforces the deadline. The highest posts are rarely filled by promotions within the service. . . . The proposal here made looks to equipping the service so that it will be able to supply within itself executives of the highest type. . . . As long as the top ranks are open only to outsiders, whether to politicians, or to lawyers, college professors and successful businessmen called in for brief periods from the outside, public administration as a career will enjoy low prestige and will fail to attract its fair share of the best ability in the country."

I conclude, therefore, that there is nothing worthy of the attention of the Thomas committee [1] in the proposal to create an administrative class in the American public service, and that the establishment of such an institution is wholly compatible with the spirit and traditions of an egalitarian society. As the Commission of Inquiry foresaw, and the Bicentennial Conference reaffirmed,

[1] Thomas was then Chairman of the Committee on Un-American Activities.—The Editor.

it must necessarily be an institution which will reflect the special characteristics of American culture. It cannot be permitted to become the private property either of the Ivy League or the several centers of higher education which purport to teach all the mysteries of the administrative inner sanctum. It will also have to make provision for the "rare bird" who is too busy getting an education to go to college. And while its prime objective is the production, recruitment, and training of generalists, it will be compelled to avoid the rigidity which would exclude from the administrative career service qualified persons whose only disability is that in the misguided enthusiasm of their youth they acquired a professional degree.

The limitations of an American career administrative service ought also to be recognized. It should not be expected to accomplish some things that the British administrative class, with its old-school-tie social coherence, has done. It cannot bear the burden of responsibility in its corporate capacity for interdepartmental and interagency coordination of program and operations in anything like the degree to which the British service is called upon to exercise this function. Although the British service is not without its institutional facilities, both in the Treasury and in the entourage of the Prime Minister, for coordination, the degree of reliance upon institutional facilities will inevitably be much greater in the United States. Moreover, administrative class officials in the United States probably will never exercise the broad degree of control over administrative operations common to the British service, if for no other reason than that the Secretary will generally be under foot, whereas his British counterpart is normally out of the way down at the House of Commons, or back home buttering up his constituency. Finally, it will be at least fifteen or twenty years after an administrative career service is established before its significant results begin to become apparent.

As a concluding observation, I should like to suggest that the establishment of an administrative career service would have a terrifically sobering effect upon instruction in American universities. For many years we have experimented gaily and irresponsibly in devising courses and reshuffling course combinations, improvising in course content and method, and generally using students for the guinea pigs many of them turn out to be. The erection of definite objective standards of comparison will inevitably affect profoundly our attitudes toward both content and teaching methods. Such a change, by and large, could not come too soon.

———◆———

In the early forties the Civil Service Assembly of the United States and Canada published a series of authoritative and forward-looking volumes dealing with the major phases of public personnel administration. The selection following is the introductory chapter of the volume titled *Recruiting Applicants for the Public Service*.

This chapter is a carefully considered and artfully presented summary of the problem of recruitment in the United States. The historical background of the problem is sketched; the guiding concepts, traditional and contemporary, are outlined and appraised; the educational, economic, and social factors that bear upon recruiting are surveyed. The chapter concludes by outlining the steps in a "positive program" of recruitment and placing the responsibility for its achievement primarily upon the "central personnel agency."

Not all students of administration would agree with the whole of the chapter—there is one school of thought, for example, that deprecates the central personnel agency and would minimize its role. On the whole, however, the chapter represents today as it did a decade ago "well-informed opinion" on the past history, present status, and desirable future development of recruiting in the United States.

Recruiting Applicants for the Public Service was produced by a committee chaired by J. Donald Kingsley, coauthor of a widely used textbook on personnel administration. The chapter reprinted here is largely from the pen of the chairman.

Recruiting Applicants for the Public Service : The Problem and Its Setting *

J. DONALD KINGSLEY

Public recruitment may be defined as that process through which suitable candidates are induced to compete for appointments to the public service. It is thus an integral part of a more inclusive process—selection—which also includes the procedures of examination and certification. Recruitment is the first step in the employment program, and in a fundamental sense the success of that entire program depends upon the efficacy of recruitment policies and upon the procedures through which they are executed. Unless candidates of capacity and character are persuaded to present themselves for examination, no amount of subsequent management will produce a high-grade public service. This fact has long been recognized, and recruitment is everywhere regarded as the core of the personnel process. "No element of the career service system is more important," concludes the Commission of Inquiry on Public Service Personnel, adding that a

* Somewhat abridged from *Recruiting Applicants for the Public Service* (Chicago: 1942). A report submitted to the Civil Service Assembly by the Committee on Recruiting for the Public Service, J. Donald Kingsley, Chairman. Reprinted by permission of the Civil Service Assembly of the United States and Canada.

recruitment policy "improperly analyzed, or inconsistently determined," can wreck the entire personnel program. . . .

The Negative Concept of Recruitment

Because the civil service commission was primarily conceived as an instrument for checking some of the graver abuses of a system of party spoils, its historic emphasis has been negative. Its first purpose was to prevent favoritism, not to improve the positive standards of the public service. Recruitment and selection were the sole fields in which the typical commission functioned. But in the exercise of even these functions civil service commissioners have traditionally concentrated, not on the recruitment of a high-grade personnel, but on "keeping the rascals out." It has been naïvely assumed that if political influence could be eliminated, able men would somehow find their way into the service of government.

We do not wish to belittle in any way the contributions made by the movement for civil service reform. They were substantial, and no one familiar with American political history would care to deny that the elimination of spoils politics was an essential step on the highroad to a career service. But because the civil service commission was first conceived as a sort of politics eliminator, and because the early reformers typically thought in terms of a moral crusade, the concept of recruitment which developed was, to say the least, a limited one. As in the days of the Revolution, the attack was once more directed against the citadels of privilege and the prime emphasis was upon the destruction of the monopoly enjoyed by the patronage dispensers. A nation which had produced Jacksonian Democracy and which, in the 1880's, was feeling the broad ground swell of Populism, remained more interested in equality of opportunity for public office than in the methods of securing a competent body of public servants. To that end, two devices were insisted upon, and they came in time to be the backbone of the recruitment program. The first was open competition; the second, the use of "practical" tests.

The first laws and the earliest commissions emphasized what was usually called the "democratic principle" of open competition. But since the goal was equality of opportunity, the stress was more largely upon the *open* than upon the *competition*. For this reason there was a general disregard of preliminary qualifications. Everyone was to have an opportunity to compete; everyone, that is, except aliens or nonresidents. These were to be excluded, because men were still thinking of public office in terms of private gain rather than in terms of public service. Each locality, it was thought, should "take care of its own." Equality was never intended for outsiders.

The "practical" emphasis is also readily understandable and arose quite naturally out of the conditions of American life. We were a "practical" people, a nation of self-made men. Our leaders in politics, in business, even sometimes in the professions, had been trained in the school of hard knocks. They mistrusted formal education and at the same time generously endowed it. They were suspicious of the thinker and skeptical of the theoretician. They were men of action, doers of deeds. They wanted immediate results, not long-range programs. What better method, then, could be devised to secure equality than to emphasize achievement rather than background? More often than not, a man owed his education to his parents. His deeds, they thought, were his own. For these and other reasons the emphasis in recruitment was upon experience rather than broad training.

The system of recruitment to which these related concepts gave rise has, we believe, proved deleterious to the development of a real career service and must be replaced by a more positive one. The reasons are not far to seek; they are inherent in the negativistic nature of traditional attitudes toward recruitment. An undue amount of time and energy was spent in keeping the rascals out; positive efforts to attract men of character and ability were virtually excluded. Civil service commissions have been inclined to rely upon the operation of the law of averages to produce high-grade candidates from among large groups, and the result has been an understandable reluctance on the part of many such candidates to compete at all. With notable exceptions, therefore, our public services have been havens for mediocrity. The rascals have been kept out, perhaps, but so have many men of vision and ability.

Secondly, the traditional concept of recruitment led to mass competitions among applicants of the most heterogeneous types and qualities. To be sure, these competitions constituted a considerable improvement over spoils methods. But whatever their value from the standpoint of the elimination of political influence, or from that of impressing the community with the democratic quality of the personnel system, it seems clear that they left much to be desired as instruments for the selection of competent personnel. The competition was more often than not of a spurious nature, in view of the variability of competitors' backgrounds, and the eligible lists founded upon it tended often to be mediocre. Then, too, the conduct of such mass contests was unnecessarily expensive and time consuming, and contributed to a chronic condition of delay in the posting of eligible lists. The result was that, when the dreary job of rating the examinations was finished and the eligible lists prepared, many of the better candidates caught up in the recruitment net were no longer interested in public employment. Under such circumstances, too, the examining process often exhausted the financial resources of the personnel agency, so that no funds were available for other important aspects of administration.

In the third place, emphasis upon apportionments and local residence requirements has, in many instances, unnecessarily restricted the area of competition and has run counter to the principle of securing the best available person for every job. To be sure, there may be times when it is desirable to restrict competition to local residents. In respect to certain routine positions which can be filled as well locally as otherwise, a case may be made for such restrictions. But the fact remains that many positions of a technical or administrative character cannot be satisfactorily filled from a restricted area of selection, and we feel strongly that local residence requirements are not justified as a matter of general policy.

Finally, the inordinate emphasis upon experience and practical tests has produced a number of undesirable results. . . . Chief among them have been a limitation of career opportunities, a stifling of promotional possibilities, leading to service stagnation, and a failure to recruit candidates with that broad training and breadth of outlook necessary to modern administration.

The Quest for Competence

The procedures based upon the traditional concepts of recruitment signally failed to produce a distinguished public service. In an agricultural society dominated by a philosophy of laissez faire this might have made no serious difference. But after the Civil War American society was no longer predominantly agricultural, and by the 1890's laissez faire was a term which described only the past. Since that time, the multiplication of governmental functions has proceeded apace and science has become a handmaiden in the service of the state. Specialization and the division of labor, characteristic of an industrial system, have necessarily developed also in the public services and all of this has spelled the eclipse of historic attitudes toward those services. The impact of two world wars within the last twenty-five years has contributed much toward dispelling the citizen's attitude of benevolent indifference toward the quality of the public service. The administration of public affairs now calls for vigor, breadth of vision, and imagination. It calls, also, for special competences, a demand that is being reflected in the educational system and in the development of curricula designed as training for public service. The day of the plainsman has gone. The old order has passed away.

Changed conditions necessitate changed policies. But there is often a lag, a time span, between the demands of a new age and a general response to them. Such, it seems, has been the case with recruitment to the civil service. The conditions have long since changed, but in many jurisdictions we are continuing the policies of an earlier and simpler day. This is not universally true. In a handful of progressive jurisdictions the quest for competence has produced an upheaval in recruitment policies and methods, but these instances are still exceptional. . . .

What is wanted, first of all, is a reconsideration of theories and methods. We need to think through our problems in the light of the new realities. In times of crisis and of social change even those not given to philosophizing must pause to consider fundamentals. Only when premises are rooted in the realities of a situation can we move forward and forget their existence. If that is not the case, if the fundamentals are wrong, little is accomplished by the development of techniques and procedures. For that reason we deal first of all with the general aspects of recruitment policy and only secondarily with questions of procedure within that framework.

A General Theory of Recruitment

There are only two basic systems of public recruitment. One is to recruit young people direct from school or university upon the basis of academic examinations; the other is to recruit more mature men and women upon the basis of practical tests related to their work experience. The first alternative has been widely followed in Europe, notably in England, the second, in the United States. The first presupposes the existence of a number of career hierarchies or ladders up which the more promising officers move throughout their public lives. The second regards the civil service as a collection of more or less discrete positions to be filled chiefly on the basis of technical qualifications for the particular job. The first emphasizes promotion and results in a fluid or mobile service. The second emphasizes techniques at entry, and results in a more static service. The first favors the promising youngster; the second, mediocre maturity. The first gears the civil service to the educational system. The second gears it to the ebb and flow of employment volume in private industry.

We believe it to be clear that neither one of these systems, considered as extremes, is adequate to the requirements of the modern public service and we are convinced that any satisfactory scheme of recruitment must combine elements of both. But the most crying governmental need in America today is for the establishment of career systems in the public services. We are in agreement with the Commission of Inquiry on Public Service Personnel as to the foundations and conditions of such a career system. A career presupposes a life work with prospects of regular advancement and it follows from this that "entrance should be limited, in the ordinary course of events, to the lowest positions within each service and to a young group of entrants." But we recognize also that there are some specialized posts for which it is desirable to recruit candidates of maturity and experience and that it may sometimes be desirable to inject a certain amount of new blood into the upper reaches of the hierarchy. Ordinarily, however, the requirement of any service for freshness of viewpoint is met, it seems to us, by the changing body of policy determining officials.

In the light of such considerations, we think that recruitment which emphasizes prior experience should be sparingly employed. The able youngster who might look forward with eagerness to a government career is likely to be much less interested after he has found a foothold in industry or a profession. Those who, in middle life, are anxious to enter the public service are all too often the ones who have been unsuccessful in the world of private enterprise. There are, of course, many conspicuous exceptions. But in general it is true that the public services fail to get their fair share of ability under a system of recruitment on the basis of experience. This is quite aside from the fact that career services can scarcely be developed under such circumstances, for the late entrance age precludes a career.

We are convinced that the failure to equate the general methods of entrance to the civil service to the various levels of the educational system has been a mistake, and that it is one which is becoming increasingly serious. It seems to us self-evident that the state as educator should serve the state as employer, and vice versa. We are struck by the illogical paradox that "the community, after spending huge sums to advance free or low cost education through high school and college, makes little or no effort to attract the best product of our educational system into civil service." Private industry long ago adjusted its recruiting to the educational structure and has benefited thereby. In the public services "uneven and halting progress must continue to be the rule until a basis for complete and permanent coordination is established."

We do not think that such articulation would be open to the criticism that can be leveled against the British system. Our educational system is enormously more democratic than that of the English, and in the relative equality of educational opportunity is to be found a partial answer to the indispensable requirement that the service be open to all classes of the population. Moreover, American education has revealed an adaptability quite unknown to the English. The necessary adjustments would not, therefore, have to be entirely on the part of the public services. Educational curricula today are extremely sensitive to the demands of new careers and would readily adjust to new opportunities in public employment.

We agree with the United States Civil Service Commission that, under these circumstances,

". . . it would be as wrong to refuse to utilize the selective process of educational training, often paid for by the taxpayers themselves, in the process of selection for government positions, as it would be to refuse to recognize the native capacities of many individuals to enter the government service at some step of the career ladder, by excluding all without education from every examination."

For these and other reasons we suggest three basic principles as the foundation for any system of recruitment; each of them stems from the fact that the modern public service must be organized on a career basis.

1. Recruitment should normally be to the bottom rungs of broadly conceived and well integrated ladders of classes of positions; the higher levels should be filled by promotion.

2. Recruitment should normally be at a relatively early age, making appropriate exception in the case of certain highly specialized positions which cannot be filled from within the service and in which maturity is a prerequisite to successful performance. The numbers of such exceptional posts should be kept to a minimum.

3. The normal method of entry should be related to the appropriate level or variety of education for the particular hierarchy involved. In determining such relationships *regard must be had to the whole range of the hierarchy*. In a career service system it is necessary to select entrants with a view to promotion and to the level they may be expected ultimately to reach. It is not enough to relate educational requirements only to those of the entrance position.

This is not to suggest the creation of a series of airtight career services, each stemming from a particular level of the educational system, and each having an impassable upper limit. It is not to suggest, certainly, the establishment of castes based upon educational background, as has been the case in England. Any changes in the American public services must be made in the light of the principle of equality in relation to public employment. But it does not follow from this that entrance to the civil service cannot be articulated with the educational structure of the country. Rather, equality of opportunity is to be sought through flexibility in the matter of transfers and promotions and through the development of in-service training programs. In the first instance, educational entrance requirements related to the normal lines of promotion in each hierarchy should be established. Thereafter, it is important that the utmost flexibility be maintained and that transfers and promotions between hierarchies be encouraged. By such means, ability may work its way to the top, regardless of the particular level of entrance, and by this means only can the principle of equality in relation to public employment be reconciled with the demands imposed upon the civil service by the requirements of an age of technology.

All of this implies, of course, a marked extension of facilities for in-service training. The change from a system of recruitment which concentrated on filling a heterogeneous collection of discrete positions to one under which we recruit to the bottom rungs of integrated career ladders must necessarily emphasize training. If it does not, there is danger that the service will harden into castes. This can never happen where training opportunities are extensive. In-service training procedures, as former United States Civil Service Commissioner Samuel Ordway, Jr., once said, "are themselves a guarantee of democracy."

We realize that the widespread acceptance of such bases of recruitment as the above will constitute a new departure in American personnel practice. But we are convinced that such a change is necessary if our public services are to be adequate to modern requirements. Of course, progress in this direction must come slowly. As a beginning, the existing classification structure should be canvassed in order to isolate those types of positions that easily lend themselves to broad recruitment techniques. We cannot reshape overnight the negativistic policies which have been developing for fifty years. Public personnel administration is a closely woven fabric and to make fundamental changes in one sector necessitates correlated alterations in the whole design. Every variation in recruitment policy has repercussions upon the whole personnel system. It involves classification and promotion policy, training, examining procedures, and all the rest. Such elaborate readjustments in the intricate machinery of public personnel administration will take time. These changes cannot be accomplished merely by the report of a committee, but they will come as a result of steady pressure by personnel administrators and others over a considerable period. Yet it seems important to set the goal and to chart in broad outline the path to be followed. When that has been done, we can proceed step by step along that route with some degree of unanimity.

The Concept of Positive Recruitment

The first step on the road to such a career service system as we have in mind is the general acceptance of a positive concept of recruitment in contrast to the traditional negative one. It is no longer enough—if, indeed, it ever was—to keep the rascals out. Rather, the personnel agency must actively engage in the quest for competence. It must take definite steps to attract the most able and best qualified potential candidates into the public service. It must cease to regard itself as a kind of policeman guarding the rectitude of the operating departments; instead, it must think of itself as primarily a service agency equipped for the positive supply of all personnel needs. It must take as its guiding rule the motto used at one time by the State of Wisconsin, "the best shall serve the State." For positive recruitment means the *active search for the best*.

To this end, a positive approach implies the adoption of practices and procedures for attracting applicants which emphasize the quality rather than the quantity of competitors. Its methods must be selective and discriminating. In comparison with traditional procedures, they are like using a rifle in place of a shotgun. A rifle is more difficult to aim; it requires greater precision. But it is also more effective and carries farther.

Characteristics of Positive Recruitment. The broad characteristics of positive recruitment are readily summarized. They include:

1. Emphasis on job and promotion ladder analysis as a basis for the recruitment program.

2. Emphasis on an aggressive search for the best qualified candidates through concentration on the most promising potential sources of supply.

3. Emphasis on the pre-test culling of obviously unfit applicants.

4. Emphasis upon close and harmonious cooperation with the operating departments.

Positive Recruitment Methods. The desirable methods of positive recruitment are those which are appropriate to these emphases. They include positive and far-reaching efforts to raise the prestige value of public employment and to shape a career system which will be attractive to able men and women. They include the use of amply attractive publicity regarding employment possibilities directed at the best potential sources of recruits. Finally, they include the development of planned work programs by the personnel agency and active cooperation with the operating officers. All of these and many more are given detailed consideration in the main body of this report.

Results of Positive Recruitment. The results which may be expected from such a program are far-reaching and important. Positive recruitment leads to test groups containing a relatively higher proportion of well-qualified candidates.

The burden of testing is somewhat reduced, and the degree of competition is intensified. Positive testing decreases the time required for the preparation of the list of eligibles and thus serves to diminish leakage at this point. It results in a group of eligibles of high average quality, characterized by a narrow range in level of relative ability. It meets the criteria of fair competition and administrative economy.

But most important, a positive recruiting policy may be expected to serve as a stimulus to careers in government. This is true because the concept of positive recruitment is a broad one, implying, as we have said, the active search for the best. The personnel agency which has grasped it recognizes that recruitment is not an isolated aspect of the personnel program, but an integral part of a closely knit system. It considers, therefore, what may be called the "recruitment aspects" of other personnel practices and the implications of factors affecting the area of recruitment. It is alive to the significance of a personnel *system*, rather than a collection of imperfectly related practices. . . .

Functional Steps in a Positive Program of Recruitment

The procedures involved in the administration of a positive program of recruitment are . . . (1) positive procedures for attracting qualified applicants, (2) the determination of personnel needs, (3) planning and developing the recruitment program, (4) application procedure in public personnel recruitment, (5) the pre-examination audit of applications, and (6) the admission of qualified applicants to competition.

Chapter 10

Classification

Classification is one of the prominent features of American personnel administration. Much of its literature concerns this subject, and many of its practitioners work in this area. More important, the system of "position-classification" favored in American public administration is unusual in principle and far-reaching in its implications.

The traditional and perhaps still most common principle of classification of members of formal organizations is that of "personal rank." According to this principle, the rank or title of the individual gives him a right to the pay, prestige, and perquisites of the rank or title; and he carries with him the title and its rights whatever role in the organization he may play at a particular time. This principle is, of course, dominant in military organizations, and it is also the dominant principle of the classification of the members of most governmental bureaucracies in other countries.

In contrast, position-classification emphasizes the particular job performed at the time rather than the rank or title of the performer. In fact, the position is conceived as a structure of duties and responsibilities that exist apart from the performer, just as a room exists whether or not it is occupied.

Position-classification, though historically and comparatively speaking a novel principle, has "swept the field" in business as well as public administration in America during the past generation. The way was prepared for its development by the equalitarian forces and sentiments of a frontier country that made Americans hostile to notions of inherent status and title. On the contrary there developed an emphasis upon "equal pay for equal work," a sentiment which has understandably been popular in both private and public administration. On the positive side, the Scientific Management movement, with its time-and-motion studies, its job analyses, and its general intense and minute study of the operations performed in organizations has contributed most of the significant concepts and techniques of position-classification.

The following is a summary statement of basic position-classification theory in public administration. It is even in a sense an official statement, for its author, Ismar Baruch, wrote as Chief of the Division of Personnel Classification of the U. S. Civil Service Commission.

The questions that will be raised in the subsequent essay are essentially two: whether position-classification is sound in basic conception, and whether as practiced it is too complicated and unresponsive. The present essay should be read with one eye upon these questions.

Basic Aspects of Position-classification *

ISMAR BARUCH

In a sizable public jurisdiction one can easily visualize the futility of any executive, legislator, or civic-minded citizen attempting constantly to remember and mentally arrange the facts about thousands of individual positions every time he is called upon to take a stand on some administrative issue, render a decision on a personnel problem, provide or expend funds for salaries, or vote upon or administer personnel laws or ordinances. In particular, he finds it impossible to

* From *Public Personnel Review*, Vol. I (October, 1940), pp. 1–17. Abridged. Reprinted by permission of the Civil Service Assembly of the United States and Canada.

know which positions are sufficiently alike to be treated alike so far as his problem or decision is concerned, and which require different treatment. If each one of several thousand individual positions has to be studied as a separate item every time that a personnel or pay policy has to be enunciated, an administrative or budgetary problem solved, a personnel procedure or rule applied, or an employee's pay rate fixed, a confused and inefficient situation results which is unsatisfactory to legislators, administrators, employees, and the public.

Also, the very nature of governmental jurisdictions places them in a position of peculiar responsibility to the public at large and makes undesirable individual actions without plan or system and based merely upon the expediency of the moment. Public personnel policies and transactions affecting positions and employees should be supportable by facts and logic in the light of broad considerations applicable to the service as a whole. Further, considerations of fairness and equity require uniform action under like circumstances in the management of public personnel affairs, particularly in the establishment of pay rates. Such uniformity is impossible of accomplishment unless it is known what circumstances are sufficiently alike to require uniformity.

For all these reasons, current facts about the duties and responsibilities of positions need to be maintained in scientifically summarized and correlated fashion: (*a*) so that the impossibility of understanding an undifferentiated mass of individual positions gives way to the feasibility of understanding a much smaller number of differentiated classes of positions; (*b*) so that positions which should be treated alike when personnel policies, problems, or actions are under consideration can easily be identified as members of a group, thus making it possible to deal with positions in like groups rather than as an undifferentiated mass; and (*c*) so that, by emphasis on an impartial, scientific approach a purely personalized treatment of work and pay problems can be avoided in favor of safeguards against favoritism and procedures for fair and equitable treatment.

Thus, effective personnel administration requires that there be applied to positions the same processes of objective classification and definition that are customarily used to bring order out of a complex array of facts in science, art, and administration generally.

Basic Nature of Any Classification

The process of classification, considered abstractly, consists of placing things in classes. We place in the same class the things that are alike in one or more respects, and we place in different classes the things that are different in those respects. These criteria constitute the *basis* of the classification.

In order to classify any aggregation of things we must decide beforehand what the basis of the classification will be. Naturally, this basis will have reference to some characteristic or quality or attribute, or combination of them, in respect to which the things to be classified are alike or different. Since most things are alike or different in more than one respect, they generally lend themselves to classification on more than one basis. The selection of the particular basis to be employed in a given instance depends, therefore, on the purpose of the classification and the uses to which it is to be put. Different purposes usually require different bases of classification.

Systematic nomenclature and definition are necessarily associated with the process of classifying any given set of objects or qualities. After the basis for classification has been selected, the various classes or groups must be segregated and must be designated by distinctive names or other means of identification to serve as common vehicles of expression. Then each such class or group must be described or defined so as to indicate its content and boundaries. The definitions, when formally recorded in writing, give each of the class or group names a standard, uniform meaning and serve as sources of future reference so that additional items may be classified in conformity with the original plan.

The Basis for Classifying Positions

Positions have various aspects or characteristics and may therefore be classified on more than one basis. Hence, as with any other group of things, in order to classify positions, we must first select that basis, from among all those possible, which effectively serves the predetermined purposes of the classification and the uses to which it is to be put. If, for example, our purposes are purely statistical, a great many bases of classifying positions are available, each of which will produce the foundation for statistical tables useful in some planning, personnel, budget, estimating, or appropriating process. Or, if we are interested in the degree of jurisdiction or control which the public personnel agency has over selections and appointments, we would be concerned with a "jurisdictional" classification of positions. On this basis, positions for which statutes, ordinances, or official orders require competitive examinations at entrance may be placed in a "competitive class"; those subject to noncompetitive tests may be placed in a "noncompetitive class"; and those entirely excluded from the jurisdiction of the central personnel agency may be placed in an "exempt class."

However, the purpose of position-classification, as the term is used in this discussion, is different from either of the two illustrations cited.

To carry on effectively over a period of time the continuous operations of personnel administration such as fixing pay, establishing qualification standards, recruiting and selecting personnel, and maintaining effective working forces, all requires certain tools of administration. One of the most important of these administrative aids is that which facilitates the establishment and current maintenance of a logical and consistent relation among: (*a*) the duties and responsibilities of positions, (*b*) the standards of qualifications to fill them and, where employment conditions are substantially the same, (*c*) the salaries paid. Position-classification is this tool. It is the purpose of position-classification to facilitate the attainment and maintenance of this relation and to serve in this and other respects as a principal tool for personnel administration.

Clearly, from a practical standpoint, the way to create and maintain this relation is to make *both* salaries and qualification standards depend on the character, difficulty, and responsibility of the work involved in the positions. In other words, the natural basis for a position-classification plan having the purpose indicated is the duties and responsibilities of the positions to be classified.

Position

A significant definition of the term "position" should emphasize those characteristics that serve as the basis for its classification. We may say, therefore, that—

A "position" is a group of current duties and responsibilities, assigned or delegated by competent authority, requiring the full-time or part-time employment of one person.

Under this definition a position is composed of assignments of duties and delegations of responsibilities. It may be part-time or full-time, temporary or permanent, occupied or vacant. It does not depend for its existence or identity upon whether or not it is occupied by an employee. It often exists as a vacancy before it is occupied by any one and it resumes its status as a vacancy when an incumbent is separated from it. It comes into existence through the action of management or other controlling authority proceeding through supervisory, operating, or legislative officials who formally or informally specify work for individuals to do and delegate responsibilities for them to exercise. At any given time a position is characterized by all its duties and responsibilities, as they exist at that time, and so long as these attributes remain the same, the position itself remains the same.

The duties and responsibilities of a position are, however, not always fixed and immutable. They may change from time to time, abruptly or gradually, and because of any one of a number of different reasons. Hence, since a position is characterized by its current duties and responsibilities, it follows that a material change in the duties or responsibilities of a position has the effect of creating a new position different, to the extent of the change, from the old one.

In order to assure proper position-classification, it is sometimes necessary to stress the distinction between the characteristics of a position and the characteristics which the employee occupying it may happen to possess or lack. The considerations having weight in position-classification should be sharply distinguished from those involved in such personnel processes as recruiting, testing, rating, and rewarding efficiency, and placement (assignment, transfer, promotion, and reassignment) in which the applicant's or employee's qualifications have an important and controlling influence.

Class of Positions

We have previously pointed out that the process of classification, abstractly considered, consists of placing things in classes; that the nature of a class of items in any system of classification implies that each individual item which the class contains shall be like every other item in certain respects; that these respects depend upon the basis of the particular classification concerned; and that in position-classification we select as the basis of classification the duties and responsibilities of the positions being classified. Hence, a class of positions is a group of positions which, irrespective of the particular operating units in which they are located, are sufficiently alike in their duties and responsibilities to justify group treatment in nomenclature, selection, pay, and other personnel processes.

A formal definition of the term "class" is as follows:

The term "class" means a group of positions established under these rules sufficiently similar in respect to the duties, responsibilities, and authority thereof that the same descriptive title may be used with clarity to designate each position allocated to the class, that the same requirements as to education, experience, capacity, knowledge, proficiency, ability, and other qualifications should be required of the incumbents, that the same tests of fitness may be used to choose qualified employees, and that the same schedule of compensation can be made to apply with equity under the same or substantially the same employment conditions.

The definition of the term "class" is the most significant of those involved in position-classification because it contains the basic principle for determining whether two or more given positions belong in the same class or in different classes. From the first part of the definition, it will be observed that if two or more positions are "sufficiently similar in respect to their duties and responsibilities," they belong in the same class; otherwise they belong in different classes. It is the decision whether or not positions are in fact "sufficiently similar" that constitutes the essence of classification. The second part of the definition establishes four concurrent conditions to govern the making of this decision.

We should especially note that equality of rank is not alone sufficient to establish positions in the same class. Two positions that may properly be paid according to the same pay-scale—one composed of stenographic work and the other statistical work—are not allocable to the same class of positions, because they do not conform to the other standards of sufficient similarity. For example, different qualification standards would be used for each of these classes.

A "class of positions" is, of course, a group concept, as contrasted with "position," which refers to duties and responsibilities performed (or to be performed) by an individual employee. In a given organization there are as many *positions* as there are employees and vacancies waiting to be filled, but there are only as many *classes* of positions as there are distinct kinds of positions, one compared with another. The duties and responsibilities making up a position may make it anything from messenger boy to head of department. The duties and responsibilities of a class of positions can, however, properly include only those having essential features of similarity.

While defined as a group of positions, a class may sometimes consist of but one position where no others of the same kind exist in the service.

In 1933 there was appointed the Commission of Inquiry on Public Service Personnel, composed of eminent students of administration and public-spirited laymen. The Commission conducted a broad and detailed study of all aspects of public service in the United States and in 1935 presented a general report of its findings and recommendations. In addition to its general report there were presented a number of the special studies made by staff members. The following selection is a chapter from one of the special studies. Its author is Lucius Wilmerding, Jr., who served the Commission as assistant to the director of research.

This essay is described in a leading book on personnel administration as a "vigorous indictment of the American system of classification." To the editor's knowledge it states the general theoretical argument against typical position-classification thinking in the most cogent as well as the most concise form. To some, however, Mr. Wilmerding's essay has a captious, querulous quality stemming from inadequate experience with the "facts of life" in American personnel work.

Query, are the arguments presented realistic or are they essentially a "debater's case," superficially plausible but really inapplicable on the American scene? What is the weight of the argument that determination of what the government *ought* to do should precede analysis and classification of what it does?

Mr. Wilmerding's essay is followed by six paragraphs quoted from a Canadian Royal Commission report on classifications in the public service. This passage will indicate that though Mr. Wilmerding's treatment may seem "academic" the issues are real and important to "men of affairs." As will be noted, part of Mr. Wilmerding's discussion concerns Canada.

Classification : Principles and Method *

LUCIUS WILMERDING, JR.

General Considerations

The Bases of Division. Classification is not an end in itself. It is only an analytic tool to be used as a means to an end. The bases upon which the civil service is divided are therefore not absolute but are determined by the purposes for which classification is used. . . .

For the purposes of recruitment it is necessary to separate the careers which may be followed by men of the same type. Doctors, for instance, must be dis-

* By permission from *Government by Merit; An Analysis of the Problem of Government Personnel*, by Commission of Inquiry on Public Service Personnel. Copyright, 1935, McGraw-Hill Book Company, Inc.

tinguished from lawyers, chemists from actuaries, geographers from geometers, and so forth, even though all are specialists performing specialist work. In general it may be said that functional subdivision is necessary wherever recruitment is based on experience and that the basis of the subdivision must be not the quality of the man, but the nature of his knowledge and experience.

Recruitment policy may also require the division of each career into grades. For if recruitment from the commercial world is permitted at all stages of experience, a number of entry points must be provided in each functional subdivision to correspond with those stages; different tests must be given to, say, the youth fresh from medical school and to the established doctor.

In any event each career must be divided horizontally for the purpose of promotion. Apprentices must be kept separate from employees in the substantive grades, and the bulk of the latter from those in controlling posts. Here the basis of division is the difficulty and responsibility of the work to be done.

This subdivision of the major kinds of work into careers and the division of careers into grades are sufficient for all the purposes of employment management. . . . Salary standardization can be gained simply by assigning a salary rate or a salary range to each grade in each career. There is nothing to be gained except a superficial uniformity by attempting to evaluate on a common basis the work of, say, dentists, veterinarians, quarantine inspectors, and pharmacognosists.

The Degree of Division. The number of careers and grades which should be recognized in the classification is likewise to be determined empirically. The number of careers will depend largely on recruitment policy. If a high degree of specialization is required for entry, it may be necessary to draw artificial distinctions between functions; clerks, for example, may have to be subdivided into mail clerks, record clerks, supply clerks, audit clerks, law clerks, correspondence clerks, clerks ad infinitum. On the other hand, a recruitment policy which is based on post-entry training will require no subdivision at all. The occupational differentiation of men of a given type can be handled as a problem in training and assignment without the cumbersome and rigid mechanism of classification.

In the same way, the grading of careers will depend on the degrees of experience required for entrance, on the extent to which central control is exercised over promotions and assignments, and on the strictness with which the doctrine of equal pay for equal work is interpreted.

The Value of Simplicity. As a general rule, however, one may say that the number of careers and grades which are recognized should be as small as possible.

The use of classification to control organization suggests the desirability of simplicity. The broader the strokes in which the picture is painted, the easier will it be for those who control organization to interpret its meaning.

The effect of classification on the conduct of official business also suggests that simplicity should be its goal. To distinguish between careers which are essentially similar and to draw the boundaries of grades too narrowly can only result in restricting unduly the power of department heads to make assignments in accordance with the necessities of their business and the capacities of their employees. The consequences are the entanglement of departmental management in red tape and the passing of official business through too many hands.

Method of Classification. These considerations indicate that the proper method of classification is, first, to decide upon the major kinds of work which ought to be done by civil servants; second, to divide each of these major kinds into occupational groups; third, to grade each occupational group to the extent required by recruitment, promotion, and salary policies; and, finally, to allocate the existing positions of the civil service to the appropriate grade and group.

Character of American Classification

Theory. Neither these principles nor this method of division have, however, commended themselves to those who have been responsible for classification in America. For they have cast classification in a somewhat grander rôle than that indicated above.

Underlying the theory and method of American classification is an analogy which is conceived to exist between the employment of men and the purchase of supplies and equipment. In the latter vast sums of money have been saved by requiring department heads to buy according to standard specifications which have been centrally drawn up for wheat, soap, lumber, steel beams, pencils, screwdrivers, and so forth. It has, therefore, been assumed that similar savings can be made by drawing up standard specifications for janitors, lawyers, junior clerks, under clerks, etc., and requiring their observance by department heads in recruitment, assignment, and promotion.

In this assumption the classifiers are fortified by a strong faith in the methods of analysis which they themselves have devised. For, as Dr. Abraham Flexner has pointed out:

"What we call personnel workers and job analysts, having ascertained the shortest possible time and the fewest possible steps required to produce a plumber or a typist, have leaped to the conclusion that the technique of job analysis enables them to unravel the higher secrets of intelligence and personality and to ascertain the precise requirements of the most highly differentiated tasks."

The goal of American classificationists is, therefore, to achieve with as much detail and scientific accuracy as possible a

"grouping together of positions sufficiently alike that the same descriptive title may be given to each; that the same qualifications may be required for the successful performance of the duties; that the same tests of fitness may be used to choose qualified employees; and that the same schedule of compensation can be made to serve with equity."

Method. In the pursuit of this goal, the specialists in classification have devised a method of analysis which is the exact opposite to that suggested [above]. That method is to build the framework of classification by combination rather than division.

The first step is to ascertain in detail the duties of each existing position; the second is to combine into classes all positions the duties of which are approximately equal in kind, difficulty, responsibility, and (consequently) value. Class specifications are then prepared to describe the duties of each class and the qualifications and experience required for their performance. The classes which are set up in this manner are then arranged hierarchically in occupational groups, usually called promotion series.

In most governments the combination of positions into classes and of classes into occupational groups completes the work of classification. It remains only for those in charge of recruitment to frame standard tests and for those who control remuneration to assign a standard range of pay to each class. But in the federal departmental service the situation is a little different. For, as Mr. Ismar Baruch explained at one of the hearings of the Commission of Inquiry on Public Service Personnel: "It was not feasible for Congress to set up classes directly, but it did set up a preliminary grouping of positions a priori in the act itself."

This preliminary grouping was into services and grades, a service being defined as "the broadest division of related offices and employments"; and a grade as "a subdivision of a service, including one or more positions for which approximately the same basic qualifications and compensation are prescribed, the distinction between grades being based upon differences in the importance, difficulty, responsibility, and value of the work."

Five services were set up. . . .[1]

The professional and scientific service is at present divided into nine grades; the subprofessional into eight; the clerical, administrative, and fiscal into sixteen; the custodial into ten; and the clerical-mechanical into four. The duties appropriate to each of these grades are defined in the act and each grade is assigned a salary range.

Into this framework the federal classifiers had to fit the classes and occupational groups which they built up from the duties of individual positions. The division into services caused them no especial difficulty, for it merely meant the grouping together of similar occupational series. But the division into grades was more inconvenient. For it meant that the upper and lower boundaries of the classes which they set up had to be coincidental with the boundaries of the arbitrary grades in order that the compensation might be appropriate. In other words, they had to provide promotional steps of uniform height for all the occupational groups in a

[1] The language of the Classification Act of 1923, quoted here in full, is omitted. The Classification Act of 1949, replacing that of 1923, sets up two schedules of grades, one for crafts and protective and custodial jobs, and another, the so-called General Schedule, for all other classes of employment. Important classes of Federal employees, however, including postal and many "blue-collar" employees, are not under the Federal Classification Act.—The Editor.

service even though common sense or a comparison with outside practice might suggest steps of different heights.

These inconveniences did not, however, affect the method of classification in the federal service. It remained fundamentally a classification by combination rather than a classification by division.

Criticism of American Classification

An Erroneous Theory. Needless to say, any theory which presupposes that men can be treated in the same manner as things is open to serious question. While supplies and equipment can be manufactured according to standard specifications, men cannot. As Professor Graham has wisely said:

"The theory underlying a classification plan is that selection is for a specific post or narrow line of development and that the organization should pay not the man but the job. But when higher positions in the supervisory scale are considered, it is difficult to separate the man from the position. His qualities make the position. He has broad responsibilities which are quite definite. But the way he works, or the steps he takes in meeting the responsibilities, are a matter properly determined by his own personality and habits. Great leeway is justifiable."

The notion that there is any value in drawing up class specifications for kinds of work which differ only in minor ways must therefore be rejected.

A Faulty Method. If the assumptions of personnel experts be erroneous, what can be said of their method? At first blush, it may appear that the difference between it and the method suggested [above] is purely formal: that to build the framework of classification by combining positions into classes and classes into occupational hierarchies and occupational hierarchies into services will give in the end the same result as a method which, taking the whole service as its starting point, classifies by division and subdivision—just as a checkerboard can be made by building it up from sixty-four separate squares or by drawing lines in the ordinary way upon a single large square.

Such an appearance is, however, deceitful, for in practice the same result will not commonly be attained. The agglomerative method can give a picture only of the work which is actually being done; it can take no account of work which is neglected. The method of division, on the other hand, presupposes a wide understanding of the kinds of work which should be done. The two can result in the establishment of the same framework only if what is being done corresponds to what ought to be being done. If conditions are otherwise the results will be different: a checkerboard cannot be perfected if some of the blocks are missing.

One may also be permitted to challenge the validity of the data upon which class specifications are drawn. The practical difficulties in the way of analyzing large numbers of positions were well described by Professor Dawson in his account of the Canadian classification of 1919, a classification made on the American plan by a Chicago firm which has had much experience in the United States:

"Sixteen distinct steps were found to be necessary in order to classify each employee in the service—making a grand total of about 800,000 operations. Cards were sent to all civil servants asking for information about their positions, and rashly adding if there were not sufficient room on the card to describe their duties another sheet might be attached. Many availed themselves of this unexpected opportunity for showing their value to the nation. It was intended that these modest accounts would be checked for accuracy by the superior officers, especially by the deputies, but the latter were for the most part out of sympathy with the whole idea, and found themselves too preoccupied to revise a couple of thousand answers apiece. From the accurate data thus obtained, aided by occasional conferences with the departments and the Commission, the experts drew up what was known officially as *The Classification of the Civil Service of Canada.* Others not so charitable dubbed it 'the joke book,' 'the yellow book,' 'the best book of short stories in the English language.' "

Bad Results. If classification were merely a game to test the human ingenuity, one might dismiss the errors in its theory and in its method as of little consequence. But classifications are made to use, and an erroneous classification may therefore lead to practical results which are bad.

The most obvious fault to be found with all classifications made on the American plan is their complexity—the great number of classes and occupational hierarchies which are set up. What seem to be the most trifling differences in function or difficulty are formally recognized and duly defined. The Personnel Classification Board, for example, in its survey of the federal field service, distinguished no less than 1,633 classes of work and 369 occupations in 104,000 positions. And these figures were exclusive of the vast postal service and several less numerous groups of positions. The standard specifications for these classes are contained in a volume of 1,327 closely printed pages.

So refined are many of the distinctions set forth in American classifications that an English student (Mr. W. J. Glenny) was led to suppose that American job analysts composed their work to the " 'sweet tetrandrian monogynian strains' of Linnaeus."

Classifications of such complexity are to be condemned because of the fetters which they place upon department heads in the management of their business. If a man cannot be advanced to work of slightly greater difficulty than that to which he was initially assigned, or if a man cannot be transferred from one kind of clerical work to another, without in the one case being formally promoted and in the other reexamined, departmental business may easily bog down in a welter of red tape.

Furthermore, it should not be forgotten that one of the objects of classification is to give those who control the civil service a bird's-eye view of its organization. With this end in view, complications should be avoided, for they do but confuse the picture and trouble the understanding of those who look upon it.

The pseudo-scientific detail of American classifications is not, however, the most serious fault which can be attributed to an erroneous theory and a faulty method. Far more evil in its consequences has been the failure of American classifiers to perceive the *major* distinctions between kinds of work. This failure is most marked in the general civil service; although it occurs also in the specialist service, where administrative work is often confused with professional, scientific, or technical work.

The clerical, administrative, and fiscal service of the federal classification . . . is not limited to one type of work, but contains all the general types from the simplest routine to the highest administrative. Yet in the federal classification the functional distinctions which exist between routine, clerical, executive, and administrative work are completely overlooked, or rather they are conceived to be hierarchical. This is extraordinary, for the difference between the ordinary administrator and the ordinary office boy must be apparent to the dullest perception. How much more apparent, then, should it be to a Congress able to tell a junior clerk from an assistant clerk, and to an administrative agency which can differentiate between an under property and supply clerk and an under storekeeper? Nevertheless the classifiers have been insensitive to the major distinctions. They have been like a singing master who, able to recognize all the half-tones, nay quarter-tones, of the chromatic scale, cannot tell a soprano from a bass voice. . . .

Recommendations

In the foregoing paragraphs I have criticized the results of the American theory and method of classification on two points: its minuteness of detail and its blindness to major distinctions. As a remedy to these errors, I suggest the inversion of the method of classification. Instead of building the classification by agglomeration from the answers to questionnaires, let the classifiers start with the whole civil service and proceed by division and subdivision. They know without making costly job analyses that government requires the services of doctors, lawyers, janitors, clerks, and so forth. Let them therefore set up out of their ordinary knowledge of government the several careers in the civil service, subdividing them to the degree which is consonant with proper recruitment and promotion policies. . . .

Unless some such recognition of the division of labor is made in the classification, defeat is certain in the attempt to organize the work of the civil service in such a way that government may concern itself with what ought to be done as well as with what must be done.

Classification in the Service *

In the years immediately following the first World War the civil service was reorganized and converted from a patronage to a merit basis. This process required an extensive review of positions, duties, and scales of remuneration throughout the service. Machinery and procedures had to be devised for grading duties and establishing standards of remuneration so as to achieve, and to maintain for the future, uniformity of remuneration for work of like quality and responsibility, in all parts of the service. The system employed to accomplish these objects was developed under the general direction of the Civil Service Commission with the technical assistance of an outside firm of experts. It was founded on a detailed, highly specialized and complex scheme of classification into which every position in the service had to be fitted. This scheme was given statutory effect by Act of Parliament in 1919 and was subsequently embodied in the Civil Service Act.

It is our considered opinion that certain of the fundamental difficulties and weaknesses of the civil service to-day are due to the persistent attempt to work within the confines of this rigid and complex system of classification. Experience in the United Kingdom, where the methods employed are far simpler and more flexible, and to a lesser extent in the United States, confirms this view.

Positions in the Canadian Civil Service are grouped, for purposes of recruitment, promotion, remuneration and general management into no less than 3,700 different classifications. Of these some 2,200 are applicable to permanent positions and about 1,500 to special wartime and other temporary positions. This very detailed differentiation results in the creation of a great number of highly specialized positions, each with its finely distinguished qualifications. Consequently, we have class titles such as Agricultural Architect, Annuities Actuary, Assistant in Fruit By-Products, Chief Record of Performance Inspector, Assistant Investigator of Values, Bath Caretaker, etc.

The implications of this system are obvious. At the gateway to the service recruitment is conducted by rating applicants on the basis of some specialized knowledge or some particular experience rather than on the basis of general intelligence and capacity. This practice has undoubtedly contributed to the failure to obtain sufficient recruits to supply the ranks out of which administrators of high calibre may be drawn. In particular it has militated against the recruitment of young men and women of capacity from those parts of the country where the educational system is not directed towards specialized types of training.

Inside the service, the classification system, through lack of flexibility, has hindered the adequate development and best utilization of high grade personnel.

* From Report of the Royal Commission on Administrative Classifications in the Public Service (Ottawa: 1946), pp. 13–14.

It has rendered difficult the transfer of individuals not only between departments but within departments. What is even more serious it has slowed down and rendered cumbersome the machinery of promotion. The career of a Canadian civil servant is bestrewn with a vast number of closely spaced blocks. The result is that many persons of ability and promise are lost in blind alleys or emerge from them too late in life. Unhappily, too, the complexity of the system entails a large amount of detailed administrative and paper work and consequently delay, with the result that important positions not infrequently remain vacant for prolonged periods.

We are firmly of the view that a simpler and more workable system of classification is essential if the Canadian Civil Service is to be fitted for the heavy and complex tasks which lie before it.

Chapter 11

Organization for Personnel Administration

Various persistent questions of organization are reflected in the problem: How to organize for personnel administration?

One of these is the question of executive control. Shall the chief executive have control of the personnel function? To what extent and in what manner? A related question is that of autonomy. Is the personnel function one which, by virtue of its scientific *expertise* or possible political misuse, should enjoy autonomous status? Another question concerns "centralization versus decentralization." What should be the relation of centrally located personnel functions (whether or not controlled by the chief executive) to the operating departments? Ought the central agency or the operating departments to perform the various personnel functions—recruiting, testing, training, and so forth? Still another question concerns democratic control and accountability. What type of organization for personnel administration is best calculated to ensure, not merely "efficiency and economy of operation," but control of the government by the people? Is such control best ensured through the legislative body, through the chief executive, or in another manner?

Such questions are not presented in the abstract. They must be viewed and answered in a context of two generations of experience; of widely accepted—but conflicting—theories; and of presently existing institutions and personalities which cannot be changed overnight.

Traditionally, personnel functions in the United States have been carried on (when consciously organized in any fashion) by a bipartisan commission enjoying substantial autonomy from executive control and rather remote from "operations." The pattern was set by the Federal government through the establishment of the Civil Service Commission in 1883. The provisions of the statute under which it was created suggest that considerable presidential control of personnel was expected, but the direction of evolution was not toward executive control but toward autonomy of operation. State and local experience tended to follow in the train of Federal.

Meanwhile there occurred, however, the rise of positive, managerial ideas in the study of public administration. These newer ideas supplemented the older philosophy of the central personnel agency: that it was essentially a policing agency to ensure political neutrality and compliance by the operating departments with all "standards." The newer philosophy, like the old, was hostile to "spoils"; but it envisaged a greatly expanded and more active personnel function. As a result, current trends in organization for personnel administration favor more control over personnel functions by the chief executive, single- rather than multiple-headed personnel agencies, and expanded responsibility for personnel matters in operating departments.

The three selections below summarize much recent thinking about organization for personnel administration. The first consists of a comparatively brief extract from the special study on personnel administration prepared by Floyd W. Reeves and Paul T. David for the President's Committee on Administrative Management; the extract presents the rationale behind the proposals which were summarized briefly above by John Fischer. The second consists of the introduction and conclusion of a 1946 essay on "The Changing Role of the U.S. Civil Service Commission" by John McDiarmid, a professor of political science who had just completed a period of service with the Commission. The bulk of this essay consists of a detailed report of activities of the Commission, designed more or less to refute the frequent charge that the Commission has been slow in operation, negative in outlook, and out of step with recent trends in the personnel field. The third consists of extracts from the report of the personnel "task force" of the Hoover Commission. Incidentally, though there was disagreement within the Commission as to the wisdom of the task force recommendations, some of the recommendations were embodied in the President's Reorganization Plan No. 5 of 1949, and present evolution is essentially along lines there projected.

Personnel Administration in the Federal Service *

FLOYD W. REEVES AND PAUL T. DAVID

Personnel administration is . . . one of the types of administrative management for which the Chief Executive has a major responsibility as the administrative head of the Executive Branch of the Federal Government. . . .

Personnel administration, however, cannot and should not be considered in isolation. It is only one phase of the larger problem of administrative management. When viewed from the point of view of the Chief Executive, it is apparent that personnel administration is one of the most important phases of administrative management and is closely related to other phases.

The effectiveness of personnel administration is a problem of vital concern to a Chief Executive who desires to increase the ability of his administration to respond to the demands made upon it. The quality of the personnel in the service is a direct reflection of the quality of past and present personnel administration. Few if any factors affect more vitally the services of government than the quality of the personnel administering those services.

Good personnel may admittedly be very ineffective in the Federal Government if placed in an organization framework that is structurally unsound. Emphasis upon good personnel should not be allowed to minimize the emphasis that properly should be given to sound organization. Both problems are of major importance, and in fact interlock. It is difficult to attract good personnel to an organization that is faulty in structure, and it is likewise difficult to improve the structure of organization without the assistance of good personnel through whom to work. The two problems must be attacked concurrently by the Chief Executive, since he is responsible for leadership in both matters. . . .

The Difficulties Faced by the Chief Executive

The Federal service is analogous in its problem of personnel administration to a large and complex private organization, but the analogy has limitations that greatly complicate the problem of personnel administration as viewed by the Chief Executive. On the one hand is the democratic ideal of equality of opportunity in accordance with merit; on the other hand is the practical political problem of the patronage.

For more than 50 years the ideal of equality of opportunity in accordance with merit has found expression in the Federal service through the selection of candidates for appointment by means of open competitive examinations. To the extent

* In Report with Special Studies, President's Committee on Administrative Management (Washington: 1937), pp. 59–133.

that the ideal of equality of opportunity in accordance with merit is rigorously adhered to, the discretion of the Executive is necessarily limited somewhat by a formalized procedure. Formalized procedures of the civil service type are rarely used in even the most efficient private enterprises. The fact that rigorous adherence to such a procedure may in some cases be inconsistent with good administration is recognized in the Civil Service Act. Provision was made in that act for exceptions at the discretion of the Chief Executive; but in those areas of the service intended to be filled on merit alone, the Chief Executive cannot allow either himself or his subordinates to exercise discretion to the extent that is typical in private industry.

The patronage areas of the service would appear to give the Chief Executive an ample opportunity for the exercise of discretion in the performance of a high type of personnel administration; but such in fact is not the case. Even aside from the limitations upon discretion in connection with the many appointments for which the confirmation of the Senate is required, the Chief Executive is faced with difficulty because of his position as a political leader.

It follows that the Chief Executive is constantly faced with conflict between his political and his administrative responsibilities in the direction of personnel activities in those areas of the service for which he has the greatest discretion in personnel administration. From the point of view of his administrative responsibilities, the tendency is to seek the best available personnel and to conduct other personnel activities on the basis of the requisites for a high type of performance. From the point of view of his political responsibilities, leadership in a legislative program of any considerable magnitude under existing political conditions requires a constant series of concessions ranging from slight favoritism toward persons with "clearance" to outright political appointments to important positions for which the appointees are unqualified and in which they exert a deadening influence over the quality of work in large areas of the service. The result is a constantly shifting pattern, occasionally marked by instances of administration of extraordinarily fine quality, but on the whole producing a grade of administration far below what it might be.

The Question of Executive Discretion

An important question that must be faced by the Chief Executive in the improvement of personnel administration thus arises: Should he seek more or less discretion over the administration of personnel matters throughout the Federal service? At the risk of appearing paradoxical, it may be ventured as a preliminary answer that he needs both more and less.

He needs restriction upon his appointing discretion over large numbers of positions. The existing number of political appointments appears to be far greater than that required for political leadership. The number should be reduced as rapidly as feasible by the extension of the formalized competitive examination procedure. This implies a considerable extension of the classified civil service.

This reform is needed not only to give the Chief Executive a buffer against political pressure in the performance of as large a part of his administrative task as possible, but also to prevent the enormous wastage of his time and strength that now occurs in making appointments open to political considerations. Pressure in connection with political appointments must be materially relieved before the Chief Executive can give adequate attention to improvement in personnel or to other aspects of administration.

Appointments, however, constitute only one aspect of the problem of good personnel administration. Other major personnel functions include the classification of positions to clarify responsibilities and duties and to permit salary standardization; the administration of status changes to improve placement and build a career service; the determination of appropriate salary levels and the administration of individual salary changes; the systematic training of employees in the performance of their duties and for advancement; the conduct of employee-management relations; the control of working conditions to promote health, safety, and efficiency; the administration of compensation for death, disabilities, and injuries in line of duty; and the retirement of superannuated and disabled employees.

All of these activities are fundamental to good personnel administration. Some of them, individually, are as important as the administration of the recruitment, selection, and initial placement of employees. Collectively, they are much more important in a mature, going enterprise than the single function of administration of original appointments. Since much improvement of techniques and procedures still remains to be achieved for each of these activities, research and investigation are also important to constructive personnel administration.

Much of the actual work of personnel administration cannot be performed by specialized personnel officers, but must continue to be performed by line supervisors. The training of supervisors at all levels in the personnel aspects of their supervisory duties is therefore an important part of any really constructive job of personnel administration.

From the point of view of the Chief Executive, the successful performance of the entire range of personnel administrative activities is essential to that efficient conduct of the business of Government for which he is responsible. His existing authority over many aspects of personnel administration is broad in theory, but in practice it comes to little because of the lack of properly organized technical assistance. To some extent he needs additional statutory authority, but in the main he needs a well-organized service of personnel administration at all administrative levels, the principal subject of this study.

The Changing Role of the U.S. Civil Service Commission *

JOHN McDIARMID

For many years, the Civil Service Commission operated primarily as a central examining agency. Along with the majority of commissions at the state and local level, its paramount job was considered that of substituting a competitive merit system for the spoils system in original appointments. Few persons were startled when additional service-wide personnel responsibilities were assigned from time to time to other units of the government. Thus, as late as 1932 position classification, efficiency ratings, and retirement were separately administered. Other major areas—such as promotion, transfer, training, health and safety, working conditions, employee relations, personnel procedures—were subject to little or no central direction or influence.

This situation, however, did not go unchallenged. In one of the most careful and constructive appraisals ever made of federal personnel work, Herman Feldman pointed out in 1931 that "the major defect is that responsibility exists nowhere for many functions which any private organization one-twentieth the size of the Federal force would have long found it imperative to delegate to responsible officials." He went on to add:

"If the purpose of the present survey is to speed the progress of Federal personnel administration, no recommendation is more important than that of establishing a central personnel authority exercising initiative in all matters affecting the Federal employees. Its responsibility should be to keep in constant touch with most of the conditions affecting the Federal service, to be ready at any time to advise the President or Congress with regard to matters of wages, hours, leaves, working conditions, incentives, causes of turnover, grievances, and similar matters, and to serve as a stimulus to administrators generally in the improvement of employment conditions."

Feldman made no recommendation as to the proper location of such a central personnel agency in the governmental structure. He found advocates of (1) a separate office in the Bureau of the Budget, (2) an enlarged and strengthened Civil Service Commission, and (3) an expanded Personnel Classification Board.

In its 1931 report, the Commission itself entered the discussion with a recommendation for combining "in one administrative body all Federal agencies which have to do with personnel in the civil service." This point of view made substantial progress with the transfer of the central activities in position-classifica-

* From *American Political Science Review*, Vol. 40 (December, 1946), pp. 1067–1096. Reprinted by permission of *The American Political Science Review*.

tion, efficiency ratings, and retirement administration to the Commission in 1932, 1933, and 1934, respecively. While these moves gave the Commission three more statutory programs to administer, they left it still quite a bit short of the goal of a "central personnel agency." They notably extended the Commission's regulatory and control authority and its contacts with operating agencies. They left untouched a wide area of non-regulatory or service functions, for which the Commission generally assumed no obligation.

The argument has frequently been advanced that a civil service commission having the responsibility for exercising controls and restrictive authority over certain phases of personnel work is not the proper agency for giving central leadership and assistance in the positive, or educational, aspects of managing employees. As early as 1922, Lewis Mayers distinguished "promotive or assisting" functions on the one hand from regulatory functions on the other, and concluded that the two should not be combined in a single agency. Similarly, Lewis Meriam stated in 1937 that "the Commission was wise in staying out of the operating field and not attempting to mix control, management, and promotion. Such a mixture would lead only to hopeless confusion and inefficiency." Even Reeves and David, in their influential report for the President's Committee on Administrative Management, threw a nod in the direction of this point of view. When citing what they considered one of the three major obstacles to the Commission's development as a satisfactory central personnel agency, they pointed to its many activities of a restrictive or policing tyype, and went on to add:

"Many friends of the Commission therefore feel that the more constructive types of personnel activity cannot be carried on effectively by an agency which necessarily must give so much attention to the enforcement of restrictive statutes. Regulatory activities such as those of the Commission are said to prevent the development of the attitudes of friendly coöperation that are necessary for other types of central personnel activity."

It would seem to me a serious mistake to attempt to limit one central personnel agency to restrictive or regulatory activities, and either set up a separate body for steady promotion and improvement of progressive practices throughout the service (as proposed by Meriam), or depend entirely on the individual operating agencies in this regard. In the first place, the line between control and promotion is almost impossible to draw. Compliance with the provisions of the Classification Act requires some central oversight and direction; far more significantly, it requires widespread understanding, and technical competence, within each department. The former is regulatory, the latter a matter of education; yet they are inextricably complementary. Similarly, the provision of a uniform efficiency rating program requires general regulations, yet depends far more for its successful operation upon the understanding and support of administrators and supervisors. The same is true of leave administration, reductions-in-force, recruitment and selection, and in fact every phase of personnel management in which public policy warrants general regulations embodying some element of restriction on the administrator's discretion. Furthermore, these control areas are intimately related to the phases of personnel work over which no central control exists.

In the second place, if it *were* possible to limit a central agency to the areas of regulation and control, the effect on both the regulators and the regulated would be disastrous. Both the quality of the regulations and the degree of real compliance could but suffer. The friction and lack of mutual understanding, some of which is inevitable in any central control function, would burgeon.

No, the combination of control and service is a prerequisite for the successful functioning of a central personnel agency. When the latter helps an operating agency meet its internal classification problems—that is, renders a voluntary service which is constructive and appreciated—three important things happen. A friendly personal basis for future relations is strengthened. The central agency gains in knowledge and appreciation of operating problems which should enlighten the formulation and administration of classification controls. The departmental officials have a further chance to clarify their understanding and appreciation of the desirable aspects of the general controls, and are more likely to exert their influence toward agency compliance. In its larger aspects, the concept of service is contagious, and helps continually to remind the central agency that its only *raison d'être* is the facilitation of the public activities of the line departments. That this reminder is constantly needed by an organization exercising restrictions and controls is, I believe, indisputable. The alternative of leaving individual operating agencies entirely without central assistance in the non-regulatory phases of personnel management is simply to overlook tremendous possibilities for the improvement of government at small cost to the taxpayer.

Fundamentally, Reeves and David assumed the need for a single organization with broad responsibilities in both control and assistance, and measured the Commission against this yardstick. They concluded that "although the Commission is now performing many of the functions of a central personnel agency in a partially satisfactory manner," there were other "appropriate and needed functions" which that agency had "not developed and is not carrying on." Areas singled out for comment as undeveloped were: transfers; promotions; central information on agency practices, with support for constructive measures and stimulation of improvements; training; responsible management-employee negotiations; interchange of personnel officials between the Commission and operating agencies.

These two observers argued that a "satisfactory central personnel agency would occupy a position exceedingly close to the Executive," and that the Civil Service Commission would never measure up as currently organized. In its stead they proposed a new agency headed by a single administrator reporting directly to the President, and combining a wide variety of control and service activities.

When Congress vetoed this proposal of a single personnel administrator as relayed through President Roosevelt, the Civil Service Commission remained, at least for the time being, the federal government's hope for an enterprising central personnel agency.

While it remained for the war emergency to spotlight this challenge, the developments of 1938 to 1941 must be recalled. June 24, 1938, was a red letter day. In two executive orders, President Roosevelt (1) thoroughly revised and modernized the Civil Service Rules, (2) extended the competitive merit system about as far as could be done without congressional action, (3) required the establishment of a division of personnel supervision and management in each department and agency, (4) revitalized the Council of Personnel Administration, with membership consisting of personnel directors and representatives of the Bureau of the Budget and Civil Service Commission, and (5) gave support to in-service training, fixing responsibility in the Civil Service Commission for coöperating with the departments in this area.

Both the content of these executive orders and the active rôle played by the Commission in their drafting broadened the influence and enhanced the stature of that agency. Creation of agency personnel divisions and an active Council of Personnel Administration provided machinery for Commission leadership in every phase of personnel management; the question remained—would it be utilized?

On September 8, 1939, another brick was laid. Executive Order No. 8248 established the Liaison Office for Personnel Management within the White House Staff, and thus signified the President's interest, and desire to extend his influence, in personnel matters of major service-wide importance. With direct access to the President, regular meetings with Civil Service Commissioners, and close relations with the Bureau of the Budget and other Executive Office arms, the Liaison Officer has dredged the channel of communication and influence in so far as the human side of personnel management is concerned. "This means has given the Civil Service Commission a new status in the government. . . ." The threshold of the war thus found the Commission with great potential influence, but with many tests to be met in its relations with Congress, the President, and the line departments and agencies. . . .

Perhaps far more than is generally realized, the recent years have seen the U.S. Civil Service Commission exercise a leadership throughout the entire range of federal personnel management. Viewing its own rôle broadly as that of a central personnel agency, it has assumed the functions of staff adviser to the Congress, the President, and the line departments on matters far afield from the "traditional civil service activities." Under aggressive leadership, in a war emergency, with adequate funds for the first time in history, it reached the pinnacle of its prestige, its influence, and its constructive contribution to the positive phases of developing human power in government.

Much of this should represent permanent gain, with widespread benefits. Current trends point to a continuation of influence, with Congress and the President, to more personal contact and coöperation with line departments, to more concentration on matters of legislative and executive policy and the establishment of general standards, and to more delegation of authority over operating details to the agencies on the firing line—all to the good.

The recurrence of the old occupational disease of civil service commissions, however, financial starvation, dampens the optimism. With huge work loads of regulatory activities which are mandatory in the statutes, drastic budget cuts could hardly result in other than the curtailment or discontinuance of many of the constructive services so long found lacking, so recently developed, and so short-lived. In addition to their intrinsic worth, these service activities enriched the Commission's philosophy, and thus paid dividends also in their indirect effect upon the day-to-day administration of restrictions and controls. Inside the Commission, the service philosophy inevitably competes with the control philosophy, and no permanent balance can result if only one army remains to occupy the field.

Also, in the control areas—for example, examining and classification—continued improvement in the quality of the Commission's performance will require adequate budgets for maintenance of competent professional staffs, and for research. Can Congress be convinced that penny wise can be pound foolish in so far as personal management is concerned?

The fact that the Commission's rôle has changed markedly in the last few years does not necessarily settle the issue as to the best form of organization for the federal government's central personnel work. Strong arguments can still be advanced in behalf of a single personnel administrator reporting directly to the President, with a board of part-time members serving in an advisory and quasi-judicial capacity. Were this step taken (and there have been some recent indications that President Truman might make the proposal), there would be the possibility of greater operating efficiency, more intimate staff work, increased delegation of authority to departments, and accelerated growth of service activities. Opponents of the change are convinced that any gains on the side of efficiency and interagency relationships are well outweighed by the weakening of the central personnel agency as merit-system protector.

This question will be reopened periodically. Whatever organization pattern finally emerges, the concept of a central personnel agency in fact as well as name seems firmly established. To the acceptance of this concept, and to the working out of the concrete steps needed to realize its potentialities, the Civil Service Commission's recent history has made notable contributions.

Program for Reorienting Efforts
of Personnel Organizations throughout
the Federal Service *

Throughout the . . . studies of Federal personnel management the Personnel Policy Committee has found that one principle should become the keynote of major revisions, present and future:

The operating agencies should be delegated maximum authority, and encouraged to assume full initiative in each principal phase of Federal personnel management: Personnel procurement, employee training and development, job evaluation and supervisor-employee relationships.

The Civil Service Commission, as the central personnel agency of the Government, should direct its efforts toward developing standards designed to secure economy and the uniform observance of Government-wide policies governing civil rights, employee loyalty, veteran preference and the protection of the merit system. It must likewise give positive assistance to the agencies in introducing these standards, as well as conduct inspections to review the compliance of the agencies with established standards.

The final studies of the Personnel Policy Committee are thus concerned with determining the form and functions of personnel organizations necessary to establish this principle of decentralized administration under centralized control. The proposals offered in this connection are grouped for ease of review under two sections: (1) Proposed revisions in the organization of the Civil Service Commission; and (2) proposed revisions in agency personnel organization.

Proposed Revisions in the Organization of the
Civil Service Commission

Dissatisfaction with certain features of the organization and program of the Civil Service Commission has apparently existed almost since its inception. In 1891, Theodore Roosevelt, then a Civil Service Commissioner, testified before the House Civil Service Committee that a single administrator could get things done more quickly. In the past 20 years observations and proposals regarding the Commission organization have been numerous. The following excerpts are representative:

"Dr. Herman Feldman in his report to the Personnel Classification Board in 1931 concluded that unless comprehensive steps were inaugurated 'toward estab-

* By the Personnel Policy Committee of The Commission on Organization of the Executive Branch of the Government. From *Programs for Strengthening Federal Personnel Management* (Washington: 1949), pp. 77–94.

lishing a central personnel authority exercising initiative in all matters affecting Federal employees . . . the personnel management of the Federal Service will remain inadequate.' "

"In 1937 the President's Committee on Administrative Management conducted an inquiry into the over-all management machinery of the Federal Government. It reported the Civil Service Commission 'poorly adapted to meet the larger responsibilities of serving as a central personnel agency for a vast and complicated governmental administration. . . .' This Committee proposed a Civil Service Administration under a single administrative officer."

"Specifically with regard to the Commission form of organization, Dr. Leonard White, after experience as a member of two commissions, pointed to their 'ineptness' as administrative agencies and observed that this experience 'satisfies the writer that the usefulness of this form of organization is exaggerated.' "

"Several proposals have been advanced in recent years for the creation of a Department of Administration in which personnel management might be integrated with budgetary control and other aspects of top management in a single organization under the President. One student of this subject sums up the problem which gives rise to the need for such integration as follows: 'Although other instruments of management have been consolidated in the Executive Office, personnel administration is represented there only through a makeshift arrangement.' "

Despite its critics, the Civil Service Commission has survived a period of 65 years, including the upheavals of 2 wars. While it has lacked the flexibility that many would desire, it has been able to maintain and steadily extend the principles of merit in the Federal civil service. Thus the recommendations which follow are not intended to minimize these substantial accomplishments but rather to remove those obstacles which appear to place unnecessary or undesirable limitations on the Commission's future development in the top-management structure of the Federal Government.

1. *The "commission form" of organization should be retained but one commissioner should be vested with full responsibility for administrative direction.*

The most frequent criticism of the "commission form" of organization is that its triple-headed structure deprives the organization of unified direction, resulting in delay in acting upon important matters of policy, lack of forward planning, inadequate follow-through on major programs and poor coordination of the work of the numerous divisions, sections, and staffs of the operating organization. The Personnel Policy Committee has found in its review of the present organization of the Commission that many of these criticisms are well-founded. It is felt, in fact, that such conditions are unavoidable in an organization of over 4,000 people with widely dispersed operations, where singleness of administration does not exist.

The issue which these problems pose has been repeatedly stated. It is the issue of whether a single-administrator form of organization is feasible in a public personnel organization which is subjected to divergent pressures and influences from many different groups. In order to answer this question, careful study has been given to various forms of organization which would "protect the merit system" and at the same time provide the desirable benefits of single administration. Three alternatives to the present "commission form" of organization have been considered. . . .

First Alternative: *The Personnel Administrator and Chairman.* This arrangement preserves in its present form the bipartisan three-member commission, but provides that the President of the United States designate one of the commissioners as chairman, and vest in him full responsibility for administering the operating organization and program of the Commission.

Second Alternative: *The Coequal Commission and Administrator.* Under this plan the three-member commission is restricted to duties in connection with handling appeals and passing on rules and regulations as they affect the protection of the merit system. A fourth commissioner is provided to administer the operating organization, but he has no formal participation in the deliberations of the three-member commission.

Third Alternative: *The Administrator-Advisory Board.* The most radical of the alternative plans provides a single administrator with full responsibility both for internal management and for all policy, judicial and appellate functions. A part-time board of private citizens, appointed by the President, is provided to investigate the administration of the merit system from time to time, and present its recommendations to the administrator and to the President.

The Personnel Policy Committee has concluded that the second and third alternatives are undesirable because they would weaken the protective functions, and sacrifice the public support which derives from a full-time bipartisan commission of three members. It is therefore recommended that the Personnel Administrator-Chairman arrangement be adopted, and that its essential characteristics be defined as follows:

a. Appointment and tenure. The three commissioners shall be chosen, as provided in the Act of 1883, by the President, by and with the advice and consent of the Senate, to serve at the pleasure of the President. No more than two may be members of the same political party. One of the three shall be designated "Personnel Administrator and Chairman" by the President.

b. Duties of the full commission. The full commission shall, by majority action:

1. Prepare rules and regulations for consideration by the President.

2. Review and recommend new or revised legislation affecting Federal personnel management.

3. Promulgate rules and regulations to preserve and strengthen the merit system.

4. Investigate any phase of the merit system.

5. Establish appellate bodies, supervise their work and act as court of final appeal.

c. Duties of the personnel administrator and chairman. . . . In addition to sharing in the duties specified for the full commission, he should be the principal point of contact between the President and the heads of operating agencies in all matters of civilian personnel management, both domestic and foreign, acting within the rules and regulations established by the full commission. In this connection he shall,

1. Originate new or revised legislation, rules and regulations for consideration by the full commission.

2. Administer a Government-wide standards program covering the procurement, compensation, training, promotion, transfer, discipline, and discharge of civilian employees.

3. Assist operating agencies in the organization and development of personnel programs suited to their individual needs.

4. Devise and present information to the public regarding career opportunities in the Federal service; and to the President and the Congress regarding the problems and achievements of Federal personnel management.

5. Administer a group of service activities for common use by the agencies in the interest of economy.

6. Prepare the budget, direct and supervise the staff, assign personnel, and coordinate the operations of the Commission.

7. Represent the Commission before the President and the Congress in his capacity as Chairman.

d. Special duties for the other commissioners. To the extent deemed desirable by the President, it is suggested that the special interests of the other two commissioners be directed along two lines:

1. Continuing study of the nature, frequency, and source of abuses of the merit system, as revealed by appeals, in order to initiate steps to prevent their recurrence.

2. Representation of the Commission before public and employee groups to secure their understanding and support.

2. *The personnel administrator and chairman should be chosen by the President with regard for his capacity as an administrator.*

The political method of appointing commissioners is felt by some not conducive to securing vigorous, informed top leadership. The President's Committee on Administrative Management in 1937 concluded that "Board members are customarily laymen not professionally trained or experienced in the activities for which they are responsible. They remain in office for relatively short periods and rarely acquire the degree of expertness necessary to expert direction." Those who make this comment hasten to add that this condition has had many exceptions in the history of the Civil Service Commission.

It is felt that the three commissioners must be policy officials, selected and appointed in the same manner as the political heads of other agencies. The Personnel Policy Committee feels, however, that it should be the objective of the President to nominate candidates for the position of personnel administrator and chairman who possess three broad qualifications:

a. Administrative ability. Of highest importance is demonstrated, widely recognized ability in the field of administrative management, either public or private. The personnel administrator should have unquestioned capacity to command the confidence of agency heads, congressional leaders, and top personnel officials throughout the Federal service.

b. Integrity and vision. The reputation of the personnel administrator for honesty, impartiality, and fair dealing should be above reproach. His ability to conceive, interpret, and present Government-wide programs should be unusual. His energy, initiative, and imagination should be vigorous.

c. Knowledge of personnel management. Specific training and experience in private or public personnel administration is desirable but of secondary importance, since these knowledges and skills will be provided by the career staff of the Commission.

3. *The internal organization of the Civil Service Commission should be realigned to place greater emphasis upon standards, inspection, and information activities.*

The central office of the Civil Service Commission is at present subdivided into 15 operating divisions and staffs, most of which perform operating services for the departments and agencies in addition to having responsibilities for standards-setting and, in several cases, inspection of agency practices. Under the proposed plan of decentralization the standards-setting and inspection tasks will become the primary duties of the central personnel agency, and operating services will diminish in size. . . .

a. Four functional divisions should be established. The principal revision proposed is the regrouping of all present functions under four functional divisions, each headed by an outstanding career personnel official. The functions to be encompassed by each division are as follows:

1. *The Standards and Research Division* should be responsible for developing standards covering all of the technical aspects of Federal personnel management; personnel procurement and placement, job evaluation and pay administration, training, personnel evaluation, and employee relations. This division will be the mainspring of the decentralization programs proposed . . . since decentralization cannot proceed until adequate standards have been developed under which the agencies can be delegated authority to act.

2. *The Management Planning and Review Division* should carry full responsibility for the inspection of agency personnel practices under the proposed program of decentralization. In addition the division should devote a large part of its efforts to assisting the agencies in developing their personnel organizations

and procedures, and in evaluating the cost and effectiveness of agency personnel programs.

3. *The Information Services Division* should plan informational programs designed to improve the prestige of Government among all groups of prospective applicants. It should likewise coordinate relations with colleges and universities, supply information to the Congress and serve as the point of contact for veteran organizations and other outside groups.

4. *The Administrative Services Division* should administer the central service activities required by the agencies, including the personnel procurement offices, the veteran preference offices, and the retirement, investigation, and service record divisions.

b. A Deputy Administrator and Executive Director should be established. The present post of Executive Director and Chief Examiner should be replaced by that of a Deputy Administrator—a career official whose time will be free to coordinate and stimulate the work of the operating divisions. This official should have a broad knowledge of personnel management throughout the Federal service. . . .

The position of Executive Director should be established to assist the Deputy Administrator in all matters of internal administration, including budgeting, personnel, internal organization and procedures, and general office services.

c. The Federal Personnel Council and the various advisory committees should be retained and brought into more effective relationship to the operating divisions of the Commission. Since its creation more than a decade ago the Federal Personnel Council has been a potent influence on the modernization and simplification of personnel procedures and the improvement of personnel policies. The several committees of the Council have conducted, in fact, an important program of personnel research and development during this period. The Commission's investment in this program has been relatively small, consisting of a staff of four technical and nine clerical employees.

During recent years another important source of advice and creative thinking has been contributed by a group of committees containing executives both from Government and private life. An especially valuable contribution to the general field of Federal personnel management has been made by the Committee on Administrative Personnel.

The Personnel Policy Committee believes that all of these activities should be retained in the revised organization, but that their contribution can be increased by:

1. Broadening the scope of the full-time staff of the Federal Personnel Council to that of secretariat for all of the advisory groups.

2. Integrating the studies of the committees of the Federal Personnel Council with the current programs of the four operating divisions of the Commission. The committees should receive their assignments from, and make their reports to the respective division heads.

3. Establishing a permanent Personnel Policy Committee, to meet periodically and discuss the programs and objectives of the four operating divisions of the Commission. This committee, composed of Federal officials and personnel authorities from private life who are interested in improving Federal personnel management, should become the successor to the present committee on Administrative Personnel.

d. The present appellate and legal advisory groups should report to the full commission since they are mainly concerned in the Commission's task of protecting the merit system. In this connection it is proposed that the chief law officer screen all matters requiring action by the "full commission."

4. *The operating divisions of the Civil Service Commission should be staffed in part by personnel drawn from the agencies.*

The effectiveness of a central staff agency such as the Commission is dependent upon the acceptance and support it receives from the agencies which it supervises and serves. If the central agency maintains a completely detached position and is staffed with individuals whose experience is restricted to work in the central agency, lack of confidence inevitably results. It is therefore recommended that there be a continuing interchange of personnel between the operating agencies and the Civil Service Commission. Such interchange is most desirable and feasible in the case of the proposed Standards and Research and Management Planning and Review Divisions, both of which will have a continuing impact upon the personnel programs of the operating agencies. As a matter of policy, it is felt that at least one-third of the positions in these divisions should be manned by personnel drawn from the operating agencies for assignments of about 1 year. Some of these assignments can be worked out as part of the proposed program of "advanced career training," to afford special training in personnel management to those who are candidates for top administrative posts in the agencies.

Proposed Revisions in Agency Personnel Organization

While there has been a top personnel-management organization in the Federal service since 1883, formal agency organizations are still rather new. For many years personnel administration was under the control of a chief clerk who was generally responsible for housekeeping and office management activities in the agency. It is said that for the most part the chief clerks were not well versed in management principles and tended to apply an unimaginative, narrow control philosophy to the tasks of hiring, paying, and administering personnel. The first major improvement in this situation occurred in 1938 when the President directed that each agency "establish a division of Personnel Supervision and Management, at the head of which shall be appointed a director of personnel qualified by training and experience . . ." (Executive Order 7916). In 1947 the President, in his Executive Order 9830, greatly strengthened the above directive by placing primary emphasis upon the responsibility of the agency head and the staff role of the personnel director:

"The head of each agency . . . shall be responsible for personnel management in his agency. To assist and advise him in carrying out this responsibility he shall maintain or establish such office or division of personnel as may be required. He shall designate a director of personnel or other similarly responsible official to be in charge of such office or division."

These two directives have provided a powerful stimulant to the establishment of competent agency personnel organizations throughout the Federal service. There are many indications, in fact, that the importance of personnel management has been accorded a satisfactory degree of recognition in most of the agencies during the past 10 years.

However, studies made in 28 agencies, including both headquarters and field installations, have revealed a wide lack of uniformity in the scope and content of agency personnel programs, and a tendency of many personnel offices to retain controls which usurp the authority of line officials and supervisors. These weaknesses contribute to unnecessary expense and, if continued, will depreciate the benefits being sought by the proposed programs of decentralizing procurement, job evaluation, employee development, and supervisor-employee relations. The principal steps necessary to correct these conditions are summarized below.[1]

1. *A concrete plan for strengthening each agency's personnel organization and program should be developed under the leadership of the Civil Service Commission. . . .*

2. *The agency director of personnel should be a member of top-management. . . .*

3. *The primary responsibilities of the Director of Personnel in each agency should parallel those of the Civil Service Commission. . . .*

4. *The primary responsibility of "operating personnel offices" should be to provide service and assistance to operating officials and line supervisors. . . .*

5. *Field installations should be subject to a minimum control by bureau personnel offices. . . .*

6. *In order to assure full participation of operating supervisors in personnel management, a definition of the responsibilities of personnel offices and line supervisors should be established by each agency head. . . .*

7. *Agency personnel offices should not be burdened with the administration of activities not directly concerned with personnel management and services, but should collaborate in the general management-improvement activities of the agency. . . .*

[1] Limitations of space make it necessary to omit the discussions following each step.—The Editor.

Chapter 12

Growth of the "Budget Idea"

Contemporary budget ideas and practices are of comparatively recent development in American government. The selections in this chapter are presented because they sketch the background against which these contemporary budgetary ideas and practices may be seen in perspective.

By the estimate of some outstanding scholars the Federal government had less of a "budget" in the early twentieth century than it had in its infancy in the eighteenth century—we had retrogressed rather than progressed. But in the past generation the changes of law, organization, spirit, and procedure have been of such magnitude that they may properly be called constitutional, though they have taken place with no change in the written document we call "the Constitution." Various influences contributed to the movement for budgetary reform which began early in the century and still continues at all levels of government in the United States. American academic study of European budgetary systems, for example, played an important role, and the writings of the early period of reform are studded with references to British and Continental experience.

Here as in other aspects of public administration the example of business organizations has been important, as the material below will disclose. The pre-First World War governmental reform movement which at its height was known as Progressivism also added strong impetus. The drive for budgetary reform, indeed, begins historically at the point at which the ideas of "efficiency and economy" of business join with the search of Progressivism for more adequate popular control of the "people's business." Budget reform has typically been advanced as simultaneously promoting both efficiency and democracy. Not a few persons, however, have argued that democracy and efficiency are antithetical. Query, has the firm belief of the reformers that budget reform would advance *both* been justified?

The first selection is taken from the famous report of the Commission on Economy and Efficiency appointed by President William Howard Taft— the predecessor of the President's Committee on Administrative Management appointed by President Roosevelt in 1936 and the Hoover Commission authorized by an act of Congress in 1947.

First in importance of the matters to which the Commission on Economy and Efficiency gave attention was Federal fiscal affairs, then unbelievably chaotic. The selections immediately below are from the document *The Need for a National Budget*, in which the Commission's findings are reported. What are reproduced here are the "Message of the President" transmitting the report to Congress and the recommendations and "Introduction" of the Commission. Together they portray well the crystallizing budget philosophy, the special problems of financial management in a separation-of-powers government, and the then chaos—matched or exceeded in both state and local governments of the day—in fiscal affairs.

Though the Congressional "spirit of antagonism" prevented the inauguration of the Commission's recommendations in the years immediately after the report was presented in 1912, the victory was ultimately to the reformers. The vastly increased expenditures which came with the First World War were in themselves a persuasive argument for more systematic finance and helped to win the victory for reform. But the Budget and Accounting Act of 1921 and subsequent developments owe much to *The Need for a National Budget*, which is an important document in American constitutional history.

The Need for a National Budget:
Message of the President *

To the Senate and House of Representatives:

I send herewith the report of the Commission on Economy and Efficiency on "The Need for a National Budget." The recommendations contained therein are approved by me. I recommend to the Congress the enactment of the legislation necessary to put them into effect.

The subject is one of fundamental importance to the Executive, as well as to the Congress. Notwithstanding the magnitude and complexity of the business which is each year conducted by the executive branch and financed by the Con-

* By William Howard Taft and the Commission on Economy and Efficiency. H. Doc. 854, 62d Cong., 2d Sess., pp. 1–5.

gress, and the vital relation which each governmental activity bears to the welfare of the people, there is at present no provision for reporting revenues, expenditures, and estimates for appropriations in such manner that the Executive, before submitting estimates, and each Member of Congress, and the people, after estimates have been submitted, may know what has been done by the Government or what the Government proposes to do.

Briefly stated, the situation is this: Under the Constitution (and subject to its limitations) the Congress is made responsible for determining the following questions of policy: What business or work the Government shall undertake; what shall be the organization under the Executive which is charged with executing its policies; what amount of funds, and by what means funds shall be provided for each activity or class of work; what shall be the character of expenditures authorized for carrying on each class of work—*i.e.,* how much for expenses, how much for capital outlays, etc.

As a means of definitely locating this responsibility the Congress was given the sole power to levy taxes; to borrow money on the credit of the United States; to authorize money to be drawn from the Treasury. To the President also has been given very definite responsibility. To the end that the Congress may effectively discharge its duties the article of the Constitution dealing with legislative power provides that "a regular statement and account of receipts and expenditures of all public moneys shall be published," and the article dealing with the Executive power requires the President "from time to time to give to the Congress information on the state of the Union and to recommend to their consideration such measures as he shall deem necessary and expedient."

Notwithstanding these specific constitutional requirements there has been relatively little attention given to the working out of an adequate and systematic plan for considering expenditures and estimates for appropriations; for regularly stating these in such form that they may be considered in relation to questions of public policy; and for presenting to the Congress for their consideration each year, when requests are made for funds, any definite plan or proposal for which the administration may be held responsible.

Regular committees on expenditure have been established by the Congress for the purpose of obtaining knowledge of conditions through special investigations. During the last century over 100 special congressional investigations have been authorized to obtain information which should have been regularly submitted, and much money as well as much time has been spent by the Congress in its efforts to obtain information about matters that should be laid before them as an open book; many statutes have been passed governing the manner in which reports of expenditures shall be made; specific rules have been laid down giving the manner in which estimates shall be submitted to the Congress and considered by it. From time to time special investigations have been made by heads of executive departments. During the last century many such investigations have been carried on and much money has been spent in the conduct of these, as well as by the Congress for the purpose of obtaining facts as a basis for intelligent consideration of methods and procedure of doing business with a view to increasing economy and efficiency. From time to time Executive orders have been issued and reorganizations have taken place.

Generally speaking, however, the only conclusions which may be reached from all of this are that—

No regular or systematic means has been provided for the consideration of the detail and concrete problems of the Government.

A well-defined business or work program for the Government has not been evolved.

The reports of expenditures required by law are unsystematic, lack uniformity of classification, and are incapable of being summarized so as to give to the Congress, to the President, or to the people a picture of what has been done, and of cost in terms either of economy of purchase or efficiency of organization in obtaining results.

The summaries of expenditures required by law to be submitted by the Secretary of the Treasury, with estimates, not only do not provide the data necessary to the consideration of questions of policy, but they are not summarized and classified on the same basis as the estimates.

The report on revenues is not in any direct way related to the expenditures, except as the Secretary of the Treasury estimates a surplus or a deficiency and this estimate is based on accounts which do not accurately show expenditures or outstanding liabilities to be met.

Instead of the President being made responsible for estimates of expenditures, the heads of departments and establishments are made the ministerial agents of the Congress, the President being called on only to advise the Congress how, in his opinion, expenditures may be reduced or revenues may be increased in case estimated expenditures exceed estimated revenues.

The estimates do not raise for consideration questions which should be decided before appropriations are granted, nor does the form in which estimates are required by the Congress to be presented lay the foundation for the consideration of: Subjects of work to be done; the character of organization best adapted to performing work; the character of expenditures to be made; the best method of financing expenditures.

The present law governing the preparation and submission of estimates, requiring them to be submitted each year in the same form as the year before, was passed without due consideration as to what information should be laid before the Congress as a basis for action, the result being that the unsystematic and confused method before in use was made continuous.

The rules of the Congress do not provide for the consideration of estimates in such manner that any Member of Congress, any committee, or either House of Congress as a whole may have at any one time the information needed for the effective consideration of a program of work done or to be done.

The committee organization is largely the result of historical development rather than of the consideration of present needs.

Inadequate provision is made for getting before each committee to which appropriations are referred all of the data necessary for the consideration of work to be done, organization provided for doing work, character of expenditures, or method of financing.

Following the method at present prescribed, the estimates submitted by each organization unit may have to be split up for consideration by appropriation committees of the Congress and be made the subject of several different bills; in few places are all of the estimates or appropriations asked for by a single organization unit brought together.

The estimates for appropriations requested for a single class of work are similarly divided, no provision being made for considering the amount asked for, the amount appropriated, or the amount spent for a single general class of governmental activity.

Generally speaking, the estimates for expenses (or cost of each definite class of services to be rendered) are not separately shown from estimates for capital outlays (or cost of land, buildings, equipment, and other properties acquired).

While the classification and summaries of estimates do indicate a proposed method of financing, these summaries do not show classes of work or the character of expenditures provided for and therefore can not lay the foundation for the consideration of methods of financing as a matter of governmental policy, as is contemplated under the Constitution.

The appropriations are just as unsystematic and incapable of classification and summary as the estimates—in fact, follow the same general form, making it difficult and in many cases impossible to determine what class of work has been authorized, how much may be spent for each class, or the character of expenditures to be made; nor does any one bill cover the total authorizations for any particular general class of work.

Bills for appropriations (the authorizations to incur liabilities and to spend) are not considered by the committee to which measures for raising revenues and borrowing money are referred, nor are revenues and borrowings considered by committees on appropriations in relation to the funds which will be available.

So long as the method at present prescribed obtains, neither the Congress nor the country can have laid before it a definite understandable program of business, or of governmental work to be financed; nor can it have a well-defined, clearly expressed financial program to be followed; nor can either the Congress or the Executive get before the country the proposals of each in such manner as to locate responsibility for plans submitted or for results.

Although the President has the power to install new and improved systems of accounts and to require that information be presented to him each year in such form that he and his Cabinet may intelligently consider proposals or estimates; although the President, under the Constitution, may submit to the Congress each year a definite well-considered budget, with a message calling attention to subjects of immediate importance, to do this without the cooperation of the Congress in the repeal of laws which would be conflicting and in the enactment of other laws which would place upon the heads of departments duties to be performed that would be in harmony with such procedure, would entail a large expenditure of public money in duplication of work.

The purpose of the report which is submitted is to suggest a method whereby the President, as the constitutional head of the administration, may lay before the Congress, and the Congress may consider and act on, a definite business and financial program; to have the expenditures, appropriations, and estimates so classified and summarized that their broad significance may be readily understood; to provide each Member of Congress, as well as each citizen who is interested, with such data pertaining to each subject of interest that it may be considered in relation to each question of policy which should be gone into before an appropriation for expenditures is made; to have these general summaries supported by such detail information as is necessary to consider the economy and efficiency with which business has been transacted; in short, to suggest a plan whereby the President and the Congress may cooperate—the one in laying before the Congress and the country a clearly expressed administrative program to be acted on; the other in laying before the President a definite enactment to be acted on by him.

Recommendations and Introduction *

The President:

If we follow the accepted usage of most civilized nations, we must conclude that a budget is a collection of documents assembled by an officer who is at the head of or is responsible for the administration and submitted to the legislative branch of the Government. Whatever else such a budget contains, in every case it carries with it an estimate of expenditures to be made by the Government during the coming financial period. While each nation has a revenue policy, the lack of emphasis which has been laid by nations in their budget upon the revenues and the relation of expenditures thereto has probably been due to the fact that by far the larger part of the revenues have come into the Public Treasury as the result of the operation of permanent law. No regular periodical action upon the part of the legislative authority has been necessary in order that revenues might be collected. As a consequence, the budget has been regarded primarily as an estimate of expenditures.

* H. Doc. 354, 62d Cong., 2d Sess., pp. 7–12. This is the supporting statement for the Recommendations, addressed to the President by the Commission on Economy and Efficiency.

Inasmuch, however, as no nation can safely adopt for a long period a policy of expenditures which has no regard to the amount of its revenues, it has been usual in most national governments to fix the amount of the expenditures in view of the expected revenue. Where, as is the case in this country, the estimates have been a matter of legislative rather than executive responsibility, the legislature has imposed upon the Treasury the duty of acquainting it with the estimated revenue for the coming budgetary period. It thus is the case that even in political systems in which revenues are based on permanent law rather than on periodical legislative action the demands of a conservative financial policy require that expenditures shall be estimated in view of revenue possibilities. We may say, therefore, that a budget should consist of estimates of revenue as well as of expenditures.

It has been said that a budget is primarily an estimate of the expenditures made necessary by the operations of the Government. That is, it is assumed that a government already exists which operates in a given way. A budget is based upon the theory that the Government for whose operations expenditures must be made is already organized and discharges certain activities whose number and extent have already been determined. The purpose of a budget is thus to finance an existing organization in order that it may successfully prosecute defined lines of work. In case it is thought desirable to have changes made in organization and in number and extent of activities, as compared with the organization and activities financed in the preceding budgetary period, these changes should be indicated at the time the budget is drawn up, and in any case, the changes must be determined before or at the time that appropriations are granted, since the appropriation is primarily a method of financing the existing organization and predefined activities.

Nevertheless since changes in organization and in number and extent of activities can hardly fail to affect expenditures, a budget, while primarily having to do with the expenditures made necessary by the defined operations of an existing governmental organization, must in the nature of things be concerned secondarily at any rate with questions of governmental organization and activities. It is, of course, to be borne in mind that other than financial considerations primarily control the decision of these questions, but it can not be forgotten that no State can enter upon an administrative program, however desirable, the expense of which its financial resources do not admit it to assume. Thus, a comprehensive naval program is entered upon for military and not for financial reasons. But if the resources of the country are insufficient the nation will have to forego the advantages of such a program, however marked they may be.

In this sense it may be said that a budget is in the nature of a prospectus and that its purpose is to present in summary form the facts necessary to the shaping of the policies of the Government so far as they affect its finances.

Budgetary practice has been influenced by the constitutional relations existing between the executive and legislative branches of government. Generally speaking, the executive authority (apart from the United States) has been conceived of as possessing powers of initiation and leadership while the legislative authority is regarded as possessing merely powers of final determination and control. In the United States, however, the legislature is usually regarded as the authority which initiates and determines a policy which it is the duty of the Executive to carry out. The effect of this conception of the relations of the Legislature to the Executive has been that the budget has been primarily an affair of the Congress rather than of the President. The Congress makes use of administrative officers in order to obtain the information which it must have to determine the important questions of policy devolved upon it by the American system. These administrative officers are acting as the ministerial agents of the Congress rather than as representatives of the President. The result is that while in most other countries the budget is in the nature of a proposal or program submitted on its responsibility by the executive to the legislature, in the United States the Book of Estimates, our nearest approach to a budget, is rather a more or less well-digested mass of information submitted by agents of the Legislature to the Legislature for the consideration of legislative committees to enable the Legislature both to originate and to determine the policy which is to be carried out by the Executive during the coming budgetary period.

Definition and Purpose of the Budget. As used in this report the budget is considered as a proposal to be prepared by the administration and submitted to the legislature. The use of a budget would require that there be a complete reversal of procedure by the Government—that the executive branch submit a statement to the Legislature which would be its account of stewardship as well as its proposals for the future. A national budget thus prepared and presented would serve the purposes of a prospectus. Its aim would be to present in summary form the facts necessary to shape the policy of the Government as well as to provide financial support. The summaries of fact included in the budget would also serve as a key or index to the details of transactions and of estimates which would be submitted with the budget or which would be contained in accounting records and reports.

An act of appropriation which follows a budget is a grant of money by the legislative branch to the executive branch of the Government. In the United States Government, in which the Congress habitually exercises the right to add to the estimates proposed by the Executive, and in which the President has no right to veto specific items in appropriation bills, items are usually found in appropriation acts which can hardly be said to have received Executive approval even where the appropriation acts containing them have been signed by the President. For, in many cases, formal Executive approval has been accorded to an appropriation act as a whole which contains items for which the Executive is not in any way responsible or to which he is positively opposed. In case the President has thus approved an appropriation act as a whole, he may, however, by instruction to his subordinates in the administration, prevent the expenditure of public money for many items of which he disapproves, since an appropriation act frequently is an authorization rather than a command.

The constitutional inhibition that "no money shall be drawn from the Treasury but in consequence of appropriations made by law" makes the budget an instrument of *legislative control* over the administration. The act of appropriation as the legal means of making funds available to the executive branch also enables the Executive, or some officer directly responsible to the Executive, to exercise *administrative control* over liabilities incurred and over expenditures made by the many officers and agents employed by the Government in the conduct of its business.

Every branch of the business of the Government is necessarily highly complex and technical. One of the most important offices of a budget is to supply the need for an effective means whereby those who are responsible for direction and control over technical processes and who understand the technical needs of the service may formally present to the Legislature and through the Legislature to the people a well-defined plan or prospectus of work to be financed in order that the Government may make provision for the needs of the country as seen by those whose duty it is to serve these needs.

The Congress, as a deliberative body, while not in a position to know what are the technical service requirements, is by reason of its representative character best able to determine questions of policy involving the expenditure of money, *i.e.,* decide what shall and what shall not be undertaken. An act of appropriation of public money should therefore be the result of the most careful consideration of both branches of the Government.

The financing of the Government calls into action both the "money raising" and the "appropriating" powers of the Congress—the one to provide funds, the other to authorize expenditures. The exercise of both of these powers affects immediately the welfare of the people. For the purpose of considering the relations of "revenue" and "borrowing" to welfare, a budget should present for the consideration of the Congress a definite financial program. For the purpose of considering the relation of expenditure authorizations to welfare, a budget should present a definite statement of the business to be done, or a work program.

The immediate relations of revenue raising to welfare have been a subject of constant national concern since the first year the Federal Government was organized. In fact, it reaches back through the Revolutionary period; it was one of the chief subjects of popular interest and agitation which culminated in the Declaration of Independence. During the entire national period a more or less definite revenue policy has been recognized. Though not presented in budgetary form, definite policies pertaining to the welfare relation of revenue raising have furnished a definite basis for appeal to the electorate for support. With respect to revenue, there has been a well-defined policy of government which may be traced from the beginning.

With respect to the relation of Government expenditure to welfare, there has been no conscious policy, nor has the subject of Government financing (the relation of revenues and borrowings to expenditures) been a matter of great public concern except in times of war, when the problem of defending our national integrity has depended on ability to finance the Government's needs. The result has been that the United States has had no definite financial program; appropriations have been regarded as special or local in their significance. It has only been within the last few years that what the Government does with its vast organization and resources has received the attention which it deserves. As was said by the President in a recent message:

"In political controversy it has been assumed generally that the individual citizen has little interest in what the Government spends. Now that population has become more dense, that large cities have developed, that people are required to live in congested centers, that the national resources frequently are the subject of private ownership and private control, and that transportation and other public-service facilities are held and operated by large corporations, what the Government does with nearly a thousand million dollars each year is of as much concern to the average citizen as is the manner of obtaining this amount of money for public use."

It is to the expenditure side of a budget that special attention is given in this report.

The second selection on the growth of the budget idea is by a distinguished authority on the subject, A. E. Buck, who had a part in the studies both of the President's Committee on Administrative Management and the Hoover Commission. The essay reprinted here is one written in the mid-twenties and is presented because it well summarizes American budgetary thinking up to that time.

Reviewed in the essay is a controvery which arose between advocates of the "executive budget" and the "legislative budget." This controversy arose because of the natural difference in interest and outlook between executive and legislative in the American system of government. Budgetary procedures both of other types of government—even if democratic—and of business organizations did not fit smoothly into the well-worn patterns of American political life. The story of the controversy between advocates of the executive budget and the legislative budget is the story of the attempt to adjust budget ideas and techniques developed elsewhere to American constitutional and political practice. This controversy, as such, has faded into the background as adjustments were made and habits established. Query, what are the adjustments that have been made, the distinc-

tively American budgetary ideas and procedures? And what are the peculiarly American budgetary (and other fiscal) problems that remain in some
sense unsolved?

The Development of the Budget Idea
in the United States *

A. E. BUCK

Twenty years ago very little attention was given to the budget idea in this country
outside of academic circles. Political leaders were not interested in the idea;
people generally knew nothing about it. Only a few persons, here and there,
had caught the significance of Gladstone's statement: *"Budgets are not merely
affairs of arithmetic, but in a thousand ways go to the root of prosperity of
individuals, the relation of classes, and the strength of kingdoms."* Our cities
were spending money, some thousands, some millions of dollars annually, with
little or no thought as to where it was coming from or what they were getting
for it. The states were "getting by" financially in even more haphazard fashion
than many of the cities. The national Government was in the heyday of the
"pork barrel" era.

So great was the general apathy in those days toward the subject of governmental finances, that newspaper men did not regard financial events as having
any news value. When a New York editor was asked to make his paper the
medium for telling the people about the city budget, he replied: "It can't be
done. We do not *make* news; we *print* news."

Perhaps the editor was right; but things have changed since then. When
President Coolidge sent his budget to Congress on December 10, 1923, newspapers all over the country carried front page news articles about it. Many of
them commented editorially on the President's budget plan for expenditures
and the reduction of taxation. Some papers reproduced certain graphs and tables
from the budget. The President's budget message seemed in many ways to over-
shadow his general message to Congress. Similar publicity, though perhaps
not so striking, has recently been given to the budgets of a number of states
and cities. Need we look for further evidence that things have changed?

How the Budget Idea Spread in This Country

How has this change been brought about? At first a few earnest individuals
began talking about the need for systematic planning in the financing of government. They pointed to the advantages of budget making in the European

* From *Annals*, Vol. 113 (May, 1924), pp. 31–39. Somewhat abridged. Reprinted
by permission of *The Annals of the American Academy of Political and Social
Science.*

countries. They explained the essentails of a good budget, and they outlined budgetary procedure as applied to our system of government. Soon other individuals got interested in the budget idea and began talking about it. Then, as the burden of local governments began to be felt, civic bodies took up the idea. Bureaus of municipal research were organized to study the financial needs, the organization and methods of city governments. The oldest one of these, the New York Bureau of Municipal Research, began immediately after it was organized in 1906 to study the budget needs of the city of New York. Among its first reports was one on "Making a Municipal Budget," published in 1907. The introductory sentence of this report ran as follows: "No document can tell in such condensed form so many significant facts about community needs and government efforts to meet those needs as a properly constructed budget." This report was perhaps the first effort, through a careful analysis of a local situation, to drive home the need for the application of budget methods to government. It may be regarded as the beginning of the campaign in this country to educate the public in the budget idea.

The largest single contribution to the literature of this campaign was that made by President Taft's Commission on Economy and Efficiency. This commission was organized in 1910 under the chairmanship of Frederick A. Cleveland. During the two years that the commission continued its work, searching studies were made of the organization, administration and financial procedure of the national Government. One of the most important of these studies was the report of the commission on "The Need for a National Budget," which President Taft sent to Congress with his approval on June 27, 1912. This report started the movement that nine years later resulted in the passage of the National Budget Law.

The work of the Taft Commission had a far-reaching influence on the states. In fact, several of the states immediately established economy and efficiency commissions to conduct studies of their administrative organization and methods. Others followed until more than half of the states had established such commissions. The more important of these state commissions, from the standpoint of illuminating reports on organization, administrative methods and fiscal procedure, were those of Illinois, New York and Massachusetts. Practically all of these commissions recommended among other things the establishment of a state budget system. This recommendation, in most instances, was the first to receive serious consideration.

With the development of the newer forms of city government, namely, the commission, the manager, and the centralized-mayor forms, the budget began to play an important rôle in municipal finances. The campaign during the last ten years for the manager form of city government has placed special emphasis upon the value of budget procedure. The rapid spread of this form of city government has given great impetus to the budget idea as applied to municipalities and even to counties.

The Different Theories of the Budget

Before the campaign for the adoption of the budget idea had proceeded very far, it became apparent that many of the developments in the organization and methods of our various governments, especially state governments, had been decidedly away from rather than in the direction of budget planning and control. It was evident to those who made a careful study of the situation that a great deal more would have to be done than just enact a budget law, if the budget procedure was to be made at all effective. So far there was an agreement; but when it came to determining just what should be done, there was a decided difference of opinion. As a result the advocates of the budget idea became divided into two groups. One group proposed that the budget should be prepared and submitted to the legislative body by the executive who is to carry out the budget plan after it is enacted and that the administrative machinery and legislative procedure should be so adjusted as to make this executive responsible for leadership. This was forthwith labeled as the "executive budget." It was contended by the other group that such a budget made for the aggrandizement of the executive and the restriction of legislative power, and since the members of the legislative body were direct representatives of the people it led ultimately to the curtailment of popular control. This group sought to make the legislative body, or a body upon which this body was represented together with the administration, the budget-making authority. A number of states and cities accepted this latter proposal, because it could be adopted without involving any serious changes in the existing organization and methods of the government. The results, however, were in most cases disappointing—so much so that the advocates of the plan sought to strengthen it by establishing a means for legislative leadership and by making the administration directly accountable to the legislative body. This device the late Charles McCarthy and his associates tried to establish in the state of Wisconsin. Although unsuccessful, the attempt brought the second group around to the point where it was essentially in agreement with the first group. Both were seeking responsible leadership in government, particularly with reference to formulating and carrying out the budget plan. This leadership might be lodged in an executive independent of the legislative body and directly responsible to the people, or it might be lodged in an executive chosen by the legislative body and responsible through that body to the people. While the former type of leadership is in harmony with our present constitutional system, the latter seems more in line with recent developments, especially in municipal government. Whatever changes may take place in this respect in the future, one thing seems certain: the executive, however chosen, will continue to occupy an important position both in formulating the budget plan and in carrying it out. This is a basic principle of the budget system that is already fairly well established in this country.

There has been considerable discussion on the question of just what an "executive budget" implies. Some have contended that a budget system is not "executive," even though the executive prepares the budget plan, unless the power of the legislature is limited in making changes in the budget proposals as submitted by the executive. Limiting the power of the legislature in passing on the executive's budget proposals is justified on the basis of English budget practices. While it is true that the English budget as proposed by the executive is never increased and rarely ever reduced by action of the House of Commons, it is also true that the relation of the English executive to the legislative body is quite different from that existing between the executive and the legislature in this country. In England the executive, that is, the Prime Minister and his cabinet, is really a part of the legislative body—a sort of dominating committee of that body. The Prime Minister, as head of this committee, is not only chief executive of the Government, but he is the responsible leader of the House of Commons. When he fails in this leadership his cabinet falls, and his place is handed to another who undertakes the responsibility of forming a new cabinet and assuming leadership. The situation, therefore, is quite different from that existing in our national and state governments. Here the executive by constitutional provision is made quite independent of the legislature. He is not a member of the legislative body; he is not directly connected with any of its committees; he may not even belong to the same political party as the majority of the legislative members; and he cannot legally control the legislative policy. Under such fundamentally different organization the English budget procedure is not applicable. If the English budget system is to be adopted in this country a new relationship, requiring basic constitutional changes, must be established between the executive and the legislature. We cannot secure the advantages of the English system by merely tacking on a budget amendment to our existing constitutions, which restricts the action of the legislature in making appropriations. . . .

Essentials of the Budget System

There are certain essentials of the budget system that may be outlined briefly. Many of these have been fairly well developed and all are more or less generally accepted. They should serve as a basis for work in the further development of the budget system.

1. *Responsible Executive Leadership.* This has been deemed the first essential of the budget system. Someone must be responsible for formulating the budget plan and presenting it for the action of the legislative body. After the budget plan has been adopted by this body, someone must be responsible for carrying it into effect. Experience has shown that the budget system is most effective when the individual, or group of individuals, that formulates the budget plan is the one that carries it out. This duty, therefore, logically falls on the executive. So it is necessary from the budget standpoint to make the executive's leadership real and effective. We know that when a person must carry out a plan that he proposes, he is likely to exercise more care in making that plan; and especially is

this true when the plan must be approved by an independent body before it becomes effective. This situation in itself tends to place a considerable amount of responsibility upon the executive for the budget program. But there are some important questions in this relation that have not yet been settled.

While the executive, especially in our national and state governments, is directly responsible to the people for the office he holds, he is not at all times responsive to the wishes of the people while in office. This is due largely to the fact that the executive is elected for a fixed term of office and is independent of the legislative body. Various proposals in harmony with our constitutional system have been made to remedy this situation. It has been suggested, as noted above in this article, that we overhaul our constitutional system so as to establish the same relationship between the executive and the legislative branches as now exists in England.

2. *Staff Assistance.* We have found that the details of budget making require special staff assistance—one person, or group of persons, depending upon the size of the government, that can give attention exclusively to the collection of the budget information and can assist the executive in the formulation of the budget plan. Such staff assistance has been provided in the Bureau of the Budget of the national Government and in the Departments of Finance and other agencies of many state and city governments.

3. *Broad and Accurate Budget Information.* This is the foundation upon which the budget plan is built. The budget information must be accurate and reliable. It should also be of such a character as to indicate clearly the scope of the work and the results of the various activities of the Government. In budget planning, we want to know four things: (1) The work the Government is undertaking to do (activity) ; (2) the agency of the Government that will do this work (organization unit) ; (3) the cost of the work (expressed in terms of purchases, operation costs, and results) ; and (4) how the cost is to be met (from revenues, borrowings, etc.).

The work that the Government is doing, or will undertake to do, is largely a matter of public policy. However, such policy immediately affects the budget, as is evident in the rapidly increasing cost of government owing to new and expanding activities. This points to an increasing need for scientific budget planning as a means of maintaining a balance between the income and the outgo of government.

The reasons for planning work with reference to a particular department or division of the Government are rather obvious. Work cannot be carried on without some agency responsible for doing it. The cost of the work cannot be definitely determined until after the performing agency and its requirements in services, commodities, and so on have been studied. The organization and methods of such agencies are of vital importance in budget making because of their direct bearing upon the cost and the character of services rendered.

In determining the cost of government work for budget-making purposes, there are three methods of approach: (1) Through an analysis of purchases, that is, the services, commodities, and so on, which are bought by the Government to carry on its work; (2) through an analysis of the operation of governmental departments, divisions, and agencies; and (3) through an analysis of the actual results of departmental and institutional service.

Up to the present time practically all the information available for budget-making purposes has been based upon an analysis of purchases. The budget estimates present in greater or less detail the departmental and institutional requirements in terms of services, commodities, properties, and obligations and compare these requirements with past and present expenditures for the same things. These estimates are based upon the information recorded by the accounting system, the greater part of which has to do only with transactions incident to purchases and payments made by the Government. Efforts in the past have been directed mainly toward classifying and systematizing this information. As a result, we know definitely just what it costs to buy the services, commodities, properties, and so on, that are required to run a department of the Government, but we have little or no information about how the department uses these things or what the results are.

An analysis of the cost of doing each of the various kinds of work under the different departments and agencies of the Government, expressed in comparable units, would be of great value in determining budget needs. Something has already been done in this direction in some fields of government work, but the information thus made available has not been used to any extent in budget making. Such information would make it possible to express the budget in terms of work to be done, as well as in terms of things to be bought. It would also be very valuable to the administrator in carrying out the budget plan.

An analysis of the actual results of governmental services seems more important than any other means of determining the cost of the various activities and of checking up the budget demands made for these activities. Citizens and taxpayers are interested not in maintaining elaborate governmental machinery, but in securing results valuable to the community. The fact that a city carries on fire prevention work, that it has a fire prevention division in the Department of Public Safety, that it employs a score of inspectors to work in this division, that the cost in salaries and other expenses is seventy thousand dollars per year, and that the inspectors make five hundred inspections each per year, is not an index to the value of the work. This index must be determined from other factors such as the elimination of fire hazards and the reduction of loss of lives and property. In other words, it is to be found in the results. Only a few attempts have been made so far to analyze the activities of governments and to measure their results. This offers a difficult, but at the same time a fruitful, field in governmental research. The value of a simple and scientific method of measuring the results of governmental activities could hardly be estimated for budget-making purposes.

4. *Complete Budget Plan.* No document can rightly be called a budget that does not set up a complete plan of proposed expenditures for a definite period and balance these expenditures with the estimated means of financing, that is, the income of the government. This is the chief value of the budget; it shows a complete picture of the Government's finances. The budget should be so set up and summarized as to make this picture quite clear to citizens and taxpayers. Considerable progress has already been made in this direction. We now have several state and city budgets that present fairly complete and understandable plans.

Some time ago there was considerable discussion on the subject of the "segregated budget," and in some sections of the country this discussion still continues. It seems to have arisen mainly from the failure to distinguish between the budget and the appropriation bill. The two should be separate and distinct documents, although they are often confounded, especially in some of the cities where the only document produced is a segregated appropriation ordinance. The purpose of the budget is to present a financial plan and give complete detailed information with regard to it; the purpose of the appropriation bill or ordinance is to present the expenditure side of the budget in the form necessary for enactment into law. The former, therefore, should be segregated; but the latter not necessarily so. Experience dictates that when proper arrangements have been made to administer and control expenditures, appropriations should be made in lump sum rather than in detailed or segregated form.

5. *Building and Improvement Program.* The budget plan extends over a definite period, namely, a year or two years. This limitation as to time is necessary in order to make the estimates of expenditures as accurate as possible and to permit the appropriation of definite amounts from available or anticipated revenues. It does not necessarily follow, however, that all financial planning for the Government should be limited to the immediate needs expressed in the budget. Indeed, a much broader view should be taken of the needs of the Government, especially those that relate to public improvements. One can find in almost every government—national, state or municipal—public works that have been constructed without regard for the public needs or that have been undertaken and never finished, a costly evidence of planless development. It is little wonder that the tax burdens continue to pile up when such harum-scarum methods are used in meeting the Government's problems. The cost of construction projects cannot be equitably distributed over a period of years without planning. And certainly a proper distribution should be made if future taxpayers are not to be overburdened.

Construction or improvement programs should be carefully worked out for the Government extending over a period of five or ten years. These should apply to all public improvements, including institutional plant development. When these programs are adopted, matters relating to the development and financing of permanent improvements are practically settled so far as the annual budget is concerned. A few cities have worked out and adopted improvement programs extending over a period of five years. Some states have made similar plans with reference to institutional development and road construction. However, on the whole, very little has been done in this direction.

6. *Open Procedure by Responsible Legislative Body.* In recent years the people have apparently lost confidence to a large extent in their legislative bodies. This is shown by the recent trend on our state governments toward increasing the importance and power of the executive. In some states it has resulted in a serious curtailment of the powers of the legislature, especially in making appropriations. But by this curtailment of the powers of the legislature we have accomplished little. The fact is we have been simply dodging the main problem. That is, a reorganization of our state legislatures by adopting the unicameral system, by providing for cooperation between the executive and the legislative branches, by reducing the number of legislative committees and organizing them along the lines of the major administrative functions, by cutting out the "red tape" of legislative procedure, and by instituting open and above board consideration of all important measures. This can be done in any state, and it will be in harmony with our present constitutional system.

Indeed, we have already made progress in this direction with our city councils. The bicameral city council is now regarded as a thing of the past. The small, single-chambered council has generally taken its place, and a noticeable improvement has resulted in our municipal legislative procedure. A properly organized legislative body, a carefully prepared budget, and wide publicity on financial matters will prevent "log-rolling" and wipe out the "pork barrel" in our state governments. Restrictions, constitutional or otherwise, will not prevent these things under our present legislative system.

7. *A Financial Calendar.* This applies more particularly to local governments. The financial calendar permits a careful adjustment to the fiscal year of the time for the preparation and passage of the budget and the assessment and collection of taxes. In brief, the budget should be adopted before the beginning of the fiscal period to which it relates, so that the necessary accounts can be set up and arrangements consummated by the executive for carrying out the budget plan. The taxes, or a first installment of them, should become payable soon after the beginning of the fiscal year. This will enable the Government to meet its bills and thus avoid temporary borrowing to finance its current expenditures. Often it is necessary to change the fiscal year in order to work out a satisfactory financial calendar. Most states have adopted the federal fiscal year—July 1 to June 30. Many cities use the same period. The calendar year, however, is more generally used by cities as their fiscal year.

8. *Effective Control over the Execution of the Budget Plan.* Important as is the making of the budget plan, it is even more important that this plan be effectively carried out. The proper executive authority and supervision should be provided to put the plan into operation. Fiscal control should be established through

accounts and otherwise to insure that the expenditures of the Government are being made in accordance with the budget plan. This control should extend to a careful checking of the revenues and receipts of the Government. As the budget plan is being carried out, information should be recorded and classified with a view to making up the next budget. The budget, when once adopted, should be rigidly adhered to throughout the period to which it applies, unless some extraordinary circumstances should arise making changes necessary. If this is not done, budget making means little and the budget plan is largely a farce.

Chapter 13

Development of Budgetary Theory

Budgetary theory and practice in the United States is roughly divisible into two phases or periods. Symbolically, if not precisely, the first of these periods ends, the second begins, with the date 1933, the year inaugurating the New Deal. The first period, the subject of the preceding chapter, had as its central concepts system, economy, honesty, and popular accountability. The second period, the subject of this chapter, has as its central concepts planning, public policy, and executive management.

In the period since 1933 the concepts and techniques of the earlier period have been, not so much discarded, as revaluated and supplemented. Several events were responsible for the altered budgetary outlook. One of these was the depression following 1929, which was responsible for the great change in political climate associated with the term New Deal, a climate much more hospitable to large-scale and vigorous governmental action. At the same time occurred the development and popularization of economic doctrines which provided a justification or rationalization for vigorous use of governmental financial powers to stimulate and regularize the national economic life. And at the same time also there occurred further development and acceptance of theories of public administration favorable to increasing the powers of the executive and providing him with adequate "tools of management."

In the climate of opinion produced by these events, older budgetary concepts underwent a change of emphasis. Economy, for example, was no longer interpreted solely in terms of small expenditures and balanced yearly budgets, but in terms of "economically desirable"—though perhaps large—expenditures, and efficient administration of functions and programs, whatever their size. At the same time newer concepts began to modify and supplement the old. "Planning," for example, though inherent in at least a rudimentary way in all budgetary thinking, now began, in years of depression and war, to seem a major function essential to personal welfare and national survival; and in this perspective budgeting became an aspect of planning, rather than the reverse. In the Report of the President's Committee on Administrative Management in 1937 the outlines of the new thinking begin to emerge clearly. And on the Federal scene the remarkable development of the Bureau of the Budget as a managerial "tool" and major focus of policy making demonstrates the realization and operation of recent thought.

The first of the two following selections, by Professor Arthur N. Holcombe, is but the introduction to his discussion of "Over-all Financial Planning through the Bureau of the Budget." But, though brief, it conveys the tone and trend of most budgetary thinking of recent years appearing in the professional literature of public administration.

The second selection is by the late Harold D. Smith, then Director of the Federal Bureau of the Budget. Written by Mr. Smith in 1944 when he was at the height of a distinguished career in governmental fiscal affairs, this essay is a notable attempt to review and reconcile new with old budgeting conceptions.

Patently, the issues raised by recent budgetary developments are deep-thrusting, reaching to the foundations of our economic and political life. On the economic side, the issues involved in recent fiscal theories often find not only the general public but competent professional economists seriously divided. On the governmental side, the problems are no less important; what may seem to the unimaginative to be matters of "mere mechanics" involve the preservation and evolution of democracy. Query, is the recent emphasis on the budget as an instrument of executive management a genuine or a spurious development of democratic government? What special terms and conditions for the proper answer of this question are set by peculiarly American factors, particularly the constitutional separation of powers?

Over-all Financial Planning through
the Bureau of the Budget *

ARTHUR N. HOLCOMBE

Speaking at the meeting of the American Political Science Association a year
ago in Washington, Harold D. Smith, Director of the Budget, described the reorganization of the Bureau of the Budget since its transfer to the Executive Office
of the President, and discussed its new role in federal administration. He squarely
repudiated the "watchdog of the treasury" view of the Bureau's function and
vigorously challenged those critics of administrative management under the present administration who would have the "watchdog" shot because it has not kept
federal expenditures down. The new role of the executive budget, he believes,
should be "to implement democracy." Conceiving the budget as a "device for
consolidating the various interests, objectives, desires, and needs of our citizens
into a program whereby they may jointly provide for their safety, convenience,
and comfort," Director Smith rightly emphasizes its position as "the most important single current document relating to the social and economic affairs of the
people."

Students of political science cannot fail to be deeply gratified with the progress
which has been made in recent years at Washington in budgetary practice. Four
years ago the President's Committee on Administrative Management noted in its
report the major defects of the system of financial administration then in operation
and recommended certain improvements. Since then the Budget Bureau has been
transferred from the Treasury Department to the Executive Office of the President, and the Budget Director has become one of the President's most intimate
administrative advisers. The appropriation for the support of the Bureau has been
multiplied fourfold, and the staff of the Bureau has been correspondingly
strengthened in numbers and quality. In consequence of these alterations and
improvements the Budget Bureau is now in a far better position than ever before
to accomplish the purposes for which it was created.

More important than the increase in the Bureau's appropriation and staff is
the change in its conception of its task. The Bureau came into existence at a time
when the emphasis at Washington was placed strongly upon retrenchment and
thrift. By example as well as by precept the early budget directors sought to give
impetus and direction to the spirit of the time. In the management of the Bureau
itself economy was transmuted into parsimony, and the larger issues of administrative efficiency in the general business of government were obscured by the
pursuit of petty savings in the budget-making process. To balance the budget year

* *Public Administration Review,* Vol. I (Spring, 1941), pp. 225–230 (pp. 225–226
quoted below). Abridged. Reprinted by permission of the author and the *Public
Administration Review.*

by year, or better still to produce a surplus of revenue over expenditure and pay off the public debt, were the objects which budget directors set themselves, regardless of the relations between public finance and the general welfare.

New Basis of Budget Policy

The present budget policy of the federal government is based upon a better understanding of the responsibilities of government in the modern world. The profits of government, unlike the profits of business, cannot be reckoned from year to year. The problem of balancing the budget merges into the larger problem of maintaining the balance of the national economy as a whole. It is not only capital outlays upon durable public works that need to be reckoned in terms of longer periods than those covered by annual budgets, but also those more speculative investments designed to maintain the equilibrium of the American economy in the successive phases of the business cycle. There may be sound political reasons for synchronizing the making of appropriations with the periodical rotation of the earth around the sun. The cycle of the seasons, however, is far too short a period for balancing the books of a government controlling an economy in which public administrative enterprise is rapidly coming to the aid of the traditional system of private enterprise.

Recognition that financial policy must be adapted to the needs of the contemporary economy and therefore must be geared to the business cycle implies the acceptance of the new role of which Director Smith has spoken for the Bureau of the Budget in federal administration. The most important decision with respect to financial policy which the President, aided by the Budget Director, is now called upon to make each year, is not whether he shall recommend that the budget be balanced, or be operated on the basis of a surplus or deficit. Under a system of energetic public administrative enterprise the investments of the state for the development of the productive plant of the country must increase year by year if the people are to enjoy the benefits of a dynamic rather than a static economy, and the budget may never be balanced in the narrow sense of the term. The important decisions in the financial policy of such a state involve a choice between the various purposes to which capital outlays may be devoted. They involve a choice also between the various rates at which present effort may be directed toward future satisfactions.

Such decisions cause reverberations throughout the whole national economy. They involve some sense of direction, some conception of what kind of society is in process of construction. There is involved even more immediately the problem of the interrelationship between the private and the governmental sector of the economy. What effect will the financial plans of the government have on the plans of farmers and businessmen, on the aspirations of salaried workers and laborers, on the flow of private funds through the channels of investment, on the general process of capital creation, on the fluctuations of the business cycle, and at last on the size and distribution of the national income? What effect will the financial plans of the government have also on the fortunes of political parties and of the candidates for public office whose interests the parties are designed primarily to promote?

To ask these questions is not to imply that there are ready answers, or that a body of highly competent advisers will always agree in their analyses or in their recommendations, or, even if they agree, that they will always be right. Omnicompetence and infallibility we cannot expect. What we have reason to anticipate is that the organization of intelligent thinking on these problems may yield more promising lines of action than the casual improvisations which the President will be compelled to rely upon in the absence of such thinking. The strategic importance of governmental financial policy in setting the conditions for the whole national economy may well justify all the ingenuity and effort which can be devoted to the planning of such policy. What an exacting task devolves upon the Bureau of the Budget as principal aid to the President in implementing democracy becomes evident when it is noted that a comprehensive program of preparation for war presents a comparatively simple problem in planning of the complex type which will become normal under a peacetime system of energetic public enterprise.

The Budget as an Instrument of Legislative Control and Executive Management *

HAROLD D. SMITH

The relationship between the legislative and the executive branches largely determines the success or failure of democratic government. Hence, the budget, because it is at the same time the most important instrument of legislative control and of executive management, is at the very core of democratic government. No one who fails to recognize this dual function can fully appreciate the true significance of budgets or appraise the difficult problems which must be solved in connection with them.

How can the budget serve both these objectives? On superficial analysis it appears that the purposes of legislative control and of executive management are in conflict. A budget which is devised primarily as an instrument of legislative control seems to hamstring administration and to impair efficiency in executive management. On the other hand, a budget which leaves wide discretion and freedom of action to execute management appears to become that much less effective as a means of legislative control.

* *Public Administration Review*, Vol. IV (Summer, 1944), pp. 181–188. Reprinted by permission of the *Public Administration Review*.

I do not deny that there is some conflict between these two objectives, but I believe that this conflict can be reconciled; that a more fundamental analysis will show that a budget which serves as an effective instrument of executive management also serves as the most effective instrument of legislative control. That is the thesis I should like to discuss.

The Budget and Legislative Control

Budgets were developed during . . . the late Middle Ages. As statements of revenues and expenditures, they were used exclusively for purposes of administration by the sovereign monarchs and their advisers. Since as a rule "the king lived of his own," that is, derived his revenue mainly from his own domain, the budget was regarded as his own business affair and was treated as a carefully guarded secret of state. In times of war, however, it became necessary to resort to taxes as an extraordinary source of revenue. In order to assure the consent of powerful taxpayers, the crown had to grant to the nobility a voice in deciding on revenue measures, particularly for financing wars. The Revolution of 1688 brought general recognition in Great Britain to the principle "no taxation without representation" but it did not yet bring all government expenditures under parliamentary control. There remained a long way to go before the principle of no expenditures without "appropriations made by law" was established in the American Constitution.

In the 250 years since the British Declaration of Rights and the 150 years of democratic governments on the European and American continents, budgetary controls have been devised in an attempt to tighten the legislative control of the executive. During this period there gradually emerged principles of budgeting designed to assure complete legislative control of the purse strings. These principles reflect various aspects of the centuries-old struggle between the crown and the parliament for democratic control of the government. While this struggle began in Great Britain, the principles themselves were developed particularly in France. The historical origin—the steady desire of parliaments to hold the crown under control—explains the onesidedness of these principles. Yet they represent standards which, with allowance for the requirements of effective management, still must be considered in a modernized approach to democratic budgeting. Therefore, I repeat them as a basis for later consideration.

These historical budget principles are substantially as follows:

1. *Publicity.* The main stages of the budget process, which include executive recommendation, legislative consideration and action, and budget execution, should be made public.

2. *Clarity.* The budget should be understandable to every citizen. As was said by a British writer in 1764: "The administration has condescended . . . to explain the budget to the meanest capacity."

3. *Comprehensiveness.* The budget should contain expenditures and revenues on a gross basis, reflecting all governmental activities without exception, and

should show the surplus available for debt retirement or the deficit to be met by new revenue legislation or borrowing.

4. *Budget Unity.* All receipts should be recovered into one general fund for financing all expenditures. This principle condemns earmarking of revenues for specific purposes of expenditure, except in cases of trust accounts, or in cases where a special and direct relationship exists between receipts and expenditures.

5. *Detailed Specification.* Receipts and appropriations should be expressed in detailed specification; transfer of items should be permitted only in exceptional cases.

6. *Prior Authorization.* The budget should be submitted, considered, and acted upon in advance of the period during which the expenditures are to be made; it should include estimates for all foreseeable needs, thus reducing as far as possible requests for supplemental and deficiency appropriations. Budget execution should stay strictly within the legislative authorization and should be checked by an auditing agency reporting to the legislature.

7. *Periodicity.* Appropriations should be authorized for a definite period of time. An appropriation not used at the end of the period should generally lapse or be reappropriated with the specific amount and purpose detailed.

8. *Accuracy.* Budget estimates should be as accurate as possible and there should be no "padding" of expenditure estimates or providing for hidden reserves by underestimating revenues.

If we look at this list of budgetary commandments and think of the budgetary practices of federal, state, and local governments here in the United States as well as abroad, we must reach the conclusion that budgeteers are hopeless sinners. Each one of these principles is frequently violated by those who prepare the budget, those who enact it, or those who execute it.

At variance with the first principle is the fact that during the war we in the federal government do not make public all details of appropriations and expenditures for reasons of military security.

We should hang our heads when we think of the second commandment, the principle of clarity. In spite of recent improvements, it is still true that the federal budget and the appropriation acts make very difficult reading for the layman and even for the expert. It is happily true, however, that several states and many municipalities are successful in presenting their budgets in a more understandable fashion.

In violation of the principle of comprehensiveness, appropriations for some types of operations are often enacted on a net basis, that is, permitting the expenditure of certain receipts without specific appropriation. This situation occurs in the federal government especially in relation to government corporations and in local governments frequently in the case of public utilities. Whatever may be said for the need of these departures from the principle, violations certainly become objectionable in those cases where *administrative* functions are budgeted on a net basis.

The fourth principle—that of budget unity—is violated in several ways. For instance, one violation occurs when the federal law requires allocation of an amount corresponding to 30 per cent of estimated customs revenues to certain agricultural purposes. The states are particular offenders against this principle of budget unity by special earmarking of revenues. In some cases the practice may be justified. In general, however, it has impaired sound fiscal planning. Some governments fail to include in their budgets receipts from borrowing and expenditures of borrowed funds, violating the principles of unity and comprehensiveness at the same time.

In a similar way we could go down the line and find violations of the other budget principles. For some of these violations there is no excuse. Others occur because these principles have been formulated exclusively from the point of view of legislative control without regard for the needs of effective management. Lucius Wilmerding, in a history of early congressional efforts to control expenditures, reached the conclusion that congressional attempts to control expenditures by narrow specifications have been "in large measure, self-defeating." He may exaggerate, but I think he is right in his belief that almost unavoidable violation results from the establishment of inflexible principles. We need a more constructive approach—one which takes into consideration the requirements of executive management.

The Budget and Executive Management

The inadequacy of the traditional budget principles became increasingly obvious with the growth of government functions and responsibilities. The issue today is no longer the struggle of a representative parliament for control of a recalcitrant crown. True, adequate legislative control must still be effectuated and vitalized—legislative control, however, of a responsible executive who must be equipped to deal with the difficult political, economic, and social problems of our time.

The Budget and Accounting Act of 1921 introduced the executive budget into the federal system. During the extensive legislative deliberations which preceded its adoption, there was considerable recognition of the budget as a basic instrument of executive management. Representative Good of Iowa, in many ways the foremost of the "founding fathers" of the national budget system, observed on the floor of Congress: "We do not appropriate money simply for the purpose of making appropriations; we appropriate money to carry out work planned for the Government. The President alone formulates this plan." Charles D. Norton, who had helped President Taft in organizing the Commission on Economy and Efficiency, in his testimony stressed the continuing functions of the central budget staff in collaboration with the budget officers of the federal agencies. He pointed out that thus "there would be created a group of associates, partners, if you please, whose particular duty was that of analysis and balancing the various projects of the administration."

Other witnesses spoke of the importance of "departmental self-study throughout the year, from year to year, by administrative officers," and of the gradual accumulation of data "to show administrative practice in performing the several functions." One of these witnesses, Assistant Secretary of the Navy Franklin D. Roosevelt, specifically referred to the budget system as "the entering wedge" toward placing "the Government on a business basis." It was for these reasons that Representative Mondell, of Wyoming, another of the "founders," proclaimed the act "the greatest measure of legislative and administrative reform in our history."

Much progress has been made since the adoption of the Budget and Accounting Act in developing the management aspect of budgeting in the federal government. A major step forward followed the 1937 report of the President's Committee on Administrative Management, which recommended a greatly increased sphere of responsibility for the Bureau of the Budget as agent of the President in the field of management. The Bureau was enabled to assume the greater part of the rôle outlined by the Committee when it was transferred to the Executive Office of the President under the Reorganization Act of 1939 and its duties subsequently defined by the President. Yet it is not to be expected that only two decades of systematic work on budget management should result in the same crystallization of thinking as has developed over a period of 150 years in the field of legislative controls. Furthermore, the principles of budget management cannot and should not be considered as graven commands, but as subject to constant development to meet the changing scope of activities and responsibilities of the federal government.

Any attempt to summarize budget principles or rules of executive management must, therefore, be of a tentative character. At the same time, the principles themselves must be dynamic. I submit such a tentative set of eight principles, referring particularly to budgeting in the federal government. These same principles can easily be modified so as to become applicable to state and local governments. One should remember, of course, that the administrative organization of the budget function depends on the fundamental organization of the government in question. In this respect a presidential form of government differs from a cabinet form; a city commission system from a council manager system. The purpose and significance of the budget are, however, the same in all types of democratic government.

These eight principles, I repeat, are designed from the point of view of executive management, and in this respect are as one-sided as those designed for legislative control. Democratic budgeting requires the reconciliation of these two distinct approaches.

1. *Executive Programming.* The budget, as recommended, reflects the program of the chief executive. When enacted it becomes the work program of the government, reflecting all government responsibilities and activities in their political, economic, and social aspects. Budget formulation, therefore, must be geared

closely and directly to the formulation of the chief executive's program as a whole. Budgeting and programming are the two sides of the same coin; both must be under the direct supervision of the chief executive. This principle holds true for all governments—federal, state, and local.

2. *Executive Responsibility.* The appropriation ordinarily authorizes, it does not direct, an agency to spend money. The executive branch is directed to fulfill the *function* established by law or implied in the language of the appropriation measure. In other words, the appropriation is not a mandate to spend, nor does it establish a "vested right" of an agency. The agency is responsible, under the direction of the chief executive, for executing the intent of the legislation in the most economical manner. The chief executive, for his part, has the responsibility of seeing that the agency programs are brought into accord with legislative intent and are executed with the greatest possible economy.

3. *Reporting.* Preparation of the budget, legislative action, and budget execution must be based on full financial and operating reports flowing up from the administrative units of the government. Current information should be furnished the executive as well as the legislative branch on the progress of work with respect to the various programs and projects, obligations incurred, expenditures made, revenues received, individuals employed, objectives accomplished, and other relevant facts. Budgeting without such reporting is blind and arbitrary.

4. *Adequate Tools.* Executive budget responsibility requires adequate administrative tools. The chief executive must have under his direct supervision a properly staffed budget organization. In addition, certain powers must be available to the executive in order to assure the most economical execution of legislative intent. These include, among others, authority to make monthly or quarterly allotments of appropriations and to set up reserves out of appropriations. The reserves are to be used in case of contingencies or are to lapse unexpended if changed conditions permit execution of the congressional intent with less than the amount appropriated. An agency reporting system, which I have just mentioned, is also an essential tool of executive budgeting.

5. *Multiple Procedures.* Modern government includes very different types of operations. Functions of every-day administration; long-run construction and developmental projects; quasi-commercial operations, such as purchase and sale of goods, or banking operations—these require varying procedures for effective management. Although all government functions, without exception, should be reflected in the budget, the methods of budgeting may vary for different types of governmental activities. Efficient management of quasi-commercial operations requires immediate response to changing market conditions and is less subject to definite advance programming than, for instance, are operations of current administration. The budgeting of quasi-commercial operations may therefore differ from the budgeting of administrative activities.

6. *Executive Discretion.* Effective and economical management may be hindered if appropriation items are too narrowly defined. The budget document must con-

tain a great amount of detail for the information and the guidance of the executive. It is desirable, however, that the appropriations be made for broadly defined functions of an agency, or subdivisions of an agency, in harmony with legislative determination of the current objectives of government. To the executive branch should be left the determination of the precise means of operation to achieve the purposes set forth by the law.

7. *Flexibility in Timing.* The budget should contain provisions which permit immediate adjustment to changing economic conditions with which fiscal policy must cope. Flexibility in timing can, for example, be accomplished if the legislature appropriates funds for certain construction and developmental programs for an extended period, say, of five years. Timing of the program can then be adjusted by the executive in accord with economic necessities.

8. *Two-way Budget Organization.* Although budget preparation and budget execution must be directed by the chief executive, efficient budgeting requires the active cooperation of each agency and its major units. There must be in each agency a budget office with functions for that agency similar to those of the government-wide budget office. The budgeting and programming work of the agency must be interrelated under the direct responsibility of the agency head. The established budget officer assists his superior in the administrative control of the subdivisions of the particular agency; he also transmits the agency's views and proposals to the central budget bureau. Budgeting is not only a central function but a process that should permeate the entire administrative structure. Traffic between the central office and the agency offices responsible for budgeting and programming should move on a two-way rather than a one-way street.

We are still at the threshold of translating these principles of budget management into reality. Just as we found many violations of legislative control principles, so we can point out many cases in which we have not yet realized the principles of budget management. Budget management in states and municipalities has made great advances in many respects. Nevertheless, it is recognized that the local and state governments, as well as the federal government, suffer from deficiencies in budgetary reporting, from frequent failures to center responsibility for budget execution in the chief executive, from lack of executive tools for budget administration, from too much detailed specification in appropriations, and from inflexibility in the timing of authorized activities. For the federal government, the Budget and Accounting Act of 1921 and the Reorganization Act of 1939 have created the basis for the development of an effective budget system. However, much can still be done and must be done in order to perfect budgeting as an effective instrument of executive management.

On the basis of an experience of more than two decades we can say now that the Budget and Accounting Act was an outstanding piece of legislation. Still, I believe that the time is approaching when the experiences of these two decades should be incorporated into that basic act by amendment. I think particularly that the powers of making allotments and establishing reserves, based on the

Anti-Deficiency Act of 1905, should be integrated with the Budget and Accounting Act and clarified.

In pointing out needed improvements in the budget system, I should also mention the much-discussed question of the desirability of the presidential "item
veto."

Harmonizing the Two Sets of Budget Principles

I have already referred to the apparent differences between the historical principles of legislative control and the new principles of executive management. The
principles of legislative control emerged from a centuries-old struggle between
parliaments and the crowns in Europe. Principles of executive management are
based largely on the experience of states and municipalities in this country. They
received a new impetus when the depression years impelled us to extend greatly
the scope of economic and social responsibilities of the federal government.

If we compare the two sets of principles which I have outlined, it appears that
there are contradictions between them. The most obvious conflict exists, for
instance, between the legislative control principle of detailed budget specification
and the executive management principle of executive budget discretion. Legislators have sometimes urged the use of a narrowly defined itemization of appropriations, while administrators claim that a broadly defined appropriation is more
conducive to economical management. Legislators have a good case when they
say that broad appropriations language may deprive them of their proper means
of control and may permit an administrator to violate legislative intent. The
answer, in my judgment, is that we should effectuate legislative intent not by
limiting the appropriations more severely but by organizing budget management
more effectively.

In the federal government, the Executive transmits to the Congress not only
proposed appropriation language but also justifications which give in detail the
programs and projects and show the way in which the agency proposes to use
the funds which are requested. It is said that sometimes justifications are used to
"sell" a program but are forgotten after the appropriation is enacted. Justifications
can play their important role in the budget procedure only if supplemented by a
reporting system.

The reports of the agency should show to what extent during the past year the
programs and projects have been executed and to what extent they have been
modified. Discretionary power within broadly defined appropriations may foster
economical management but also may lead to misuse. Therefore, it must be supplemented by accountability. The management principle of executive budget discretion, if supplemented by budget reporting and independent auditing, really
serves the ends for which the control principle of budget specification was designed.

Another example of apparent conflict with the historical principles occurs in
the management principle of flexibility in timing. Budget flexibility with respect

to timing is of decisive importance if fiscal policy is to play its role as an instrument of economic development. I mentioned as an example the possibility of providing for a five-year program of construction and developmental projects, and of allowing executive discretion with respect to the timing of such expenditures within the limits of the appropriation. Again it appears that such a policy would violate the orthodox rules of legislative control, especially the demand of periodicity. This principle implies that unused appropriations should lapse or be reappropriated at the end of each fiscal year. The purposes of budget flexibility and legislative control can be reconciled in this case if (*a*) the program for the next five years is subject *annually* to legislative consideration and enactment, the procedure followed with respect to the capital budgets of several cities; (*b*) the appropriation language directs that only under specified conditions may the executive spend more than the intended proportion in one year; and (*c*) the executive transmits an annual report on the progress of the five-year program in relation to the development of economic conditions during the preceding year. A third example is the apparent conflict between legislative interest in budget clarity and management need for budget procedures adapted to various types of government operations. Variations in methods of budgeting add complications to the budget which, at best, is never simple. Yet the variation in budget procedures is necessary to take account of the different types of operations. The simplicity which would be attained by uniform treatment may be more apparent than real. True clarity may actually require multiple procedures.

I believe it is possible to reconcile each case of apparent conflict between the purposes of legislative control and the needs of executive management. Such reconciliation requires, however, that those concerned with budgeting be fully aware of both of these aspects of budget policy. Further, if they realize the fundamental unity of purpose, then these apparently conflicting principles can be made to supplement and reinforce each other. Legislative control and executive management serve one end—the same end which the budget is designed to serve—better government for all.

There may be some who still believe that weak budget management facilitates strong legislative control. There may be some who still feel that the executive should not have those essential budget tools which I have mentioned. History prior to the Budget and Accounting Act has demonstrated, I believe, that legislative budget control is practically impossible without effective budget management. With the development of an executive budget and executive budget management, legislative controls have become more effective. Legislative budget control can become *most* effective when it operates through a fully developed system of executive budget management.

No budget system can eliminate all conflict in budgeting. Various regional or economic groups in the population have different concepts of the general welfare which their government is to serve. These differences are reflected in both the legislative and the executive branches of government. There is no scientific determination of the "proper" content of a budget. Struggle and compromise are the very essence of the democratic process and are necessarily reflected in the budget. In the President's program the problems of the nation as a whole are focused. The budget process itself serves as a method to channel and balance the conflicting views and to assure that whatever compromise is reached will be effectuated. A budget cannot be measured by any mechanical rule but only by its usefulness as an adaptable instrument of legislative control as well as of executive management. The real test of a budget lies in its ultimate effectiveness to carry out the will of the community.

How can a budget which is compiled, considered, and acted upon once a year be an instrument of management when management requires daily responses to changing conditions? The answer is that though we compile and enact the budget once a year, all those concerned with budget preparation, budget legislation, and budget execution can and should use their heads each day of the year and each hour of the day. We must learn to think of the budget not as an incomprehensible book but as a living process of democratic policy formation and policy execution. Then, and then only, will the budget serve equally well the purposes of legislative control and executive management.

———◆———

Certainly among the most important developments in the field of budgeting in recent years is "performance budgeting." The following selection explains performance budgeting and distinguishes it from the traditional method. On first notice the difference may seem a technical matter of importance only to those with a deep professional interest in budgeting. But, as with many technical matters, if we take the trouble to understand them, we find that important problems of collective life and personal happiness are involved.

This selection is from the report on budgeting and accounting submitted by the "Hoover Commission," the familiar name of the body officially titled the Commission on Organization of the Executive Branch of the Government. This Commission, chaired by ex-President Herbert Hoover, was created by Act of Congress in 1947 to survey Federal organization and administration and to make recommendations designed to further economy, efficiency, and responsibility. The purpose of the Hoover Commission was thus similar to that of the earlier President's Committee on Administrative Management—often called the Brownlow Committee, after its Chairman, Louis Brownlow. While the Hoover Commission followed the main lines of administrative theory and policy laid down by the Brownlow Committee, there were nevertheless some significant differences in their respective emphases and recommendations. These differences stem from differences in the composition and outlook of the two bodies, as well as from the changed political circumstances. The Brownlow Committee and its staff consisted of "academicians and civil servants with academic leanings" and was relatively homogeneous; the Hoover Commission and its staff consisted of "public office holders, business men, academicians, and civil servants," and was relatively heterogeneous. In style of presentation and in tenor of its recommendations, this selection is typical of the many reports submitted by the Hoover Commission.

This selection consists of Part One of the report titled "Budgeting and Accounting"; and an illustration from Part Five, the "Annex" to the report, in which performance budgeting principles are applied to the Forest Service budget. Some of the "Recommendations' " quoted go beyond performance budgeting, strictly speaking, but they serve to indicate the relationship of performance budgeting to related matters, both fiscal and constitutional.

Query, is performance budgeting congruent in every way with the line of developing budgetary thought given in the preceding selections? Are there any advantages in "old style" budgeting which are lost in performance budgeting? Are there disadvantages or limitations of performance budgeting which are glossed over in this attempt to "sell" it?

Reform of the Budget *

The budget and appropriation process is the heart of the management and control of the executive branch.

There is a great need for reform in the method of budgeting and in the appropriation structure.

The Federal budget is an inadequate document, poorly organized and improperly designed to serve its major purpose, which is to present an understandable and workable financial plan for the expenditures of the Government. The document has grown larger and larger each year as the Government's requirements have increased, but its general framework and method of presentation have not changed. The latest budget document, that for 1949–50, contains 1,625 closely printed pages, with about 1,500,000 words, and sums covering thousands of specific appropriations.

There is no uniformity in the schedules of appropriations. Some appropriations represent huge sums, others small amounts. Appropriations for the same service appear in many different places. Much of this results from historical accident.

* By the Hoover Commission. Washington, 1949, pp. 7–17, 80–84.

The Bureau of Indian Affairs, for example, had approximately 100 appropriation titles and subtitles for the expenditure during the fiscal year 1947–48 of about $50,000,000. The largest appropriation item for this bureau amounted to more than $11,000,000, while the smallest item was $114.53.

At the other extreme, perhaps, is the Veterans Administration, which has an appropriation item of more than a billion dollars for "salaries and expenses," a title which indicates nothing whatever of the work program of that organization.

A Performance Budget

Recommendation No. 1:

We recommend that the whole budgetary concept of the Federal Government should be refashioned by the adoption of a budget based upon functions, activities, and projects; this we designate as a "performance budget."

Such an approach would focus attention upon the general character and relative importance of the work to be done, or upon the service to be rendered, rather than upon the things to be acquired, such as personal services, supplies, equipment, and so on. These latter objects are, after all, only the means to an end. The all-important thing in budgeting is the work or the service to be accomplished, and what that work or service will cost.

Under performance budgeting, attention is centered on the function or activity —on the accomplishment of the purpose—instead of on lists of employees or authorizations of purchases. In reality, this method of budgeting concentrates congressional action and executive direction on the scope and magnitude of the different Federal activities. It places both accomplishment and cost in a clear light before the Congress and the public. . . .

To indicate the deficiencies of existing practices, we may cite here the National Naval Medical Center at Bethesda. This hospital now receives allotments from 12 different Navy appropriation titles such as:

Secretary's Office—Miscellaneous Expenses, Navy
Bureau of Ships—Maintenance
Bureau of Ordnance—Ordnance and Ordnance Stores
Bureau of Supplies and Accounts—Pay, Subsistence, and Transportation
Bureau of Supplies and Accounts—Maintenance
Bureau of Supplies and Accounts—Transportation of Things
Bureau of Medicine and Surgery—Medical Department, Navy
Five Other Similar Appropriation Titles

We propose, for instance, that by using performance budgeting, the costs of operating the Bethesda Center, along with those of other comparable Naval hospitals, would be shown as an identifiable program under one appropriation title for "Medical Care." . . .

The idea of a performance budget is not new. It has been adopted in the modernization of budgets by some States and several municipalities.

The performance budget does not change or shift legislative responsibility; control by the Congress still lies in the power to limit expenditures by appropriations. Performance budgeting gives more comprehensive and reliable information to the President, the Congress, and the general public, and helps the individual congressman to understand what the Government is doing, how much it is doing, and what the costs are. Supporting schedules can be fully provided, and in more understandable and effective form.

One of the primary purposes of the performance budget would be to improve congressional examination of budgetary requirements. Such examination should be largely on the level of accomplishment, and for this reason the Congress needs to know clearly just what the whole of the expenditures is and what the executive and administrative agencies propose to do with the money they request. In the Bethesda case mentioned above, the Congress under the new system would have presented the cost of operating the hospital in detail, so that the Congress might readily compare such cost with that of the preceding year or with the costs of other comparable hospitals.

The Bureau of Ships in the Navy Department, for example, is financed by 27 appropriations, many of which, as shown in the budget, have no apparent connection with the Bureau. Efforts have been made to resolve this confusion through the working out of an adequate budget structure. The ideas thus developed have been applied in part to the new Air Force estimates as set forth in the budget in 1949–50.

In a detailed example, given at the end of this part of the report, of the effect of performance budgeting on the Forest Service, our task force points out that the real operating cost of the Forest Service for the management and protection of the national forests does not appear in full under that heading in the budget, but actually is included in several other places. The total operating cost for the national forests, as displayed by the performance budget, would be shown as about $43,000,000 instead of only $26,000,000 as indicated under the present appropriation headings in the budget.

The New Approach

Indeed, the first task of the Appropriations Committee is to review what has been accomplished and what is proposed for the future period, the latter always being examined in the light of the past experience. The approach which we propose should enable these committees more easily to decide the basic expenditure issue each year; namely, just what should be the magnitude of the many Federal programs.

The performance budget would make it possible for the budget document to be submitted and acted upon in a shorter length of time. It would not delay or hamper the action of the Congress on the Budget. It would assure more complete expenditure estimates and more accurate revenue figures for the next budget period.

Executive and legislative review of functional estimates and program justifications under the performance budget should center around two basic questions:

First: What is the desirable magnitude of any major Government program or function in terms of need, relation to other programs, and proportion of total governmental expenditures? This is essentially a question of public policy, and must be answered by the responsible officials of the executive branch and eventually by the Congress.

Second: How efficiently and economically can an approved Government program be executed? In other words, can the same amount of work be performed satisfactorily under different arrangements or through improved procedures at less cost?

The performance budget would enable administrators to place responsibility upon subordinate officials for the clear execution of the provisions made by the Congress. It would also simplify the reporting and accounting system.

Appropriation Structure and Performance Budgeting

The present appropriation structure underlying the budget is a patchwork affair evolved over a great many years and following no rational pattern. In some areas of the budget, there are entirely too many appropriation items; in others perhaps too few. Some appropriation items are exceedingly broad in scope; others are narrow on account of excessive itemization. Appropriations for a particular function appear in different places. In spite of recent simplifications, the language of some appropriation items remains a jungle of detailed provisions. Many of these detailed prescriptions would seem to be susceptible of more or less uniform treatment in codified form.

The appropriation structure not only affects the presentation of the budget estimates, but runs to the root of management and fiscal responsibility. Departmental management is complicated and fiscal responsibility is diffused when single bureaus or functions are financed from diverse appropriations.

The appropriation structure is further complicated by several different kinds of authorizations such as annual, no-year, and permanent appropriations, reappropriations, contract authorizations, and appropriations to liquidate contract authorizations. Congress, the press, and the public are therefore often confused about the total amount of appropriations in any major appropriation bill. Certainly a comprehensive survey of existing appropriation practices looking towards simplification of appropriation structure, language, and procedure is long overdue. The revision of these practices should be made along the general lines and in accordance with the underlying purpose of the performance budget.

Recommendation No. 2:

We recommend to the Congress that a complete survey of the appropriation structure should be undertaken without delay.

Checks against Deficits

The Congress has long been interested in seeing that agencies so spend their appropriations as not to incur deficits. Various actions have been taken both by the Congress and Presidents to achieve this end. These have finally resulted in a system of apportioning appropriations.

This system requires the spending agencies to submit to the Budget Bureau for its approval their requests for quarterly apportionments of their appropriations. Any revisions in the original apportionments require supplementary forms to be submitted to the Bureau for approval. A copy of the apportionments and any revisions goes to the Treasury for its information.

Each month the spending agencies are required to report on the status of their appropriations, including obligations and balances. But these reports on the status of appropriations are often misleading, since the spending agencies may report their obligations as they see fit. Neither the Budget Bureau nor the Treasury seems to have any direct check or control over what these agencies report. Furthermore, the administrative accounts, as prescribed by the Comptroller General, do not provide properly for the keeping of obligations under apportionments. Under these circumstances, the authority of the Budget Bureau to approve all apportionments on behalf of the President means very little in actually preventing current deficits.

This is the most glaring weakness of the present system of apportionments.

Much needed control cannot be effectively applied under the system of accounting presently employed by the operating departments and agencies. This is an important reason for our subsequent accounting recommendations.

Separation of Capital Outlays

There is, at present, constant confusion in Federal budgeting and accounting because current expenditures and capital outlays are intermingled. These two types of expenditures are essentially different in character, and should, therefore, be shown separately under each major function or activity in the budget. This is an important feature of performance budgeting.

The appropriations for capital purposes, provided each year, are usually only a part of the total cost of the numerous projects which the Federal Government is initiating or has under way. Many of these appropriations are made for a year's work on a given project without an adequate understanding of the total previous expenditure and the cost commitment which has been authorized in order to have a completed structure or improvement. This is not good business on the part of the Federal Government.

While capital projects may be carefully analyzed for usefulness, timeliness, and total probable costs at the time of original authorization, the total remaining costs of all capital projects should be set forth in the budget each year, together with costs incurred to date. These costs should be revised in succeeding years to keep them current with later developments.

Recommendation No. 3:

We recommend that the budget estimates of all operating departments and agencies of the Government should be divided into two primary categories— current operating expenditures and capital outlays.

This Type of Budget Already in Use

The use of this type budgeting has been demonstrated by the budgeting of Government corporations under the Government Corporation Control Act of 1945. Government corporation budgeting practice at the present time amounts to a partial adoption of many of these simplifications based upon functional budgeting, accrual accounting and separation of capital outlays from current expenditures. It has greatly added to flexibility of management and to simplification of budgeting, accounting and audit.

Reductions in Appropriated Expenditures

Present law and practice are not clear on whether or not the Budget Bureau and the President have the right to reduce appropriated amounts during the year for which they were provided.

Recommendation No. 4:

We recommend that it is in the public interest that this question be clarified and, in any event, that the President should have authority to reduce expenditures under appropriations, if the purposes intended by the Congress are still carried out.

To illustrate . . . the application of the performance budget, we take the Forest Service in the Department of Agriculture and show (1) how it is budgeted at present in the 1949–50 budget document and (2) how it can be budgeted on a performance basis.

The Present Method of Budgeting the Forest Service

As budgeted at the present time, the estimates of the Forest Service cover 18½ closely printed, quarto pages of the budget document. The estimates are built around 16 separate items, each of which constitutes an appropriation. Each item has an average of about a page of supporting schedules, setting forth detailed information, principally according to an object classification.

These 16 items or groups now making up the estimates are more or less chance creations; they do not follow either organizational or functional lines. They do not specify accomplishments or indicate performances. Only as one can read meaning into three vertical columns of figures set up on the objective basis can one have any idea of the essential programs, the extent to which these programs succeed or fail, and the effect of changing conditions upon the future character of the programs.

The 16 groups do not make any distinction between current operating costs and capital outlays. Some headings indicate that the amounts requested are to be spent mainly for capital acquisitions; others clearly signify operating costs but, when analyzed, show capital outlays to be included.

The Forest Service has about $24,000,000 of receipts annually which should be indicated in connection with its budget, since percentages of these receipts enter into certain appropriation items, as noted below.

Finally, the 16 items of appropriations made to the Forest Service do not carry all the funds which are required for its operation. Several other appropriations, some of them made directly to the Secretary of Agriculture, contribute to the funds of the Forest Service. By reason of these additional funds the operating requirements of the Service are much larger than actually indicated in the budget. This administrative transfer of funds which takes place on a wide scale within all large governmental departments and agencies makes the present method of budgeting more or less meaningless and defeats the present scheme of appropriations which Congress follows. Only functional budgeting will expose this situation, and allow it to be corrected.

FOREST SERVICE

As Set Up in the Present 1949–50 Budget

(Material in italics below is the Commission's comment and does not appear in the budget quoted.)

1. General administrative expenses..............................$ 655,000
   (This item does not by any means include all administrative expenses of the Service. It has not increased appreciably for several years.)
2. National forests protection and management.................... 26,489,500
   (This item contains the bulk of the Service's operating expenses, and it includes considerable capital outlays.)
3. Fighting forest fires.......................................   100,000
   (This is a nominal figure. Receipts from payments for the suppression of forest fires on State and private lands are also made available.)
4. Forest research into forest and range management.............. 2,812,500
   (This item covers research into fire control, silviculture, watershed control, and forest and range management. Receipts from the rental and sale of equipment and supplies to non-Federal agencies which cooperate with the Forest Service in fire control are included.)
5. Forest products 1,172,000
   (This item includes the operation of the great Forest Products Laboratory located in Wisconsin, but there are no indications as to

the volume and general character of its work, the nature of the ex-
periments and tests being conducted, or the discoveries which have
resulted.)

6. Forest resources investigations................................   866,000
    (This item provides for a comprehensive forest survey and investi-
    gation of forest economics. Receipts are also available, as under
    Item 4 above.)

Subtotal annual specific appropriations.......................... 32,095,000

7. Forest development roads and trails.......................... 9,752,000
    (This item is for the construction, reconstruction, and maintenance
    of roads and trails, not main thoroughfares, in national forests. Re-
    ceipts are also available, as under Item 4 above.)

8. Forest fire cooperation...................................... 9,000,000
    (This item is the contribution of the Federal Government to the
    States for fire control in timbered and cut-over lands.)

9. Farm and other private forestry cooperation...................   814,500
    (This item is for advice to farmers and other private forest owners
    on sustained-yield management and proper utilization of timber re-
    sources.)

10. Acquisition of lands for national forests......................   401,000
    (This item is for the acquisition of forest lands under the Weeks Act,
    1911. It includes the costs of surveys.)

11. Acquisition of forest land, Superior National Forest, Minnesota...   100,000
    (This item is for the acquisition of forest lands, including surveys,
    under an Act of 1948.)

12. Acquisition of lands (in connection with seven National forests
    in three western states, Utah, Nevada, and California)........   142,000
    (This item includes land appraisal and other work in acquiring
    lands.)

(Transfers of funds to and from the Forest Service require four pages of schedules
at this point.)

Total annual specific appropriations............................. 52,304,500

13. Payment to school funds of Arizona and New Mexico...........   55,000
    (This is a permanent appropriation from the general fund.)

14. Payment to States and Territories........................... 5,995,000
    (This is a permanent appropriation, consisting of 25% of the net
    revenue from National forests, paid to states in which the forests
    are located.)

15. Roads and trails for States................................. 2,398,000
    (This is a permanent appropriation, consisting of 10% of the net
    revenue from National forests, paid to states in which the forests
    are located.)

Total Permanent appropriations.................................. 8,448,000

Total Forest service, general and specific accounts.................... 60,752,500
16. Cooperative work 5,300,000
    *(This item is from privately contributed (trust) funds by users of
    the forests. It is used for various purposes that benefit both the
    National and privately owned forests.)*

Grand Total, Forest Service...................................... $66,052,500
    (The above numbered headings are supported by schedules, mostly on an object
basis, amounting to about 18½ closely printed quarto pages of text.)

Suggested Performance Budget for the Forest Service

It is proposed in the outline below that the two major functions of the Forest Service should be (1) the protection and management of the National forests and (2) forest research.

As far as possible from the facts and figures in hand, all expenditure estimates for each of these functions have been assembled. The first major function has been roughly divided between current operating costs and capital outlays, to illustrate how such a division may be made. The current operating costs, under "protection and management," have then been divided into 10 operating functions or programs. Many of these may be subdivided for purposes of showing important sub-programs. In each case, the nature of the work should be explained briefly, the elements involved in carrying it on, some appraisal of results, and the scope or trend of future work. This explanation or justification of the operating programs should be satisfactorily set forth on 4 or 5 pages of the budget document.

The headings under capital investments and improvements indicate the general classes of outlays for which the Forest Service spends funds. It has not been possible to segregate maintenance and other expenses which are frequently included in the capital items; hence the figures are only approximate.

In the total for the national forests, we do, however, show a figure that includes approximately all of the operating costs and oulays in connection with these forests. Some of the programs, like white pine, blister rust, pest control, and flood control, are now financed from appropriations made elsewhere in the Department of Agriculture.

Under the second major function of the Forest Service, that of forest research, we show the major subfunctions or subprograms. These are to be treated in the same way as the operating programs under National forests.

Two other major items make up the grand total under the Forest Service. These are (1) cooperative work with the private users of the national forests, and (2) payments under acts relating to State and private cooperation in the forestry field. These items are set up separately because the first involves the use of private or trust funds, and the second is in the nature of a subsidy for promoting certain work with the States and private owners of forests.

FOREST SERVICE

Suggested Set-up Under a Performance Budget
(Figures used are approximate)

I. The national forests   1949–50 Figures
   A. Protection and management   Redistributed
     1. Over-all managerial and custodial activities..............$ 7,300,000
     2. Forest fire control.................................... *7,400,000
     3. Insect pest and disease control......................... 2,276,650
     4. Timber management (growing and cutting)............. 4,300,000
     5. Range management (grazing).......................... 1,097,000
     6. Recreation use (health and safety measures)............. 599,000
     7. Land-use management................................. 620,000
     8. Water resources management......................... 44,000
     9. Maintenance of improvements........................ 13,297,000
     10. Payments to states in lieu of taxes...................... 6,050,000

Total protection and management................................ 42,983,650
   B. Capital investments and improvements
     1. Acquisition of lands for national forests.................. 1,225,750
     2. Flood control works................................... 1,941,600
     3. Construction of roads and trails........................ 1,752,000
     4. Construction of other improvements..................... 213,000
     5. Reforestation of forest lands........................... 1,268,000
     6. Revegetation of forest lands........................... 758,000

Total capital investments and improvements...................... 7,158,350
Grand Total national forests 50,142,000
Revenues, national forests, from use of lands and sale of products.....
                                   $23,980,000

II. Forest research
   A. Forest and range management research.....................$ 2,862,000
   B. Forest products utilization............................... 1,200,950
     1. Forest Products Laboratory ($858,000)
   C. Forest resources surveys................................. 885,300

Total forest research.. 4,948,250
III. Cooperative work—Forest Service and private users of national forests
   A. Protection and management
     1. Forest and range management......................... 275,000
     2. Custodial services.................................... 109,000
     3. Forest fire control................................... 985,000
     4. Maintenance of improvements......................... 550,000

* Estimated supplement of $4,000,000 additional needed for fire control.

5. Timber management	2,736,000
6. Refunds to cooperators	100,000

Total protection and management............................. 4,755,000
    B. Capital improvements
       1. Construction of improvements......................... 520,000
       2. Reforestation 25,000

Total capital improvements.................................... 545,000
Total cooperative work (trust account)......................... 5,300,000
IV. State and private cooperation
    A. Forest fire prevention and protection (Clarke-McNary Act).... 9,000,000
    B. Farm and other private forestry (Clarke-McNary and Norris-
       Doxey Acts)... 814,500

Total State and private cooperation............................. $9,814,560

Each of these programs or projects is to be accompanied by appropriate explanatory text and supporting schedules.

PART FIVE : MANAGEMENT

Chapter 14

The Executive

In the literature of public administration a great and perhaps still increasing amount of attention has been directed to the powers, functions, and methods of the executive. In these writings one discernible trend is related to what is said elsewhere in this book about the tendency to depreciate the role of the "top man." In some quarters there is nowadays less attention than formerly to legal powers and formal status, and more attention to working methods, to noncoercive aspects of the position, to influence rather than to power. But on the other hand a persistent strain throughout the growth of public administrattion has been the argument that responsibility in a democracy can best—perhaps *only*—be achieved by uniting strong powers with full, formal responsibility, in an executive who can be called to account by the people. Recently this point of view has been further developed and extended by able exponents.

The following selection is taken from some of the most pungent writing in the field of public administration, the "letters" of the late Lent D. Upson. During his later years Mr. Upson was Dean of the School of Public Affairs and Social Work of Wayne University and Director of the National Training School for Public Service; back of this lay a rich experience in practical public administration.

Wishing to keep open his lines of communication with his former students and wishing to pass on to them a type of information that is "not always in the textbooks," he circulated a number of "letters from a dean to his graduates." These letters were so well received that a number of them were collected and published in 1947. The letters have a personal father-to-son quality that sharply distinguishes them from the formal essay. Their chief characteristic is a ripe worldly wisdom which occasionally crosses the line into a more or less genial cynicism. As will be observed

329

the letter sometimes strays from a strict interpretation of its title "Being an Execuive," but never from the subject of effectiveness in administration.

Being an Executive *

LENT D. UPSON

Your education for executiveship has been the process of telescoping other people's adventures (along with some untried theories) into a short space of time, or to quote Dean Will E. Mosher: "Education is hastened living." But don't believe that academic education is a complete substitute for practice. . . .

You will fall in love with your profession—we all do, and it is one in which there are few divorces. But fall in love with its virtues—the frontiers to explore, its excitement, the satisfactions of major, though often anonymous, accomplishment. Do not become enamoured with the rouge and fingernail polish of phrase making, those adolescent poses to which every new profession resorts in order to appear grown up, even sophisticated.

The first catch in your being a good executive or administrator (some pundits believe there is a difference) is to be able to get criticism of the conduct of the job that doesn't come from "yes" men; or perhaps you will be one of those administrators who believes your subordinates are smart because they know the same things and think the same things as you do. If you are, it is going to be pretty tough on the sub-administrator who tries to keep you from tripping over your own feet. Tough—because every observing subordinate has seen some underling "yes-yes" himself right up into the surtax brackets—and if he's as smart as he ought to be, will act accordingly.

Corollary to this, a good administrator hires people who are smarter than he is. Certainly, there is some danger that one of the smart ones may get your job, but if an administrator is smart enough to hire smart people, he probably will be smart enough to keep his job in spite of them.

Still another corollary is to remember that most of the successful things you have done were not by premeditation but largely by chance—even if it hurts your vanity to do that remembering. Probably many administrators are where they are because they happened to be on the grabbing side of the street when the heiress' horse ran away. Few rich men would admit they got that way by accident; and no successful administrator would.

Give your subordinates as much credit as you can and still not build their reputations beyond their capacities. In appraising the capacities of subordinates, it is well to remember that they are usually much larger than you believe. Every

* From *Letters on Public Administration—From a Dean to His Graduates* (Detroit: 1947). Somewhat abridged. Reprinted by permission of the Estate of Lent D. Upson.

administrator instinctively measures his associates by the yardstick of his own personality and his own methods. Insofar as characteristics deviate from that yardstick, he too often assumes them to be inferior. They may be only different— and that very difference may be a superior asset. At any rate, give the subordinate a chance to do a bigger job. He may do it differently from your way. It may be a better way.

Keep your lines of authority straight. Don't make somebody responsible for a job and then give the same task or one in his bailiwick to his subordinate. The best way to wreck the morale of any organization is to pass out orders like campaign buttons regardless of who gets them, making privates believe that they are majors, and majors believe that they are nothing at all. The obverse of this rule is: find and keep your own place within the frame-work of authority; and learn not to criticize a superior except to his face.

Relationship to your immediate boss turns up another problem of administration for which the experts have no solution—yet.

Untoward circumstances may precipitate the most potentially disastrous of situations—whether your allegiance is to your boss or to your institution; to an often friendly, likeable incompetent or to an insensate pile of masonry peopled by comparative strangers, but which in combination represents a purpose to which you devote your energies far beyond payroll necessities.

What is your move when things are wrong in your particular jurisdiction and your superior refuses to permit anything to be done about it? Or when things could be better done and he wants well enough left alone? Or to complicate the problem further, suppose the issue involves moral turpitude—over and above philandering with the office help, which is his business and hers and his wife's. If you are real bright you won't know about that until it gets into the newspaper.

In cases of downright dishonesty you have no alternative but to take your job in your hand, and go over the boss' head to his superior. That's bible and ethics and law unless you want to be an accessory before, during, and after the fact. You may find yourself pounding the pavements and ringing doorbells again as a result—because your boss' boss may be equally mixed up in the matter. But that's the price you may have to pay in order to live with your conscience.

If the issue has to do with efficiency and economy and progress—your handling of it may be a test of your capacity to be an administrator. You can educate and cajole your chief with nerveless patience; you can ask his permission to talk to his chief; as a last resort you can tell him you are going to go around him and that he and you can both take the consequences. There's only one rule—never go around your superior to the higher ups without telling him you are going. . . .

But don't bank on the cataclysmic theory of progress. Few superiors ever hang themselves even when given enough rope. Incompetency is the last offense men are fired for.

Don't try to handle details yourself—which is another way of saying don't know facts you don't need to know, but be very sure of the ones you do need to know. You cannot know and are not supposed to know the multiplicity of detail involved in carrying on a considerable enterprise. To try to know these things means unintentional misstatements and eventual embarrassment. Let subordinates do that remembering for you—and accurately. It is no detriment to good administration to consult a subordinate when information is required, or to present him to a group of outsiders when necessary, and it may help his ego and your business.

Most administrators supplement their formal reporting systems with departmental gossip. Gossip has to be handled gingerly else your employees become a bunch of factionalists and tattle-tales. Barroom gossip is, of course, public property; bed-room gossip is and should be confidential.

Don't ask your superior to approve of plans you are sure of. The mere asking raises the question of expediency. If it is necessary to discuss a subject with a superior, it is usually well to bring a gang with you. One of your associates will think up the right answer while you are stumbling over it—or at least will confuse the issue so thoroughly that your superior will remain in the dark. Loud talk and confusion may snatch victory out of defeat. This administrative technique is particularly good at public hearings.

An alternative is always to bring in two plans—a good one and a bad one. Your boss will spend half the morning tearing your bad plan apart and then be so tired he will approve the good one without change.

Your subordinates have doubtless already learned these techniques. But what to do if one of them gets out on a limb indulging in them? Yank him back if he is a good man, a mayor's appointee or the nephew of a heavy stockholder. Otherwise, saw off the limb after about the third error—or resign yourself.

Don't be "busy." A good executive has learned either to delegate his work or not to take on more than he can do well. And a hard cure for "pressure" is to get down an hour earlier in the morning; an easy one is to cut out part of the idle office gossip about acquaintances, friends, and colleagues—who appear always to be doing something meriting condemnation. There is little merit in after-office hours work, except on routine. Somewhere a good idea may have been cerebrated after six o'clock in the evening, but I have never met up with it.

If you haven't already done so, learn to write and speak the King's English. Mental capacity in university circles is fairly common; but the rarest quality is ability to write and speak so that other people can understand you.

Except for emergencies don't reply to letters at the time you receive them. Your mind is then full of the subject and you are likely to be garrulous. It will relieve you, your secretary, and your correspondents if you devote only a couple of mornings a week to letter-writing and the rest of your time to useful work.

Whenever practical let your subordinates answer the office mail over their own signatures—which will also save your time and give them personal satisfactions that are compensations.

When you find yourself writing uninvited letters to editors and notables, have your blood pressure taken and be looked over for other signs of senility. . . .

If a project is in the offing, make preparations for its happening. If it doesn't happen, you can usually push your chess men back where they were without too much loss of time and money.

Never stand in the way of promotions. Losing a key man hurts sometimes. It may injure an organization and leave highly important jobs unfinished. Under those circumstances, is the loyalty of an administrator due his job or his colleague? In my opinion, the loyalty runs to the man and an administratior who steals his subordinate's opportunities to do bigger and more remunerative things is as reprehensible as if he had stolen his purse or his wife's affections.

Selfishly, the reputation of every administrator is enhanced no end by capable associates who have gone into upper ranks, ambulant witnesses of training and opportunities.

Staff loyalty, next to competency, is the most necessary ingredient of effective administration. By loyalty I mean a feeling by the staff that they are working *with* what is, or is going to be, the best outfit of its kind, and by their actions intend to keep or make it so.

There are two methods of getting loyalty, or the appearance of it—the fear technique and the decency technique. The first method is the easier if you have the disposition of a bully. You can scare many employees into doing their jobs, into working unreasonable hours, and into leaving your employment at the first opportunity. This last item is known as "turn-over" and is greatly deprecated by efficiency experts, though perhaps a modicum of it would be good for most universities.

The decency technique is more difficult to handle, but gets the same or better results with less wear and tear on everybody's disposition. But don't confuse being a considerate boss with the role of a patronizing old "softy" who expects a potted geranium from the staff every time he falls into a sewer.

Once a year, at least, look over your staff and ask yourself what they are worth. That saves them the embarrassment of asking for a raise in pay or accepting another job, and saves you the embarrassment of realizing that some subordinate is worth more than you are paying him and that you have been stealing from him for the benefit of your organization. When an employee has to threaten you with another offer to get a raise—he'd better accept the other offer on the theory that he's working for the wrong man or wrong organization.

Occasionally ask the advice of your colleagues and subordinates on some current problem. It will flatter them and they may surprise you.

Always acknowledge the books and reprints of articles authored by associates and of which they have sent complimentary copies. A good non-committal form letter can be devised—"Thank you for your book (or article) which I had already seen noted (or reviewed) in the *Saturday Review of Literature* (or the *Collegian* or the *Trivia*). It is a further evidence of your industry and scholarship. (This sentence should be deleted if it can be used as a lever for a promotion.) I am looking forward to an examination of the book (or article) in detail. Sincerely." Every statement is correct except the "sincerely."

Don't waste time trying to impress either your help or your clients with your importance. If your subordinates are as smart as they ought to be they will know how good you are without having your greatness rubbed in seven hours a day with time and half for overtime. When you find yourself calling an assistant into your office when it's more convenient for everybody that you go into his, then you can start wondering whether you shouldn't trade offices permanently. . . .

A sibling of the foregoing bounder is the executive who utilizes the telephone technique for self-aggrandizement. Bad manners are international but are full flowered when fertilized by science with such media as the telephone, automobile, and electric doorbell. You can show your total lack of good breeding by telling off your listener over the telephone, knowing he can't smack you. Then you can brag to your secretary about your heroism.

You wouldn't do that—but you may have your secretary call someone on the phone and leave him getting a tin ear while you get around to finishing something you started before you answer. That helps you believe you are impressing somebody but all the while that somebody knows you are a conceited ass. . . .

Be willing to stick your neck out. The dangers you worry about probably will never materialize—and courage is so rare that a little of it will bring chances you never thought of. The repercussions of a mistake are never as great as you fear when you are in the "shall I" or "shall I not" mood. A good rule: when in doubt, go ahead.

Of course, physical courage is often the result of lack of imagination; moral courage is always a by-product of intellectual honesty.

Rules are excellent substitutes for thinking and for the stamina necessary to make decisions. That's why rules are so popular with officials of governments, of universities, and with bureaucrats generally. When in a tight spot, drag out the book of rules—and, abracadabra, you're out of it without using a scintilla of thought or courage. Thus, you save your strength for great crises.

If you are an administrator for a public utility, a social or civic agency, or a government, a big help to your job is a "good press." In fact a "good press" may give you the repute of a good administrator even if you aren't one.

Provided your boss isn't mad at the editor-owner of the newspaper or vice versa, think up some scatterbrain Utopian idea for each of the Sunday issues of the newspapers and you are made. The City Hall reporters will bless you as a source of news, the public will learn to think of you as great and won't remember that most of your suggestions went to the limbo of forgotten things.

But newspaper men must be cultivated and their idiosyncrasies catered to. Originally, they were young fellows like you, just across the campus studying journalism, English, or something else and writing for the *Collegian*. Through the years they have become cynical because they know so many fakers, ticket fixers, and prominent citizens with too many latch keys. They are zealous for the underdog and suspicious of anybody who owns two pairs of pants. This socioeconomic attitude is not congenital. It results from what the mathematicians tell me is a universal ineptitude at guessing the last card dealt. . . .

Always in appraising the actions of men you will wonder whether they were motivated by cunning or by chance. When there is the slightest doubt, give the decision to chance. Elementary strategy may be planned but successful development is usually a matter of fortuitous circumstances. Incidentally, the most baffling of all cunning in the world is downright honesty; it is so often mistaken for something else.

Don't believe more than half you hear about graft in public business—and only one-half of that when it comes to amounts or men. Most of the graft you will learn about will be pretty petty stuff—some protection money from bawdy houses and gamblers, some buying through "right" brokers, some campaign contributions from questionable people, a part of which may go into the pocket of the campaigner and not into the campaign. Much big corruption will be open and above board and offends no law save that of common decency. Some nascent Machiavelli has yet to write a manual on how to graft—which should be dedicated to such impecunious groups as reformers, preachers, and school teachers. . . .

However strong your opinions may be on an issue or whatever you think privately about your opponents, do not impute improper motives to them or make them enemies beyond the day that the issue is settled. Politics does make queer bedfellows and tomorrow you may want to do some political bundling with your severest critics of yesterday. In public service you can't afford to make enemies beyond those people who probably have good reasons for not liking you anyway.

As an executive, you must expect some people to disagree with you—some who are smarter than you are and honestly object to both your methods and objectives; some who are less smart than you are and out of that inadequacy damn what you are doing in an effort to make themselves appear big; some who dislike or misunderstand your motives and who will fight everything you try to do simply because you are doing it. Of these groups, respect the first, ignore the second, and fight the third—and fight them without compromise, winner take all. Don't be too disturbed that the "againsts" always have more and better cards than the "fors." It is easy to be against change—"now is not the time," "these points should have been clarified," "there is concealed danger in this," "prove specific advantages." It is dangerous to advocate anything new—there is always the possibility of your ship sailing into the sunset and off the precipice at the end of the earth. No, for a presumed easy life be content with the *status quo*. You will not find the Indies or Livingstone, or introduce a merit system, or write a new city charter—but there won't be the tension and disappointments that go with reform. But remember that your arteries may harden as quickly sitting in a rocking chair and listening to the noises of the city streets as they will from worthwhile effort.

Be objective and broadminded—hear both sides before you arrive at a decision —even on matters that appear to have only one side. Do not make the decisions over the telephone or at the behest of casual callers. But do make decisions—and then for your own peace of mind forget that the other side has a side at all. Don't be so broadminded that you are wishy-washy and neither side can see you when the fight's on or won.

People against you will say things about you and about what you are doing. You can take easily the criticism that arises from honest disagreement. It is difficult to take lies, exaggerations and innuendoes from persons who exude personal abuse as do all skunks. Over the centuries, various generalizations have been evolved for these situations—which, like most generalizations, are false. You will have to evolve your own philosophy—but, in general, don't reply to criticisms unless your name is misspelled.

Stave off the putting of your office practices into writing for as long as you can. As soon as you formalize regulations governing vacations, sick leaves, and employment policies generally, you have to live up to them, no matter how unjust that may be to some valued associate. Yet some employees may insist on getting their rights at the price of giving up their privileges which often means swapping elephants for rabbits.

Red tape has strangled more men and institutions than ever has hemp rope. Red tape is always woven with the best of intent—committees to advise, forms (pink and blue) to be filled out to prevent errors, routines to be followed to keep nincompoops from doing something they oughtn't. Then some important project goes wrong because some other nincompoop has authority beyond his ability, some official's feelings have been hurt by unintentional over-sight, some coordinator substitutes his opinion for those of his betters, somebody didn't know or somebody forgot.

All we know about red tape is that its effectiveness increases at about the square of the physical distance between the bureaucrat and the individual affected—and that's why federal red tape is reddest and stickiest; that it appears spontaneously when institutions start to jell intellectually; that the only antidote is a combination of hell raising and abject resignation.

Be patient with the limitations imposed by men's environments. Remember that street cleaners, club women, deans of colleges all handle the little chores imposed upon them with the same seriousness and rhetoric with which other men have built pyramids.

Always speak considerately of your colleagues. Adorn your addresses with their names and accomplishments—hoping that they will have a decent sense of reciprocity. This technique is particularly good in academic circles and not bad in many others.

Don't bother too much about being "practical." Too often that merely means doing the job the way it was done in 1880.

In spite of cynicisms to the contrary, committees are useful—useful to encourage group participation, to minimize group opposition, to temper individual enthusiasms. But remember with Ely Culbertson that "no committee has ever been known to create a system of philosophy or of economies, to write a poem or to compose a symphony." Committee thinking is different from individual thinking, but committee findings are seldom the true consensus of the members. Rather such findings are the thinking of one easily imposed upon person dragooned into writing a report—and then only to the extent that these conclusions can be foisted upon the others. Early in a committee meeting present a preliminary sketch of a possible committee report as a means of circumventing otherwise endless talk.

Never give personal advice to anyone—about getting married, getting a divorce, buying a home, or trading jobs. Review the facts objectively so that your enquirer misses none of them. Then he must make his own decisions according to his preference for blonds, brunettes, climate, geography, salary, work, and the state of his glands.

All of which sums up: About a quarter of being a good administrator is knowledge of the tools of administration; the other three-quarters is skill with people. Some civil service authorities believe that it is all the first; some administrators, all the second.

In any event, it is a fair conclusion that the larger the organization you head the more you must know about people and politics and the less you need to know about the tools of administration.

The president of a nation or the mayor of a great city must be first of all a politician. They can delegate their administrative authority. The manager of a medium or small sized city or organization must be an administrator, in fact as well as in name.

Delegation of administrative authority means actually delegating it—not merely saying that you do, and then trying to outsmart your subordinates on every technical subject that comes up. If you do, they will quit trying to be competent on the general theory that you are General Know It All and will make the decisions anyway.

So the bigger your organization and the farther you are removed from detail—the more you must learn to depend on the capacities of your subordinates and your skill with people—and take the consequences.

Seriously, though,—whether your first line administrators number two or twenty—their capacity as a group, and also the capacity of the subordinates of every one of them, will depend much on your ability to develop group spirit and to stimulate group-interaction. You may have fun using your administrators as a silent back drop for the exhibition of your egotism. But you will get more accomplished if you develop group enthusiasm and a lively flow of intra-group suggestions. The way of doing this is often called "the conference method." Some say this method can be learned. More likely, group leadership is something you have to be born with.

Knowledge of the tools of administration you can acquire. Skill with people means leadership—that indefinable something that consists of elements of physical appearance, vitality, honest thinking, ability to talk just enough, tact, courage, and cultivation of the right people.

The last of these requirements may be something of a bore. And speaking of the right people, always be nice to secretaries—or at least to the other fellow's. You can never tell when they are going to make up the boss' mind for him, loose your most important communication in the waste basket, or neglect to telephone your appointment.

Executiveship carries prerogatives and privileges but also responsibilities. It isn't a one way ticket. On the asset side is respect for your office if not for yourself, sometimes use of an official car, always personal errands run and personal chores done by your staff. There is the accompanying liability to that staff to see that salaries are adequate, that family emergencies are met with a minimum of hardship, that good nature and convenience are not imposed upon.

My colleagues who are addicted to psychology say that the foregoing admonitions are a waste of effort and ink—that executives are not only born and not made, but that many of those so born are unmade because their families pushed them around too much or too little before and immediately after they crawled out of the cradle. In consequence they demand affection, attention, and status and so become irksome to superiors, subordinates and equals—and have other mental quirks too numerous to mention. These traumata of infancy, childhood, and adolescence are said to be too serious to be remedied by reading a few rules that only impinge on a mental blind spot.

———◆———

The following selection on the role and methods of the governmental executive supplements the foregoing "letter" by Dean Upson and affords an interesting comparison in style and perspective. The author, Donald C. Stone, was introduced above as the author of "Washington-Field Relationships."

Mr. Stone's essay is an excellent summary statement of recent thought on the executive. It will be noted, for example, that the practical limitations on the formal authority of an executive are stressed; the naïveté of early administrative theory on this point, it will be remembered, was treated in a humorous vein by Professor Latham in a selection in Part 2. "Communication," an aspect of administrative endeavor that is receiving more and more attention, is also emphasized.

The difference in tone between Dean Upson's letter and Mr. Stone's essay is obvious. Query, are there significant differences in analysis and recommendations?

Notes on the Governmental Executive: His Role and His Methods *

DONALD C. STONE

This discussion of the job of being a successful governmental executive is predicated on the assumption that the product of any organization is an institutional product, not the executive's personal product. What the executive can accomplish —his impact on the organization—at any one point in time is conditioned by the state of his organization, and what he achieves is largely the product of his influence rather than his command. Therefore, in long range terms, the job of an executive is to create an environment conducive to concerted effort in pursuit of the organization's objectives. In short run terms, his job is to know what is going on in the organization and to be in a position to act on the issues which require his personal attention and still to retain sufficient freedom to deal with those outside his organization—superiors, legislators, public. Stated differently, the executive's job is one of maximizing his influence throughout his organization as distinguished from relying exclusively upon his formal authority and the power of command. . . .

Whatever may be the notions of what executives do and how they do it, the bedrock fact is that the executive must rely on his staff for the achievement of his objectives. Most issues in his organization will be settled without ever reaching him. And on those that do reach him his choice will generally be a restricted one. By the time a report or instruction has been developed, worked over, revised, reviewed, level by level, what finally remains for the executive to say in most cases is "O.K." He may be inclined to make some changes, but he will soon learn that something else will demand his attention before he is through. Unless what comes to him involves an issue of great importance, he will, therefore, frequently have to accept what he considers to be an inferior product. When the issue is a crucial one for the organization's program and involves high level judgments on the consequences of a given course of action, the executive may be called upon to choose among two or three alternative solutions, but secondary questions are likely to have to go by the board. Consequently, unless the executive's objectives are wholeheartedly accepted by his organization, the chances that they will be achieved are problematical.

* From *New Horizons in Public Administration: A Symposium* (University, Alabama: 1945). Somewhat abridged. Reprinted by permission of the University of Alabama Press.

Failure on the part of the executive to seek aggressively his organization's support may leave him in a precarious position. The forces militating against an effective working together toward a common goal are many and powerful in any large organization: unreconciled points of view, tradition and routine, inertia, the distortions that grow out of specialist interests, personal ambitions. These internal resistances singly or in combination can cancel out the executive's efforts. To be sure, some of the drives in any established organization represent forces of stability that will keep the organization running when there is no leadership and will save the new executive from many mistakes. Furthermore, the necessary adjustment of the executive to the facts of his environment can contribute to his development by increasing his understanding of how he can function in relation to what goes on around him. On the other hand, if the executive is entirely unsophisticated in the ways of institutional behavior and does not consciously and continuously take steps to offset the divisive elements in his environment, he will find himself dominated by rather than dominating his organization.

The executive is often seen as the man sitting at the top of the organization, possessed of a dangerous amount of authority, hiring and firing at will, whose every suggestion or order is responded to promptly and completely. This view reflects one of the greater misconceptions about the nature of executive work. The government executive may have a large grant of legal authority, but he will find that in actual fact it must be used in an economical fashion. If he lacks discrimination in the use of his power, he will debase its value and perhaps find himself impotent at a moment of crucial importance. He must guard against destroying the organizational support on which he must depend in executing his program. As Paul Appleby has often remarked, the new executive in an organization may fire a few persons but not very many. Reducing the point to an absurdity, he can't issue an order, "Now and henceforth all employees shall wear red neckties," and expect to get a response. By persuasion, by indoctrination, by leadership—in other words by influence—he may, however, be able to accomplish what he cannot accomplish by fiat. This is by no means a universally understood truth. There are too many executives who fail to recognize that because the members of their organizations are creatures of reason, their positions would be strengthened if they bolstered their formal authority with the support that comes from conviction.

I do not mean to suggest, however, that awareness of the importance of influence as a method of reaching institutional goals is a strictly milk and honey proposition of dubious effectiveness in moments of crisis. If the executive is skillful and knows how to establish his position, he can be the decisive element in determining the character of the organization, and he can exercise his authority with telling effect when the occasion demands it. The point is he cannot "bull his way through" any and all situations; he cannot run against the tide of organization opinion. He may buffet his way by sheer force on occasion or on specific issues, but if he does it too often he may pay for his gains by failure to carry his organization with him over the long run.

I have already commented that the executive's job has to be viewed in long range terms as well as on a day-to-day basis. His aim will be to use his own time and talents on the activities and issues that will contribute the most to the organization's forward movement and to develop a supporting team to the point of optimum production. His success in reaching it will be, in important measure, determined by his success in developing a body of commonly shared ideas. This is a prerequisite if his staff are to have guide posts against which to judge their general direction and their specific actions and if he is to have some assurance of reliable performance. Without this kind of institutional environment, the executive will be unable to mold the organization into something more than the sum of its parts. Furthermore, cultivation of such an atmosphere is essential if the members of the organization are to have a sense of participation in an enterprise bigger than themselves and secure the satisfactions necessary to good staff work. Only then do the fragmented jobs that are the lot of most people in large organizations become a source of stimulation.

The importance of an institutional environment and of indoctrination in its meaning has long been understood by the Army and Navy, but in large part has been neglected by civilian governmental organizations. It has often been observed that indoctrination permits West Point and Annapolis trained men to function, and function well, even though the commonly accepted rudiments of good organization may be missing in a given situation. Some of the civilian organizations such as the Farm Credit Administration, the New York City Police Force, and the Tennessee Valley Authority are conspicuous for their high morale—the natural by-products of a consciously fostered environment. More often than not, however, this basic source of organization strength has been given too little attention by governmental executives in this country.

Awareness of the problem does not mean prompt solution. Almost any executive is likely to find that the contribution he can make to an organization's environment can be made only over an extended period of time. Rapid adjustments, such as customarily take place in the Army and Navy at the outbreak of war, or in a relief agency in time of distress, are the exception rather than the rule. The recently appointed chief of a Federal bureau with many years of tradition and precedent behind it has estimated that his job of redirection is at least a ten-year one. On occasions in the Federal Government when time considerations were crucial and other factors permitted, this problem has been solved by setting up a new agency, thus short circuiting the process of retooling a staff steeped in earlier programs and methods. This is a principal reason why some of the new war agencies were set up to do jobs which on the face of it might have been assigned to existing agencies. Normally, however, a government executive is likely to find it necessary to work with what he inherits and to develop a plan of action that can be followed without too much disruptive pulling and hauling. This may mean focusing his developmental efforts on future rather than on current activities, so that the daily work of the organization can move ahead with a minimum of uncertainty and interruption.

What the executive accomplishes over the short run will depend upon the state of the institutional environment at any one time and upon the external circumstances affecting his program. His day-to-day activities and decisions may be directly in line with his long range plans or he may be forced on occasions to accept situations or proposals that do not measure four square with his ultimate objectives. Whether the executive's job is viewed in long range or short range terms, however, the ways in which he can seek to maximize his influence and close the gap between present reality and the ultimate ideal of smoothly integrated activity are the same. It is on these that I shall comment briefly for the remainder of this discussion.

How He Spends His Time

The executive's concept of what his job is and the way this affects the scheduling of his time and talents will be a primary factor in the results he secures. In large part this can be encompassed under the head of "operating at his proper level." In his recent book, *Big Democracy*, Paul Appleby develops the point at some length. By this he means that no head of a government department or other subdivision should do work or make decisions that should be the responsibility of officials at a lower level in the organizational hierarchy. Not only does this disrupt and confuse his subordinates but it prevents the executive from doing what is properly his job.

Dealing with People. The executive job is one of dealing with people, of judging, adjusting to, and working around personalities both inside and outside his organization. This is at the core of the business of getting people to apply their energies in harmony with each other and getting things done. I recall a case of a city manager who was extremely unpromising at the time of his appointment. He had no apparent experience or interest in such matters as working out arrangements for delegations of authority or subdivision of labor, he probably had never heard of the follow-up principle, and he was completely baffled by theoretical discussions of management. He had, however, an abiding interest in people. He attracted people, and he had an uncanny sense of whom he could trust. Anyone looking at his organization and how he functioned would say it couldn't work. But it did. He had a feeling for what it took to provide the cohesion and the central pull necessary for turning out services to the community.

This is in part a reflection of the fact that the executive should use a major portion of his time and talents in being the catalyst who assimilates and draws together the ideas of others, resolves lines of action, gets agreements nailed down, sees that action gets taken. He must develop and rely on his staff for the carry through on the specific elements of his program, and must carefully restrain himself if tempted to dip into technical work. If he does not, he will never have time for his part of the institutional job—the never-ending one of bringing about a consensus on the one hand and on the other of seeing that discussion does not protract interminably, that something decisive happens.

In doing this, he will need to take care not to go off on his own without regard for his organizational resources. If he forgets or ignores his staff in the course of operations, he runs the risk of dispensing off-the-cuff opinions which will not stand close analysis or making commitments which his organization cannot fulfill, not to mention the fact that such actions leave the staff in thin air. Unfortunately, not all governmental executives are like the one who commented to me recently that he doubted that he crossed up his staff as often as they did him. There are too many who operate as if the chief function of staff was to keep the executive from the embarrassment of explaining away their errors. This can only lead to a frittering away of strength in checking up on many small and relatively unimportant episodes.

The public arena character of the executive's responsibilities will draw upon his resources day and night, and he will find that in varying degrees, depending upon his status in the governmental scheme of things, he will not be able to live his life according to his personal choice but must govern himself in the light of the demands upon him. Nor will he be able to compensate for this by pointing at the end of the day to specific accomplishments and saying, "I did such and such." He may be able to think of a number of things that his organization did and how he tried to influence his organization and perhaps provide the capstone to some enterprise, but he can't look upon the results as his own.

It is because of these characteristics of executive life and routine that the appointment of good technicians to administrative posts is often a failure. Unless the specialist happens to possess the rare quality of administrative aptitude he cannot be remade into an executive with satisfaction to either himself or his staff. Anyone who has observed governmental operations has seen many instances of the unfortunate consequences of moving to administrative posts persons who are first and last technicians—making a physician a public health officer, a design engineer a commissioner of public works, a social case worker a welfare director, a program idea man in a Federal department an assistant secretary.

Not as a Technician. The need for the executive to eschew the technical and stick to the level where adjustments get made and judgments about the implications of surrounding circumstances are applied is one of the oft repeated dictums of the public administration fraternity, but the point too frequently is oversimplified. For one thing the dividing line can never be determined with finality. The extent to which the executive concerns himself with specific issues will always be affected by such factors as the age of his organization, outside circumstances, and the extent to which he may have to compensate for failure at lower levels.

In any event, the executive must know enough of the general field not to get lost in the labyrinth. If he does not know the program at the outset, he must master quickly its major substantive elements. Otherwise he will be unable to command the loyalty and respect of his specialists and weld them together as a team. He must have sufficient understanding of the basic issues involved in his program to be able to judge whether the necessary steps have been taken to arrive at a proper conclusion. In the early days of the Federal Bureau of Old Age and Survivors Insurance, for example, the way in which individual participants were to be enumerated and their accounts identified—now numbering approximately seventy million—was one of the major technical issues. With many contending proposals advanced, members of the Social Security Board as well as the head of the Bureau had to go into the problem sufficiently to be assured that the staff had developed the best answer.

The more background the executive develops with the passage of time, the more discriminating will be his judgments that have technical ingredients. He will learn to know when he should overrule his specialists (seldom on technical grounds) and how far he can rely on them, and he will know enough not to be cowed by them. Although the executive must be able to find his way among the technicians, his dominating concerns are more likely to be the non-technical factors affecting the resolution of a problem, particularly the general implications and potential outside acceptance of what is done. While the state highway commissioner, for example, will need to keep up with major changes in specifications or design which may become centers of controversy, he will find that his main headaches will arise out of such questions as the right of way for a road or the location of a bridge.

External Affairs. This necessary concentration of the executive on what is feasible and on judging what is in the public interest should affect materially the amount of time the executive spends in becoming sensitive to and influencing the outside environment. It is the executive's job to cultivate relationships with the heads of other government agencies, with members of legislative bodies, with private institutions, and with the public, so that his staff will have a favorable climate within which to function. In this way he can increase his awareness of the ways in which programs and ideas must be carried out if they are to be accepted. The job of running interference for his organization is one that only the executive can do, and the effectiveness with which it is done will be a significant determinant of what his organization can accomplish.

His success in this part of his job will be affected in part by whether the executive confines his contacts to those that come to him or whether he consciously seeks to direct the character of these relationships. The government executive too often restricts himself to persons of his own social background or of the particular group with which his agency deals. He needs to mix with those who are against as well as for his program. If his agency's function is concerned with aids to business, he needs to understand the viewpoint of labor; if it is social welfare, he needs to mingle enough with the rugged individualists to see life from their angle. If his outside contacts are not well rounded or if he neglects them altogether, he may find that he will end up with a distorted view of the outside environment.

The executive's success in meeting these outside responsibilities will also be in part a by-product of his reaction to what his job demands of him as an individual. The broader and more generalized it is, the more important it will be for him to know what is going on not only in his general field, but in the community, in the nation, and in the world. He will need to broaden his own horizons, stretch his mind, and develop new ideas from which his whole organization can benefit. I know one Federal department head, for example, who met at regular intervals with people of ideas both inside and outside his organization, thus doing comprehensively what every executive should do at least in some degree. As a basic minimum, he should find time to keep up-to-date on the journals and books that give perspective to government enterprise, and I do not mean here administrative literature, important as that may be. If he lets himself become so preoccupied with his immediate problems that he fails to keep up with life that is going on about him, he lets slip one of the best ways through which he can have an impact on his organization—by helping to bridge the gap between it and the world at large.

How He Saves His Time

I trust these comments on the level of activity on which the executive's energies should be focused do not give the impression that all the executive need do is have a bit of insight into what is demanded of him and proceed forthwith. It will unfortunately be an inevitable part of his lot that people and things will press for his attention far beyond his capacity to deal with them. His life will be a succession of meetings, telephone calls, documents. He cannot escape spending appreciable time handling many problems which will seem small in themselves but which may have serious implications for the status of the organization: persons who are not performing, staff troubles and worries, some aggrieved citizen, a press release. Many persons outside his organization will seek him out—citizens, legislators, newspaper men, old friends, *ad infinitum*.

Although he will need to take the greatest care not to appear inaccessible either to his staff or to those outside his organization, he must face the very practical problem of deciding whom he will see and of maintaining a balance among the competing demands for attention. If he holds himself open to deal with any problem that comes to him, he will become inaccessible to his operating chiefs and he will neglect his outside responsibilities. Decisions will be delayed. He will lose perspective on both his organization and the world and will fail to provide the upward pull and unifying influence that his position requires. With a little firmness and careful planning, however, there are a number of steps he can take to conserve his time, and he can establish controls that will in reality increase rather than decrease his accessibility.

Personal Staff. Judicious use of personal assistants is one of the best of these. In a large department or office, the executive may have several such assistants. Former Secretary of State Stettinius, in announcing new appointments in the State Department, designated fifteen persons to various types of assistant positions, in addition to the regular staff officers of the Department. For some of these, special areas of concern were indicated, *e.g.*, International Organization and Security Affairs, Press Relations, Broad Management Matters; for others no special assignment was mentioned. This is probably far too many for the ordinary situation. The city manager of a city of 50,000 inhabitants, the head of a department of a medium-sized state, or a Federal division chief, for example, may find that a single administrative assistant will be sufficient.

One of the most important uses of the executive's personal staff, including his secretary, is in meeting the problem of seeing people. They can help him arrange his calendar, determine whom he should see, control the length of time he spends with visitors. They can frequently do much to satisfy those whom the executive is not able to see or arrange for their business to be disposed of by other officials. To meet the needs of subordinates they can often secure spot information or decisions from the executive. They can arrange meetings between the executive and persons both within and without the organization according to relative urgency.

The personal staff can also identify the most pressing problems requiring the executive's attention and can pave the way for their speedy disposition by being sure that all necessary information is at hand and in order. They can sometimes pinch hit for the executive on spot jobs. They can give assistance in writing speeches and articles and can accompany him on trips when they can be useful. They can keep him up-to-date with what is going on. Sometimes one of them serves as an intimate adviser and will help select key officials and evaluate the performance of subordinates who seem to be falling down on their jobs. Obviously, each of the executive's personal assistants is not assigned to all of these tasks, as there will be specialization among them. But until his immediate office is staffed with aides who can do some or all of these things for him, he will be unnecessarily handicapped.

On the other hand, he must guard against overdoing it. A large number of personal assistants may mean that there are deadheads or blanks in the organization for whom the executive is seeking to compensate by increasing his personal staff. This can only muddy up the regular lines of communication and command and cause confusion in his organization. Personal assistants can also be a source of uncertainty if the executive fails to define their jobs so that their roles are understood by the rest of the organization.

An executive's personal assistants must not function as palace princes, accessible in varying degrees to other organization officials and pleading the cause only of favorites. They must be the same to all men, and the executive must kill any tendency to manipulate the organization or to afford an entrance through the "back door." Equally fatal is reliance on them by the executive to the point that his outlook becomes limited and warped.

Operating Aides. In addition to what the personal staff can do to save the executive time and energy, there will also be need in any large organization for the kind of assistants who can share his principal operating burdens. If the executive chooses such aides judiciously he can compensate for talents which he may not have and multiply several times the impact of his leadership.

If the job of the executive requires a high level of public leadership, extensive dealing with a legislative body, a large number of outside contacts, or the devotion of much time to evolving a program or to negotiations with other executives, or if his talents do not lie in the management of an organization, a general deputy responsible in the line of command for internal administration will be needed. A permanent deputy position is likewise desirable when the executive post is one that changes with political fortunes. To be sure, it is not possible to have such a deputy in all the situations where one could be used advantageously. In most city manager cities, for example, it is not often feasible for the manager to share his principal duties. The extent to which public attention is fixed on the centralization of responsibility in *the* city manager almost precludes the use of a double, although not of other types of assistants.

Short of a general deputy, the executive may utilize a principal assistant either as an operating aide or as a chief of staff, giving him varying degrees of responsibility, or he may divide his managerial duties with one or more such assistants in a manner mutually compatible with the persons involved. The specific arrangements must be based upon the systematic analysis of tasks to be performed and of the personalities of the executive and the persons that can be secured to perform them. But even the best possible person will never fill the job as theoretically conceived.

However the matter is arranged, and it will always be difficult to work out smoothly, such assistants must think and act in terms that are appropriate to the organization at large. If they do not deal with matters that cut across the entire organization, they no longer serve as aides to the executive in his general leadership and management job but rather as operating heads of a group of specialized units. They then become preoccupied with segments of the organization and their work does little to contribute to the achievement of balance among the different parts. In the Federal Government, assistant secretaries in the departments are frequently used in this fashion—in the Interior, Commerce, Post Office, and Justice Departments among others. Generally speaking, there has been under-development of the general deputy or assistant type of post I am describing here, in state and local government as well as in the Federal Government.

Time Saving Procedures. Apart from the help the executive can get by providing himself with staff to supplement or complement his own efforts, there is much that can be done to save his time if careful attention is given to the way in which documents, information, problems, issues are presented to him.

With a little ordinary care the amount of time the executive need spend on strictly informational material can be reduced to manageable dimensions. Summaries can be prepared for reports, lengthy memos can be briefed to one page, papers dealing with related subjects can be brought together. . . .

The way in which this can be done in a vast organization is illustrated by the manner in which information is packaged and presented to the Army Chief of Staff and other principal officers in the War Department. A log of selected, important messages to and from the War Department and points in all parts of the globe is the first order of business each day, taking from 15 to 45 minutes. This is followed by a meeting, attended by the Chief of Staff and his Deputy, the Secretary of War, and the Commanding General of the Army Air Forces, at which material on military operations throughout the world and on enemy developments and capabilities is presented and discussed. The data are organized by the Operations and Intelligence Divisions of the General Staff, and the discussion consumes from one-half to two hours. These daily informational routines are supplemented by a comprehensive system of briefing the Chief and Deputy Chief of Staff on all matters on which they must make decisions or on which they should be informed. . . .

Governmental executives generally could do much to simplify their lives by insisting upon the adaptation and development of this idea to meet their particular needs. More often than not, full implementation of a plan or recommendation will take a series of steps or actions. Each of these should be set up in a fashion to permit the executive to take action quickly. It is more economical of time for the executive to send documents back for change if need be than to try to make a decision on other than a specific basis. Too often executives are confronted with the statement, "Here's a problem," rather than, "I propose that you do this for these reasons."

This process of simplification should not, however, be carried to the point that the executive is deprived of the opportunity of deliberation on the facts surrounding the proposal with which he is confronted. It is not always feasible nor is it necessarily desirable to reduce proposals to one recommended course of action. When there are non-technical factors entailing judgment and perspective of a level to warrant careful attention by the executive, cut and dried solutions will handicap rather than aid him. He should have the opportunity to consider well thought-out alternative recommendations.

How He Communicates His Ideas

It will not profit the executive a great deal to be a genius in the management of his time, if he does not take steps to forge strong links between himself and the other elements in his organization. In this connection, the mobilization and indoctrination of his team of key subordinates must be near the top of any executive's agenda. When the executive sees to it that the persons in positions of responsibility have been selected and trained for the function of leadership, the way will be open for securing response to new objectives, policies, and methods. Without such a staff he will have a mob, not an organization.

If there is a free and open channel through which ideas and information can move both down and up, the influence of the executive can be felt all the way through the organization. This is not, of course, a one way process. If the executive is skillful he will take pains to develop to the utmost the ideas and suggestions coming from his staff, both because this is the way to strengthen the net product and because only in an atmosphere where there is mutual respect are the executive's views likely to carry their maximum weight.

The kind of person the executive happens to be also has a good deal of bearing on the amount of influence he has. He is a symbol to his organization, and in the case of the higher posts, to the public as well. His attitudes and actions, both private and public, will have an effect—indirect and subtle perhaps, but nonetheless important—on the attitudes of all within his organization. If his characteristics and actions excite admiration, his staff will unconsciously be motivated to respond to his leadership and ideas. If the contrary is true, the natural reluctance of individuals to adapt themselves to the requirements of organized activity is likely to be thrice compounded.

Oral Communication. In small sessions with key officials, the executive has his best opportunity for putting over his ideas. The values of such sessions can be multiplied if, when feasible, the officials primarily concerned with the resolution of an issue bring with them a principal subordinate or two, and if appropriate staff officers are included in important discussions with line officers. Any such devices that will increase the likelihood of cross-fertilization of ideas without setting undue obstacles in the way of the expeditious handling of business should be encouraged by the executive. Furthermore, to the extent that the executive makes the most of his opportunities for meeting with groups of people rather than individuals, he will be able to extend the area over which his influence is directly felt. It is not always necessary for the executive to be present in person for this result to be achieved. One of his staff officers or assistants thoroughly familiar with his point of view and attitude can often represent him.

Meetings of this character are of enormous importance as a means of facilitating the forward movement of an organization. If as issues come to the top they can be thrashed out by the principals involved, all points can be brought out on the spot and the most effective answer nailed down. This speeds the handling of important business, and through the process of dealing in unison on organization-wide matters, the principals get to know each other and how to work together. The more this understanding is developed, the more readily they will team up voluntarily when special problems confront two or more of them.

Staff Meetings. General staff meetings, if well planned and confined to subjects that are of common interest and concern, can do much to aid communication. They can bring about fuller recognition by each individual of his relationship to the larger whole, and the executive can use them to bring about a common perspective and to help him in knitting the organization together. Anyone who has attended an effectively conducted meeting has observed how much more readily ideas take shape and are acted upon when an easy means of exchange is developed.

I do not wish to suggest, however, that general staff meetings are of exceptional importance. They are only one of many tools in the management kit. It is often taken for granted that every executive should get his key subordinates together—the department heads of a city or state government—as a cabinet, at frequent, regular intervals. The only useful purpose of group meetings of this character is discussion of matters of common concern. There is no merit in bringing diverse officials together to consider matters that can be settled in the line of command. In a meeting of department heads with the governor, any discussion of the welfare director's problems would put the director of public works to sleep. If the head of the agriculture department started to bring up his problems, most of the rest would be bored stiff. The reason for calling key subordinates together should be to dispose of issues requiring their collective judgment.

Written Communications. Written communications are a generally understood although not too well applied method of conveying the executive's ideas from one level to another in an organization, and they can be an aid to his long range efforts to develop his institution. In many organizations subordinates down the line are deluged with detailed instructions and regulations on every aspect of institutional life. Failure to credit staff with a certain amount of common sense and ingenuity will not generate mutual understanding and more likely than not will lead to complete indifference. In either event, the executive is not helped by the result.

On the other hand, there is only too apt to be a grievous lack of well thought-out statements issued by the executive outlining specific objectives, schedules of operating requirements, and definitions of responsibilities. However good a job the executive may do in dealing with his principals and however conscientious they may be about passing on the information they get from the top, this will not cover the situation entirely. Written communications are an important supplement in getting to the entire organization the basic outlines of policies and objectives.

As important as it is that policies, and also programs and methods, be translated into clear, written communications, these should not be relied upon to get an essential thought over without the assistance that comes from personal comment on their application. Furthermore, this is the only way there can ever be assurance that staff members read or at least become aware of the written word. Written communications are useful chiefly as a point of departure and serve their primary purpose, after the actual labor of thinking them through is completed, as a basis for a discussion or series of discussions with staff of the ideas or directions contained therein. They are particularly useful for the orientation and instruction of new members of the organization.

How He Harnesses His Organization

My comments to this point have been focused on the ways in which the executive uses and extends his personality, ideas, and time. This has largely left out of account the institutional framework through which he must function. None of his personal activities, negotiations, or dealings will amount to much if his institution is not so organized that he can get a firm grip on it at crucial points and at crucial times.

Keeping up to Date. Essential number one is that he must know what is going on in his organization. If he organizes for the purpose, he can keep track of the trend of affairs—weak spots and strong spots, emerging problems, bottle necks, opportunities for progress. If he does not, he is likely to be at a loss in attempting to pursue a balanced program.

In the normal course of events he will be confronted with a vast array of paper: actions or letters requiring his signature, drafts of orders and regulations, proposed plans of work, reports of inspections or organizational studies, program appraisals, reports of progress, statistical summaries and interpretations, personnel documents, budget and fiscal analyses, *ad infinitum.* With the help of his assistants in organizing and controlling these materials, they can provide him with much grist for appraisal of the organization's operations.

The picture the executive gets in this fashion will be only a partial one and will lack a good deal of realism if he does not supplement these sources of information with others. Many of the gaps the executive can fill in for himself, through conversations and dealings with his subordinates, and in some fields of governmental work, through inspections. The state conservation commissioner can see at first hand what is being done in the way of development and use of state parks and in the management of state forests. On the other hand, the head of an agency engaged in activities having little tangible or physical expression cannot rely very heavily on this device. A commissioner of internal revenue, for example, cannot learn much about the product of his organization by looking at the files of paper in process.

The executive's personal staff can help keep him posted on what is going on by passing on information that he might pick up himself if he could see more people. What I am referring to is spot news that may affect the organization and its work, information on breakdowns in the organization, on personnel maladjustments, reactions of particular persons to actions by the executive, new proposals or ideas in the making, complaints with which the executive may have to deal. They may learn of these things informally by contacts below the upper crust of the organization, and they may pick up some of them from conversations with or reports by both staff and line officers. The executive needs to differentiate between the significant and unimportant in this kind of stuff, which may often be little more than rumor or gossip. He must keep a check rein on it, and not let it offset the solid help which his general staff divisions can give him directly.

Staff Divisions. Perhaps the most important single tool the executive has in harnessing his organization and keeping it in focus is his general staff—the budgeting, program planning, personnel, organization and methods planning divisions. I do not include here service or auxiliary units such as statistical, procurement, and office services, as important and necessary as these may be. Neither do I include here accounting and legal services which, while providing control mechanisms for the executive, are otherwise more akin to the service units than they are to the general staff divisions. It is true, however, that because of personal competence, as well as the fact that they engage in some general staff activity, the accounting and legal chiefs are often used by the executive for a variety of general staff responsibilities.

The staff divisions provide resources for the analysis and development of solutions of problems common to the whole organization. They provide a source of highest counsel and advice on matters about which the executive is uncertain or has reason to doubt the solution offered by an operating subordinate. They provide a general rather than a specialized viewpoint both in reviewing proposals made by the operating subdivisions and in evaluating the results of the work of such subdivisions. They can do much to help the executive bring the objectives of the organization into focus and get consistency of action. In addition, the employees of such divisions circulate around the entire outfit and provide one of the most fruitful means of gathering information and of securing understanding and acceptance of policy.

The executive needs the benefit of a group of staff advisers functioning in this fashion to help him in anticipating tasks to be done, in planning to meet contingencies that may be around the corner, in mapping out policy and program, and in working out fundamental organization and methods. Their value depends, however, on the way in which they function. They must stay in the staff role of advising, consulting, and coordinating and must avoid imposing their personal judgment on line officials on operating matters. Staff divisions can become a burden rather than a help if they diffuse the executive's line of command by dipping into operating work and if they insulate the executive from other sources of counsel. That the temptation to move outside the staff realm frequently is not resisted is reflected in the common practice of having a large number of detailed transactions referred to the budget office or personnel office for review, transactions that involve no new policy questions. Perhaps the reason staff officers often insist on this is because it is easier to review the activity of others than to do creative work, or because they do not have the capacity to do staff work, or because they have never learned what real staff work is.

The staff divisions cannot fulfill their roles to the maximum if they move off on their own in separate directions. It is, therefore, essential that general staff activities be coordinated with each other. The executive or his general deputy may be able to supply this coordination. Sometimes this can be more readily achieved by placing the staff units under an executive officer or a chief of staff.

The various staff elements can in this way be brought into focus by someone concerned with the management of the organization as a whole, and the total resources are more available to the executive. Furthermore, there will then be less likelihood of non-productive competition for the attention of the executive, and the number of organizational units the executive must keep track of personally will be reduced.

But regardless of the arrangement, general staff functions must be directed by high level officers who have a considerable amount of free access to the executive, with the executive officer performing a facilitating function and providing the environment in which the executive can most easily tap the reservoir of ideas of the individual staff officers.

Arrangement of Line Units. The way in which the executive arranges the subdivisions of his agency or bureau will also have a lot to do with whether he is on top of or at the mercy of his organization. There is much common knowledge of how to organize operating subdivisions, and I shall not go into the question in detail. I should like to comment particularly on the relationship between the way in which the organization is put together and the executive's opportunity to act on significant issues.

For example, a small number of operating divisions will not necessarily mean that the executive is sufficiently free of detail that he can contribute the element of over-all perspective and influence. When there are so few or the establishment is so arranged that the executive is walled off from operations by many layers of supervision or the job of harmonizing and coordinating on major issues is pushed down to a subsidiary level, he may become the slave rather than the master.

Related to the question of too few operating units and the layers of supervision that this may entail, is that of the excessive independence that statutory provisions often give subordinate operating officers. When the functions of major division heads are defined by statute, the top executive is placed under a severe handicap in trying to manage what frequently become independent principalities. I recall the vivid comment of a Federal executive who complained that he had the impossible task of administering a federation of bureaus rather than a department.

In a different category are the complications that may ensue if there is too fine a breakdown of activities. Not only is he unable to hold the separate units within his span of attention, which leaves them floating on their own, but those issues that do reach him may get one-sided or unbalanced consideration. Functions need to be so arranged that, to the maximum extent possible, varied points of view will be brought to bear and reconciled along the way. In recognition of the dangers of over specialization, up-to-date city health departments, for example, have moved away from the system of organizing public health nursing services on the basis of specialized types of work: tuberculosis, venereal disease, infant care. Units or districts consisting of a group of nurses able to meet varied problems and situations are in large measure self-coordinating and thus reduce the burden on higher administrative positions.

There is another disadvantage in agencies or units set up with relatively narrow functions. If the agency commands the support of a specialized or single purpose type of interest or pressure group, undue influence in one direction may be exerted on the executive, and it will be more difficult for him to keep his organization in proper focus. . . .

Is He a Success?

This discussion has touched on some of the things that the executive can do to harmonize and get the most out of the other elements in his organization. I have emphasized that this is the way that he builds up his influence in his organization and guides it toward its objectives. In closing, I should like to reiterate my earlier point that although the executive is not likely to succeed if he approaches his organization as something that is his own to command, he is at no disadvantage as he takes up the role of leadership.

The fact that he is the repository of formal authority in his organization is a powerful asset in the business of developing his titular position into one of genuine force and strength. Furthermore, it is up to him at any one point in time to determine the issues which he wants to have referred to him for decision. Although he may not decide much in his organization, quantitatively speaking, his choice of the decisions that he should make will determine how his organization meets its major difficulties. The point is that for the most part, he must depend upon others; therefore to the extent that the entire organization moves within a commonly accepted framework it will develop some speed and assurance in its forward movements.

Chapter 15

Departmental Management

Between the subject of the preceding chapter and the present one there is obviously considerable similarity. There is nevertheless a significant change in focus, bringing under scrutiny narrower, more technical problems. There is also some change in subject, though just what the change in subject is precisely it is difficult to say.

The difficulty arises over an acceptable definition of "department." What is a department? An airtight definition is impossible—at least from the point of view of a school of philosophy different from that of the definer.

A working definition satisfactory for present purposes is: A department is that part of an organization for which an executive (or administrator) immediately below the chief executive in the chain of command is formally responsible. "Departmental management" as ordinarily understood thus concerns the relationships between the chief executive and his immediate subordinates, the department heads; but it concerns also and in more detail the methods and devices by which the department heads manage their parts of the organization.

The following selection presents the problem of departmental management in its broadest aspects, in the American system of government: the department head's dual role with respect to his superior and his subordinates, his dual concern with policy and administration, and his dual responsibility with respect to the chief executive and the legislative body. The selection is taken from the "Task Force" report on departmental management, prepared for the so-called Hoover Commission. Part II of this report, from which this selection is taken, was drafted by John D. Millett, professor of public administration at Columbia University. The part reproduced here is only the introduction to a more detailed discussion of such matters as "The Need for Staff" and "Role of Assistants."

Purpose and Organization of Departmental Management *

JOHN D. MILLETT

Officials' Dual Responsibility

The actual functioning of our administrative structure reveals that department and agency heads in the executive branch have two basic responsibilities which they ought to fulfill—one political and the other administrative. First of all, the department head is the President's outpost in an assigned field of administrative activities.

The department head must be regarded as an extension of the President's personality. He is expected to carry out any basic instructions which a President may provide for his guidance. As a consequence of campaign promises, after consultations with various party and congressional leaders, or as a matter of firm personal conviction, a President may hold certain basic beliefs about foreign

* From *Departmental Management in Federal Administration: A Report with Recommendations*, prepared for the Commission on Organization of the Executive Branch of the Government (Washington: 1949), pp. 38–42.

policy, agricultural policy, fiscal policy, welfare policy, the conservation of natural resources, or any one of a host of vital public issues. He may then convey his point of view to a department head. It is the obligation of the department head to insure that these broad policy instructions are translated into appropriate action by the department.

The department head is also an adviser to the President, both on specific issues which arise within the field of his assignment and also within broadly related fields. Out of department activities may emerge various problems on which the department head desires presidential guidance. Particularly, any suggestions about new major legislation are almost certain to require some presidential consideration. Outside groups may bring some matter to the attention of the President, or legislative leaders may suggest to the President the desirability of some kind of action. In all these circumstances a department head must be prepared to advise the President about the desirability of proposals.

Furthermore, a department head is expected to provide a certain political point of view to departmental operations. He must be more than a mere channel of communication between the department and the President for vital matters on which the latter must make a decision. The department head should bring a political attitude to all departmental affairs. Such a political attitude is not to be defined in terms of a narrow partisanship concerned with either the appointment of loyal party workers or the realization of special privileges. Rather, a political attitude reflects prevailing beliefs on broad public issues, beliefs about the scope and magnitude of Government activities, about both the ends and means of governmental action. A department head is an interpreter of prevailing public attitudes to the permanent officials under his direction. A department head must create an atmosphere for the guidance of public effort.

The department head is an indispensable link in providing political responsibility for present-day administration. Today there is general acceptance of the belief that Government service must be essentially a career service, that all but a handful of Government positions must be filled upon the basis of technical competence and experience. Any other practice is notoriously wasteful. In a time when Government economy is more essential than ever before, such conspicuous waste as the spoils system cannot be afforded. But by the same token, a Government career service can become a dangerous bureaucracy if the means of political responsibility are not clearly defined and vigorously enforced. Here the role of the department head today takes on new and far-reaching importance. In the vast structure of administrative activity, the department head has become the essential link between a career service and a President elected by the majority of the people and accountable to them.

To be sure, the Congress also provides a check upon the danger of politically irresponsible administration. But this check by its very nature cannot be a continuing one. Congress must decide the general content, the scope, and the magnitude of Government effort. Congress may also criticize what is done and modify basic instructions, but the day-to-day direction of administrative effort must necessarily remain with the President and with department heads.

In a sense the relations of a department head to Congress are merely the projection of the relations of the President to Congress. Yet it would be entirely unreal to look upon a department head as nothing more than a Presidential lieutenant. Department heads have oftentimes cultivated their own independent relationships with congressional committees and influential congressional leaders. Such a situation may be both an advantage and an embarrassment to a Chief Executive. When new legislation and modified programs become essential, the department head usually presents the principal justification both to Congress and to the public at large. The department head is the primary point of contact between the executive and legislative branches in requesting appropriations. Thus, the President's formulation of policy and program for legislative consideration must usually be presented in detail to the legislature by the department head.

To be sure, concerned as he may be with a special point of view, a department head, with legislative encouragement, may present attitudes or even specific recommendations which are contrary to those of the President, concerned as he is with a broader point of view. In such instances the relationship of the department head to the Congress may prove to be a cause of friction with the Executive. If the friction becomes sufficiently troublesome, the President may, of course, find a new department head.

But in any event, the relationships between the department head and the legislature are real and vital. The department head must first of all present the Presidential point of view to the legislature. If he personally holds a different point of view, he may suggest the area of disagreement, provided the President first approves. Otherwise, good taste and a proper regard for our governmental processes require a department head to resign when he is in fundamental and irreconcilable conflict with Presidential wishes.

On the other hand, the department head is an important channel for the communication of the legislative point of view to the President. Having as an ordinary rule more intimate and detailed knowledge of legislative opinion, the department head should be able to keep the President informed about congressional attitudes. Such information is vital in the formulation of Presidential policies and programs.

The department head must also serve as a connecting link between the permanent officials of Government and the legislature. Here the task is one of insuring both the proper consideration of the legislative point of view in the preparation of departmental policies and programs for Presidential approval, and of insuring that legislative instructions conveyed in substantive statutes and appropriation laws are faithfully executed.

It is no easy position which a department head must occupy under our system of government. As a member of the executive branch his first constitutional obligation is to the President. He is at all times an assistant to the Chief Executive.

But as a part of the executive branch, he has also the constitutional obligation both to consult with and inform the legislature, as well as to see that legislative intentions expressed through statutes are realized.

Administrative Duties

The second major task of a department or agency head is to serve as the administrative leader of the agency to which he is assigned.

This role of administrative chief is no small responsibility, especially in a time of large-scale governmental activities. Certainly as an effective department leader the department head must combine many different qualities. Necessarily he must possess or develop some general knowledge about the substance of the work done. He must know something about administrative processes and techniques. He must learn the capabilities and peculiarities of subordinate personnel. He must supply not only the essential link between the department and the White House but also a vitalizing influence upon internal operations.

To be sure, the department head finds immediately at hand an extensive going concern. Usually the department has a tradition based upon long historical evolution. In addition, it has an accustomed method of operation. The Administrator, moreover, will find key subordinates and key assistants ready to help him— within certain limits. It is one of the paradoxes of large-scale Government administration that the ineffective department head by no means brings the performance of Government services to a halt, while the effective department head may over a period of time introduce a new enthusiasm, a new energy, and a new efficiency into the performance of an agency's work.

In its broadest terms the administrative role of the department head is to provide a sense of unity or common purpose for the agency as a whole and to insure the effective performance of the programs with which his agency is charged. No administrative challenge is so great as that of building and maintaining a sense of common purpose. Supervision is likely to be regarded as essentially negative and restrictive unless it is exercised in the context of identifying inter-relationships and promoting adherence to some general objective. And unless the department head himself gives thoughtful attention to the possibilities of administrative improvement, no continuing, sustained effort in that direction will result.

Perhaps a word should be added about the meaning of improvements in the performance of Government services. These improvements may be reflected in one or two ways. They may mean expanded service to the public without any increase in the personnel and other resources required to perform that service. Or improvements may be evident in an actual reduction of the resources required to render a particular service. In a growing society of more people and expanding material wealth, Government services may also be expected to increase. Administrative efficiency then does not mean a reduction in operations; rather it means an increasing output from the resources devoted to a particular purpose.

Improvements in the performance of Government service should realize increasing efficiency by greater output per unit of input.

To amplify somewhat, we may say that the administrative role of the department head involves the performance of these various duties:

1. He must review the basic purposes of a department's effort in the light of the statutory instructions and the general discretion which they confer. Within the limits of these legislative instructions he may modify purposes because of presidential desires or commitments or because of changing circumstances. And he may suggest changes in the statutory authorization and congressional approval. But he must be sure that basic purposes are being accomplished.

2. He must build a sense of loyalty to a common purpose or a general goal for the agency as a whole. He must be alert to interrelationships among bureau activities and seek to insure effective collaboration in the realization of a common purpose.

3. He must provide a positive sense of leadership for the department. In general, he must be available for consultation and consideration of issues with his immediate associates and his operating subordinates. He must be willing to make decisions in the light of the best available information and within the basic policy framework of the department. He must encourage initiative and enterprise among his associates and subordinates and cultivate a sense of teamwork. He must be ready to acknowledge and recognize able performance. He must possess the courage to insist upon loyalty to a common purpose, even through necessary disciplinary action.

4. He must constantly be alert for opportunities to insure the more efficient performance of departmental services. Here especially there are many techniques at hand to assist him in answering a variety of questions. How detailed and how adequate are advance preparations for administrative performance? What work is no longer vital or even useful? What work tends to overlap other work? Could housekeeping services be reduced or performed for less cost? What organization changes if any would contribute to more satisfactory or efficient performance of service? What work methods could be simplified or improved? What information is needed and used about the volume and quality of the service rendered? What information is needed and used about the efficiency of work methods? To be sure, no administrator can personally undertake to find out the answers to these and similar questions. It is not the task of the departmental head to become immersed in management detail. But the department head must insist that such questions be asked and answered.

The department head has associates to help him in fulfilling his own leadership role and subordinates to carry out operating details. Yet only he himself can provide the constant personal influence which makes the difference between ordinary and extraordinary performance of Government services.

The author of the following selection, Paul H. Appleby, was introduced in Part 1 as author of the selection "Government Is Different." His extensive experience in the "front office" of the Department of Agriculture and his later tour of duty in the Executive Office of the President make his opinions especially weighty on the subject to which he here addresses himself, "Organizing around the Head of a Large Federal Department."

The questions that are posed by this essay are many and challenging. Has Mr. Appleby's extensive experience at the "top" of administration led him to overvalue integration, manageability? Is there an "interest" of the nation at large? If there is a national interest other or different from that of specific individuals or groups, what is it and how is it identified?

In the past few years there has been a searching critical look at accepted theories about "staff" organization and functions. Is the analysis of staff organization and functions here presented valid?

Query, to what extent are the theories and recommendations advanced here proper and advisable in state and local government? Are there qualitative as well as quantitative differences?

Organizing around the Head of a Large Federal Department *

PAUL H. APPLEBY

Professor Carl Brent Swisher in his recent book, *The Growth of Constitutional Power in the United States*, makes the point too often forgotten that the primary purpose of written constitutions, including our own, is to grant adequate power to govern. Checks on the power to govern, important as they are felt to be, follow —they do not precede. In a very similar way, consideration of administrative organization begins with the arrangements essential to authority and responsibility. Delegation, decentralization, and all of the techniques making for a diffusion of influence and for zealous and reciprocal collaboration enormously enrich administration—but they are secondary. True and effective decentralization can only follow effective centralization.

In this paper I wish to discuss organization around the head of a great governmental department in the primary terms of his needs as an important factor in the process of governmental integration. These needs, like the primary purpose of a constitution, are too often forgotten. Any citizen—of whatever degree of acquaintance with government—is aware of *his* needs to influence the course of government and to modify the impact of government on him. Any government

* From *Public Administration Review*, Vol. 6 (Summer, 1946), pp. 205–212. Reprinted by permission of the author and the *Public Administration Review*.

employee of whatever rank is aware of the need for the wind of authority to be tempered to his sensitive individuality. In a democracy these awarenesses work constantly for the betterment of certain important aspects of our organized society. But few are so constantly alert to the competing but complementary need for adequate organization. And too often even those functionally assigned to the business of supporting the essential centralized authority go through their labors in an unthinking manner—throwing away necessary controls with one hand and holding tenaciously to unfruitful routines with the other.

In one sense, consideration of the administrative aspect of government begins, of course, with the people for whom the government exists. In another sense, its consideration begins with the means by which government in administration may do effectively that which it is required to do. In this sense, consideration of public administration in the national government begins with the fact that the executive government must be *manageable* by the President who is held responsible for the executive government. There would be little national profit from assigning responsibility to the President if we were to equip him insufficiently with authority and with other means by which he may act responsibly. Ultimate controllability by the President is the keystone of the arch—if we are to have an arch: coordinated, integrated government within the bounds covered by the executive process; responsible executive action responsive as a whole to the whole people and not merely responsive in its parts to special-interest groups.

The phrase "ultimate controllability" requires elucidation. I am speaking, of course, about executive controllability as a necessary preliminary to congressional and popular controllability. Even with respect to programs of acknowledged political content any President can exercise usually only a general control. He must delegate much of his responsibility for control. He must rely generally upon the principal executive to whom he has delegated responsibility until that executive is felt to be unsatisfactory; when the unsatisfactory executive is replaced, similar general reliance must be placed on the new appointee. Yet when the delegated responsibility can be clearly concentrated in one person and the power to replace is unhampered, this power is the basis for essential presidential control. There are areas where administrative control can be relatively lax; these are areas where programs have become controversial and operations stable. Presidential power in practice, with respect to such areas, will be more remote—at any moment more in reserve, more of an ultimate power, less of a present and direct power—than in the case of new or newly controversial programs.

There are some other areas in which presidential powers may need to be somewhat restricted in law—forcing the President to exercise a more general, more reserved, more "ultimate" power of control, a less quick and direct control. It is my belief that such areas are much smaller than they commonly are believed to be and that legal restrictions on the President's control should be less drastic than they frequently are. The areas in question include those of "administrative law"—the regulatory process involving "quasi-judicial" functions. These particular areas are actually to be distinguished somewhat from areas of other types of action programs, but I believe that even with respect to them the tendency has been to restrict presidential powers too much. "Ultimate controllability" here takes on a very important meaning. But both here and in still other areas where there is less justification, the tendency has been to deprive the President and his responsible executives of even an ultimately real control. These are areas where the cry is to "take administration out of politics." In such instances the unconscious effort is actually to take administration out of democracy. Laws in some of these instances would force administration for a long time to continue in accordance with the ideas of the pressure group sponsoring the original enactment. In other specific cases the effort is to throw policy control away from the people and into the hands of a specific group of experts—lawyers, scientists, military men, etc.

With or without bases in laws, sub-administrators do seek and do develop administrative autonomy. This tendency is dangerously effective principally as it is supported by practices that permit particular private interests or groups of private interests largely to dominate the bureaus or programs concerned. The proper influence and ultimate control of the whole people are violated by such autonomous administration. Coordination and integration are difficult, intricate, and important means by which all programs of the government are brought under the influence and control of the nation at large. Don Price has stated it this way: "The real issue of representation and responsibility is not between the chief executive and the legislature, but between the chief executive and the legislature on the one hand, and on the other hand, the departments, bureaus and legislative committees that seek to go their own ways." The subject of organizing around the head of a department must be approached first of all in terms of the relationship of a department head to the central business of securing representative and responsible government—making democracy effective. Bureau autonomy is a denial of democracy. Departmental autonomy is an even more thoroughgoing denial.

II

In this paper, then, we begin our consideration of the situation of a department head by thinking of him in the executive level next below the President. It is a familiar picture of Cabinet members, but I wonder how much we—or they— reflect upon the picture. The Cabinet member who consciously and systematically organizes his department so as positively and imaginatively to contribute to the presidential function of governmental integration is yet to appear on the scene. The usual performance is so markedly in another direction as to lead one of the profoundest observers for our government to declare seriously that Cabinet members are characteristically "the President's worst enemies."

Certainly among themselves and individually in relationship with the President it is true that Cabinet members are more competitive than cooperative. They are champions of special and competing private interests, of groups functionally specialized. They are competitors with respect to appropriations, authority, and prestige. Seeking to simplify and make manageable *their* jobs, they resent and resist efforts directed toward governmental integration. Quietly, even carrying their differences with the President to congressional committees, they may at any time block his proposals. (If an example is required, consider the history of reorganization efforts.) Congressional committee structure reflects special interests in much the same way as do the executive departments. On the Hill as in the Executive Branch, the need is to translate special policy into better general policy; cross-lots dealing of bureau and department personnel with congressional committees tends to prevent this translation. Department heads, then, throw into the presidential lap a very great many more differences than they prevent from landing there. Probably this would be true in the best of circumstances, but no one can doubt that the government would profit from a greater effort by and under department heads to work imaginatively toward a better fulfillment of presidential, government-wide needs.

I am not speaking about any particular Cabinet, of course, and I intend no extravagant laboring of the point. I wish simply to indicate that proper organization around a department head needs to be pointed upward to the President and outward to the rest of the government—not merely downward for the sake of the secretary's own essential controls. Indeed, the downward flow of authority assumes a new significance if adequate integration of a department is seen as preliminary to adequate integration of the government. Often the worst sins of competition between departments are committed without the participation or knowledge of department heads. So far as department heads are concerned, these are sins of omission; commission is within the bureaus.

The problems of integration in terms both of policy and of administration are more staggering today than ever before because of the enormously increased complexity of our society. The intertwining of interests on the part of various governmental departments is akin to the increased intertwining of, let us say, physics and chemistry. But the most vivid and urgent development is the way in which so many domestic policies now impinge upon and require reconciliation with international relations. In the future, domestic policy simply cannot be permitted to develop without the check of international considerations, and foreign policy cannot be permitted to develop in a vacuum unrelated to the thousand and one relevant domestic policies. Here is the most compelling new requirement for integration of manifold matters. It cannot be achieved by a President individually, or by heads of departments singly or together, or by the State Department alone. It requires intricate, institutional coordination and wholly new methods of governmental organization. The trenches of isolationist sentiment are no longer out in the country. They are held in Washington by officials who *believe* internationally but who *act* less than nationally—departmentally or bureau-mentally. How to overcome this isolationism is the supreme problem in public administration today. This is so because the translation of many segmented, special interest policies into sound national policy and the translation of national policy into effective international policy is the supreme public policy problem today. Organization and administration are means by which we produce policy as well as the means by which we carry it out.

Departments of the future, then, must be better and especially organized for inter-departmental functioning and for better projection of policy and administration into presidential, whole-public-interest terms. This can be done at the department level, I feel confident, by an administrative program having generally this form: staff organisms around department heads whose sole reason for being rests in the functions of projecting policy and administration into governmental and international terms; behind these, staff agencies adequate to develop bureau policy and administration into departmental terms and into forms sufficiently controllable by the secretary to be capable of the still higher projection.

Coordination and adequate centralization, then, are words reflective of the administrative aspect of the primary function of government: the provision of means by which 140,000,000 people reach common action, the parts related to the whole, the whole related to the parts. The responsibility is by no means wholly within departments. We are very inadequately organized as a *government*. Aside from the lack of adequate governmental institutions, we have many specific lacks. We tend, for example, to have departmental or bureau career services and not much of a governmental career service. But if it is true at the presidential level, as I have suggested it to be, that the Chief Executive cannot effectively administer the government simply through department heads, it is equally true that no department head can administer his department adequately simply through his bureau chiefs. One reason why department heads take positions hostile to presidential needs and policy is in the fact that they defend or are governed by bureaus they themselves do not control. To a degree they are merely "fronts" for bureaus.

It would require another paper to discuss as it merits the tendency to autonomy in organizational segments of which the bureau is a chief example. And it would require still another paper to suggest the more specific and detailed ways by which loose federations of bureaus might be knit into actual departments. Here it is impossible to do more than to present some general thought by way of orientation. But it is necessary to recognize that it is much easier to unify a division than it is to unify a bureau, very much easier to unify a bureau than it is to unify a department, and very, very much easier to unify a department than it is to unify the Executive Branch. Most of the persons engaged in public administration are at levels or in segments where this problem is insufficiently revealed. They need better to understand it if for no other reason than to be able more equably to adjust to it. I am indicating belief in need for greater departmental unification; if it is achieved it will be at the cost of considerable emotional strain on the part of those who have been working in relatively autonomous isolation.

On the other hand, it should be recognized that the choice is not between this stress and an absence of stress; it is between stresses. The stress that results from governmental confusion produces frustration in citizens generally, including government personnel, and it has a special, additional impact on workers within government.

The secretary who does not have essential control of his department does have many real powers the exercise of which can work havoc within the organization. Adjustments to succeeding secretaries in ways not warranted by policy change or by mere personality differences are perhaps as destructive of individual and organizational performance and morale as any other single phenomenon. After adequate unification, therefore, I am inclined to rank administrative continuity through institutional means as only second in importance. Perhaps it is only the obverse side of the same coin.

Most heads of departments come—and probably will continue to come—to their posts without some of the most desirable qualifications. We have no system by which young men of political promise are given experience and trial in administration. By the time members of Congress come to Cabinet posts, they are likely to be set in a nonadministrative pattern of individual performance. Business executives usually have come to dominate particular organizational situations rather than having developed a flexible general administrative ability that might enable them to adjust to the wholly strange political environment. Bankers and farmers, insofar as they are qualified for specific Cabinet posts, are qualified in technical familiarity with some aspects of the subject matter rather than as political leaders and administrators. Editors, lawyers, and educators tend to have more general policy understanding but are primarily individualists without actual administrative understanding.

Even in a particular case where a department head may prove to be a competent administrator, it is difficult for him to bequeath anything of administrative value to a successor. He tends to build a structure wholly reflective of his own way of working, and its very novelty and history invite early abandonment of it.

In a broad way, then, the problem seems to turn upon setting up a permanent basic structure for departmental administration so firmly that it cannot readily be disregarded or dispensed with, yet elastic enough to provide for the injection of a few personally selected aides to help insure policy shift and to permit change in keeping with changes in administrative needs. A large part of the machinery for departmental management and policy integration must exist ready-made, so placed as not readily to be ignored, and not exclusively dependent on the favor of the incoming secretary. If they are to be at the same time a responsive and useful tool, the organic arrangements must be nicely made by custom and the weight of administrative arrangements, and not by law.

If it is true, as I have asserted, that no secretary can administer a department wholly through bureau chiefs, I think it is also true that no secretary can administer his department wholly through career aides. He needs a few aides—two or three or four or five—who as distinctly personal selections extend his reach.

Such aides usually are amateurs and usually they act in a semidetached manner that invites disorder and whimsy. It has seemed to me important that their yeasty interest in policy innovation should be associated quickly and directly with organic staff entities. Assuming responsibility for continuing administrative functions, the new aides could be expected to draw more quickly upon the wisdom of experience and at the same time to have at their command the most effective controls and tools for effecting change. A definite provision for new persons to be given responsibility for career staffs should make room for both dynamics and continuity.

I am inclined to believe that heads of staff units under these personal appointees should have a special recognized status on a special register of key government administrative personnel with eligibility for transfer under general controls exercised by the Executive Office of the President and a special board. All of the necessary arrangements can and should be made under existing laws; a rigid, special corps must be avoided. Properly safeguarded, the maintenance and development of such a register should effect a considerable improvement in public administration; it should result in building more and better administrators, and they, because of government-wide status and opportunity, should contribute to greater administrative unification.

III

We come, then, to specific consideration of the form and utilization of *departmental* staffs. It should begin with thought about the nature of the policy and action to be served and developed. It therefore also has to do with qualifications needed for high staff personnel.

Speaking with an English friend recently I remarked casually, "Perhaps you will be surprised to hear me say it, but I believe that the thing in shortest supply in Washington is *political* sense." He said in reply that he agreed with me, but that he would say it differently: "The thing in shortest supply in Washington is ability to think—to think in whole terms encompassing all of the elements of the scene, all of the relationships, including especially the human and social factors; people in Washington are equipped to think and do think in too highly specialized ways." I could agree with no statement more completely than with this one of my English friend.

We very much want breadth in the levels around the secretary and in all levels of staff serving the secretary. The primary staff purpose is to help translate the specialized thinking, specialized policy, and specialized administration of departmental segments and individuals into *public* policy and *public* administration.

There is a great tendency on the part of budget people to see all policy as budgetary policy or fiscal policy, all administration as budgetary control. There is a similar tendency for attorneys to see all policy as legal policy. There is a similar tendency for personnel officers to see all administration as administration of personnel. There is a tendency for economists to see all policy as economic policy.

There is a tendency for politicians to see all policy as partisan policy or to see it in other narrowly political terms. All of these things are simply some of the aspects of public policy. Of all the terms used, the term political is the broadest and the one most difficult for the more narrowly specialized to accept. Really sound and effective political policy comes very close to describing really sound and effective public policy. In general understanding, however, the phrase has some connotations that drag its meaning to a lower level of abstraction. For purposes of this paper, then, let me minimize the truly, properly, and necessarily political nature of both policy and administration by saying again that the staff function is to help translate narrower, more specialized thinking and action into terms that will enable the secretary in his sphere and auxiliary to the presidential function to develop and maintain truly public policy and truly public administration.

If this is the staff function, it follows that no staff member especially responsible for a specialized segment of the staff function should have dominance over the total staff function. This is to say that the budget officer, the director of administrative planning, the director of personnel, the solicitor, the economic adviser, the head of any economic policy group, and the head of any planning group—important as they all are—should be excluded from any position analogous to chief-of-staff. Although a political staff function should be broader than any of the others, I believe that in practice any specialized political aide, such as one responsible for congressional, national committee, state, and local government contacts, also should be excluded from the post of staff leader.

Actually, I believe that the staff leader should be merely that—a chairman whose only preeminence is in his responsibility for staff cross reference and synthesis.

It follows, of course, that no staff leader should have a monopoly on the function of staff representation to the secretary.

The preliminary purpose of the staff is to synthesize its product and the product of the bureaus. Without explicit *authority* to do so, it does it within the limits fixed by an absence of authority. Beyond these limits, the staff purpose is to serve the authority of the secretary by providing him with perspective in terms of his interests, functions, and responsibilities. Reporting and recommending from their several vantage points—all at the secretarial level—they equip him with various views and judgments from which—in connection with the reports and recommendations from bureau heads, and in the light of his dealings with the President, the Congress, and the public—he is enabled to arrive at the best judgment of which he is capable. Where there is sharp controversy, one view would provide him with nothing more helpful than a picture of head-on collision. A three-dimensional view is a minimum for internal perspective.

There is at least one other important aspect to the limitation of the chairman of the secretary's staff. Chester I. Barnard, in *The Functions of the Executive*, indicates that all of the executives reporting to a single executive should be as nearly as possible equal to each other, and that all of them together are roughly equal to their superior officer. It may be that in some respects all of the second-level executives are greater than the superior executive; they might, for example, by common action easily ruin their chief. But in another respect the superior executive ought to be equal to a little more than the sum of the next-level-executive parts. The staff, at least, certainly should not usurp the whole role of the principal executive, but since their function is based on his function there is always some tendency toward usurpation. Staff plus bureau chiefs should equal a little less than the secretary, and staff minus bureau chiefs should, of course, equal a good deal less. The two military departments of our government have had a great part in developing the staff idea, but in recent years they have appeared to me to have violated many basic principles of organization and administration. Neither of these departments has balanced departmental organization, and in both, staff and operations have been so combined as to minimize secretarial functions. This latter situation constitutes a victory of the technician, the specialist, over the generalist, and results, I believe, in less truly public policy. The staff should not usurp the role of the operating chiefs. The staff and the secretary together should definitely be superior to, greater than, and different from, the sum of the operating chiefs. The chairman of the staff should be less than the whole staff, and, of course, less than the secretary.

A few other thoughts I would suggest dogmatically as desirable rules: the staff should have a collegial character in which the principal discipline would be in the enforcement of cross reference. The principal responsibility of the staff chairman should be this enforcement of cross reference and as much synthesis as could be derived from it. No staff aide should have a function or field coextensive with that of a single bureau; preferably the function and field of each principal staff aide should be department wide as a contribution to the process of translating material into secretarial terms. No staff organization should be permitted to get into an operating position where it is competitive with an operating agency. The regular staff function should not involve the review of bureau judgment in the same terms, but review and anticipation in terms above the field of special bureau competence.

To go further than this into the detailed arrangements for staff functions would go much beyond the purpose of this particular paper. Here begin knotty problems so involved with particular program situations, so in need of flexibility with which to meet changing conditions, that they would require very detailed analysis. The kinds of activities by means of which a secretary does his job are surprisingly few: he sees people—individual citizens, representatives of organized groups, members of Congress, other national officials, state and local officials, party leaders, his own executives; he signs letters, orders, documents; he issues statements, makes speeches, testifies before congressional committees, sees the press; he reads newspapers, gets news and opinion reports, reads memoranda, reports, and recommendations. The staff organization needs to take account of all these things, for here is where confusion or integration takes place. These things involve the whole departmental policy and administration in secretarial terms. They suggest staff organization giving attention to these things: personnel selection and utilization; budgetary and financial management; interdepartmental and Executive Office relationships; international relationships; congressional and party relationships; general public relationships and information; coordination of the department's procedures in terms of law; coordination in terms of operating programs; administrative organization and practice; program development and planning; review of public papers; interviews and conferences. The management of these things *in their interrelationships* and *in terms of the secretary's responsibilities* is the business of departmental—as distinguished from bureau—personnel.

Chapter 16

Morale and Leadership

The selections in this chapter are from writers identified primarily with business administration rather than with public administration. This is because morale and leadership were of earlier interest to business administration, and hence have had there the fullest and—generally speaking—most fruitful development.

The following selections are, indeed, but samples of a very large literature in the field of business administration which, though not limited to consideration of morale and leadership, comes to a focus in this area of interest. This body of literature can best be described by the term "industrial sociology," though "industrial psychology" does nearly as well. Industrial sociology is perhaps essentially an extension and refinement of the Scientific Management movement, a concentration of attention upon the "human" element in management in the spirit of inquiry associated with the name of Frederick W. Taylor. But it owes a debt to and has been enriched by concepts, tools of analysis, and trained personnel from the fields of psychology and sociology—and to a lesser extent other disciplines and inquiries. In fact, it must be stated that industrial sociology, though close in spirit to Frederick W. Taylor, has been largely led by persons whose professional training was not in "management" as such. Preeminent among such persons was the late Elton Mayo of Harvard University, whose training and first writing were in psychology.

The following selection is an account of experiments dealing with morale, the so-called "Hawthorne studies," conducted over a period of sixteen years at the Hawthorne plant of the Western Electric Company. These studies are probably the most famous consciously planned experiments in the history of social science to date; much of the development of industrial sociology has centered upon them. Paradoxically, though the results of the studies concern morale, their original focus was on productive efficiency. As will be seen, what began as a study of lighting in its relation to worker productivity ended with a broad inquiry into the conditions of worker happiness and effectiveness in modern industrial society.

The writings in industrial sociology, as in business administration generally, are of considerable importance to the student of public administration. But the differences between public and private administration—hard to delineate as they are—must ever be borne in mind. He whose interest is public administration must ask as he reads the following material: Does comparability between this situation and one in public administration exist? What is the same and what is different? Is the "value system" in which the data are placed appropriate in *public* administration? Is the value system one that should be accepted uncritically? Some writers, for example, have criticized as incompatible with democratic ideals what they have described as a "paternalism" or "elitism" in the writings of the industrial sociologists. Query, are the values of the writer of the following selection acceptable for public administration in a democratic society?

The following selection is the major part of a chapter in a widely read little book titled *Management and Morale* by Professor F. J. Roethlisberger. The author has been an active member of the faculty in business administration at Harvard University, which has been a leading center in the development of industrial sociology. Professor Roethlisberger participated in the Hawthorne studies, and was an associate of the late Elton Mayo.

The Road Back to Sanity *

F. J. ROETHLISBERGER

Too often we try to solve human problems with nonhuman tools and, what is still more extraordinary, in terms of nonhuman data. We take data from which all human meaning has been deleted and then are surprised to find that we reach conclusions which have no human significance.

* Reprinted by permission of the publishers from Fritz Jules Roethlisberger, *Management and Morale*, Harvard University Press, Cambridge, Mass. Copyright, 1941, by The President and Fellows of Harvard College.

It is my simple thesis that a human problem requires a human solution. First, we have to learn to recognize a human problem when we see one; and, second, upon recognizing it, we have to learn to deal with it as such and not as if it were something else. Too often at the verbal level we talk glibly about the importance of the human factor; and too seldom at the concrete level of behavior do we recognize a human problem for what it is and deal with it as such. *A human problem to be brought to a human solution requires human data and human tools.* It is my purpose to use the Western Electric researches as an illustration of what I mean by this statement, because, if they deserve the publicity and acclaim which they have received, it is because, in my opinion, they have so conclusively demonstrated this point. In this sense they are the road back to sanity in management-employee relations.

Experiments in Illumination

The Western Electric researches started about sixteen years ago, in the Hawthorne plant, with a series of experiments on illumination. The purpose was to find out the relation of the quality and quantity of illumination to the efficiency of industrial workers. These studies lasted several years, and I shall not describe them in detail. It will suffice to point out that the results were quite different from what had been expected.

In one experiment the workers were divided into two groups. One group, called the "test group," was to work under different illumination intensities. The other group, called the "control group," was to work under an intensity of illumination as nearly constant as possible. During the first experiment, the test group was submitted to three different intensities of illumination of increasing magnitude, 24, 46, and 70 foot candles. What were the results of this early experiment? Production increased in both rooms—in both the test group and the control group—and the rise in output was roughly of the same magnitude in both cases.

In another experiment, the light under which the test group worked was decreased from 10 to 3 foot candles, while the control group worked, as before, under a constant level of illumination intensity. In this case the output rate in the test group went up instead of down. It also went up in the control group.

In still another experiment, the workers were allowed to believe the illumination was being increased, although, in fact, no change in intensity was made. The workers commented favorably on the improved lighting condition, but there was no appreciable change in output. At another time, the workers were allowed to believe that the intensity of illumination was being decreased, although again, in fact, no actual change was made. The workers complained somewhat about the poorer lighting, but again there was no appreciable effect on output.

And finally, in another experiment, the intensity of illumination was decreased to .06 of a foot candle, which is the intensity of illumination approximately equivalent to that of ordinary moonlight. Not until this point was reached was there any appreciable decline in the output rate.

What did the experimenters learn? . . . One thing was clear: the results were negative. Nothing of a positive nature had been learned about the relation of illumination to industrial efficiency. If the results were to be taken at their face value, it would appear that there was no relation between illumination and industrial efficiency. However, the investigators were not yet quite willing to draw this conclusion. They realized the difficulty of testing for the effect of a single variable in a situation where there were many uncontrolled variables. It was thought therefore that another experiment should be devised in which other variables affecting the output of workers could be better controlled.

A few of the tough-minded experimenters already were beginning to suspect their basic ideas and assumptions with regard to human motivation. It occurred to them that the trouble was not so much with the results or with the subjects as it was with their notion regarding the way their subjects were supposed to behave—the notion of a simple cause-and-effect, direct relationship between certain physical changes in the workers' environment and the responses of the workers to these changes. Such a notion completely ignored the human meaning of these changes to the people who were subjected to them.

In the illumination experiments, therefore, we have a classic example of trying to deal with a human situation in nonhuman terms. The experimenters had obtained no human data; they had been handling electric-light bulbs and plotting average output curves. Hence their results had no human significance. . . .

The Relay Assembly Test Room

Another experiment was framed, in which it was planned to submit a segregated group of workers to different kinds of working conditions. The idea was very simple: A group of five girls were placed in a separate room where their conditions of work could be carefully controlled, where their output could be measured, and where they could be closely observed. It was decided to introduce at specified intervals different changes in working conditions and to see what effect these innovations had on output. Also, records were kept, such as the temperature and humidity of the room, the number of hours each girl slept at night, the kind and amount of food she ate for breakfast, lunch, and dinner. Output was carefully measured, the time it took each girl to assemble a telephone relay of approximately forty parts (roughly a minute) being automatically recorded each time; quality records were kept; each girl had a physical examination at regular intervals. Under these conditions of close observation the girls were studied for a period of five years. Literally tons of material were collected. Probably nowhere in the world has so much material been collected about a small group of workers for such a long period of time.

But what about the results? They can be stated very briefly. When all is said and done, they amount roughly to this: A skillful statistician spent several years trying to relate variations in output with variations in the physical circumstances of these five operators. For example, he correlated the hours that each girl spent in bed the night before with variations in output the following day. Inasmuch as some people said that the effect of being out late one night was not felt the following day but the day after that, he correlated variations in output with the amount of rest the operators had had two nights before. I mention this just to point out the fact that he missed no obvious tricks and that he did a careful job and a thorough one, and it took him many years to do it. The attempt to relate changes in physical circumstances to variations in output resulted in not a single correlation of enough statistical significance to be recognized by any competent statistician as having any meaning.

Now, of course, it would be misleading to say that this negative result was the only conclusion reached. There were positive conclusions, and it did not take the experimenters more than two years to find out that they had missed the boat. After two years of work, certain things happened which made them sit up and take notice. Different experimental conditions of work, in the nature of changes in the number and duration of rest pauses and differences in the length of the working day and week, had been introduced in this Relay Assembly Test Room. For example, the investigators first introduced two five-minute rests, one in the morning and one in the afternoon. Then they increased the length of these rests, and after that they introduced the rests at different times of the day. During one experimental period they served the operators a specially prepared lunch during the rest. In the later periods, they decreased the length of the working day by one-half hour and then by one hour. They gave the operators Saturday morning off for a while. Altogether, thirteen such periods of different working conditions were introduced in the first two years.

During the first year and a half of the experiment, everybody was happy, both the investigators and the operators. The investigators were happy because as conditions of work improved the output rate rose steadily. Here, it appeared, was strong evidence in favor of their preconceived hypothesis that fatigue was the major factor limiting output. The operators were happy because their conditions of work were being improved, they were earning more money, and they were objects of considerable attention from top management. But then one investigator —one of those tough-minded fellows—suggested that they restore the original conditions of work, that is, go back to a full forty-eight-hour week without rests, lunches and what not. This was Period XII. Then the happy state of affairs, when everything was going along as it theoretically should, went sour. Output, instead of taking the expected nose dive, maintained its high level.

Again the investigators were forcibly reminded that human situations are likely to be complex. In any human situation, whenever a simple change is introduced—a rest pause, for example—other changes, unwanted and unanticipated, may also be brought about. What I am saying here is very simple. If one experiments on a stone, the stone does not know it is being experimented upon—all of which makes it simple for people experimenting on stones. But if a human being is being experimented upon, he is likely to know it. Therefore, his attitudes toward the experiment and toward the experimenters become very important factors in determining his responses to the situation.

Now that is what happened in the Relay Assembly Test Room. To the investigators, it was essential that the workers give their full and whole-hearted coöperation to the experiment. They did not want the operators to work harder or easier depending upon their attitude toward the conditions that were imposed. They wanted them to work as they felt, so that they could be sure that the different physical conditions of work were solely responsible for the variations in output. For each of the experimental changes, they wanted subjects whose responses would be uninfluenced by so-called "psychological factors."

In order to bring this about, the investigators did everything in their power to secure the complete coöperation of their subjects, with the result that almost all the practices common to the shop were altered. The operators were consulted about the changes to be made, and, indeed, several plans were abandoned because they met with the disapproval of the girls. They were questioned sympathetically about their reactions to the conditions imposed, and many of these conferences took place in the office of the superintendent. The girls were allowed to talk at work; their "bogey" was eliminated. Their physical health and well-being became matters of great concern. Their opinions, hopes, and fears were eagerly sought. What happened was that in the very process of setting the conditions for the test —a so-called "controlled" experiment—the experimenters had completely altered the social situation of the room. Inadvertently a change had been introduced which was far more important than the planned experimental innovations: the customary supervision in the room had been revolutionized. This accounted for the better attitudes of the girls and their improved rate of work.

The Development of a New and More Fruitful Point of View

After Period XII in the Relay Assembly Test Room, the investigators decided to change their ideas radically. What all their experiments had dramatically and conclusively demonstrated was the importance of employee attitudes and sentiments. It was clear that the responses of workers to what was happening about them were dependent upon the significance these events had for them. In most work situations the meaning of a change is likely to be as important, if not more so, than the change itself. This was the great *éclaircissement*, the new illumination, that came from the research. It was an illumination quite different from what they had expected from the illumination studies. Curiously enough, this discovery is nothing very new or startling. It is something which anyone who has had some concrete experience in handling other people intuitively recognizes and practices. Whether or not a person is going to give his services whole-heartedly to a group depends, in good part, on the way he feels about his job, his fellow workers, and supervisors—the meaning for him of what is happening about him.

However, when the experimenters began to tackle the problem of employee attitudes and the factors determining such attitudes—when they began to tackle the problem of "meaning"—they entered a sort of twilight zone where things are never quite what they seem. Moreover, overnight, as it were, they were robbed of all the tools they had so carefully forged; for all their previous tools were nonhuman tools concerned with the measurement of output, temperature, humidity, etc., and these were no longer useful for the human data that they now wanted to obtain. What the experimenters now wanted to know was how a person felt, what his intimate thinking, reflections, and preoccupations were, and what he liked and disliked about his work environment. In short, what did the whole blooming business—his job, his supervision, his working conditions—mean to him? Now this was human stuff, and there were no tools, or at least the experimenters knew of none, for obtaining and evaluating this kind of material.

Fortunately, there were a few courageous souls among the experimenters. These men were not metaphysicians, psychologists, academicians, professors, intellectuals, or what have you. They were men of common sense and of practical affairs. They were not driven by any great heroic desire to change the world. They were true experimenters, that is, men compelled to follow the implications of their own monkey business. All the evidence of their studies was pointing in one direction. Would they take the jump? They did.

Experiments in Interviewing Workers

A few tough-minded experimenters decided to go into the shops and—completely disarmed and denuded of their elaborate logical equipment and in all humility—to see if they could learn how to get the workers to talk about things that were important to them and could learn to understand what the workers were trying to tell them. This was a revolutionary idea in the year 1928, when this interviewing program started—the idea of getting a worker to talk to you and to listen sympathetically, but intelligently, to what he had to say. In that year a new era of personnel relations began. It was the first real attempt to get human data and to forge human tools to get them. In that year a novel idea was born; dimly the experimenters perceived a new method of human control. In that year the Rubicon was crossed from which there could be no return to the "good old days." Not that the experimenters ever wanted to return, because they now entered a world so exciting, so intriguing, and so full of promise that it made the "good old days" seem like the prattle and play of children.

When these experimenters decided to enter the world of "meaning," with very few tools, but with a strong sense of curiosity and a willingness to learn, they had many interesting adventures. It would be too long a story to tell all of them, or even a small part of them. They made plenty of mistakes, but they were not afraid to learn.

At first, they found it difficult to learn to give full and complete attention to what a person had to say without interrupting him before he was through. They

found it difficult to learn not to give advice, not to make or imply moral judgments about the speaker, not to argue, not to be too clever, not to dominate the
conversation, not to ask leading questions. They found it difficult to get the person
to talk about matters which were important to him and not to the interviewer.
But, most important of all, they found it difficult to learn that perhaps the thing
most significant to a person was not something in his immediate work situation.

Gradually, however, they learned these things. They discovered that sooner or
later a person tends to talk about what is uppermost in his mind to a sympathetic
and skillful listener, and they became more proficient in interpreting what a person is saying or trying to say. Of course they protected the confidences given to
them and made absolutely sure that nothing an employee said could ever be used
against him. Slowly they began to forge a simple human tool—imperfect, to be
sure—to get the kind of data they wanted. They called this method "interviewing." I would hesitate to say the number of man-hours of labor which went
into the forging of this tool. There followed from studies made through its use
a gradually changing conception of the worker and his behavior.

A New Way of Viewing Employee Satisfaction and Dissatisfaction

When the experimenters started to study employee likes and dislikes, they
assumed, at first, that they would find a simple and logical relation between a
person's likes or dislikes and certain items and events in his immediate work
situation. They expected to find a simple connection, for example, between a
person's complaint and the object about which he was complaining. Hence, the
solution would be easy: correct the object of the complaint, if possible, and
presto! the complaint would disappear. Unfortunately, however, the world of
human behavior is not so simple as this conception of it; and it took the investigators several arduous and painful years to find this out. I will mention only a
few interesting experiences they had.

Several times they changed the objects of the complaint only to find that the
attitudes of the complainants remained unchanged. In these cases, correcting the
object of the complaint did not remedy the complaint or the attitude of the
person expressing it. A certain complaint might disappear, to be sure, only to
have another one arise. Here the investigators were running into so-called
"chronic kickers," people whose dissatisfactions were more deeply rooted in
factors relating to their personal histories. For such people the simple remedy of
changing the object of the complaint was not enough.

Several times they did absolutely nothing about the object of the complaint,
but after the interview, curiously enough, the complaint disappeared. A typical
example of this was that of a woman who complained at great length and with
considerable feeling about the poor food being served in the company restaurant.
When, a few days later, she chanced to meet the interviewer, she commented
with great enthusiasm upon the improved food and thanked the interviewer for
communicating her grievance to management and for securing such prompt

action. Here no change had been made in the thing criticized; yet the employee felt that something had been done.

Many times they found that people did not really want anything done about the things of which they were complaining. What they did want was an opportunity to talk about their troubles to a sympathetic listener. It was astonishing to find the number of instances in which workers complained about things which had happened many, many years ago, but which they described as vividly as if they had happened just a day before.

Here again, something was "screwy," but this time the experimenters realized that it was their assumptions which were screwy. They were assuming that the meanings which people assign to their experience are essentially logical. They were carrying in their heads the notion of the "economic man," a man primarily motivated by economic interest, whose logical capacities were being used in the service of this self-interest.

Gradually and painfully in the light of the evidence, which was overwhelming, the experimenters had been forced to abandon this conception of the worker and his behavior. Only with a new working hypothesis could they make sense of the data they had collected. The conception of the worker which they developed is actually nothing very new or startling; it is one which any effective administrator intuitively recognizes and practices in handling human beings.

First, they found that the behavior of workers could not be understood apart from their feelings or sentiments. I shall use the word "sentiment" hereafter to refer not only to such things as feelings and emotions, but also to a much wider range of phenomena which may not be expressed in violent feelings or emotions —phenomena that are referred to by such words as "loyalty," "integrity," "solidarity."

Secondly, they found that sentiments are easily disguised, and hence are difficult to recognize and to study. Manifestations of sentiment take a number of different forms. Feelings of personal integrity, for example, can be expressed by a handshake; they can also be expressed, when violated, by a sitdown strike. Moreover, people like to rationalize their sentiments and to objectify them. We are not so likely to say "I feel bad," as to say "The world is bad." In other words, we like to endow the world with those attributes and qualities which will justify and account for the feelings and sentiments we have toward it; we tend to project our sentiments on the outside world.

Thirdly, they found that manifestations of sentiment could not be understood as things in and by themselves, but only in terms of the total situation of the person. To comprehend why a person felt the way he did, a wider range of phenomena had to be explored.

Output as a Form of Social Behavior

That output is a form of social behavior was well illustrated in a study made by the Hawthorne experimenters, called the Bank Wiring Observation Room.

This room contained fourteen workmen representing three occupational groups —wiremen, soldermen, and inspectors. These men were on group piecework, where the more they turned out the more they earned. In such a situation one might have expected that they would have been interested in maintaining total output and that the faster workers would have put pressure on the slower workers to improve their efficiency. But this was not the case. Operating within this group were four basic sentiments, which can be expressed briefly as follows: (1) You should not turn out too much work; if you do, you are a "rate buster." (2) You should not turn out too little work; if you do, you are a "chiseler." (3) You should not say anything to a supervisor which would react to the detriment of one of your associates; if you do, you are a "squealer." (4) You should not be too officious; that is, if you are an inspector you should not act like one.

To be an accepted member of the group a man had to act in accordance with these social standards. One man in this group exceeded the group standard of what constituted a fair day's work. Social pressure was put on him to conform, but without avail, since he enjoyed doing things the others disliked. The best-liked person in the group was the one who kept his output exactly where the group agreed it should be.

Inasmuch as the operators were agreed as to what constituted a day's work, one might have expected rate of output to be about the same for each member of the group. This was by no means the case; there were marked differences. At first the experimenters thought that the differences in individual performance were related to differences in ability, so they compared each worker's relative rank in output with his relative rank in intelligence and dexterity as measured by certain tests. The results were interesting: the lowest producer in the room ranked first in intelligence and third in dexterity; the highest producer in the room was seventh in dexterity and lowest in intelligence. Here surely was a situation in which the native capacities of the men were not finding expression. From the viewpoint of logical, economic behavior, this room did not make sense. Only in terms of powerful sentiments could these individual differences in output level be explained. Each worker's level of output reflected his position in the informal organization of the group.

What Makes the Worker Not Want to Coöperate

As a result of the Bank Wiring Observation Room, the Hawthorne researchers became more and more interested in the informal employee groups which tend to form within the formal organization of the company, and which are not likely to be represented in the organization chart. They became interested in the beliefs and creeds which have the effect of making each individual feel an integral part of the group and which make the group appear as a single unit, in the social codes and norms of behavior by means of which employees automatically work together in a group without any conscious choice as to whether they will or will not coöperate. They studied the important social functions these groups perform for their members, the histories of these informal work groups, how they spontaneously appear, how they tend to perpetuate themselves, multiply, and disappear, how they are in constant jeopardy from technical change, and hence how they tend to resist innovation. In particular, they became interested in those groups whose norms and codes of behavior are at variance with the technical and economic objectives of the company as a whole. They examined the social conditions under which it is more likely for the employee group to separate itself out in opposition to the remainder of the groups which make up the total organization. In such phenomena they felt that they had at last arrived at the heart of the problem of effective collaboration. They obtained a new enlightenment of the present industrial scene; from this point of view, many perplexing problems became more intelligible.

Some people claim, for example, that the size of the pay envelope is the major demand which the employee is making of his job. All the worker wants is to be told what to do and to get paid for doing it. If we look at him and his job in terms of sentiments, this is far from being as generally true as we would like to believe. Most of us want the satisfaction that comes from being accepted and recognized as people of worth by our friends and work associates. Money is only a small part of this social recognition. The way we are greeted by our boss, being asked to help a newcomer, being asked to keep an eye on a difficult operation, being given a job requiring special skill—all of these are acts of social recognition. They tell us how we stand in our work group. We all want tangible evidence of our social importance. We want to have a skill that is socially recognized as useful. We want the feeling of security that comes not so much from the amount of money we have in the bank as from being an accepted member of a group. A man whose job is without social function is like a man without a country; the activity to which he has to give the major portion of his life is robbed of all human meaning and significance.

If this is true—and all the evidence of the Western Electric researches points in this direction—have we not a clue as to the possible basis for labor unrest and disputes? Granted that these disputes are often stated in terms of wages, hours of work, and physical conditions of work, is it not possible that these demands are disguising, or in part are the symptomatic expression of, much more deeply rooted human situations which we have not as yet learned to recognize, to understand, or to control? It has been said there is an irresistible urge on the part of workers to tell the boss off, to tell the boss to go to hell. For some workers this generalization may hold, and I have no reason to believe it does not. But, in those situations where it does, it is telling us something very important about these particular workers and their work situations. Workers who want to tell their boss to go to hell sound to me like people whose feelings of personal integrity have been seriously injured. What in their work situations has shattered their feelings of personal integrity? Until we understand better the answer to this question, we cannot handle effectively people who manifest such sentiments.

Without such understanding we are dealing only with words and not with human situations—as I fear our overlogicized machinery for handling employee grievances sometimes does.

The matters of importance to workers which the Hawthorne researches disclosed are not settled primarily by negotiating contracts. If industry today is filled with people living in a social void and without social function, a labor contract can do little to make coöperation possible. If, on the other hand, the workers are an integral part of the social situations in which they work, a legal contract is not of the first importance. Too many of us are more interested in getting our words legally straight than in getting our situations humanly straight.

In summary, therefore, the Western Electric researches seem to me like a beginning on the road back to sanity in employee relations because (1) they offer a fruitful working hypothesis, a few simple and relatively clear ideas for the study and understanding of human situations in business; (2) they offer a simple method by means of which we can explore and deal with the complex human problems in a business organization—this method is a human method: it deals with things which are important to people; and (3) they throw a new light on the precondition for effective collaboration. Too often we think of collaboration as something which can be logically or legally contrived. The Western Electric studies indicate that it is far more a matter of sentiment than a matter of logic. Workers are not isolated, unrelated individuals; they are social animals and should be treated as such.

This statement—the worker is a social animal and should be treated as such—is simple, but the systematic and consistent practice of this point of view is not. If it were systematically practiced, it would revolutionize present-day personnel work. Our technological development in the past hundred years has been tremendous. Our methods of handling people are still archaic. If this civilization is to survive, we must obtain a new understanding of human motivation and behavior in business organizations—an understanding which can be simply but effectively practiced. The Western Electric researches contribute a first step in this direction.

———◆———

The author of the following selection, T. N. Whitehead, is also a professor at Harvard University, an associate of F. J. Roethlisberger. Whitehead as well as Roethlisberger has been influenced by Elton Mayo, and their general outlook is similar. This selection is a chapter from a book which also gives an account, in an early chapter, of the Hawthorne studies.

As background to Professor Whitehead's essay it may be well to recall the essay of Professor Latham's (in Part 2) in which he satirizes the "God-Chief" theories of organization—the rather naïve ideas of some earlier organization theorists that organizations and their component members can be manipulated at will by those holding formal authority. A number of factors have combined in recent years to induce in administrative students a feeling of the great complexity of large-scale formal organizations in modern society and a keen sense of the difficulties of the manager or administrator. One of these factors is the Hawthorne studies and the great amount of thought and further studies they have provoked. Another factor is the impact of psychology upon administrative study. Since recent psychology has emphasized nonrational and irrational aspects of human nature, theories of organization and management are now being reconstructed to accommodate these aspects. Another factor is the impact of anthropological and sociological concepts and data, which have added new colors and dimensions to the administrative world.

These three factors—the Hawthorne studies, psychological concepts, and anthropological-sociological concepts—can be seen interacting in Professor Whitehead's essay. We now appreciate, as he indicates, that organizations as well as individuals have a "subconscious," a large area in which communication is difficult and motives are obscure and—in terms of traditionally accepted ideas—nonrational. It is obvious, for example, that the rationalism of classical economic theory, with its shrewdly self-calculating "economic man," led us to expect a rationalism in organizational behavior which has proved to be false. We have learned also that not only are there "societies" and "classes" within an organization, but that organizations exist *within* societies or cultures and must be studied and construed always in relation to their environment. In an expressive metaphor, a formal organization is an iceberg, only one-eighth of which is visible above the surface.

One of the results of these recent currents of thought has been a focusing of attention upon leadership. If the obstacles to coordinated effort are large, if institutional inertia is so great that the issuing of an order by the administrator or executive is, at best, but the mere beginning of coordinated effort to achieve official organizational goals, then the administrator or executive must be a "leader." That is to say, he must have the capacity not just to issue orders but to influence the behavior of the members of his organization. The conditions under which, and the means by which, this can be accomplished have recently been the subjects of intense study. One result of this interest, for example, has been the adding of the area of "communication" to administrative study.

The following essay is a brief but concentrated and suggestive treatment of some of the themes that enter into current treatments of the subject of leadership. In it the author directs his attention to private organization.

Query, what changes, if any, are necessary to make his generalizations true and relevant for public administration?

The Evolution of Modern Leadership *

T. N. WHITEHEAD

Originally, a leader was one who showed the way and was followed by others; he quite literally led by performing some activity which was copied faithfully by his followers. In this sense, one man may lead others on a country walk. There is little implication of an organizing function in such leadership; the leader is an example to follow. It is doubtful whether a pure example of such primitive leadership could be found in any society, however simple, but much leadership does approximate to this type. And, in fact, the element of imitation is never entirely absent in any case. In a small industrial group, such as the relay test group, that member will obtain ascendancy over the others who, among other qualities, shows an unusual aptitude in an activity which the others also desire to exercise. If the group is interested in its work, then its natural leader will be that member who performs his work best, according to the group's criterion. In any case the leader will be one of the better workers. If the group be in violent opposition to its management, it will act in such a manner as to thwart the latter, and the most successful trouble maker becomes the leader or, in the current phrase, becomes the "ringleader."

A leader is in some sense chosen by the rest of the group as one who is both able and willing to assist them in doing that which they already wish to do. This act of choosing is not necessarily deliberate or even recognized by the group.

So leadership in its simple form has certain well-marked characteristics whether it be found in industry, among primitive tribes, or in the cities of modern society. In the first place, the leader is selected by the joint inclinations of the candidate himself and of the society or group of which he is a member. Secondly, he is selected for his skill in specific activities. His skill, in a simple community, is usually a manual technical skill. Thirdly, the exercise of the given skill, and the objective promoted, accord with the social sentiments of the group.

Thus, the leader's function is such as to assist the group in maintaining its customs, its purposes and its attitudes undamaged by the chance ineptitudes of the less experienced or less skilful members. This is a conservative function calculated to maintain the society in an unvarying circle of procedures. A group so maintained may be expected to display integration in a high degree. Not only are human relations shielded from external shock, but the social "meaning" of every activity, and of the physical accessories to those activities, takes on the

* Reprinted by permission of the publishers from Thomas North Whitehead, *Leadership in a Free Society*, Harvard University Press, Cambridge, Mass. Copyright 1936, by the President and Fellows of Harvard College.

vivid colour of absolute ultimate fact. Nothing is more certain to a primitive than that his horn, or maybe his hearthstone, has some very real, though not accurately definable, relation to himself, to customs in which the article is involved, and to some legendary episodes or persons. Everything stands in a close and absolute relation to everything else.

If we analysed the attitudes of a typical English country squire of the recent past, we should find something like the following among those facts fundamental to his thinking.

1. To trap a fox is a bad act.
2. To hunt a fox is a good act.
3. Good men hunt foxes.
4. Good men believe (unquestioningly) in the Established Church of England. They attend divine service.
5. The Church shows people what's what, and teaches the lower orders their place; it makes them good.
6. Bad members of the lower orders trap foxes.
7. To trap a fox is a bad act.

And so we go round and round the circle of a closed, integrated system of social actions, sentiments and beliefs. The system is emotionally self-consistent; it relates everything to everything else by a series of non-logical moral judgments and sentiments, each of which must be, and in fact is accepted as fundamental and absolute. It is a characteristic of such a society that thinking is in terms of absolute values, that hypotheses are not readily entertained, that problems are not argued on the basis of intellectual considerations but are judged in the light of an elaborate ethical code. This code rests on a myth, a mystical account of some sort, or on a formed religion which, being ultimate, is not itself open to rational investigation.

The social values and sentiments of any industrial group of workers, in so far as that group is integrated, will be found to run a course not unlike that just depicted. Persons, social acts and things all have their interlocking "meanings"—judgments of good and bad conduct are accepted with unthinking conviction, although if questioned they will be defended by a string of rationalizations. To a considerable extent this is the thinking and sentiment of every individual but, as we shall see later, other elements may serve to modify the picture.

Clearly, leadership within a simple non-intellectual group is not a progressive affair if left to itself; on the other hand, it is highly competent from a certain point of view. It achieves two objectives: it integrates its groups, and it secures the future by a perpetuation of the best standard techniques of the community. From the standpoint of a modern code of values, this leadership has one capital defect: it is not progressive. The rise of this explicit urge for designed, technical progression is one of the unexpected developments of primitive leadership.

The primitive leader is well exemplified by the highly skilled mechanic. Such a man has by long application acquired an unusual skill in his art. He is also in possession of a traditional set of methods, or sequences of operations, with which he tackles his technical problems. Perhaps the outstanding characteristic of the mechanic-leader is his intense pride in, and unswerving loyalty to the detailed procedure by which he exercises his skill. Any attempt on the part of his "boss" to modify these by one hair's breadth will evoke the most unmeasured anger. It is as though a brutal assault had been made on his household gods. And that is exactly what it amounts to. The simple leader is above all things loyal to his skill and to its accompanying procedures. Every act of discriminating attention, every guarding and controlled movement has been practised a thousand times and is the basis of a deep sentiment; these *are* his ways of life, and on them his ultimate values are grounded.

But a sympathetic study of a skilled worker over a sufficient period will reveal an apparently erratic streak in his behaviour. Sooner or later in his work, our friend will surmount some particular difficulty by an elegant device, and he will explain with pride that "in his young days" they were taught to do such and such, but that he had subsequently "thought of" the procedure just demonstrated. No loyalty is shown towards the discarded traditional procedure, and his common sense would be outraged at the bare suggestion that any value could adhere to the inferior method. In all these respects, he would be followed without question by his group.

The fact is that our mechanic, for once in his life, is thinking for himself and he has temporarily discarded the whole lumber of social sanctions and taboos. Up to that moment he was possessed of an implicit skill in action—a practical wisdom below the level of speech. But in the continual practice of his art, he was learning to notice the connection, the causal relations, between the various operations involved. He began to understand the reasons why, and to be able to give a few logical explanations for some of his actions. He would have once declared that he did such and such because "that was the way to do it"—an appeal to social sanction. Now he can say that too heavy a feed on his lathe will result in "chattering," *because* of lack of rigidity in the construction of the slide. And a designing engineer would, by suitable calculation or experiment, be able to endorse the mechanic's logical deduction, based as it was on discriminating observation of the facts.

This is the first step in an individual liberty of thought; a liberation from the guidance of social custom. Having once achieved this enormous stride, it is a second and almost inevitable step, human nature being what it is, to practise these logical processes with small imaginary variations; what would happen if I stiffened the tool holder on the slide in such and such a way? The mechanic tries this out and is the proud inventor of an improved process.

To a university-trained engineer, the whole affair seems out of proportion. He is filled with respect for the mechanic's skills of operation, but as for the so-called "invention"—why, his day is spent in the habitual exercise of far more elaborate constructions than that! However, the engineer would be wrong:

the achievement of independent logical thought is one of the major successes of mankind, and in a greater or lesser degree it is achieved afresh by every individual at some stage in his life.

This, or something like it, is the story of technical advance in primitive communities, as well as amongst many industrial groups. And it is observable that the changes in non-progressive groups are in the first instance improvements in technical procedures; social changes arise as the unwitting consequences of these technical advances.

The steps leading to a technical advance are roughly as follows:

1. The leader shares with his group a profound loyalty to the technical procedures by which they prosecute their purposeful tasks. These procedures are their "way of life."

2. The leader is trusted as one who has unusual skill in these technical procedures. He is the guardian of the social customs and in these matters his word is final.

3. The leader, being genuinely a man of intelligence in this respect, obtains an unusual insight into the causal relations involved in his procedures. He begins to reflect upon his technical actions and on the behaviour of the material he operates upon.

4. He continues in his traditional procedures, but less because of society's sanction and more because he sees the "reason why." He has partly shifted the grounds for his pattern of behaviour, unnoticed by himself and by the group.

5. Sooner or later, the leader, in his semi-rational reveries and reflections, stumbles on a technical improvement. He adopts this without misgiving because the group has accorded him the right to make decisions in technical matters— [this is my rationalization, not his].

6. The group follow their leader, and adopt the improved process without question; the leader is the right man to show the way, and the group's lesser but real insights with respect to their procedures dimly indicate the underlying logic.

Since technical procedures are part and parcel of a group's social structure, it follows that even a small technical advance will result in a modification of the structure. The dependence of society on its procedures is naturally not explicit in the minds of the group, and they may simultaneously adopt the new procedure and deplore the change or loss of "meaning" involved in the departure from the "good old ways." The degree to which this sentiment is shown by all groups and societies is amazing. One manifestation of this sentiment consists in faking up new things or procedures to appear like the old.

For instance, some of the very earliest stone churches to be built in England have the stone worked in such a manner as to suggest a wooden structure; wood in those days (roughly, 8th century) being the traditional material. Similarly, there exists in Nova Scotia, or there did a year or two ago, a wooden bridge the piers of which were constructed of roughly hewn stone, shaped and piled on one another in crisscrossed fashion like wooden logs in imitation of the more usual bridges of the neighbourhood. To this day, some of the ocean-going motor ships have quite unnecessary funnels in imitation of the traditional steamers. And the latter at one time were fitted with spars reminiscent of sailing ships, although they did not carry corresponding sails. I confess that an electric locomotive is not so "real" to me as the steam locomotive with which I was familiar as a child, and I regret the manner in which the chimneys of the latter have been losing their original majestic height. Almost every new substance and many structures are introduced as more or less successful imitations of those they are supplanting. The same thing applies to human procedures and customs. On parade, Army officers present themselves in the guise of swordsmen, but on active service these parade swords are never taken into the trenches; hand-grenades and firearms are the modern instruments of warfare.

However, in modern industry most workers are quite explicitly aware of the connection between technological advance and change in social structure, and in consequence the former is often strenuously opposed. This opposition is explained on rational grounds, and frequently this is genuinely the real and sufficient basis for the action; but this explanation is not invariably the only motive.

In the absence of modern leadership, such as is typical in industry today, the pace of technological improvement in society would be sufficiently deliberate to prevent any radical break with the immediate past, and in his own thinking each man would carry on the traditions of his father. Primitive leadership is thus an instrument for holding a group closely to its norm, but in the course of generations the norm is subject to a slow wandering in the direction of technological improvement together with the consequent social adaptation. Such leadership is typical of unprogressive groups, whether these be agricultural societies of the Atlantic countries, some societies in the Far East, or many small employee groups in so far as they are not directed from above. Naturally, the extent to which any given group approximates to this type is a matter of degree; and in modern industry the trend of employee mentality is away from the manually skilled worker towards that of the mentally adaptable thinker. This shift is perhaps not quite so emphatic as many would have us suppose. Observers are apt to be misled by their own sentiments; the hammer, the cold chisel and the file are still the symbols, for elderly mechanics, of manual skill, just as the sword is still symbolic of the warrior, and they are sceptical of a skill which seems to consist in controlling the levers of an automatic machine.

We have in outline traced the evolution of explicit logical skill from the implicit skill in action of the superior man, and we have noticed that skills to this day, and specifically in industry, are largely of the more primitive type. But explicit logical skill in itself will result in nothing more than sporadic bursts of change, arising directly from a contemplation of the current procedures. The final step which mankind has so far achieved is deliberately to organize logical thinking in such a way as to lead to a stream of improvements. Broadly speaking, what has been evolved is a direction of the thinking processes towards a continual evolution of better and better technological procedures.

It has been already noticed, as an exceptional trait, that the simple leader, in spite of an intense emotional loyalty to traditional techniques, showed no particular regret in deserting an old technique for a better one which he understood in terms of familiar fact. In so far as thought takes the form of pursuing the causal relations of accepted terms or things, *i.e.,* in so far as thought is logical, the process arouses no particular sentiment. Emotional resistance makes its appearance when recognition is demanded for some fact or thing which is incompatible with an existing sentiment. Apparently small technical advances occasionally introduced by an accepted leader, based as they are on logical processes (not necessarily quite explicit), do not seem to involve a sufficient area of accepted practice to arouse resentment.

Resentment, and emotional resistance generally, is the guardian of those attitudes and behaviours which cannot be investigated by logical procedures, given the mental development of the individual in question. The simple details of working tasks are matters about which leading men of all ages have been able to reflect, and for this reason they have been able to make comparisons between alternative possibilities without violating social sanction. This of course does not mean that such men conceived of reflection per se as being a virtue; exceptional people have shown this trait from early days, but as a widespread phenomenon, the evolution from the cheerful acceptance of sporadic technological advances to the deliberate quest for systematic development is a matter of comparatively recent history.

Socially guided thinking in simple groups or societies depends on the absolute "reality" of social verdict. This *is* bad, that *is* good, and no doubts are entertained. However, logical thinking involves, or makes probable, a comparison of this with that. Two or more concepts or procedures are simultaneously entertained as possibilities. Neither is regarded as absolutely good or bad a priori, but the relative merits of the two are critically considered.

Such mental activities inevitably weaken the force of social sanction, at least with respect to those matters towards which this attitude is habitually adopted. Those matters first and chiefly liberated from social control in this way were the technological procedures; not until very recently were the social customs and attitudes themselves habitually subjected to the same process, and even now this is only possible to a much smaller extent than is sometimes supposed.

For the most part, social change has been the unwitting outcome of technical advance. However, the pace of the latter has been so great that in industrial societies people have found themselves living under conditions obviously different from those of their parents, and even changing unmistakably within their own lives. This not only prevents the individual from being closely conditioned for his present social situation, it also invites comparisons as between situations. Thus the modern intellectual tendency is to regard customs and procedures as having relative degrees of merit rather than as possessing the absolute force of a sanction. The merits of everything from reciprocating steam engines to marital relations are open to investigation, and opinions are held as hypotheses subject to modification. Moral and social sentiments, whilst in some sense "believed" and acted upon, are held as being the current attitudes and as possessing merit relative to some other sentiments, but their foundations are no longer supposed to rest on a rock of absolute ultimate truth. This, at least, is what intellectualism would like to think of itself, and it contains some measure of truth as compared with less restless communities and groups.

However, society, or social behaviour in any form, would be quite impossible without fairly accurate expectations regarding the sentiments and behaviour of others, and these imply social tradition in some shape or other. Social custom with its accompanying moral and ethical codes performs the function of rendering the activity of human beings at once predictable and fitting to each other.

It is not difficult to see that the modern restless, experimental attitude is a natural outcome of sporadic reflection on well-practised routines, but we must beware of supposing that this evolution is in any sense necessary, or even very probable. The Chinese have been socially cultivated for centuries without exhibiting any great tendency towards a systematically sought progression. At the present time, impact from the West does seem to have started this process.

However that may be, the present industrial communities do appear to be committed to an explicit systematic development of their scientific and technological procedures, with whatever that may imply in the matter of social change. Great changes have already taken place in social function and structure, and more may be expected to follow. For instance, in any community of a few generations ago, and in many communities now, industrial occupations were not properly distinguishable from social life in general. Purposeful activities of all kinds represented the ordinary procedures of mankind as they lived their lives. The distinction between a man tilling his field and his wife doing the housework was not profound either in his thinking or in ours. Both were guarding the total situation by the performance of interlocking and, to a large extent, overlapping activities. The leaders of such a community were similarly engaged.

In a modern society, a part of the purposeful activities are, as before, performed as social living, and are regulated, though in a lesser degree, by social usage. But another part of these purposeful activities has become singled out for a very different form of organization. These activities have been withdrawn from the main stream of social living and are highly organized from the standpoint of technological efficiency. This fraction of the purposeful activities is known as industry, or, more broadly, as business. The division of social activity into ordinary living on the one hand and business on the other was not the result of custom or of the direct needs of human intercourse; it depended on the chance evolution of technological procedures. The industrial organization is controlled, without adequate regard for the social lives of those involved, by a type of man highly skilled in the logical, reflective thinking suitable to the rapid evolution of technology. This does not imply that the modern executive is indifferent to the welfare of those beneath him, but it is true that this welfare has not been the primary force in moulding the industrial organization. So long as industry formed a relatively small part of the total activities, this situation was perhaps not dangerous to social integrity; but at the present time so much activity is industrial that society is becoming seriously and increasingly disorganized.

The modern executive is indeed in a peculiarly difficult situation. Let us review his functions and see how they compare with those of a leader of an unprogressive group. In the first place, an executive does not literally lead his human material, he organizes it. It is broadly true to say that he cannot compare with his employees in the performance of any one of their several tasks. The occupation of an executive is different, not only in detail but also in kind from that of his men; their respective sentiments and attitudes are based on radically different experiences. The modern "leader" is no longer quite a member of his group, working by their side and sharing their daily lives.

Secondly, it follows from this that the social organization of the group is not oriented primarily towards their executive, but toward some informal leader of their own choosing—one of themselves. For every group has its leader, or an inner ring of leaders, a miniature aristocracy. Thus, whether he realizes the fact or not, the executive is in danger of directing a formed society from without; a society that will evolve defense mechanisms and sentiments of antagonism, if its social living appears to be in danger of interruption.

Thirdly, the executive is himself a social being and his general attitudes are oriented by his society, but this society is not the group he is directing and his attitude is not moulded by them. The executive is a member of a highly competitive "progressive" society anxious for its preservation and for its advancement, and his more general outlook necessarily conforms to this social pattern. I say "necessarily conforms" because this society chose him for that very reason. Thus his activities are directed by his society's desire for "economic progress" rather than by any needs of his employees. It is true that these latter are also members of the society outside, though they may well come from a different stratum, but as a working group they have little part in forming and sharing their executives' social sentiments.

Fourthly, the control which the executive exercises over his group has no explicit relation to their social life. Its purpose is simply to organize their activities with a single eye to their technological efficiency, and with the intention of elaborating and introducing improved procedures as quickly as may be.

In the sense previously employed, it may be said that the modern executive is only too apt to stand in a secondary, rather than in a primary relation to his group; and the purpose of that relation is a logical one. We saw that the primitive leader promoted the integration of his group, guarded its future economic position, but was essentially unprogressive. The modern executive endangers the integration of his group, evolves procedures designed to improve their future economic position, and is thus progressive. The business man's functions come near to disintegrating the society whose economic future he is providing for. Naturally, this picture is softened in many respects; human situations always overflow any simple formula. For instance, it is obvious that executives are anything but indifferent to the sentiments of those beneath them; and narrow logical motives are always diluted with a greater or lesser measure of ordinary human decency, or in other words with social wisdom.

This review of executive functions is in no sense a criticism of individuals, but an attempt to analyse the actual structure within which executives have to operate. The situation may be summed up by stating that industry is built up of small employee groups, having many of the characteristics of simple communities: a great dependence on social sanction, a tendency to relate things and sentiments by customary ties supported by an uncritical belief in their absolute truth or value, occupations easily leading to set "ways of life" with appropriate emotions, and so forth. These groups are directed by men from outside whose intellectual training and bias is above all things experimental and "progressive." Moreover, these men are under pressure from society to organize and direct their groups from precisely this standpoint.

And finally, we should have the candour to admit that hardly any of us could tolerate a society which did not display intellectual curiosity and a restless tendency towards experimental behaviour. In other words, there is no going back; the problem is not how to construct yet one more primitive community, but how to combine progress with immediate social satisfaction. One thing is apparent: social integrity can no longer be trusted to look after itself. In the past, slowly developed ways of life possessed inherent stability, and the processes by which this stability was maintained were never explicitly recognized. But progress gives no time for the gradual development of instinctive wisdom, and the price of stability in the future will be the exercise by society of a critical self-knowledge.

Chapter 17

Planning

The author of the following selection, Sir Henry N. Bunbury, is a distinguished British public servant who is recognized as an outstanding writer on the subject of governmental planning. He has been also an intelligent and sympathetic observer of the American public scene and has contributed much to an exchange of administrative experience.

This essay, addressed to British readers and appearing in the British journal *Public Administration,* was written in the late thirties and bears some obvious marks which "date" it. It remains, however, what it was when first penned: a balanced, concise introduction to the subject of governmental planning.

In explaining the origins and nature of governmental planning Sir Henry in effect presents an argument *justifying* a certain amount of governmental planning of national life, especially on the economic side. Most American students of public administration would be in general agreement with his treatment of the subject. The subject of planning, however, is not only extraordinarily complex (as will appear below, some types of planning of special concern to administrative students are not even mentioned in this general statement), it is extremely controversial; and what seems good ethics and obvious logic to some Americans is tendentious ideology to others.

Query, is Sir Henry demonstrably incorrect in any statement? Has the passage of time invalidated either a statement of fact or a judgment of value?

Governmental Planning *

SIR HENRY N. BUNBURY

. . . In many countries the scope of governmental activity, in relation to the social and economic life of the people, has in recent years been greatly enlarged. There has been a strong, though by no means a uniform, reaction against the principles of *laisser faire.* Many forms of activity which formerly were left as a free field for individual or corporate enterprise, or for voluntary and wholly unguided action, have become matters of active community interest. The State has intervened to guide, to stimulate, to control, to forbid, to buy and sell, to operate. The causes which have led to this development are many and various, and it is unnecessary to discuss them here: let it suffice to say that, for various reasons, the prospects of a return to the free, spontaneous, self-regulating economy, and to the negative, non-interfering State, which was, if not the achievement, at any rate the objective of liberal nineteenth century statesmanship, seem somewhat remote to-day.

* From *Public Administration* (October, 1938), 381–398. Abridged. The full title is "Governmental Planning Machinery"; only the introductory part of the essay is reproduced here. Reprinted by permission of the Institute of Public Administration.

If, however, the scope and content of government is thus enlarged, appropriate administrative mechanisms and personnel to enable it to carry out its new tasks are needed. And, as we should expect, such mechanisms have in recent years appeared in many countries, mostly in a more or less experimental form. What is the function and structure of these various mechanisms; how well, or ill, do they in fact operate; can any conclusions yet be drawn as to what features are suitable and promote efficiency? . . .

These new or enlarged functions of the State or the community have come to be associated in many circles with the term "planning." The term is comprehensive and convenient, but it is also overworked, and has come to carry with it varying connotations and emotional associations, both of which make for confusion rather than clarity. . . .

Planning is, strictly, a process, with its associated techniques. It is a *method* of arriving at some desired result. When applied to the field of social and economic activity it is, fundamentally, a process for securing continuity in time, and internal consistency, in the governmental policies operating in that field. It implies a general objective. It may be said that these are things to which all governments which are worthy of the name direct their efforts. To this, the planners will answer that, in the complex conditions of to-day, without conscious planning they largely fail to achieve them, for two reasons. In the first place, under a private enterprise economy, the particular enterprise, compelled to seek, and to seek only, its own maximum advantage, will not take into account the effect of its own economic activities, either on other enterprises or on the social welfare of the community in which it operates. For example, a road transport undertaking may by its policies take from the railway so much traffic that the latter, compelled still to maintain its system, is threatened with insolvency. It is for this reason that in many countries we may observe attempts by governments to plan their transport services as an organic whole. And again, an enterprise which has acquired the right to exploit some material resource will be likely to exploit it without regard to the social obligations which its activities create, or the social losses which will arise when the resource is exhausted. Hence the demand for the orderly development and exploitation of resources by means of a comprehensive long-term plan. This applies conspicuously to the land in many of its uses.

In the second place, in the absence of planned policies, democratic government tends to be ruled by the pressures of "pressure groups" representing particular interests, and to follow the line of least resistance to those forces from time to time. Planning is essentially, from this point of view, an attempt to create, in concrete form, an alternative to this process: to present a known and accepted objective, to which policies can be directed and co-ordinated, and which represents the general and more permanent interest of the community.

In short, when once the belief is abandoned that if every independent individual and particular interest is free to pursue its own interests, the advantage of all will be most fully realised, planning in some form or another becomes essential. Planning, however (which, as has been said, is a process), may not only be directed towards different objectives, but may vary greatly in extent and character.

The principal distinction to be drawn is between planning in a private enterprise economy and that of a collectivist economy. In the former case, the questions arise, which activities should be taken out of the field of private enterprise and assumed by the State, and what should be the nature and form of the guidance or control to be imposed on private enterprise by the State? In the latter case these questions do not arise. Now, as regards State guidance and control, a casual survey of the situation in various countries will exhibit great differences both in the methods of approach and in the degree and character of the control or planning which actually operates. Everything, it would seem, is experimental. We are all searching for solutions. We are trying to find something better than casual interventionism wandering uncertainly from expedient to expedient, from crisis to crisis.

It has been said that planning implies a general objective. In the modern world it would seem (as indeed is to be expected) that by far the strongest and most general demand is for stability and security of livelihood for all the people at a reasonably high level. In a recent investigation among the employees of three English factories it was found that, among various desiderata of the employees, "security of employment" was the first choice of nearly 90 per cent. of the voters, while "high wages" occupied a much lower place. This is, I believe, the general experience. Now this security of livelihood generally—*i.e.*, for all the people— appears to be unattainable by private enterprise by itself, however highly it may be organised and with whatever powers it may be endowed. It appears to be essential that government, representing the community collectively, and controlling as it must the so-called strategic factors of monetary and fiscal policy, external trade policy, the development of communications, etc., shall play its part. Again, it is obviously desirable that the national resources of a country, both material and human, should be developed, conserved and used so as to provide the maximum of wealth. Further, that that wealth should be so used and distributed as to secure for all a reasonable living standard and reasonable social amenities. This objective involves planning by direct action on the resources themselves, as well as by indirect action through the "strategic factors." It will include town and land planning, the control of the exploitation of particular resources by private interests, the provision of particular facilities and amenities, and so on.

Thus social and economic planning is a many-sided process, demanding a high efficiency in the agencies and mechanisms through which it is carried out. When applied to an economy based on private enterprise, and carried out under the conditions of democratic self-government, the problem becomes still more complex and delicate. For, on the one hand, private enterprise must continue to function efficiently within the limits assigned to it, and, on the other, the planning agency has to achieve its ends by the processes of persuasion. It is these considerations which make the problem of planning mechanisms one of special interest and importance and, it may be added, of difficulty, in the countries where private enterprise is valued and encouraged.

So far we have assumed, as the sole general objective, the achievement, for all the people, of the maximum security of livelihood, the maximum continuing production of wealth (including the amenities of social life) and their most equitable distribution. Of such a case, the United States is typical. There is also the case of those economies which preserve private enterprise, that is, production, and the employment of labour, for profit, but direct it to some purpose other than that to which it would tend to direct itself if left relatively free from control. It may be called the State-controlled private economy. Of this type, Germany and Italy offer the best known examples.[1] The general purpose, to which all economic activity is subordinated, is to attain the maximum degree of national self-sufficiency, partly for reasons of "national defence," partly to minimise the risk of disturbance to the economy through the policies and actions of other countries in the commercial and monetary fields. This system also presupposes a complete control in principle, by the State, of all economic activity, though no doubt in practice a considerable latitude to enterprise is permitted, so long as the requirements of State policy are not contravened. The organisation for planning is appropriate to this modified purpose. Organisations of producers, distributors and employees play an important part in the working of the system. Production appears to be based largely on quantitative control, made effective by the use of various control devices and priorities to secure the fulfilment of the major objective. Unfortunately, in those countries where this system has been developed, national defence and armament have played so large a part in the planning bodies that no judgment as to the possibilities which might be achieved if it were directed wholly to the welfare and prosperity of the people and the raising of their standards of living, appears to be possible. The material for an objective comparison from this point of view between this system and that of the liberal enterprise economy does not exist.

Lastly, there is the economy in which private enterprise as above defined finds no place at all. Here planning takes on a different form and becomes, in the hands of organs of government, an integral and essential part of the economic and cultural life of the nation. It *must* plan, or collapse and probably starve. It is perhaps sufficient to say here that the technique of planning for collectivist production and a collectivist culture is materially different from that required where private enterprise is, within limits, demanded and encouraged.

It would be a profound mistake to suppose that the planning of the economic and social activities of a community is something new. On the contrary, it has always existed since man began to live a civilised and ordered life. Rather, it is the circumstances that are new. The movement for planning is a demand that we adjust ourselves to a new situation. The world has grown smaller. Communica-

[1] This refers to the Nazi and Fascist regimes of the late thirties.—The Editor.

tions and transport have been vastly improved and cheapened. The impacts of communities on each other have been amplified. The production of material wealth, and still more its potentialities, have greatly increased. With these things has also come the development of new financial, corporate, stock-market and accounting techniques which, if capable of social benefit, are also capable of grave anti-social abuse. If security of livelihood for all people, and an equitable distribution of wealth are the objectives, there is, it would seem, a need for a new adjustment—a new co-ordination of economic and social activities which apparently is unlikely to arrive without conscious and deliberate effort in that direction.

For let us be clear what the issue is. In many situations the particular enterprise or group, seeking its own maximum advantage, *cannot* take account of all the factors which enter into the situation, and which will be affected by its decision. It will take account only of those which affect itself. For example, a lumber company, left to itself, will cut down its timber as rapidly as it can find a market for it at a satisfactory price: what happens afterwards to the land, the surrounding region and the population which drew its livelihood from its activities, is not its concern. A town may become derelict through the removal of a factory, but the effect of the removal on the town is not a matter which the factory owners are required or expected to take into their financial calculations. The essence of planning is that all the factors, and not only some of them, are taken into consideration before a decision is arrived at.

Clearly this task is, in any highly developed state, and whatever the general objective, one of great difficulty and complexity. In a wholly free economy, production and distribution depend on the initiative and judgment of a great number of individuals working independently of each other. In these circumstances some individuals are making mistakes at any time and all individuals at some time: but the work of production and distribution in the aggregate goes on, and the worst that happens are some wasted resources, the fluctuations of the trade cycle, and a highly unequal and to some extent inequitable distribution of the wealth produced. These are bad enough. In a planned system, on the other hand, to the extent to which planning actually operates, initiative waits on governmental decision: thus the organization needed in order to secure that, within the limits of human capacity, the right decisions are taken at the right time is no light matter. The danger is a gradual slowing down of productive and distributive effort, accompanied by efforts to increase it which may be a menace to the liberty desired by every man. The cake may be more equitably distributed but it might be a very much smaller cake.

———◆———

H. S. Person, author of the following selection, has designated himself as a "Consultant in Business Economics and Management," but he has also been a prominent contributor to the literature growing out of the Scientific Management movement as well as a successful practitioner. Like several of the other most eminent Scientific Managers his interest in and contribution to public administration has been very large.

In this essay Mr. Person views the subject of research and planning nearer at hand and from a different perspective. Sir Henry Bunbury wrote as a public administrator viewing planning trends and national planning machinery comparatively. Mr. Person writes of planning as a "function of administration and management." He writes from the "inside," as a professional, and on the more technical aspects of planning.

But this, while true, is somewhat misleading. For the important thing about Mr. Person's view of planning, as will be seen, is that it is to him an all-pervasive aspect of good administration and management, both a process and a quality that together equal "intelligent direction" of collective enterprise; not an activity that can be taken on and put off as might a special piece of equipment, and not necessarily identified with specially named planning organs.

Query, does Mr. Person's analysis of the planning function apply as fully to government as to private enterprise? Has he dealt adequately with the problem of how *in the American system of government* the planning function should be organized and controlled?—with the question of who plans the planners?

Research and Planning as Functions of Administration and Management *

H. S. PERSON

I take planning to include definition of the objective of an enterprise, formulation of policies governing its achievement, designing of a system of procedures whereby the objective is achieved precisely and with minimum waste of the energies employed, and in most instances giving initial direction to execution, in which respect it overlaps execution. Planning is dynamic; it is a continuous process. Although in certain matters a plan may appear to be made once and for all time, as in the design of a public park, even in such instances permanence is relative because unforeseen variables eventually enter and there must be rearrangement.

The planning with which we are here particularly concerned—that of a live and active business enterprise or public agency—is dynamic in the highest degree

* From *Public Administration Review,* Vol. 1 (Autumn, 1940), pp. 65–73. Abridged. Reprinted by permission of the *Public Administration Review.*

because it involves continuing adjustment of and to a ceaseless stream of variables, some of which are unforeseeable and others foreseeable but indeterminate. The beginning of the understanding of planning is the realization that it is concerned generally with dynamic situations and is a procedure for minimizing the frictions, confusions, and losses arising out of variability. Its purpose is to substitute pre-determination for casualism insofar as particular circumstances and human capacity make this practicable. If foreseen, some variables can be avoided, others modified, and the remainder prepared for.

The term research used in connection with planning means primarily purpose-ful, *ad hoc* research, but it does not neglect fundamental research. Of course, fundamental research is essential to the definition and redefinition of an objec-tive and to the discovery of new ways and means of achieving it; but the great bulk of the research involved in day-to-day and week-to-week planning is homely *ad hoc* research stimulated by a succession of specific problems arising out of the constant impact of variables on the situations being managed.

Also we must be generous and permit the term research to cover some very simple fact-finding—superficial, some scientists might say. But we must be realistic; the purpose of research for planning is not primarily to discover funda-mental truths but to make each of the stream of acts constituting management the best possible under the circumstances. A problem arises in the morning in respect of which an executive must make a decision before he leaves his desk for the day. That problem can be given only six or eight hours of intensive study, although it is known to be of a nature that calls for six weeks or six months of study. But the best study of it that can be made within the six or eight hours should be made. The time factor in a dynamic situation determines the nature and direction of the research. Those investigations that have time limits of a day, a week, or a month are functionally of the highest rank in planning and should be given appropriate recognition.

Planning expresses no preference for a particular mode of research. It is con-cerned with variables; its problems vary, and therefore the modes of research vary. Planning employs as required every known mode of investigation. It draws on the techniques of all the sciences. The specific problem and the time factor determine the type of research employed at a particular moment. Planning tries always to be inductive, but at times it may have to be deductive. It may inspect many units of observation or it may take samples. It may make superficial observa-tions, or a vast array of quantitative measurements. It may conduct a few try-outs, or it may employ truly scientific experimentation. Let us say that it strives to employ in any instance the most pertinent and satisfying modes of research, but is governed by the time factors of its dynamic environment. . . .

Administration and Management

When the title of this paper was first suggested it included the word adminis-tration but not the word management. I added the word management purposefully. I believe a clear understanding of the differences between administration and management is essential to fruitful discussion of the nature and technique of planning.

Three terms would perhaps be more precise: direction, administration, management.[1] By direction I mean determination of the objective and of most general policies. In a large business it is the function of the board of directors as representative of entrepreneurial interests. In government it is the function of the Congress and the President as representative of the citizenry; in a state, of the legislature and the governor. At the other extreme is management—from a good old Latin word meaning fingering, or manipulation. Management manipulates facilities—plants, tools, machines, materials, and labor. It is concerned with the detailed conduct of operations. In a position between direction and management is administration—also from a good old Latin word identifying the function of the representative of a central government in a province, not concerned with the management of the province but with guardianship of the interests of the empire. The president of a business enterprise, the executive offices of a government, or the head of any public agency is the administrator. He is the connecting link between direction and management. He sees to it that management is conducted within the frame of the direction. He translates direction and general policies into more specific policies and programs. However, because many presidents of business enterprises are on boards of directors and are at the same time general managers—are really three functionaries in one person—it appears expedient to limit our terminology to two words—administration (including direction) and management.

While I believe that clear thinking about planning is possible only with such intellectual tools as are represented by these words, identifying clearly defined concepts, it must be admitted that there are difficulties attending their use. Among businessmen, and in government as well, all these words are used, but without uniformity of meaning. In one place administration, for instance, is given a meaning as I have defined it; in another place it is used to identify the functions of a chief clerk.

Also in government confusion is made worse confounded by such factors as these: a constitution with its division of responsibilities and authorities and its checks and balances; court decisions; and customs that have developed in the relations among the flexible parts of organized government. Yet if one thinks of government as the organization of a people for the conduct of public affairs, and thinks of it in terms of functions, the three basic functions of direction, administration, and management stand out clearly. We should think and plan in terms of logical functions, but in implementing plans we must translate our scientific

1 Many writers would disagree with Mr. Person's terminology; often management and administration as here defined are essentially reversed. But the important thing is the analysis behind the words rather than the words themselves.—The Editor.

language into the language of those on whom we must rely for execution, and we must even modify our plans to meet established and stubborn habits.

Administrative and Managerial Planning

Both administration and management plan, but their plannings are on different levels and generally employ different techniques. The planning of administration establishes a frame within which management plans. Administration does not concern itself with details of operations; on the other hand management accepts administration's frame of objectives and basic facilities. General Motors administrative planning establishes a frame for Buick or Delco or Yellow Cab managerial planning. Each of these within its frame plans its operations. In turn, Buick local general administration plans a frame within which the several departments do their managerial planning. The head of a government department establishes, or should establish, a frame or field of action for each bureau; within that frame the bureau should plan its operations in detail. It is the development of this technique of frame-within-frame of planning during the past quarter century that has made possible a harmonizing of centralization and decentralization, and the successful conduct of huge enterprises. Where huge enterprises have failed or faltered, the incompetence of the planning in respect of one or more of these frames has been responsible and has neutralized effective planning in the other frames.

While every mode of research that the sciences have devised is available to both administration and management, particular modes of research are more suitable for the one than for the other. Because management is concerned especially with physical facilities and their manipulation, with human facilities and their supervision, and with innumerable unit situations, it employs the experimental method more than administration can. Management, being concerned with operations and with the constant flow of variables and their problems, must frequently resort to hasty investigations because of time factors. Administration, on the other hand, because of its concern with direction, general policies, the long run, and situations of wide scope, cannot employ the method of experimentation widely, but it can utilize the historical method and quantitative measurement of trends more than can management. Any mode of research is available to both administration and management, but the function of each and the attendant circumstances make a particular mode the more suitable or expedient.

Personnel for Planning

This distinction between administration and management leads to an additional consideration. What type of individual is most suitable for one or the other field of planning, for designing the planning, and for executing the planning? Of course planning, wherever its locus, calls for a different type of individual from that called for by executive work, but not so different as many people assume. The planner must be temperamentally interested in details, and have capacity for analysis and synthesis. He must be an artist with an instinct for design. He must perceive and understand the meanings and relations of things. This vision must extend beyond the immediate situation. The executor, on the other hand, is concerned primarily with the problem of the moment and with getting things done. He must be dynamic and capable of persuading people. Generally he is impatient of details; his eyes are always on the time factor and the result.

Yet it is superficial to say that the executive must be an extrovert and the planner an introvert. I believe the planner also should be an extrovert, an artist with the temperament of a Whistler. We must distinguish three subfunctions within the function of planning: research, design, and implementation. Now the finding of facts and their analysis is a suitable responsibility for the introvert, but design should be done by one on the border line at least between introvert and extrovert; and I believe the implementation (which is dynamic because it adjusts plans to concrete situations, the initial step of execution) is best done by one fairly extroverted, one who can inject into the plan and the planning procedures that dynamic quality which comes from joyous contact with variable persons and variable things. Planning is as dynamic a function as is execution. We distinguish properly for convenience between planning and execution, but the final stages of planning are the first stages of execution.

As a nation we have educated and trained a staff of fact-finders and fact-analysts, but not of plan designers and implementers. The profession involving all-round capacities does not yet exist because education, training, and experience have not yet integrated into a sufficient number of particular individuals all the essential capacities. I believe that those trained in the political and economic sciences are more competent to design plans on the level of general administration than on the level of management; those trained as engineers, more capable on the level of management than on the level of general administration; and those trained in schools of business administration on the whole more capable than either of the others where both levels are combined in one responsibility.

When it comes to the dynamic final stages of planning—the actual planning that directs towards accomplishment of objective the constant flow of variables in an operating situation—there is the rub. No formal training yet devised gives the experience, discipline, and aptitude for this phase of the work. The best school for development of this capacity is service in the planning department of an industrial concern, which may thus afford a graduate school for candidates formally trained in fact-finding, analysis, and design. As for public agencies, the best move today for any of them is to follow the practice of industrial concerns and bring in as part-time consultants industrial engineers of proved competence. These experts could soon create out of personnel represented by the graduates of universities and technical schools a personnel for public service of real ability in the conduct of planning operations, as distinguished from fact-finding and analysis and the designing of plans. I know of one public agency that has pursued this policy successfully. Some day we shall, I hope, have in our government bureaus skilled technicians in planning whose education and training have been an integration of the social sciences, and engineering and industrial experience.

Postulates of Planning

I should like now to bring to those interested in public affairs some of the experience of private industry in planning. This should be worth our while, for in the final analysis there is no more technical operating difference between a public and a private undertaking than between some kinds of private undertakings—than between, for instance, an automobile plant and an insurance company or bank. Of course, as I have already said, the constitution, laws, and customs have developed other technical operating differences. But if industry has generalized its experience in a manner that covers both the automobile factory and the insurance company, these generalizations should have very great value for public enterprise. After all, purposeful effort is purposeful effort, whatever its particular objective and external form. For the sake of brevity I shall present this experience somewhat in the form of postulates.

1. The beginning—the foundation, the *sine qua non*—of effective planning is complete and clear specification of objective by general administration. The unknown cannot be planned; that which is not clearly understood cannot be well planned. Effectiveness of planning varies directly with completeness and clearness of understanding of the goal. The beginning of good general administrative planning is a clear definition of objective; and the remainder of it rests on that definition. And there can be good managerial planning only if there is a directive frame of good general administrative planning.

This postulate reminds us at once of a basic difference between public and private enterprise. The private enterprise defines its objective with a considerable degree of precision—an automobile company intends to produce automobiles; a textile mill, certain kinds of textiles; a bank, profits from service as custodian of funds, exchange, short-term loans, and investment. In contrast, read an act of the Congress establishing a department of the government or some other public enterprise. How vague it is; how much is left to the imagination of the first chief, and of each succeeding chief, modified by guesses and opinions of the General Accounting Office and the Attorney General's office. Not only does the head of a department have to guess, but the chiefs of his bureaus have to guess, and a greater or less degree of guessing passes all the way down the line. The starting point of effective planning and improved management in public affairs is on this level and at this point—more specific statements of objectives in the acts of the Congress, within this frame a much more comprehensive and definite statement of objective by each head of an agency, and within this frame very definite statements of subobjectives by the chiefs of the component bureaus.

The public agencies in which a considerable degree of planning and of economical management has been developed are those whose objectives lend themselves to relatively precise definition; for instance, the Army, the Navy, the special activities of the Corps of Engineers, the Tennessee Valley Authority, the Public Works Administration, and the Rural Electrification Administration. Planning is possible, to a greater degree than is at present attained, in all public agencies. I believe that, as a consequence of the pressure of circumstances, there is a ferment of planning thought and endeavor in many of the agencies in which at superficial glance it may appear impracticable.

2. After the objective has been defined the next step in effective planning is for general administration to formulate broad policies governing its achievement. Every enterprise has relationships; these relationships must be evaluated and policies regarding their continuance or modification must be established. For instance, you decide to make a low-price automobile—what is your policy of labor relations and wage rates? Or the government decides to build a dam to promote navigation and incidentally generate electric energy—what is its policy of relationship with private industry? We may perhaps say that this second stage of planning is the determination of relations and the adjustment to environmental factors affecting or affected by achievement of objective.

3. The third step in planning is the joint analysis, in the large, by general administration and management of the technical ways and means of achieving the objective within the frame of formulated policies. There are variables and alternatives, different ways of reaching a goal. If an industry has decided on one policy of labor relations, the sweat-shop system is not an available factor. If a government has decided to maintain the farmer's independence of action in the management of his farm, certain ways and means of aiding him are shut off. If a government does not believe that capacity for offense is the best defense, or does believe that it has dangers which should be avoided, the ways and means of building and operating a military establishment are different from what they would be if other views were held.

4. Following this analysis of ways and means in the large comes a task of synthesis as the next major step in planning. Administration, with the technical advice of management, sets up an organization. Organization is a resultant of the general analysis of ways and means. It is a frame of relationship of basic essential functions. Individuals are not yet involved. This is the frame of the functional structure within which management is to carry on its operations, and it defines the area of management's operations. It is a tool of management, as Oliver Sheldon has said, but it is also a limitation on management's field of activity. Observe that organization follows analysis of ways and means in the large, but is functional and precedes the assignment of individuals to particular responsibilities.

5. Then follows the most detailed analysis of ways and means by management and subsequent additional synthesis. This synthesis results in specifications of the flow of work and of procedures. These procedures are given qualitative, quantitative, and time characteristics. This is the sector of planning design identified in management literature by the term standardization. There result standard com-

ponent objectives, standard facilities for producing them, and standard modes of manipulation—all with standard qualities, standard quantities, and standard timing. At this stage are designed and incorporated every gear and rod of the organization or machine that management is to operate.

6. Next is the assignment of responsibilities to individuals. To be sure, there have been preceding assignments as different inclusive functions and responsibilities at higher levels have been determined; but it is at this stage that assignments are made to most of the individuals concerned, on whose qualitative and quantitative suitability precision and economy of actual operations ultimately depend. It is the people at machine, bench, and desk whose individual precisions and economies make in the aggregate institutional precision and economy. One may organize and reorganize and again reorganize at the top or in respect of the general frame but, except through modification of objective, he will not thereby effect major economies in doing the things to be done until he has studied and analyzed every detailed activity and established a standard and commonly understood flow of work and system of integrated procedures. Procedural relations and technical organization, and economies resulting from the aggregate of unit economies, are built from the bottom up.

7. Responsibilities having been assigned under the conditions herein set forth, the dominant force becomes the sense of *responsibility* to perform in accordance with predetermined procedure instead of *authority* to perform in accordance with individual guess and whim. Where such responsibility becomes dominant, the need of complete and clear understanding also becomes dominant, and management becomes chiefly a process of giving clear understandings. Background education of workers becomes important to management; specific training and instruction become a major part of its responsibility; the issuing of daily instructions as to what, how, how much, when, and where—all processes of giving clear understanding—constitutes the essence of management. Every worker is a cooperating executive, executing his part of the whole, because he understands what the part is and what part it is. He is part of a cooperative group in which each member is engaged in an individual activity, but in which the individual activities are supplemental one to another and contribute precisely and economically to a predetermined result because all are coordinated through design. From detailed work of this kind, not from over-all manipulations of structure, comes precision and the greater economy. There are two points at which important economies may be effected: at the administrative level in decisions concerning objectives and the elimination of undesirable or unnecessary or too costly objectives; and at the management level in the establishment of a continuous, precise flow of work in which every detailed act is in itself the most precise and economical possible, and in which every separate act is given its proper relationship.

8. Finally, planning must provide for measurement of results of operations and for publicity of the results—unit by unit, section by section. This checking

of progress is of major importance in two respects. First, it shows where misunderstandings are and gives management its opportunity to correct them before
they have seriously affected the quality and volume of work. Second, it serves as
the stimulus to qualitative and quantitative excellence. Publicity, through daily
output analyses and similar documents, awakens one of man's strongest impulses
—pride of achievement. In planned management, provided standards are reasonable and just and measurements objective, the individual's pride of performance
takes the place of the old type foreman's pressure technique with its tongue
lashing or blow of the fist.

Planning and Execution

It is admitted that I have at moments been discussing planning as a function of
administration and management as though it were administration and management. This is not entirely an accident. Planning and managing are as vitally inter-
connected as are Siamese twins.

There is too prevalent a habit of thinking about planning and execution as
wholly distinct: that the planning unit plans some line of action and then forgets
about it, the executors taking up where planning ended. Such thinking is unrealistic and misleading.

At this point a distinction should again be made between the research for
planning and design of a plan, and the implementing or planning itself. The
research must be detached and objective; and the procedures and standards
established by it must be the best in terms of the factors of the situation, and
impersonal. The researchers for planning may assume the attitude that they are
through when they have established the standards in terms of factors of the situation; but they soon discover that a dynamic situation is always changing and they
must always be on the jump to keep up with circumstances which compel the
modification of established standards and the establishment of new ones. But
they are through once standards are established, in the sense that they are not
concerned with the actual operations.

There is, however, a part of the planning function which is actively concerned with operations, and which functionally overlaps execution, although it is
commonly assumed to be distinct. For instance, incoming orders in a business—
to which correspondence, memoranda, other documents, and other impulses to
action in a government bureau may be considered analogous—come first to the
planning room and from there are sent on to the functionaries commonly identified with execution. The supervisors in the planning room in scientific management are rated as foremen, above the men at machines in the shops, and on a
par with the foremen actually in the shops.

This executive aspect of the planning function is made necessary by the fact
that the input of impulses into the organization is full of variables, while the
flow of work and the procedures of the operating organization demand a minimum of variables. The control sector of the planning function is, as it were, an

analyzing and synchronizing chamber into which flow the variable impulses—orders or documents—and which analyzes them, puts them into homogeneous groups, and passes them on to operatives. For an oversimplified example: if orders for ready-made suits of clothes went one at a time directly to the cutting room, that room would be overwhelmed by variability, and would find itself in a jobbing business. But if all orders for suits go first into a planning unit and are there analyzed and grouped, the cutting room can be given instructions for finishing suits in lots of a hundred or more to the style and size. Variability has been analyzed and synthesized out. Thus execution really begins under the aegis of the planning function.

Chapter 18

The Nature and Measurement of Efficiency

No concept has been more central and important in American study of administration than "efficiency." In the essay which marks the birth of public administration as a self-conscious inquiry, namely, Woodrow Wilson's essay on "The Study of Administration," it is argued that we can learn from European autocracies their more efficient administrative methods without importing also their autocratic spirit and ends; indeed that we *must* do so if democracy is to be able to meet the challenge of chaos from within and of force from without.

From Wilson's day to the present most writers on administration have taken the achievement of efficiency as the central objective of their discipline. In often quoted lines of Professor Luther Gulick, the idea is expressed thus: "In the science of administration, whether public or private, the basic 'good' is efficiency. The fundamental objective of the science of administration is the accomplishment of the work in hand with the least expenditure of manpower and materials. Efficiency is thus axiom number one in the value scale of administration."

The idea that the central objective of administrative study is achievement of efficiency is closely related to two other ideas—as has already been suggested. One of these is that administration is a science, or can be made a science if properly approached. The other is that as a matter of logical analysis, means and ends in cooperative human endeavor can be separated; and as a matter of the proper method of treating either, *should* be separated.

The association of efficiency with science is easily understood. The central concern of pure science is not with efficiency as such; its central concern might be stated as: "What is the nature of physical reality?" However, when one moves from the realm of pure science into the realm of applied science, questions of efficiency come to the fore. Typically, applied science is concerned with problems of how knowledge of physical phenomena may be used to realize some human goal more efficiently. There seems thus implicit in the manner in which science becomes meaningful for everyday life a distinction between ends and means, between the goals or values human beings seek to realize and the methods by which they may be realized.

Following this line of thought, the seeming clear *logical* distinction between ends and means was transformed early in the modern period of the "scientific" study of administration into a *methodological* distinction. The realm of administration was conceived to be a "value-neutral" realm in which the methods of science are applicable in the same manner as they are in a field of applied mechanical science. Ends or values, on the other hand, though determining the direction of administrative endeavor, lie outside the area of administrative science.

This viewpoint was rationalized and defended in a general political theory which held that all governmental activity is divisible into two parts, decision and execution: first deciding what is to be done, and then executing the decisions. The first of these is "politics," the second administration. Politics belongs to the realm of philosophy or ethics—or what not. Administration belongs to the realm of science.

This general view of the methods, significance, and relations of administrative study has had a distinguished lineage and wide acceptance. Clearly sketched by Woodrow Wilson in 1887, it was ably developed in 1900 in a book famous in the history of administrative study, *Politics and Administration* by Frank J. Goodnow. Goodnow's chief concern was with politics rather than administration; the book was primarily an argument for such political reforms as would forward popular control of administration through political parties. But that part of the argument which seemed to divide the governmental process into two realms distinguished by different problems and methods became for students of administration a justification for concentrating on problems of efficiency and slighting questions of values. For a period of a generation there was in the professional literature no important dissent from this point of view.

Increasingly during the past two decades, however, these once firmly held ideas have been either modified or abandoned. While the idea of efficiency remains, for most students, at the center of administrative study as the goal or measure of achievement, there has arisen considerable doubt as to what, precisely, efficiency is, and about how—and even whether—it can be measured in human affairs. Science remains a respected word, but even those most ardent in belief in the applicability of the methods of natural science in administration have lost the optimistic belief of the early writers that the conquest by science will be simple and rapid. A wealth of careful observation and analysis of the administrative process has meanwhile convinced all students of administration that many of the beliefs of the early writers concerning the separation of politics and administration were unrealistic or erroneous.

The selections in this chapter have been chosen to illustrate some of the recent and contemporary thinking about efficiency and related ideas. The first selection, "The Criterion of Efficiency," is from one of the most important and influential books on administration published in recent years, Professor Herbert A. Simon's *Administrative Behavior; A Study of Decision-making Processes in Administrative Organization.*

Administrative Behavior might be characterized as a restatement of the "classical tradition" in public administration. For Professor Simon presents in modern dress many of the essential notions concerning efficiency, science, and the separation of politics and administration enunciated earlier by such eminent men as Woodrow Wilson, Frank Goodnow, Charles A. Beard, and F. W. Willoughby. Professor Simon's writings on administrative theory, both critical and constructive, are distinguished by careful, logical— even mathematical—argument from clearly delineated philosophical premises. He has refined the "classical tradition" by the elimination of errors and inconsistencies which had weakened it, and he has pushed forward the logical development of its essential ideas. For example, he recognizes as error what many early students maintained: that policy making or politics can be separated from execution or administration in the sense that each is performed, or would be performed in a properly constructed government, by separate organs of government. But he argues cogently that there is nevertheless a clear-cut distinction between questions of value and questions of fact, though both types of judgments are made by each of the branches or organs of government. Questions of value are not subject to scientific determination. In the field of cooperative human endeavor, factual judgments relating to the efficiency of means to ends constitute the area of administrative science.

The selection which follows—approximately half of his chapter on "The Criterion of Efficiency"—should be viewed in such a perspective. It must be read carefully, for there are many ideas in small compass. In addition to a defense of his idea of efficiency as the "common denominator of value" there is an explanation of the relationship of efficiency to economy, as measured in money. There is also a review of some of the recently expressed criticisms of efficiency as a goal or basis for administrative

THE CRITERION OF EFFICIENCY

decision making, and an attempt to show the invalidity of these criticisms against a proper conception of efficiency.

Query, is the "criterion of efficiency" valid? Can it be applied to real administrative problems—or is it merely an interesting piece of abstract logical analysis? Can a choice between alternative means, assuming they involve the same cost or "application of resources," be made without entering the realm of "values"? What are the implications of Professor Simon's statement that though the criterion of efficiency supplies a common denominator for the comparison of administrative alternatives, it "does not supply a common enumerator"?

The Criterion of Efficiency *

HERBERT A. SIMON

The criterion of efficiency is most easily understood in its application to commercial organizations that are largely guided by the profit objective. In such organizations the criterion of efficiency dictates the selection of that alternative, of all those available to the individual, which will yield the greatest net (money) return to the organization. This "balance sheet" efficiency involves, on the one hand, the maximization of income, if costs are considered as fixed; and on the other hand, the minimization of costs, if income is considered as fixed. In practice, of course, the maximization of income and the minimization of cost must be considered simultaneously—that is, what is really to be maximized is the difference between these two. . . .

The simplicity of the efficiency criterion in commercial organizations is due in large part to the fact that money provides a common denominator for the measurement of both output and income, and permits them to be directly compared. The concept must be broadened, therefore, if it is to be applicable to the process of decision where factors are involved that are not directly measurable in monetary terms. Such factors will certainly be present in noncommercial organizations where monetary measurement of output is usually meaningless or impossible. They will also be present in commercial organizations to the extent that those controlling the organizations are not solely directed toward the profit motive—*i.e.* where they are concerned with questions of the public interest or employee welfare even when those factors are not directly related to the profit-and-loss statement. Moreover, nonmonetary factors will also be involved in the

* From *Administrative Behavior; A Study of Decision-making Processes in Administrative Organization* (New York: 1947). This selection is an abridgment of Chap. IX. Copyright, 1947, by The Macmillan Company, Publishers, and used with the permission of The Macmillan Company.

internal operation even of purely commercial organizations where specific activities are concerned whose relation to the profit-and-loss statement cannot be assessed directly. For example, decisions in a personnel department cannot always be evaluated in monetary terms, because the monetary effect of a particular personnel policy cannot be directly determined.

The Cost Element in Decision. In both commercial and noncommercial organizations (except for volunteer organizations) the "input" factor can be largely measured in money terms. This is true even when the organization objectives are broader than either profit or conservation of the organization. That is, even if the organization is concerned with the cost *for the community*, this cost can be fairly valued in terms of the goods and services that the organization buys.

This point may not be entirely evident in the case of the evaluation of the services of employees. The tasks to which employees are assigned are not all equal with respect to agreeableness, hazard, and the like; and, to the extent that they are not, the money wage (unless this accurately reflects these elements—which it usually does not) is not an accurate measure of input in an organization where employee welfare takes its place among the organization objectives. In such cases, organization decisions must balance not only money input against output, but money input against output *and* employee welfare.

There are other cases, too, where input is not accurately measured by money cost to the organization. An industrial concern, for example, which is not penalized for the smoke and soot it distributes over the community has a cost factor, provided the organization objectives include concern for community welfare, that does not appear in the accounts.

When the decision is being made for a public agency that embraces among its objectives the general stability and prosperity of the economy—the Federal government, for example—still other considerations must enter in. In the case of a private business, interest on invested capital, at the market rate, must be included in calculations as a cost. In the case of government, if the effect of spending is to employ investment capital that would otherwise be idle, the interest on this capital is not really a cost from the standpoint of the economy as a whole. Moreover, the "output" of government investment may include effects of this investment on the level of income and employment in the economy, and these effects must be included in the measurement of product.

Likewise, when a private business employs an unemployed person his wage is an ordinary cost; while when the government employs such a person it makes use of a resource that would otherwise not be utilized, and hence the wages of those employed do not involve any real cost from the standpoint of the community.

These comments are not intended to defend any particular concept of the role of government spending in a modern economy—a subject that evokes sufficient controversy among the various competing schools of modern economists—but merely to point out that the criterion of efficiency cannot be applied to decisions in governmental agencies without consideration of the economic effects that the activities of these agencies may have. In the language of the economist, the problem of efficiency in the public agency must be approached from the standpoint of the general, rather than the partial, equilibrium.

Positive Values in Decision. While the negative values involved in decision can usually be summarized in terms of time or money costs, the positive values present a somewhat more complex picture. As we have seen, in a commercial enterprise, money value of output plays somewhat the same role as cost of production (input) in summarizing the value element involved. From a positive standpoint the kind of product manufactured is a valuationally neutral element. Not so in the case of public services. Hence, some substitute must be found in public administration for money value of output as a measure of value.

This substitute is provided by a statement of the objectives of the activity, and by the construction of indices that measure the degree of attainment of these objectives. Any measurement that indicates the effect of an administrative activity in accomplishing its final objective is termed a measurement of the *result* of that activity.

DEFINITION OF OBJECTIVES. The definition of objectives for public services is far from a simple task. In the first place, it is desirable to state the objectives so far as possible in terms of values. That is, only if they are expressions of relatively final ends are they suitable value-indices. When objectives are stated in terms of intermediate goals, there is a serious danger that decisions governed by the intermediate ends will continue to persist even when that end is no longer appropriate to the realization of value. The proliferation of forms and records in an administrative agency, for instance, frequently evidences a failure to reconsider activities which are aimed at some concrete end in terms of the broader values which that end is supposed to further.

On the other hand, however, the values which public services seek to realize are seldom expressible in concrete terms. Aims, such as those of a recreation department—to "improve health," "provide recreation," "develop good citizens"—must be stated in tangible and objective terms before results can be observed and measured. A serious dilemma is posed here. The values toward which these services should be directed do not provide sufficiently concrete criteria to be applied to specific decisional problems. However, if value-indices are employed as criteria in lieu of the values themselves, the "ends" are likely to be sacrificed for the more tangible means—the substance for the form.

Further difficulty arises in the lack of a common denominator of value. An activity may realize two or more values, as in the case of the recreation department mentioned above. What is the relative importance of the various values in guiding the department's activities? The health department provides an illustration of the same problem. Shall the department next year redistribute its funds to decrease infant mortality or to increase the facilities of the venereal disease clinic? Observations of results, measured in terms of value-indices, can merely tell the extent to which the several objectives are realized if one or the other course of action is taken. Unless both activities are directed toward exactly the same value, measurement of results cannot tell which course of action is preferable. Rationality can be applied in administrative decisions only after the relative weights of conflicting values have been fixed. . . .

ACCOMPLISHMENT A MATTER OF DEGREE. Defining objectives does not exhaust the value element in an administrative decision. It is necessary to determine, in addition, the degree to which the objective is to be attained. A city charter or ordinance may define the function of the fire department as "protecting the city from damage due to fire"; but this does not imply that the city will wish to expand the fire-fighting facilities to the point where fire damage is entirely eliminated—an obviously impossible task. Moreover, it begs the question to say that the fire department should reduce losses "as far as possible," for how far it is possible to reduce losses depends on the amount of money available for fire protection and fire prevention services.

Value questions are not eliminated from the fire protection problem of that city until it has been determined that (1) the fire department should aim to limit fire losses to x dollars per capita, and (2) the city council will appropriate y dollars which, it is anticipated on the basis of available information, will permit (1) to be carried out. Values are involved, then, not only in the definition of objectives, but in the determination as well of the level of adequacy of services which is to be aimed at. Attainment of objectives is *always* a matter of degree.

The processes of "policy determination," as they take place in our governmental institutions, seldom cope with these questions of degree in determining the objectives of governmental services. It will be urged in later sections of this chapter that extension of policy determination to such questions is of fundamental importance for the maintenance of democratic control over the value elements in decision. It will be shown that a large measure of this procedural reform can be attained by a modification and extension of budgetary techniques.

DISTRIBUTIVE VALUES. Thus far, the discussion has centered on values which are "aggregates." That is, the community measures its fire loss in terms of total dollars of destruction during the year. It does not distinguish the loss of $1,000 in Smith's store from a loss of $1,000 in Jones' store. The police department, in attempting to reduce the number of robberies, does not give a robbery on Third Street a different weight from a similar robbery on Fourth Street.

Nevertheless, questions of "distributive" value enter into almost every administrative decision—if in no other way than in an assumption of "equal weight" like those cited above. A playground built on the West Side will not serve children on the East Side. If chess classes are offered at the social center, there may be no facilities available for persons interested in social dancing.

Many distributive questions are geographical, but they may involve social, economic, or innumerable other "class" distinctions. The importance of such considerations in administration can be appreciated when it is recognized that agencies for assessment administration, administrative tribunals, and even welfare agencies are concerned primarily with questions of distributive rather than aggregate value. . . .

Distributive questions are also of great importance when the work of an organization is specialized by "area" or by "clientele." In these cases, the objective of the organizational unit is immediately restricted to a particular set of persons, and interjurisdictional problems of the greatest consequence may arise.

A Common Denominator for Value—the Criterion of Efficiency. A fundamental problem involved in reaching a decision is the discovery of a common denominator between the two values which have been mentioned: low cost and large results. How is the choice made when the two conflict? Four relations are conceivable between choices *A* and *B*. If I_A is the input for *A*, and I_B for *B*, and O_A and O_B are the respective outputs, then these four possible relations may be expressed as follows:

1. I_A is less than I_B, and O_A is greater than O_B.
2. I_B is less than I_A, and O_B is greater than O_A.
3. I_A is less than I_B, and O_A is less than O_B.
4. I_B is less than I_A, and O_B is less than O_A.

In cases 1 and 2 the choice is unequivocal; but not so in cases 3 and 4. That is, when possibility *A* involves a larger cost than possibility *B*, but produces a smaller result, *B* obviously is preferable. But when possibility A involves a lower cost as well as a smaller result than B, cost must be weighed against result before a choice can be made.

The path to the solution of this difficulty has already been indicated. Underlying all administrative decisions is a limitation—a "scarcity"—of available resources. This is the fundamental reason why time and money are costs. Because they are limited in quantity, their application to one administrative purpose prevents the realization of alternative possibilities. Hence, the administrative choice among possibilities can always be framed as a choice among alternatives involving the same cost, but different positive values.

An administrative choice is incorrectly posed, then, when it is posed as a choice between possibility *A*, with low costs and small results, and possibility *B*, with high costs and large results. For *A* should be substituted a third possibility *C*, which would include *A* *plus* the alternative activities made possible by the cost difference between *A* and *B*. If this is done, the choice resolves itself into a comparison of the results obtainable by the application of fixed resources to the alternative activities *B* and *C*. The efficiency of a behavior is the ratio of the results obtainable from that behavior to the maximum of results obtainable from the behaviors which are alternative to the given behavior.

The criterion of efficiency dictates that choice of alternatives which produces the largest result for the given application of resources.

It should be noted that this criterion, while it supplies a common denominator for the comparison of administrative alternatives, does not supply a common numerator. Even though all decisions be made in terms of alternative applications of the same resources, the problem still remains of comparing the values which are attained by the different courses of action. The efficiency criterion neither solves nor avoids this problem of comparability.

Note on the Term "Efficiency." The term "efficiency" has acquired during the past generation a number of unfortunate connotations which associate it with a mechanistic, profit-directed, stop-watch theory of administration. This is the result of the somewhat careless use of the term by overenthusiastic proponents of the "scientific management" movement. Nevertheless, no other term in the language comes so close as "efficiency" to representing the concept described in this chapter. The term has therefore been employed, with the hope that the reader will understand the criterion in the sense in which it has just been defined, and will be able to dissociate from it any unfortunate connotations it may have had in his mind.

Until practically the end of the nineteenth century, the terms "efficiency" and "effectiveness" were considered almost as synonymous. The Oxford Dictionary defines "efficiency": "Fitness or power to accomplish, or success in accomplishing, the purpose intended; adequate power, effectiveness, efficacy."

In recent years, however, "efficiency" has acquired a second meaning: the ratio between input and output. In the words of the *Encyclopaedia of the Social Sciences:*

"Efficiency in the sense of a ratio between input and output, effort and results, expenditure and income, cost and the resulting pleasure, is a relatively recent term. In this specific sense it became current in engineering only during the latter half of the nineteenth century and in business and in economics only since the beginning of the twentieth."

The use of the term by leaders of the scientific management movement added still a third meaning. Again quoting from the *Encyclopaedia of the Social Sciences:*

"The foundations of modern scientific management may be dated from F. W. Taylor's paper, *A Piece Rate System*, in which he described his pioneer method of establishing standards of job performance at the Midvale steel plant. When such standards were set, it became customary to refer to the ratio of actual performance to the standard performance as the efficiency of labor, a use somewhat different from that of the mechanical engineers, who apply the term to the ratio of actual output to an actual input."

Harrington Emerson, another pioneer in the scientific management movement, and one who preferred the term "efficiency engineering," is reported to have defined efficiency as "the relation between what is accomplished and what might be accomplished." In this connection, he speaks of the "efficiency percent of the employee."

It must be noted that there is a difference in computing an output-input ratio in the physical and in the social sciences. For the engineer, both output and input are measured in terms of energy. The law of conservation of energy tells him that the output of useful energy cannot exceed the input. In the social sciences, output and input are seldom measured in comparable units; and even when they are, as in a comparison of cost of fire protection with dollar losses from fire, there is no "law of conservation of energy" which prevents the output from exceeding the input. Hence, the concept of perfect efficiency, if it is used at all, must be redefined. As a matter of fact, the concept of perfect efficiency will not be required in the present study. Actual problems, as they present themselves to the administrator, are always concerned with *relative* efficiencies, and no measure of *absolute* efficiency is ever needed. Moreover, the theory does not require a numerical measure of efficiency, but merely a comparison of *greater* or *less* between the efficiencies of two alternative possibilities. Under these circumstances, the definitions of efficiency as ratio of output to input and as ratio of the actual to the maximum possible amount to the same thing. . . .

Criticisms of the Efficiency Criterion

Criticisms of "efficiency" as a guide to administration have been frequent and vociferous. One group of criticisms need not concern us here, for they refer to definitions of the term different from the one proposed here. In this category must be placed attacks on efficiency which equate the term with "economy" or "expenditure reduction." As we have used "efficiency," there is no implication whatsoever that a small expenditure—or, for that matter, a large expenditure—is *per se* desirable. It has been asserted only that if two results can be obtained with the same expenditure the greater result is to be preferred. Two expenditures of different magnitude can, in general, be compared only if they are translated into opportunity costs, that is, if they are expressed in terms of alternative results.

"Mechanical" Efficiency. Others have objected to "efficiency" on the ground that it leads to a "mechanical" conception of administration. This objection, too, must result from the use of the term in quite a different sense from that proposed here. For a mere criterion of preference among possibilities does not in any manner limit the administrative techniques which may be employed in attaining the possibilities, nor, as we see in the next section, does it in any way reduce the role of the administrator's judgment in reaching decisions. Furthermore, the efficiency criterion is in the most complete accord with a viewpoint that places the social consequences of administration in the forefront of its determining influences.

"The Ends Justify the Means." Two other lines of criticism assert that the criterion of efficiency leads to an incorrect relationship between "means" and "ends." On the one hand it is alleged that, in the interests of efficiency, ends are taken to justify any appropriate means. As we have noted . . . the terms "means" and "ends" must be employed carefully in order to avoid contradictions; and for this reason we have preferred to talk of the value and factual aspects of

alternatives. Suffice it to say that if the evaluation of the results of administrative activity takes into account *all* the significant value elements of the administrative alternatives, no undue subordination of "means" to "ends" can result.

"Ruthless" Efficiency. On the other hand, it is charged that efficiency directs all attention to the means, and neglects the ends. This charge has already been answered in pointing out the integral role which valuation plays in the employment of a criterion of efficiency. It may be freely admitted that efficiency, as a scientific problem, is concerned chiefly with "means," and that "efficient" service may be efficient with respect to any of a wide variety of ends. But merely to recognize that the process of valuation lies outside the scope of science, and that the adaptation of means to ends is the only element of the decisional problem that has a factual solution, is not to admit any indifference to the ends which efficiency serves. Efficiency, whether it be in the democratic state or in the totalitarian, is the proper criterion to be applied to the factual element in the decisional problem. Other, ethical, criteria must be applied to the problem of valuation.

Common to all these criticisms is an implication that an "efficiency" approach involves a complete separation of "means" and "ends." We have already seen that, strictly speaking, this is not the case—that the only valid distinction is one between ethical and factual elements in decision. Yet, in the actual application of the efficiency criterion to administrative situations, there is often a tendency to substitute the former distinction for the latter, and such a substitution inevitably results in the narrower, "mechanical" efficiency which has been the subject of criticism.

How this substitution comes about may be briefly explained. The ethical element in decision consists in a recognition and appraisal of all the value elements inhering in the alternative possibilities. The principal values involved are usually expressed as "results" of the administrative activity, and, as we have seen, the activity itself is usually considered as valuationally neutral. This leads to the isolation of two values: (1) the positive values expressed as "results," and (2) the negative values, or opportunity costs, expressed in terms of time or money cost.

In fact, to consider the administrative activity itself as valuationally neutral is an abstraction from reality which is permissible within broad limits but which, if carried to extremes, ignores very important human values. These values may comprehend the remuneration and working conditions (using these terms broadly) of the members of the group which carries out the activity.

We may enumerate some of these value elements more explicitly:

1. If cost is measured in money terms, then the wages of employees cannot be considered as a valuationally neutral element, but must be included among the values to be appraised in the decision.

2. The work pace of workers cannot be considered as a valuationally neutral element—else we would be led to the conclusion that a "speed-up" would always be eminently desirable.

3. The social aspects of the work situation cannot be considered as a valuation-ally neutral element. The decision must weigh the social and psychological consequences of substituting one type of work situation for another.

4. Wage policies, promotional policies, and the like need to be considered not only from the viewpoint of incentives and result-efficiency, but also from that of distributive justice to the members of the group.

It must be emphasized, then, that when a choice between alternatives involves any valuationally significant difference in the work activity this difference must be included among the values to be weighed in reaching a decision.

Valuational Bias. A closely related fallacy in the application of the efficiency criterion is to include in the evaluation of alternatives only those values which have been previously selected as the *objective* of the particular administrative activity under consideration. The effects of some administrative activities are confined to a rather limited area, and indirect results do not then cause much difficulty. The activities of the fire department usually have an effect on fire losses (unless ardent fire fans form a large part of the community). Hence the fire chief does not have to take recreation values into consideration in reaching his decisions. It is very fortunate that the consequences of human activities are so strictly segregated; if they were not, the problem of reaching rational decisions would be impossible. But the mere fact that activities do not *usually* have valuationally significant indirect effects does not justify us in ignoring such effects if they are, *in fact*, present. That is, the fire chief cannot, merely because he is a fire chief, ignore the possibility of accidents in determining the speed at which his equipment should respond to alarms.

This all seems commonplace, yet . . . in actuality, administrators in reaching decisions commonly disclaim responsibility for the indirect results of administrative activities. To this point of view we oppose the contrary opinion that the administrator, serving a public agency in a democratic state, must give a proper weight to *all* community values that are relevant to his activity, and that are reasonably ascertainable in relation thereto, and cannot restrict himself to values that happen to be his particular responsibility. Only under these conditions can a criterion of efficiency be validly postulated as a determinant of action. . . .

Factual Elements in Decision

We have seen that the criterion which the administrator applies to factual problems is one of efficiency. The resources, the input, at the disposal of the administrator are strictly limited. It is not his function to establish a utopia. It is his function to maximize the attainment of the governmental objectives (assuming they have been agreed upon), by the efficient employment of the limited resources that are available to him. A "good" public library, from the administrative standpoint, is not one that owns all the books that have ever been published, but one that has used the limited funds which are allowed it to build up as good a collection as possible under the circumstances.

When a decision is made in terms of the criterion of efficiency, it is necessary to have empirical knowledge of the results that will be associated with each alternative possibility. Let us consider a specific municipal function, the fire department. Its objective is the reduction of the total fire loss, and results will be measured in terms of this loss.

The extent of the fire loss will be determined by a large number of factors. Among these are natural factors (frequently of high winds, heavy snowfall, severe cold weather, hot dry weather, tornadoes, hurricanes and cyclones, earthquakes, and floods), structural and occupancy factors (exposure hazards, physical barriers, density of structures, type of building construction, roof construction, contents, and risk of occupancy), the moral hazard (carelessness and incendiarism), and finally the effectiveness of the fire department itself. The fire chief must know how the activities of his department affect the loss if he is to make intelligent decisions.

How does the fire department perform its task? It inspects buildings to eliminate fire hazards, it carries on campaigns of education against carelessness, it fights fires, it trains firemen, it investigates and prosecutes incendiaries.

But we can carry the analysis a step farther. Of what does fire-fighting consist? A piece of apparatus must be brought to the scene of action, hose laid, water pumped and directed upon the flames, ladders raised, and covers spread over goods to reduce water damage. Again, each of these activities can be analyzed into its component parts. What does laying a hose involve? The hose must be acquired and maintained. Firemen must be recruited and trained. The firemen must spend a certain amount of time and energy in laying the hose.

A final level of analysis is reached by determining the cost of each of these elements of the task. Thus, the whole process of fire-fighting can be translated into a set of entries in the city's books of accounts.

The problem of efficiency is to determine, at any one of these levels of analysis, the cost of any particular element of performance, and the contribution which that element of performance makes to the accomplishment of the department's objectives. When these costs and contributions are known, the elements of performance can be combined in such a way as to achieve a maximum reduction in fire loss.

There are at least four rather distinct levels at which the analysis of the administrative situation may be carried out. At the highest level is the measurement of results, of the accomplishment of agency objectives. Contributing to these results are the elements of administrative performance. Subordinate to these, in turn, is input measured in terms of effort. Effort, finally, may be analyzed in terms of money cost.

The mathematically minded will see in this structure a set of equations— strictly identical with the economist's "production functions." The first equation expresses the results of government as a function of the performance of certain activities. Further equations express these performance units as functions of less immediate performance units, the latter in terms of units of effort; and finally effort is expressed as a function of expenditures. The problem of efficiency is to find the maximum of a production function, with the constraint that total expenditure is fixed.

———◆———

The theme of the closing paragraphs above—that efficiency can be analyzed or measured at different "levels"—is enlarged upon in the following selection. This idea of different types of efficiency achieved and measured by different methods is one of the important aspects of contemporary thinking about efficiency.

The following selection is but an excerpt from an essay on "Institutionalizing Administrative Controls," by the late Professor Harvey Pinney. That Professor Pinney felt obliged to devote several pages to an analysis of efficiency in an essay on administrative controls illustrates the centrality of the concept of efficiency in the study of public administration: the significance of administrative controls is deemed to lie in their contribution to efficiency, and they are judged good or bad, desirable or undesirable, according to their presumed contribution to efficiency.

The current disposition to think of efficiency as differing at different levels undoubtedly represents an increasing subtlety in the analysis and sophistication in the use of the concept. The question which must now be asked is whether at the "higher levels" it is really a valid or useful concept. For example, the expression "social efficiency" has often occurred in recent writings, to indicate that administration must be measured not according to narrow monetary or mathematical standards, but in broad human terms. Query, does this represent the transference of an idea from mechanics (and perhaps economics) where it is valid or useful, to a realm in which it is at best distorted or diluted, at worst wholly inappropriate?

In the following selection note especially the use of the phrase "social accounting" and "subjective criteria." Is social accounting a meaningful notion? Can efficiency be measured by subjective criteria?

Levels of Measurement of Efficiency *

HARVEY PINNEY

The efficiency of a governmental administrative unit is a problem in social accounting—a complex of many factors. It is a mixture of objective and subjective criteria. The objective standards should be approached first.

When the units of energy input are identical and infinitely divisible, and when the units of output are likewise, it is possible to get an objective statement of efficiency. This is true of the material and energy factors in the production and distribution of electric power. Similar evaluations can be made for various types of engines. On a comparative basis, it is possible to approach measuring human energy inputs and the product thereof in the same way. In a given operation, a man-hour of energy input should produce a certain quantum of output. Obviously, the nearer the total operation approaches that of a machine, the more accurate such measurements become. Thus there are large numbers of operations for which standards of efficiency can be constructed. Where the product of a total unit is a physical quantum—steel ingots, automobiles, baby carriages, or what not—efficiencies of individual operations underlie the efficiency of the plant, although they alone do not make it.

In this objective sense, organization is a machine. Improved organization is as much technological advance as is improved machinery. The mass production industries have struggled constantly for better integration, more continuous flow of processes, reduction in number of operations, shortening the distances of material movements, and so on. Wherever operations become standardized, it is possible to arrive at standardized units of organization for the performance of such operations—units of organization that, other things being equal, are the most efficient possible for the performance of these particular operations. The larger the number of distinctly diverse operations to be integrated into a unified total process, the more difficult, obviously, is the objective determination of over-all efficiency.

From this objective engineering level we may rise to the next—that of economics. Here, to a fair degree, objective judgment may prevail (within the price system), but the element of the subjective becomes more pronounced. It may be scientifically possible to construct an internal combustion engine of a certain maximum degree of efficiency, but the cost may be out of proportion to the results in terms of money income produced. It might cost two to three times as much to have an engine fifty per cent efficient in fuel consumption as to have it thirty-five per cent. This is the eternal problem of the business man: What

* Excerpted from "Institutionalizing Administrative Controls," *American Political Science Review*, Vol. 38 (February, 1944), pp. 79–88. Reprinted by permission of the *American Political Science Review*.

quality of material should go into his product? What combination of raw material costs will net the largest profit? What quality of machinery is most economical (not necessarily most productive in physical terms) for him? In so far as units of materials are standardized in both quality and price, and machines likewise, the entrepreneur can reach fairly objective judgments (assuming market stability).

So also he can reach rough approximations of labor costs in terms of ultimate profits. That is, assuming that the entrepreneur is strictly rational in the matter (which he rarely is), he can estimate on a cost basis the quantities, kinds, and conditions of labor which will net him the largest return within the period in view. The organization of men, equipment, and materials into a productive process faces the same problem: Is the most productive (physically) organization also the most economic in terms of the given conditions? The perfection of organization may have to stop short of its goal because of deficiencies in materials, personnel, or capital—short even of the ideally most economic organization. The business man must make these judgments in terms of his own interest. He is all too frequently handicapped on the side of organization by not having standardized forms suitable to his operations, or the personnel to apply such forms.

The efficiency of the business organization has certain over-all checks (as well as those of analysis of specific operations). Profit is the central criterion, but profit is only a function of sales income in relation to costs. If profits fall, the business man has certain definite checks: volume of sales (considering prices) ; inspection of advertising and sales operations; return of defective articles and other complaints about his product; costs of raw materials; costs of various operations in the productive process. He may, of course, discover that the difficulty lies with factors external to his management of his business. Nevertheless, the price system offers him certain fairly objectively checks on the efficiency of his operations in terms of profit economy.

The third level does not leave entirely the area of objective judgment, but it emphasizes subjective and imponderable factors. Whether or not consumers are satisfied with commodities depends on a number of factors, chief of which is the availability of alternative choices of which the consumer is aware. Under such circumstances, the business man has an objective negative factor revealing consumer dissatisfaction—falling sales. In fields where fashion, styling, and branding play an important part, it may give the business man no end of headaches trying to find wherein he is failing to please. When the business man himself leaves the rational foundations of strictly economic competition and indulges in power politics, in attempts to monopolize a market, in efforts to wreck a competitor or a labor union, the criteria of efficiency are reduced to elements in his personal satisfaction. He may, on occasion, sacrifice millions to get control of some other company or put it out of business. Efficiency may lie in legal manipulation or financial legerdemain rather than in productivity.

In monopoloid situations where prices and production are to some degree matters of administrative policy as contrasted with matters of market determination, other difficulties enter in. The complexities of accounting involved in joint costs in large-scale operations face the monopolizer with extremely difficult problems of determining efficiency. He must rely on consciously contrived administrative devices. This does not mean that prices cease to play an important part; monopoly price may be, economically, a highly rational device in terms of profit-making. But it may also be highly complex, as an examination of the relations between A. T. & T. and Western Electric has shown.

In short, the monopolist is frequently in the position where he is not obliged to keep his costs down; and when the relentless pressure of open competition is removed, costs tend to rise through the accumulation of inefficiencies, rigidities, lags in adaptation. Under such circumstances, the maintenance of a high degree of productive efficiency depends on devising supervisory mechanisms which constantly check unit and over-all productivities. Such supervisory devices may be standardized for stable operations and regularized through periodic reports, inspections, conferences. Administrative pressure for technological improvement (mechanical and organizational) can be, and has been, institutionalized in research divisions and staff agencies, so that a monopoly or monopoloid business is not necessarily a stagnant one. Organized initiative capitalizing on co-ordinated skills may be substituted for sporadic individual initiative.

In a unit of public administration, or the administration as a whole, this third level of efficiency is complicated by the fact that there frequently is not even the profit check available to the monopoly. The efficiency of educational, library, police, health, and many other administrative units cannot be measured in either engineering or economic (price) terms. Consideration must always be given to public satisfaction, to somewhat imponderable statistics (crime control), to intangibles such as educational achievements. The "service" character of public administration, combined with security of tenure in civil service and the large portion of the public actually present in public personnel, makes the evaluation of an administrative unit consider the effects of its functioning upon its personnel and the consequent relations of that personnel to the outside public. Social accounting in public administration is achievement accounting with due regard for engineering efficiency, cost economy, and the intangibles of human satisfactions and dissatisfactions.

To organize an administrative unit for efficient achievement in terms of social accounting involves a series of steps (in planning and thinking) proceeding from the objective to the more subjective levels. The over-all organization is naturally governed by the character of the function which the unit is to perform. That function having been defined, an analysis of the machinery necessary to perform it can be made. Unless the function involves a large proportion of the novel, it will be possible to select large areas of operations in which there are standardized, efficient procedures. The organization of office units, filing units, accounting, budgeting, personnel, and a substantial number of other operations will involve primarily the adaptation of already proved procedures. Standards for evaluating the efficiency of these specific operations will be both engineering and economic, tempered by the established and discovered factors for maintaining morale which affects over-all efficiency.

The organization of specific operations on a basis of efficient unit productivity must be followed by the organization or the integration of all operations into a going concern efficiency. The problems in this area are manifold, and proved techniques to use on them are fewer. They involve ordering the flow of materials, information, ideas; the determination of the size of units appropriate to supervisory levels; the grouping of units for overhead supervision; the determination of appropriate horizontal relations between units; the allocation of power and authority to centers of decisions; and many other problems. The fact that this is an area of complex and difficult problems does not mean that the instrument of objective analysis cannot be used. Analyses of the flow of processes with a view to reducing waste motion; analyses of time spent in specific operations (including supervisory), and the relation of time to quantity and importance of accomplishment; analyses of personal fatigue at bottleneck positions; and other analyses of objective character can aid in the evaluation of efficiency and in improving procedures.

These internal analyses involve the study and evaluation of end operations (delivery of mail, apprehension of violators, prevention of violations, achievement of graduates, circulation of books, elimination of disease, and so on, in terms of work unit efficiencies) ; the examination and testing of the adequacy and economy of auxiliary services (budget, purchasing and supply, accounting and audit, personnel) ; the measuring of the effectiveness of staff operations (supervision, co-ordination, planning, research). These internal evaluations must then be placed in the light of over-all achievements and over-all costs. Substantively, what has the unit accomplished and with what public benefits? What have been the costs—in money, in personnel, in public dissatisfaction or resistance? A new organization will be built up with these considerations in mind; a going concern will be interested in devising means for making such evaluations.

It is obvious, of course, that the assumption of stable operations must be highly qualified. Conditions external to the administrative unit are constantly changing; new tasks are laid upon it, old ones taken away; technological advance in equipment and organization is constantly taking place; the unit itself is constantly learning more about itself and its functions. Stability of function is therefore a matter of degree. The administrative institution is a dynamic organism which must give much conscious attention to the preservation of its youth—that is, to its capacity for adaptation.

There therefore appear two problems in the institutionalizing of controls relevant to the application of social accounting. One is the devising of techniques for the preservation of the efficiency of unit operations and their co-ordination into an efficient going concern; the other is the devising of techniques for constantly improving the efficiency of unit operations and of over-all social achievement.

———◆———

The following selection illustrates a current tendency of many administrative students to emphasize the "relativity" of efficiency—to insist that there has been much hasty and unproved generalization about efficiency which we need to reexamine. The author, Paul Appleby, now Dean of the Maxwell School of Citizenship and Public Affairs, was introduced earlier in the book.

Much of the essay concerns the relative efficiencies of private and public enterprises, and the thesis is developed that there is "no absolute, universal, and intrinsic difference" in degree of efficiency between the two, but rather that they are not wholly comparable entities. Quite apart from the truth or falsity of the thesis, it is important that this attitude is now assumed by leading students of administration—of private administration as well as public. For one of the prominent features of the public administration movement a generation ago was an ardent conviction that business is more efficient than government and that governmental efficiency can be increased by the adoption of forms of organization, methods, and procedures successful in business. Dean Appleby has been prominent among those who insist that government must be measured, not by standards of monetary profit or mechanical efficiency, but according to its ability to meet "political" tests of responsiveness and acceptability to the people.

Query, is this a correct viewpoint? Is the proposition that "there is no objective test for broad efficiency except survival" true?

The Relativity of Efficiency *

PAUL H. APPLEBY

One of the rights of American citizenship most frequently exercised is that of criticizing the inefficiency of government, but it is difficult to find many references to the lack of governmental efficiency that reflect genuine thoughtfulness. Almost no one, however, indulges in similar glib generalizations about the efficiency of other institutions or organizations. Few persons attempt to judge, for example,

* Reprinted from BIG DEMOCRACY by Paul H. Appleby, by permission of Alfred A. Knopf, Inc. Copyright 1945 by Paul H. Appleby.

the general efficiency of Bethlehem Steel or of General Motors. Most of us need to develop a corresponding restraint in evaluating the efficiency of government. It is dangerous to be dogmatic about efficiency of administration in any field, public or private, big or little. Who would venture to assert that the printing plant producing the *New York Times* every day is more or less efficient than the plant producing the *Saturday Evening Post* every week? Presumably the *Times* plant is the most efficient plant known for producing the *New York Times*. Presumably the *Post* is the most efficient one known for producing the *Saturday Evening Post*. The question is: what objectives is the organization trying to accomplish? What means are available to obtain the desired end? In short, what are the criteria?

Evaluation of Efficiency

Fashion merchandise does not lend itself to assembly-line production. Small shops can spring into action and serve a market for such goods before a big one can even get organized. Clearly an item chiefly dependent on some rare manual craftsmanship can be most efficiently produced in a small shop. Nor are these the only advantages that go with smallness in size. The owner of a printing plant doing a million-dollar business once told me that any printing job amounting to less than a hundred dollars costs him money because it costs that much merely to get a job going in his establishment. Yet certainly there are hundreds of small plants which can earn a profit even from five-dollar jobs.

Some years ago an industrialist described to me the difference in efficiency in two plants he operated, both manufacturing similar products. One had been in production only three years. It employed three hundred persons. The other had been in operation for thirty years and employed thousands. Yet similarity in their functions offered a basis for computing comparative efficiency. What he had found was that the new plant was not nearly so efficient as the old one; it was, as he said, too new to be highly efficient. It is my observation that this factor of age is equally important in government. From the standpoint of operations per se, a new governmental agency simply cannot be expected to be as efficient as an old one. New organizations, whether in or out of government, are likely to be more efficient in terms of "drive," imagination, and bold policies, but they are almost necessarily less efficient than older ones in effectuating their purposes. Obviously any big and complex new unit with a big and complex new function will be less efficient in its operations than a new unit with a small and simple function. But it is also a safe assumption that small new agencies will ordinarily be less efficient than big ones that are older.

These considerations illustrate the futility of most references to governmental inefficiency as contrasted with the efficiency of private industry. Patently the government is more efficient as a political agency than is private industry. Even with all its modern interest in public relations and its growing appreciation of personnel administration, industry does not have to be nearly so political as government. And surely government is more efficient at providing minimum educational advantage, organizing road systems, and many other things including coining, issuing, and regulating the value of money. Some of these functions are of the essence of government and are so completely accepted as such that there is today no argument whatsoever as to the propriety of these things being handled by government. Yet it was not always so and the fact that it was not should help us appreciate that the real question with regard to new uses of government is simply this: has the function involved come to have a sufficient public-interest character to be in the field of what must be handled governmentally? There is no clear limiting principle for governmental action in a democracy. The range of public power and activity will and should differ at different times in history.

Efficiency Is Relative

There is no absolute, universal, and intrinsic difference in efficiency as between public and private management or between big and little business that may serve as a safe guide in determining, on that basis, whether or not any particular function should be entrusted to government. But there are other objectives and considerations according to which governmental management of that particular function will be adjudged by the people to be more or less *desirable* than continued private management. These other objectives and considerations change from time to time and they are certain to change in the future as they have in the past. These things are the vitally important factors; they count for more in the scales of democracy than the relative efficiency of government—though this too is important—in the performance of a function that could conceivably have been left in private hands.

Even if one should believe that government is more efficient than other forms of enterprise, there are other values than the values of efficiency about which one should be concerned. Our descendants may espouse socialism in some form or other; whatever they do, it can be set down with certainty that they will insist that their society shall foster and protect in new and special ways values more imporant than mere efficiency. Man never will live by bread alone. The argument, however, should be made on the points of our real concern. Are there new and better ways of maintaining old values we know to be good? If so, let them be developed, considered, and adopted. This is the hope of gradualism, as contrasted with revolution.

Against this background, however, there are many things that could be said about specific aspects of the relative efficiency of government and business. Is there, for instance, more or less nepotism in business than in government? Are appointments in the one field more a reflection of pull and privilege than in the other? No one knows. My *guess* is that in these respects government is superior. Yet it may be otherwise; the subject is certainly debatable. Is purchasing as done by government more or less a matter of favoring friends as compared with purchasing as done by corporations? No one knows. Again my guess is that government has the better record. Do the personal, irrelevant interests of executives determine their decisions more often in business or in government? No one knows. But here too my guess is that because of the public-interest atmosphere surrounding it government normally gets a more completely disinterested judgment from its executives than does a commercial corporation.

Countless similar questions could be posed. The answers to them would doubtless underscore anew the fact that people are capable of reacting to different stimuli in many different ways. The profit motive is not the beginning and end even of self-interest. Enlightened self-interest often becomes astonishingly altruistic. It is by no means uncommon for businessmen to work every bit as hard at things involving no material self-interest as at their businesses. The selfish desire to be well regarded often flowers in truly social attitudes. Persons in government are characteristically among those who seek other than monetary returns and rewards. Perhaps scientists carrying on research in government laboratories furnish the clearest examples; they carry on significant and zealous work without being moved by anything like the profit motive.

The Dynamic of Competition

The principal advantage commonly attributed to private enterprise is that of dynamics. "Individual initiative" and "free competition" are popular slogans because we have believed that they have been the principle of our rapid progress. Even with respect to these factors, however, we have more sentiment than cold analysis and measurement. Take, for example, the rather common charge that we have an "economy of waste"; that waste has been blandly defended, or discounted, as good economics, as being on the whole profitable. But no one seems to have attempted to compute a balance sheet, a careful, factual estimate of the total cost of our wastes and total dynamic return from them.

Probably we shall never make a determination on any such basis, but it is worth while to ponder the question a bit. Before the war a friend who is in the oil business told me that if a motorist started from Richmond to drive to Los Angeles and bought a pint of gasoline at each filling station he passed, he would, on arriving at Los Angeles, have not only a full tank of gas but enough in addition to fill two tank trailers. This is just one aspect of a situation treated popularly some years ago in a series of articles in *Collier's Weekly*, "Too Many Retailers." It is a familiar story to anyone who visits his old home town and observes the effects of mortality among business houses. The once familiar Main Street has become a strange place—and this despite the fact that he cannot know of other changes between the visits which have left no trace at all.

Notwithstanding all we hear about "duplication" in government, it is my observation that this is no more a major problem in public administration than it is in any other field. Bureaucracy is its own check against duplication—and for much the same reason that businessmen would, if they could, end competition. Duplication exists in almost all non-governmental fields, and though it is generally believed to be a blessing, it is not so regarded by businessmen as they come directly up against it. On the contrary they do their best to get away from the "free competition" they loudly espouse during political campaigns.

One of our national business journals called two or three years ago for suspension by the Department of Justice of its enforcement of the anti-trust laws. The writer did not attack Congress and demand repeal of the laws. Instead he attacked Thurman Arnold for trying to enforce them! He did it by questioning the national belief in free competition and by insisting on the inevitability of bigger and bigger business. Here are three of his paragraphs:

"The old theory of competition was that it lowered prices down to a point just far enough above the cost of production to assure a small margin of net profit and continuance of the business. Actually, as we have learned over and over again from experience, unrestricted competition forces prices down to a level which is less than the actual cost of production.

"In any competitive price war, which so many politicians seem to think should be encouraged, the lowest price level is from 10% to 20% under the real cost of production. This means that a corporation with the greatest resources is bound to win at the end of any competitive struggle. It also means that in a price war, competitors would fight on, gradually exhausting their strength until, like roosters in a cock fight, one or both die. Unlike roosters, however, industrialists have intelligence and judgment. So they do their best to bow to the law; at the same time they get together somehow to prevent suicides. . . .

"With every good intention, they attempted by legal enactment to resurrect and revitalize it. They sought to upset an economic trend and to break up combinations by law. Of course, they did not succeed. Natural law made cynical jokes of our man-made anti-trust laws. Within the past 50 years, and since the passage of the Sherman law, there has been a veritable slaughter of small units. Corporations and combinations of them have grown by leaps and bounds, until the so-called independent is today the exception. Officially we have not yet recognized the immutability of the natural law. The fight against it is kept up at great and wasteful legal expense."

After this defense of big and bigger business, the writer opposed big government. Consider his argument: "Ideas and progress come from individual minds, not from the mass. The crowd can feel, hate, consume and destroy, but it cannot build." Here he seems to be on Thurman Arnold's side! He applies this latter thought to government. It could as well be applied to business.

The problem of dynamics in big business is not inherently different from the problem of dynamics in government. Socially we have relied less on progress brought about by a single big company than on progress made by a variety of companies, both big and little. Yet big business is capable of making many important contributions to society. So, too, is government, which is one entity and yet many. But both of them can perfect their organization to ensure greater dynamism—and both need to do so. Increasing giantism in our major corporations will simply mean that this will become more and more of a common problem for business and for government.

It has been said that Congress causes government to be inefficient by ordering the doing of things that are not required. According to whose judgment? By what criteria? Who is to say that Congress is "wrong" in interpreting popular sentiment as indicating a need for a certain action? Wherein does such a Congressional determination differ essentially from that of the board of directors of a commercial corporation? The board has the criterion of corporate profit; Congress, the criterion of national need and sentiment. Is the criterion of corporate profit a superior and more efficient criterion? Are all executive and board decisions in business good decisions?

Anatomy of Efficiency

The most persistent and most thoughtful argument respecting the relative efficiency of government and business is that competition, presumably present in business and lacking in government, guarantees efficiency in business and that therefore private enterprise is naturally more efficient than public enterprise. But it may be questioned whether competition is absent from governmental administration. Each of thousands of budget estimates competes strenuously with all others for appropriations. Each bureau, each program, each project, has to fight for life and funds. A section head is under tremendous pressure in preparing estimates to justify his askings; he has to play down, skimp, or reduce estimates for projects that he cannot hope to justify effectively in contrast with other items from other sections. Throughout the year that follows he must continuously watch and review so that he can adjust any part of his work that would make his section competitively vulnerable. The division chief goes through the same process, coming up at the end of the year with a budget request he knows he can fight for against askings of other divisions in the bureau. The bureau chief functions similarly in handling requests from all his divisions, accepting those he feels able to justify in the departmental competition with other bureaus. So with the department. It presents to the Bureau of the Budget only what it feels able to justify in competition with other departments. The Budget Bureau goes through the same process in preparing submissions to the President and to the Congress. Finally Congress itself holds lengthy hearings, criticizing and scrutinizing the budget in detail in terms of the probable reactions of constituents back home. Invariably these hearings result in definite cuts; yet these reductions may not represent the end of the gantlet. Even when the chambers are unable to decide on specific ways to make reductions, they may order horizontal cuts, leaving it to agencies to find ways of making particular reductions.

This process resembles very much what happens in business. There the drive behind the process may come from competition in the sense of the urge for profit, whereas in government the drive behind the process comes from desire for public acceptance and approval. But the process is essentially the same. Can anyone be sure that these different urges working through similar administrative processes will produce essentially different results?

It is to be questioned, too, whether competition is by any means so constant a force in private business, or so clearly a force in the direction of efficiency, as many assume.

A perfect monopoly would obviously be free from the immediate and most drastic pressures of competition. But there are many degrees and kinds of monopoly, so that competition is minimized in countless ways and in varying degrees. It is in the nature of business to want to eliminate competition. It is in the nature of business also to try to set its own competitive stage by focusing attention on points other than those calculated to encourage objective comparison between its products and those of its competitors. What is to be said of the intrinsic efficiency of investing huge capital and a great volume of manpower in the manufacture and sale of such products as chewing gum, nail polish, lipstick, Dr. Kwack's Gout Router, and other similar trivia? Even with government restraining the inefficiency of free enterprise through a Food and Drug Administration empowered to exclude many deleterious goods from the channels of trade, there is in the market a terrific amount of what-of-it merchandise. Wasteful and unimportant features become the basis of competition in many instances. Department-store overhead has tended to go up steadily for years because of a competitive race to provide costly services and features. Two nationally known inventor-industrialists asserted in my hearing several years ago that the way to make money is to invent a doodad rather than to expend effort on more fundamental research. These are some of the aspects of competition that disqualify it as a force making for efficiency.

What is an "economic good" after all? Is it not anything that satisfies a human desire or a desire people can be made to have? Wherein does it differ from a "political good" which is the basis for Congressional action and governmental administration? What is more efficient than what? Who says so? What is efficiency anyway? These questions, it seems to me, all fall before another, greater question: What do the people want to do? That is a political question. Politics determines the basis on which economics lives and moves. There is therefore no easy way to compare efficiency in government with efficiency in business. The president of the New Jersey Bell Telephone Company, Mr. Chester Barnard, in *The Functions of the Executive* declares that there is no objective test for broad efficiency except survival. There is no real point to glib assertions concerning relative efficiency of government and business. There is much point to efforts directed toward making both government and business better able to survive, more adjustable, more satisfactory in their functioning.

Chapter 19

Administrative Responsibility in a Democracy

Whenever one person performs an act for or in the name of another the problem of "responsibility" is posed. Was the act performed on the instructions of the principal? If not, on what grounds, by what theory, was the act justified as one for or in the name of the principal? How can the principal ensure that an act performed in his name represents his precise wish or his "real will"?

These questions are but a few of the many which pertain to the relationship between two persons when one acts for or in the name of the other. Usually, such questions are "private." That is to say, they arise in human relationships commonly regarded in our tradition as of no direct or legitimate concern to the State. They are thus posed as problems in manners or morals; or as problems in law, but still "private" law in the sense that neither party is the government.

But often and increasingly the problems of responsibility are public. As the area of government functions broadens there is a corresponding increase in the problem of the responsibility of the government, including the "public servants" or bureaucrats, to the citizens; and of various organs and agencies of government to one another. On the satisfactory solution of these problems depends in large part the answer to the question whether government functions have been undesirably expanded, or might, on the contrary, be further expanded with profit and without danger.

The problems of responsibility in public administration, if pursued in their theoretical aspects, lead one into the major categories, the perennial problems, of political theory. They raise questions as to the origins of political authority and what it is that can make political power legitimate. They lead to consideration of the nature of Justice, Individual Rights, and Public Welfare, and to the further consideration of who has the right and competence to make such determinations. They induce reflection on the implications of social structures, of economic systems, and of religious doctrines.

Pursued in another fashion, the problems of responsibility become what might be called problems in social mechanics. Given satisfactory resolutions of the problems of theory, how shall these resolutions be implemented? What forms of organization, what particular administrative procedures, and precisely what legal forms and personal relationships are most likely to result in the desired end?

The following essay on "The Responsibility of Public Administration" gives a historical and theoretical perspective on the problems of responsibility in the modern democratic state. The author is John M. Gaus, who was introduced earlier as the author of "American Society and Public Administration." Professor Gaus displays once again those qualities of breadth of view, insight, and balance that have made his writings on administration of especial value.

The Responsibility of Public Administration *

JOHN M. GAUS

The contribution of the United States to the idea of responsibility in administration was made by requiring the chief executive—and later, many minor executives—to submit directly or indirectly to popular vote. At the time of the Revolution and of the Constitution-making which the Revolution made necessary, the responsibility of the major executive officials to the legislature in the older states of Europe, including Great Britain, was not yet established. Indeed, in the very decade of the Revolution, Edmund Burke, in his *Thoughts on the Cause of the Present Discontents,* was describing for the first time a consistent theory of party government in which the responsibility for the direction of administration is vested in the leaders of the majority party of the legislature. When the American leaders rejected the responsibility of their governments to the King of England, they did not transfer the responsibility of the executive to the new legislatures which were set up. Thus we developed a kind of triple responsibility in our administration. It is viewed as responsibility to the people through the elective chief executive. It is also responsible to the ordinary courts for observing both procedural and substantive requirements of the fundamental constitutional law and of the statutory law, through which the administration is established and empowered to act. It is responsible also to the legislature for the proper use of the powers conferred upon it by the legislature through statutes, and for the proper expenditure of the money granted to it by legislative act. Whereas responsibility to the people is enforced through elections, and to the courts through judicial review, secured through various forms of procedure, the responsibility to the legislature, although not so obvious and complete as in the forms of the

* From *The Frontiers of Public Administration* (Chicago: 1936), pp. 26–44. Abridged. Reprinted by permission of the University of Chicago Press.

cabinet system which have evolved in Europe, particularly in France and England, is nevertheless enforced through financial measures and control of the establishment and organization of administration by statutes, through legislative investigations, and through the confirmation of appointees.

The rise of the party system has added a further complication. While in theory it may be held that popular election of a chief executive makes the administration responsible to the people directly, and indirectly also that responsibility is enforced through the action of the legislature in law-making and other forms of control, actually the immediate master is a party or a factional machine. This situation is similar to that in the medieval system when a theoretical responsibility of the government to God was actually enforced—when it was enforced—by an interested Papacy.

Nor is this the only complexity. The responsibility of an individual civil servant to the hierarchy of his superiors—to the legislature, to the courts, to citizens generally—is confused. Are the particular acts called into question in a particular dispute discretionary or ministerial? Does the issue involve a political question? Does the public servant hold an office or an employment? Is he personally liable for a tort, or is his employer, the state? Is the function which he is performing governmental or proprietary? While the French administrative tribunals have developed a case law in which these issues have been given some definition, our own law, at least, is complex and confused.

Thus, the concept of the responsibility of public administration after this development of the centuries is not clear-cut and consistent. The characteristic functions of government today are such that neither the electorate nor the legislature can express in concrete detail the specific policy which it desires the administrative organization to enforce. Suppose, for example, we wish to regulate the movies or the radio in the interest of public morals. Neither the electorate nor the legislature can anticipate the kind of situation for which detailed provision should be made. If we assume that it will, at least, be possible to submit the action of the administration to a judicial review, we are met with fresh difficulties. Neither the electorate nor the legislature in their desire to regulate the movies in the interest of public morals can go much beyond fixing a general principle which is to be applied to all specific cases by an administrative staff which will preview every movie which the producers wish to present to the public. If these producers feel aggrieved at what they believe to be an abuse of this discretionary authority given by the electorate and the legislature to the administrative officials, the theory is that they may appeal to the courts for a review of the decision. If the power delegated to the administrative authority is too general, the theory is that it may be attacked as an unconstitutional delegation of legislative authority to the executive.

But what, actually, do we find? Confronted with this situation, with the claim that the general principle laid down in the statute is so broad that it practically confers legislative power, the Supreme Court has held, through one of its members, that in any event such general principles must get their meaning from "the sense and experience of men." Thus one may ask again what responsibility the administrator has today in view of the relinquishment by electorate, legislature, and court, at so many points, of the power and the function of determining or defining policy. While recent decisions of the courts have challenged this trend, the nature of our problems of government prevent its reversal.

Indeed, it is hardly desirable or possible for the electorate to determine policy except in the most general way and on the most infrequent occasions. At best it can only indicate which of various competing political leaders it would prefer to place in office over a period of time. This means that so far as the responsibility of the administration to the electorate is concerned, it will at best be vague. At the next election the electorate will have a general notion as to whether or not the administration of the public business during the preceding electoral period has, on the whole, been acceptable as compared to what it might be under the alternative rival leadership during the next electoral period. We choose the ins or the outs. There is here an element of responsibility which is not to be ignored, and which must remain an essential attribute of any system of representative government. Yet it will be agreed that this form of responsibility is, nevertheless, very general and, on the whole, clumsy unless other forms of responsibility are developed whereby the ultimate responsibility of the great mass of public servants to the state as a whole can be made vivid and effective.

Legislatures are in a more effective position for giving content and meaning to the responsibility which the Constitution vests in them. There is general agreement among students of administration that generally legislatures have done far more harm than good by too detailed control of the organization of administration. Legislatures have been forced, from the nature of the problems concerning which they legislate, to confer wide discretion upon the administration in the enforcement of statutes. This has been true, regardless of the political party controlling the legislature or of the cultural complexion of the state. It was during the Harding administration, for example, that Congress conferred upon the President the power to raise or lower tariff rates upon the advice of the Tariff Commission, in accordance with changes in the differences of the cost of production between the United States and any foreign country. One does not need to be a trained economist to know that differences in cost of production are not so clear-cut as to offer a usable standard that can be impartially applied. Within the past few years similar wide discretionary authority over tariffs has been conferred upon a British administrative agency. In 1934 the Reciprocal Tariff Act gave a Democratic president powers to make international tariff agreements. In both countries, in other words, the legislatures without regard to party have turned over to the executive a wide range of power to change taxes—the power which historically they wrested from the executive at the cost of civil war. This policy is even more striking in the many fields of governmental regulation forced by scientific and technological developments.

With every increase in governmental intervention in the past hundred years it has been necessary to develop a form of intervention in which emphasis might be placed upon a sensitive and flexible adjustment of a general principle laid down in the statute to the peculiar circumstances of a trade, a locality, or other contingent and differentiating factors. Thus, the responsibility of administration to the legislature, while not so vague as toward the electorate, is nevertheless best confined to general policy, and it is the specific application after all which really counts with the average citizen affected by the enforcement of the law in question.

Time has dealt harshly not only with the responsibility of the administration to the electorate and to the legislature. It has laid an unholy hand upon responsibility to the courts as well. Indeed, certain administrative agencies have been established for the purpose of avoiding the inadequacies of judicial treatment of the problems concerned, and we are likely to see more of this transfer. There is, for example, the development of such special administrative agencies as those dealing with the problem of industrial accidents. Probably we shall have a development of administrative agencies which will replace the work of the courts in dealing with automobile accidents and traffic problems generally. The advantage of administrative treatment of certain questions (already forced by technological developments, as in transportation) would be rendered impossible if controversial cases were to be reopened *de novo* by the courts generally. Should this occur, as was pointed out by one harassed member of the United States Supreme Court, "the wheels of government would be stopped." It is, indeed, because we wish to have the advantage of the special knowledge of experience of experts, and the simplicity and economy of investigation and procedure of the administrative agency, that we have turned over many problems of regulation to the new administrative tribunals. Thus there has grown up a wide area of discretion in which finality of decision by the administrative authority is accepted. The courts may, on occasion, indeed, intervene, to "try the trial." They may intervene from time to time to substitute their judgment as to what the law requires in the way of factors in valuation or appraisal generally, of which the administrator must take account. But in the day-to-day work of most administrative agencies the administrative decision is likely to be final.

But why, it may be asked, does the problem of administrative discretion concern us in our inquiry into administrative responsibility? The connection between these two aspects of administration is very clear when we examine such an argument as that advanced by Brand Whitlock in his discussion of *The Enforcement of Law in Cities*. In that little book the former mayor of Toledo discusses the difficult problem of the enforcement of laws which may conflict with customary views concerning alcoholic drink and Sunday observance. As a matter of fact and of common observance, we know that policies of enforcement of such legislation vary widely within a single political area, under different administrators. To whom is the administrator responsible in this situation? The assumption is that he is not responsible to the legislative authority since this very flexibility in the application of the statute is applauded. If we then say that he is responsible to the electorate, we are only confronted with the question, what portion of the electorate? And if we say, finally, that he is, in any event, responsible to the courts in this matter, we are met again with a wide range of attitudes taken by and through the courts, which, indeed, try to avoid this issue by withdrawing from their jurisdiction those questions which they conveniently designate as "political." . . .

In a state in which the powers of government intermesh widely with those of industry, commerce, and finance the traditional restraints upon the discretion of the administrator through making him responsible to the electorate, the courts, and the legislators are inadequate. The injurious policy or action is taken long before review can attempt to undo the damage. It is only by having the interest which might be injured present and on the spot when the policy is determined and the action taken that substantial justice can be secured. And even more significant is the fact that increasingly public administration concerns itself directly with seeing that that interest is organized, so that it may resist coercion. Labor is given the right to organize, and the state polices the election in order to safeguard its fairness. The state has had to create consumer organization, hitherto non-existent, and has drawn upon the small number of those who have concerned themselves with the consumer's interest and point of view and associated them with the day-to-day administration. Thus, in the end, we find this fundamental problem of the formulation of policy out of the clash of group interests and their reconciliation woven into the fabric of administration because of the inadequacy of traditional forms of securing administrative responsibility.

The effort to establish . . . agencies whereby the interest groups directly affected may be consulted and the administrators reminded of their responsibilities to them is not, of course, the only example of this effort to solve the problem of responsibility. In a valuable review of the employment of private associations and interest groups and their representatives in collaboration with public administration Lane Lancaster remarks that

"much of our public administration is conditioned by the attitude of so-called private associations . . . in fact a substantial portion is actually conducted by such organizations. . . . The work of society is in reality the task of a collaboration; it is not accomplished by 'public' agencies if, in using that term, we carry in our minds notions of sovereign commands and willy-nilly compliance. And a realistic view of the administrative machinery of a state reveals not an official group on the one side and an obedient public on the other, but a situation in which the community in its helplessness turns to those with competence and confirms, by making them officials, a social responsibility which is not in fact increased by the conferring of an official status. . . ."

Authority, in short, follows the successful exercise of function; the role of the administrator is to achieve a reconciliation of the interests involved, and requires the winning of consent by the accumulation of exact and relevant knowledge.

In tracing these institutional changes I may seem to have lost sight of the lone civil servant upon whom, in the last analysis, responsibility falls. If, out of necessity, there has developed so wide a measure of discretionary power for an administrative organization, what has been his fate? Does this discretion fall to him, and, if so, to whom is he responsible? Traditionally and legally he has been responsible to his superior officer and to the law. But here, again, there is a tendency to make the political head dependent upon his staff, as the nature of the problems increasingly requires for their solution an experience and training which the political head rarely possesses. Just as administration has been invaded by the interest group in order to secure an effective responsibility to the knowledge and experience of the groups most affected, so the individual civil servant is at last wondering whether he may not need some protection in an organized way for the responsibility which his knowledge and professional training place upon him. The responsibility of the civil servant to the standards of his profession, in so far as those standards make for the public interest, may be given official recognition. Thus, through his superior officer and through the consultative committees of interest groups associated with his department, his responsibility to the electorate and legislature is enforced; while, through some organization representative of the civil servants and of the professional groups from which they are recruited, his responsibility to a profession is also given recognition.

In recent years a combat has been waged in various literary journals in the United States between various factions over the use of the term "humanism." One aggressive band, upholding its own style of humanism, employed the term, "the inner check." Without committing ourselves to any position in the literary struggle we may, at least, borrow this term for application in the present discussion. Certainly in the system of government which is now emerging, one important kind of responsibility will be that which the individual civil servant recognizes as due to the standards and ideals of his profession. This is his "inner check." This is not so new or rare an attitude as the average person might seem to suppose. More than a quarter of a century ago John R. Commons pointed out, in a discussion of "Unions of Public Employees," that,

"in this country, with universal suffrage, the workingman in public employment does not need to strike. He forms a clique and goes in with the politicians. He has the suffrage. We cannot get away from organization. These employees will organize, in one way or another. The real solution is, not to try to destroy the organizations of public servants, but to give them official recognition, to give them a part in the administration of the department, and then to hold them to that responsibility."

An illustration which Professor Commons is able to supply from the Seth Low administration in New York City is the valuable co-operation in improvements in administration achieved through the organization of the Street Cleaning employees, encouraged by Colonel George Waring, the distinguished engineer appointed to the Commissionership. Through the ten members of the Board of Conference, which included five executive bureau chiefs and five spokesmen chosen by the organization of the employees, over eleven hundred grievances, which ordinarily would have been the materials from which the local factional boss would develop an irresponsible organization, were dealt with through a procedure which stimulated a new and creative attitude on the part of the civil servants toward their work. One is inclined to agree with Professor Commons' statement, "I consider that this invention of Commissioner Waring in the Street Cleaning Department of New York is the most important practical contribution that has been made to Civil Service reform in a democratic government." The statement of employment policy adopted by the Tennessee Valley Authority is a recent illustration of the same principle.

During the past twenty-five years we find many other indications of the growth of this new type of responsibility in public administration. There is, for example, the rise of new professions such as that of social work. The American Association of Social Workers has for many years fought to raise the standards of training, recruitment, and working conditions of social workers throughout the United States. A relatively new profession of this kind is peculiarly dependent upon the "inner check" of the pride of its members in undertaking pioneer work and developing, of their own initiative, higher standards of all kinds, because the general public and its average representatives on a lay board or legislature are likely to have very little knowledge of the possibilities and conditions in this field. Equally striking is the rise of such organized efforts at improving administration from within as the many state leagues of municipalities now federated into the American Municipal Association, the International City Managers' Association, and kindred groups; or the valuable co-operation in improvement of administration that is achieved by the United States Public Health Service, through its joint conferences and exchange of research and information through publications and other means with the state and local public health officers. . . .

We have by no means reached the limits of possibility of experimentation in the older types of responsibility. Indeed, we are only beginning to study carefully questions of public opinion and problems of political responsibility generally. Much more effective methods and instruments of civic education and political control are needed as administrative discretion increases. It may be that in the United States, for example, we may find it desirable to return to the system of party and political responsibility of the period prior to Jackson, in which party organization was found in the members of the party having membership in elective legislative and executive positions; that is, those possessing responsibility with legal power to make that responsibility good in actual legislation and administration. Such a division of party organization would be an improvement over the present convention system, and one could retain the use of a primary election as a means of general control over the personnel selected to represent the party in these posts. This would meet the legitimate criticisms aimed at the perhaps overcircumscribed and rigid governing class which the party conventions displaced, yet it would avoid the even more serious aspects of irresponsibility because of complicated convention and committee arrangements within the party, which the Jacksonian movement introduced. Also, we could undoubtedly improve greatly the relations between the administration and the legislature in the direction of clarifying their respective shares of responsibility. Those of us who have been, perhaps, unduly critical of our own system may well note that parliamentary countries are also dissatisfied on this point. The late Senator Bronson Cutting proposed, at the Progressive Conference held in Washington in 1931, that in view of the wide delegation of power by Congress to administrative agencies, there should be established a continuing joint committee of Congress for the purpose of watching the application of these general provisions by administrative authorities. This and other detailed proposals that might be mentioned have much value. They would reduce the risks of narrow and selfish professionalism in the civil service.

There are possible developments in the field of judicial review whereby the responsibility of the civil servant and the administrative department respectively, or of the state, may be clarified either by the ordinary courts or by special administrative tribunals. I refer only briefly to these matters, not because I think them unimportant, but rather because I feel that it is in the attitude of the civil servant as an individual toward his work and his profession, as an integral part of the complex society gradually taking form before our eyes, that the most important aspect of responsibility is to be explored in this period of the development of the state.

The note of a corporate sense pervading the whole administrative organization is to be found not only in government as the term is usually employed, but also in the supplementary governments and civil services of business and industry, particularly where internal pressures of participating groups have been given regular and stable channels through which to be registered and adjusted. Jennie Turner, in her discussion of "Democracy in Administration" has emphasized this, as have Commons, Perlman, and other students of economic institutions. Just as the officials in the medieval chancery developed into something of a guild, thus limiting the arbitrary discretion of king or minister, so the machinery of negotiation over hours, wages, and conditions of work in the clothing industry, for example, elevates the casual relationship of employer and employee into something of the public status of persons engaged in the responsible conduct of joint enterprise which has public implications. "The state is as its officials are," says Dewey. The fact of being an official has its own overtones. They may be detected, also, in an interdependent economy and society wherever some stability and security, some stake in a kind of property right to a job properly done, have developed. Unless this sense of responsibility is encouraged, the responsibility of administration is incomplete, negative, and external. . . .

———◆———

The following essay on "Gauging Administrative Responsibility" by Arthur A. Maass and Laurence I. Radway of the Harvard University Department of Government covers much of the same ground as did Professor Gaus in the preceding essay. The approach and the style are much different, however; they present not a review and commentary, but an enumeration and argument.

As indicated in Professor Gaus' essay, the rationale and methods of achieving responsibility in administration in the modern democratic state are various, and, to some extent, confused and conflicting. Responsibility to the people at large, to the people organized in "interest groups," to the legislative body, to the chief executive, to political parties, to professional spirit and ethical standards, and to the courts—all these are part of the American political system as operating today. The following essay, viewing the diversity and conflict, attempts to establish criteria of responsibility and argues the relative values of the various types of responsibility.

The essay is closely knit. The argument must, in fact, be approached as though it were a demonstration in geometry. Each paragraph, however, bristles with argument.

Are the authors on sound ideological and methodological grounds? Is the treatment of each type of responsibility "fair"? Does the essay delineate criteria that can be used "in the field"?

Gauging Administrative Responsibility *

ARTHUR A. MAASS AND LAURENCE I. RADWAY

Method of Approach

The following discussion is an effort, albeit tentative and incomplete, to establish criteria which will be useful in determining the extent to which any administrative agency conducts itself as a responsible instrument of government. It is

* From *Public Administration Review*, Vol. 9 (Summer, 1949), pp. 182–192. Reprinted by permission of the authors and the *Public Administration Review*.

not primarily addressed to the related problem of how best to sustain the state of mind that issues in responsible administrative conduct. The emphasis here is rather on appraising degrees of responsibility on the basis of criteria applicable to particular functioning agencies.

Much has been written on the "principles" of administrative responsibility. Students have engaged in lively controversy over their nature and validity. But these principles are frequently equivocal; and though mutually incompatible, they are often equally applicable to the same administrative situation. It is therefore believed desirable to use the more modest language of "criteria" of responsibility, some of which may indeed conflict with others, but all of which must be weighted and applied together in any attempt to gauge the responsibility of a specific administrative agency.

Of course, these criteria have not been formulated *in vacuo*. They rest on certain points of view or biases which must be made explicit. Necessarily these biases are cast in normative terms. But they are held as tools for the task, not as dogma for the ages. In particular, the analysis assumes large-scale federal organization in the context of contemporary American society; and this context is taken to include both constitutional government in its presidential form and prevailing democratic ideology.

Responsibility—A General and Historical View

To appreciate the general nature and importance of administrative responsibility it is necessary to understand the significance of bureaucracy in the modern state. Logically, of course, constitutional government presupposes a functioning bureaucracy; for until an administrative machine exists there cannot be efforts to subject it to popular influence and control. But more than this, bureaucracy is the very core of constitutional democracy in the sense that no modern government can long survive without an efficient administrative organization. "It is . . . not a question of *either* democracy *or* bureaucracy, of *either* constitutionalism *or* efficient administration," but of "a combination of the two, of a working balance between them, in short, of a responsible bureaucracy."

Historically, the responsibility of officials has been enforced more often, and perhaps more easily, through religious than through secular sanctions. The only way to escape religious responsibility and its restraints is to emancipate oneself from religious faith itself. This is what happened in Renaissance Italy. Deviations from the religious norm seemed necessary to meet the practical requirements of government. They were made in the name of *raison d'état*. The Christian mind, still clinging to its ideological traditions, attempted to rationalize such conduct by deifying the political order. In the seventeenth century, government by and responsible to divine law thus became government by and responsible to kings ruling by divine right. But ultimately the religious sanction lost its force, and modern government has on the whole been obliged to seek other means for enforcing responsibility. These means are summed up in the term "modern constitutionalism," which is essentially "an effort to produce responsible conduct of public affairs without religious sanctions."

Constitutional democracy thus seeks to restrain bureaucracy by secular devices. And administrative responsibility under such a regime has been termed the sum total of the constitutional, statutory, administrative, judicial, and professional practices by which public officers are restrained and controlled in their official actions. But it is not possible to identify the *criteria* for gauging administrative responsibility by relying on such general language. It becomes necessary, therefore, to relate the general concept of responsibility to the specific functions of power (i.e. responsibility to whom?) and purpose (i.e. responsibility for what?).

Responsibility for What?

Working Bias: An administrative agency should be responsible for formulating as well as executing public policy.

It has been popular in the past for American political scientists to assume that administrative officials are responsible only for the execution of policy and not at all for the formulation of policy. The distinction between policy making and policy execution may have a great deal of practical value as a relative matter. By accepting such a distinction, we have been enabled, for example, to develop many of the detailed techniques for the conduct of personnel, budget, and related functions in government. But as an absolute form, any such distinction between politics (the making of policy) and administration (the execution of policy) is unrealistic and leads to incomplete, if not incorrect, analyses of the conduct of responsible government. Public policy is being formed as it is being executed, and it is being executed as it is being formed. Politics and administration are not two mutually exclusive processes; they are, rather, two closely linked aspects of the same process.

Administrative hierarchies have a profound influence on public policy formulation in two ways: (1) in the exercise of the discretionary powers allowed in everyday operations; (2) in the process of developing specific proposals for legislative consideration.

With respect to everyday operations, the extent to which an administrative agency determines policy depends largely on the nature of the discretionary powers which the legislature has assigned to the agency. These powers may be classified according to the legislature's disposition regarding its mandate:

a. Technical Discretion. Here the legislature states the desired results or assumes that the administrator knows them. Its mandate is clear, and the administrator plays the role of a technical expert in fulfilling it.

b. Discretion in Social Planning. Here the legislature does not know in fine detail what results it seeks. Its mandate is vague or general, and the administrator is authorized both to work out definite rules for action and to plan goals for government activities.

c. Discretion in Reconciliation of Interests. Here the legislature in effect asks the administrator to break a political deadlock. Its mandate is in dispute, and the administrator acquires a certain discretion to mediate and to facilitate negotiations between pressure groups.

Administrative hierarchies may also formulate specific proposals for legislative approval, amendment, or rejection. That they do in fact play such a role has been established by careful studies of the origin of legislation in both federal and state governments. That they should play such a role is coming to be accepted by most political scientists and practitioners, though the ritual of partisan politics often appears to require denunciation of bureaucratic influence on legislation. Accordingly the administrator has a responsibility to seek a legislative policy that is clear, consistent, feasible, and consonant with basic community values. It is his obligation to anticipate problems, to devise alternative policies for meeting them, to estimate the probable consequences of each alternative, and, through the chief executive, to transmit this information to the legislature along with his own recommendations.

The bureaucrat is peculiarly well equipped for this task by virtue of his opportunity to develop professionally accepted techniques and standards; his opportunity to observe at first hand how policies work out in practice; his capacity for tempering enthusiasm for theory with a shrewd appreciation of what is practical and what is not; and his ability to represent interests which are not well represented by organized pressure groups, for example, the consumers.

Responsibility to the People at Large

Working Bias: An administrative agency cannot and should not normally be held directly responsible to the people at large.

In the last century direct official responsibility to the entire electorate was encouraged by requiring that many administrative officials be elected at the polls. But the long ballot secured hardly more than an ill-defined and intermittent responsibility to the general public at the expense of an unfortunate dispersion of authority and an undue responsiveness to private interests. Popular election has given way therefore to an integrated administration governed by the power of appointment and the principle of hierarchical subordination. Other devices for holding the bureaucracy directly accountable to the electorate, such as the recall, the initiative, and the referendum, have not been conspicuously successful, and none is used in the federal government. In general it is becoming clear that direct control by the public at large cannot insure administrative responsibility and that the influence of John Doe can be exerted effectively only through the legislature, the executive, and special interest associations.

More recently, some governmental programs have come to depend significantly on voluntary cooperation of the general public for their administration. Good examples are selective service and consumer rationing. In such cases the information function of the government agency becomes of central importance. The people at large need to be informed of available administrative services. They must also be notified of what is expected of them in conformance to government rules and regulations. The agency's intelligence service must in turn pick up from the public the attitudes and information necessary to the successful development and execution of policy—"where the shoe pinches," how it can be made to fit better, what is felt to be unnecessary red tape, and so on. Thus it is possible to state one's criterion for gauging administrative responsibility to the people at large—the extent to which the voluntary cooperation of the general public is sought for programs whose success depends significantly on such cooperation. Application of this criterion requires an evaluation of methods for disseminating, collecting, and utilizing the type of information discussed above.

Responsibility to the People—Pressure Groups

Working Bias: An administrative agency should be responsible to pressure groups so far as necessary to equalize opportunities for safeguarding interests, to acquire specialized knowledge, and to secure consent for its own program.

It has been argued that the responsibility of all government is the free and effective adjustment of group interests. Certainly the administrator as well as the legislator operates within a context of intense intergroup activity. Indeed, the legislator often confers upon the administrator a specific responsibility for consulting with groups and reconciling their respective interests. He may do this either because group conflict is so intense that he is unable or unwilling to make the necessary reconciliation, or because the issues are so complex that he lacks the time and information to resolve them and has, therefore, to delegate to administrators the authority to make the necessary rules and regulations. In either case the responsibility of the administrator is clear: to recognize what the legislature has required of him and to conduct his operations accordingly. The extent to which he does this is, then, the first of the possible criteria of responsibility which relates the administrator to pressure groups.

But the administrator will undoubtedly have to work with special interests even in the absence of a specific legislative mandate. His agency and the laws which he administers are usually the product of the pressures and rivalries of organized groups. Naturally, these groups will continue to seek a voice in the development of programs which affect them; and as the scope of the administrator's activities continues to increase, group attention will tend to shift from legislator to bureaucrat in conformity to the adage, "where power rests, there influence will be brought to bear."

This growing tendency for interest groups to participate in the formulation and execution of policy, irrespective of legislative provision, can be supported on at least three grounds: first, that such group representation is desirable to equalize opportunities for protecting and promoting respective interests; second, that the preparation of detailed regulations on complicated matters requires exact knowledge which even the best informed official may not possess and which interest groups can supply; third, that group participation in policy decisions makes possible the winning of consent for the agency's program. This last proposition is not, of course, intended to imply that the agency should attempt to win consent at any price. The desires of the legislature, the chief executive, and other agencies, relevant professional standards, and the dictates of ordinary morality set limits which must be respected in any program which pretends to further the public interest. But within these limits there is ample margin for the agency to seek consent by anticipating the reaction of affected interest groups, by keeping them informed of agency activities, and by permitting them to be notified in advance, to be heard, and to be informed of the basis of emerging policy. In this manner the official can avoid foolish mistakes; he can resolve differences with less "loss of face" on the part of all; and he can impart to the people organized as pressure groups both a sense that they are respected and a conviction that they are playing a valuable role in the process by which they are governed.

The effectiveness with which an agency discharges the aforementioned obligations to special interests furnishes the three criteria of responsibility which follow:

a. The extent to which an agency equalizes opportunities to safeguard interests. Do the groups dealt with represent all major interests affected by the program? Is each given equitable treatment? Have steps been taken to assure that group spokesmen fairly reflect the views of those whom they claim to represent?

b. The adequacy of the means employed and the results achieved in securing from interest groups technical knowledge necessary to policy decisions.

c. The extent to which an agency succeeds in winning group consent in the sense discussed above. This includes an appraisal of its methods and its effectiveness in forecasting the reaction of interested groups to contemplated measures and in exchanging with these groups factual data and attitudes of mutual concern.

Application of these criteria, so far as they involve an appraisal of the methods by which an agency maintains contact with interest groups, requires some study of the precise *form* of the relationship between agency and interest group. Often, groups are represented in the very structure of government, as when an organization is created to benefit a special category of citizens. The Veterans Administration, Women's Bureau, and Bureau of Indian Affairs are generally cited as examples of such clientele agencies. When a number of different interest groups is involved, resort is sometimes made to "staffing for point of view," *i.e.,* appointing officials on the basis of special vocational affiliation or experience. A more direct device is interest representation on multi-headed boards; and occasionally interest groups are even authorized to nominate members of such boards. Finally, public power may actually be delegated to private organizations, although this practice is not generally in accord with our constitutional traditions.

Perhaps more often, however, interest groups maintain merely an advisory or consultative status in their relations to administrative agencies. They present their views in the process of legal or less formal procedures of investigation, notice, and hearing. Some agencies create special staff units to maintain contact with outside groups and present their grievances and suggestions. A common technique is to establish advisory committees composed of the relevant special interests. Wartime experience with such advisory bodies, particularly in the War Production Board and the Office of Price Administration, was on the whole successful, and from that experience improved techniques for the utilization of advisory bodies have been developed.

A general bias is here stated in favor of the advisory devices. An incentive should be placed upon the administrator to win group assent; and group representation should be free to withdraw or criticize as they see fit. To build interest representation into the governmental structure, at least on a piecemeal basis, is to invite the extremes of hierarchical suppression of group demands or of undue responsiveness thereto. Furthermore, the advisory relationship should be formalized or legalized, since an informal relationship opens the way to invisible exertion of pressure with consequent danger of action that is irresponsible in the eyes of all third parties. It is conceded, however, that these results need not necessarily follow in each situation; that a general preference for formalized consultation may derive from an uncritical acceptance of traditional democratic ideology; and that each case must be examined on its own merits. With this approach, a finding that pressure groups have been directly integrated into the administrative structure, or at the other extreme, that complete informality exists in the relationship between bureaucrat and group spokesman, should be regarded only as a red flag indicating possible lack of responsibility ahead.

Responsibility to the Legislature

Working Bias: An administrative agency should be responsible to the legislature, but only through the chief executive, and primarily for broad issues of public policy and general administrative performance.

Representative bodies are the institutional embodiment of democratic theory, and an administration responsible to the legislature is of the very essence of democratic government. Yet many political scientists fear that representative bodies are losing both power and prestige because of the compelling necessity to delegate to administrators broad discretion in the initiation and execution of public policy. There is no reason, however, why delegation of power need necessarily result in loss of power provided the legislature devises techniques for holding the administration responsible for the exercise of its discretion. If it is true that Congress has lost power and prestige, that is because Congress has not adapted its organization and procedures to the needs of the time, not because such adaptation is inherently impossible within our present form of government.

Moreover, it has been pointed out that the problem of responsible government today is not so much that of legislative-executive relations as of the relationships between the legislature and chief executive on the one hand, and the administrative agency, often allied with pressure groups and legislative blocs, on the other.

The administrative agency must be answerable in some sense to *both* the chief executive and the legislature. The real question is how to structure such dual responsibility under our present constitutional system. Should the agency be responsible directly to the legislature, or should it be responsible to the legislature through the chief executive?

The advocates of direct responsibility point out that the legislature creates, defines the powers of, and appropriates the money for each administrative agency. Also, they note that many agencies exercise sublegislative and quasi-judicial functions which they feel should be supervised by legislature and courts respectively. And perhaps most important, they argue that the direct responsibility of an agency cannot end with the chief executive because the chief executive himself cannot be made answerable to the legislature in quite the same sense as under parliamentary government. In its relationships with the President, Congress lacks the ultimate sanction: authority to force resignation when the President no longer commands the confidence of the Congress.

Advocates of indirect responsibility argue that it is of supreme importance to focus responsibility sharply, and that if the legislature attempts to hold each agency directly accountable, responsibility for the coordinated conduct of government programs in broad areas of public policy will become too diffused to be made effective. It is contended: (1) That there must be unity of ultimate command and clearly formulated lines of authority in any such hierarchical organization as a public bureaucracy. Lack of clarity gives rise to uncertainty, conflict, and irresolution, making it difficult to enforce responsible conduct. It is asserted that this can best be prevented by running the line of authority from agency to chief executive to legislature. (2) That careful coordination of the often conflicting programs of different agencies is required if the official is to be kept from an unduly narrow view of the public interest. The legislature alone cannot accomplish such coordination, particularly if it attempts to hold each agency directly responsible. However, the chief executive, if assisted by adequate staff, is in a position to develop clear and balanced programs for areas of public policy which cut across organizational lines. He is also in a better position to insure effective execution of such programs. (3) That legislators must have balanced programs responsibly placed before them if they are to be able to make intelligent policy decisions. It is the chief executive who is best equipped to prepare such programs and assume responsibility for placing them before the elective body. (4) That the legislature is not equipped to hold the many individual officers and agencies of government to a detailed responsibility. On the other hand, the interposition of the chief executive can reduce the pressure on the legislature. He can devise procedures for settling matters too trivial for legislative attention, for eradicating administrative parochialism, and for controlling the executive agencies in such a manner as to simplify the task of legislative surveillance. (5) That direct responsibility to the legislature nearly always means direct responsibility to individual members of particular legislative committees which happen to have jurisdiction. In such cases the legislature often finds it difficult to check its own entrenched and un-coordinated minorities. This is less likely to occur when the legislature considers integrated policies submitted by the chief executive. (6) That the difficulties of executive-legislative relationships under a system of separated powers are reduced by the presentation, through the chief executive, of an internally consistent and coherent legislative program. (7) That sublegislative powers are really similar to the policy making powers of regular executive agencies, and as such should be exercised under direct responsibility to the chief executive, while judicial functions should be independent of both legislature and executive. (8) That a single responsible chief executive to manage the departments in accordance with statute is an essential part of our republican system and was clearly intended by the framers of the Constitution.

On balance, it is believed that the advocates of indirect responsibility have the better of the argument. Of course, there is no question but that a determined legislature can in fact control individual agencies directly if it wishes to pay the price; the general position taken here requires rather the evolution of a custom of legislative self-restraint where direct controls are concerned. Nor is it meant to imply that the legislature should be denied the *authority* to prescribe the duties and procedures of administrative agencies in detail. No more is meant than that the requirements for a truly effective responsibility today will call for sparing use of such authority. The legislature can neither determine a national policy nor maintain effective supervision over the executive branch unless it focuses on the great issues and rests content with having laid out general lines of policy for the executive branch. To impose mandatory and minute specifications for the organization and operation of the administrative machine is to absolve "first the bureau chief, then the Secretary of the department, and then the President . . . from part of his executive responsibility, and in consequence the Congress is foreclosed from adequately criticizing the conduct of the business." Accordingly, administrative agencies should be responsible to the legislature, but only through the chief executive, and primarily for the broader questions which arise in formulating and executing policy.

If an agency can be controlled effectively only when Congress focuses on major issues of integrated policy, a major criterion of its responsibility is the success with which that agency, in reporting to Congress through the President, points up the broad policy questions which require legislative determination and plays down administrative details. The remaining criteria of indirect responsibility to the legislature can be derived in the process of examining the nature of the business which draws legislator and bureaucrat together.

First, agencies give legislative committees professional assistance and advice that leads to the drafting of statutes. Here the criterion of their responsibility is the effort which they make, by producing competent advice, to encourage the passage of laws containing a careful definition of the agencies' obligations and authorities. An official cannot proceed to a wise and democratic use of his discretion unless the legislature has indicated the general nature of the standards which should guide his action; and it is his responsibility to present the professional information available to him to the legislature, through the chief executive, in a way to insure the writing of competent standards into law. A corollary of this criterion is the extent to which the agency presses for revision of vague or overly ambitious statutes when it has access to technical information for the determination of more satisfactory standards. Yet another corollary is the response of legislative committees to the agency's recommendations. However, this last criterion does not have wide application. It is based on the assumption that committees generally respond more favorably to recommend legislation that incorporates professionally determined standards than to other recommendations. Though this may be true, there are so many other factors which enter into legislative response that it will usually be difficult to isolate this one.

Second, agencies are required to come before appropriation committees annually to present their plans for the ensuing year, to account for activities and expenditures for the current and past years, and generally to satisfy these committees that the legislature's purposes are actually guiding their operations. Review of the budget is the most important of the regular legislative controls over the executive branch. Even though changes in items may be relatively small, it should not be thought that this review is ineffective. Departments and budget officers are keenly aware of legislative attitudes and prepare their budgets to meet them. In this activity the criterion of responsibility is the effectiveness with which the agency (*a*) reports and justifies projected work, and (*b*) reports and accounts for accomplishments. A corollary measure is the treatment accorded the agency's budget by the appropriations committees, but here again there are too many other factors conditioning legislative response to permit any but extremely guarded conclusions.

Third, an agency is constantly subject to legislative investigations; and though it may never have undergone such an investigation, the threat of one is a continued sanction by which the legislature insures conformity to its own policies and safeguards against abuses which run counter to community values. The agency must always be prepared to answer; its record must be good; and it must be prepared to spread that record before the legislature. The criterion of responsibility is thus the willingness and ability of an agency to provide investigating committees with a complete, accurate, and clear record of its activities. A corollary, again to be used with extreme care because of the vagaries of "politics," is the extent to which an investigating committee indicates satisfaction with its findings.

Fourth, the accounts of agencies are regularly audited by an independent instrumentality of the legislature. The criterion of responsibility is here self-evident.

Fifth, agencies conduct business with the legislature which involves the appointment and removal of personnel, both personnel whom the agency appoints directly and personnel whom it recommends to the President to be confirmed with the consent of the Senate. The criteria of responsibility here are also difficult to apply because of the supervention of "political" factors, but they can be enumerated as the success of the agency in obtaining confirmation of appointments which it has in fact initiated, absence of legislative efforts to impeach or by other means remove or place obstacles on the removal of agency personnel, and general evidence of legislative satisfaction with the agency's staff.

Finally, agencies often maintain a network of informal contacts with individual legislators and committees. In some form such relationships are inevitable, and in fact indispensable. But in their pathological form, a single legislator or committee may occupy a position of influence so commanding in matters affecting the agency that responsibility to the remainder of the legislature is prevented. Accordingly, a final criterion of responsibility to the legislature is whether an agency conducts its relationships therewith in a manner to prevent minority control over its affairs.

Responsibility to the Chief Executive

Working Bias: An administrative agency should be directly responsible for conforming to the general program of the chief executive and for coordinating its activities with other agencies of the executive branch.

To the extent that the chief executive is held responsible by the legislature and by the public for the administration of a government-wide program, he will in turn try to establish the responsibility of administrative agencies to himself. In so doing he must define the duties for which they are held accountable and the means by which this accountability is to be effectuated.

Both in formulating and in executing programs, agencies usually operate under the general policies or philosophy of the Administration. The broad lines of such policy are normally laid down by the chief executive. But he cannot be expected to provide detailed direction on all matters. He is entitled to expect that, within the limitations of specific legislative determinations, agencies will adapt their activities to his general policy directives and to the broad philosophy of his Administration. The extent to which such adaptations are made is one major criterion of an agency's responsibility to the chief executive.

Moreover, nearly all agencies operate in fields in which they also effect the programs and interests of other organizations immediately subordinate to the chief executive. If the purposes set by the President are to be achieved with maximum effectiveness, it is essential that these agencies act in concert. To be sure, it is becoming fashionable to observe that a sophisticated executive may prefer something less than complete coordination of his establishment on the ground that occasional conflict between subordinates enables him to keep posted and insures that policy conflicts will be brought before him for resolution. But a decision to adopt this strange substitute for an effective intelligence service should rest with the superior, not with the subordinate. Generally, an agency subordinate to the chief executive has an obligation not to take action which has not been carefully checked with other interested agencies through the established means for coordination. Thus, a second major criterion of responsibility to the chief executive is the extent to which an agency coordinates its work with that of other agencies. A closely related criterion is the extent to which controversial matters of detail, unworthy of legislative attention, are settled within the executive branch.

The remaining criteria of responsibility to the chief executive relate to the means for attaining concerted conformance to his program. They involve techniques for departmental and overhead organization designed to provide public leadership. These techniques include not only unity of ultimate command and clearly formulated lines of authority, but also the existence of effective staff organs at appropriate levels in the administrative hierarchy. Some progress has been made in recent years in securing such staff organs, especially for administrative staff services (budget and personnel) and long-term planning. The development of policy general staff has lagged behind. By direction of the President, the Bureau of the Budget performs a central clearance function for the programs of executive agencies. But though central clearance has proved effective in a large number of instances, the procedure is notoriously less adequate for those important cases which involve highly controversial subjects. On broader issues interdepartmental committees have been used to eliminate conflicts in policy. Such committees, however, especially when unsupported by secretariat, are too often stultified by the "veto power" and by the presence of members more concerned with defending their positions than with reaching genuine agreement.

More recently, there has grown a general awareness that negative and piecemeal review of individual proposals flowing up from agencies to the chief executive cannot produce an integrated governmental program at the time it is required. It is becoming clear that top level executives require policy staff organs to formulate general programs which subordinate units cannot evolve because of limited terms of reference, inertia, organizational or professional bias, or inadequate factual information. Such a policy general staff, by supplying common premises for action, can help insure coordination "before the event," that is, by prior indoctrination.

From this discussion it is possible to derive the following additional criteria of responsibility to the chief executive: (1) the existence of unity of ultimate command and clearly formulated lines of authority within an agency; (2) the availability and effectiveness of administrative staff organs, intra-agency committees, and liaison or other devices for insuring concerted conformance with the chief executive's policies; (3) the extent and genuine sincerity of agency cooperation with staff, liaison, interdepartmental, or other coordinating mechanisms established by the chief executive; (4) the extent to which an agency conforms to the chief executive's program in information transmitted to the legislature or to the public; (5) as a measure of successful adjustment of program conflicts, the extent to which evidence of such conflicts with other agencies fails to appear in information transmitted to the legislature or to the public; (6) so far as can be ascertained by rough estimate, the extent to which an agency demonstrates a "sense of administrative discipline" in its conduct.

Responsibility to Political Parties

Working Bias: An administrative agency cannot be held independently responsible to the organization or policies of political parties.

If responsibility to political parties exists at all in the federal government, it is largely indirect and can be included within the criteria already developed. For example, for some purposes the political party can be considered an interest group. Furthermore, political parties dictate the organization of the legislature and the selection of the chief executive and his top aides, so that the manner in which responsibility to the legislature and chief executive is effectuated will reflect whatever responsibility to political parties exists. In contrast to cabinet government and to British society, the structure of American government and of American society has not encouraged the development of party organization or policy to which administrative agencies can be held responsible.

Responsibility to Profession

Working Bias: An administrative agency should be responsible for maintaining, developing, and applying such professional standards as may be relevant to its activities.

An administrative agency can be held responsible for adherence to the standards of technical knowledge, craftmanship, and professionalism applicable to the function administered. In other words, it can be said that objective standards of professional performance are one technique for insuring responsible conduct. Where such standards exist, the official often sacrifices his personal preference to the compulsion of professional group opinion. Should he fail to do so, he faces a loss of professional status or possibly affirmative action by executive, legislative, or judicial agents based on use of professional standards as a measure of conduct.

It is generally agreed that the professional sanction does not of itself provide an adequate guarantee of responsibility in our society. Some students have even emphasized the special dangers of any heavy reliance on professional standards. It is held that there can be no real responsibility unless it is an obligation to someone else (X being responsible to Y for Z), and that this condition cannot be fulfilled by the relationship of a man and a science or by an inward personal sense of moral obligation. It is also feared that professional responsibility leads to group introversion, undue emphasis on technique and inflexibility. It is felt that agency traditions based on a sense of narrow monopoly of expertness often harden into a pattern that resists alteration. Finally, there is the traditional democratic aversion to the efficiency which is one of the objectives of professional standards. The maxim that "men who think first and foremost of efficiency are seldom democrats" is of hoary, if not wholly palatable, vintage.

But most of the objections cited above are not really objections to reliance on professional standards. They are objections to the fact that the bureaucracy often has a monopoly of skill in modern governments, and that the indispensability of skilled administrators tends to make such a bureaucracy autonomous. Professionalization may actually play an important role in transforming the quasi-autonomous bureaucracy into a subservient tool. Conversely, responsibility is often most conspicuously absent where objective professional standards either do not exist or are not applied.

For present purposes it is enough that the professional responsibility recognized by an agency must be supplemented by responsibility to interest groups, legislature, and chief executive, and that it must be convincing to persons not associated with the profession or agency concerned. Whether or not it will be convincing depends in part on the status of the profession involved, *i.e.*, the extent to which the profession has developed or can be made to develop objective standards which are generally recognized and respected, and in part on evidence that the agency recognizes and has taken steps to insure fidelity to such standards by its personnel.

Accordingly the criteria for gauging the responsibility of an agency to professional standards includes: (1) the extent to which it recognizes such generally accepted standards and utilizes them to formulate policies and to anticipate problems which a technically qualified man knows will arise; (2) the extent to which it makes an effort to develop additional standards, especially when it possesses a near monopoly of skill in its field; and the extent to which such standards gain the respect of competent professional personnel outside the agency; (3) the extent to which it takes into account the professional education and experience of personnel in its recruitment, advancement, and separation policies; (4) the nature and extent of in-service training programs designed to improve professional skills; and (5) the nature and extent of its cooperation with outside organizations which attempt to keep their members up-to-date on professional developments and to promote devotion to the highest professional standards.

Beyond the standards of any one profession or craft, there are also standards common to the whole body of public servants considered as a distinctive social group—*i.e.*, as "bureaucracy." These standards usually reflect (*a*) the fiduciary relationship in which bureaucracy generally stands to political authority and (*b*) the norms of the wider social order. Consequently in a democracy they will include the demand for honesty, efficiency, courtesy, and impartiality in public acts, and an insistence that administration, both as to policy and procedure, be conducted in accordance with the prevailing democratic values. The extent to which these requirements are met furnishes the major criteria of the responsibility of public officials regarded as a single identifiable profession.

Responsibility to the Courts

Administrative responsibility will not be discussed in any detail, nor will criteria for this type of responsibility be developed. Administrative law has recently been the subject of so many specialized studies that the limited examination that might be made here would add nothing.

Failure to develop criteria for judicial responsibility is not intended to detract from its importance. All responsibility of public officials is, of course, responsibility under law; and in the United States it is generally to the regular courts that administrative agencies must prove, when challenged, that they have not abused their discretion, overstepped their jurisdiction, or committed an error of law, fact, or procedure. It should be noted, however, that such administrative abuses as excessive red tape or offensive conduct toward the public are beyond the reach of the courts. Moreover, judicial review is largely a negative, *post hoc*, and unduly ritualized check addressed to errors of commission, whereas administrative irresponsibility in the modern state is just as likely to arise from errors of omission.

For these reasons it is necessary to supplement the legal accountability of administrative agencies with responsibility to the people organized as interest groups, to the legislature, to the chief executive, and to relevant professional standards. Ordinarily, the analysis of a genuinely responsible agency will reveal a high positive correlation on all the criteria developed in connection with these relationships. But such a multiplicity of responsibilities may occasionally impose mutually contradictory obligations on an agency; and in such cases, as was suggested at the outset, the criteria of responsibility herein developed may well conflict. In this event there is a residual responsibility for the agency to evidence rational policy and good faith in seeking a resolution of the impasse, primarily through the chief executive.

Index